SCIENCE IN ELEMENTARY EDUCATION

METHODS, CONCEPTS, AND INQUIRIES

Tenth Edition

Joseph M. Peters
The University of West Florida

David L. Stout
The University of West Florida

PEARSON

Merrill
Prentice Hall

Upper Saddle River, New Jersey
Columbus, Ohio

Library of Congress Cataloging-in-Publication Data
Peters, Joseph M.
    Science in elementary education: methods, concepts, and inquiries/Joseph M. Peters,
David L. Stout.— 10th ed.
        p. cm.
    Includes bibliographical references and index.
    ISBN 0-13-171601-8
    1. Science—Study and teaching (Elementary) I. Stout, David L. II. Title.
LB1585.G4 2006
372.3'5044—dc22   2005040826

Vice President and Executive Publisher: Jeffery W. Johnston
Senior Editor: Linda Ashe Montgomery
Senior Editorial Assistant: Laura J. Weaver
Senior Development Editor: Hope Madden
Production Coordination: Jolynn Feller, Carlisle Publishers Services
Senior Production Editor: Linda Hillis Bayma
Design Coordinator: Diane C. Lorenzo

Photo Coordinator: Monica Merkel
Cover and Text Designer: Kristina Holmes
Cover photos: Nature Picture Photos
Production Manager: Pamela D. Bennett
Director of Marketing: Ann Castel Davis
Marketing Manager: Darcy Betts Prybella
Marketing Coordinator: Brain Mounts

This book was set in Goudy by Carlisle Communications, Ltd. It was printed and bound by Courier Kendallville, Inc. The cover was printed by Phoenix Color Corp.

Photo Credits. Chapters 1-8: Courtesy of Uncle Milton Industries: 2; Silver Burdett Ginn Needham: 8; Israel Office of Information: 13; Ken Karp/PH College: 20; Jet Propulsion Laboratory/NASA Headquarters: 30; Anne Vega/Merrill: 42; Michael Newman/PhotoEdit: 46; Cary I. Sneider/Great Explorations in Math and Science: 72; James Kudlack and Barb Eldridge/Onekama Elementary School: 80; Tim Daniel/ODNR/Division of Wildlife: 91; Kenneth P. Davis/PH College: 100; Scott Cunningham/ Merrill: 110, 183; Richard Hoyt/Great Explorations in Math and Science: 116; Anthony Magnacca/Merrill: 126, 160, 173; Barbara Schwartz/Merrill: 138; Joseph M. Peters: 142; T. Hubbard/Merrill: 152; LWA–JDC/Corbis/Stock Market: 164; Diasuke Morita/ Getty Images, Inc.–Photodisc: 177; KS Studios/Merrill: 192; Alan and Sandy Carey/Getty Images, Inc.–Photodisc: 201; David J. Sams/Getty Images, Inc.–Stone Allstock: 206.
Inquiry Unit chapters 1-12: Anthony Magnacca/Merrill: 4, 118, 152, 216, 264, 298, 330; Anne Vega/Merrill: 38, 182, 368; Irene Springer/PH College: 62, 307; Cindy Charles/PhotoEdit: 66; Spencer Grant/Stock Boston: 84; Harold E. Edgerton/USDA/NRCS/ NCGC/National Cartography and Geospatial Center: 85; Sybil Shelton/PH College: 96; U.S. Department of Agriculture: 206, 313; Bruce Roberts/Photo Researchers: 207; National Institutes of Health: 227; Runk/Shoenburger–Grant Heilman Photography: 232, 251 (bottom); American Museum of Natural History: 233, 238; W.P. Taylor/U.S. Department of the Interior: 234 (left); Modern Curriculum Press/Pearson Learning: 234 (right); Silver Burdett Ginn: 251 (top); USDA Soil Conservation Service: 312; U.S. Geological Survey/U.S. Department of the Interior: 323(A, C), 324(E, H), 325(I, J, K, L); Richard M. Busch: 323(B); USGS/Courtesy James B. Stevens: 323(D); U.S. Geological Survey, Denver: 324(F, G); National Oceanic and Atmospheric Administration: 363(A, B, C); Courtesy of All Weather Inc., Sacramento, CA: 364.

Pearson Education Ltd.
Pearson Education Singapore Pte. Ltd.
Pearson Education Canada, Ltd.
Pearson Education—Japan

Pearson Education Australia Pty. Limited
Pearson Education North Asia Ltd.
Pearson Educación de Mexico, S.A. de C.V.
Pearson Education Malaysia Pte. Ltd.

10 9 8 7 6 5 4 3 2 1
ISBN 0-13-171601-8

This book is dedicated to Darlene, Joseph B., and
Brenda Peters and Patty, Danny, and Kelly Stout
for their inspiration and support throughout this project.

PREFACE

Elementary and middle school teaching is a rewarding and exciting career. Your future as a professional educator includes the responsibility to help your students meet the demands and challenges of society, and the elementary and middle school classroom is where it all begins. It is your job to build the skills, content knowledge, and desire for inquiry that will allow your students to function in a society that will be highly scientific and technologically developed. This new edition of *Science in Elementary Education: Methods, Concepts, and Inquiries* has been crafted to help you do just that. It is designed to help you prepare your students to understand science concepts through active learning experiences. It accomplishes this by modeling inquiry teaching, engaging you in constructivist science inquiry, and providing you with the materials you need to successfully organize and manage your own science classroom.

Organization of the Text

This book combines practical methods, subject matter, and inquiry on how to teach science to elementary through middle level learners.

Part I: Methods for Teaching Elementary School Science

Focusing on the methods of teaching elementary and middle school science, Part I centers on why science education is basic to children's schooling and explains the foundations that give it form and substance. Each of the eight chapters develops a broad concept or a cluster of related teaching skills through descriptions and the use of many real-life examples.

The chapters and special features should enable you to do the following:

- Decide what areas of science are basic, useful, and curious to children.

- Recognize and assess differences in children's thinking.

- Use open-ended and closed-ended teaching activities in planning and implementing lessons and units.

- Improve children's scientific skills.

- Develop technological applications.

- Locate and use a variety of resources to teach science.

- Arrange and manage learning centers, computer centers, and projects.

- Assess science teaching.

Each chapter focuses on an overall concept such as learning, assessment, or technology. Practical teaching tips are highlighted and sprinkled throughout each chapter, and teaching concepts are aligned to the National Research Council's *National Science Education Standards*. In addition, learning objectives are linked to the American Association for the Advancement of Science (AAAS) *Benchmarks for Science Literacy*, which are cited throughout the text when applicable. To help summarize and extend the content, each chapter includes a summary, reflection, and additional readings.

Part II: Concepts and Inquiries for Teaching Elementary School Science

Building on the foundational methods of Part I, the second section of the text focuses on inquiry activities and related conceptual information. Its 12 inquiry units utilize the constructivist learning model (Yager, 1991) and the learning cycle model—concept exploration, conception invention, and concept explanation (Barman, 1989)—presented in Part I of the text to help model constructivist applications for science teaching and learning.

Each inquiry unit begins with a brief introduction, followed by sample benchmarks and standards, and inquiry activities grouped by topic. Each science inquiry will help you apply the skills developed in the first eight chapters. For example, the constructivist approach developed in Part I is illustrated through in-context examples. The inquiry investigations also offer chances for you and your students to inquire, as co-investigators if you wish, into open-ended problems and topics. The learning experiences use everyday, easy-to-get materials and can also enrich school science programs. Engaging in the inquiry activities in Part II can help you gain confidence in conceptual knowledge even as the concept explanations located at the end of each inquiry unit will help you solidify your science background knowledge. The scientific concepts that are tied to the inquiry experiences provide useful, everyday examples of scientific principles at work.

A Closer Look at the Text's Features

Modeling Inquiry Teaching

By taking you into successful inquiry-based classrooms, we contextualize the concepts being covered and help you envision your own constructivist science classroom:

- *Focus on Inquiry* vignettes beginning every chapter and peppered throughout provide you with a glimpse of meaningful science lessons.

- *Free CD-ROM Science in Elementary Education: Visit an Inquiry Classroom,* containing footage of master teacher Glenn McKnight, models constructivist teaching and successful inquiry-based science classroom management.

- *Visit an Inquiry Classroom* features throughout chapters integrate the chapter content, CD footage, and the text's Companion Website.

- Portfolio questions relating to the CD are found at the end of each Part I chapter.

- More CD-related activities are available on the text's Companion Website.

Addressing Today's Science Teaching Realities

Today's science teachers must be accountable to state and national standards as they ensure their teaching meets the needs of every learner in their classroom:

- *Benchmarks and Standards* features throughout chapters help you see how to integrate the *National Science Education Standards* in your own teaching.

- *Scaffolding for English Learners* features in the inquiry units help you adapt your instruction to benefit English learners.

- *Adapting for Students with Exceptionalities* features in the inquiry units help you adapt your inquiry lessons to better support students with exceptionalities.

Providing the Materials You Need

To truly prepare you for your classroom, we have created tools that will build your own understanding of inquiry science teaching and become meaningful tools for your own classroom.

- *Twelve Inquiry Units* model constructivist applications, build conceptual knowledge, and provide a bank of classroom-tested lessons to use in your own science classroom.

- *Teaching Tips* throughout chapters provide starting points, suggest activities, and consider safety to help you master constructivist science teaching.

Supplements

CD-ROM Science in Elementary Education: Visit an Inquiry Classroom

By modeling a constructivist, inquiry approach to teaching science, master teacher Glenn McKnight and his lively fourth graders illustrate science teaching and learning at its best and most effective.

CD Features

The CD footage helps you envision all aspects of inquiry science teaching by exploring the following:

- Model inquiry unit
- Nature of science
- Constructivist pedagogy
- Lesson planning and classroom management

Each topic illustrates its component parts through nine video clips. To help you truly understand the construction and implementation of a model inquiry, for example, we provide you with footage of the following:

- Instructional planning
- Preparing resources
- Invitation to explore
- Team formation
- Inquiry exploration
- Concept invention
- Concept application
- Ongoing assessment
- Putting it all together—4 days of science

Accompanying every piece of footage are the perspectives of text author Joseph Peters, teacher Glenn McKnight, a teaching colleague, and fourth-grade students. Each voice interprets what he or she sees in each clip, helping you notice the details of teaching and learning. Quotes from the professional literature identify research that supports McKnight's teaching discussions, stimulating further thinking about the video contents.

Additional Features

- Bonus lessons on the CD provide you with meaningful lessons you can use right in your own classroom.

- Links to the Internet allow you to move back and forth between the CD and the Companion Website, where more questions and lessons connect the footage to the text material and to your own classroom.

- Look for CD icons throughout the text to point you toward features, reflection questions, and applications that will help you make the most of this meaningful media.

- *Visit an Inquiry Classroom* features in the text lead you to reflect on specific clips in terms of their relation to the chapter concepts. Answer questions about these clips on the Companion Website.

- Chapter-ending questions help you make connections between the material you learned in the chapter and the footage you find on the CD.

Companion Website

This robust online support system offers many rich and meaningful ways to deepen and expand the information presented to you in the text:

- *Focus Questions* provide a useful advanced organizer for each chapter's online companion.

- *Meeting the Standards* provides *National Science Education Standards* integration, delivered through adaptable lessons that can be saved to your hard drive or disk. This module provides you with lessons to take right into your own classroom that align with both national and state standards.

- Praxis Practice questions help pre-service teachers prepare for the Praxis 2 exam.

- Additional CD-ROM activities help you continue to deepen your understanding of inquiry science teaching.

- Self-assessments help you gauge your understanding of text concepts.

- Web Links provide useful connections to all standards and many other invaluable online literacy sources.

Visit this online supplement at **www.prenhall.com/peters**

Electronic Instructor's Manual

This useful tool for instructors, available online at **www.prenhall.com** with an instructor's access code, provides the following rich instructional support:

- Test bank, including multiple choice and essay tests

- PowerPoints® specifically designed for each chapter

- Chapter-by-chapter materials, including chapter objectives, suggested readings, discussion questions, and online integration

National Science Education Standards Sampler

This document works in tandem with the text to help you learn, fully understand, and apply the *National Science Education Standards*.

Where the Web Meets Textbooks for Student Savings!

SafariX Textbooks Online™ is an exciting new choice for students looking to save money. As an alternative to purchasing the print textbook, students can subscribe to the same content online and save up to 50% off the suggested list price of the print text. With a SafariX WebBook, students can search the text, make notes online, print out reading assignments that incorporate lecture notes, and bookmark important passages for later review. For more information, or to subscribe to the SafariX WebBook, visit *http://www.safarix.com.*

Additional Titles of Interest

For your convenience, this text is also available as a split set of two texts:

- *Methods for Teaching Elementary School Science*, Fifth Edition, 0-13-171599-2

- *Concepts and Inquiries for Teaching Elementary School Science*, Fifth Edition, 0-13-171598-4

References

Barman, C. R. (1989). A procedure for helping prospective elementary teachers integrate the learning cycle into science textbooks. *Journal of Science Teacher Education*, 1(2), 21–26.
Yager, R. (1991). The constructivist learning model. *The Science Teacher*, 58(6), 52–57.

Acknowledgments

We thank the many people who helped with the tenth edition of *Science in Elementary Education*, especially editors Linda Montgomery and Hope Madden of Merrill/Prentice Hall for their extensive editorial support, insight, encouragement, continued assistance, and constructive comments.

This edition of *Science in Elementary Education* includes many *Focus on Inquiry* vignettes. We extend our sincere thanks to Norman Lederman, Ken Tobin, Jerry Mayernik, George O'Brien, Angela Alexander, Christine Peters, Kata McCarville, Pam Northrup, Charlotte Boling, and Sue Dale Tunnicliffe for sharing their experiences with us in the methods chapters.

We also acknowledge the external reviewers of this text: Mary Margaret Capraro, Texas A&M; Huabin Chen, Saint Martin's College; Raymond W. Francis, Central Michigan University; Karen Ivers, California State University, Fullerton; Robbie V. McCarty, Southwestern Oklahoma State University; James T. McDonald, Central Michigan University; Leah M. Melber, California State University, Los Angeles; Michael Odell, University of Idaho; John Shimkanin, California University of Pennsylvania; Lori-Anne Stelmark, Teachers College Columbia University; and Rita K. Voltmer, Miami University, Oxford, Ohio.

EDUCATOR LEARNING CENTER: AN INVALUABLE ONLINE RESOURCE

Merrill Education and the Association for Supervision and Curriculum Development (ASCD) invite you to take advantage of a new online resource, one that provides access to the top research and proven strategies associated with ASCD and Merrill—the Educator Learning Center. At **www.educatorlearningcenter.com,** you will find resources that will enhance your students' understanding of course topics and of current educational issues, in addition to being invaluable for further research.

How the Educator Learning Center Will Help Your Students Become Better Teachers

With the combined resources of Merrill Education and ASCD, you and your students will find a wealth of tools and materials to better prepare them for the classroom.

Research

- More than 600 articles from the ASCD journal *Educational Leadership* discuss everyday issues faced by practicing teachers.
- A direct link on the site to Research Navigator™ gives students access to many of the leading education journals, as well as extensive content detailing the research process.
- Excerpts from Merrill Education texts give your students insights on important topics of instructional method diverse populations, assessment, classroom management, technology, and refining classroom practice.

Classroom Practice

- Hundreds of lesson plans and teaching strategies are categorized by content area and age range.
- Case studies and classroom video footage provide virtual field experience for student reflection.
- Computer simulations and other electronic tools keep your students abreast of today's classrooms and current technologies.

Look into the Value of Educator Learning Center Yourself

A four-month subscription to Educator Learning Center is $25 but is **FREE** when packaged with any Merrill Education text. In order for your students to have access to this site, you must use this special value-pack ISBN number **WHEN** placing your textbook order with the bookstore: 0-13-195431-8. Your students will then receive a copy of the text packaged with a free ASCD pincode. To preview the value of this website to you and your students, please go to **www.educatorlearningcenter.com** and click on "Demo."

CONTENTS

NOTE: Every effort has been made to provide accurate and current Internet information in this book. However, the Internet and information posted on it are constantly changing, and it is inevitable that some of the Internet addresses listed in this textbook will change.

METHODS FOR TEACHING ELEMENTARY SCHOOL SCIENCE

CHAPTER 1

SCIENCE INQUIRY AND THE NATURE OF SCIENCE

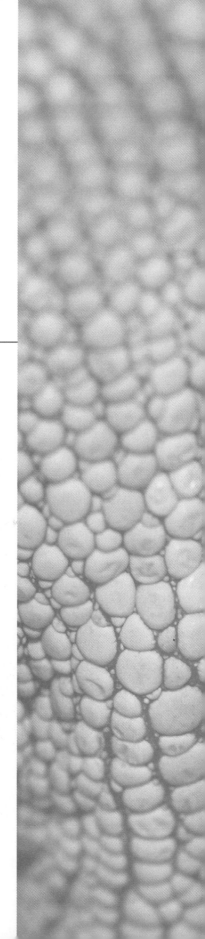

FOCUS QUESTIONS

- What is the "nature of science"?
- Can you use an inquiry approach to demonstrate the nature of science with your students?
- What guiding documents and other societal concerns will you incorporate into your teaching of children?

Focus on Inquiry

Teaching the Nature of Science

Dr. Norman Lederman,
Illinois Institute of Technology

The year is 1971, and Peter is a typically self-conscious high school sophomore. Like several of his friends, Peter has a slight acne problem. After trying several creams and ointments available at the local drugstore, he convinces his parents that the problem requires the help of the family physician. The physician tells Peter and his parents that the cause of his problem is an abundance of oil production by the glands on his face and that this extra oil provides a good nutritional source for common bacteria. She also tells Peter that eating less chocolate, among other things, might solve the problem but that there is a more reliable approach. Naturally, Peter and his parents are anxious to listen further. The physician recommends that Peter's parents purchase a sunlamp. The U.V. rays emitted by the sunlamp do an excellent job of "drying" the skin and eliminating acne problems. In fact, the physician adds, sunlamps are generally good for most people's skin regardless of whether they have an acne problem. Peter would only have to use the sunlamp about 10 minutes per day and, in addition to relieving his acne problems, he can have a desirable tanned look year-round. So, Peter, with his parents' permission, did what thousands of Americans did in the 1970s.

Thirty years later, the medical profession has recognized the possible carcinogenic effects of ultraviolet radiation. Acne patients are no longer advised to use sunlamp therapy. Indeed, the current advice regarding U.V. rays is to avoid them as much as possible. Consequently, the availability of sunscreen lotions and sunglasses designed to protect both the skin and the eyes from harmful light rays has increased significantly. The physician's advice to Peter and his parents in the 2000s would be much different from what it was in 1971.

How does the general public react to this "change of heart" by the scientific community? Although we have seen a proliferation of ointments and creams designed to block the harmful rays of the sun, tanning is as popular as ever in the United States and, indeed, around the world. A significant number of individuals have decided to ignore the advice of the scientific community. It is not uncommon to hear people say, "Why can't scientists make up their minds? One day something is good for you, and next day you hear that it causes cancer. It seems that everything causes cancer. I'm not going to do anything different until they decide once and for all."

See the Chapter 1 Web Destinations on the Companion Website (*http://www.prenhall.com/peters*) for links to documents such as *Inquiry and the National Science Education Standards* (National Research Council, 2000) that contain information to further illustrate the nature of science as it applies to science teaching.

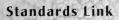

The case of U.V. rays is not unique. "Flip-flops" in the opinions of scientists and physicians have occurred with respect to aspirin, alcohol, cold fusion, and vitamin C, and many foods. Indeed, such changes have become the object of jokes.

THE NATURE OF SCIENCE

What does the idea of scientific flip-flops have to do with teaching elementary and middle-level students about the nature of science? These flip-flops we so often see are really not weaknesses of science. They are not reasons for the general public to disregard scientific knowledge or to lose faith in the scientific way of thinking. These flip-flops constitute one of the most important strengths of science—in fact, they *are* science. That is, scientific knowledge is self-correcting on the basis of new empirical evidence or new ways of interpreting data. The knowledge, though tentative, is based on volumes of data and should not be disregarded. Disregarding scientific knowledge severely limits the quality of decisions that we each make about our lives.

See the Web Destinations for Chapter 1 of the Companion Website for a link to *Teaching About Evolution and the Nature of Science* (National Academy of Sciences, 1998).

What is the nature of science? There are as many answers to this question as there are books; however, at the level of generality that will be useful to you as an elementary or middle school teacher there is a strong consensus. Strictly speaking, *science* can be defined as a body of knowledge, a process, and a way of knowing or constructing reality. The *nature of science* refers to six characteristics of scientific knowledge that derive directly from how the knowledge is developed. Of importance to you as an elementary or middle school science teacher are the following characteristics.

1. There is no single set or sequence of steps that always directs a scientific investigation. There is no such thing as "the scientific method."
2. Scientific knowledge, both theories and laws, is subject to change. All scientific knowledge is tentative.
3. Scientific knowledge must be at least partially supported by empirical evidence. Scientific knowledge must involve the collection of data, be consistent with what we "know" about the world, and be testable.
4. Scientific knowledge is partially the product of the creative imagination of the scientist. All scientific knowledge combines both empirical evidence and the creative interpretation of data by scientists.
5. Given the importance of scientists' individual creativity, scientific knowledge is necessarily subjective to some degree. Scientific knowledge is not totally objective as is commonly believed.
6. Scientific knowledge is a product of both observation and inference.

In your future classroom, you will need to carefully address the characteris-

---

tics of scientific knowledge as you teach. You will also need to consider the developmental level of your students. Then, you will be able to help your students develop the understandings that will guide them in making decisions for the rest of their lives. In particular, your students will begin to develop a more balanced view of the truth of scientific knowledge. They will take the so-called truth of science with an informed "grain of salt." This means your students will heed the notion that the sun's rays can cause cancer. It also means they will not disregard all future knowledge about the effects of the sun's rays if the scientific community alters its current position.

As you begin to explore your own teaching of the nature of science, keep your learners in mind. Developing content knowledge and inquiry skills with your students is helped by their inherent natural curiosity. Children enjoy observing the world around them. Picture a group of students on a playground during lunch, as they watch ants move about on the pavement. Looking at the ants, the students begin to ask the following questions.

Why do ants follow each other?
Why do the ants live in the ground and not above the ground?
How can the ants carry things twice their size?

How thoughtfully did *your* teachers handle questions that you asked in school? Were you able to explore some of your own interests in the classroom, or was learning more restricted? Were you guided to think through some problems for yourself, or were standard answers always given? How your teachers worked with you and your classmates reflected their notions about science and science teaching. We hope that what you learn through this methods course will affect how you will teach science. Take time to question your beliefs and your understandings as you explore science and science teaching in this course.

> Find the complete text of the *National Science Education Standards*, as well as your own state's standards, in the Web Destinations for Chapter 1 of the Companion Website (*http://www.prenhall.com/peters*).

Visit an Inquiry Classroom
The Child as a Scientist

As you view *The Child as a Scientist* video in the "Nature of Science" section of the Companion CD, notice how Mr. McKnight involves the students in thinking about the activity. One of the goals of science teaching is for every child to experience inquiry in the classroom similar to the way a scientist experiences inquiry in the field. You see evidence of this in how the children identify questions or hypotheses to explore and then carry out their investigations.

Review the video and ask yourself the following:

- How would your beliefs about the nature of science affect how you would teach this lesson?
- How would you modify this lesson if you were to teach it to elementary or middle school students?

Do a web search and find a sample science lesson plan. Compare the approach in that plan to how Mr. McKnight teaches. Record your ideas and the answers to the previous questions in your portfolio or use the Companion Website to share your ideas.

Visit an Inquiry Classroom
Science as Inquiry

View the *Science as Inquiry* video in the "Nature of Science" section of the Companion CD. We see Glenn promoting inquiry by working with children to identify problems to solve.

Review the video and ask yourself the following:
- How does Mr. McKnight interact with the students when they are developing questions to explore?
- Why doesn't Mr. McKnight just tell the students what to do with their experiments?
- We talk about promoting "process over product" in the narrative of this video. What does this mean and what example do you see in the video?

CW   Think about a science lesson you will teach in your field placement. What are some ways you will promote process over product? Record your ideas and the answers to the previous questions in your portfolio or use the Companion Website to share your ideas.

Your school or district office will probably give you some instructional materials for teaching science, but your own concepts and values about science teaching will strongly affect what children actually learn in your science classroom. If you desire to understand **the nature of science, scientific concepts,** and **scientific processes,** this desire to learn more about the world around you will be transferred to your students.

How you and your students learn science will be related to your desire for inquiry and the nature of science. You will need to "[i]mplement approaches to teaching science that cause students to question and explore and to use those experiences to raise and answer questions about the natural world" (National Science Teachers Association [NSTA], 2004). In the following sections, we use contrasting teaching approaches to show how your teaching can affect students' curiosity about the nature of science. As you read, think about the National Research Council (NRC) History and Nature of Science Standard in the Standards Link box.

The nature of science means those characteristics of scientific knowledge that derive directly from how the knowledge is developed.

Scientific concepts relate to the knowledge of science, or what scientists have found out as a result of their work.

Scientific processes are the skills that students develop, such as observation, classification, inference, and measurement.

See the Web Destinations for Chapter 1 at *http://www.prenhall. com/peters* for links to supporting documents on the nature of science, inquiry, educating teachers, and instructional materials as they relate to the *National Science Education Standards.*

THE NATURE OF INQUIRY

Imagine that you are sitting in on two teachers as they use a teachable moment to engage students in the topic of "ants." Students from Martin Luther King Jr. Elementary School have just come back from their noon recess. While walking back from the playground, students from the classes discussed what they had witnessed: fire ants attacking a baby bird that could not fly. They are now wondering why ants behave the way they do, why they eat what they eat, and what their underground homes may look like.

Grade 3 Examples

Two teachers draw off of the students' natural curiosity, and introduce a lesson on ants. Compare each of the two approaches.

Mr. Bryant's Class

In his classroom, Mr. Bryant captures an opportunity to follow up the ant discussion with the classic story *A Bug's Life* (Steiner, 1998). Over the next few days, he substitutes reciting from the reading series for *Ant Cities* (Dorros, 1987) and *It's an Ant's Life* (Parker, 1999). They discuss the anthills and tunnels and the worker ants, males, and queens. Later, they make a homemade Ant Farm® as suggested in *Ant Cities*. Mr. Bryant introduces ants to the farm, and the children periodically feed them. During free time for the next few weeks, the students intermittently observe the ants to see what they are doing.

Ms. Davis's Class

Ms. Davis begins asking her students what they observed outside. She has students take turns recording this information on a flip chart. She also includes questions about what the students would like to know about ants. Later, she reads the fable *The Little Red Ant and the Great Big Crumb* (Climo, 1995) to begin a discussion on which foods ants eat. She then reads *The Magic School Bus Gets Ants in Its Pants* (Cole, 1996) and *Hey Little Ant* (Hoose, Tilley, & Hoose, 1998) to initiate conversation on ant behaviors and habitats. Her class discusses the anthills and tunnels and the worker ants, males, and queens. Next, the students set up an Ant Farm® as outlined in *The Practical Entomologist* (Imes, 1992). After students build the farm, Ms. Davis asks them to predict what will happen as the ants are introduced to the ant habitat and what will occur over the next few weeks. Students hypothesize that the ants will develop small sections of the farm into colonies.

Ms. Davis's students write these predictions and the accompanying observations on the flip chart. They also record brief daily observations and compare these against their predictions. Ms. Davis's students infer what kinds of food ants like. They place different containers of food near the ant mound outside the classroom to see what will happen (see Cole, 1996). They predict which food will be found first and infer which food the ants will appear to like best. They periodically have class discussions to communicate the facts they find out about ants. Ms. Davis ends the lessons by returning to the students' questions to see if they were all answered. She also follows up to be sure the students have no **misconceptions** about ants.

Classroom Comparisons

In the previous two situations, the teachers discuss ants. Mr. Bryant and Ms. Davis both expand on the opportunity presented to them by the students. They answer questions about ants and integrate children's natural wonder with their literature, activities such as building Ant Farms®[1], and opportunities for observation. Mr. Bryant uses this activity as a fun way to see ants in their habitat and to learn about ants in general. Ms. Davis, however,

Misconceptions are mistaken ideas that students have about how something works or how it is otherwise unlike what the scientific community has found to be true.

1. Ant Farm® is a registered trademark of Uncle Milton Industries, Inc. Used with permission

Visit an Inquiry Classroom
Approaches to Teaching

Watch the *Learning to Think* video in the "Constructivist Pedagogy" section of the Companion CD. Mr. McKnight interacts with students as they explore earthworms.

Review the video and ask yourself the following:
- How will you use questioning to promote ideas in your own science teaching?
- How does Mr. McKnight's approach to teaching about earthworms compare to Ms. Davis's approach?
- Based on Mr. McKnight's lesson, what suggestions would you make to Mr. Bryant?

 Think about the advantages to Ms. Davis's approach to science as compared to Mr. Bryant's approach. Based on the video, what suggestions could you make to Mr. Bryant? Record your ideas and the answers to the previous questions in your portfolio or use the Companion Website to share your ideas.

sees this as not only a fun learning activity but also an opportunity for her students to make systematic observations of ants and to develop other related scientific skills. She wants her students to infer, predict, communicate, experiment, and form tentative theories as scientists would in similar situations. Ms. Davis also wants her students to understand that scientific knowledge is based on observation and inference as with their ant studies—all part of learning the nature of science.

Grade 5 Examples

Students in two fifth-grade classrooms at Martin Luther King Jr. Elementary School have also witnessed the ants. Their teachers are preparing ant lessons, too.

Mrs. Brown's Class

Mrs. Brown begins with reading to the class *Life Story: Ant* (Chinery, 1991). They discuss anthills, ant life cycles, and ant food behaviors. She has Tanezia read *Those Amazing Ants* (Demuth, 1994). This book offers interesting information, such as the mating dance, cleaning habits, and the way ants use secretions to mark food trails. The students discuss this information. Guided by the activity "A Special Plot" from the **AIMS** book *Field Detectives: Investigating Playground Habitats* (Gazlay, 1998), Mrs. Brown completes a skill-development activity with her students. They observe and sketch several ant mounds near the school and develop **Venn diagrams** of the commonalties and differences in the habitats. The students then discuss what they found out from their diagrams.

Mrs. Malloy's Class

Mrs. Malloy's fifth-grade class decides on ants as a study theme for the next few days. Karolyn reads aloud the story *The 512 Ants on Sullivan Street* (Losi, 1997); Taylor reads *A*

AIMS   (Activities for the Integration of Mathematics and Science) are hands-on/minds-on integrated activities found in a series of books available from the AIMS Foundation. (See http://www.prenhall.com/peters for links and further information.)

Venn diagrams,   named after John Venn, use circles inside of a rectangle to represent sets of objects, to show relationships between the objects.

Children discuss animals that live underground as part of their research related to the study of ants.

Remainder of One (Pinczes, 1995); and Rochelle reads *One Hundred Hungry Ants* (Pinczes, 1993). These stories incorporate number sense and division to lay the foundation for related mathematics activities. Casen then reads aloud the story *Antics!* (Hepworth, 1992), and Hoa reads *There's an Ant in Anthony* (Most, 1980). These alphabetical anthologies lend themselves to language activities during which Mrs. Malloy's students try to find as many words as possible with *ant* in them. Finally, they explore "Ants Around the World" from the book *Ants* (Teacher Created Materials, 1997).

Continuing the ant theme, Mrs. Malloy asks the students what they have already found out about ants and what else they would like to know about ants. They generate a list of topics such as the following, to copy into their science journals.

> *How do ants tunnel? Are all tunnels alike?*
> *What is the ant's body structure? Is it different for males, females, and queens?*
> *How do ants reproduce and grow?*
> *What is a scent trail, and how is it made?*

Mrs. Malloy makes available for her students resource materials, including *AIMS Field Detectives* (Gazlay, 1998), *Ant Homes Under the Ground* (Lawrence Hall of Science, 1996), and *Project WILD* (Council for Environmental Education, 1992). She also arranges a table with several other activity and field identification books and materials for making an Ant Farm®. Her students use these in small groups to plan science activities. She also bookmarks an Internet ant cam (online video camera) and movie site for her class to use in their studies.

 Teaching Tips Project WILD, Project Aquatic WILD, Project Learning Tree, and Project WET are national programs that enhance environmental education. (See http://www.prenhall.com/peters for links to these and related programs.)

Mrs. Malloy loads *SimAnt* (Broderbund/Maxis) onto the classroom computer. Students take on roles of ants with this program. They learn ant behaviors, including how to communicate with one another and how to avoid being "done in" by fierce red ants, ravenous spiders, and heavy human feet. Students use scientific information to develop strategies to survive, increase the size of their colony, and finally reach the ultimate reward—a safe home with a food supply.

See *http://www.prenhall.com/peters* for ant cam and related links.

Mrs. Malloy facilitates and provides other resources as her class works in small groups to plan and participate in numerous activities related to ants. Later, they share what they have discovered about ants. They conclude when they have answered the questions in their science journals.

Classroom Examination

Mrs. Malloy generates interest in ants through mathematics and language activities. She uses the ant theme as a starting point to help her students generate ideas for experiments and other hands-on activities. These activities will help her initiate student discussion, seek answers to their related questions, and develop scientific skills. In this less teacher-directed approach, the children act like scientists as they explore and experiment with ants—constructing understandings and answers to their questions. They find that there is no one correct way to explore ants. They also see that their theories related to ants often change with new observations and inferences that better explain things. In short, they not only are learning about ants but also are experiencing the nature of science through inquiry, a connection with other school subjects as suggested in the NRC's *Science Program of Study Standard*.

Questions as an Invitation to Learn

In exemplary classrooms, teachers carefully use questioning techniques to engage the students. Let's look at two more classrooms building on their students' interest in ants. Compare the examples to see how each teacher began his or her lesson.

Science Program of Study Standard

The program of study in science for all students should be developmentally appropriate, interesting, and relevant to students' lives; emphasize student understanding through inquiry; and be connected with other school subjects.

- **The program of study should include all of the content standards.**

- **Science content must be embedded in a variety of curriculum patterns that are developmentally appropriate, interesting, and relevant to students' lives.**

- **The program of study must emphasize student understanding through inquiry.**

- **The program of study in science should connect to other school subjects.**

(Program Standard B, National Research Council, 1996, p. 212.)

Teacher 1

- A queen ant is usually bigger than the other ants, and new queens and males have wings.
- Ants may eat honeydew from aphids or juices from insects and plants.
- An ant develops from an egg, to a larva, to a pupa, to an adult that will emerge from a cocoon.

Teacher 2

- Why did some ants look different from others in the ant nest we observed?
- I wonder if the ants we observed today and last week all eat the same food.
- Why did we find eggs, grubs, and cocoons in the ant nests?

The first teacher simply states what will be taught. For example, in her first lesson, children will learn that queen ants are bigger than worker ants and new queens and males have wings. Once the initial teaching is accomplished, the lesson is completed.

The second teacher always begins his lessons with a question referring to children's everyday experiences. This teacher agrees with current reform efforts that ask teachers to base science on students' everyday lives. This method supports the notion that science is

Visit an Inquiry Classroom
Questioning

Watch the *Questioning* video in the "Planning and Management" section of the Companion CD. Mr. McKnight uses questioning in this video as he often does with his class. Did you notice that many of his questions are open, meaning they have no one right or predetermined answer?

Review the video and ask yourself the following:
- Why does Mr. McKnight ask so many questions?
- What would make you think that Mr. McKnight's questions were not predetermined (i.e., written down in a lesson plan)?
- How do Mr. McKnight's questions indicate children's concept development and concept attainment?

 The authors of the *National Science Education Standards* (1996) suggest teachers "ask a question about objects, organisms, and events in the environment" in order to promote inquiry. What are some specific examples of Mr. McKnight doing this? Record your answers in your portfolio or use the Companion Website to share your ideas.

a human endeavor. Science principles, or concepts, typically have many real-life applications. They are a result of the creative imagination of the scientist. Beginning and ending lessons with applications enable children to reflect on their own experiences, to interpret their observations creatively, and to construct new knowledge. The second approach also takes the pressure off the teacher to know everything about the topic under study. The teacher can explore the subject *with* his or her students.

You probably see by now that the second way of teaching is likely to be more interesting and productive to you and your students. Yet, if you're like most college students who select elementary or middle school teaching as a profession, science is probably not your strongest subject. You may not feel confident about teaching science. Do not worry about this; you and your class will learn together. What's important is to develop an awareness of the nature of science and how you can develop scientific skills and understandings with the students. Let's look at how you would teach the nature of science.

How Can You Demonstrate
the Nature of Science?——————

Figure 1–1   **Inside view of the oatmeal container.**

Although the current reforms in science education place a strong emphasis on students' understandings of the nature of science, there are not abundant resources to help you share that concept. The following idea has been found to be successful for teaching students about each of the six characteristics of scientific knowledge. This activity requires virtually no scientific background on the part of the students. Consequently, it is relatively risk free.

Creating the Tube

1. Re-create the tube pictured in Figure 1–1. I suggest that you obtain a mailing tube from the post office, the map room at a local library, or a store that sells posters. You may also use a meter-long piece of PVC pipe or an empty oatmeal container. Clothesline, twine, or rope from a local hardware store will do for the rope. The ring holding the ropes together is plastic; you can buy one at a craft store. If a ring is not available, the lower rope can simply be looped over the upper rope. The ends of the tube can be sealed with rubber stoppers or be taped.
2. Make an overhead (and class set of handouts) of what is pictured in Figure 1–2.

Figure 1–2   **Outside view of the oatmeal container.**

Teaching the Concept

3. Have the students carefully observe several sequential pulls of the various rope ends. It makes no difference which rope ends you choose to pull.
4. Have individual students, pairs, or groups speculate about what is inside the tube in an effort to explain what they have seen. After several minutes, allow students to manipulate the ropes. At this point, they will be testing their hypotheses about the contents of the tube.
5. Allow the students several more minutes to revise their speculations on the basis of the additional data that they have just collected.
6. Allow several volunteers the opportunity to share their hypotheses with the rest of the class on the overhead diagram. There are a variety of workable explanations; allow the sharing of ideas until at least two alternatives are

presented. If the students seem to be fixed on only one approach, be prepared to offer other possibilities. Be sure not to imply that any one of the explanations is correct or better than the others.

7. You and the students can discuss the ideas presented. Restrict the focus of the discussion to the relationship between the inferred ideas and the data collected through your demonstration.

8. Have the students construct models of the tube they developed, using a toilet paper or paper towel roll. Provide string, scissors, and paper tubes, or direct students to bring these from home.

9. After construction of the models, have the students follow along as you pull various ropes on your model. This gives the students a chance to see how consistent their models are with the actions of your model.

10. Some students' tubes will not "behave" the same way as yours, but most probably will. Stress two ideas at this point: First, lead the class to the idea that there are several ways to construct the tube so that it functions like yours. Second, ask the students if they can now know for sure what is in your tube, just because their model "behaved" the same as yours. The primary point is that we are never certain whether the proposed explanation is correct unless the tube can be opened.

Depending on the grade level of your students, the following ideas should be discussed.

- The tube is analogous to the universe; what your students did is analogous to what scientists do. But we have no way of actually opening the universe to see how it really works.
- Students collected empirical data and developed inferences to explain the data. These activities are similar to the way scientists collect data and develop inferences

Visit an Inquiry Classroom
Collecting and Using Data

Watch the *Collecting and Using Data* video in the "Nature of Science" section of the Companion CD for examples of students collecting data. They are engaged in both data collection and inference based on the data.

After looking at the video, read Mr. McKnight's perspective on collecting and using data. Can you answer the following questions?
- What is Mr. McKnight's primary reason for having the children collect data?
- How does Mr. McKnight want the children to use the data?
- It would be much easier if all of the students did the exact same experiment and collected the same data which could be compared for accuracy. Why doesn't Mr. McKnight use these "cookbook" type activities instead of allowing students to explore their own questions and collect and interpret their own data?

     Think about an elementary or middle school teacher you had who taught science. What was this person's questioning technique? How does it compare to Mr. McKnight's technique? Record your ideas and the answers to the previous questions in your portfolio or use the Companion Website to share your ideas.

to explain the data. In essence, the speculations about the contents of your tube are theoretical models used to explain necessarily limited data. What your students have done is analogous to what a scientist does all the time. What your students have done is not very different from what the scientists of the 1970s did when they observed acne and inferred possible explanations and solutions for the problem.

- Finally, explicitly discuss with your students how each of the six characteristics of scientific knowledge is evident in the activity.

Take a moment to see if you can identify the six characteristics of science in this activity.

The pulling of the rope in the container clearly points out some tenets of the nature of science. In *Benchmarks for Science Literacy* (American Association for the Advancement of Science [AAAS], 1993), the authors make the following point about the study of science.

When people know how scientists go about their work and reach scientific conclusions, and what the limitations of such conclusions are, they are more likely to react thoughtfully to scientific claims and less likely to reject them out of hand or accept them uncritically. Once people gain a good sense of how science operates—along with a basic inventory of key science concepts as a basis for learning more later—they can follow the science adventure story as it plays out during their lifetimes. (p. 3)

Visit the standards module on the Companion Website at *http://www. prenhall. com/peters* for a link to *Benchmarks for Science Literacy*.

Children's curiosity is enhanced through science experiences such as the exploration of ant environments.

Visit the Companion Website for an overview of the concepts and process of science that are in the *National Science Education Standards and Benchmarks for Science Literacy*, which will be at the core of your science teaching. Scientific processes are also discussed in Chapter 4 of this textbook, and concepts are found in the inquiry chapters.

This passage means that it is critical for students to understand how the scientific process works in order to be good science consumers and lifelong learners. Students must see science as a human enterprise, not as a body of knowledge to be memorized. When they read and appraise an item in the newspaper or have a problem to solve, the students' past scientific experiences will assist them.

Like the examples in the rope and container activity, you may also wonder about some scientific "changes of heart," or new theories. Your knowledge of the nature of science will assist you in understanding the scientific information as presented. Remember that the products of science are constantly changing with new experimentation. Lederman (1992) asserts that "the nature of science is as tentative, if not more so, than scientific knowledge itself" (p. 352), meaning that the nature of science itself develops over time. What remains constant is that good science education originates with your understanding of the nature of science and your ability to teach science to children. How will you teach children about science?

TEACHING CHILDREN

Applying concepts and processes of science to society's problems is the reason why science education is such an important subject in school. Because we are dealing with elementary and middle-level students, however, we need to match what is taught with the students' interests and developmental levels.

You may have heard the expression, "To a child who's discovered the hammer, the entire world is a nail." This idea illustrates children's broad curiosity and inner need to try things for themselves. Science education encourages and rewards this natural curiosity; but science educators need to guide the learning, keeping the instruction developmentally appropriate.

Generalizations can be seen as principles or statements that have a general application to a specific body of knowledge.

For example, broad **generalizations** and skills are useful in science study. As a generalization or process approaches the most advanced scientific model, however, it is less likely that children can learn it or will even want to try. To persist is simply to have them bite off more than they can chew. So, teaching generalizations about molecules in the primary years, for example, or insisting that all variables be controlled in experiments, is likely to be self-defeating. Our elementary students will understand that ants may bite and are male and female. They may have trouble understanding the hymenopteran's specialized mouthparts or the concept of how males originate from unfertilized eggs and females from fertilized eggs.

It is unlikely that any publisher or curriculum office can develop a program that suits every child or class. It will be your responsibility to create a suitable match between students and the curriculum. This task will require understanding how children learn science, children's developmental levels, and what is required of your science education program.

It is important for children to understand and see the purpose of what they are doing. Children also need to reach short-range goals as they progress toward goals that are farther away. Children usually learn best when working with concrete or semiconcrete materials and limited generalizations. Keep this key factor in mind when working with young students.

Guiding Documents for Science Education

How can you tell what is appropriate for your students to learn? One way to see the types of processes and concepts with which students at a particular grade level should be familiar is to look at two of the guiding documents in science education. We have already referred to *National Science Education Standards* (NRC, 1996) and *Benchmarks for Science Literacy* (AAAS, 1993). The benchmarks were developed as part of Project 2061 (AAAS, 1989), which was an undertaking of the American Association for the Advancement of Science to help reform science, mathematics, and technology education. They focus on the science that should be learned by all Americans. The standards were a national collaborative headed by the National Research Council, again with the focus on scientific literacy for all. There is a high level of correlation between the two projects. Many states have adopted the benchmarks, the standards, or a state-specific variation of one of the projects as their own statewide standards for which you will be accountable in your classroom. We refer to the benchmarks and the standards throughout the text.

Are there other considerations besides process and content? The authors of Project 2061 and the standards both discuss societal perspectives as they relate to science education.

Refer to the Companion Website (*http://www.prenhall.com/peters*) for links to the online versions of the standards, benchmarks, and other documents.   **CW**

Societal Considerations

We began this chapter with a discussion of the nature of science and how students observed ant mounds in the schoolyard. These observations provided the basis for deeper exploration into ants—allowing students to further construct concepts of ants and their behaviors, as well as scientific process skills. A well-planned and flexible curriculum usually contains many of these everyday applications.

It is important to educate people and thus change attitudes in order to cope with today's challenges. Naturally, the education system plays a major role in this process. For example, the focus of science education centers on such topics as AIDS, endangered species, wetlands, energy exploration and conservation, environmentally safe food, uncontaminated drinking water, multicultural career opportunities, and gender equity in science-related careers.

Every society wants its contributing members to be literate, that is, to have enough background knowledge and ability to make informed decisions, communicate, produce, and improve the general welfare. In a society as advanced and dynamic as ours is today, the amount of information increases at an accelerating rate. Under such conditions, people need a common core of knowledge. A common ground allows us to communicate more efficiently with one another and facilitates public policy.

Literacy serves as the common ground for discussing and understanding diverse and complex issues. Issues such as toxic waste dumps, in vitro fertilization, AIDS, nuclear accidents, the hole in the ozone layer, the greenhouse effect, genetically altered foods, and artificial body parts are examined in our everyday encounters with the media. Knowledge of specific technical information may be considered when making purchases. For example, when buying a car, it is helpful to have some knowledge of horsepower, fuel economy, and antilock brakes. To secure a job, we are expected to know something about the nature of the position we are seeking. The ability to function and survive in our society is linked to literacy.

Science literacy is imperative in a society that leans heavily on science and technology. The AAAS (1993) views literacy in the following way.

See Chapter 1 Web Destinations on the Companion Website (*http://www.prenhall.com/peters*) for links to Nova Science in the News and the National Academies Science in the Headlines.   **CW**

> Project 2061 promotes literacy in science, mathematics, and technology in order to help people live interesting, responsible, and productive lives. In a culture increasingly pervaded by science, mathematics, and technology, science literacy requires understandings and habits of mind that enable citizens to grasp what those enterprises are up to, to make some sense of how the natural and designed worlds work, to think critically and independently, to recognize and weigh alternative explanations of events and design trade offs, and to deal sensibly with problems that involve evidence, numbers, patterns, logical arguments, and uncertainties. (p. XI)

All children need a rich array of firsthand experiences to grow toward a full measure of science literacy. Quality science programs make it possible for advanced study, which can

Standards Link

Science Program Equity Standard

All students in the K–12 science program must have equitable access to opportunities to achieve the *National Science Education Standards*.

(Program Standard E, National Research Council, 1996, p. 221.)

lead to many occupational choices and benefits for all society. An important area related to societal considerations is equity as suggested by the NRC Program Equity Standard.

Equity

Think for a moment about what the world would be like if women cultivated half of the technological developments. What advances would be made? What current problems would be minimized? What if minorities developed an equivalent proportion of scientific discoveries? How might the world be different? Some estimates indicate that 85% or more of the workforce is composed of minorities, persons with disabilities, and women (e.g., Florence, 1992). How is this new workforce affecting science?

Current science education reforms promote scientific literacy for all students—or equity—as their central theme (AAAS, 1998). The belief is that science should be comprehensible, accessible, and exciting for all students from kindergarten through grade 12. In reality, these goals are rarely achieved, especially for underrepresented populations. The National Science Foundation (NSF, 1996) reports the typical pattern indicates that males score higher than females and white students score higher than black or Hispanic students on national assessments.

Science has long been studied in the traditions of the white, Anglo-Saxon male. This focus makes it difficult for females or minorities to place science in an understandable social context. Think about a living scientist. Is this person male or female? Is this a person of color or white? What does this person look like? Stop for a moment and consider your image of a scientist. Is your image stereotypical?

Teaching Tips You can begin to remediate stereotypical images by bringing local minority and female scientists into the classroom.

Children often view a scientist as a white male with a lab coat, a pocket protector full of pencils, and unkempt hair—a nerd with glasses. This view furthers the problem of equity. Not only do most boys not want to be this "scientist," but also what woman or minority would want to be perceived as this image? As a teacher, you will probably pass your views of a scientist on to your students. Make sure that your view is consistent with the diverse group represented in the scientific community. View your children as scientists, too. This further ensures equity since your curriculum is based on your children's experiences as "scientists." Equity can even become a function of the diversity of the children that you teach, because your classroom will have children of mixed gender and cultural backgrounds.

The Language of Science

Another way to help correct the imbalance of science achievement is to think about how science is taught at the elementary level. If science is just rote learning of disjointed facts, it becomes an especially difficult enterprise for minorities who do not have a strong command of the language. It is no wonder that these students do not elect to take more than the required minimum of science courses as they go on to high school. It's surprising that every student is not eventually turned off by this language-intensive, fact-only approach.

In an attempt to help students understand the "language" of the scientist, the National Science Teachers Association published *The Language of Science* (Mandell, 1974, p. 1). The author of this book equates the language of science to a foreign language and stresses the importance of knowing the language in order to be a participant in the science classroom. Along these lines, Gallas (1995) discusses why "science talk" is so important for children and why teachers need to help them develop the language of science. Lemke (1990) states:

> It is not surprising that those who succeed in science tend to be like those who define the "appropriate" way to talk science: male rather than female, white rather than black, middle- and upper-middle-class, native English speakers, standard dialect speakers, committed to the values of Northern European middle-class culture. (p. 138)

What Mandell, Gallas, Lemke, and many other authors are saying is that teachers need to understand that the language of science is often a barrier to equity in the classroom.

Another major consideration in the development of a quality elementary or middle school science program is the matter of gender equity. As an educator, it will be your responsibility to select science textbooks, teaching materials, and methodologies that present realistic role models for men and women in all walks of life. In addition to arranging for female role models to visit your classroom, you may want to try assigning student biographies of famous female scientists. The importance of this issue cannot be understated as we go into an era where we will need a growing number of science and technology professionals who are women.

The current science literacy problem that exists in many minority populations may be a forewarning of an increasing science literacy problem with all students. Your contribution in the classroom will have a major impact on the types of career decisions your students make.

> One way to become a better teacher is to investigate your own teaching. See the "Teacher as Researcher" Links on the Companion Website for more information.
> CW

Summary

- The nature of science suggests that (1) there is no single set or sequence of steps in a scientific investigation; (2) scientific knowledge is subject to change; (3) scientific knowledge must be at least partially supported by empirical evidence; (4) scientific knowledge is partially the product of the creative imagination of the scientist; (5) given the importance of scientists' individual creativity, scientific knowledge is necessarily subjective to some degree; and (6) scientific knowledge is a product of both observation and inference.
- Scientists use tools and organized ways to search for patterns in objects and events. They generalize the

data they collect and form explanations in the form of principles, theories, and laws. Elementary and middle school students can construct and refine their own concepts by using similar methods.

- Children need to experience the processes of science by making observations, interacting with objects, testing hypotheses, working with data, and experimenting.
- An interrelationship exists between science and society. It is important to understand the roles of women and minorities in the scientific enterprise as you plan and facilitate science lessons.

Reflection

Companion CD

1. Based on your understanding of the nature of science, what changes would you make to the "Importance of Food and Nutrients" lesson linked to the *Child as Scientist* video on the Companion CD?

2. Look at the "Earthworm's Cousin—Espinal" lesson linked to the *Questioning* video on the Companion CD. Identify any misconceptions you may have had about worms based on this lesson. Would your students have similar misconceptions?

3. Look at the "What Is Anatomy" lesson linked to the *Science as Inquiry* video on the Companion CD. What generalizations can be made about earthworms, humans, or other animals with respect to the digestive, reproductive, circulatory, respiratory, muscular, and skeletal systems?

Portfolio Ideas

1. One way to begin exploring how you will teach elementary or middle school science is to investigate your attitudes toward science. Do you feel science is exciting, rewarding, and fun or monotonous, boring, and discouraging? Is it important or trivial? Were your science experiences inclusive or exclusive of certain populations? If you have time, compare your attitudes with those of your parents, friends, or study partner and record these in your portfolio.

2. In your portfolio, record your memories of elementary science experiences. Which of these experiences are hands-on activities that promote the nature of science and scientific understanding? Which are entertainment, show-and-tell, or memorization activities? Be ready to share with others the implications of why you would remember one experience more than another, or which have helped more with later science experiences.

3. Observe an elementary or middle school science class at your practicum site and note how the teacher provides equity in terms of gender. Does the teacher call on boys more than girls? Are the boys dominating the experiments? Are the girls afraid to answer questions or provide explanations? Think of ways to promote equity in your classroom, and share these ideas in your portfolio.

4. Use the resource *Multicultural Women of Science: Three Centuries of Contributions* (Harris-Stewart, 1996) to enhance your own understanding of the contributions of multicultural women to the field of science. This book contains many hands-on activities. An increasing number of other related resources are available for use with your students. The books *From Sorceress to Scientist: Biographies of Women Physical Scientists* (Nies, 1990) and *From Priestess to Physician: Biographies of Women Life Scientists* (Nies, 1996) include biographies, demonstrations, and lab activities. Use aids from these two books to help promote positive female role models with your practicum class and future elementary or middle school students. Record ideas in your portfolio.

5. *Teaching About Evolution and the Nature of Science* (National Academy of Sciences, 1998) is available online (*http://books.nap.edu/html/evolution98/*) and includes activities that relate to the nature of science. Try some of these activities and share them through your portfolio.

References

American Association for the Advancement of Science (AAAS). (1989). *Science for all Americans*. Washington, DC: Author.

American Association for the Advancement of Science (AAAS). (1993). *Benchmarks for science literacy*. New York: Oxford University Press.

American Association for the Advancement of Science (AAAS). (1998). *Blueprints for reform*. New York: Oxford University Press.

Chinery, M. (1991). *Life story: Ant*. New York: Troll Associates.

Climo, S. (1995). *The little red ant and the great big crumb: A Mexican fable*. New York: Clarion Books.

Cole, J. (1996). *The magic school bus gets ants in its pants*. New York: Scholastic.

Council for Environmental Education. (1992). *Project WILD*. Bethesda, MD: Author.

Demuth, P. D. (1994). *Those amazing ants*. New York: Simon & Schuster.

Dorros, A. (1987). *Ant cities*. New York: HarperCollins.

Florence, P. (1992). *Northwest women in science: Women making a difference—a role model guide*. Richland, WA: Northwest College and University Association for Science, Northwest Women in Science.

Gallas, K. (1995). *Talking their way into science: Hearing children's questions and theories, responding with curricula*. New York: Teachers College Press.

Gazlay, S. (1998). *Field detectives: Investigating playground habitats*. Fresno, CA: AIMS Education Foundation.

Harris-Stewart, C. (Ed.). (1996). *Multicultural Women of Science*. Maywood, NJ: The Peoples Publishing Press.

Hepworth, C. (1992). *Antics!* Los Angeles: Putnam & Grosset.

Hoose, P. M., Tilley, D., & Hoose, H. (1998). *Hey little ant*. Berkeley, CA: Tricycle Press.

Imes, R. (1992). *The practical entomologist*. New York: Simon & Schuster.

Lawrence Hall of Science. (1996). *Ant homes under the ground*. Berkeley, CA: Author.

Lederman, N. G. (1992). Students' and teachers' conceptions of the nature of science: A review of research. *Journal of Research in Science Teaching, 29*, 331–359.

Lemke, J. L. (1990). *Talking science: Language learning and values*. Norwood, NJ: Ablex.

Losi, C. A. (1997). *The 512 ants on Sullivan Street*. New York: Scholastic.

Mandell, A. (1974). *The language of science*. Arlington, VA: National Science Teachers Association.

Most, B. (1980). *There's an ant in Anthony*. New York: Mulberry Books.

National Academy of Sciences. (1998). *Teaching about evolution and the nature of science*. Washington, DC: National Academy Press.

National Research Council (NRC). (1996). *National science education standards*. Washington, DC: National Academy Press.

National Science Foundation (NSF). (1996). *The learning curve*. Washington, DC: Author.

National Science Teachers Association (NSTA). (2004). *Scientific inquiry. A position statement*. Washington, DC: Author. Retrieved October 1, 2004, from www.nsta.org/positionstatement&psid=43

Nies, K. A., (1990). *From Sorceress to Scientist and Biographies of Women Physical Scientists*. Tarzana, CA: California Video Institute.

Nies, K. A. (1996). From *Priestess to Physician: Biographics of Woman Life Scientists*. Tarzana, CA: California Video Institute.

Parker, S. (1999). *It's an ant's life*. Pleasantville, NY: Reader's Digest.

Pinczes, E. (1993). *One hundred hungry ants*. Boston: Houghton Mifflin.

Pinczes, E. (1995). *A remainder of one*. Boston: Houghton Mifflin.

Steiner, T. J. (1998). *A bug's life*. Burbank, CA: Mouse Works.

Teacher Created Materials. (1997). *Thematic unit: Ants*. Huntington, CA: Author.

Suggested Readings

Alcoze, T., Bradley, C., Hernandez, J., Kashima, T., Kane, I. M., & Madrazo, G. (1993). *Multi-culturalism in mathematics, science, and technology: Readings and activities*. Menlo Park, CA: Addison-Wesley. (a teacher resource for exploring many cultures and global perspectives)

American Association for the Advancement of Science (AAAS). (1993). The nature of science. In *Benchmarks for science literacy* (pp. 3–21). New York: Oxford University Press. (explores the nature of science in the context of various grade levels)

Barr, B. B. (1994). Research on problem solving: Elementary school. In D. L. Gable (Ed.), *Handbook of research on science teaching and learning* (pp. 237–247). New York: Macmillan. (problem-solving research to apply to future teaching)

Dunbar, R. (1995). *The trouble with science*. Cambridge, MA: Harvard University Press. (a history of science and the nature of science)

Hatton, J., & Plouffe, P. B. (1997). *Science and its ways of knowing*. Upper Saddle River, NJ: Prentice Hall. (a collection of essays showing the relationships between fact and theory and the nature of science)

National Research Council (NRC). (1998). *Every child a scientist: Achieving scientific literacy for all*. Washington, DC: National Academy Press.

National Research Council (NRC). (1999). *Selecting instructional materials: A guide for K–12 science*. Washington, DC: National Academy Press.

National Research Council (NRC). (2000). *Inquiry and the national science education standards*. Washington, DC: National Academy Press.

National Science Resources Center, National Academy of Sciences, Smithsonian Institution. (1997). *Science for all children: A guide to improving science education in your school district*. Washington, DC: National Academy Press. (a comprehensive book on how science education can be changed at the elementary and middle school level)

CHAPTER 2

CONSTRUCTING SCIENCE EXPERIENCES

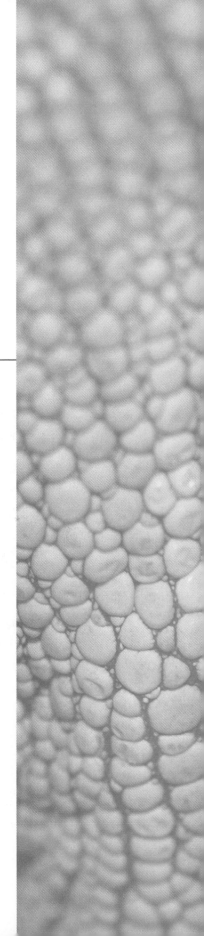

FOCUS QUESTIONS

- What is a paradigm for science learning?
- What is meant by constructivism and how do children construct knowledge?
- How do Piaget and Vygotsky provide the theoretical foundation for constructivism?
- What is meant by a constructivist approach to teaching?
- How can the constructivist learning model be integrated into your planning?

Focus on Inquiry

How Do Children Learn?

Dr. Ken Tobin,
The Graduate Center of City University of New York

"Hold it! Hold it! Oh, no! Ana, you've got to hold it while I connect the roof on." Michael is agitated with Ana. They have been working on building a castle for 3 days now, and still the walls will not stay up. They planned to build a castle that had strong walls and two stories. Their drawings looked good but the materials Ms. Roberts had given them to build their castle with were not working.

Losing confidence in their ability to succeed, Ana is feeling grumpy about this whole activity. The walls will not stay up. Every time she holds them up, the sewing pins connecting the straws come loose. Why can't they use glue anyway? "Castles are not made out of pins and straws!" she asserts.

Ana and Michael's teacher, Ms. Roberts, is pleased with the castle-building activity. The students are busy and they are doing science. The activities she has planned for students engage them in the use of manipulatives, problem solving, an opportunity to exchange ideas, and the ability to integrate writing, social studies, and literature. The idea of building castles arose from the class's study of Germany. Most importantly, students are engaged in problem solving. Ms. Roberts perceives her role to be that of a facilitator: closely observing her students, listening to their ideas, and offering support to help them meet their goal of building castles.

Teachers like Ms. Roberts have long accepted that a hands-on approach is an appropriate way to teach science. Recently the term *hands-on/minds-on* has become a popular way to describe school science. Ms. Roberts's grade 3 science lesson is typical of what can be observed in many elementary classrooms. The activity is consistent with a hands-on/-minds-on metaphor and the teacher's role as facilitator. Problematic, however, is that even though Ms. Roberts's students are involved in an extensive hands-on activity that promotes communication and problem solving, the development of scientific ideas is absent.

Problem solving as a way to engage students in constructing their own understanding of science concepts must be connected to specific science learning goals. Scientific knowledge does not reside in the materials students use. Rather, scientific knowledge needs to be co-constructed in interactions in which students and teacher converse verbally, using a shared language during the activity. For example, the realization that a structure can be made rigid through the use of triangular braces is a reasonable goal for the activity described. In this castle activity, however, it is unlikely that Ms. Roberts's students will construct that understanding. Even if some students include triangular braces in their structures, it is unlikely that they will associate that inclusion with increased rigidity of the structures they are trying to build. Manipulation of materials is a context for rich conversations in which those who know science can facilitate the learning of those who do not know. It is essential to student understanding and quality science instruction that the teacher mediate the language of the child and the language of science. This does not imply a return to the days when teachers transmitted facts in lectures with prescribed language, but it does require engagement in problem-solving experiences that promote conversation. Student understanding is facilitated when students talk science in ways that connect their experiences with other subject areas. It is at this point that students will begin to see the relevance science plays in their lives both in and outside of school.

SCIENCE LEARNING

Teaching is seen as the actions or methods used by an educator to create an environment that will promote learning by students.

Learning is a process by which students' knowledge, attitudes, behaviors, and beliefs are formulated or modified.

Think back to your elementary school experiences. Was **teaching** viewed as a class reading of the textbook, a daily student worksheet, a predetermined outcome type of activity, or a lecture where the teacher handed down the "body of knowledge"? Was your **learning** about scientific ideas and concepts the focus of your classes? Or, consistent with the science inquiry standard, did your teacher actively engage you in seeking new knowledge, team you up with others to help one another learn, and guide you by emphasizing scientific understanding and inquiry? Were your scientific understandings useful in other situations, both in school and outside school? Answering these questions provides you an indication of a teaching perspective and a perspective of how children can learn science more effectively.

Effective science learning is crucial for your future elementary and middle school students. Today's global society is experiencing explosive changes in scientific knowledge and the application of scientific knowledge in the form of technology (National Science Teachers Association [NSTA], 2003). Predictions once indicated that the total amount of knowledge doubles every 18 months or less and that 80% of the scientists who have ever lived are alive right now (Petersen, 1994, 1997). Current studies show that stored information grows so rapidly that in 2002 alone, print, film, magnetic, and optical storage media produced about 5 exabytes of new information (School of Information Management and Systems University of California at Berkeley, 2003). In perspective, 5 exabytes is equivalent to the information contained in 37,000 new libraries the size of the Library of Congress

Standards Link

Science Inquiry Standard

As a result of activities in grades K–8, all students should develop

- **Abilities necessary to do scientific inquiry**

- **Understandings about scientific inquiry**

(Content Standard A, National Research Council, 1996, pp. 121, 143.)

book collections. We are in the information age and to be able to utilize this ever-growing pool of information, our students will need to know how to access and apply this information in meaningful ways.

The science experiences you provide will develop the foundation your students need to continue meaningful learning experiences throughout their lives. Thus, a first step to successful science teaching is to consider your own views of science and science learning.

Paradigms

> Teachers should be aware that science is not just a body of knowledge but a paradigm through which to see the world. (American Association for the Advancement of Science [AAAS], 1998, p. 202)

Take a moment to think about how you currently view the nature of science and science learning. Is it different now from when you were in elementary school? If so, what changed your viewpoint? Maybe you are science phobic because of past experiences. If you are, then what could have been done differently to dispel your fear of science? What influences how science is currently taught and how you will teach science? The current paradigm for teaching and learning science is seen as integral to helping students better realize the nature of science and the value of understanding science concepts. This new paradigm is leading educational reform.

Understanding Paradigms

Where did the idea of paradigms begin? Thomas Kuhn (1962) first defined a **paradigm** as a commonly accepted viewpoint. He defined a *paradigm shift* as a radical change in this viewpoint. For example, the paradigm of a sun-centered solar system replaced the paradigm of the earth-centered solar system. Paradigm shifts occur because scientists use experimentation and new technologies to better explain observed scientific phenomena.

Scientific discussion, experimentation, and publication generally center on current paradigms. Deviating from the paradigm is apt to place a scientist's research funding and acceptance of publications in jeopardy. Ideas that are inconsistent with current paradigms are generally dismissed. Occasionally, however, because of advances in technology or new research, a paradigm shift and an accompanying revolution in the scientific community occur. Old ideas are discarded as a new theory emerges and becomes the dominant paradigm. An example is the presentation of the plate tectonics theory in 1956. Scientists explaining this theory discussed how continental land masses were resting on a small number of "plates" or semirigid sections of the earth's crust. Earthquakes and volcanoes occur primarily at the margins of these sections as the plates drift together, apart, or alongside each other. The plate tectonics theory changed how scientists viewed the movement of continents and seafloor spreading. Even as paradigms in science change our perspectives and understanding of how the world works, they also transcend science education and our understanding of how to better teach science.

Paradigms of Science Education

Looking at the research related to the National Science Education Standards of the National Research Council (NRC, 1996) and Project 2061 of the American Association for the Advancement of Science (AAAS, 1993), we find that **constructivism** is the current

Paradigm is a typical viewpoint or ideal example that provides a model for all related processes or systems.

Constructivism is an approach to teaching based on research about how people learn. Many researchers say that each individual constructs knowledge rather than receiving it from others. Constructive teaching is based on the belief that students learn best when they gain knowledge through exploration and active learning. Hands-on materials are used instead of textbooks, and students are encouraged to think and explain their reasoning instead of memorizing and reciting facts. Education is centered on themes and concepts and the connections between them, rather than isolated information. (McBrien & Brandt, 1997)

Standards Link

Science Teaching and Learning Standard

Teachers of science guide and facilitate learning. In doing this, teachers

- Focus and support inquiries while interacting with students.

- Orchestrate discourse among students about scientific ideas.

- Challenge students to accept and share responsibility for their own learning.

- Recognize and respond to student diversity and encourage all students to participate fully in science learning.

- Encourage and model the skills of scientific inquiry, as well as the curiosity, openness to new ideas and data, and skepticism that characterize science.

(Teaching Standard B, National Research Council, 1996, p. 3.)

Inquiry is a term used to describe the activities that students engage in to help them construct knowledge and understanding of scientific ideas.

paradigm in science education. This paradigm supports inquiry teaching and is reflected in the Science Teaching and Learning Standard in the Standards Link.

The authors of the Science Teaching and Learning Standard provide a research-based explanation of how children engage in inquiry to construct personal knowledge and learn science. They underscore the need for teachers to guide and facilitate learning in science and to provide inquiry experiences for their students. They also emphasize the importance of student discourse.

You will notice that **inquiry** is a strand throughout the Science Teaching and Learning Standard, as it is throughout the standards document. Figure 2–1 contains characteristics of classroom inquiry.

As you read about different perspectives of teaching and learning science in this chapter, consider the ability of each perspective to support scientific inquiry as outlined in Figure 2–1.

Children's Learning and Your Classroom

Pause for a moment and contemplate yourself teaching science in an elementary or middle school classroom. What methods will you employ to be consistent with the standards? Will the continuous need to infuse science and technology in your curriculum make it impossible for you to teach science as you learned it in school? Will you be able to engage students effectively in understanding science?

Thinking about and sharing your viewpoints related to the questions and statements presented here may bring about many new questions. As you continue to read and reflect on this chapter, you will come to understand constructivism and inquiry. You will see why constructivism has emerged as the paradigm for the construction of knowledge in science education.

Figure 2–1   **Essential features of classroom inquiry.**

- Learners are engaged by scientifically oriented questions.
- Learners give priority to evidence, which allows them to develop and evaluate explanations that address scientifically oriented questions.
- Learners formulate explanations from evidence to address scientifically oriented questions.
- Learners evaluate their explanations in light of alternative explanations, particularly those reflecting scientific understanding.
- Learners communicate and justify their proposed explanations.

Source: From *Inquiry and the National Science Education Standards: A Guide for Teaching and Learning* (p. 25). Copyright © 2000 by the National Academy of Sciences. Courtesy of the National Academy Press, Washington, DC.

CONSTRUCTIVISM

What does it mean to know?
What does it mean to be a knower?
Is there a relationship between the knower and the known?

These questions may be too philosophical for you at first glance. They are, however, at the heart of the constructivist-learning paradigm. The knower–known relationship is also the basis for the current reform movement in education. This movement emphasizes *the active role of the learner* as constructing her own knowledge. It also places the teacher in a more facilitative role in the learning process.

Those who adhere to the constructivist paradigm hold the belief that all knowledge is constructed by an individual, not passed on from the teacher to the student (Driver, 1995; McBrien & Brandt, 1997; Tobin & Tippins, 1993). Using constructivism as a referent for science teaching maximizes student learning, because the teacher's role is to *facilitate* the learning process, as opposed to transferring knowledge. The teacher's purpose is to provide the best materials and learning situations to make learning individually meaningful for each student. Students change in some way as a result of the learning. They may replace a prior belief about a science concept, add to their existing knowledge, or modify something they already know. The learning, or construction, takes place in a context of what learners already have in their own mental store.

Cobern (1993) likens the constructivist approach to a construction site where existing structures are the foundation upon which to build new knowledge. To get a better idea of constructivism in general, study the following teaching example. As you think about the

Visit an Inquiry Classroom
Inquiry Learning

View the *Four Days of Science* video in the "Model Inquiry Unit" section of the Companion CD. Note the constructivist approach to teaching and learning, and that the inquiry seen in the video involves a *learner-centered* process. The once popular listen-to-learn paradigm of the classroom has been replaced with an inquiry approach. You will see a process of exploring the world that leads to asking children questions and their making discoveries in the search for new understandings.

Review the video and ask yourself the following:
- Are the children passive or active in the video?
- What specific indicators are they learning?
- What evidence is there that Mr. McKnight is probing the students' understandings of earthworms?
- What evidence is there that the children are learning?

Go to the Companion Website's Web Destinations for Chapter 2 and look at the *Field Guide to Earthworms* from NatureWatch at the *http://www.naturewatch.ca/ english/ wormwatch/about/guide/intro.html* link. Students could also learn about earthworms through this medium. Compare and contrast Mr. McKnight's and NatureWatch's approaches to learning about earthworms. Would Nature-Watch's approach also be considered a constructivist approach to teaching and learning? Record your ideas and the answers to these questions in your portfolio or use the Companion Website to share your ideas.

example, ask yourself, "Will this activity provide a meaningful learning experience for the students?" or "How will the children learn?"

A General Constructivist Approach to Teaching

Ms. Terrell, a fourth-grade teacher, refers to the K–4 Earth and Space Content Standard D (see Standards Link), to develop this lesson objective: "The students will discover the observable changes in the moon as it travels across the sky over the coming months." As she prepares for the phases of the moon activity, she asks the students what they have observed in relation to the moon as it appears in the sky.

Ms. Terrell then asks the students to assemble a science journal with blank pages. Today there is a new moon, and she instructs students to look at the moon each day or night, as it becomes visible. Students should date each journal page and draw and describe the moon as they observe it in the sky. Each day, they will compare their pictures with one another and with the predictions they find on the Internet and in the newspaper. They will also explore children's books such as *The Moon Seems to Change* (Branley, 1987) and *Day Light, Night Light* (Branley, 1975). At the end of this exploration period, Ms. Terrell will have the students discuss what they found out and generate ideas about this phenomenon.

To test students' ideas, Ms. Terrell brings in a homemade **astronomy dome.** Her instruction with the class about this subject takes place from inside the dome. There, she has one student hold up a spotlight to indicate the sun. Other students hold up a model earth (basketball) and moon (tennis ball). Together, they replicate the motions of the earth, the sun, and the moon. They demonstrate what happened throughout the month as the moon circled the earth. Ms. Terrell asks the students to explain what is going on and whether this matches their moon drawings. As an informal assessment, students shade in a series of blank circles that represent moon images as the sun would light them. Finally, the class discusses the vocabulary associated with the phases of the moon.

As you may infer from this constructivist-based lesson, students learn the material in a context that they can understand. They will readily recall the information in the future and apply the processes they learned in this and other situations.

Students have observed the process of the **waxing** and **waning** of the moon and recorded it in illustrations. (See Inquiry Unit 12, "Moon Phases," for an activity and related concepts.) The terms, such as *new, full, crescent, quarter,* and *gibbous,* as well as processes such as observation of the earth–moon–sun interactions, make sense because this relevant context is provided. The learners engage in activities that relate to their own previous experiences. To better understand constructivism, let us look at early influences on research that led us to a constructivist approach to teaching and learning.

Standards Link

K–4 Earth and Space Content Standard D

As a result of their activities in grades K–4, all students should develop an understanding of

- **Properties of earth materials**
- **Objects in the sky**
- **Changes in the earth and sky**

(K–4 Earth and Space Content Standard D, National Research Council, 1996, p. 130.)

An **astronomy dome** is made from black painter's plastic taped on the side with box tape to form a "dome." The 20-foot by 100-foot sheet can be cut to fit the available classroom space. A box fan is taped to one end to inflate the dome, and the other end is sealed shut. A class of 25 students can sit inside the dark dome. Other versions use cardboard and binder clips (see *http://www.cccoe.net/stars/*). Also see the Companion Website for teaching ideas in the dome.

Waxing   refers to increasing in size.

Waning   refers to decreasing in size.

THEORETICAL FOUNDATIONS FOR CONSTRUCTIVIST TEACHING

The 18th-century work of the Neapolitan philosopher Giambattista Vico was an early form of constructivism, in that he believed humans can clearly understand only what they have themselves constructed. Contemporary constructivism has its origins with John Dewey, who theorized that education depends on action. Dewey believed that knowledge and ideas emerge from a situation in which learners draw them out of experiences of meaning and importance (see Dewey, 1966). Dewey saw learning as occurring in a social context where students manipulate materials, thus creating a community of learners building their knowledge together. Today, constructivism is a broad-based theory about learning that includes such areas as the *cognitive* constructivism associated with Jean Piaget and the *sociocultural* constructivism linked with Lev Vygotsky.

Piaget and Cognition

Often viewed as an early constructivist, Jean Piaget focused his research on children's construction of knowledge through **equilibration** (Bettencourt, 1993; Bybee & Sund, 1990). Piaget's theory involves mediating mental processes for mental cognition (Labinowicz, 1980). To understand these processes, it is important to understand the notion of a schema.

Equilibration is a process by which a learner compensates for a mental dilemma and constructs new knowledge.

Schemata

A **schema** is viewed as a concept, pattern of action, theory, model, or idea that is part of our cognitive repertoire. Schemata (the plural of *schema*) are "meaningful units" that are used repeatedly (Henriques, 1990, p. 143). Schemata can be specific, sequential, or elaborate and often involve an entire network of context-specific bodies of knowledge that learners apply to specific situations. For example, we may have a "hammering" schemata. At the novice level, this involves identification of the tool (e.g., scheme of a hammer) and how to use it to pound a nail (e.g., schemata of striking the nail). At an expert level, it may involve knowledge of explicit types of hammers for specific uses (e.g., claw, roofing, ball-peen, finishing, tack, brick, drywall), understanding of the numerous types of nails (e.g., common, box, finishing, flooring, concrete, wallboard, roofing), and advanced techniques for driving in the nails (e.g., using more wrist than elbow and more elbow than shoulder for good rhythm, toenailing to join studs, spacing of reroof nailing to prevent wind damage).

Schema is a cognitive framework used to store and organize information such as knowledge and experiences.

Schemata become relevant as we need them. They help us function on a daily basis and deal with new experiences. For schemata to be effective, they need the capability to be modified to fit new experiences through the processes of **assimilation** and **accommodation.** We assimilate when we adjust our schemata to include new details; we try to transform incoming information so that it fits with our existing way of thinking (Siegler, 1986). Accommodation means restructuring our schemata so that we can make sense of situations.

Assimilation can be seen as the way we adapt new information into existing mental structures so that our minds can seek equilibration.

An example of assimilation is when a child has a schema that involves birds such as robins, sparrows, and pigeons. When the child sees a new type of bird, like an osprey or hawk, she may need to adjust the schema to assimilate the new information of a much larger bird that is flying overhead. Later, if the child sees a penguin or an ostrich at the zoo, assimilation may not be as useful. This new information includes birds that do not fly. The child may not be able to simply assimilate the new information. Now the child must adapt her way of thinking to new experiences (Siegler, 1986). This process is called accommodation, because the schema can now accommodate the new information.

Accommodation is a circumstance where no preexisting mental structures are available for assimilation and children must adapt their own mental structures to accommodate new information.

The result of the accommodation is that the child's schema can now accept birds that fly and birds that do not fly. Equilibration is primary to children's construction of reality, as it involves both assimilation and accommodation. It is the overall interaction between existing ways of thinking and a new experience (Siegler, 1986). For example, with the phases of the moon activity, the students may not have known that the moon reflects light. Their schema may have been that all objects in the night sky give off light. Certainly assimilation and accommodation are useful in resolving this **disequilibrium.**

In general, Piaget sees cognitive development as resolving the disequilibrium that may exist in the child's mind. In his theory of development, equilibration, through assimilation and accommodation, is the foundation for significant developmental changes in the child. What does this say to us as future teachers? We can assist children in building their neural connections. To better understand how, it is helpful to take into consideration Piaget's stages of children's cognitive development.

Piaget's Stages of Development

Piaget developed his theory based on his observations and studies regarding scientific conceptions of children. With this, Piaget proposed stages in the development of thought at different ages. The three stages that elementary teachers are most concerned with are the preoperational stage, from about 2 to 7 years old; concrete operational stage, from about 7 to 12 years old; and the formal operational stage, from about 12 years old and beyond (see Appendix E).

Children who are preoperational are not yet able to do the kind of thinking Piaget calls **operations,** or mental tasks. The latter part of the stage, which lasts from about ages 4 to 7, is known as the *intuitive thought substage*. Because this is the time when most children begin school, we start our study of children's thinking at the intuitive period of their mental development.

"Intuitive thought" describes how 4- to 7-year-olds think. They typically use their sense impressions or intuition rather than logic in forming judgments. They also tend to remember only one thing at a time. A common activity to demonstrate intuitive thought is to have a child roll out a ball of clay and then to ask the child about what happened. Children at this stage will suggest that there is "more clay" because it is rolled out and appears longer.

Children who are concrete operational, in contrast, are logical thinkers, but the ideas they consider must be tied to concrete materials they can manipulate. They must have some firsthand experience with the materials to think about them. Specific examples, models, and detailed explanations are needed with concrete operational children.

In the stage of formal operations, older children are able to think much more abstractly. They have far less need to refer to concrete objects. This stage generally occurs after elementary or middle school. It is considered the summit of cognitive development because students can handle formal logic and abstract reasoning.

A Piagetian Approach to Teaching

Returning to Ms. Terrell's students, they are not yet at the formal operations stage. Their teacher is engaging them in concrete activities during which they are actually manipulating materials versus thinking about them abstractly as they will later do in the formal operations stage. In class, the children are building a "moon phaser" with a paper dial, downloaded from the Internet. They will use the moon phaser to predict when the next full and new moons will occur and to study related terms. Ms. Terrell's objectives for the students are as follows:

1. Locate the horizon and zenith with their moon phaser.
2. Determine the current moon phase.

Disequilibrium   is when a child's conception of a thing or event is no longer adequate and the child seeks to establish a balance through assimilation and accommodation.

Operation,   as described in this textbook, is a mental action such as adding numbers or classifying objects.

To better understand the preoperations and concrete operations stages, see the related activities for Chapter 2 at the *http://www.prenhall. com/peters* website.

3. Find the moon's approximate position in the sky for a given date and time.
4. Determine the approximate time of moonrise and moonset for eight moon phases.

This activity meets all of these objectives and appears to be at an appropriate developmental level for her students. Because her students have never used a device like the moon phaser, Ms. Terrell anticipates that they will be very active assimilating and accommodating new information. Later, her students will apply the information from this activity as they work with balls and flashlights to re-create the phases of the moon in a different way.

Throughout the stages of development, concrete activities play an important role in the process of cognitive growth. Assimilation, accommodation, and equilibration all require thought processes. As teachers, we must facilitate learning that keeps the mind active, as we see done with the moon activity (particularly when students are unable to manipulate "real" space objects such as in space science activities). We also need to keep in mind that reality is something children construct from their own actions. It is not something waiting to be found or discovered (Piaget, 1954; Piaget & Inhelder, 1969).

Go to *http://www.prenhal.com/peters* for links related to resources for a lesson on moon phases and earth and space science sites.

But is it solely a teacher's activities that cause children's development and construction of meaning? What other factors or influences may come into play in children's development, such as social or cultural influences? Some theorists believe that culture and social exchange are important in the knowledge development process.

Vygotsky and Social Constructivism

Is the role of others important to our learning? Lev Vygotsky's sociocultural constructivist theory involves the role of culture and society. Vygotsky believed that behavior must be studied in a social and historical context, giving rise to the term *sociohistorical*. Vygotsky theorized that children do not simply reproduce what is said or shown to them, rather they undergo socially mediated cognitive constructions.

See *http://www.prenhall.com/peters* for additional information on Vygotsky.

Vygotsky was born in the same year as Piaget. Although he died at the age of 38 and was not well known in the United States, English translations of his more than 180 writ-

Visit an Inquiry Classroom
Social Learning

View the *Social Learning* video in the "Constructivist Pedagogy" section of the Companion CD. The video shows a group of students huddled around computers viewing content and online movies about earthworms. The students are exchanging ideas and information.

Review the video and ask yourself the following:
- Many educators believe that children learn from other children at least as well or better than they learn from the teacher. What evidence is there on the video segment to support or refute this claim?
- What is the teacher's role in social learning?

Recall a lesson that you have observed in your field placement. Was there an exchange between students? Was it similar to what was seen with Mr. McKnight's class? Did this social interaction promote learning? Explain your answer in terms of Vygotsky's sociocultural constructivist theory. Record your ideas and the answers to these questions in your portfolio or use the Companion Website to share your ideas.

Children look at the
moon as it appears in
space to help construct
understandings of the
phases of the moon.

ten works indicate that Vygotsky understood an important facet of cognitive development. For Vygotsky, cognitive development is a matter of an individual's social interaction within the environment (Vygotsky, 1978).

Vygotsky Versus Piaget

How does Vygotsky compare to Piaget? Although both theorists believed that learners construct their own knowledge, the two theories held a major difference. Piaget was a developmental constructivist and saw development as leading learning, which he described in his stages of development. Piaget emphasized the child's internal thinking processes. Vygotsky, however, saw learning as leading development. Students who are engaged in learning **spontaneous concepts** with their peers later restructure these same concepts into **scientific concepts** within their own cognitive structures. In other words, a concept such as "light" begins in an informal social setting as children talk about light and darkness (e.g., a child telling her peers that she thinks she needs a nightlight because her bedroom is too dark). Later, through time and repeated use, this concept and related spontaneous concepts become better organized in the child's cognitive structure as a more systematic "scientific concept." The child will better understand the nature of light and be able to apply this concept as needed to make sense of her world (e.g., light sources penetrate the dark because of the movement of electromagnetic waves).

Spontaneous concepts
are acquired informally from
everyday life experiences.

Scientific concepts
are represented by a
systematically organized body
of knowledge and are usually
learned through formal
instruction.

Social Construction of Scientific Concepts

According to Vygotsky (1986), as a child grows, words begin to take on meaning and communication begins to develop. The child finds names for objects; and informal, spontaneous concepts begin to develop as a result of verbal exchange with others. These concepts are often vague and tend to be illogical and unsystematic, but they are further developed through the use of **psychological tools** or signs.

Psychological tools are the culturally developed signs used in mental and social activities; examples are letters, words, numbers, speech, and pictures.

Using Psychological Tools and Semantic Mediation

Psychological tools are used like the tools that any craftsperson uses to perform tasks better. Psychological tools, as mental tools, allow us to improve our communication and to adapt to our environment. They can be either external or internal. Writing notes in a notebook is an example of an external psychological tool; these notes help to augment the mind's capacity. Internal psychological tools, such as the formulas and rhymes we call mnemonic devices, also assist in mental development.

Signs, as a kind of mental tool, assist in regulating our thinking and are part of Vygotsky's theory. For instance, if we write a note and stick it to the refrigerator or if we place a name in an appointment book, we are creating a sign. These activities help us remember important dates or information. Vygotsky's term **semantic mediation** refers to how we, as humans, use tools and signs to assist us in remembering. Mental tools, such as signs, are representative of our culture and are unique to humans. All animals share mental behaviors such as attention and perception (lower or biological forms); however, semantic mediation provides a level of understanding that separates human thoughts from those of other animals. This higher order thought process is known as *cultural mental behavior,* as opposed to the *natural mental behavior* common to all animals (Vygotsky, 1981).

Semantic mediation is the transformation of lower forms of mental behavior to higher forms of mental behavior through the use of signs.

Social Collaboration

The main difference between lower biological forms and higher social forms is the shift that occurs from outside control (teacher and peer-supported activity) to self-directed (autonomous) control. Social collaboration is gradually lessened as a child takes on more responsibility for her own learning. To put it another way, the development of higher forms of mental processes occurs through a child's enculturation into society as a result of the educational process. Instruction is a principle source of the child's concepts. For Vygotsky, as for Piaget, the stages of concept development reflect a maturation process. Figure 2–2 illustrates the stages of concept development from simple labeling of objects to abstract and systemized knowledge of scientific concepts (Dixon-Krauss, 1996).

Figure 2–2 **Vygotsky's stages of concept development.**

Heaps	Child groups objects into random categories.
Complexes	Traits of objects are analyzed and concrete factual relationships among diverse objects are established.
Potential Concepts	Transition from the concrete and spontaneous to the abstract and scientific concept.
Genuine Concepts	Abstract and systematic concepts that are common to a culture.

Source: From Table 1.1, p. 12, *Vygotsky in the Classroom* by Lisbeth Dixon-Krauss. Copyright © 1996 by Longman Publishers USA. Reprinted by permission of Addison-Wesley Educational Publishers Inc.

Note the similarities and differences between the stages proposed by Vygotsky and those proposed by Piaget. You can see that Piaget focused on children's mental development as they pass through the stages of development that lead to higher learning. For Piaget, moving into higher development levels also leads to the ability for more advanced learning. Vygotsky, conversely, emphasized learning as leading development. He saw learning on a continuum of simply naming things, to developing spontaneous concepts, to refining the spontaneous concepts as scientific concepts. For Vygotsky, opportunities for learning lead to higher developmental levels.

Teachers as Mediators

Can we, as elementary or middle school science teachers, maximize learning by taking advantage of social collaboration? Is group work important in the classroom?

Vygotsky (1978) noted that when children were placed in groups that were under the guidance of an adult or when they collaborated with a more experienced peer, they could perform at levels higher than were possible when working on their own. Furthermore, what was possible in the group situation now would be possible on an individual basis later. For instance, if a child was able to complete a classification of leaves based on common properties with the assistance of a more knowledgeable classmate, this same child could later complete this classification task independently.

Social constructivists would argue that the only good kind of instruction is that which marches ahead of and leads development. Vygotsky (1962) saw instruction not as the *ripe,* finished product, but as the *ripening* product in development. So with group or teacher assistance, a child's instruction should always be slightly ahead of what was possible for that child on her own level. If the student can already complete a classification based on two properties but not on three, instruction should be directed at classifying with three properties under the guidance of the teacher or learning group. For example, a student may be able to perform a dichotomous classification of objects that are either animals or plants. This same child may not be able to classify objects that are plants, animals, or monerans.

Teaching Tips

The importance of working with others supports the use of cooperative learning in the classroom.

Zone of Proximal Development

Zone of proximal development is the gap between a child's current level of development and potential level of development when supported by collaboration with a more capable peer.

Scaffolding is when an adult first structures a learning task and then provides the dialogue needed to guide a child's successful participation in that task.

The term **zone of proximal development** indicates the difference between what a child can do with the help of a more knowledgeable person and what the child can do independently. The goal of instruction is to actively engage the student in solving problems within the zone of proximal development. The teacher's role is that of a facilitator or mediator. The teacher provides an environment where learning in the zone of proximal development is maximized. The teacher, through **scaffolding,** provides just the right amount of support to accomplish the developmental goal. Alternatively, the teacher can arrange a cooperative learning group in which another student will be the knowledgeable other.

Scaffolding and Teacher Support

The scaffolding support that a teacher provides is analogous to the scaffolding that painters use. Painters may reach many areas independently, but when they cannot reach an area on their own, painters require a scaffold to assist them in performing the task. Correspondingly, painters would not use high scaffolding to paint a baseboard or normal wall. The implication here is that the teacher should not provide more guidance than is needed for developmental support; too much support will not promote the development of independent thought in children.

Visit an Inquiry Classroom
Zone of Proximal Development

View the *Zone of Proximal Development* video in the "Constructivist Pedagogy" section of the Companion CD. Robert receives assistance from Ashley and Josh with the earthworm activity. With the help of these "more knowledgeable people," Robert is able to complete an activity that he would not otherwise be able to complete independently.

Review the video and ask yourself the following:

- What are other examples of students working within the zone of proximal development?
- What is the function of communication in this lesson?
- What role does Mr. McKnight play in this lesson?

 Some educators argue that computer software works as the "knowledgeable other," allowing children to work in their zone of proximal development. Look at the Virtual Worm lesson at the *http://www.naturewatch.ca/english/wormwatch/virtual_worm/Introduction.html* link. Do you agree or disagree that this medium can work as a knowledgeable other, much like his peers assisted Robert in the *Zone of Proximal Development* video on the Companion CD? Record your ideas and the answers to these questions in your portfolio or use the Companion Website to share your ideas.

A Vygotskian Approach to Teaching

As an extension to their moon activities, Joshua's class discusses the principles of light, mirrors, and reflection. As Joshua shares his newfound knowledge with his sister, Melanie, she becomes curious about light, how it travels, and its everyday effects. She decides to aim their new laser pointer near the cat and see if the cat will chase the light beam. Joshua instructs Melanie not to look at the light beam directly and not to let the cat see her pointing the laser. He also describes for her how light travels in a straight line and how light is reflected by a mirror.

Melanie tries out many different ideas but is now using a large mirror in the hallway and some hand mirrors borrowed from her parents' bathroom. She got the idea to try the mirrors from her brother talking about reflections. She also saw how the light reflected from her own vanity mirror as she tried different ways to make the light shine into another room.

Melanie is involved in experimentation here. She is looking at the relationship among mirrors, reflections, and pathways of light. She is also engaged in dialog with her older brother. She asks questions and tries out some new ways of doing things to answer her question about the light beam and the cat. She is absorbed with the activity and motivated to figure out how the light beam can be redirected to reach her goal. Together, the children are engaged in an interactive learning situation.

Application of the Vygotskian Approach

Think about how scientists, engineers, physicians, computer technicians, and other professionals carry on activities within the workplace. Do they work independently or as a team? Do physicians imply that, to be effective, they must know the answer to every question and not rely on others? It is the same with the laser activity. For example, a child's concept of a mirror tends to be that of an object used to see themselves and not that of an instrument to reflect light. Melanie relies on her brother for guidance. He leads her into thinking about mirrors in new ways.

Has Melanie changed in her knowledge of mirrors? As Melanie communicates, she begins to have a more logical and systematically structured verbal definition for the mirror. She uses psychological tools and signs to assist her in controlling her mental behavior. It is now more in keeping with culture's accepted body of knowledge related to mirrors. Melanie now has the beginning of a scientific concept. Her previous spontaneous concept becomes a part of this new scientific concept, making the new concept more meaningful. Melanie is eventually able to complete the task with the laser pointer because she received some assistance from her older brother. Her brother became the scaffold for her learning in this situation.

Our role as teachers is to assist students in developing tools and signs, as well as in maximizing the integration of spontaneous concepts and their related concrete experiences into scientific concepts. When this happens, spontaneous concepts can be logically defined, retrieved, and used by the child.

Collaborative learning and thinking, as seen with the laser activity, is the foundation of Vygotsky's theory. It is the very means by which a child learns the fundamentals of society. It is the method of moving from lower learning to higher learning and is the system by which activities within a child's zone of proximal development are successful. Scientific experimentation and problem-centered activities, or those that have multiple-solution paths, provide the framework for successful science experiences. Much like scientists and engineers engaged in collaborative research, your interactions with students will promote learning.

Your role as a teacher will be to facilitate this type of activity and to adapt the curriculum to meet your students' needs. Like the physician who must consult on many cases, you will not be an expert in all areas and will rely on others, including students, to assist you in knowledge acquisition. Just as the physician cannot be available at all times for every patient and needs to employ the help of nurses, technicians, and others, you cannot be available at all times for every student, and will need to employ the help of others, including students. These knowledgeable others will assist in the scaffolding process, communicating the terminology and processes to their peers.

Visit an Inquiry Classroom
Scaffolding

View the *Scaffolding* video in the "Constructivist Pedagogy" section of the Companion CD. Mr. McKnight ensures that students have the things they need to be successful with the activity. He also provides verbal prompts to guide the students in the activity.

Review the video and ask yourself the following:
- Patricia Mason Spigarelli's perspective of this video clip includes the statement, "We don't want to give them all the information, we just give them enough help so that they can do it for themselves and I think that's what scaffolding is and how it works in science." Do you agree or disagree with this statement? Explain your viewpoint.
- What might happen with this activity if Mr. McKnight was not there to provide verbal guidance? Discuss specific statements made by Mr. McKnight and the effect on the students.

How have you provided scaffolding to another student in your field placement or in your methods class? Was it successful? Explain your activity and its effect on the other individual's learning. Record your ideas and the answers to these questions in your portfolio or use the Companion Website to share your ideas.

The Role of Language

Because language is central to Vygotsky's theory, it is important that students understand and use the language of science (Gallas, 1995; Lemke, 1993). Science is a foreign language for them—one with comparatively more new terms than found in a foreign language text. Social constructivist theory suggests that a child constructs an understanding of language from the whole to its parts. If this is the case, then the classroom should surround children with information on science topics so that the children are exposed to the content of science through a whole language or integrated approach to learning. Vocabulary should remain in the context of what is read, not be encountered as a separate, out-of-context, memorization drill. Science instruction should be a model of how science is performed by scientists. Figure 2–3 presents further suggestions for teaching within a social constructivist framework.

 Teaching Tips | Peer tutoring, when a high-achieving student tutors a lower-achieving student, is an excellent application of Vygotsky's theory.

Figure 2–3   **Social constructivist teaching suggestions.**

Planning the Curriculum	• Plan to assess student's preconceptions through class and individual discussions, drawings, writing activities, and other assessment procedures.
	• Plan to build on student's prior knowledge to take advantage of spontaneous concepts.
	• Plan to keep students involved in the lesson through the use of challenging and open-ended activities.
Opportunities to Develop Scientific Concepts	• Provide as many chances as possible for students to explore phenomena and communicate with each other.
	• Use concrete examples whenever possible.
	• Organize many opportunities for oral and written language so that students share meanings and construct concepts.
Time and Classroom Management	• Provide ample time for small-group activities.
	• Leave plenty of time after instruction for reflection and questions by the students.
	• Arrange the classroom to maximize peer interaction and small-group activities.
	• Use reading, writing, and science centers effectively and not just as a management tool for those who get their work done early.
Listening and Questioning Skills	• Ask questions before the lesson to evaluate student's prior knowledge and to assist students in recalling the information.
	• Listen carefully to students as they are talking to you and others so that you can adjust their lessons to fit their zone of proximal development.
	• Ask open-ended questions and encourage elaboration of student's answers.
Planning and Facilitating Classroom Activities	• Develop lessons that offer multiple pathways to learning, such as reading, writing, listening, and small-group activities.
	• Plan activities that connect in-school learning to out-of-school learning.
	• Construct lessons that are culturally diverse.
	• Use creative writing and subject-specific journals.
	• Use assessment procedures that can show where a student is on the continuum of learning.
	• Vary assessment procedures to check for student understanding.

Driver, Asoko, Leach, Mortimer, and Scott (1994) sum up the learning of science as follows:

> [Science learning] involves being initiated into scientific ways of knowing. Science entities and ideas, which are constructed, validated, and communicated through cultural institutions of science, are unlikely to be discovered by their own empirical enquiry; learning science thus involves being initiated into the ideas and practices of the scientific community and making these ideas and practices meaningful at the individual level. The role of the science educator is to mediate scientific knowledge for learners, to help them to make personal sense of the ways in which knowledge claims are generalized and validated. (p. 6)

As you can see, social constructivism has important implications for the teacher. Students construct new knowledge within a sociohistorical framework, where language is an important component.

> **Teaching Tips**
> Activities in the classroom should promote the use of language, which is central to a child's development.

A CONSTRUCTIVIST APPROACH TO TEACHING

A constructivist model describes the learning process in terms of the student, not the teacher. We cannot prescribe a curriculum for everyone. Notwithstanding, when students are actively engaged, they are constructing knowledge. Learning is taking place, not as a result of the transference of knowledge from teacher to student via text or a personal knowledge base, but as students interpret and make sense of their surroundings.

Similar to the social constructivist theories, as the students interpret their surroundings, the new interpretation is influenced by their prior knowledge. It is therefore the teacher's role to facilitate activities that will guide the learner into developing meaningful concepts. Constructivists generally agree that discourse is especially important in negotiating meaning and developing socially agreeable constructs. Therefore, open-ended questioning is important before, during, and after activity periods.

> **Teaching Tips**
> A constructivist approach implies that the use of a variety of activities in the classroom promotes a child's making sense of the world and developing scientific concepts.

Constructivist Teaching Promotes Active Learning

If knowledge is the result of constructive activity, then it cannot be transferred effectively to a passive receiver. The construction of knowledge must be an active process by the individual learner. The role of the teacher is to orient the learner in a general direction and then attempt to prevent the learner from going in directions that would be inappropriate. This is exactly what we find with the following luneometer activity.

As they continue their moon studies, Ms. Terrell's class looks at the question, "What kind of information can we collect in order to predict when the moon will appear tomorrow evening?" From a page in the *Out of This World* activity guide (shown on page 37), students document the angle of elevation of the moon every 30 minutes for a total of 5 hours. They build luneometers with rulers and protractors to measure the moon's angle as it rises. They also graph the results of their observations and actively engage in making sense of the data.

How can we make today's science classrooms better than those in the past? One way is to change our perception of teaching from promoting rote learning proposed by behav-

Children determine the angle of elevation of the moon as part of their exploration of the phases of the moon.

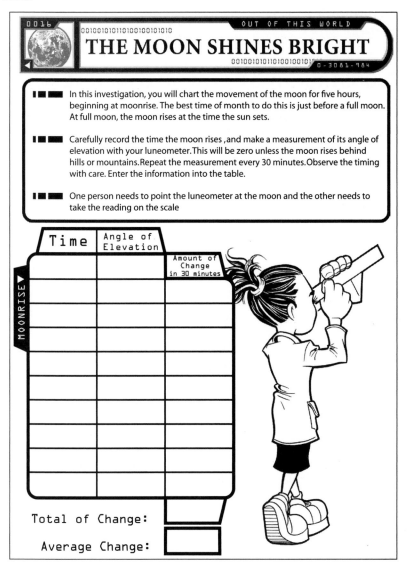

Source: Reprinted by permission of the AIMS Education Foundation from *Out of This World* Copyright © 2005 AIMS Education Foundation. All rights reserved.

iorists to engaging students in a series of well-thought-out logical steps. Teachers should scaffold a child's growth in building conceptual knowledge from the child's prior knowledge to that which is the cultural development of society.

The teacher's role as a facilitator of the curriculum is to provide the resources for learning, to engage students actively, and to refocus students' activity when appropriate so that they remain productive in the learning process. For example, Ms. Terrell provided the luneometer template and then guided students in making sense of the data as they were collected. Her role in the activity was to pose a problem to solve and invite students to make observations that accomplish the task. She then steps aside and allows the students to interact with the environment and each other. Ms. Terrell intervenes only when necessary. Intervention is used to refocus student discussion in a more productive way, initiate a new pattern of activity, or begin an assessment activity for the students to express their personal understanding.

THE CONSTRUCTIVIST LEARNING MODEL

Yager (1991) described the constructivist learning model (CLM) as a promising new model in learning. It focuses on the learner instead of the teacher. Building on the work of researchers at the National Center for Improving Science Education, Yager introduced a set of constructivist strategies for teaching, which are provided in Figure 2–4.

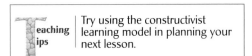

Teaching Tips | Try using the constructivist learning model in planning your next lesson.

As you can see, the CLM is an ongoing four-part process. First, you get the students to think about a phenomenon in a new way (invitation part). Then, they explore the phenomenon (exploration part) and develop explanations or solutions (constructs; proposing explanations and solutions part). Fi-

Figure 2–4   **Constructivist strategies for teaching.**

Invitation
- Observe surroundings for points of curiosity
- Ask questions
- Consider possible responses to questions
- Note unexpected phenomena
- Identify situations where student perceptions vary

Exploration
- Engage in focused play
- Brainstorm possible alternatives
- Look for information
- Experiment with materials
- Observe specific phenomena
- Design a model
- Collect and organize data
- Employ problem-solving strategies
- Select appropriate resources
- Discuss solutions with others
- Design and conduct experiments
- Evaluate choices
- Engage in debate
- Identify risks and consequences
- Develop parameters of an investigation
- Analyze data

Proposing Explanations and Solutions
- Communicate information and ideas
- Construct and explain a model
- Construct a new explanation
- Review and critique solutions
- Utilize peer evaluation
- Assemble multiple answers/solutions
- Determine appropriate closure
- Integrate a solution with existing knowledge and experiences

Taking Action
- Make decisions
- Apply knowledge and skills
- Transfer knowledge and skills
- Share information and ideas
- Ask new questions
- Develop products and promote ideas
- Use models and ideas to elicit discussions and acceptance by others

Source: R. Yager, "The Constructivist Learning Model." Reprinted with permission from NSTA Publications, September 1991, from *The Science Teacher,* National Science Teachers Association, 1840 Wilson Blvd., Arlington, VA 22201-3000.

Visit an Inquiry Classroom
Invitations to Learn

View the *Invitation* video within the "Model Inquiry Unit" section of the Companion CD. Mr. McKnight asks the children questions to stimulate their curiosity of earthworms and set the stage for future activities. This is in keeping with the first stage of the constructivist learning model, invitation.

Review the video and ask yourself the following:
- What specific questions could be used to cause students to want to engage in the exploration stage of the constructivist learning model?
- How can Mr. McKnight best transition into the exploration stage of the constructivist learning model?

 "The search for meaning is innate" is the third brain/mind learning principle (*http://cainelearning.com/pwheel/*). The authors suggest that "we are born to function as scientists, discovering what our world is about." How does the constructivist learning model support this brain/mind learning principle? Record your ideas and the answers to these questions in your portfolio or use the Companion Website to share your ideas.

nally, they share their new ideas with others or reexplore the phenomenon in a new way (taking action part).

When constructivist theories such as the CLM are used, the focus is on the learner and the learning environment. This makes your job as a teacher–facilitator different from what you may have experienced from your teachers in elementary or middle school. As you read through the remaining chapters of this text, think about how you can use the tenets of constructivism to enhance the learning environment for your students.

Summary

- Piaget's work helps provide insight into how children grow intellectually. He defined the stages that children go through as they develop and the characteristics of these stages. Piaget also explained the learning process as a dynamic balance between assimilation and accommodation and a result of seeking equilibration because of new experiences. Piaget was a developmental constructivist who viewed development as leading learning.
- Vygotsky's constructivism is a sociohistorical theory in which behavior is studied in a social and historical context. In this theory, children undergo socially mediated cognitive constructions. Psychological tools and signs assist us in semantic mediation and the development of scientific concepts. The zone of proximal development allows a child's instruction to be slightly ahead of her development. Later, what she could do with the assistance of another, she can now do on her own. Vygotsky was a sociohistorical constructivist who saw learning as leading development.
- In either constructivist theory, the curriculum is not a set of right answers and truths to be taught, rather a set of culturally accepted ideals used to guide learning. Elementary and middle school science teachers must understand the goals of the curriculum guided by science standards, the individual children in their classrooms, and how to structure the learning environment to meet these individual needs in the elementary and middle school science classroom.

Reflection

Companion CD

1. Look at the "Living Versus Nonliving Things" lesson linked to the *Planning* video on the Companion CD. Does this lesson support an inquiry approach to science teaching and learning? Support your answer with references to the science standards.
2. Look at "The Reproductive System" lesson linked to the *Moral Dimensions* video on the Companion CD. Why might the fact that earthworms are both male and female cause disequilibrium with elementary students? How could you use assimilation or accommodation to resolve this disequilibrium?
3. Look at the "Classification of Living Things" lesson linked to the *Preparing Resources* video on the Companion CD. Apply the constructivist learning model to this lesson. What changes would you make with this lesson based on the CLM?

Portfolio Ideas

1. Discuss with your classmates the following common ideas related to scientific knowledge, teaching, and learning.
   * Elementary students already have conceptions of science when they arrive at the elementary classroom.
   * Every child is a scientist.
   * Teachers and students can learn science together.
   Record your findings in your portfolio.
2. Try some Piagetian tests on children at your practicum site (see the Companion Website). What observations can you make? Record your observations and compare these with others made by students in your methods class. What do you note?
3. Discuss constructivism with a teacher at your practicum site. What is her or his viewpoint? Discuss it with your educational psychology professor. What is her or his viewpoint? The current science education research trend, or paradigm, is toward a constructivist perspective. Why do you think this is so? Mathematics educators also operate under a constructivist paradigm. What does your mathematics methods instructor have to say about constructivism? What are some views of your other methods instructors? Record your ideas in your portfolio.
4. Observe students in a classroom working together to solve a problem. Does it become clear that some students could not have completed the problem on their own? What is the teacher's role as students engage in the collaborative activity? How can you, as an outside observer, tell whether the students are learning? How will the teacher know whether learning has occurred? Share your findings with classmates and in your portfolio.

References

American Association for the Advancement of Science (AAAS). (1993). *Benchmarks for science literacy.* New York: Oxford University Press.

American Association for the Advancement of Science (AAAS). (1998). *Blueprints for reform.* New York: Oxford University Press.

Bettencourt, A. (1993). The construction of knowledge: A radical constructivist view. In K. Tobin (Ed.), *The practice of constructivism in science education* (pp. 39–50). Washington, DC: AAAS Press.

Branley, F. (1975). *Day light, night light.* New York: HarperCollins.

Branley, F. (1987). *The moon seems to change.* New York: HarperCollins.

Bybee, R. W., & Sund, R. B. (1990). *Piaget for educators* (2nd ed.). Prospect Heights, IL: Wavelend Press.

Cobern, W. W. (1993). Contextual constructivism: The impact of culture on the learning and teaching of science. In K. Tobin (Ed.), *The practice of constructivism in science education* (pp. 51–69). Washington, DC: AAAS Press.

Dewey, J. (1966). *Democracy and education.* New York: Free Press.

Dixon-Krauss, L. (1996). Vygotsky's sociohistorical perspective on learning and its application to Western literacy instruction. In L. Dixon-Krauss (Ed.), *Vygotsky in the classroom: Mediated literacy instruction and assessment* (pp. 7–24). White Plains, NY: Longman.

Driver, R. (1995). Constructivist approaches in science teaching. In L. P. Steffe & J. Gale (Eds.), *Constructivism in education* (pp. 385–400). Hillsdale, NJ: Lawrence Erlbaum Associates.

Driver, R., Asoko, H., Leach, J., Mortimer, E., & Scott, P. (1994). Constructing scientific knowledge in the classroom. *Educational Researcher, 23*(7), 5–12.

Gallas, K. (1995). *Talking their way into science: Hearing children's questions and theories, responding with curricula.* New York: Teachers College Press.

Henriques, A. (1990). Experiments in teaching. In E. Duckworth, J. Easley, D. Hawkins, & A. Henriques (Eds.), *Science education: A minds-on approach for the elementary years.* Mahwah, NJ: Lawrence Erlbaum.

Kuhn, T. (1962). *The structure of scientific revolutions* (2nd ed.). Chicago: University of Chicago Press.

Labinowicz, E. (1980). *The Piaget primer: Thinking. Learning. Teaching.* Menlo Park, CA: Addison-Wesley.

Lemke, J. L. (1993). *Talking science: Language, learning, and values.* Norwood, NJ: Ablex.

McBrien, J. L., & Brandt, R. S. (1997). *The language of learning: A guide to education terms.* Alexandria, VA: Association for Supervision and Curriculum Development.

National Research Council (NRC). (1996). *National science education standards.* Washington, DC: National Academy Press.

National Research Council (NRC). (2000). *Inquiry in the national science education standards.* Washington, DC: National Academy Press.

National Science Teachers Association (NSTA). (2003). *Beyond 2000—Teachers of science speak out. A position statement.* Washington, DC: Author. Retrieved October 1, 2004, from www.nsta.org/positionstatement&psid=17

Petersen, J. (1994). *The road to 2015.* Corte Madera, CA: Waite Group Press.

Petersen, J. (1997). *Out of the blue: Wild cards and other big future surprises—How to anticipate and respond to profound change.* Arlington, VA: Arlington Institute.

Piaget, J. (1954). *The construction of reality in the child.* New York: Basic Books.

Piaget, J., & Inhelder, B. (1969). *The psychology of the child.* New York: Basic Books.

School of Information Management and Systems University of California at Berkeley. (2003). *How much information 2003.* Berkeley, CA: Regents of the University of California. Retrieved October 1, 2004, from www.sims.berkeley.edu/research/projects/how-much-info-2003/execsum.htm#summary

Siegler, R. S. (1986). *Children's thinking.* Upper Saddle River, NJ: Prentice Hall.

Tobin, K., & Tippins, D. (1993). Constructivism as a referent for teaching and learning. In K. Tobin (Ed.), *The practice of constructivism in science education* (pp. 3–21). Washington, DC: AAAS Press.

Vygotsky, L. (1962). *Thought and language* (E. Hanfmann & G. Vakar, Eds.). Cambridge: MIT Press.

Vygotsky, L. (1978). *Mind in society: The development of higher psychological processes* (M. Cole, V. John-Steiner, S. Scribner, & E. Souberman, Eds.). Cambridge, MA: Harvard University Press.

Vygotsky, L. (1981). The genesis of higher mental functions. In J. V. Wertsch (Ed.), *The concept of activity in Soviet psychology* (pp. 144–188). Armonk, NY: Sharpe.

Vygotsky, L. S. (1986). *Thought and language* (A. Kuzulin, Ed.). Cambridge: MIT Press.

Yager, R. (1991). The constructivist learning model. *The Science Teacher, 58*(6), 52–57.

Suggested Readings

Bodrova, E., & Leong, D. J. (1996). *Tools of the mind: The Vygotskian approach to early childhood education.* Upper Saddle River, NJ: Merrill/Prentice Hall. (a guide to incorporating Vygotsky's ideas into teaching)

Brooks, J. G., & Brooks, M. G. (1993). *In search of understanding: The case for constructivist classrooms.* Alexandria, VA: Association for Supervision and Curriculum Development. (a guide to developing classrooms that encourage understanding of concepts)

Chaille, C., & Britain, L. (1991). *The young child as scientist: A constructivist approach to early childhood education.* New York: HarperCollins. (an overview of how children construct knowledge)

Dixon-Krauss, L. (Ed.). (1996). *Vygotsky in the classroom: Mediated literacy instruction and assessment.* White Plains, NY: Longman. (an overview of Vygotsky's theory, including the zone of proximal development and scaffolding)

Duckworth, E. (1987). *"The having of wonderful ideas" and other essays on teaching and learning.* New York: Teachers College Press. (a Piagetian view of education)

Tobin, K. (Ed.). (1993). *The practice of constructivism in science education.* Washington, DC: AAAS Press. (an edited compilation of the nature of constructivism and what it means for teachers)

von Glasersfeld, E. (1995). *Radical constructivism: A way of knowing and learning.* Washington, DC: Falmer Press. (a comprehensive work on radical constructivism)

CHAPTER 3

PLANNING
FOR INQUIRY

- How can you use the national standards in science program, unit, and lesson planning?
- What is involved in unit planning?
- How do you plan for inquiry-based teaching?
- What is involved in lesson planning?
- What are some planning models that support scientific inquiry?

Focus on Inquiry

Divergent Thinking Activity

Jerry Mayernik,
Northway Elementary School, North Hills School District, Pennsylvania

A thin stripe of yellow tape in the school hallway marks the starting line for the test track. In a few minutes, colorful cans of many sizes will clink, clank, and thump their way down the long, narrow test course, with students whispering encouragement to their carefully constructed devices as the cans slow down, wiggle, and begin the trip back to the starting line. At no time is science terminology, textbook pages, or vocabulary words referred to as the children test, refine, and retest their "comeback cans."

In my science class, the school year begins with a demonstration of "Herbie, the Wonder Can," a 3-pound coffee can rigged with a rubber band and a large fishing sinker inside.

Before the "comeback can" activity, you may want to use the "rolling cans" activity: Try rolling a full can of sand, an empty can, and a half-full can of sand down a ramp.

When Herbie is carefully rolled across the classroom, it magically slows, stops, and returns to its starting point. After students are shown how to construct a similar device, they are challenged to build their own comeback cans and test them against the best efforts of Herbie. The next day, cans of all sizes and construction litter the windowsill, ready to challenge Herbie in a test of endurance.

Which can will roll the longest distance and return to the yellow stripe? After several cans traverse the track, students begin to realize that variations exist in their methods of construction. Some cans have thicker rubber bands, some thinner. Some devices are larger, some fatter, some longer. The masses inside are small, huge, and everywhere in between. Which of these variables are critical to can performance? What are the optimal can size, rubber band width, and mass? Students are encouraged to study the construction of the leading cans and to modify or refine their cans, as they like. Finally, after weeks of testing and retesting, trial and error, and elation and frustration, the top cans compete in the

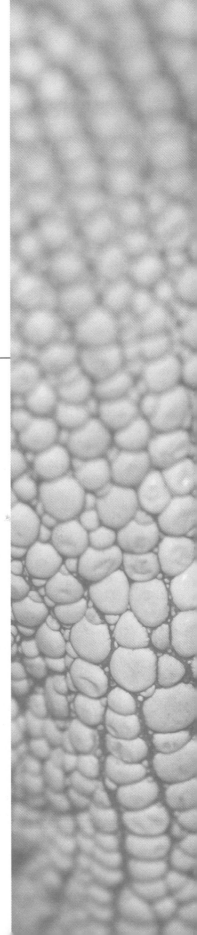

See *http://www.prenhall.com/peters* for links to the comeback can and similar activities.

Comeback Can Derby. The five winning can-builders are awarded small trophies in honor of their efforts.

This activity promotes divergent thinking. Although the comeback cans have a common construction, the task encourages a wide variety of responses. The winning cans have never been constructed in quite the same way. This activity allows students to explore, analyze, and adapt. It encourages children to attempt a novel approach (like a "Bigfoot" can, with Plexiglas "wheels" twice the diameter of other competitors'). The experience provides the "mental hooks" upon which learners will hang physics concepts in high school.

NATIONAL STANDARDS AND PLANNING

In the "Focus on Inquiry: Divergent Thinking Activity," Mr. Mayernik's class is involved in a challenging inquiry activity. How will you plan for inquiry activities in your own classroom? What considerations did Mr. Mayernik make as he prepared for this activity?

To help you think about planning and your classroom activities in a different way, envision yourself working in a manufacturing company that makes sport utility vehicles (SUVs). Your job is to assist in developing a new SUV. As you think about your new job, consider that you cannot talk with any other employees throughout the day. More experienced employees do not help you in any way. You also have to separate the workday into time periods. First, you will complete all the scientific undertakings, then the mathematical duties, some people-related responsibilities, and finally the language-type assignments. You spend the same amount of time each day on the four categories of tasks, regardless of how successful you are with any one type of task. You never spend very much time on reflection. You do not consider why the new vehicle needs to be built, whom it is being built for, or how it can be made differently. Nor do you spend any time trying to make the process or product better. You just want to meet a minimal standard for the construction of a new vehicle.

How successful will you be in your job with these constraints? Now, think how successful elementary or middle-level students will be with similar constraints. As a teacher, you assist children in constructing new knowledge. A big part of this process is planning. Good planning will produce a better automotive product just as it worked to promote inquiry with the students in Mr. Mayernik's class.

The authors of the *National Science Education Standards* (National Research Council [NRC], 1996) provide specific guidelines for how you can plan a science program. These are illustrated in the Inquiry Planning Standard shown in the Standards Link box.

Standards Link

Inquiry Planning Standard

Teachers of science plan an inquiry-based science program for their students. In doing this, teachers:

• **Develop a framework of yearlong and short-term goals for students.**

• **Select science content and adapt and design curricula to meet the interests, knowledge, understanding, abilities, and experiences of students.**

• **Select teaching and assessment strategies that support the development of student understanding and nurture a community of science learners.**

• **Work together as colleagues within and across disciplines and grade levels.**

(Teaching Standard A, National Research Council, 1996, p. 30.)

As you may have determined from reading the Inquiry Planning Standard, the National Science Education Standards, like most state and district standards, provide a flexible framework for the "yearlong and short-term goals" to be taught. They recommend a general sequencing of topics from the early elementary through high school levels. As we begin to think about and apply the standards to our own planning, first we discuss the big picture of a unit plan, and then we can talk about individual lesson plans.

See *http://www. prenhall.com/peters* for links to all National Science Education Standards.

PLANNING UNITS

When you begin a unit, keep the following questions in mind.

See *http://www.prenhall. com/peters* for a link to the document *Inquiry and the National Science Education Standards: A Guide for Teaching and Learning*.

*   Is the unit based on a small number of concepts?
*   Do the lessons relate to students' experiences, provide feedback about their current knowledge, and move smoothly into the first activity of each sequence?
*   Are open activities included?
*   Can a variety of science processes be used in the activities?
*   Are the activities appropriate for the students' abilities?
*   Are useful activities from other subject areas integrated into learning sequences?
*   Do students apply their knowledge in assessments, or simply recall it?
*   Does the unit plan allow enough time for students to learn what is proposed?

In deciding how to make your units, you must know the following three things.

1. How to determine which generalizations to use
2. How to gather more activities, if needed, to teach each generalization
3. How to introduce, or bridge into, each generalization's sequence of activities

Determining Generalizations

The chapters or units of most textbooks are organized around up to 10 main generalizations or concepts. Make a tentative list of such generalizations. Then, go through the chapter to see whether your list reflects the main parts of the chapter. Change your list of generalizations as needed to match what you find in the chapter if you want to stick closely to the textbook's contents. Alternatively, you may want to supplement the chapter's concepts with other generalizations found in ancillary materials. You may also want to look for science generalizations in thematic resources. In any event, your task is to wind up with as few big ideas as possible without combining unrelated ideas. When making a unit, you need to know the generalizations in order to compile extra activities.

Whether you use text chapters or a main integrated theme as a base for a unit, it is important to think through the basic organization. This sort of analysis boosts your confidence by providing a sense of direction. It leads to the feeling that, if needed, you can make a few changes and add some ideas. It helps you decide what is important and what is not.

Finding Activities

Activities can come from a wide variety of sources, including trade books and the teacher's guide to the student science text. Many other activity books are available from the National Science Teachers Association (1840 Wilson Blvd., Arlington, VA 22201, *http://www.nsta.org/*). A series of activity books are also available from the Activities Integrating Math and Science (AIMS) Education Foundation (P.O. Box 8120, Fresno, CA

See *http://www.prenhall.com/peters* for other activity source links.

93747-8120, *http://www.aimsedu.org/*) and the Great Explorations in Math and Science (GEMS) group (Lawrence Hall of Science, University of California, Berkeley, CA 94720, *http://www.lhs.berkeley.edu/GEMS*).

How many open investigations should you plan for? The number depends greatly on the diversity of your class. Cultural diversity and disadvantaged populations in the classroom may require more experiences to make connections.

After you have researched the topic and grouped good learning activities under each generalization, arrange them in a logical teaching order. The sequence of content in the class textbook can provide the overall direction here. Remember to cluster concrete activities ahead of reading and other secondhand activities when possible.

Determining Bridges or Introductions

Now that you have located some activities for each generalization, you will need a way to introduce each of these main parts of the unit to students and move smoothly into each accompanying set of activities. Teachers call this phase "bridging" because it takes the children from where they are now to the beginning of where they need to go next.

Children use an earthquake activity as a supplement to a textbook unit on the earth's changing surface.

A useful introduction, or bridge, relates to students' experiences and current understandings. It stimulates them to use their current constructions as you interact with them. Students' responses and questions give you insight into what the students already know about the generalization or topic to be studied, including their misconceptions. The last part of the bridge also leads into the first activity in each sequence.

You may want to introduce your students to the entire unit at one time by asking questions based on all the generalizations. Many teachers believe, however, that it is easier and more meaningful to the children to introduce only one section at a time. Of course, a brief statement about the overall unit topic should be made in any case.

Ideas for bridging into each set of activities usually can be found in the textbook, a text's teacher's edition, or an activity book. Most programs reflect the constructivist view. They are likely to begin a unit or lesson with an opportunity for the teacher to find out what children already know and relate this to what they will learn.

When supplementing a textbook unit, consider the following suggestions.

1. Thoroughly read the unit to grasp what it is about.
2. Look for places where you can use local resources.
3. Look for opportunities to integrate reading, mathematics, language, and other subjects into lessons.
4. Look for chances to use concrete activities.
5. Estimate the total time needed to teach the unit and then fit the text's lessons into the block of available time.

Some teachers feel restricted by the book format. Without the publisher's full array of multimedia resources as aids, teachers see mostly closed activities that illustrate ideas in the book rather than broad chances for real inquiry. They see relatively short, tightly controlled lessons when they want students to ask more questions and pursue strong interests over longer periods of time. These teachers are aware of some ways to augment the book unit, but for them these measures do not go far enough. They want the book to be one tool among several, rather than the main event. What they really want is a practical way to design their own multimedia unit and a format that allows them to work flexibly with their students.

See *http://www.prenhall.com/peters* for links to the *Atlas of Science Literacy* (AAAS). This document is a collection of strand maps that show how students' understanding of the ideas and skills that lead to scientific literacy grow over time.

A Sample Unit

For a sample unit developed in this way, see Figure 3–1. The unit is written on index cards, which is a convenient way to keep track of generalizations, activities, and bridges. Suggestions for using the format follow.

Write one broad generalization at the top of each 5-inch by 8-inch card. This is for your reference only, not for teaching to the children. Sections of the book may be headed by problems, topics, or themes. If one seems useful, you might prefer to first write this heading, then the generalization. Next, write your sequentially arranged activities under each generalization, leaving a space for the bridge. Then write the bridge. Be sure to relate the last part of the bridge to the first activity so that you can move smoothly into it.

The use of cards has advantages. Cards can be shuffled in any desired sequence. It is easy to add and take away generalizations and activities. Special sections can be added: bulletin board ideas, news clippings, notes, whatever else is desired to make the unit complete and easier to teach.

Notice the marginal notes for science processes written next to some activities. These can remind you of what to stress in such activities. Several "open" notes serve the same function. Open activities are often the easiest and best way to meet students' individual differences in unit teaching.

Figure 3–1   Sample unit: Volcanoes.

Earth's Changing Surface

This is a fourth-grade unit on the forces that tear down and build up the earth's surface. Children also learn how rocks are formed and several ways soil is conserved. Fifteen periods of about 50 minutes each are planned for the unit. (See block plan on back of this card.)

(Front of card)

	April 6–10	April 13–17	April 20–24
Monday	Generalization I, Activity 1 (Ask class for materials for Act. 2.)	Gen. II, Act. 1	III, Act. 3 (Ask for rocks and jars Gen. IV, Act. 2, 4.)
Tuesday	I, Act. 2 (See custodian for materials for Act. 3.)	II, Act. 2	III, Act. 6, assess. (Ask for rocks and jars, IV, Act. 2, 4.)
Wednesday	I, Act. 3 (Ask class for materials for Act. 6.)	II, Act. 3 or 5	Gen. IV, Act. 1, 2
Thursday	I, Act. 4 or 5	II, Act. 4, assess.	IV, Act. 2, 3
Friday	I, Act. 5 or 6, assess. (Ask for materials for Gen. II, Act. 1, and milk cartons from cafeteria.)	Gen. III, Act. 1, 2 (Ask volunteers to bring materials for Act. 3.)	IV, Act 4, 5 assess. (Follow up on crystal growth next week.)

Order library books. Also AV materials by March 6 for I (4), II (3), III (1, 2). Phone II (5), III (4).

Gen. I. Weathering and erosion constantly wear down the earth's surface. (Class text pages 61–68.)

Bridge

How far down do you think the soil goes? What is beneath the soil? What are some ways rock may get broken up? How might broken up rocks and soil be removed? What does *weathering* mean? What is *erosion?*

Activities

(obs.)   1. Define weathering and erosion. Tour school grounds for examples. (Open-ended.)
(exp.)   2. Plants break rocks experiment, text p. 63. (Open-ended.)
(infer.)   3. Dirt mountain erosion demonstration, Schmidt p. 56.
            4. Films: Face of Earth (15 min.), Work of Rivers (10 min.).
            5. Read text pp. 61–68 and library books. SUMMARIZE weathering and erosion forces.
(class.)   6. Kids find and sort picture examples of forces that bring change. Display. (Open-ended.)
            7. Haiku poetry on forces that change the earth's surface.

(Front of card)

Materials

Act. 2. Plaster of paris; bean seeds; paper cups.
Act. 3. Shovel; hose. (See custodian.)
Act. 4. MP204; MP206 (AV center).
Act. 6. *Nat'l Geographic, Arizona Highways* back issues; scissors; construction paper; paste.

Assessment

How many examples of weathering and erosion can you find on the school grounds? Find some examples we did not observe on our first tour. Make a record. Also use end-of-section questions, p. 68.

(Back of card)
(continued)

Figure 3–1 (*continued*).

Gen. II. Topsoil is composed of mineral, vegetable, and animal matter; topsoil is conserved in several ways. (Pages 69–77.)

Bridge

What are some reasons farmers might be interested in erosion? How might they guard against soil erosion? What makes up soil? Let's see for ourselves.

Activities

(class.) 1. Small-group analysis of soil samples. Sort objects found. (Open-ended.)
(exp.)   2. Plant seeds in poor and good soil samples, text p. 72. (Open-ended.)
          3. Introduce six study points on soil erosion. See "Conserving Our Soil" videotape.
          4. Read text, pages 69–77, and library books. SUMMARIZE ways to conserve soil.
          5. Possible visit by agent, Soil Conservation Service. (Practice interview and listening skills.)

(Front of card)

Materials

Act. 1. Magnifiers; old spoons; sack of good topsoil; newspapers; clean pint milk cartons.
Act. 2. Bean seeds; sack each of good and bad soil; milk cartons.
Act. 3. SP (set of 6) 117; Vid. 440.1 (AV center).
Act. 5. Bill Johnson, Soil Cons. Service, 555-6600.

Assessment

What are some ways you might prevent erosion on our school grounds? Think about the examples you found before. Discuss these ways with two partners. Then give a report.
We don't live on farms. What difference would it make to us if most farm soil erodes? Also use end-of-section questions, p. 77.

(Back of card)

Gen. III. Lava flows and crustal movements continually build up the earth's surface. (pages 77–84.)

Bridge

Does anyone know what a volcano is? What do you think makes a volcano happen? What is an earthquake? Has anyone been where there was an earthquake? Let's find out some surprising ways the earth's surface changes.

Activities

1. Film: *Earthquakes and Volcanoes* (30 min.).
2. Explore Internet for related information (25 min.).

(meas.) 3. Make clay models of volcanoes, p. 79. Also "seismograph," special project Hone, p. 28. (Art and construction.)

4. Guest speaker with northern California earthquake slides. (or locate earthquake pictures).
5. Use maps to locate active volcanoes.
6. Read text, pages 77–84, and library books. SUMMARIZE how mountains are formed.

(Front of card)

Materials

Act. 1. MP 254 (AV center).
Act. 2. Internet-connected computer.
Act. 3. Two colors of clay; newspapers; rulers; scissors. (Seismograph volunteers, check Hone book for materials.)
Act. 4. Orville McCreedy, 286-6147. (or, past *Nat'l Geographics,* 1989 issues).

Assessment

Children will construct cutaway models of volcanoes and, using the models, explain how volcanoes may happen. Also use end-of-section questions, p. 84.

(Back of card)

(continued)

Figure 3–1 *(continued).*

Gen. IV. Three kinds of rocks are formed as the earth's surface wears down and builds up.

Bridge

Thank you for bringing so many different rocks. What makes them look different? Which of these might have come from volcanoes? How else might some have been made? Before we find out, let's see how many different properties of these rocks you can observe.

Activities

(comm.) 1. Partners do rock description game. (20 questions—lang. develop.)
(exper.) 2. Crystal growing activity, p. 91. (Open-ended.)
     3. Read text, pages 85–93, and library books.
(class.) 4. Sort rocks as to basic type, p. 90. (Open-ended.)
     5. SUMMARIZE Gen. IV and whole unit.

(Front of card)

Materials

Act. 2. Baby food jars; string; paper clips; sugar; hot plate; teakettle; newspaper.
Act. 4. Children's rock samples—stress variety; heavy paper sacks; several hammers.

Assessment

Children will be able to control the size of "rock" crystals by varying the cooling rates of hot sugar solutions. Children will be able to identify some properties of rocks and explain how these are clues to the rock's formation. Also use unit test questions, p. 93.

(Back of card)

Note also the specific assessment section for each of the four main parts of this unit. For generalizations I and II, assessments are stated as questions. For generalizations III and IV, they are stated as student behaviors to observe.

The next step in the planning process is to take your overall unit plan and begin to develop individual lessons. Consistent with the Inquiry Planning Standard found on page 44, individual lessons should promote inquiry in the classroom. Remember the third concept of the Inquiry Planning Standard: "Select teaching and assessment strategies that support the development of student understanding and nurture a community of science learners." To do this, we will need to plan for daily inquiry teaching.

INQUIRY TEACHING

Think back to Mr. Mayernik's comeback can activity. Remember that inquiry teaching and learning is a dynamic process. Students are naturally curious and enjoy inquiry. Your job is to further develop their ability to solve problems, transform information into meaningful knowledge, and become lifelong learners. You, as an elementary or middle school teacher, can convert your classroom into a better learning environment through a variety of inquiry activities. Table 3–1 shows the diversity of inquiry tasks available to you as you plan your activities.

Teacher-Directed Versus Learner-Directed Activities

You will find that variations in the far left column of Table 3–1 require more direction from you as a teacher. They have only one correct answer or one specific pathway to an answer. Variations to the right in Table 3–1 are less teacher directed and more learner centered. These variations are increasingly divergent. They will have more than one answer or pathway to an answer. Let's look at an example. In the following scenarios, both teachers are planning to teach about **food chains.** See whether you notice any differences.

Food chains refer to the organisms in an ecological community that provide a continuation of food energy from one organism to the next as each one consumes a lower member in the chain and is, in turn, preyed upon by a higher member in the chain.

Visit an Inquiry Classroom
Learner-Centered Teaching

View the *Active Learning* video in the "Constructivist Pedagogy" section of the Companion CD. Mr. McKnight, in an active learning situation, questions students about their findings related to earthworms. They are sharing their ideas and proposing explanations and solutions about earthworms consistent with the constructivist learning model.

Review the video and ask yourself the following:
- Why would this video segment be considered an illustration of learner-centered teaching when the teacher is asking questions?
- We suggest that learner self-direction is high in this community of science learners. Do you agree or disagree? Support your viewpoint with specific examples from the video and Table 3–1.

  What learner-directed activities have you seen in your field placements? Have you seen any teacher-directed activities that could be changed into learner-directed activities? Explain how these activities could become more learner centered. Record your ideas and the answers to these questions in your portfolio or use the Companion Website to share your ideas.

Table 3–1

Essential Features of Classroom Inquiry and Their Variations

Essential Feature	Variations			
Learner	Self-Direction: Less ————————————————————→ More			
Learner engages in scientifically oriented questions	• Learner engages in question provided by teacher, materials,or other source	• Learner sharpens or clarifies question provided by teacher, materials, or other source	• Learner selects among questions, poses new questions	• Learner poses a question
Learner gives priority to evidence in responding to questions	• Learner given data and told how to analyze	• Learner given data and asked to analyze	• Learner directed to collect certain data	• Learner determines what constitutes evidence and collects it
Learner formulates explanations from evidence	• Learner provided with evidence	• Learner given possible ways to use evidence to formulate explanation	• Learner guided in process of formulating explanations from evidence	• Learner formulates explanation after summarizing evidence
Learner connects explanations to scientific knowledge		• Learner given possible connections	• Learner directed toward areas and sources of scientific knowledge	• Learner independently examines other resources and forms the links to explanations
Learner communicates and justifies explanations	• Learner given steps and procedures for communication	• Learner given broad guidelines to sharpen communication	• Learner coached in development of communication	• Learner forms reasonable and logical argument to communicate explanations
Less	↔	Amount of _Learner_ Self-Direction		↔ More
More	↔	Amount of Direction from _Teacher_ or Material		↔ Less

Source: Adapted from _Inquiry and the National Science Education Standards: A Guide for Teaching and Learning_ (p. 29). Copyright © 2000 by the National Academy of Sciences. Courtesy of the National Academy Press, Washington, DC.

Teacher-Directed Example

Mrs. Steen plans her activities to begin with reading _The Magic School Bus Gets Eaten_ (Cole, 1996). This story gains student interest and initiates discussion. Next, she asks her students to list the plants and animals found in the story. The students list these in their notebooks. Now, she directs the students to arrange the organisms according to a food chain illustrated on the chalkboard. The students list phytoplankton, zooplankton, anchovies, tuna, and people as a food chain. Mrs. Steen then asks about the source of energy for the food chain.

In this example, students are engaging in questions and activities directed by the teacher. Learner self-direction is low, and teacher direction is high (see Table 3–1).

Learner-Directed Example

Mr. Mitchell plans his lesson to start with reading *What Do You Do When Something Wants to Eat You?* (Jenkins, 1997). The students read about how certain fish, reptiles, amphibians, and other animals escape danger. Mr. Mitchell asks why the animals need to defend themselves in the examples provided in the book. The students respond in a variety of ways, and Mr. Mitchell allows them to ask about examples of animal defenses not found in this story. Soon, students are posing questions about why animals would want to eat one another. Mr. Mitchell continues the lesson by reading *Who Eats What?* (Lauber, 1995). Various food chains are described in the book. The students give other possible examples when prompted by Mr. Mitchell about what food chains may have been a part of their dinners last night.

As the discussion continues, the students come to realize that there are many kinds of food chains, that food chains are part of food webs, that plants are the basis of a food chain, and that the sun is an important part of every food chain. Learners are more self-directed in this example, often asking new questions or providing a variety of answers. The teacher direction is low, as is reflected in Table 3–1.

Convergent and Divergent Questions

In Mrs. Steen's teacher-directed lesson, inquiry is generally focused on one correct answer, such as the sun being the ultimate source of energy. Students are provided specific examples and **convergent questions** related to the food chains for plants and animals. The problem that students are working on is considered closed. Closed problems and activities foster convergent thinking. They converge on a common single response.

Mr. Mitchell's learner-centered lesson encourages students to seek many answers. The correct response is considered open because there is more than one possibility for a correct answer. Students in Mr. Mitchell's class answer **divergent questions** based on their understanding that there are a variety of food chains and these food chains play a key role in ecosystems. Open problems and activities lead to a wide variety of responses and produce divergent thinking. With open problems, answers and other possible experiences diverge from one initial experience, question, or problem. A balance of both open and closed problems and activities are needed for scientific inquiry during the elementary and middle school years.

Convergent questions are asked with predetermined answers in mind.

Divergent questions do not have single answers, are used to promote discussion, and allow for creative thinking.

Closed Activities

Closed activities tend to be short and tightly focused. Open activities are usually longer and branch out into many related questions. Both are appropriate to use in inquiry teaching; however, closed and open activities differ in other ways. To see how, let's study each type in more depth. We begin with some common closed activities involving children. In each case, the students are active; they do things.

Grade 2 Example

In Mrs. Imat's second-grade class, children work on the "Mouth Map" activity from the book *Gobble Up Science* (Johmann & Rieth, 1996). Using sugar, salt, tonic water, and lemon juice, they find the taste buds on their tongues: The tips of their tongues sense sweet, the back of their tongues sense bitter, and they discover salty and sour taste buds on the sides. The activity ends with children discovering what Mrs. Imat knew they would experience.

Grade 4 Example

The AIMS-produced *Fun with Foods* book contains many other food activities that can be adapted for use in the elementary and middle school grades.

In Ms. Bagui's fourth-grade class, children are learning about acids and bases with the "Red-Cabbage Indicator" activity found in the book *Science Experiments You Can Eat* (Cobb, 1994). They find that cabbage juice solution is an indicator and changes color, depending on whether the substance is an acid or a base.

Grade 6 Example

In a sixth-grade class, Mr. Uvah's adolescents learn about variables through the "Popcorn Comparison" activity in *Fun with Foods: A Recipe for Math + Science* (Alfving et al., 1987). Students find that the moisture content of popcorn kernels has an effect on the volume of popped corn that is produced.

Notice that each of these closed activities illustrates some idea or procedure with concrete materials. Working with concrete materials helps the children to form realistic concepts and learn useful investigative techniques. Once a closed activity has made its point, there is no need to continue. Closed activities, when taught well, help children construct a solid subject-matter background that is rooted in experience and often lays the foundation for more open inquiry.

Open Activities

As noted earlier, open activities are usually longer and branch out into many related questions. Students are provided multiple pathways to learning. Let's look at some examples.

Grade 2 Example

Mrs. Bell places a few food items, some balloons, and various other items such as beakers and jars on a table and challenges her second-grade students to blow up a balloon by using the food. This activity is based on the "Blowing Up a Balloon with a Banana" activity found in *Icky, Squishy Science* (Markle, 1996). The activity is a result of informal class discussions after finishing a weather unit by reading *Cloudy with a Chance of Meatballs* (Barrett, 1978) and its sequel, *Pickles to Pittsburgh* (Barrett, 1997). Students were discussing things food could do other than be digested. Mrs. Bell challenged them to try blowing up a balloon with the food items provided. Later, the students will discover some properties of food, including the presence of bacteria.

Food activities are excellent ways to introduce diversity and multiculturalism to elementary and middle school students.

Grade 4 Example

In his fourth-grade class, Mr. Pettis allows students to discover their own ways to cure meat, based on suggestions from the books *More Science Experiments You Can Eat* (Cobb, 1979) and *Silly Science* (Levine & Johnstone, 1995). The students complete this activity based on questions originating with the reading of *Stone Soup* (Brown, 1997), *Eating the Plates* (Penner, 1991), *Corn Is Maize* (Aliki, 1976), and other stories. Their study of the foods eaten by Pilgrims and American Indians generated possible discovery activities that could promote further inquiry.

Use of Open Activities

Most exemplary teachers provide a foundation and then encourage children to try their own ideas about how to investigate and organize objects or events. This is seen in Mr. Mayernik's

"Focus on Inquiry: Divergent Thinking Activity" at the beginning of the chapter. Students are allowed to discover things for themselves. When students are given some autonomy, some suggestions lead to others and there is almost no end to what may be investigated.

Open activities allow students to study objects and events in two very useful ways: (1) observe similarities and differences in the properties of things, and (2) discover conditions that can produce or change properties (thus the name *discovery learning*).

Note the contrast in this pair of questions:

What materials will rust?
In what ways can you get some objects to rust?

When children examine the properties of comparable things, they learn that properties usually exist in varying degrees. As students inspect these variable degrees of properties, they will observe, describe, contrast, measure, and classify them. This is why open-ended investigations of things with comparable properties are so well suited for intuitive-level students and others who lack experience with the materials being examined. A common way to facilitate open activities is through the guided discovery approach.

PLANNING LESSONS

Teacher education students are exposed to lesson planning early in their professional preparation. Planning is an important component of science education. How will you plan a lesson? Will you simply write a page number from a teacher's guide? What are some ways to plan more effectively?

Developing a Lesson Plan

Many models for planning a lesson have been designed. The "objectives, materials, procedure, and evaluation of students" general format is an example of one type of lesson plan. Figure 3–2 presents an enhanced format. It is designed to help you think about the science lesson in a new way. It challenges the teacher to look at the activities from multiple perspectives.

The first part of the lesson model includes an overview of the lesson in your own words, as well as lesson topic, a specific grade level, any curricular objectives, and applicable performance objectives. In this area are the science themes. These originate in the benchmarks (AAAS, 1993). Science themes are needed to see the so-called big picture of science and how the lesson fits into the themes. Specifically, your lesson should support the development of one or more common science themes. These include systems, models, consistency, evolution, scale, and patterns of change. For each lesson, consider how you address one or more of these themes.

Next, provide any applicable standards or benchmarks. Use the *National Science Education Standards*, the *Benchmarks for Science Literacy*, your state standards, or any district standards that may apply.

Scientific process skills—such as classification, observation, measurement, inference, prediction, communicating, and experimentation—should also be addressed as part of the contextual framework. The last thing to consider as part of the contextual framework is the curricular integrations. Think about various ways to integrate social studies, language arts, reading, mathematics, art, music, or physical education into the lesson.

See *http://www.prenhall.com/peters* for a link to the science themes from *Science for All Americans* (1989) by the American Association for the Advancement of Science.

Figure 3–2   **Inquiry lesson plan format.**

Overview of the Lesson

Science Themes (From *Science for All Americans,* 1989, AAAS)

Standards (Use appropriate standards or benchmarks based on local requirements)
- Science Benchmarks (From *Benchmarks for Science Literacy,* 1993, AAAS)
- Science Standards (From *National Science Education Standards,* 1996, NRC)
- State Science Standards
- District Science Standards

Scientific Process Skills
    Curricular Integrations

Materials
    Supplies (what, how many, how much, etc.)
    Equipment

Procedure
    Steps to Follow or Problem to Solve
    Closed or Open Questions

Assessment
    Student Assessment
    Teacher Assessment

Bibliography
    Sources for Content Information and Children's Literature

Source: Adapted from Briscoe, Peters, & O'Brien, An elementary program emphasizing teachers' pedagogical content knowledge within a constructivist epistemological rubric. In *Excellence in Educating Teachers of Science,* P. Rubba, L. Campbell, & T. Dana (Eds.). Copyright © 1993 by ERIC Clearinghouse, Columbus, OH.

Materials

The second section in the lesson plan is a listing of materials. Both consumable and non-consumable supplies and equipment should be listed here. Remember to list materials for the teacher demonstration and student participation.

Procedure

The procedure of a direct instruction lesson plan is very specific, whereas a problem-centered lesson will be more generalized in its procedure. A guided discovery lesson is a blend of the two types of lessons. A direct instruction lesson has numbered steps logically arranged to meet time and curricular requirements. Write out and follow every step so that you do not forget anything. Give careful thought to what you want to say and do during the class period. Write these thoughts in an expanded outline form. Specific teacher questions can also be placed here. This ensures that you will not forget to ask something important. In a problem-centered lesson, the procedure may simply be a listing of the problem to solve and sample approaches to a solution.

Visit an Inquiry Classroom
Lesson Materials

View the *Finding and Organizing Materials* video in the "Planning and Management" section of the Companion CD. Mr. McKnight organized his classroom to maximize available workspace and traffic flow. Behind the scenes, he carefully selects appropriate materials and has these available for students in accessible locations. He then arranges the students in workgroups.

Review the video and ask yourself the following:
- How does Mr. McKnight manage the class and materials to ensure that students have what they need to carry out the activities?
- What is the role of the "materials person"?

 Have you observed a teacher engaging students in a lesson involving science materials and/or equipment? Describe the activity and materials and/or equipment needed. How did the teacher manage these materials? Record your ideas and the answers to these questions in your portfolio or use the Companion Website to share your ideas.

Visit an Inquiry Classroom
Pacing a Lesson

View the *Pacing and Time Allocation* video in the "Planning and Management" section of the Companion CD. As Mr. McKnight finishes a science lesson, he allows time for cleanup and begins to ask students about what activities would be appropriate in the future. He provides students with a preview of what they will do in the next lesson.

Review the video and ask yourself the following:
- Given the limited time for science in a busy school day, how can a teacher most effectively plan lessons that include investigations such as the earthworm activities Mr. McKnight plans?
- What is Mr. McKnight's perspective on the limited amount and use of time in the classroom? How does this compare to your view?

 Look at a lesson plan used by a teacher in your field placement. How does this lesson's procedure compare with the one described in the text or with Mr. McKnight? Why would there be differences, if any? Record your ideas and the answers to these questions in your portfolio or use the Companion Website to share your ideas.

Assessment

Next, a lesson plan must address assessment. How will you assess your students? Chapter 5 provides an in-depth view on student assessment. Teacher self-assessment should also be considered in this section of the lesson plan, especially for beginning teachers who need to practice reflecting on their instruction. You may want to videotape or audiotape the lesson, have a peer teacher or administrator observe the lesson, seek student feedback in some way, write personal observations in a journal, or use a school-based assessment form.

Bibliography

The lesson plan concludes with a bibliography. All sources used in planning should be listed here, including audiovisual support, computer-based tools, and applicable Internet links. Also include any fiction or nonfiction literature you will make available to students. The Lesson Model: The Planets on page 62 provides an example of a lesson plan.

Visit an Inquiry Classroom
Student Feedback

View the *Feedback* video in the "Planning and Management" section of the Companion CD. Mr. McKnight first uses questioning as a way to check for understanding before continuing with his lesson.

Review the video and ask yourself the following:
- What other ways does Mr. McKnight assess students?
- Is all feedback a form of assessment? Why or why not?

 Does your science methods professor use feedback? Does the professor also provide ongoing assessment? What are some specific examples? Record your ideas and the answers to these questions in your portfolio or use the Companion Website to share your ideas.

See *http://www.prenhall. com/peters* for links related to the use of children's literature in science.

Visit an Inquiry Classroom
Planning Integrations

The *Thematic Plan and Integration* video in the "Planning and Management" section of the Companion CD shows students exploring *Your Gross and Cool Body* (*http://yucky.kids. discovery.com/flash/body/*). This videoclip is an expansion of the "Worm World" activities that they were completing as part of their class project (*http://yucky.kids.discovery.com/ flash/ worm/index.html*). Both sites are located at the Discovery Communications *Yuckiest Site on the Internet* (*http://yucky.kids.discovery.com/flash/index.html*). Students will be able to expand their science activities to writing activities about their own body functions as they relate to worms.

Review the video and ask yourself the following:
- In what other ways could this website be used to expand the earthworm activities?
- Could the "Roach World" (*http://yucky.kids.discovery.com/flash/roaches/*) also be used?

 What other integrations can you think of for an earthworm lesson? Record your ideas and the answers to these questions in your portfolio or use the Companion Website to share your ideas.

Lesson Model
The Planets
(Direct Instruction Lesson Plan Example)

Overview of the Lesson

This lesson centers on the names of the nine planets and their relationship to the sun. The students will be asked to name the planets in order, give an approximation of their size, and be able to understand the concept of a satellite of a planet.

Science Themes

Systems —The solar system is a common example of a system. It is a group of planets and their satellites. It also includes solid, liquid, and gaseous material in an interrelated organization.
Models —The idea of a model is established as students create models of the solar system.
Consistency —The planets rotate in consistent patterns in the solar system.
Patterns of Change —Patterns of change are modeled as stars are formed and the visibility of planets changes throughout the year.
Evolution —There is a lot of verified data on the evolution of the solar system. The launching of new spacecraft to study the solar system and beyond brings relevancy to this topic.
Scale —Scale is established as the various sizes of the planets are compared.

Benchmarks for Science Literacy

By the end of fifth grade, students should know that

- Planets change their positions against the background of stars.
- Earth is one of several planets that orbit the sun, and the moon orbits the Earth. (AAAS, 1993, p. 63)

National Science Education Standards

As a result of their activities in grades K–4, all students should develop an understanding of

- Objects in the sky
- Changes in Earth and the sky (NRC, 1996, p. 130)

Scientific Skills

Classification —Classification activities are promoted as students develop classification systems for the planets (by composition, temperature, and size).
Observation —The students will observe the night sky and record data.
Measurement —The students will measure and re-create a scale model of the solar system.
Inference/Prediction —The students will infer why the temperature of Venus is high, based on that planet's characteristics.

Curricular Integrations

Measurement activities integrate *mathematics* into this lesson.
Art is incorporated into this lesson as students draw planet and star models.
Social studies is integrated into this lesson as students discuss ancient theories of an Earth-centered solar system.
Reading is integrated into this lesson as students read *The Magic School Bus Lost in the Solar System* (Cole, 1990).

Materials

Supplies

Large sheets of paper; crayons, markers, or paints.

(continued)

Equipment

Inflatable planetarium (two large sheets of black painter's plastic with both sides taped together lengthwise to form a large dome). A box fan is taped to one end and turned on to inflate the dome.

Procedure

Steps to Follow

1. Introduce the vocabulary: *Mercury, Venus, Earth, Mars, Jupiter, Saturn, Uranus, Neptune, Pluto, moon, satellite, orbit, asteroid, rotation,* and *revolution.* (Use definitions from end of the chapter and have students repeat the words. Write the definitions on the overhead for them to copy.)
2. Read the chapter on the planets from the student text. Discuss origins of the solar system. Read *The Magic School Bus Lost in the Solar System.*
3. Demonstrate the relative distances between planets by creating a model with students acting as the sun, planets, and satellites (see specific measurements in the text).
4. Demonstrate the rotation of Earth and the moon and their revolution around the sun by using students to represent the sun, Earth, and the moon (see picture in supplemental materials).

Closed Questions

A. What is the center of the solar system? Describe its characteristics.

B. What is the first planet from the sun? Describe its characteristics. (Repeat for the rest of the planets.) What is the difference between the moon and a satellite? (Note: The moon is Earth's satellite. We call other moons by their proper name, *satellite.*)
C. Define an orbit.

Open Questions

A. Which planets are colder? What is a possible cause for their low temperature?

B. Give some possible reasons for Venus being so hot. (Discuss greenhouse effects.)

5. Develop three planet classifications (Monday).
6. Redraw the scale model of the planets from the text, measuring exactly from the book (Tuesday).
7. Draw a picture of the night sky (Wednesday).
8. Find pictures of the winter and summer night sky from other books and magazines (Thursday).
9. Take students into the planetarium and demonstrate the position of the stars and planets by using the portable star projector (Friday).

Additional Homework Activities (select one)

10. Research what causes eclipses of the sun or moon.
11. If you started today and traveled 1000 miles per hour to Jupiter, determine how old you would be when you reached your destination (see adaptation of AIMS activity from *Out of This World*) (Lind et al., 1994).
12. Most people incorrectly believe that the distance from the Northern or Southern Hemisphere of the Earth to the sun causes the seasons. Research the real cause of the seasons.
13. Research the planets on NASA Internet sites.
14. Research and discuss why the International Astronomical Union, the official body for naming astronomical objects, would want to reclassify Pluto as a "trans-Neptunium asteroid" instead of a planet.

Assessment

Student Assessment

1. Design a mnemonic sentence to remember the order of planets (e.g., My Very Excellent Mother Just Served Us Nine Pizzas).
2. Describe in your journal what life would be like on Jupiter. How would it compare to life on the moon?
3. Write to NASA for more information on space exploration and present it to the class.

Teacher Assessment

Videotape the lesson and review it at home.

Bibliography

Branley, F. M. (1987). *The planets in our solar system.* New York: Thomas Crowell.

Cole, J. (1990). *The magic school bus lost in the solar system.* New York: Scholastic.

Lauber, P. (1982). *Journey to the planets.* New York: Crown Publishers Inc.

Lauber P. (1990). *Seeing the Earth from space.* New York: Orchard Books.

Lind, M., Knecht, P., Dodge, B., Williams, A., & Wiebe, A. (1994). *Out of this world.* Fresno, CA: AIMS Education Foundation.

National Geographic Society (Producer). (1987). *The planets* [laserdisc]. Washington, DC: National Geographic Society.

Scholastic. (1994). *The magic school bus explores the solar system* [CD-ROM]. Redmond, WA: Microsoft Corporation.

INSTRUCTIONAL LESSON MODELS FOR INQUIRY TEACHING

Inquiry is seen as a teaching and learning method where students "develop knowledge and understanding of scientific ideas, as well as an understanding of how scientists study the natural world" (National Research Council, 1996, p. 23). Although there are various ways to develop understandings, all inquiry methodologies have essential features as identified by the National Research Council (2000) and shown in Table 3–1. These include the learner doing the following:

- Engaging in scientifically oriented questions
- Giving priority to evidence
- Formulating explanations
- Connecting explanations to scientific knowledge
- Communicating and justifying explanations

As we explore methodologies such as direct instructions learning, guided discovery learning, and problem-centered learning, see if you can identify the NRC's characteristics of inquiry.

Direct Instruction

A common way to engage in closed activities is through **direct instruction.** Direct instruction generally involves carefully sequenced steps that include demonstration, modeling, guided practice, and independent application (Lokerson, 1992). In direct instruction, the teacher employs lectures, worksheets, recitations, demonstrations, or specific-answer type questions in a prearranged sequence. A detailed lesson plan is generally used for a direct instruction experience. The teacher is in control of the lesson and true student inquiry is limited.

Direct instruction is a teacher-centered, well-structured approach to teaching.

Advantages to Using Direct Instruction

One advantage to direct instruction is that the teacher can arrange the sequence of activities ahead of time and thus reduce the number of teaching decisions to be made during a lesson. This is especially helpful for inexperienced teachers who are preoccupied with activity or classroom management issues or who want to be sure they cover a certain curriculum. It is also helpful when introducing a new skill such as classification or engaging children or adolescents in the use of a new piece of science equipment. Direct instruction can also be useful when safety issues must take precedent over student exploration.

A more important advantage is that direct instruction can be used to help students construct a knowledge base for future learning. As noted by Tweed (2004): "Teachers must teach students an experimental design process before students can be asked to conduct their own experiments when studying science concepts . . . Teaching an experimental design process often occurs using an exploratory experiment or using direct instruction, but the teacher should guide the process."

When teaching through a direct approach, teachers can spend as much time as needed to plan beforehand. This allows them to think through which analogies, metaphors, activities, and questions will best support the concept they want to develop before the lesson. The direct approach also allows instruction to continue systematically until the teacher feels comfortable that most students understand some basic concept.

Disadvantages to Direct Instruction

One disadvantage to direct instruction is that students construct their knowledge at an individual pace. Therefore, the teacher's pace may not match the pace of each student. Also, students learn to perform science activities more remotely and are not free to explore topics further on their own. They are subject to what the teacher selects as themes or important concepts. Problem solving and higher order thinking skills are better developed through more independent learning experiences.

Another disadvantage of direct or teacher-centered instruction is that the teacher may have gender, cultural, or other biases that will limit learning for some students. In other words, the students are subject to everything from the teacher's point of view—not their own. For example, if the teacher unconsciously believes that boys are better suited for science than girls, he may call on boys more often to answer a question or to assist in a demonstration. This behavior reinforces the cultural disadvantage girls have in the sciences (Kahle & Meece, 1994).

See *http://www.prenhall.com/peters* for links related to promoting activities that encourage girls to engage in science learning.

In review, direct instruction is a method of learning that involves closed activities. Outcomes are predictable and specific. Children follow someone else's ideas or procedures. What should you do to promote children's ideas? To boost children's thinking processes, independence, and creativity, you should offer more open experiences such as guided discovery learning.

Guided Discovery Learning

Guided discovery learning is a less teacher-oriented and more student-oriented instructional method. It would fall midpoint in the classroom inquiry continuum found in Table 3–1. In this approach, students are guided in exploration of materials. They observe phenomena, gather data on their own, make comparisons, draw inferences, and arrive at conclusions. Teachers follow up on what has been discovered and point out any misconceptions. Students are then free to explore once again. This method is especially valuable in making connections between science vocabulary and scientific concepts.

Remember the lesson plan components from Figure 3–2 on p. 58. The same general procedures are used here as well. Students are provided time to discover concepts based on initial information. In guided discovery, follow-up discussion and questioning is crucial. The direct instruction approach spells out exactly what is to be learned. Guided discovery, in contrast, allows students more time to explore on their own.

In guided discovery activities, it is crucial to follow up after student exploration and determine whether the students have made correct assumptions. The following Lesson Model presents a guided discovery lesson for electricity.

Problem-Centered Learning

Problem-centered learning moves us even further from teacher-control to learner-control lesson models (refer back to Table 3–1). Now, students become more involved in the planning and implementation of lessons. Following the development of an initial question, students continue their investigation until they solve a problem.

> **Problem-centered learning** is a method of teaching and learning that focuses on children's ability to construct their own meaning for concepts.

Start with a Problem

In *Science for All Americans* (AAAS, 1989), there is a message to all science teachers that good teaching starts with questions about nature or explorations of phenomena that are interesting to students and at their level. The authors go on to say that as students become familiar with the things around them, they will begin to question and find answers to these questions. This idea is at the very heart of problem solving in elementary and middle school science. Children are very inquisitive during the elementary and middle school years. Promoting and developing this inherent trait will provide lifelong skills in solving everyday problems. One way to increase problem-solving ability is through problem-centered learning.

Through problem-centered activities, children learn to view science as a meaningful, dynamic activity. They see science as a human endeavor in which they can participate. You will notice that the lesson plan is similar to the other lesson plans, except that its procedure section contains a problem for the students to solve, as opposed to a specific procedure. Generally, a problem-centered lesson will also have more open questions, because the teacher is not presenting specific concepts or definitions that are repeated by the students.

> See *http://www.prenhall. com/peters* for links related to *Blueprints for Reform* (AAAS, 1998).

Problem-Centered Learning: Making Science Relevant

It may not come as a surprise to you that elementary and middle school teachers see a value in their students learning science. What you may not understand is why these same teachers do not teach more science throughout the week. One reason commonly given is increasing pressure from parents and administrators to have students score high on standardized reading and math tests. One way to satisfy both worlds is to teach more science without detracting from reading and mathematics. In other words, integrate other content areas with science as suggested by the National Science Teachers Association (NSTA, 2003) and the authors of the Science Program Standard in the Standards Link box.

Standards Link

Science Program Standard

The program of study in science for all students should be developmentally appropriate, interesting, and relevant to students' lives; emphasize student understanding through inquiry; and be connected with other school subjects.

- **The program of study should include all of the content standards.**

- **Science content must be embedded in a variety of curriculum patterns that are developmentally appropriate, interesting, and relevant to students' lives.**

- **The program of study must emphasize student understanding through inquiry.**

- **The program of study in science should connect to other school subjects.**

(Program Standard B, National Research Council, 1996, p. 212.)

Lesson Model
Guided Discovery Lesson Plan for Electricity

Overview of the Lesson

Electricity has become very important to modern humans. The commonplace nature of electricity makes it an excellent topic of discovery in the elementary or middle school classroom.

Science Themes

Systems —The activity requires the investigator to create a system that includes a power source, a power transmission, and a power consumer.

Models —This activity is done on a small scale but is representative of a much larger system. Through the creation of series and parallel circuits, students will be better able to understand how/where electricity is generated, transported, and used.

Consistency —Electrical systems require consistency. Dry/wet cells are designed to provide a constant voltage so that a device is not damaged by surges or suppressions in current. Likewise, the power derived at power stations requires a feedback system of substations, switching devices, transformers, and monitors to ensure that constant voltage is maintained.

Patterns of Change —Power generation undergoes many changes as new technologies are created to maximize the amount of energy produced from fossil fuels while limiting harmful effects to the environment. Nuclear and solar technologies are changing the way electricity is generated. Batteries are also changing as new materials are being tried to create longer lasting, more powerful, rechargeable, less expensive batteries.

Evolution —The production and use of electricity may have important evolutionary significance. Animals, including humans, may undergo evolutionary change in response to electromagnetic fields, or may have already changed in response to the availability of light and heat from electricity.

Scale —Scale is inherent to a study of electricity. Large-scale generators and transformers produce high-voltage electricity at power stations. Next, the power is transmitted through high-tension lines to substations. From the substations, electricity is scaled down and sent to neighborhoods, where it is again stepped down into a usable voltage for home use. Generally, a house has three wires coming into it. One is a common ground and two are hot wires, at 110 volts each. From there, electricity may go to electrical appliances, where it is further scaled, or transformed, into a much lower voltage, such as 9 volts.

Benchmarks for Science Literacy

By the end of fifth grade, students should be able to

- Make safe electrical connections with various plugs, sockets, and terminals. (AAAS, 1993, p. 293)

National Science Education Standards

As a result of the activities in grades K–4, all students should develop an understanding of

- Light, heat, electricity, and magnetism. (NRC, 1996, p. 123)

Scientific Skills

Classification —Students will be able to classify various types of circuits into either series or parallel.

Observation —Students will observe the various ways that light (or do not light) the bulb.

Measurement —Students check individual batteries to ensure that they are producing a current.

Inference/Prediction —Students will predict various ways to light the bulbs and then test the predictions. Students will infer that their house circuit is a parallel circuit as they discover the differences between the two circuits.

Communication —Communication skills will be developed as students interact in small groups to solve the problem. Communication of results will also occur as groups share their findings.

Experimenting —Students will have to identify the variables that cause the bulb to light up. They will also explore relationships among the batteries, wires, and bulbs. Students will construct hypotheses about the differences between series and parallel circuits. They will have to design a solution to the batteries and bulbs problem.

Curricular Integrations

In *language arts,* numerous stories and poems are based on electricity themes. Most children have experienced the lack of electricity in their homes at one time or another, opening up possibilities for creating short stories.

In *mathematics,* experiences can be related to meter readings/billing and electrical usage, comparisons of electrical usage among appliances, and measuring voltages.

Art can be incorporated into an electricity activity in a variety of ways. Students can draw pictures of their experiences during an electrical blackout.

Music could become part of the lesson as a discussion of how instruments have evolved through the use of electricity.

Social studies is important to the study of electricity. American communities all depend on electricity. A comparison between cultures based on the availability of electricity is important.

Safety is vital to any discussion of electricity. Local power companies are excellent sources for materials on safety topics.

Materials

Supplies

Light bulb–shaped paper for student stories; pamphlets on safety precautions about electricity.

Equipment

Class set of batteries, wires, and bulbs.

Procedure

Steps to Follow

1. The introductory activity/advance organizer includes stories and poems based on electrical themes as a way to introduce the topic. A brief discussion of power outages will also be done as appropriate.
2. The first activity is to light the bulb. Students are provided one battery, one wire, and one light bulb and are instructed to design an investigation that individually would result in lighting the bulb. Guide them in defining a complete circuit and explain the path of electricity through the bulb, if necessary. Remind them that the electrons have to go into and back out of the light bulb for it to function.

Closed Questions for Lighting the Bulb

A. What do you notice about the light bulb? (It has a base, filament, and glass enclosure.)
B. What makes the bulb light? (Electrons flow through the filament.)

Open Questions for Lighting the Bulb

A. What were some probable ways that the light bulb was invented?
B. What are some creative ways to light a bulb?

Steps to Follow (continued)

3. The second activity is to create a circuit with two dimly lit bulbs and another circuit with two brightly lit bulbs. Students are provided two light bulbs, one battery, and four or more wires to produce a series and parallel circuit. Note that the materials only provide for one circuit to be produced at a time. Once the first one is designed, students will have to diagram the finding and then continue with the other circuit. Provide the following diagram if necessary.

(continued)

Series Circuit

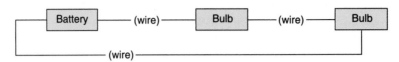

Parallel Circuit

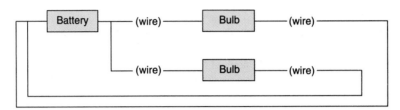

Closed Questions on Circuits

    A.   How are the lights in this room wired? (parallel)

    B.   What happens to the old-style Christmas tree twinkle lights when a bulb is removed? (They all go out because it is a series circuit.)

Open Questions on Circuits

    A.   Why do you think buildings are wired in parallel instead of series circuits?

    B.   What are some ways to create a parallel circuit?

Steps to Follow (continued)

    4.   Science/Technology/Society extension activity on determining appliance power consumption and reading a power meter from power company handout. Discuss how cultures rely on energy.

    5.   Discuss how electricity is produced and various types of fuel. Discuss the impact on the environment (thermal pollution from steam cooling, greenhouse effect from giving off carbon dioxide, acid rain from burning sulfur, electromagnetic fields from electricity transmission).

Closed Questions on Electricity Production

    A.   What form of fuel does our local power company use?

Open Questions on Electricity Production

    A.   If we were to close down all the electrical generation plants that use fossil fuels, what impact would that have on society?

    B.   What are some ways people could conserve energy?

    C.   How did you feel when the power was out last time? How did it change your life?

Assessment

Student Assessment

    1.   Students will complete a written story based on their experiences with electricity.

    2.   Students will go to a hardware store and check types of wire and fuse boxes to determine which would be most appropriate for their house.

    3.   Students will actually make a series and parallel circuit (light the bulbs).

    4.   Students will interview family and friends to see which type of fuel (fossil, solar, nuclear) they prefer when generating electricity and why.

    5.   Students will record in their science notebooks the various ways they lit the bulbs.

Teacher Assessment

Invite a peer teacher to come into the room and observe questioning technique, particularly with regard to teacher dominance of questions versus students' independent inquiry.

Bibliography

Bains, R. (1982). *Discovering electricity.* Mahway, NJ: Troll.
Berger, M. (1989). *Switch on, switch off.* New York: Franklin Watts.
Fife, J. (1996). *Watered-down electricity: Using water to explain electricity.* Huntington, WV: University Editions.
Gosnell, K. (1994). *Thematic unit: Electricity.* Huntington Beach, CA: Teacher Created Materials.
Johnston, T. (1988). *Energy: Making it work.* Milwaukee, WI: Gareth Stevens.
Markle, S. (1989). *Power up: Experiments, puzzles, and games exploring electricity.* New York: Antheneum.
Mayes, S. (1989). *Where does electricity come from?* Tulsa, OK: EDC Publishing.
Siegel, B. M., & Stone, A. H. (1970). *Turned on: A look at electricity.* Englewood Cliffs, NJ: Prentice Hall.

Benefits of a Problem-Centered Approach

When science is done in an integrated, problem-centered format, children begin to value science because they see its relevance. They can read about science in an interesting context. Science activities based on literature build on familiar contexts and further reinforce a positive attitude toward science and other subjects (see Tchudi & Lafer, 1996, for examples). Other advantages for an integrated approach to science are as follows:

* Children learn in a social environment that fosters rich language activities.
* Scientific concepts are put into a meaningful context by connecting them with literature and other content areas.
* More time is spent on learning science because it becomes a part of the normal reading and mathematics curriculum.

Another benefit of an integrated, problem-centered approach to science is that science becomes less of a disconnected collection of facts and more of a "coherent, meaningful body of knowledge" (Keig, 1994, p. 79). Students use their prior knowledge and new experiences to form bridges between the known and the unknown. In *Blueprints for Reform* (AAAS, 1998), the authors indicate that "providing a link to the student's own world through contextual learning can be a powerful motivating factor" (p. 126).

Integrated, problem-centered instruction is also beneficial because it is intrinsically cooperative (Post, Ellis, Humphreys, & Buggey, 1997). Small groups of students are engaged in inquiry, and this can result in a successful learning experience for the group and for each of its members (Jones, 1990). Cooperative methods promote interaction between students. This interaction has the potential to involve students in clarifying, defending, elaborating, evaluating, and even arguing (Tobin, Tippins, & Gallard, 1994). Although cooperative learning may not always lead to the teacher's predetermined learning goal, the consensus building and negotiation are valuable learning tools.

Another benefit of an integrated, problem-centered approach is that this method is a direct application of the multiple intelligence theory provided by Howard Gardner (Charbonneau & Reider, 1995; Sunal et al., 2000). Because children learn in different ways, an integrated curriculum that promotes various approaches to learning will support the various learning styles. Students can benefit from the "multilevel instruction" and "multitasking" inherent in integrated approaches to the curriculum (Roberts & Kellough, 2000, p. 3).

A final benefit of an integrated, problem-centered approach is that it generally includes a variety of children's books. Children's literature is captivating to young people and useful in developing emerging concepts. Children's books help place new vocabulary in a context that makes constructing meaning easier. For example, if a student looks at a selection of dinosaur books, he will begin to develop the concept or scheme of "dinosaurness" or an even more relevant science concept that living things transform over time to adapt to changing environments.

See *http://www.prenhall. com/peters* for the International Reading Association and other links related to the use of children's literature.

Problem-Centered Lessons and Children's Literature

Remember some of the food-related science activities found earlier in this chapter? These activities incorporated the food theme in children's books as an integral part of the lesson. The food topic could have been extended into other content areas to further integrate the lessons and help children and adolescents identify problems to explore that are relevant to their own needs or address their own questions. Consider the following content areas.

- In mathematics, the teacher can read *Spaghetti and Meatballs for All!* (Burns, 1997) as an introduction to geometry, *Each Orange Had 8 Slices* (Giganti, 1992) in order to promote counting skills, or *Gator Pie* (Mathews, 1979) as a means to study fractions.
- Language skills and poetry can be introduced through the story *Never Take a Pig to Lunch and Other Poems About the Fun of Eating* (Westcott, 1994).
- Social studies can be brought in through *Everybody Cooks Rice* (Dooley, 1991) or *The Tortilla Factory* (Paulsen, 1995).
- Other activities can originate from the *Food* (Willrich, 1993) or *Food and Nutrition* (Sterling, 2000) thematic unit books or the countless other children's books related to the food theme.

Although each of the abovementioned books is associated with other content areas, they all support science concepts in one way or another.

When choosing books to use in your science program, keep the following points in mind.

- **Is the book appropriate for your students' developmental level?**   Do not use a book just because it has the same title as the unit you are currently studying. Check that it is written at an appropriate reading level. If you are not going to read it to the class, make sure that your advanced readers can read it to other students.
- **Is the content appropriate?**   Before placing a book out for students to read, be sure that the content will not develop further misconceptions about the topic under study. Students have many false notions about scientific phenomena, and you do not want to reinforce these or add to them. Preread each book and note any inconsistencies; eliminate nonsupportive books.
- **Will the book be interesting to your students?**   Select a wide variety of books (if possible) to ensure that you meet the individual needs of your students. Consider gender and cultural diversity when selecting books. Look for colorful illustrations and a good story line.
- **Does the book encourage scientific investigation?**   Your purpose for starting with children's literature is to provide a baseline for further knowledge and process skill development. Select books that are good springboards to further learning.

For additional teaching ideas by using children's literature, explore the resources identified in Figure 3–3.

Figure 3–3   Resources for teaching science with children's literature.

Bosma, B., & DeVries, Guth, N. (1995). *Children's literature in an integrated curriculum: The authentic voice.* New York: International Reading Association & Teachers College Press.
Butzow, C., & Butzow, J. (1989). *Science through children's literature: An integrated approach.* Englewood, CO: Teacher Ideas Press.
Butzow, C., & Butzow, J. (1994). *Intermediate science through children's literature: Over land and sea.* Englewood, CO: Teacher Ideas Press.
Butzow, C., & Butzow, J. (1998). *More science through children's literature: An integrated approach (through children's literature).* Englewood, CO: Teacher Ideas Press.
Butzow, C., & Butzow, J. (1999). *Exploring the environment through children's literature: An integrated approach (through children's literature).* Englewood, CO: Teacher Ideas Press.
Butzow, C., & Butzow, J. (2002). *The world of work through children's literature: An integrated approach (through children's literature).* Englewood, CO: Teacher Ideas Press.
Flagg, A., Ory, M., & Ory, T. (2002). *Teaching science with favorite picture books: Grades 1–3.* New York: Instructor Books.
Fredericks, A. (2001). *Investigating natural disasters through children's literature: An integrated approach (through children's literature).* Englewood, CO: Teacher Ideas Press.
Fredericks, A., Meinbach, A., & Rothlein, L. (1993). *Thematic units: An integrated approach to teaching science and social studies.* New York: HarperCollins.
Gertz, S. E., Portman, D. J., & Sarquis, M. (1996). *Teaching physical science through children's literature.* New York: McGraw-Hill Trade.
Hefner, C., & Lewis K. (1995). *Literature-based science: Children's books and activities to enrich the K–5 curriculum.* Phoenix: Oryx.
Jagusch, S. A., & Saul, W. (1992). *Vital connections: Children, science, and books.* Portsmouth, NH: Heinemann.
Keane, N. J. (2002). *Teaching science through literature: Grades 4–6.* Worthington, OH: Linworth Publishing.
Keane, N. J., & Wait, C. (2002). *Teaching science through literature: Grades 6–8.* Worthington, OH: Linworth Publishing.
LeCroy, B., & Holder, B. (1994). *Bookwebs: A brainstorm of ideas for the primary classroom.* Englewood, CO: Teacher Ideas Press.
Shaw, D. G., & Dybdahl, C. S. (1996). *Integrating science and language arts: A sourcebook for K–6 teachers.* Boston: Allyn & Bacon.

An Integrated, Problem-Centered Lesson Example

An example of an integrated, problem-centered lesson is one based on *Bartholomew and the Oobleck* (Geisel & Geisel, 1977). The students' stated problem to solve is to determine and describe the properties and behavior of the cornstarch and water mixture and communicate why the substance behaves in this way.

The teacher begins by reading the story. After the story is read, students receive a mixture of cornstarch and water (made beforehand) for their exploration. The students

Children interact with a cornstarch and water mixture as part of an integrated, problem-centered lesson.

Source: Reprinted from the Great Explorations in Math and Science (GEMS) teacher's guide entitled *Oobleck: What Do Scientists Do?*, copyright by The Regents of the University of California, and used with permission. The GEMS series includes more than 70 teacher's guides and handbooks for preschool through eighth grade, available from LHS GEMS, Lawrence Hall of Science, University of California, Berkeley, CA 94720-5200. (510) 642-7771. *http://www.lhsgems.org*

interact with the mixture and problem-solve to determine its properties. Through this experience, students work on many scientific skills. Students also explore content knowledge as they discuss new words and ideas, as they communicate their results in a small-group social setting. Finally, students develop values and attitudes as they begin to use their natural curiosity to explore scientific phenomena.

Curricular Integration Examples

Mathematics can be integrated by measuring the amounts of water and cornstarch it takes to make a "good" mixture. The subject matter of social studies is integrated in a discussion of kingdoms because the story is based on a king. Art can be integrated when students create mosaics with water-based paints and the cornstarch mixture. The sourcebook for arranging this experience is *Oobleck: What Do Scientists Do?* (Sneider, 1985).

Assessing Integrated, Problem-Centered Experiences

The assessment of this integrated experience should be in keeping with its constructivist nature. Students should be assessed on the product (knowledge), process (skill), and attitude (value) of the experience. Literature/language activities can become an assessment exercise as students write (or orally present) a creative story. Students could also write descriptive adjectives about the mixture. These are used to create poetry, such as cinquains or diamantes.

Scientific attitudes can be assessed as students are asked how they feel about the fact that even scientists cannot agree on why the mixture acts the way it does. Students should also be challenged to come up with their own explanation as to why the material behaves the way it does.

Concept maps (see Chapter 5) would be an appropriate way to determine content knowledge in this case (i.e., the properties of the substance). Students can be provided a key word such as *mixture* and asked to develop links based on what they know. See the Lesson Model for exploring and communicating the properties of a substance.

Misconceptions Occurring During Problem-Centered Lessons

As you think about the various ways to plan and teach lessons, it becomes evident that not every student will learn exactly what you want them to learn. Sometimes students form misconceptions during explorations. Misconceptions are ideas a person has that something is one way but it is really another. This tends to happen in the lessons when students have more control over their learning.

Misconception Examples

In the cornstarch and water lesson, students often think that the material hardens when kneaded in the hands because all of the water is removed by their skin. In fact, just allowing the material to rest in the hands will show that it readily softens again without the skin supplying the moisture.

Here's another example of a misconception. Suppose you ask a child what would happen if an astronaut "dropped" something like a pen on the moon. The child may reply that it would float away. You may then ask why the astronaut does not "float away." Students may answer that the astronaut's heavy boots weigh him down and keep him from floating away. Of course, the moon does have gravity, and this is what keeps the astronaut from floating away. The pen actually does fall toward the moon as it would on the earth. Because the moon has less mass, however, the pen falls with less force than here on the earth. In synopsis, everything on the moon is attracted to it; otherwise, the rocks and dust would also float away.

See *http://www.prenhall. com/peters* for links related to science misconceptions and other specific examples.

Lesson Model

Integrated, Problem-Centered Lesson
for Exploring and Communicating the Properties of a Substance

Overview of the Lesson

Children can become scientists as they explore the world around them. When they encounter a new situation, children can observe, classify, measure, infer, predict, communicate, and experiment to solve problems and gain new information or ideas. Children's curiosity is stimulated as they complete activities. This activity is designed to acquaint children with a substance that does not behave as other substances do. Specifically, the mixture gets harder as it is manipulated and softer when it is left alone. This is in direct opposition to materials such as play dough (flour, water, salt, cream of tartar, dye) or clay.

Science Themes

Systems—The cornstarch and water mixture is a physical/chemical system of molecules that interact with each other and the environment. To understand the nature of the substance, we must consider its behavior as an integrated system of interacting parts and energy.

Models—In considering the way molecules or atoms are arranged in the mixture, students will create pictorial or mental models of the structure of this particular type of matter.

Consistency—Although we can cause temporary changes in the substance by inputting energy in one form or another, students will notice that the system tends to maintain its properties and reorganize itself into the same physical consistency and structure as before the system was disturbed.

Patterns of Change—The cornstarch and water mixture seems to be both solid and liquid at the same time. It can be compared to other substances, and the patterns of change that are represented as liquid and solid states are interchanged.

Scale—The behavior of the mixture may be caused by scale. The sizes of the molecules allow them to interact in ways that a larger substance cannot.

Benchmarks for Science Literacy

By the end of fifth grade, students should know that

- Heating and cooling cause changes in the properties of materials. Many kinds of changes occur faster under hotter conditions.
- When a new material is made by combining two or more materials, it has properties that are different from the original materials. For that reason, a lot of different materials can be made from a small number of basic kinds of materials. (AAAS, 1993, p. 77)

National Science Education Standards

As a result of the activities in grades K–4, all students should develop

- Abilities necessary to do scientific inquiry
- Understanding of properties of objects and materials (NRC, 1996, pp. 121, 123)

Scientific Skills

Classification—Students will compare this substance and other materials in an attempt to classify it according to its properties.

Observation—Students will use all their senses to observe the substance (provide a caution against tasting the material).

Inference/Prediction—Students will infer from the collected data such non-observable properties of the mixture as what it is made of or how the atoms might be arranged.

Communication—Students will communicate their findings to the group. They will also communicate with each other when developing theories of why it behaves the way it does.

Experimenting—Students will design and carry out experiments to alter the mixture, to find its properties, and to explain its behavior.

Curricular Integrations

For *language arts,* the teacher can record the words used to describe the mixture and discuss descriptive adjectives. Descriptive poetry, such as cinquains or diamantes, can be developed.

Mathematics activities can be developed as students compare densities of other substances to that of the mixture. Art can be integrated into this lesson as students experiment with water-based paints and the mixture.

Physical education is promoted as students act out the behavior of a substance's molecules.

Social studies is a natural integration as kingdoms are discussed. Also, the interaction between science and society can be stressed.

Safety during the activity is stressed when using heating devices. Also, caution against eating the substance or getting it on clothing.

Materials

Supplies

Two or three boxes of cornstarch; green food coloring; water; small objects such as marbles, coins, rubber stoppers; other common substances or materials that can be used to explore. (Note: Prepare the mixture by placing one or two boxes of cornstarch in a mixing bowl and mixing in small amounts of green-colored water. Continue until the consistency is like a thick plaster.)

Equipment

Thermometers, heat source (microwave), balance, graduated cylinders

Procedure

Problem to Solve

1. The problem to be solved is (1) determine and describe the properties and behavior of the cornstarch and water mixture, and (2) successfully communicate a theory as to why the substance behaves the way it does. Record the words used to describe the properties of the mixture in a concept map.

[Note: While students explore, walk around the room, questioning students about what they are doing, why they are doing it, and what else they can do to gain information about the mixture.]

Closed Question

A. What happens to the mixture as you continue to squeeze it in your hands? (It hardens.)

Open Questions

A. What did you find out about the mixture?
B. What do you think causes the mixture to behave this way? Have students explain why it behaves as it does and suggest what materials it might be made from.
C. What possible explanations do you think scientists give for the behavior of the substance? Discuss scientific theory and why scientists cannot completely agree on why it behaves as it does. Discuss the tentative nature of science theoretical models and their use, and the scientific search for explanations.
D. How could the king have eliminated this material from the kingdom?

2. Extension activity. Problem: Can you find other materials that behave the same way as the mixture?

(continued)

Open Question

    A.   What other substances do you think behave like this substance?

    3.   Art/PE extensions. Problem: Why would it be unlikely that this material would cover an entire kingdom?

Closed Question

    A.   What is a kingdom?

Open Question

    A.   Since America is a democracy and not a kingdom, would we handle the situation differently than the king did in the story?

Assessment

Student Assessment

1. Develop a concept map on the properties of the mixture.
2. Assign group reports that explain why the mixture behaves as it does. Require such items as a hypothesis, data collected, a summary of the data, and conclusions.
3. Write a story about your own day in the kingdom as the messy substance fell. What did you find out?
4. Take a small amount home and ask a parent or friend to provide thoughts on the mixture.
5. Find out more about Newtonian and non-Newtonian fluids.
6. Leave the mixture out for 1 week. What effect does this have on the substance? Explain why this happens.
7. Use descriptive adjectives to develop poetry, such as cinquains or diamantes.

Teacher Assessment

Audiotape the lesson and review it with the following questions in mind: How did the students react to the investigation? What percentage of the time was I dominating the discussion and how often were students actively discussing the mixture?

Bibliography

Geisel, T. S., & Geisel, A. S. (1977). *Bartholomew and the Oobleck.* New York: Random House. (original work published in 1949 by Dr. Seuss)

Kerr, D. A. (1983). Quick clay. *Scientific American, 209*(5), 132–142.

Sneider, C. I. (1985). *Oobleck: What do scientists do?* Berkeley, CA: Lawrence Hall of science.

Walker, J. (1978). The amateur scientist. *Scientific American, 239*(5), 186–198.

Walker, J. (1982). The amateur scientist. *Scientific American, 246*(1), 174–180.

Summary

- When planning a unit, the main things you must know are (a) how to determine which generalizations to use, (b) how to gather more activities to teach each generalization, and (c) how to introduce, or bridge into, each generalization's sequence of activities.
- Closed problems and activities lead to a single response. They foster convergent thinking. Open activities and problems lead to a wide variety of responses. They produce divergent thinking.
- Children can be taught using direct instruction, guided discovery, or problem-centered lessons. As you reduce teacher control and increase student autonomy, students are required to take charge of their learning. More meaningful relationships can be formed with problem-centered learning.

Reflection

Companion CD

1. Look at the "Earthworm Family" lesson linked to the *Thematic Plan and Integration* video on the Companion CD. Can you identify aspects of this lesson that are high in "teacher direction"? How could you modify the lesson to make it more learner centered?
2. Look at the "Earthworm Waste" lesson linked to the *Curiosity and Interest* video on the Companion CD.

How could you make this lesson into more of a "guided discovery" format?
3. Look at the "What Is Vermicomposting" lesson linked to the *Teacher Attributes* video on the Companion CD. How could you make this lesson into more of a "problem-centered" lesson format?

Portfolio Ideas

1. Take a lesson plan that you have recently completed and rewrite it in the form of a problem-centered lesson to share in your portfolio and with the class.
2. Search the Internet for some lesson plan databases. A good starting point is to use the key words *lesson, plan, elementary,* and *science.* Record findings in your portfolio.
3. Observe the next five science lessons while at your practicum site. Note in your portfolio the use of open and closed activities. How could more open activities be incorporated?
4. Ask several adults one of the misconceptions questions. Do you notice any pattern in their answers? Did your classmates have similar experiences? Record findings in your portfolio.
5. Read *Multiple Intelligences in the Classroom* (Armstrong, 1994, Alexandria, VA: ASCD),

Teaching with the Brain in Mind (Jensen, 1998, Alexandria, VA: ASCD), or *Use Both Sides of Your Brain* (Buzan, 1989, New York: Plume) and research ways that curriculum and planning can be modified to better meet students' needs. Enter findings in your portfolio.
6. Integrate multiple intelligences activities into your curriculum by using a resource such as *Celebrating Multiple Intelligences: Teaching for Success* (Faculty of the New City School, 1994, St. Louis, MO: Author), *Succeeding with Multiple Intelligences: Teaching Through the Personal Intelligences* (Faculty of the New City School, 1996, St. Louis, MO: Author), or *If the Shoe Fits . . . How to Develop Multiple Intelligences in the Classroom* (Chapman, 1993, Arlington Heights, IL: IRI/Skylight). Compile a listing of activities in your portfolio.

References

Alfving, A., Eitzen, L., Hyman, J., Patron, R., Holve, H., & Nelson, P. (1987). *Fun with foods: A recipe for math + science*. Fresno, CA: AIMS Education Foundation.

Aliki. (1976). *Corn is maize*. New York: HarperCollins.

American Association for the Advancement of Science (AAAS). (1989). *Science for all Americans*. Washington, DC: Author.

American Association for the Advancement of Science (AAAS). (1993). *Benchmarks for science literacy*. New York: Oxford University Press.

American Association for the Advancement of Science (AAAS). (1998). *Blueprints for reform*. New York: Oxford University Press.

Barrett, J. (1978). *Cloudy with a chance of meatballs*. New York: Aladdin Paperbacks.

Barrett, J. (1997). *Pickles to Pittsburgh*. New York: Atheneum Books.

Briscoe, C., Peters, J., & O'Brien, G. (1993). An elementary program emphasizing teacher's pedagogical content knowledge within a constructivist epistemological rubric. In P. Rubba, L. Campbell, & T. Dana (Eds.), *Excellence in educating teachers of science* (pp. 1–20). Columbus, OH: ERIC Clearinghouse.

Brown, M. (1997). *Stone soup*. New York: Aladdin Paperbacks.

Burns, M. (1997). *Spaghetti and meatballs for all! A mathematical story*. New York: Scholastic.

Charbonneau, M., & Reider, B. (1995). *The integrated elementary classroom: A developmental model of education for the 21st century*. Boston: Allyn & Bacon.

Cobb, V. (1979). *More science experiments you can eat*. New York: HarperTrophy.

Cobb, V. (1994). *Science experiments you can eat* (Rev. ed.). New York: HarperTrophy.

Cole, J. (1996). *The magic school bus gets eaten*. New York: Scholastic.

Dooley, N. (1991). *Everybody cooks rice*. Minneapolis, MN: Carolrhoda Books.

Geisel, T. S., & Geisel, A. S. (1977). *Bartholomew and the Oobleck*. New York: Random House.

Giganti, P. (1992). *Each orange had 8 slices: A counting book*. New York: Mulberry Books.

Jenkins, S. (1997). *What do you do when something wants to eat you?* Boston: Houghton Mifflin.

Johmann, C., & Rieth, E. (1996). *Gobble up science*. Santa Barbara, CA: Learning Works.

Jones, R. (1990). *Teaming up!* LaPorte, TX: ITGROUP.

Kahle, J., & Meece, J. (1994). Research on gender issues in the classroom. In D. Gabel (Ed.), *Handbook of research on science teaching and learning* (pp. 542–557). Arlington, VA: National Science Teachers Association.

Keig, P. (1994). Introducing elementary teachers to thematic science instruction. In L. Schafer (Ed.), *Behind the methods class door: Educating elementary and middle school science teachers* (pp. 79–88). Columbus, OH: ERIC Clearinghouse.

Lauber, P. (1995). *Who eats what?* New York: HarperCollins.

Levine, S., & Johnstone, L. (1995). *Silly science: Strange and startling projects to amaze your family and friends*. New York: John Wiley.

Lokerson, J. (1992). *Learning disabilities: Glossary of some important terms*. Arlington, VA: The ERIC Clearinghouse on Disabilities and Gifted Education.

Markle, S. (1996). *Icky, squishy science*. New York: Hyperion.

Mathews, L. (1979). *Gator pie*. Littleton, MA: Sundance.

National Research Council (NRC). (1996). *National science education standards*. Washington, DC: National Academy Press.

National Research Council (NRC). (2000). *Inquiry and the national science education standards: A guide for teaching and learning*. Washington, DC: National Academy Press.

National Science Teachers Association (NSTA). (2003). *Science education for middle school students. A position statement*. Washington, DC: Author. Retrieved October 1, 2004, from *www.nsta.org/positionstatement&psid=20*

Paulsen, G. (1995). *The tortilla factory*. New York: Voyager Books.

Penner, L. R. (1991). *Eating the plates: A pilgrim book of food and manners*. New York: Aladdin Paperbacks.

Post, T., Ellis, A., Humphreys, A., & Buggey, L. (1997). *Interdisciplinary approaches to curriculum: Themes for teaching*. Upper Saddle River, NJ: Merrill/Prentice Hall.

Roberts, P., & Kellough, R. (2000). *A guide for developing interdisciplinary thematic units* (2nd ed.). Upper Saddle River, NJ: Merrill/Prentice Hall.

Sneider, C. I. (1985). *Oobleck: What do scientists do?* Berkeley, CA: Lawrence Hall of Science.

Sterling, M. (2000). *Food and nutrition*. Westminster, CA: Teacher Created Materials.

Sunal, C., Powell, D., McClelland, S., Rule, A., Rovegno, I. Smith, C., & Sunal, D. (2000). *Integrating academic units in the elementary school curriculum*. New York: Harcourt College Publishers.

Tchudi, S., & Lafer, S. (1996). *The interdisciplinary teacher's handbook: Integrating teaching across the curriculum*. Portsmouth, NH: Heinemann.

Tobin, K., Tippins, D., & Gallard, J. (1994). Research on instructional strategies for teaching science. In D. Gabel (Ed.), *Handbook of research on science teaching and learning* (pp. 45–93). New York: Macmillan.

Tweed, A. (2004). Direct instruction: Is it the most effective science teaching strategy? *NSTA Reports*. Arlington, VA: National Science Teachers Association.

Westcott, N. (1994). *Never take a pig to lunch and other poems about the fun of eating*. New York: Orchard Books.

Willrich, L. (1993). *Food*. Westminster, CA: Teacher Created Materials.

Suggested Readings

Eby, J., & Martin, D. (2001). *Reflective planning, teaching, and evaluation for the elementary school: A relational approach* (3rd ed.). Upper Saddle River, NJ: Merrill/Prentice Hall. (a book that promotes reflective thought in the planning process)

Freeland, K., & Hammons, K. (1998). *Curriculum for integrated learning: a lesson-based approach*. New York: Delmar. (a guide to K–8 integration based on an integrated lesson plan structure)

Mason, C., & Markowsky, J. (1998). *Everybody's somebody's lunch: Teacher's guide*. Gardiner, ME: Tilbury House. (a book of activities and information on food chains, predators, and prey)

National Science Teachers Association (NSTA). (1996). *Pathways to the science standards: Guidelines for moving the vision into practice*. Arlington, VA: Author. (a practical guide to help put the national standards into practice during teaching and assessment)

Shymansky, J. A. (1996). Transforming science education in ways that work: Science reform in the elementary school. In J. Rhoton & P. Bowers (Eds.), *Issues in science education* (pp. 185–191). Arlington, VA: National Science Teachers. (discusses curriculum and instruction in the light of science education reform)

CHAPTER 4

DEVELOPING INQUIRY SKILLS

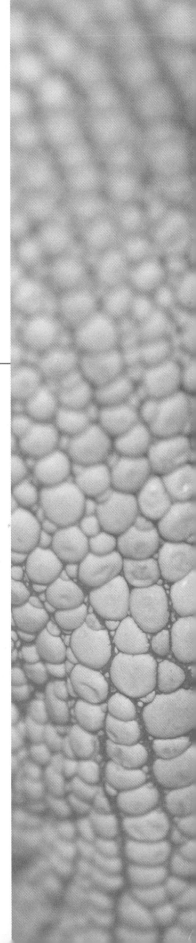

FOCUS QUESTIONS

- How can an "active" approach to science make it more meaningful?
- What are the components of the learning cycle?
- What are the scientific skills?
- What are some examples of scientific attitudes?

Focus on Inquiry

Scientific Skill Development

Dr. George E. O'Brien, Miami,
Florida International University
Angela M. Alexander,
Pine Villa Montessori School, Dade County (Florida) Public Schools

Picture a small community school just 30 miles from downtown Miami but in a rural, farm region of south Florida. This particular day, Ms. Alexander has arranged her students into cooperative learning groups, and they are excited, curious, and anxious about what is going to happen in the science lesson.

Each group receives plastic gloves, dissecting needles, hand lenses, and an oval-shaped object wrapped in aluminum foil. Can the students predict and/or infer what the objects are? They unwrap the foil from the objects carefully and inspect the objects. An initial reaction from many students is, "Wow, I don't know if I really want to touch this." These reactions fade fast. The students use dissecting needles to separate parts that make up the oval-shaped objects and then to record observations and make inferences concerning what the objects or their contents might be and why they think so. Quickly, some students discover or infer that they are working with bones. Some say they are working with wishbones, and one student says these are hog bones (because hogs have a lot of bones). Some students think they can make out a bird's head, and one student thinks she can see parts of a hamster. Some students guess that they are working with dinosaur teeth, human teeth, or some kind of fossil.

The students from each group sort the bones. The task of sorting and organizing the bones into recognizable entities is a problem-solving challenge. The challenge of discovering the mystery objects piques the students' curiosity. Although on this day no one infers the objects to be owl pellets, the pieces of bones lead to more discoveries about the animals that are consumed by barn owls.

At the University

Back in Miami, Dr. O'Brien, a professor of elementary science methods at the university, sets up the activity in the same way as Ms. Alexander. He leads his students through the same challenge of identifying the contents of owl pellets. As bones are uncovered and carefully removed and placed to the side on sheets of plain white paper, university students use dichotomous keys (classification) to identify skulls removed from the barn owl pellets. There is much debate and negotiation (communication) in the cooperating groups concerning the identity of the skulls. As skulls of small mammals, including moles and shrews (Order Insectivora), and rats, voles, and mice (Order Rodentia) are identified, the students take pride in their individual and group accomplishments. As a follow-up activity, the students are to diagram food webs with a barn owl at the highest trophic level and grass seeds at the lowest level. The sequence of activities helps the students construct knowledge of diets of barn owls and other birds of prey, food webs showing that energy passes from one organism to another on a higher level through consumption of that lower organism, and other ecological concepts.

Learning Science Is an Active Process

In the fourth-grade classroom, Ms. Alexander brings books for her students to research owls. Can the students identify the contents of the owl pellets? Yes. In much the same ways that the university students identified prey, the children are able to identify the skulls of different animals. All the students—at the elementary school and university—solved the mystery of finding out the contents of the pellets. The students, by collecting information from the evidence (in this case, produced by barn owls about 12 hours after consuming a meal by casting, or regurgitating, indigestible hair and bones as a pellet) and using science process skills (in this activity, analyzing, communicating, observing, inferring, classifying, predicting, extrapolating, synthesizing, evaluating, measuring, interpreting information, and making conclusions) enjoyed participation in the active, intellectual process of science. Science surveys and interviews conducted by the instructors, after these lessons emphasized hands-on, inquiry-based science, revealed positive attitudes toward science (in both groups) and positive attitudes toward science teaching (in the university group).

Teachers of science—whether at the elementary school or the university—should believe that learning science must be an active process. Learning science is something students do, not something that is done to them. When an instructor focuses on actively engaging students in doing science, then a natural connection of learning concepts, scientific skills, and attitudes follows. In such classrooms, a focal question in planning science lessons is, "What will the students be doing?" They will be observing, classifying, measuring, predicting, inferring, collecting data, graphing, experimenting, and/or communicating. The better the teacher understands the level of skill development that the students have, the better she can choose activities to match the needs of her students.

Making Connections

Just as it is important for students to be active in their learning, it is equally important for the teacher to be an active inquirer and a visible partner to the students during the instructional process. Following are comments from Ms. Alexander, who taught the lesson on owl pellets.

"I approach teaching science in a way that empowers the students. The students will be given the power to create their own learning environment, and these ideas on what to teach come from discussions I have with my students many times a day."

"When the children are working on activities that require an experimental design, I go to each group to discuss how they will set up the experiment. While the students are working on this task, I go from group to group and question the groups on why they chose to set up their experiment this way. Some experimental setups will be better than others. Each group of students will be working from what their group knows. They will be exposed to all the other groups' experiments, which will encourage them to consider other variables in their next exploration. I feel it's also important for the students in the group to self-evaluate their group's experiment. This helps me to know where the group is in the learning process and what they should be focusing on in the next experiment."

"Before they begin the experiment, the groups predict what they think will happen; they may also predict why they think it will happen. When the children start the experiment, I go from group to group, asking each questions about their experiment so I can understand their thinking and/or explanations. I keep notes on each group and record their responses to questions and any misconceptions that I detect. Each group devises a plan and collects data according to that plan. Then the students explain what they think happened in the experiment and share any data collected and recorded with other groups."

"In my class, I feel the students are in charge of their own learning. The teacher sets up and manages situations in which the students can discover and invent on their own to reach understanding. Science process skills are important in my classroom, as is development of critical thinking. The students are encouraged to reach understandings that allow them to be better able to explain their theories. I encourage students to reconsider any misconceptions they might have, and I have students discuss different opinions to see if a consensus can be reached."

The classroom setting Ms. Alexander describes includes the following characteristics:

- Students are engaged in a motivating classroom environment that provides encouragement and frequent student–teacher interaction.
- Students can integrate science processes and problem-solving skills.
- Students are encouraged to actively construct knowledge and explanations.
- Students can use familiar objects in real-life settings.
- Students are given the opportunity to encounter natural phenomena through firsthand experiences.
- Students are involved in varied classroom settings, including individualized instruction, cooperative learning, whole-class demonstrations, and interest centers.
- Students employ risk taking, divergent thinking, and self-initiated questioning.
- Student activities are developmentally appropriate and capitalize on student interest.
- Students are encouraged to create a learning community where everyone's opinions, questions, and conceptions are valued.

Obviously, an elementary or middle school teacher preparing a science lesson has to focus on the question, "What will the students do?" Just as important, however, the teacher needs to be aware of other vital factors, including the selection of instructional materials, physical limitations of the students (e.g., in using manipulatives), choice of management strategy, assessment techniques, cognitive developmental levels of the students, decisions on prerequisites and hierarchy of tasks, and relevant or related science misconceptions. The selection of the overall instructional strategy (e.g., learning cycle or constructivist learning model) is also an important part of inquiry-based hands-on/minds-on science (Flick, 1993).

MAKING ACTIVE SCIENCE MEANINGFUL

The Focus on Inquiry: Scientific Skill Development discusses how the use of scientific skills makes science active and meaningful. What did you notice about the use of the skills of observation, classification, measurement, communication, inference, prediction, and experimentation?

In 1929, John Dewey noted that education emphasized the learning of *fixed conclusions* rather than the advancement of intelligence as a *method of action.* He went on to say that schools *separate knowledge from the very activities that would give the knowledge meaning.* By this, he meant that teachers concentrated on teaching facts and conclusions. They were not teaching concepts through experimentation. Students were not developing the skills necessary to investigate facts or to develop new knowledge.

In a more recent discussion of how science should be taught, National Research Council (NRC) members explain the necessity and interaction of activities and content even more specifically. Their views are summarized as follows:

> Those developing the national standards were committed to including inquiry as both science content and as a way to learn science. Therefore, rather than simply extolling the virtues of "hands-on/minds-on" or "laboratory-based" teaching as the way to teach "science content and process," the writers of the *Standards* treated inquiry as both a learning goal and as a teaching method. (NRC, 2000, p. 18)

In this millennium, educators should take seriously the NRC's suggestion and Dewey's advice. Teachers need to continue the practice of inquiry teaching in their own classrooms. As the authors of both *National Science Education Standards* (NRC, 1996) and *Benchmarks for Science Literacy* (American Association for the Advancement of Science [AAAS], 1993) indicate, inquiry teaching is essential to scientific literacy for all students.

> **Standards Link**
>
> ## Science Inquiry Standard
>
> As a result of activities in grades K–8, all students should develop
>
> - **Abilities necessary to do scientific inquiry**
>
> - **Understandings about scientific inquiry**
>
> (Content Standard A, National Research Council, 1996, pp. 121, 143.)

See the Chapter 4 Web Destinations on the Companion Website (*http://www.prenhall. com/peters*) for links from the National Research Council on the application of the standards in teaching and learning.

The Goal of a Science Program

The goal of all science programs should be problem solving and developing the inquiry skills necessary for competing effectively in the global marketplace. Scientific ventures such as genetic engineering, drug research, telecommunications, nuclear fusion, and environmental monitoring are increasingly done as cooperative ventures between many nations. Today, more than ever, educators must prepare a diverse workforce capable of scientific research, investigation, and informed decision making.

To paraphrase Dewey, intelligent action is the lone definitive resource of humankind (1929). This action of education refers to such entities as the science process skills. These are what scientists, adults, and children use to do science.

What skills were being taught in the owl pellet activity? How would you use this activity in your classroom? Are the instructional strategies consistent with the Science Inquiry Standard, as listed in the Standards Link box? Is the strategy consistent with the constructivist learning model as presented in Chapter 2? What is the **learning cycle** approach to inquiry mentioned in the owl pellet activity? How could the learning cycle be used in teaching skills to children?

The assumption behind the learning cycle is that it is consistent with the ways students learn and can modify false beliefs (see Rosenthal, 1993).

Learning cycle   is an inductive approach to instruction involving exploration, concept introduction, and concept application phases.

USING THE LEARNING CYCLE

The learning cycle is based on an *inquiry* approach to learning consistent with the standards (see the Science Inquiry Standards Link) and an effective strategy for bringing explorations and questioning into the classroom (National Science Teachers Association [NSTA], 2004; Karplus & Their, 1967; Odom & Settlage, 1996). The learning cycle helps students develop a quest for knowledge, data, or truth. All students are naturally curious, and this approach to learning scientific skills leads to a *conceptual understanding* (Karplus, 1977). An advantage of the learning cycle is that it is a methodology that can translate the skills and vocabulary used by scientists into a more meaningful learning experience for students.

See the Chapter 4 Web Destinations at *http://www.prenhall. com/peters* for links to programs that use the learning cycle.

Barman (1989) has modified the original terminology of the learning cycle to make it more understandable for elementary and middle school teachers. He suggests the following three phases.

1. *Exploration Phase. The first phase of the cycle is student centered; the teacher plays the role of a facilitator, observing, questioning, and assisting students as needed. The students interact with materials and each other during this phase.*

In our owl pellet story, this phase occurred when the students were interacting with the owl pellets. For example, they were observing the contents of the owl pellets, classifying the bones with a key, and communicating with each other what they had found. In both the elementary and university classrooms, students were actively involved in inquiry, with the teacher playing the role of facilitator.

2. *Concept Introduction Phase. This teacher-centered phase is characterized by naming things and events. The teacher's function is to gather information for students that pertains to their explorations in the first phase. The teacher works with students to develop vocabulary and to introduce pertinent information.*

During the owl pellet activity, Ms. Alexander brings in books for the students to begin naming things and events surrounding the formation of the pellet. Dr. O'Brien's class also engages in learning new names such as Rodentia and Insectivora as students continue the lesson.

3. *Concept Application Phase. This activity-oriented phase is, again, student centered and allows students to apply freshly learned information to new situations. The teacher presents a new problem to solve, allowing more time for the students to apply what they have learned.*

The university students depict this phase as they diagram food webs to illustrate the barn owl's diet. They are applying what they have found out in the second phase. The fourth-grade students also begin to apply what they have learned as they further research the characteristics of the owl through children's literature and nature books.

As shown in Figure 4–1, this cycle also has an evaluation and discussion aspect. This is an interactive component throughout each phase. The evaluation and discussion help identify current false beliefs and prevent the construction of new misconceptions. In each of the phases, the teacher may rely on various means of assessment (see Chapter 5) to assist in student understanding. Clearly, the cycle is supported by a continuous evaluation. That way, there can be a return to a previous phase, when needed, or an appropriate further application in a new phase.

See the Chapter 4 Web Destinations at *http://www.prenhall. com/peters* for additional learning cycle links.

In the previous examples, both Ms. Alexander and Dr. O'Brien facilitated discussions throughout the owl pellet activity. They were careful to monitor what the students were

Figure 4–1   **The learning cycle.**

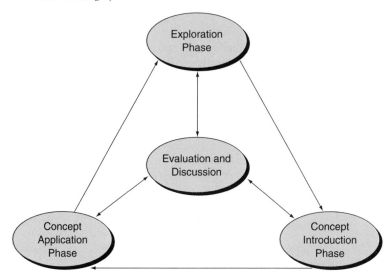

Source: Adapted from a figure by Charles Barman in "A Procedure for Helping Prospective Elementary Teachers Integrate the Learning Cycle into Science Textbooks," *Journal of Science Teacher Education,1*(2), p. 22.

saying and to ask pertinent questions wherever they thought misconceptions were present. The ongoing assessment allows for a holistic, or complete, approach to evaluation that includes activity-based evaluation. Consider other possible evaluation strategies as we further explore the three phases.

Exploration Phase

As we discussed earlier, the **exploration phase** is a student-oriented phase. Remember the constructivist model presented in Chapter 2? The exploration phase of the learning cycle is similar to the exploration component of the constructivist learning model in which students are *actively engaged.* The teacher's function in either model is to scaffold the learning environment based on the concepts she believes are important for the students to learn at that time.

Students can be involved in observing, classifying what they have observed, measuring, making informal inferences based on their observations, conducting experiments, collecting and organizing data, and communicating their findings to their peers in the learning cycle exploration phase. It is important for you as the facilitator to build the foundation by making the connections between the activities and the students' everyday lives.

Exploration Example

For example, if you want to develop an understanding of floating and sinking, you could first discuss the students' trips to a pool or the beach by asking, "What floated on the water? What sank?" Next, have the students observe pictures of various objects either floating or sinking. Then, ask a series of questions designed to engage the students in a discussion of the phenomena. Students will begin to make inferences about why objects float or sink. It is important for you to identify students' inferences, noting similarities and differences in their perceptions or explanations. The students could even test several objects during this

---

Exploration phase   of the learning cycle allows children the opportunity to experience events to initiate their thought processes.

Visit an Inquiry Classroom
The Learning Cycle–Exploration

View the *Exploration* video in the "Model Inquiry Unit" section of the Companion CD. Mr. McKnight moves throughout the classroom facilitating student interaction as they observe earthworms and record their findings.

Review the video and ask yourself the following:
- What specific examples show this is a "student-oriented" phase of the learning cycle?
- What is Mr. McKnight's role in this lesson?

Reread the owl pellet activity at the beginning of this chapter. Compare and contrast Mr. McKnight's explorations with those of Ms. Alexander. Record your ideas and the answers to these questions in your portfolio or use the Companion Website to share your ideas.

phase and make a chart of which ones float or sink. Assessment during this phase could be as informal as open questions or as structured as individual student interviews.

Concept Introduction or Invention Phase

During the **concept invention phase,** the teacher is a facilitator. She begins to focus the questioning, to organize the information, and to guide the class into an agreed-upon concept. This process of making connections and sense of things is termed *concept invention*. The teacher assists the students in naming the objects and concepts (vocabulary development) and in experimenting with the newly formed concepts, relating them to the experiences from the exploration phase. In terms of the constructivist model, students are now in the "proposing explanations and solutions" phase and are looking for ways to construct new explanations.

> **Concept invention phase** of the learning cycle allows children the opportunity to determine relationships among the objects or events that they explored in the exploration phase.

Concept Invention Example

In the floating and sinking example, the teacher would introduce terminology and concepts such as *weight, surface tension,* and *density.* Specific definitions would accompany these terms and relate to the students' explorations. Questioning why the students think some objects float and some sink would be based on both the new vocabulary and definitions and the explorations. Students would measure various densities in support of concept development. Finally, the students would construct the notion that objects that are denser than water will sink in water and those that are less dense than water will float in water.

Concept Application Phase

Now it is time for the students to apply their new knowledge and skills in the **concept application phase.** Students are provided similar situations and challenged to implement their new concepts. In terms of the constructivist model, the students are now taking action on what they have learned. They make decisions about the new explorations and apply newly learned knowledge and skills.

> **Concept application phase** of the learning cycle allows children the opportunity to apply the concept or skill that they developed in the concept invention phase.

Visit an Inquiry Classroom
The Learning Cycle–Concept Invention

View the *Concept Invention* video in the "Model Inquiry Unit" section of the Companion CD. Mr. McKnight questions the students and helps them to think about their earthworm explorations and to form concepts. Notice how students are making connections between their current activities and past observations and experiences.

Review the video and ask yourself the following:
- What concepts are the elementary or middle school students forming?
- What is the role of teacher questioning in a student's concept development?
- Many times, elementary or middle school teachers have students engage in a fun science activity but then do not follow up with concept invention. Why is the concept invention stage so important?

In the NSTA's *Position Statement on Scientific Inquiry* (2004), the authors make the statement, "Scientific inquiry is a powerful way of understanding science content." Explain what they mean by this statement and the role that the concept invention stage of the learning cycle might play in supporting scientific inquiry and understanding science content. Use specific examples from the video on the Companion CD. Record your ideas and the answers to these questions in your portfolio or use the Companion Website to share your ideas.

Concept Application Example

In terms of the floating and sinking example, the teacher may provide new items for students to hypothesize about and test. The teacher may also complete a performance-based evaluation (see Chapter 5) at this point, checking how many objects the students can correctly identify as "floaters" and "sinkers." Different experiments may test the new knowledge or lead back to the exploration phase of the cycle. For example, the teacher may ask the students to float a paper clip in a cup of water. The students know that the paper clip is denser than water, so now they have to experiment with surface tension, bringing them back to the exploration phase.

A Variation of the Learning Cycle

One way to make the learning cycle more complete is through the addition of stages to capture the students' attention and assess what the students have learned after instruction (Staver & Shroyer, 1994). A variation of the learning cycle with these additions is the five-stage model developed by BSCS (Bybee et al., 1989). This five-stage model incorporates the engage, explore, explain, elaborate, and evaluate stages. The *engage stage* is matched with the invitation stage of the constructivist learning model. Students observing surroundings and looking for interesting phenomena are characteristics of both models. Here, teachers begin with questions to capture students' attention.

The *explore, explain,* and *elaborate stages* are equivalent to the original learning cycle. The added *evaluate stage* provides additional opportunity for assessment. It allows the teacher to find out what the students have learned and sets the stage to begin the cycle once again.

The Learning Cycle and Textbooks

In many elementary and middle schools, a textbook series makes up the science program. Such books contain many activities whose purpose is to illustrate ideas presented in the

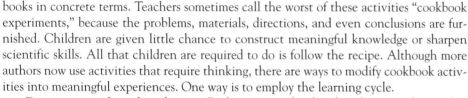

Visit an Inquiry Classroom
The Learning Cycle—Concept Application

View the *Concept Application* video in the "Model Inquiry Unit" section of the Companion CD. Students gather again to discuss their newly developed concepts with Mr. McKnight. Later, they will engage in further earthworm activities to apply their knowledge in new ways.

Review the video and ask yourself the following:
- What activity would you do as a follow-up to the discussion shown in this video segment?
- As the students finish their study of earthworms, how could you transition into a study of round worms or flat worms as a way to apply what they have learned in previous explorations?

In the article, "Less Is More: Trimming the Overstuffed Curriculum," Fratt (2002) supports the American Association for the Advancement of Science's Project 2061 position that teachers should teach fewer topics but teach them in greater depth to promote better understanding. Do you think that the learning cycle approach supports the idea of promoting better understanding? Explain your answer and include specific examples from the video on the Companion CD. Record your ideas and the answers to these questions in your portfolio or use the Companion Website to share your ideas.

books in concrete terms. Teachers sometimes call the worst of these activities "cookbook experiments," because the problems, materials, directions, and even conclusions are furnished. Children are given little chance to construct meaningful knowledge or sharpen scientific skills. All that children are required to do is follow the recipe. Although more authors now use activities that require thinking, there are ways to modify cookbook activities into meaningful experiences. One way is to employ the learning cycle.

Do not start with reading the text. Rather, start with related explorations designed to invite students to want to explore more. Try an experiment out of the book as a discovery activity and not as a set of directions to follow. Then, use the text to develop the related language and reinforce the concepts. Finally, try some associated experiments from the text or supplemental materials.

If you are involved in selecting the textbook for your science program, pay attention to the ways authors lead into the activities and the comments following them. Look for questions that are posed before the experiment, with extending information following the experiment. This enables you to use the author's questions to explore beforehand, and then introduce the experiment, and finally use the book's information to extend the children's learning after the experiment is completed.

The Learning Cycle and Skill Development

In short, we want to use the learning cycle to develop students' scientific understandings and skills. The learning cycle is generalized as a *do-talk-do* cycle (Ramsey, 1993). In the "do" parts of the cycle, skills are being used. What specifically are the scientific skills? Which skills are appropriate for the elementary or middle school students? What are other ways to develop these skills?

In preparing for your own first elementary or middle school science unit, like the authors of Focus on Inquiry: Scientific Skill Development you may decide to use owls as a theme. You will want to focus on scientific skills. You will probably begin to ask yourself the following questions about skills.

How will the scientific skills fit into my elementary or middle school curriculum?
Do I fully understand the skills?
Am I prepared to teach scientific skills to children?
What are some examples of activities I can do to promote specific scientific skill?

SCIENTIFIC SKILLS

The learning cycle explains *how* you will teach scientific skills. In their respective publications, the NRC (1996) and the AAAS (1993) explain *why* you need to teach the how-tos of teaching scientific skills. Now we look at the *what* question. What are the scientific skills of observation, classification, measurement, communication, inference, prediction, and experimentation? Let's begin with observation.

Observing

Observation is defined here as carefully exploring the properties of an object or phenomenon, such as texture, color, sound, taste, smell, length, mass, or volume.

The process of **observation** is the taking in of sense perceptions. It is our job to help students use all their senses when they observe similarities, differences, and changes in objects or events. Students can learn that each of the senses is a gateway to observing different properties of objects. Seeing allows them to notice properties such as size, shape, and color of objects and how the objects may interact. Hearing makes knowable properties of sounds, such as loudness, pitch, and rhythm. Touching teaches the meaning of texture and is another way to discover sizes and shapes of objects. Tasting shows how labels such as bitter, salty, sour, and sweet can be used to describe foods. Smelling allows students to associate objects with odors, such as smells "like perfume" or "like cigar smoke."

Properties enable children to compare and describe likenesses and differences among objects. This leads to explorations that require several of the other processes, such as classifying and communicating. You can ask broad and narrow questions to guide learning in such science processes as observation.

In keeping with our owl theme, you may want to begin with a children's literature approach to the study of owls. *Owl Eyes* (Gates, 1994) is a good starting point. This story describes a Mohawk legend in which animals can choose their own colors and body form. It assists the students in observations of the owl and its characteristics. *Owl Moon* (Yolen, 1987) is another story rich in observation that describes a walk in the woods in search of owls. *Good-Night Owl!* (Hutchins, 1972) is a story about animal noises and would be a good introduction to student observations of animal sounds in the schoolyard.

See the Chapter 4 Web Destinations on the Companion Website at *http://www.prenhall. com/peters* for links related to owl pellet availability and activities.

As you begin to explore the owl pellets with children in a primary-level class, invite everyone to observe by saying, for example:

What do you notice about the object wrapped in foil?
Does it make any noise?
What do you think you will see inside?
Is what you see inside different from what you expected to see?

Later, pose more questions:

How does the object feel?
How many bones did you find?
What do the bones look like?
What does it smell like?

An owl rests in its natural habitat as children observe its characteristics.

In a middle-level class, begin to make observations more specific:

What animal skeletons in the guide compare to the skeletons that you found?
How many animal remains did you find in the pellet?

In an upper-level class, explore with even more specific observations:

In what specific ways are the bones alike?
How do the skulls that you found compare with the ones shown in the guide?

Classifying

Most primary students can select and group real objects by some common property. **Classification** imposes order on collections of objects or events through characteristics such as color, shape, and size. Dichotomous classifications divide objects or events into two groupings. Elementary students should be proficient at dichotomous classification and multigroup classifications in which they observe and group items on the basis of different properties.

Classification is seen as constructing an order based on similarities and differences between objects or events.

With our owl lessons, we can introduce *The Book of North American Owls* (Sattler, 1995) and *Owls* (Kalman, 1987). The students can classify the owls on the basis of habitat or physical features. Through reading *Town Mouse & Country Mouse* (Brett, 1994), the students can set up a dichotomous key listing comparisons of the two types of habitats that the mice—and accompanying owl and cat—live in as presented in the story.

Primary-Level Example

In a primary-level class, students can look over the contents of the pellet and sort them by properties. The teacher can prompt the students with the following:

> Think of one property, such as hardness. Sort all the objects that have that property into one pile. Leave what's left in another pile.

Later, to expand on the activity, the teacher can say:

> What other properties can you use to sort your objects?

In another primary-level class, students look over the contents of the pellet and sort them into animal and plant remains.

Middle- and Upper-Level Examples

Many middle-level students can classify an object into more than one category at the same time and hold this in mind. In a middle-level class, some students have classified owls into three groups, based on the geographic range of their habitat, with two subgroups each: urban and rural. They completed this independently in response to their teacher's question:

> How can you group owls by habitat?

Next, the teacher will explore owl coloration subgroups. Some upper-level students can also reclassify according to other properties that fit their purposes. In an upper-level class, students have a collection of pictures of animals that owls may prey upon. They start off by dividing them into groups by order but then decide that this will not fit their purpose. They have to reclassify according to the prey's location on the food chain. This example demonstrates a major point about classification: It is done to fit a purpose. What works to fulfill the intent of the classifier is what counts. Objects can be classified in many ways.

Measuring

Measurement is the specific determination of the length, mass, volume, speed, time, or other property of an object or event. See the Companion Website for additional information.

Thinking about properties in a quantitative way naturally leads to measuring them. **Measurement** is used to compare things. At first, at the primary level, children may be unable to compare an object with a standard measuring tool, such as a meterstick or yardstick. Instead, they find out who is taller by standing back to back. They find out which of two objects is heavier by holding each object in their hands. Eventually, they begin to use nonstandard measuring devices, such as paper clips or lengths of string, to measure their desks.

There is good reason to start off measuring in this way. Remember that primary students may not conserve several concepts that deal with quantity. Changing the appearance of an object still fools them. Children who think that merely spreading out some material gives them more, for example, have to be taught differently than children who conserve quantity. Most young children find it difficult to work meaningfully with standard units of measurement such as centimeters and inches until about age 7.

Primary students can build readiness for working with standard units by using parts of their bodies or familiar objects as arbitrary units to measure things. A primary child may say, "The classroom is 28 of my feet wide."

Concrete Referents and Improvised Tools

One way to improve the ability of children to measure and estimate accurately is to have numerous concrete objects in your classroom for them to refer to as needed. Metersticks, yardsticks, and trundle wheels are useful for thinking about length. Containers marked with metric and English units are good for measuring liquid volumes.

Similar references are needed for other concepts involving quantity. A kilometer is a round trip from the school to the police station. A mile is the distance from the school to the post office. Meanings associated with time can be developed by many references to water or sand clocks (containers with holes punched in the bottom) and real clocks. Temperature differences become meaningful through using several kinds of thermometers.

Measurement Motivators: From Dinosaurs to Decimals (Palumbo, 1989) and *Measurement: 35 Hands-On Activities* (Garcia, 1997) can be helpful resources when developing meaningful measurement experiences with your students. The concept of measurement as a part of everyday life is also seen in *How Big Is a Foot?* (Myller, 1990), in which a foot is used to measure a bed. As students become interested in more detailed information, refer to such sources as *The World of Measurements* (Klein, 1974). This source contains details on units, their history, and their use.

By the time they leave elementary school, most children will have had some experience with a variety of measuring instruments such as the ruler, meterstick, yardstick, balance, clock, thermometer, graduated cylinder, protractor, directional compass, and wind gauge. When possible, children themselves should choose the right measuring tool for the activity underway. Sometimes they can make their own tools when they need them. Inventing and making a measuring instrument can be challenging and interesting.

Measurement and the Metric System

Scientists everywhere have long used the metric system because, like our number system, its units are defined in multiples of 10. The three basic units most commonly used in the metric system are the meter, liter, and gram.

A meter is used to measure length, a liter is used to measure liquid volume, and a gram is used to measure weight or mass. Strictly speaking, the terms *mass* and *weight* mean different things in science. Mass is the amount of material or matter that makes up an object. Weight is the gravitational force that pulls the mass. On the moon, for example, an astronaut's weight is only about one sixth of what it is on the earth, but the astronaut's mass stays unchanged.

The Celsius (C) thermometer, named after its inventor, Anders Celsius, commonly measures temperature in the metric system. It has a scale marked into 100 evenly spaced subdivisions.

Prefixes are used in the metric system to show larger or smaller quantities. The three most common prefixes and their meanings are as follows:

- *milli-:* one thousandth (0.001)
- *centi-:* one hundredth (0.01)
- *kilo-:* one thousand (1000)

Take a closer look at Figure 4–2 to see how prefixes are used in combination with basic units.

Before your students use different metric standards, have them consider the right standard for the job. Children will usually discover that the metric system is easier to use than the English system. Conversions from or to the English system should be avoided because they are confusing. If your curriculum calls for work with both metric and English measures, give your students a lot of practice with concrete materials for both systems. Try to treat each system separately instead of shifting back and forth. For example, when the students are comparing indoor and outdoor Fahrenheit temperatures as part of a weather

Figure 4–2   Comparison of length, volume, weight, and temperature.

Length

1 millimeter (mm)	= The diameter of paper clip wire
1 centimeter (cm)	= The width of a formed paper clip
1 meter (m)	= 1000 millimeters (mm)
1 meter (m)	= 100 centimeters (cm)
1 kilometer (km)	= 1000 meters (m)
1 kilometer (km)	= About the length of nine football fields
1 kilometer (km)	= About six tenths of a mile

Volume

1 milliliter (ml)	= About one fifth of a teaspoon
1 liter (l)	= 1000 milliliters (ml)
1 liter (l)	= 100 centiliters (cl)
1 liter (l)	= Slightly over a quart
1 kiloliter (kl)	= 1000 liters (l)

Weight (Mass)

1 milligram (mg)	= About 1/1000 of the mass of a paper clip
1 gram (g)	= 1000 milligrams (mg)
1 gram (g)	= 100 centigrams (cg)
1 kilogram (kg)	= 1000 grams (g)
1 kilogram (kg)	= About 2.2 pounds

Temperature

0 degrees Celsius	= Freezing point of water
100 degrees Celsius	= Boiling point of water

activity, do not automatically ask what the temperature would be in degrees Celsius. Instead, at a later time, develop a chart of Celsius temperatures outside over the period of a month and discuss the temperatures and any temperature changes.

The story *A Toad for Tuesday* (Erickson, 1998) can be a starting place for measurement activities related to the owl theme. Potential measurement activities could include the distance of the toad's journey through the woods before meeting the owl, the time the owl waits before changing his mind about his vow to eat the toad, the potential temperatures of the woods, the relative sizes of the toad and owl, and the appropriate weights of the owl and toad.

Communicating

Communication is the sharing of information through written or spoken means such as an oral report, charts, graphs, reports, and publications.

Communication is putting the information or data obtained from our observations into some form that another person can understand or some form that we can understand at a later date. Children learn to communicate in many ways. They learn to draw accurate pictures, diagrams, and maps; make proper charts and graphs; construct accurate models and exhibits; and use clear language when describing objects or events. The last of these activities is usually stressed in elementary science.

It is important to say things or show data in the clearest possible way. We can help our students learn this by giving them many chances to communicate and by helping them to evaluate what they have said or done.

The book *The Man Who Could Call Down Owls* (Bunting, 1984) is a good introduction to communication. *Turtle in July* (Singer, 1989) also involves month-by-month communication from animals' points of view, including a poem from an owl.

Think of a primary-level class where some students are seated on a rug. They are viewing a series of pictures of the life cycle of an owl from an LCD projector. The teacher has scanned the pictures into the computer from *See How They Grow: Owl* (Ling, 1992) and is projecting them for all the students to see. She suggests a game in which a child communicates the properties of a life stage, such as "I am fluffy, hunched over, and my eyes are closed." Others try to identify the stage. The child who identifies the growth period first gets to be the new describer. Reminding the children to carefully consider the description discourages guessing. After each student's identification, the teacher asks questions, for example:

What did she say that helped you figure out this stage?
What else would be helpful to say?
Did anyone get mixed up?
How do you think that happened?

The teacher summarizes the communications activity by reading *Owl Babies* (Waddell, 1994) and having the children describe the owlets.

In an upper-level class, the students want to find out the locations of owls. They are collaborating with students from throughout the region via the Internet. Students are collecting real-time data on sightings of owls and hearing owls' screeches. Together they will make maps, charts, and graphs on their findings and communicate the results.

In another upper-level class, students want to find out the warmest time of the day. Temperature readings are made on the hour from 10 A.M. until 3 P.M. for 5 days in a row and then averaged. They decide to record their results on a line graph, but they do not know whether to put the temperature along the side (vertical axis) or along the bottom (horizontal axis) of the graph. Is there a "regular" way? The teacher helps them see how graphs are arranged in their mathematics text. Scientists call the change being tested the *manipulated variable*. In this case, time is usually placed along the horizontal axis. The change that results from the test is called the *responding variable*. In this situation, temperature is the responding variable and is placed along the vertical axis.

See the Chapter 4 Web Destinations on the Companion Website at *http://www. prenhall.com/peters* for links related to graphing and graphing activities.

Defining Operationally

Defining operationally is a subprocess of communicating, usually introduced after the primary grades. To define a word operationally is to describe it by an action (operation) rather than by other words. For example, suppose you invite some students to hold an evaporation contest: Who can dry water-soaked paper towels fastest? They begin to speculate excitedly. But there is just one thing they will have to agree on before the fun begins: How will everyone know when a towel is "dry"? This question stumps the students, so you pose another open question that hints at *actions* they could take: What are some things they could do to the towel to tell if it is dry? Now, they start coming up with the following operations (actions) to try.

Squeeze the towel into a ball and see if water comes out. Rub it on the chalkboard; see if it makes a wet mark. Tear it and compare the sound to a dry towel you tear.

Hold it up to the light and compare its color to an unsoaked towel.

See if it can be set on fire as fast as an unsoaked towel. Put an unsoaked towel on one end of a balance beam; see if the other towel balances it.

The children agree that the last operation is easiest to observe and the least arguable. It is stated as an operational definition: "A towel is dry if it balances an unsoaked towel from the same package." Now the activity can begin.

Had the open question not worked, a narrow question such as, "How would squeezing the towel show if it is dry?" could have been posed, followed with a broad question such as, "What else could you do to the towel to tell if it is dry besides squeezing it?"

When operational definitions are not used, it is easy to fall into the trap of **circular reasoning:** What is the condition of a dry towel? It contains no moisture. What is the condition of a towel that contains no moisture? It is dry. Or, to borrow from children's humor, consider this example:

> He is the best scientist we've ever had.
> Who is?
> He is.
> Who is "He"?
> The best scientist we've ever had.

There are some predictable times when the need for operational definitions will come up. Watch the children's use of relative terms such as *tall, short* (How tall? short?), *light, heavy, fast, slow, good,* and *bad* (What is "bad" luck?).

Circular reasoning is like a specious argument where the child's answer is plausible to a child but the argument has a logical flaw.

Creating a Record of Activities

Recording is another subprocess of communicating. When activities require time to gather data (e.g., growing plants over many weeks) or when there are many data to consider (e.g., discovering how much vitamin C many juices contain), it is often sensible to make a record of what is happening. Without a record, it is difficult to remember what has happened and to draw conclusions. In a way, recording can be considered communicating with oneself. Many teachers ask their students to make records in a notebook or data log. Records can be in picture or graph form, as well as in writing. Whichever way the data are recorded, they should be clear.

In a primary-level class, some children are recording the growth of their plants with strips of colored paper. Every other day, they hold a new strip of paper next to each plant and tear off a bit to match the plant's height. They date the strips and paste them in order on large paper sheets. A growth record of the plants is clearly visible to all the students.

Other children in the class have drawn pictures of their plants at different stages, from seed to mature plant. These pictures are made into record booklets at the teacher's suggestion. The children describe each picture for the teacher, who swiftly writes their short statements on paper slips. The children paste these beneath their pictures. The result is a "My Plant Storybook" for each child, who can proudly read it to impressed parents.

In a middle-level class, five groups are at work with narrow strips of litmus paper. (This chemically treated paper changes color when dipped into acidic or basic liquids.) The children want to find out whether five mystery liquids in numbered jars are acidic, basic, or neutral. Each group has a recorder who notes the findings on a data sheet. At the end of the work session, the teacher asks how the results of all the groups should be recorded on the chalkboard. It is decided as outlined in Table 4–1. Notice that by having a code (A: Acid, B: Base, N: Neutral) written to one side, the teacher cuts down on the time needed to record the findings. The data are now compared, differences noted, and possible reasons discussed. Careful retesting is planned to straighten out the differences.

In an upper-level class, some students want to find out whether there is a pattern to the clouds passing over the city in the spring. They have made a chart that has three columns: one each for March, April, and May. In each column is a numbered space for each day of that month. Next to about half of the days, the students have drawn the weather

Table 4–1						
Acidity of Mystery Liquids						
Group	**1**	**2**	**3**	**4**	**5**	
Miranda	A	B	N	B	A	A: Acid
Tasha	A	B	N	B	A	B: Base
Evan	A	A	N	A	A	N: Neutral
Brian	A	B	N	A	A	
Britton	B	B	N	B	B	

bureau cloud symbols for the cloud cover, if any, on those days. Even though the record chart is only partly completed, a sequential pattern is taking shape. After the chart is completed, the students will compare it with data gathered by the local weather bureau office for the same months in previous years.

Inferring

The usual meaning of **inference** is to interpret or explain what we observe. If Wallie smiles when she greets us (observation), we may infer that she is pleased to see us (explanation). The accuracy of our inferences usually improves with more chances to observe. Several like observations may also lead us to the *prediction* that the next time we see her, Wallie will smile (observation) because she will be pleased to see us (explanation). For convenience, then, view the process of inferring as having two parts: We may make an *inference* from what we observe, and we may predict an *observation* from what we infer. Let's now look at children explaining observations and then, later, in another section, predicting them.

Inference is an explanation of an observation based on the available information.

Inferring as Explaining

In at least three common ways, we as educators can help children infer properly from observations. Primary-level students, however, may have a very limited overall understanding of this process.

First, we can get students to distinguish between their observation and an inference. In a middle-level class, two children are looking at a picture of shoeprints in the snow. One set of prints is much smaller than the other (observation). One child says, "One of these sets of shoeprints must have been made by a man and the other by a boy" (an inference). The other child says, "That's true" (another inference). Hearing this, the teacher asks an open question to make them aware of other possibilities:

> In what other ways could these prints have been made?

They think for a moment and come up with other inferences: Perhaps two children made the prints—one wore his father's shoes; or maybe it was a girl and her mother; or it could have been a girl and her older brother.

The teacher points out that what they have observed is still the same but that there is more than one way to explain the observation. If the children look at the tracks closely, they may conclude that one of their inferences is more likely than the others. A *conclusion* is simply the inference in which one has the most confidence after considering all the evidence.

Second, we can get students to interpret data they have observed or recorded. Remember the students who were using litmus paper to identify mystery liquids? When several groups recorded their data, they noticed that some data were inconsistent. Some liquids were labeled both acidic and basic. The children inferred from this that the litmus test was done incorrectly by one of the groups. After the tests were redone, all the data became consistent. So, the children inferred that their final labeling of the mystery liquids was probably correct.

Recall the cloud data study. The sequential pattern the children saw when they examined their data was an inferred pattern. Later, when they compare their pattern with the weather bureau's report, they will be able to evaluate the quality of their inference.

Third, we can let students observe and interpret only indirect evidence or clues. Scientists must often depend on clues rather than clear evidence in forming possible inferences. For example, no scientist has visited the middle of the earth, yet earth scientists have inferred much about its properties.

Children can learn to make inferences from incomplete or indirect evidence, and they can also learn to become wary of hasty conclusions. In a primary-level class, some students are working with two closed shoeboxes. One box contains a smooth-sided, cylindrical pencil; the other box contains a six-sided, cylindrical pencil. The children's problem is, "Which box contains which kind of pencil?"

They tip the boxes back and forth and listen intently, inferring correctly the contents of the two boxes. When the teacher asks students what made them decide as they did, one child says, "You could feel which one was the bumpy pencil when it rolled." The other child says, "The bumpy one made more noise."

Later, the teacher puts into the boxes two pencils that are identical except for length. The students now find that correct inferring is more difficult, so they become more cautious. What observations must they rely on now?

In the middle and upper grades, students can do an excellent job of inferring the identity or interactions of hidden objects from indirect observational clues. In science, this way of inferring is called *model building.*

Explore owl inferences with your students. Why is the owl's beak a particular shape? Why are the feathers of one owl different than those of another? How do owls differ from eagles or other birds of prey? Read *A First Look at Owls, Eagles, and Other Hunters of the Sky* (Selsam & Hunt, 1986) to follow up on your inferences.

Predicting

Prediction is an estimate of a future observation.

A **prediction** is a forecast of a future observation based on inferences from the available data. The more data that are available, the more confidence we have in the prediction; the reverse is also true. We can be confident that spring will follow winter, but not at all confident that spring fashions this year will be exactly like those of a year ago. Without some data, we can only guess about future observations; to predict is impossible. When students put their data in graph form, they usually have many chances to predict.

Upper-level students measure and record on a graph the time candles burn under inverted glass jars. After they have recorded the times for 100-, 200-, and 300-milliliter jars, the teacher asks, "How long do you think the candle will burn under a 250-milliliter jar?"

Notice that predicting the time for a 250-milliliter jar would require the students to read the graph between the current data—they have the times for a 200- and a 300-milliliter jar. This is called *interpolating.* If the teacher had asked the students to predict the candle-burning time of a 400-milliliter jar, the students would have needed to go beyond the current data. This is called *extrapolating* from data. Using these processes to predict is more accurate than guessing.

Children often need assistance when predicting. Simple diagrams can help them reason through data. If they cannot calculate precise predictions, just asking them to predict the direction of change is useful to them. Primary-level students might be asked, "Will more or less water evaporate when the wind blows?" Middle-level students might be asked, "Will a *higher*, *lower*, or the *same* temperature result when these two water samples of different temperatures are mixed?"

Experimenting

Experimentation is the quintessence of inquiry teaching. Authors of the Inquiry Teaching Standard in the Standards Link box list investigations, inquiry, accessibility of science resources, and the learning environment as important teaching considerations. When we think of inquiry, we often think of experiments. But just what is involved with an "experiment"?

To a child, experimenting means "doing something to see what happens." Although this definition is overly simple, it does capture the difference between experimenting and the other six science processes. In experimenting, we change objects or events to learn how nature changes them. This section is about how children can discover the various conditions of change. Experimentation builds on the concept of open investigations.

Experimenting is often called an *integrated* process skill because it may require us to use some or all of the other process skills: observing, classifying, inferring and predicting, measuring, and communicating. That is one reason some curriculum writers may reserve experimentation for upper-grade activities; but experimental investigations can vary in difficulty. With guidance, even primary students will benefit from experimentation. This does not mean any hands-on activity may properly be called experimenting. Two generally accepted criteria that separate hands-on activities from experimentation are as follows:

> **Experimentation** is finding a conclusion to a hypothesis through the integration of all the scientific skills.

Standards Link

Inquiry Teaching Standard

Teachers of science design and manage learning environments that provide students with the time, space, and resources needed for learning science. In doing this, teachers:

- **Structure the time available so that students are able to engage in extended investigations.**

- **Create a setting for student work that is flexible and supportive of science inquiry.**

- **Ensure a safe working environment.**

- **Make the available science tools, materials, media, and technological resources accessible to students.**

- **Identify and use resources outside the school.**

- **Engage students in designing the learning environment.**

(Teaching Standard D, National Research Council, 1996, p. 43.)

> Children should have an idea they want to test (hypothesizing).
> Children should vary only one condition at a time (controlling variables).

To many educators, almost any investigation is experimenting, as long as the child changes an object for a purpose and can compare its changed state to the original one. This is the position taken in this book.

Hypothesizing

How do we get students to form ideas they want to test before they manipulate objects? There are several ways of getting children to state operations that they want to try. For elementary students, stating operations as questions such as, "Will dropping a magnet make it weaker?" or "Does adding salt to water make objects float higher?" is a clear and easy way

Students discover the properties of a parachute as part of an extension to a parachute lab.

for them to state hypotheses. It makes them focus on what they want to do to produce some effect, or on what effect to observe and connect to a cause.

In science, a hypothesis is often stated in an "if–then" manner: If I do this, then I believe this will happen. If a magnet is dropped, then it will get weaker. You may want to use the if–then form with upper-level students. For most children, however, stating a hypothesis as an operational question is easier and more understandable.

Allowing students to explore the properties of real objects stimulates them to suggest their own ideas for changing the properties. Their curiosity usually prompts them to state operations they want to try or to be receptive to broad or narrow questions that you ask. For example, in a primary-level class, some children have been making and playing with toy parachutes. They tie the four corners of a handkerchief with strings and attach these to a sewing spool. Some release their parachutes while standing on top of the playground slide and watch them fall slowly to the ground. Others simply wad the cloth around the spool and throw their parachutes up into the air.

A few children have made their parachutes from different materials. They are quick to notice that some parachutes stay in the air longer than others. After they go back to the classroom, they discuss their experiences. Then, the teacher says:

> We have plenty of materials to make more parachutes on the science table. How can you make a parachute that will fall more slowly than the one you have now?

The children will respond in different ways: "Make it bigger," "Make it smaller," "Use a lighter spool," or "Make it like Martha's." These are the children's hypotheses. Some children may say nothing, but peer intently at the materials. They are hypothesizing, too, only nonverbally. The children's ideas need testing so that they can find out what works. Now the children have purposes for doing further work with parachutes.

Where did the children's hypotheses originate? When the children were first observing their parachutes in action, they did much inferring. ("Jimmy's parachute is bigger than mine. It stays up longer." "Corinne has a big spool. Her chute falls fast.") It is natural for people to be curious about the correctness of their inferences. *Hypotheses are simply inferences that people want to test.*

Exploring the properties of concrete materials provides the background that most children need to construct new concepts. They may not be able to offer broad explanatory hypotheses to test concepts or theories. This calls for additional scaffolding and prior knowledge and experience. For this reason, some *what* questions (What makes a ship float?) are difficult for children to answer. Instead of broad, general hypotheses, elementary students are likely to offer limited hypotheses based on the objects they have observed or manipulated.

Primary students are far more limited in this ability than upper-elementary or middle school thinkers. Scaffolding is more effective with real materials to think about during their discussion, instead of relying on discussion alone. Most primary students can only think about one variable at a time. This limits the experimenting they can do, because they are unlikely to control other variables that might affect the outcome. So, primary-level investigations usually lean more heavily on the other six science processes.

Controlling Variables

To find out exactly what condition makes a difference in an experiment, we must change or vary that condition alone. Other conditions must not vary; in other words, they must be controlled during the experiment.

Suppose you think that varying the size of a parachute will affect its falling rate. A good way to test the variable is to build two parachutes that are identical in every way except size. These could then be released at the same time from the same height. After repeated trials, you can infer whether size makes a difference in the test.

Grade 2 Example

Do not expect primary-level students to reason in this way. They will not think of the many variables or conditions that can influence their experiment. They may unwittingly change several variables at the same time. Their intent is simply to make a parachute that will fall more slowly than another, not to isolate variable conditions. Older children, in contrast, will grasp the need to control some variables. Typically, they will insist on releasing their parachutes from the same height and at the same time. Otherwise, "It won't be fair," they will tell you.

The parachute experiment is more than just a trial-and-error activity. The children have observed parachutes and have done some inferring about their observations. The changes they try will reflect thinking we can call hypothesizing. And although they may not think of controlling all the possible variables, they are conscious of some. This is the nature of children. How well they do and how fast they progress is influenced by how we as teachers scaffold their experiences. Following are more examples of teachers helping their students construct the idea of experimentation.

Grade 4 Example

In Mr. Li's fourth-grade class, the children have worked with seeds and plants for about 2 weeks. The teacher says:

> We've done well in getting our plants started. But suppose we didn't want our seeds to sprout and grow. Sometimes in nature seeds get damaged or conditions are not right for seeds to grow. What could you do to keep seeds from sprouting and growing?

Figure 4–3   **Things that may keep a seed from growing.**

Squashing it	Cutting it in half
Chewing it	Not watering it
Freezing it	Watering it with saltwater
Boiling it	Microwaving it

The children begin suggesting operations to try, as shown in Figure 4–3. These are their hypotheses; at this point, they need not be framed as operational questions. The teacher writes all of these on the chalkboard, regardless of content. The teacher then has the class screen the hypotheses for those that may have possibilities:

> With which conditions might the seed have some chance to live? Suppose Matoteng squashed his seed just a little. Would the seed sprout? Would the plant look squashed? Would this happen with any kind of a seed? How about some of the rest of these conditions?

This mixture of broad and narrow questions is posed slowly to give the children time to think. The children discuss a number of possibilities. After a while, the teacher says:

> How can we test our ideas?

It soon becomes obvious that some children are going to do several things at one time to their seeds, so the teacher says:

> Suppose Hongmei squashes her seed and also freezes it. How will she know which one stopped the seed from growing?

The children decide to change just one condition at a time. Pairs of children quickly form operational questions from hypotheses they want to test:

> Will squashing a bean seed keep it from sprouting? Will cutting a bean seed in half keep it from sprouting?

Interest is high as experimenting begins.

Grade 6 Example

In Ms. Xu's sixth-grade class, students are working in pairs. They are testing their reaction time by catching dropped rulers. In each pair, one student holds the ruler just above his partner's hand. When he releases the ruler, the partner catches the ruler between her thumb and forefinger. The ruler number closest to the top of her pinched fingers is recorded. This is her "reaction time." After a few minutes, the teacher asks the students to give their reaction times. He writes these on the board in the form of a histogram, as shown in Table 4–2. Histograms are used to classify data in a way that encourages thinking about the differences in the data.

After a few moments, in a discussion with the students on how the scores are distributed, Ms. Xu says:

> Suppose everything and everyone were the same in our experiment. How would the histogram look? Well, are there differences that may have given us these results? What conditions might affect reaction time?

The students start forming hypotheses:

> Not everybody did it the same way.
> Some people have faster reaction times.

Table 4–2

Reaction Time Histogram

```
                              X
                              X
                              X
                    X         X
                    X    X    X    X
          X         X    X    X    X
          X         X    X    X    X    X    X
 X        X         X    X    X    X    X    X              X
 1    2   3    4    5    6    7    8    9    10   11   12
```

Some kids have more practice.
I was tired today.

After a discussion to narrow down and clarify different ideas, Ms. Xu says:

How are you going to test your ideas?

The students state their ideas as operational questions: Will people have the same reaction time if they do the experiment in exactly the same way? Does practice give you a faster reaction time? Do people who feel "tired" (defined as having fewer than 8 hours of sleep) have slower times than when they don't feel tired? Everybody agrees that they must do the experiment in the same way each time to control the test variables. Then each question is tested separately under the controlled conditions.

Experimentation and Scientific Attitudes

According to the National Science Education Leadership Association (2001), "Teachers should base their teaching of elementary science on process and inquiry skills such as observing, classifying, measuring, interpreting data, proposing hypotheses and conclusions." Experimentation incorporates all of the process and inquiry skills. Another positive outcome of promoting experimentation and scientific skills in your classroom is in the area of student attitudes toward science.

SCIENTIFIC ATTITUDES

As seen in the Inquiry and Attitudes Standard in the Standards Link box, an important part of inquiry is acquiring positive scientific attitudes. Experimentation and other skills are not fully developed if they are completed in a negative framework or only finished to "get it over with." Science is different from such activities as learning to spell, in which the task is simple and there is only one correct answer. Science includes developing attitudes and

> **Teaching Tips**
>
> Exploring your students' attitudes and resolving any negative attitudes toward science will assist in positive teaching experiences throughout the school year.

questioning those attitudes. The development of these attitudes is part of the job for elementary and middle school teachers. We will consider five categories related to attitudes.

Curiosity

"To be a child is to touch, smell, taste, and hear everything you can between the time you get up and when your parents make you go to bed. I don't have to teach curiosity. It's there already." The kindergarten teacher who made this statement about curiosity echoes the feeling of many of her elementary school colleagues. Yet, in some classes, there are children who lack interest in science.

Walk into two adjoining classrooms: one with a hands-on science program and another where students just read and do worksheets during science time. Handing concrete materials to children is like rowing downstream or cycling with the wind at your back. Making children sit still and be quiet for long periods is like rowing upstream or riding into the wind: You can do it, but it is better to avoid it. Children lose much of their curiosity unless they are allowed to do what comes naturally.

Teachers who maintain or spark students' curiosity apply science to everyday life. These teachers also use several open-ended investigations during a teaching unit. As you can see, we often use children's literature as a way to initiate curiosity about a topic. For example, reading *Poppy* (Avi, 1995) explores the relationship between an owl and a deer mouse. Students will immediately begin to wonder about the relationship between these two animals.

Standards Link

Inquiry and Attitudes Standard

Teachers of science develop communities of science learners that reflect the intellectual rigor of scientific inquiry and the attitudes and social values conducive to science learning. In doing this, teachers:

- **Display and demand respect for the diverse ideas, skills, and experiences of all students.**

- **Enable students to have a significant voice in decisions about the content and context of their work and require students to take responsibility for learning of all members of the community.**

- **Nurture collaboration among students.**

- **Structure and facilitate ongoing formal and informal discussion based on a shared understanding of rules of scientific discourse.**

- **Model and emphasize the skills, attitudes, and values of scientific inquiry.**

(Teaching Standard E, National Research Council, 1996, pp. 45, 46.)

Inventiveness

To be inventive is to solve problems in creative or novel ways. This is contrast to simply taking a known solution and applying it to a problem at hand: It's good to apply what you know about a car jack to change a flat tire, but what do you do when there's no jack? Inventive people may apply their knowledge to solve problems much as other persons do, but they are more likely to show **fluency, flexibility,** and **originality** in their thinking.

Critical Thinking

To think critically is to evaluate or judge whether something is adequate, correct, useful, or desirable. A judge does this when she decides whether the evidence is adequate to find guilt; the judge has a standard in mind against which she makes a judgment. This is the key to critical thinking: Know the accepted standard and decide whether or to what degree it is being met.

Fluency   refers to the number of ideas a child gives when challenged with a problem. We can promote fluency by asking open-ended questions.

Flexibility   is the inclination to shift one's focus from the usual.

Originality   is shown when children generate ideas that are new to them. We can promote originality by encouraging children to use their imagination and combine others' ideas in new ways, and by withholding evaluative comments until we have all the ideas.

Visit an Inquiry Classroom
Curiosity

View the *Curiosity and Interest* video in the "Nature of Science" section of the Companion CD. Mr. McKnight asks students questions to stimulate their curiosity. More importantly, however, he has the students identify questions that they would like to explore.

Review the video and ask yourself the following:
* Why doesn't Mr. McKnight simply provide a written question and have all the students explore that question?
* Mr. McKnight does not readily answer the question of "how do they have babies" but instead tells Josh, "When you learn the answer, you won't believe it." Why didn't he simply provide a brief answer to this question?

Novak (1977) suggested that inquiry is a student behavior that involves activity and skills, but with the focus on the active search for knowledge or understanding to satisfy students' curiosity. Explain why you agree or disagree with this idea.

 CW Record your ideas and the answers to these questions in your portfolio or use the Companion Website to share your ideas.

A problem we face as teachers of elementary and middle school children is the numerous standards of behavior in science. Many are highly sophisticated. Let's see if we can reduce them to a manageable few and restate them on a level that makes sense to young minds.

Science has three overall standards for critical thinking that most children can gradually understand and learn to assimilate: open-mindedness, objectivity, and willingness to suspend judgment until enough facts are known.

The *open-minded* person listens to others and is willing to change his mind if warranted. An *objective* person tries to be free of bias, considers both sides in arguments, and realizes that strong personal preferences may interfere with the proper collecting and processing of data. Someone who *suspends judgment* understands that additional data may confirm or deny what first appears. Looking for further data improves the chances for drawing proper conclusions.

Try having several groups work on the same activity and then report and compare findings. The degree of open-mindedness soon becomes obvious when people refuse to listen to others, push their own ideas, or jump to conclusions before all groups have their say.

Critical and creative thinking go hand in hand—it is artificial to separate them. When problem solving or experimenting, for example, children should be encouraged to generate several possibilities, rather than just consider the first idea suggested. You also want them to appraise all the ideas critically so that they can tackle what looks most promising. Controlling variables in experimenting gives students another chance to generate suggestions, but they must also think: "Will these controls do the job?" Later, if groups come up with different findings, critical thinking is again needed to answer why. Perhaps one or more variables were not controlled after all. You can see that creative and critical thinking are different sides of the same coin.

When students seek information, a variety of sources are available to them, including each other, printed matter, audiovisual materials, electronic information, and knowledgeable adults. Certainly, students can be cautioned to check copyright dates and agreement with what is known, to consult more than one source, and to note conflicts in fact. This is especially important when exploring the Internet, where information can be posted from anyone who has access to it. Children often do not critically appraise information. As educators, we can help children learn ways to consult these sources efficiently and to understand what the sources say.

Spend time reading fictional materials with your students. *Owls in the Family* (Mowat, 1981) is a humorous tale of two owls. Critical thinking is promoted as students begin to separate fact from fiction in this story.

Persistence

Most elementary and middle school science activities can be completed within a short time, but some require a sustained and vigorous effort. To do our best work often takes persistence. Children sometimes lack the persistence to stick with a worthwhile goal. Primary-level students often want instant results. Their short attention span and need for physical activity can easily convert into impatience. You can combat this impatience by arousing children's interests with meaningful science activities.

Uncertainty

Another important attitude to develop is the ability to understand or accept uncertainty. Much of this attitude centers on students understanding the nature of elementary statistics. Some events can be predicted well; some cannot. We do not always know all the variables in a given situation, nor do we always have representative data of a population. For instance, the weather announcer on television only predicts rain tomorrow on the basis of the percentage of times it has rained with similar weather conditions (e.g., air pressure, wind patterns, cold and warm fronts).

Elementary and middle school students should be aware that evidence is not always complete and that therefore predictions may not always be precise. Experiments are influenced by the lack of an accurate observation, missing information of compounding factors, or a model to explain the variables effectively. Scientists do not always have all the answers, but must theorize on the observations and experimental results they do have.

Visit an Inquiry Classroom
Teacher Modeling of Attitudes

Watch *Glen McKnight's Perspective with the Teacher Attributes* video in the "Nature of Science" section of the Companion CD. What does Mr. McKnight specifically say that indicates he possesses positive scientific attitudes and passes these on to his students?

Review the video segment and ask yourself the following:
- If I were being interviewed, what would I say about my attitudes toward science?
- We state that "early learning of attitudes begins with imitation" and that "the open-minded, accepting teacher who reflects positive attitudes is more likely to influence students in positive ways." From your own experiences, do you find this to be true? Provide specific examples.

Corsaro (2003) discusses how we as a society may be losing our parental influences on children and that more influence may come from the school environment. If he is accurate with this idea, what would that suggest to you as a future elementary or middle school science teacher? Record your ideas and the answers to these questions in your portfolio or use the Companion Website to share your ideas.

Developing Attitudes

Early learning of attitudes begins with imitation and later comes from experiences with the consequences of having or not having the attitudes. The open-minded, accepting teacher who reflects positive attitudes is more likely to influence students in positive ways than one who lacks these qualities.

Open-ended activities bring out positive attitudes. Success in science is bound up with curiosity, inventiveness, critical thinking, persistence, and tolerance for uncertainty. Children learn, in a more limited way, the same habits of mind as scientists and other reflective people. Successfully practicing these attitudes helps build self-esteem.

Summary

- In *observing*, students learn to use all their senses, note similarities and differences in objects, and become aware of change.
- In *classifying*, students group things by properties or functions. Students may also arrange them in order of value.
- *Measuring* teaches students to use nonstandard and standard units to find or estimate quantity. Measurement is often applied in combination with skills introduced in the mathematics program.
- *Communicating* teaches students to put observed information into some clear form that another person can understand.

- By *inferring*, students interpret or explain what they observe. When students infer from data that something will happen, usually the term *predicting* is used. When people state an inference they want to test, usually the term *hypothesizing* is used. Therefore, predicting and hypothesizing are special forms of inferring.
- In *experimenting*, we often guide students to state their hypotheses as operational (testable) questions and help them control variables within their understanding.

Reflection

Companion CD

1. Look at "The Earthworm's Body: Digging It" lesson linked to the *Learning to Think* video on the Companion CD. Can you rewrite this lesson to be more consistent with the learning cycle?
2. Look at "The Earthworm and Water" lesson linked to the *Cognitive Apprenticeship* video on the Companion CD. How could you modify the "Extended Practice" section to have students apply their new knowledge and skills as part of the concept application phase?
3. Look at "Mechanics of the Digestive System" lesson linked to the *Scientific Method* video on the Companion CD. Observation is not identified as a skill to be taught in this lesson. In what ways could you modify this lesson to include developing observational skills?

Portfolio Ideas

1. Safety is an important consideration when experimenting or developing other scientific skills in the elementary and middle school classrooms. Purchase a copy of *Safety in the Elementary Science Classroom* (National Science Teachers Association, 1997, at http://www.nsta.org) and identify potential safety hazards in your practicum classroom. Record these in your portfolio and discuss them with the teacher. Also visit the Companion Website (http://www.prenhall.com/peters) for more safety information.
2. What other scientific skills can you think of to teach children? What approaches could you take to develop these skills in elementary or middle school students? Record findings in your portfolio.

3. How well do you know the science processes? Experiment with one of the activities from the books listed in the Suggested Readings. Repeat your experiment with students at your practicum site, document findings in your portfolio, and compare their results with those of your classmates.
4. Interview an elementary or middle school student and compare her scientific attitudes with those in this chapter. Share these results in your portfolio and with the class or your instructor.
5. Try some activities in *Floaters and Sinkers* (Cordel & Hillen, 1995) as an initial source to learning cycle activities related to mass, volume, and density. Enter findings in your portfolio.
6. A fun way to introduce the metric system is to have a classroom or schoolwide Olympics. The book *Math & Science: A Solution* (Ecklund & Wiebe, 1987) has metric measurement activities related to the Olympics. *Olympic Math* (Vogt, 1996) also has measurement and graphing activities. The *Math Counts* series (Pluckrose, 1995) has titles that relate to introductory measurement, such as length, weight, time, and capacity, that can assist students in identifying concepts as part of the Olympics experience. Record how your event turned out in your portfolio.
7. Try using the "Deliver Woodsy's Message" activity in the *Woodsy Owl Activity Guide* (Children's Television Network, 1977) as a communication activity. Students can make posters, create mobiles, write poetry, or perform a play based on a "lend a hand—care for the land" theme. Record what you find in your portfolio.

References

American Association for the Advancement of Science (AAAS). (1993). *Benchmarks for science literacy.* New York: Oxford University Press.

Avi. (1995). *Poppy.* New York: Orchard Books.

Barman, C. R. (1989). A procedure for helping prospective elementary teachers integrate the learning cycle into science textbooks. *Journal of Science Teacher Education, 1*(2), 21–26.

Brett, J. (1994). *Town mouse & country mouse.* New York: G. P. Putnam.

Bunting, E. (1984). *The man who could call down owls.* New York: Macmillan.

Bybee, R. W., Buchwald, C. E., Crissman, S., Heil, D. R., Kuerbis, P. J., Matsumoto, C., & McInerney, J. D. (1989). *Science and technology education for the elementary years: Frameworks for curriculum and instruction.* Washington, DC: National Center for Improving Science Education.

Children's Television Network. (1977). *Woodsy Owl Activity Guide.* Washington, DC: USDA Forest Service.

Cordel, B. & Hillen, J. (1995). *Floaters and Sinkers.* Fresno, CA: AIMS Educational Foundation.

Corsaro, W. A. (2003). *We're friends, right?: Inside kids' culture.* Washington, DC: National Academy Press.

Dewey, J. (1929). *The quest for certainty: A study of the relation of knowledge and action.* New York: G. P. Putnam.

Ecklond, L. & Wiebe, A. (1987). *Math & Science: A Solution.* Fresno, CA: AIMS Educational Foundation.

Erickson, R. E. (1998). *A toad for Tuesday.* New York: Lothrop, Lee & Shepard Books.

Flick, L. B. (1993). The meaning of hands-on science. *Journal of Science Teacher Education, 4*(1), 1–8.

Fratt, L. 2002. Less is more: Trimming the overstuffed curriculum. *District Administrator, 38*(3). Retrieved December 23, 2004, from www.districtadministration.com/page.cfm?p=228

Garcia, A. (1997). *Measurement: 35 hands-on activities.* Cypress, CA: Creative Teaching Press.

Gates, F. (1994). *Owl eyes.* New York: Lothrop, Lee & Shepard Books.

Hutchins, P. (1972). *Good-night owl!* New York: Macmillan.

Kalman, B. (1987). *Owls.* New York: Crabtree.

Karplus, R. (1977). Science teaching and the development of reasoning. *Journal of Research in Science Teaching, 14*(2), 169–175.

Karplus, R., & Their, H. D. (1967). *A new look at elementary school science: Science curriculum improvement study.* Chicago: Rand McNally.

Klein, A. (1974). *The world of measurements.* New York: Simon & Schuster.

Ling, M. (1992). *See how they grow: Owl.* New York: Dorling Kindersley.

Mowat, F. (1981). *Owls in the family.* New York: Bantam.

Myller, R. (1990). *How big is a foot?* New York: Dell.

National Research Council (NRC). (1996). *National science education standards.* Washington, DC: National Academies Press.

National Research Council (NRC). (2000). *Inquiry and the national science education standards: A guide for teaching and learning.* Washington, DC: National Academies Press.

National Science Education Leadership Association. (2001). *Elementary science education. Position statement.* Raleigh, NC: Author. Retrieved December 23, 2004, from www.nsela.org/nselapositionpapers.pdf

National Science Teachers Association. (1997). *Safety in the elementary science classroom.* Washington, DC: Author.

National Science Teachers Association (NSTA). (2004). *Scientific inquiry. A position statement.* Washington, DC: Author. Retrieved October 1, 2004, from www.nsta.org/positionstatement&psid=43

Novak, J. (1977). *A theory of education.* Ithaca, NY: Cornell University Press.

Odom, A. L., & Settlage, J., Jr. (1996). Teachers' understandings of the learning cycle as assessed with a two-tier test. *Journal of Science Teacher Education, 7*(2), 123–142.

Palumbo, T. (1989). *Measurement motivators: From dinosaurs to decimals.* Torrance, CA: Good Apple.

Pluckrose, H. (1995a). *Math counts: Capacity*. Chicago: Childrens Press.

Pluckrose, H. (1995b). *Math counts: Length*. Chicago: Childrens Press.

Pluckrose, H. (1995c). *Math counts: Time*. Chicago: Childrens Press.

Pluckrose, H. (1995d). *Math counts: Weight*. Chicago: Childrens Press.

Ramsey, J. (1993). Developing conceptual storylines with the learning cycle. *Journal of Elementary Science Education, 5*(2), 1–20.

Rosenthal, D. (1993). A learning cycle approach to dealing with pseudoscience beliefs of prospective elementary teachers. *Journal of Science Teacher Education, 4*(2), 33–36.

Sattler, H. R. (1995). *The book of North American owls*. New York: Clarion Books.

Selsam, M. E., & Hunt, J. (1986). *A first look at owls, eagles, and other hunters of the sky*. New York: Walker.

Singer, M. (1989). *Turtle in July*. New York: Macmillan.

Staver, J. R., & Shroyer, M. G. (1994). Teaching elementary teachers how to use the learning cycle for guided inquiry instruction in science. In L. Schafer (Ed.), *Behind the methods class door: Educating elementary and middle school science teachers* (pp. 1–11). Columbus, OH: ERIC Clearinghouse.

Vogt, S. (1996). *Olympic math*. Grandview, IL: Good Year Books.

Waddell, M. (1994). *Owl babies*. Compton, CA: Santillana.

Yolen, J. (1987). *Owl moon*. New York: Philomel Books.

Suggested Readings

Council for Environmental Education. (1992). Owl pellets. In *Project WILD K–12 activity guide* (pp. 144–145). Bethesda, MD: Author. (a guide to owl pellet activities)

Gabel, D. L. (1993). *Introductory science skills* (2nd ed.). Prospect Heights, IL: Waveland Press. (a comprehensive workbook of scientific skill development and assessment)

Goldsworthy, A., & Feasey, R. (1997). *Making sense of primary science investigations*. Hatfield, Herts., UK: Association for Science Education. (a guide to primary science investigations and the skills involved)

Ostlund, K. (1992). *Science process skills*. Menlo Park, CA: Addison-Wesley. (ways to assess each of the science processes, with material lists and reproducible worksheets)

Ostlund, K., & Mercier, S. (1996). *Rising to the challenge of the national science education standards: The process of inquiry*. Fresno, CA: S & K Associates. (36 activities that promote the processes of science inquiry)

Rezba, R. J., Sprague, C., Fiel, R. L., Funk, H. J., Okey, J. R., & Jaus, H. H. (1995). *Learning and assessing science process skills* (3rd ed.). Dubuque, IA: Kendall/Hunt. (a workbook of scientific skill development and assessment)

Ruchlis, H. (1991). *How do you know it's true? Discovering the difference between science and superstition*. Buffalo, NY: Prometheus Books. (an easy-to-follow account of how scientific theories are based on facts and observations)

Smith, B. (1989). *Measurement motivators: From dinosaurs to decimals*. Torrance, CA: Good Apple. (a book of measurement activities)

CHAPTER 5

ASSESSMENT

- How is assessment different today than when you were in elementary or middle school?
- What are some types of authentic assessment?
- How can you effectively assess attitudes in the science classroom?

Focus on Inquiry

Portfolios

Christine Peters,
Harborcreek School District, Pennsylvania

During the last several years, I've been using portfolio assessment more and more. At first, I felt somewhat uncomfortable with the notion. I worried whether I'd find the time in our hectic day to collect, sort, choose, meet, and interview. Now that I've been using this form of individualized assessment, I see that my students are the ones who are responsible for the selection process. This is actually the most important aspect of using portfolios. By involving the children in the decision-making process, they achieve a deeper sense of pride, a feeling of ownership about their work, and a desire for excellence.

In building portfolios, I am concentrating on the process of the child's learning, as well as the product. My students are better able to focus on a specific goal, rather than on a letter grade. I am also promoting a closer relationship with my students because my assessment focuses on the development of a student's work over time. Not only do my students feel a great sense of pride, but I feel like the world's best teacher when I compare one of their spelling assessments from September with one from May, or when I listen to one of my student's oral reading cassettes from the first week of school—when she knew very few words and didn't have enough skills to sound them out—and compare it with the middle or end of the tape when she is able to read anything she picks up from the library.

The toughest part of using portfolio assessment is deciding when to fit the interviewing and selection process into your day. I have tried many approaches, and what I like the best is what I call "free choice time." Every other Friday afternoon, the boys and girls in my classroom are free to do what they would like to do. Of course, I give them some guidance in choosing options, and if there is any unfinished work for the day or week, that must be completed first. I will often invite one or two other adults into my classroom to help with the interviewing and selection process. Administrators, instructional and learning support teachers, and parents have all been involved in this process in my classroom in the past. It

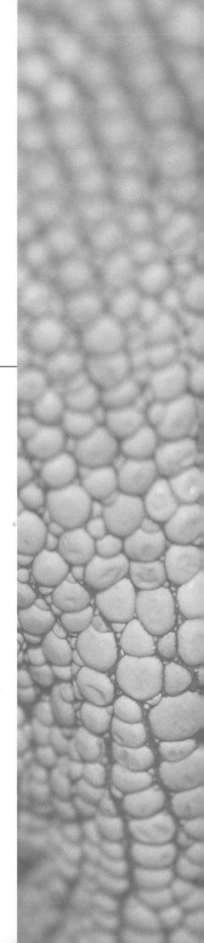

is valuable to use the same volunteers so that little time will be respent on "training," even though this is not always possible.

A typical free choice time in my classroom will look like this:

- A small group works in the science center on a food pyramid with pictures they've cut out of magazines; several children play *Pictionary* using the sand trays and shaving cream boards in the corner; a group of children make numbers out of clay to take to another classroom; two children tape themselves reading one of the big books our class wrote, entitled *Ten Black Dots*; and several children read books from our classroom library that they will then present to their classmates by using puppets or posters.

- At the same time, I and my adult volunteers will meet individually with each of my 22 students. Before the students are individually interviewed, they are told what materials are required for their meeting. They have an idea of which works (products) they will want to place into their portfolios, and they have thought about why they have chosen such pieces. During their interviews, I go over the selected pieces and together (later in the year, the students fill this out independently) we write out a "Portfolio and Goals Survey." This survey states the date, the title of the piece, why the piece was chosen, the favorite part of the piece, what the piece shows, what the child has learned so far, what he wants to learn next, and things that will help him learn better.

- If I have several adult helpers and if time permits, then I also find it valuable to go over one of my checklists with each child. One week, I may share each child's oral reading checklist with him or her, and the next week I'll share the writing or cooperative learning checklists. These are forms that I keep in students' portfolios to record learning skills and behaviors that I observe in their daily work and in how they work with each other.

I love using portfolios in my elementary classroom! The students enjoy having a collection of their work that progresses throughout the year. Even my students with learning difficulties can't help but see the progression of skill in their work. They all feel successful and are always trying to do their best, hoping that what they are currently working on will be added to their portfolio. Parents are even excited about the portfolio assessment going on in my classroom. They can see their child's learning in concrete terms and become partners in the learning process. Parents are invited in often to view their child's works, and a few times a year, the portfolio is sent home along with a letter in which the parents are encouraged to give feedback.

It doesn't take much preparation to begin using portfolios in your classroom. All you need are some file and pocket folders, composition books, cassette and/or videotapes, large manila envelopes, and lots of stick-on notes. To store the portfolios, I use a large plastic crate. A cardboard box would even fit the purpose.

Some of the items that go into my students' portfolios are my observations; their writing samples; journals; reading, writing, math, and cooperative learning inventories; artwork; parent surveys; rubrics; book evaluations; and child-selected samples of daily work.

Portfolio assessment teaches students how to learn and teaches teachers how to slow down, get to know each student and his or her strengths and needs, and develop a curriculum that appeals to each student's multiple talents. It encourages students—and teachers—to strive for excellence in all they do.

THE CHANGING PRACTICE OF ASSESSMENT

The portfolio process discussed in the Focus on Inquiry: Portfolios is representative of **assessment** practice changes in our schools. To better understand the need for these changes, let's use an industry metaphor.

Throughout most of the 20th century, school, like industry, was conceived of as a manufacturing process in which raw materials (students) were operated on by the machinery (teachers). Some of the products were worked on for longer periods of time than others, but in the end, we molded a finished product (a literate citizen).

Education in the 20th century certainly moved beyond the agrarian practices of the 19th century. Students were no longer in one-room schoolhouses where education was planned around harvest and planting seasons. Children of this era learned in unison as they progressed through the assembly line (curriculum). The primary process used to shape the final product was expository teaching. The bosses (school administrators) told the workers how to run the assembly line under rigid work rules (behavioral aims, goals, and objectives) that gave them little or no stake in the process (see Rubba, Miller, Schmalz, Rosenfeld, & Shyamal, 1991).

Assessment practices, the "quality control" of the educational allegory described above, were consistently used to seek out the degree of factual knowledge students were able to absorb. It is well documented that educators of this generation were in the "we teach what we test" mode. Unfortunately, tests of this nature were "fundamentally incompatible" with reform efforts such as those we now associate with constructivism (Resnick & Resnick, 1989).

> **Assessment** involves the collection and interpretation of information about what students know and can do as it relates to the curriculum.

> See the Chapter 5 Web Destinations on the Companion Website (*http://www.prenhall.com/peters*) to explore current assessment research and practice.

Assessment Today

This chapter reflects the view that the primary purpose of assessment is to improve opportunity to learn and the student's construction of knowledge and that quality assessments should be designed to reflect excellence in science curriculum and instruction (National Science Teachers Association [NSTA], 2001). One way to do this is to match the assessment with the learning paradigm of constructivism. We hope to make the linkage between what we want students to know and the assessment tool used to find the answer. Assessment should not be something we do *to* children, but something we can do *with* children. Look at the Consistency of Assessment Standard in the Standards Link box. This standard is a good beginning example. Does this standard cause teachers to think about assessment in a different way? Why would they use one procedure or another? What question would they hope to answer through the data collected? How will they analyze the data collected? Is the scoring rubric fair and consistent? Will this approach be helpful to the students and lead to good instructional decisions?

As you read this chapter, think about your own assessment practices. Consider how your beliefs and practices may be different from what you find here and why you and your students should be more involved

---

Standards Link

Consistency of Assessment Standard

Assessments must be consistent with the decisions they are designed to inform.

- **Assessments are deliberately designed.**
- **Assessments have explicitly stated purposes.**
- **The relationship between the decisions and the data is clear.**
- **Assessment procedures are internally consistent.**

(Assessment Standard A, National Research Council, 1996, p. 78.)

in assessment. A good starting point is to see why we use assessment, what assessment involves, and how it is changing.

Assessment of Science Learning

The following are good reasons for using assessment in your classroom:

For many beginning teachers, it is easier to concentrate on two assessment areas—the knowledge and skills of the students.

- Monitoring students' progress
- Increasing communications with students
- Improving instruction and the learning environment
- Determining the best science program and opportunities to learn
- Enhancing teacher accountability

You will find that assessment techniques can check students' process skill development, factual knowledge, conceptual knowledge, problem-solving ability, and higher level understanding.

Knowledge Objectives

Knowledge objectives, the content and concepts of science, can be overwhelming if you concentrate on discrete facts and definitions. Instead, work toward encompassing concepts and generalizations. For example, instead of focusing on learning every item that a magnet will attract, work toward the generalization that magnets attract objects made of iron and steel.

Skill Objectives

Skill objectives, or the process skills of science referred to in Chapter 4, are also easier to work with if they are kept to a manageable level. During the elementary and middle school years, focus on observation, classification, measurement, inference, prediction, communication, and experimentation.

Changing Emphasis

In keeping with the standards-based reform efforts, assessment is one of the most important revisions to the learning environment. The authors of *National Science Education Standards* sought a changing emphasis in the area of assessment (National Research Council [NRC], 1996). They envisioned less emphasis on assessing discrete or scientific knowledge and more emphasis on assessing scientific understanding, reasoning, and well-structured knowledge.

Today, this means we no longer place as much importance on teacher-tested vocabulary and definitions related to a topic under study. Rather, we look for teacher- and student-assessed genuine understanding. We look at how the phenomenon under study fits into the child's current and future thought processes. With changing assessment procedures, we no longer look at what students do not know, but what opportunities students have had to learn and what they do know or have achieved. We can build on the knowledge that our children already have, and thus expand the possibilities.

Look at the Achievement and Opportunity to Learn Standard in the Standards Link box. The authors make an interesting point that assessment of the **opportunity to learn** is as important as assessing the learning itself. This means that assessment should be an ongoing process. Meaningful connections should take precedence over "covering the curriculum." In *Benchmarks for Science Literacy* (American Association for the Advancement of Science [AAAS], 1993), authors call for reducing the amount of material being covered

Opportunity to learn   is the concept that assessment should go beyond individual achievement and include the teacher's presentation of the content and skills through quality instructional delivery.

Visit an Inquiry Classroom
Ongoing Assessment

View the *Ongoing Assessment* video in the "Model Inquiry Unit" section of the Companion CD. Mr. McKnight uses an "investigation record" as a tool for assessing his students.

Review the video and ask yourself the following:
- What evidence is there in the video that this form of assessment is working?
- Would you want to rely solely on the investigation record as an assessment tool? If so, justify your answer. If not, what other types of assessment would you use?

In the year 2000, the National Assessment of Educational Progress presented a survey of fourth- and eighth-grade student achievement in *The Nation's Report Card: Science* (2003). The authors noted that between 1996 and 2000, there was no statistically significant difference observed in the average science scores of fourth- or eighth-grade students. Given the national testing requirements under No Child Left Behind, do you think there is an increase in the average science scores in 2005? Why or why not? Record your ideas and the answers to these questions in your portfolio or use the Companion Website to share your ideas.

in science classes. Their goal of "teaching less, but teaching it better" does not mean to teach science less often. It means to teach fewer unrelated facts and to spend more time making connections, refining skills, and providing in-depth study of a topic. Part of this goal is to spend time before, during, and after instruction on assessment, including identifying and resolving misconceptions.

This assessment picture can be more difficult but provides a better indication of the true learning occurring in your classroom. To see how assessment can be more student centered and related to understanding, follow along with the students as they study the effects of water on the environment.

Mr. Correa's Water Lesson

Mr. Correa reads *A Drop of Water* (Wick, 1997) to his fifth-grade class and sparks an interest in how water travels through the water cycle. The next day, a student follows up the discussions by telling the class about a book she recently read called *Water Dance* (Locker, 1997). The student tells the class the story of how water travels throughout the environment.

Later in the week, Mr. Correa facilitates from the *Project Learning Tree* an activity called "Water Wonders" (American Forest Foundation, 1996). Students become drops of water and cycle through clouds, mountains, oceans, streams, plants, animals, and groundwater stations set up in the classroom. At each stop, they pick out a slip of paper that leads them to the next randomly selected station. They keep track of their journey by taping the slips of paper

---

Standards Link

Achievement and Opportunity to Learn Standard

Achievement and opportunity to learn science must be assessed.

- **Achievement data collected focus on the science content that is most important for students to learn.**

- **Opportunity-to-learn data collected focus on the most powerful indicators.**

- **Equal attention must be given to the assessment of opportunity to learn and to the assessment of student achievement.**

(Assessment Standard B, National Research Council, 1996, p. 79.)

Children experiment at a laboratory streamed as part of their river erosion activities.

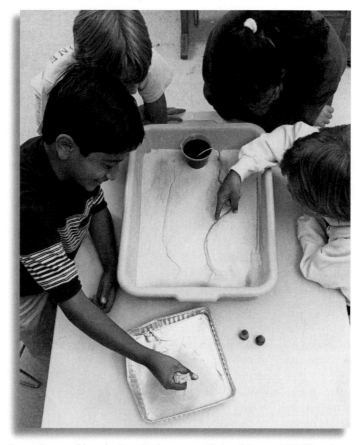

Source: Reprinted from the Great Explorations in Math and Science (GEMS) teacher's guide entitled River Cutters, copyright by The Regents of the University of California, and used with permission. The GEMS series includes more than 70 teacher's guides and handbooks for preschool through eighth grade, available from LHS GEMS, Lawrence Hall of Science, University of California, Berkeley, CA 94720-5200. /(510) 642–7771. http://www.lhsgems.org

they select at each station onto a scorecard. After they finish, students each tell a story about their adventures. In the follow-up discussion about streams, one student mentions a stream near his house. He informs the class of hearing his father's concern over a new tax to assist the county with erosion and drainage problems. Taking the discussion a step further, Mr. Correa decides to model the situation with the students.

He engages the students in an activity from *River Cutters* (Lawrence Hall of Science, 1989). The students work together to set up a streambed with diatomaceous earth inside. They place a rubber tube connected to a water source that allows drops of water to flow onto the surface. They carefully observe this model of the effects of water on the earth.

Next, students draw pictures of what happens with the models. Using tags that Mr. Correa places alongside specific features, students label the streams, rivers, valleys, and other features that form in the diatomaceous earth. They discuss the features in the

 Teaching Tips *River Cutters* is one in the Great Explorations in Math and Science (GEMS) series of thematic activity books based on a hands-on/cooperative learning format (see *http://www.prenhall.com/peters* for the link to GEMS materials).

streambeds with their small groups and later with their teacher. Mr. Correa asks the students what other experiments they could do with the streambed apparatus.

Mr. Correa now looks on as the students generate ideas for further study. They write a description of what they would like to find out, propose ways to model the situation, and predict outcomes. They want to demonstrate what is occurring near Ninth Street. The students begin to work with the streambeds. They are adjusting the water flow to create the correct model of their neighborhood.

Where has the assessment occurred with the stream activities? What type of assessment was done? Could Mr. Correa have employed **authentic assessment** as part of his water lessons? To answer these questions, let's look further into what is meant by authentic assessment.

> **Authentic assessment** is seen as measuring or testing what the student really knows about a concept or skill, as opposed to testing something inconsistent with what was taught or the goals of the science program.

The Use of Authentic Assessment

When you were asked about the water cycle and erosion in elementary and middle school, was it similar to how Mr. Correa assessed his class? If so, you participated in authentic assessment. The authors of the *National Science Education Standards* (NRC, 1996) and Project 2061 (see AAAS, 1998) indicate that assessment should be authentic or genuine. They want the data to measure what they are supposed to measure. This view of assessment is indicated in the Quality of the Data and Interpretations Standard, as described in the Standards Link box.

Assessment should be "similar in form to tasks in which [students] will engage in their lives outside the classroom or are similar to the activities of scientists" (NRC, 1996, p. 83). The term *embedded assessment* refers to how assessment should be "part of the activities that naturally occur in a lesson or a logical extension of the lesson's central activity" (National Science Resources Center, 1997, pp. 103, 108). Examples of authentic assessment are included in Figure 5–1.

You can infer from the different types of assessment practices noted in Figure 5–1 that assessment is not just for assigning a grade. In fact, there are two types of assessments according to the Project 2061 authors (AAAS, 1998): *internal purpose assessments* and *external purpose assessments*.

Internal purpose assessments are administered to convey expectations about what is important to learn, to provide information on progress, to help students judge their learning, to guide and improve instruction, and to classify and select students (AAAS, 1998). Examples are the child-developed, teacher-made, and textbook series–provided assessment tools used by teachers as part of the normal classroom experiences.

External purpose assessments include examinations given to provide information for accountability, to guide policy decisions, to gather information for program evaluation, to

> **Internal purpose assessments** are classroom-based assessments used by the teacher to measure the progress of students within their class.
>
> **External purpose assessments** are standardized assessments generally initiated by a school district or state to compare intact classes within a larger system.

Standards Link

Quality of the Data and Interpretations Standard

The technical quality of the data collected is well matched to the decisions and actions taken on the basis of their interpretation.

- **The feature that is claimed to be measured is actually measured.**

- **Assessment tasks are authentic.**

- **An individual student's performance is similar on two or more tasks that claim to measure the same aspect of student achievement.**

- **Students have adequate opportunity to demonstrate their achievements.**

- **Assessment tasks and methods of presenting them provide data that are sufficiently stable to lead to the same decisions if used at different times.**

(Assessment Standard C, National Research Council, 1996, p. 83.)

Figure 5–1   **Examples of authentic assessment practices.**

- Student observations
- Student interviews
- Written reports or journals
- Portfolios
- Performance measurements
- Concept or vee maps
- Multiple-choice tests
- Essay tests
- Short-answer tests
- Attitude surveys
- Creative assessments
- Projects and laboratory experiences

sort and classify people for admissions, and to certify or hire (AAAS, 1998). This is the standardized type of assessment resulting from achievement, placement, or certification tests such as the Iowa Test of Basic Skills, Scholastic Aptitude Test, or a standardized state exam for elementary or middle school students.

Today, both internal purpose and external purpose forms of assessment are receiving much attention. Internal purpose assessment is a key to the reform effort, because the assumption "we teach what we test" still holds true in many classrooms. External purpose assessment is likewise becoming increasingly important for teachers at a personal level. Suggested initiatives such as linking assessment results to teacher performance portfolios, or teacher pay raises, are now being proposed or implemented in some states. The ability to provide quality assessment is also a consideration in National Board Certification (National Board for Professional Teaching Standards, 1997). In either internal purpose or external purpose assessment situations, it is important to understand what good assessment is and the many forms of authentic assessment.

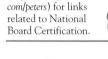

See the Chapter 5 Web Destinations at the Companion Website (*http://www.prenhall. com/peters*) for links related to National Board Certification.

Characteristics of Good Assessment

A good rule of thumb for assessment is that it is *reflective*, not *reflexive*. Assessment should not be an automatic, end-of-the-chapter reflexive routine. It should be an everyday experience that is increasingly indistinguishable from the classroom learning activities themselves. It is not a multiple-choice test that comes at the end of the chapter, waiting for our response. Rather, it is a *teacher- and student-selected* means to show that learning has occurred.

Assessment data should support reasonable conclusions of learning that has occurred as seen in the Sound Inferences Standard in the Standards Link box. The information should help both teacher and students reflect on what they have or have not learned. It should also help the teacher reflect on what future lessons or activities will assist in student understanding of the concepts being learned. Appraisal of learning should account for the students' individual differences and varied experiences. Figure 5–2 contains some good assessment characteristics.

Standards Link

Sound Inferences Standard

The inferences made from assessments about student achievement and opportunity to learn must be sound.

- **When making inferences from assessment data about student achievement and opportunity to learn science, explicit reference needs to be made to the assumptions on which the inferences are based.**

(Assessment Standard E, National Research Council, 1996, p. 86.)

Figure 5–2   Characteristics of good classroom assessments.

- They indicate an opportunity to learn.
- They allow for the student to select the best approach to a task.
- They are relevant to the student and are not just a correct answer.
- They accommodate the student's developmental level.
- They account for the student's prior knowledge.
- They are consistent and reliable for the student.
- They generally take more time to complete than tests.
- They are relevant to the learning goal.
- They promote transfer of learning into new situations.
- They produce measurable evidence of learning.
- They include both individual and group efforts.
- They are a continual process.

TYPES OF AUTHENTIC ASSESSMENT

Essay Items

Essay items provide a bridge between traditional assessment procedures and authentic assessment practices. Essay questions are useful in evaluating whether students are able to express personal ideas clearly. This type of question can be designed to assess higher order thinking, the ability to solve problems, or the capability to reason about the interrelationships between concepts.

As a caution, essay questions can be very subjective because there is not one right or wrong answer. The questions may be too vaguely worded for students to understand exactly what answer the teacher wants. Or, they may be too obvious for students and so the questions are not effective in measuring learning.

Also keep in mind that disabilities, language differences, and cultural diversity will affect students' abilities to answer questions, as pointed out in the Fair Assessment Standard in the Standards Link box. Students with poor language skills will often do poorly on these items, regardless of content knowledge. Likewise, students with good language skills may be able to bluff through answers that they do not fully understand. Cultural differences are also an important consideration.

As with other tests, careful construction of items will help make the test more meaningful. Compare the following two test items:

> What are the phases of the moon?
> Explain what we would observe here on Earth as the moon goes through its phases.
> Explain why it appears this way to us on Earth.

The first item is open for your students to interpret. They could respond by just listing "new, first quarter, full, last quarter." The second item requires your students to provide an explanation for why the phases occur and what they would look like, as well as the names of the phases. Essay tests that are well constructed match what was learned in class. They also ask well-defined, explicit questions that are understandable to all students. Additionally, good essay questions indicate, either in writing or through discourse, exactly what the teacher is looking for as an acceptable response.

 Teaching Tips | Creating a rubric for essay test questions provides a fair and consistent method when grading essay items.

Visit an Inquiry Classroom
The Teacher's Role in Assessment

View the *Teacher Withitness* video in the "Planning and Management" section of the Companion CD. At the beginning of the video sequence, Mr. McKnight works with groups of students as they complete the activities. He asks questions and allows students to fill in their investigation record. This is his form of authentic assessment.

Review the video and ask yourself the following:
- Are there other ways Mr. McKnight could assess students?
- Will the investigative records show that Mr. McKnight's students are learning? Explain your answer.

In *Classroom Assessment and the National Science Education Standards* (NRC, 2001), the authors define *authentic assessment* as "assessments that require students to perform complex tasks representative of activities actually done in out-of-school settings." Explain what they mean and include the teacher's role in the assessment process. Record your ideas and the answers to these questions in your portfolio or use the Companion Website to share your ideas.

The teacher should set and communicate to the students his expectations for length, detail, and spelling prior to the test. A grading rubric should also be developed that lists the specifics of what is expected. Use of a checklist will eliminate most subjectivity.

Are essay questions and other paper-and-pencil tests the best indication of learning? Could the students actually *do something* as part of the assessment?

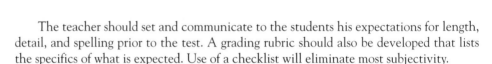

Performance-Based Assessment

Reflecting back on Mr. Correa, his students are being assessed as they complete the activities. How? The students are challenged to create a model streambed that is consistent with the severe erosion patterns in their neighborhood. Their *performance* on this task is one form of authentic assessment.

A performance-based assessment will generate an answer by the students. This type of assessment will also indicate the process used by the students to arrive at that answer. Performance-based assessment is often associated with the phrase "know and be able to do" (Ochs, 1996). Because students are doing something, we can assess the procedure as well as the product. There are ways to assess the procedure a student uses to arrive at an answer. This procedure is often more important than the answer itself. In fact, many times more than one answer will be correct.

The streambed example, as in other performance-based measures, provides three basic steps to follow (McMillan, 1997). The first step is *to construct the performance task* for students. In our example, Mr. Correa wanted his students to apply what they learned about erosion, so he asked the students themselves to generate or identify an idea for a task. Brainstorming ideas leads into the second step, which is *to develop a task description*. This is often done as a group effort but can also be completed individually. Third, with Mr. Correa's assistance, the students were asked *to write a task question*. Their specific "problem to solve" was to model what was going on in their neighborhood.

> **Teaching Tips**
>
> Assessment of the performance task can be done through teacher observation, student interviews, a written outline for the students to complete, or daily journal entries.

Was this the best question to explore? It was meaningful to the students, but other questions are certainly possibilities. Other examples of products that could be developed through this type of assessment include models based on scientific concepts, written material, or a formal decision. Products could also be applications of process skills, such as experiments with definite or undetermined conclusions.

When used, journals should be written in daily and checked often so that a dialogue can occur between the student and the teacher. This will indicate whether the student has misconceptions or whether the teacher needs to adjust instructional practice in any way or to encourage students to explore further.

Assessing Process Skills

Process skills should also be addressed. Assessing these operations requires students to be placed in contexts that allow them to gather and process data. To help yourself better track your students' achievement of process skills, develop a recording chart similar to the one in Figure 5–3.

In its purest form, a performance measure has a child demonstrate process skills with concrete materials. For instance, the inquiry may ask the child to measure several irregularly shaped rocks to find the one with the greatest volume. Materials for this task include various types of rocks, a wide-mouthed clear plastic cup, a spoon, a marking pen, and a container of water. To demonstrate this process, the child could partly fill the cup and mark the water level with the pen. Next, he will carefully submerge each of the various rocks into the cup with the spoon, taking care each time to mark the water level and not spill any water. If the process is performed properly, the child identifies the rock with the highest water level as having the most volume.

See the Chapter 5 Web Destinations on the Companion Web (*http://www.prenhall.com/peters*) for links related to assessing student performance in science.

Another example of a performance measure is to ask a child to infer the identity of three unknown leaves by consulting a chart with descriptions of leaves. A variation of the task is to ask the child to classify a small collection of leaves. Can the child put them into two or more groups and state the observable property or properties used to group them? Will the groupings be consistent with the stated properties?

Working with concrete materials may not always be possible. Performance-based measures can also use representations of things. For instance, students can classify pictures

Figure 5–3   **Process skill checklist.**

Name	Classify	Observe	Measure	Infer	Communicate	Experiment
ROSE	(A-C-T)	(A-C-T)	(A-C-T)	(A-C-T)	(A-C-T)	(A-C-T)
DAVE	(A-C-T)	(A-C-T)	(A-C-T)	(A-C-T)	(A-C-T)	(A-C-T)
NINA	(A-C-T)	(A-C-T)	(A-C-T)	(A-C-T)	(A-C-T)	(A-C-T)
JOSH	(A-C-T)	(A-C-T)	(A-C-T)	(A-C-T)	(A-C-T)	(A-C-T)

Note: A = Achieved Skill, C = Continuing to Improve, T = Trouble Applying

of leaves or animals. Another idea is to supply a chart that shows data from an investigation and to ask the child to interpret the data and draw a conclusion.

When children are capable writers, some performance measures may be completed entirely with words. For experimenting, this problem might appear as follows:

> Suppose you want to find out whether bean plants will grow faster with fertilizer A or fertilizer B. How could you set up an experiment to find out?

The problem could also address a specific part of the experiment:

> What variables do you need to control in the plant experiment?

In either instance, it is important to place an emphasis on assessing the performance of the students. But if you have a good science program, isn't that enough?

Using Performance-Based Assessment

Some teachers with active, hands-on/minds-on science programs bypass performance measures. They believe that they get all the assessment data they need by observing their students at work and interacting with them during regular activity times and follow-up discussions. This may be possible with a wide array of process-rich activities and systematic observing; but mandated performance explorations are becoming more prevalent at school district, state, and national levels. Avoiding them entirely in the regular science program may cause students to do poorly on such assessments. Reliability of your personal assessments may also be affected if you leave out **performance-based assessment.** This could be due to bias of your observations of certain students because of their personality or prior success. One way to complete this type of assessment and decrease bias is through an instrument such as the example in Figure 5–4.

Note that the particular checklist in Figure 5–4 is for a small-group assignment. You will have to modify the checklist to use on an individual basis or in different learning situations. Also, if you are working with early grades, you will find that teacher observation is the primary means of gathering assessment data. In these situations, it is important that you track progress over longer periods of time and record progress as students develop new skills.

Project-Based Science Assessment

Whether exploring on an individual basis or as a small group, **project-based science** assists students in investigating authentic questions based on scientific phenomena. The principle behind project-based science is that young learners engage in exploring important and meaningful questions through a process of investigation and collaboration (Krajcik, Czerniak, & Berger, 1999). The result of this approach is that students learn fundamental science concepts and principles that they can apply to their daily lives.

It's a good idea to view science projects as normal and regular extensions of concepts and generalizations studied by the whole class. Projects can be individual self-directed activities, similar to a science fair project. They can also be small-group projects during which students collaborate in learning. One way or the other, they make assessment simpler, less formal, and more frequent. Extended investigations can be useful in pursuing knowledge in greater depth or in focusing on a particular area of interest. But what makes a good project?

Characteristics of a Good Project

An ideal project usually requires self-assessment from start to finish. If guidelines are simple and your comments regarding success are consistent, students will develop judgment in assessing their efforts during projects and when reporting them. The components of a good project are found in Figure 5–5.

Performance-based assessment is a form of testing that requires students to perform a task rather than select or provide answers on a test. The teacher then judges the quality of the student's work based on an agreed-upon set of criteria. An example would be asking a student to generate scientific hypotheses.

Project-based science organizes science experiences around an authentic question. The students focus on all of the class activities to answer this driving question.

See the Chapter 5 Web Destinations Companion Website (*http://www. prenhall.com/peters*) for a link to project-based science and the PIViT software from the University of Michigan.

Figure 5–4 **Performance-based assessment checklist (upper elementary).**

Completed by the Student

Student Names
(List the names of the students in your group.)

Problem to Be Solved
(State the problem you are investigating in your own words.)

Method or Strategy
(How will you go about solving the problem?)

Skills
(Identify how you used the following skills while investigating this problem: classifying, observing, measuring, inferring/predicting, communicating, and experimenting)

Results
Written Response
  What did you find from your investigation?
Pictures
  Can you illustrate your findings?

Verification and Communication
Did you compare your answer with other groups? Did you verify it with the teacher?

Teacher Checklist

_____   Students understood the problem.
        (0—no; 1—somewhat; 2—completely)
_____   Students developed a method/strategy to solve the problem.
        (0—no; 1—somewhat; 2—completely)
_____   Students used scientific skills in solving the problem.
        (0—no; 1—somewhat; 2—completely)
_____   Students were able to come to a conclusion.
        (0—no; 1—somewhat; 2—completely)
_____   Students communicated and verified their results.
        (0—no; 1—somewhat; 2—completely)
_____   Total (possible 10)

Remember that good projects also give students many chances to display the scientific attitudes of critical thinking, such as persistence, inventiveness, curiosity, and questioning techniques. Sample questions for you to keep in mind during the assessment process are as follows:

1. Are the parts of the report or presentation logical and consistent?
2. Does the display or model show evidence of learning?
3. Is there evidence that the child overcame difficulties or was successful at problem solving?
4. Was the child resourceful in substituting materials as needed?
5. Does the child or other children ask further questions based on the project?

When you notice behaviors like these and give positive comments, you will reinforce the students' success at projects. Returning to our situation with Mr. Correa, he plans to continue the learning situation with individual projects.

As a springboard for ideas, next week, Mr. Correa's students will independently read a variety of children's literature, including *Bringing the Rain to Kapiti Plain* (Aardema, 1992), *Mendel's Ladder* (Karlins, 1995), *Peter Spier's Rain* (Spier, 1997), *A Rainy Day* (Markle, 1993), and *The Rains Are Coming* (Stanley, 1993). These and other books related to rain will help initiate creative ideas for individual projects. Keep in mind that as the students design the projects, they can also design complementary assessment procedures.

Peer or Individual Assessments

Do you want your students involved in the assessment process? Try experimenting by allowing your students to design an authentic assessment procedure. Of course, student assessments may not be as elaborate as some procedures that you may design, but they have certain advantages. Often, students will become more involved in the learning process if they are included in the evaluation and decision making that occur in the classroom. Additionally, students are creative and can develop some interesting and useful assessments.

There are some considerations to keep in mind with regard to individually created assessment procedures. First, consider that this is a **low stakes assessment.** By this, we mean that it is only one piece of the assessment package for that student. In contrast, a **high stakes assessment** affects a student's future to a much higher degree. A student's final grade should be determined through a combination of procedures, including different forms of teacher-based assessments.

A second consideration in peer- or self-constructed assessment procedures is to be clear with the directions that are given related to the assessment. Make sure that everyone knows what is required. Ask questions to ensure that your students understand the requirements. Provide guidance to be sure that the students are not undertaking a procedure they cannot complete. Finally, encourage the students and assist them in reaching their goals. A follow-up interview may assist in clarifying the assessment procedure and results.

Interviews

Are you having learning or assessment difficulties with your students? Interviews are an effective way to get information directly. They can be especially useful with early elemen-

Low stakes assessment is a tool to assist in finding out what a student knows, in determining future curricula, or in diagnosing a student's skills.

High stakes assessment is used to determine passing or failing, to place a student in a remedial or advanced program, to decide on graduation, or otherwise to compare students, classrooms, schools, districts, states, or even nations.

Figure 5–5   Components of a good project.

- **Title:** Name of the investigation that is being considered.
- **Problem:** A brief description of the problem to be solved. The student or teacher can determine the problem.
- **Materials:** A listing of what is needed for the investigation.
- **Hypothesis:** A statement that explains what will happen during or as a result of the investigation.
- **Experiment:** The steps that will be taken to investigate the hypothesis. Includes specifics on variables and how measurements will be taken.
- **Data:** An organized listing of the data collected in charts and graphs.
- **Results:** A data-specific explanation of what happened as a result of the experiment.
- **Conclusion:** An explanation of what happened in your own words.
- **Research Results:** A summary of the background information collected as part of the investigation.
- **Communication of Investigation:** A report, display, presentation, or other means to share the results of the investigation.

tary students who cannot express their thoughts in writing. Interviews are also helpful for assessing students with special needs. Keep in mind that the specific answers provided by the children are less important than the reasons why they responded as they did. Try to look for trends in thinking patterns and to identify misconceptions.

When using interviews as an assessment tool, keep in mind that you should be accepting of all answers and value each child's thoughts and opinions. Put yourself in the child's perspective and ease the sometimes uncomfortable situation by using the following techniques:

Know and use the child's name.

Select nonconflicting times to interview.

Sit at floor level.

Talk in a cheerful tone.

Inform the child before the interview what you are doing.

Intervene only as necessary to keep the discussion focused on the topic. Ask questions such as the following to promote further discussion:

What can you tell me about . . . ?
What do you think about . . . ?
How do you feel about . . . ?
Can you explain why . . . ?
How would you describe . . . ?
How did you discover . . . ?

Maintain the discussion with questions such as the following:

What else can you say about . . . ?
What if you were to . . . ?
How is this related to . . . ?
Is there another way to explain . . . ?
How could we change . . . ?
What question should I ask the next student about . . . ?

General questions should be prepared ahead of time; nevertheless, ask additional clarifying questions as needed. Also make sure to provide enough time for the interview.

Try to make students feel relaxed with the interview process. Allow them to create illustrations or to use models as needed. Some early elementary students may even want to "speak" through a teddy bear or other object if they are too shy to speak directly to you. Do not mistake a child's being afraid to speak as a sign that he or she is unfamiliar with the concept discussed.

> **Teaching Tips**
> If you are using other students or parent volunteers as interviewers, make sure that you have a checklist of interview questions for them to fill out.

Another use for interviews is to supplement regular testing for culturally and linguistically diverse students. For instance, you can do these things:

Provide additional clues to failed test items.

Change the language of test items in an interview.

Ask probing questions in the student's own dialect.

Focus on how the student is attempting to solve a problem. (Gonzalez, Brusca-Vega, & Yawkey, 1997)

Using interviews to help meet the needs of diverse students will not only allow you to better find their strong and weak areas but also will be a boost to their self-confidence when

A child composes her daily notes as part of her science journal.

they can understand the assessment procedure. Complement interview discussions with journal writing as the students are able to express themselves with written discourse.

Journals

Do you remember keeping a science notebook when you were in school? Journals similar to the one you may have kept can assist students in recording observations, outlining procedures, drafting hypotheses, developing inferences, writing the results of experiments, or reflecting on what they have done. You know that recording data in a notebook or log is usually necessary when observations occur over time. Doing so makes it more likely that the students will keep track of changes, observe more carefully, and think about what they are doing. Teachers may also ask their students to respond in writing to questions in activities for similar reasons. These recordings are best kept in a journal.

Notice how often questions appear in properly constructed activities. This practice is typical of elementary school science. Students can appraise their recordings by comparing them with those of other group members. It's natural for students to pursue reasons, when experimental data conflict. Journals can be a way to develop this dialogue with students who want to learn more about a topic. Remember to be flexible and consider that not every journal should look the same.

Today the concept of writing to learn is applied in all subjects. It holds much value for science. Many teachers have their students keep science journals. A journal offers opportunities to improve science learning and to practice important writing skills at the same time. Writing requires thinking, which changes with different purposes.

Descriptive writing can be used, among other possibilities, to identify things:

> Can you describe an animal (plant, habitat, etc.) so well, without naming it, that your partner can tell what it is? Make a chart that shows the properties of these rocks. Can your partner match the rocks to your descriptions?

Assessing these writings is straightforward. If a problem with a conflicting answer arises, the partners can work together to figure out a solution.

Defining concepts in writing, before and after instruction, enables children to assess for themselves what they have gained from their studies. The questions, "What is soil, and what is it made of?" may yield quite different results before and after lessons.

Creative writing should also be linked to concepts being studied. If your students are writing stories about an imaginary visit to an outer planet, you might ask them to use recently learned words correctly, such as *orbit, acceleration,* and *zero gravity.*

Use cooperative learning groups in judging whether concepts are used correctly in journals or creative writing activities. Your students should consult with you as needed.

You can also ask students at different developmental levels to write summaries of what they have learned in a lesson, give opinions and defend them, write persuasive letters, and compose interview questions. Each form can be assessed for clarity, logic, and completeness. Journals are also a valuable tool with students who are too shy to express answers publicly. Journals provide a secure channel of communication with the teacher.

It is important to have your students assess their own writing as much as possible through clear directions and standards. You should evaluate or sample their writing often, but at the same time allow them to do most of the work. The following methods will help you provide guidance for them to self-evaluate their work:

> How would you describe your level of participation in the activity?
> What contributions did you make to the solution of the problem?
> What best describes your role in the group (leader, recorder, materials manager, maintenance crew, liaison, or bystander)?
> How effectively do you manage time while completing tasks?
> What are you learning in science?

One way we use journals in our own work is to include them as part of a folder or three-ring notebook that is a student's **portfolio.**

Portfolios

Would you like to cultivate more self-assessment abilities like those described in the Focus on Inquiry: Portfolios at the beginning of the chapter? Would you like to motivate your students to increase their effort in learning? Can you show parents tangible and understandable evidence of what their children are learning? If you would like to improve your assessment procedures, consider a portfolio for each child. A portfolio is a "container of evidence of someone's knowledge, skills, and dispositions" (Collins, 1991, p. 293).

The collection can be a student or personal portfolio where children show accomplishments and learning over a long period of time. An example is a graduation portfolio or a yearlong, grade-level portfolio. Another type is the project portfolio where a student demonstrates the sequence of steps that go into a project or independent study. Other examples are graded portfolios, integrated portfolios, cooperative group portfolios, multiyear portfolios, multiple intelligences portfolios, portfolios of intelligent behavior, class profile portfolios, school profile portfolios, time capsule portfolios, and district portfolios (Williams, 2000).

Portfolio is a sampling of work over time that gives observable evidence of knowledge, processes, and attitudes gained by a student over one or more subject-matter units.

Visit an Inquiry Classroom
Authentic Assessment

View the *Authentic Assessment* video in the "Constructivist Pedagogy" section of the Companion CD. Students share their findings from the earthworm activities.

Review the video and ask yourself the following:
· Based on what you have learned thus far, is this representative of authentic assessment? Explain your answer.
· Could Mr. McKnight use the computer in other ways to assess students?

In *Classroom Assessment and the National Science Education Standards* (NRC, 2001), the authors state, "Journals kept by the students become the stimulus for regular reflections on learning and the connections between their topic to the bigger picture." Explain what they mean in this statement. Record your ideas and the answers to these questions in your portfolio or use the Companion Website to share your ideas.

Mr. Correa, from our streambed example earlier in this chapter, uses project portfolios as part of the evaluation of his students. In his view, project portfolios are good assessment tools during the 4-week study of the water cycle.

What should go into a portfolio? Both the child and you should select items, or **artifacts,** for the portfolio. When the child selects artifacts to demonstrate learning, he can also jot down why he selected the item. This will make the learning and assessment more relevant. You will also find that to have diverse student portfolios, you must have diverse learning opportunities in the classroom. Otherwise, the portfolio becomes a collection of the standard science tests and vocabulary sheets. Collins (1991) warns:

> There is no guarantee that portfolios always will be a mode of authentic assessment; they can become folders in which teachers plunk the same tired stuff they have been doing because they have been instructed by the administration to use portfolios for assessment. (p. 299)

Mr. Correa avoids the misuse of portfolios discussed in this quote by having students select artifacts to include in the portfolios. Following are examples of artifacts that Mr. Correa's students will include:

- Tests—end of lesson, unit, performance
- Activity log pages
- Project or book reports
- Concept maps, vee maps, other graphic organizers
- Charts
- Graphs
- Science journal pages
- Creative stories
- Science words learned
- Artwork
- Out-of-class assignments
- Computer resources or data
- Videotaped resources or data
- Cartoons and analysis or explanation

Artifacts are typical products or results of a student's learning, such as a student story, lab report, or picture of a scientific phenomenon.

Figure 5–6   Portfolio artifact form.

Name: _____
Date: _____

Portfolio Artifact: (name of item)

I am including this item because . . .

_____

_____

_____

_____

This is how the item shows what I learned . . .

_____

_____

_____

_____

The next time I do this activity, I will change . . .

_____

_____

_____

_____

In addition to items that the students will include in their portfolios, Mr. Correa will have his students include an artifact form, as shown in Figure 5–6, for some of the items. The form will assist the students in determining what items to place in their portfolios.

What are some other points to keep in mind? Everything should be dated so that items in a category can be put in order by time and progress observed. Guide the children to look for improvements in their work and to discuss with their groups the examples they have selected. Encourage them to pair an original effort with an improved version when possible; this can make them more conscious of their progress and help develop a sense of pride in their work.

How should the artifacts be arranged? Materials may be stored in a standard expandable folder or a larger folder cut from poster board. Storage considerations may prompt you to consider electronic portfolios. The advantage of electronic portfolios is that they can be easily stored on disk, reducing the amount of paper in the classroom. The disadvantage is that students' keyboarding skills may be inadequate or computer access may be limited in the elementary classroom.

Should the science portfolio be separate? Or is it better to reserve a section for science in a more comprehensive portfolio? Primary-level teachers lean more toward comprehensive portfolios. Upper elementary and middle school teachers generally arrange portfolios by content area. Either type gets overstuffed and difficult to store or manage

Teaching Tips

To help your students set goals for themselves, periodically have them review and think carefully about the work samples they include in their portfolios. This can be done monthly or at the end of a unit.

Figure 5–7   **Parent or guardian portfolio assessment rubric.**

Parent or Guardian Name: _____

Date: _____

Portfolio Assessment Questions

The item I think is my child's best work is . . .

_____

_____

The item I think my child could improve on is . . .

_____

_____

Overall, I see evidence of my child learning because . . .

_____

_____

_____

I would like to see my child . . .

_____

_____

unless some material is sent home periodically or discarded. Some teachers ask their students to write thoughtful responses to these two questions:

What do I feel good about?
What do I want to improve?

Responses to the second question can make it easy to set goals with children. At the next periodic review, they can examine their portfolios for evidence that shows whether the goals were met. Also have parents assist in evaluating portfolios. This assistance helps develop better teacher–parent, teacher–child, and parent–child communications. A form such as the one in Figure 5–7 can be used for parent portfolio assessments.

Teacher scoring of the portfolio is also a consideration. Figure 5–8 shows a typical scoring method for elementary science portfolios.

See Chapter 5 Web Destinations at the *http://www. prenhall.com/peters* Companion Website for links related to the public domain concept map software from the Institute for Human and Machine Cognition at the University of West Florida.

CW

Concept Maps

One message from researchers in human learning is especially clear: Organization and meaning go together. The better we are able to relate new information to what we already know, the easier we are able to remember and use it. Science programs now commonly employ several different graphic organizers to help children construct meaningful relationships among the facts and concepts they learn. The **concept map** is probably the most used organizer, and an excellent means to assess conceptual knowledge.

Figure 5–9 shows a concept map that was developed by a student independently studying chameleons. It was generated with a computerized concept map program. As you can see from the map, it contains **nodes** representing the individual concepts and **links** connecting the concepts in a meaningful way. This type of assessment provides a richer view of the student's knowledge than typical objective tests.

Concept maps are hierarchical graphic organizers of a person's concepts.

Nodes are the specific locations where the concepts contained on the map are located.

Links or cross-links are the relationships between concepts in different nodes of the concept map.

Figure 5–8 **Portfolio assessment scoring rubric.**

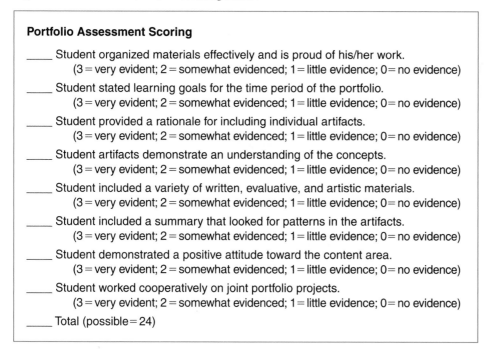

Portfolio Assessment Scoring

_____ Student organized materials effectively and is proud of his/her work.
(3 = very evident; 2 = somewhat evidenced; 1 = little evidence; 0 = no evidence)

_____ Student stated learning goals for the time period of the portfolio.
(3 = very evident; 2 = somewhat evidenced; 1 = little evidence; 0 = no evidence)

_____ Student provided a rationale for including individual artifacts.
(3 = very evident; 2 = somewhat evidenced; 1 = little evidence; 0 = no evidence)

_____ Student artifacts demonstrate an understanding of the concepts.
(3 = very evident; 2 = somewhat evidenced; 1 = little evidence; 0 = no evidence)

_____ Student included a variety of written, evaluative, and artistic materials.
(3 = very evident; 2 = somewhat evidenced; 1 = little evidence; 0 = no evidence)

_____ Student included a summary that looked for patterns in the artifacts.
(3 = very evident; 2 = somewhat evidenced; 1 = little evidence; 0 = no evidence)

_____ Student demonstrated a positive attitude toward the content area.
(3 = very evident; 2 = somewhat evidenced; 1 = little evidence; 0 = no evidence)

_____ Student worked cooperatively on joint portfolio projects.
(3 = very evident; 2 = somewhat evidenced; 1 = little evidence; 0 = no evidence)

_____ Total (possible = 24)

A concept map, according to Novak and Gowin (1984), is a "schematic device for representing a set of concept meanings embedded in a framework of propositions" (p. 15). The **propositions** are used to link the concepts, and the map in its entirety is like a snapshot of the person's conceptual understandings. Concept maps can be used before, during, or after a learning activity to assess development of understandings. They encourage reflective thinking and foster development of scientific concepts (Mason, 1992).

Concept maps are also an effective small-group project. When done by groups, communication and negotiation among members help in identifying student misunderstanding. Working together, they can resolve their misconceptions.

How can you get your students started with concept mapping? So that students can see how concepts maps are formed, it may be good to start with showing students maps related to the context you are teaching. Next, provide the students maps in which some of the words are already filled in. Have the students complete these maps by filling in other words of their choice. Later, provide just the words for them to use in developing their own concept map. For example, Mr. Correa could have provided the following words:

water cycle

clouds

streams

oceans

mountains

plants

animals

groundwater

> **Propositions** are the connecting words, such as _has, can be,_ or _is part of._

Figure 5–9   Concept map.

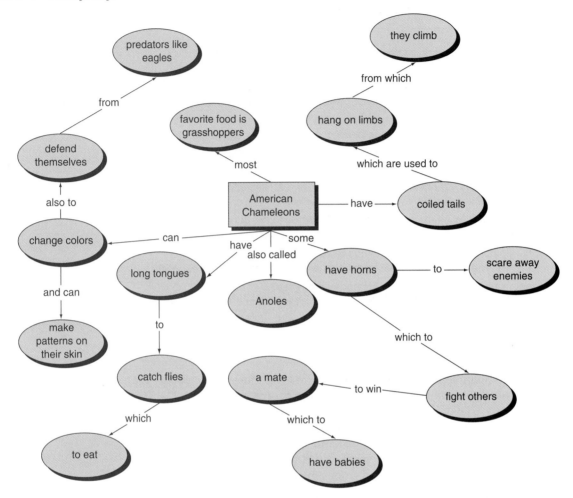

Beginning students could map just these words. Advanced students could add more words as appropriate to complete the concept map. In time, students will be proficient at reflecting their knowledge with concept maps with little assistance from the teacher.

Note that students often make different concept maps after receiving the same instruction. This happens even when they understand all the concepts in the way that you intend. They may simply view relationships among the concepts differently. It is important for them to compare their maps on a regular basis with partners and to interact with you to more fully assess what they have learned.

Vee Maps

Vee maps are similar to concept maps but have two sides: a conceptual side (the "knowing" side that may contain a concept map) and a methodological side (containing results and actions).

Vee maps, similar to concept maps, are useful in developing and conducting investigations. They are a less-structured approach to activities, likened to a "road map showing the route from prior knowledge to new and future knowledge" (Roth & Verechaka, 1993, p. 25).

Vee maps are arranged with the "knowing" words and phrases about a topic on the left and the "doing" or skills and activities on the right. In the center is a large V that represents the interplay and interdependence between the knowing and doing. The following quote summarizes the use of vee maps:

The left and right sides of the Vee emphasize two interdependent aspects of science learning: knowing and doing, respectively. What students know at any one moment—their existing conceptions, the investigative tools available to them, and their ideas—will determine the quality and quantity of the questions they ask. Conversely, the answers students obtain to their questions will affect what they know, by changing, adding to, refining, or reconfiguring their knowledge. The Vee should lead students to discover the relationship between doing and knowing science. (Roth & Bowen, 1993, pp. 28–32)

Teacher Observations

The job of teaching is inexact at best. We view it as a series of consecutively developed hypotheses. That is, each thing we do or say is a kind of hypothesis that we are uncertain will be accepted (learned) by the children. If much teaching takes place before receiving specific feedback, learning has occurred, and then we can make many unwarranted assumptions about what has been learned by the children.

We can observe, and often help students stay on track, in whole-class settings, but the most productive times are likely to be in individual and small-group situations. There are many chances for informal teacher–child contacts during the activity times in lessons. Notice what your students say and do when they interact with you, a partner, or other members of a small group. What you observe gives you data for fast self-correction or for assisting individual students, if needed.

The quickest way to find out whether students understand the concepts and processes being taught is to ask questions and listen carefully to their responses. Forming follow-up questions to responses may help in detecting misconceptions so that you can quickly address these errors in thinking.

Open-Ended Questions

An open-ended question has more than one correct response or pathway to a response (Carter & Berenson, 1996). The response may be an answer to a question, a procedure to arrive at a solution to a problem, or an opinion about something. The value of this type of question is that each student can answer it differently.

> **Teaching Tips** | Open-ended questions are useful in identifying misconceptions or in promoting divergent thinking.

Assessment of open-ended questions often lies in the completeness of the response. A clear, complete response that includes accurate information and/or the student's opinions is desirable. A rubric for scoring this type of question could simply be a six-point scale based on information provided by the student, as shown in Figure 5–10.

Following are guidelines for writing open-ended questions:

- Make sure that the question is understandable to students.
- Do not lead students to an answer; let them construct one on their own.
- Make the questions interesting when possible.
- Match each question with the content or process being studied.
- Allow sufficient wait time for students to respond.
- Allow multiple students time to answer and ask further questions before going on to another question.
- Attempt to get at deeper levels of understanding through increasingly complex questions.
- Maintain students' interest through meaningful, thought-provoking questions.

Figure 5–10   **Open-ended question scoring rubric.**

Use the following list of five areas to assess a student's response to an open-ended question.

- Understands the question
- Provides a complete response
- Provides accurate information
- Justifies the response as needed
- Provides additional information as requested

Award one point for each objective demonstrated by the student. The scoring ranges from one to five points for each response, as follows:

Scoring rubric:

5—all five areas complete
4—one of the above five is missing
3—two of the above five are missing
2—three of the above five are missing
1—four of the above five are missing
0—five of the five are missing or no response

Weather Concepts

Name	Sunshine	Wind	Rain	Snow	Hail	Hurricane	Tornado
Bonnie Total:____	____	____	____	____	____	____	____
Doug Total:____	____	____	____	____	____	____	____
Shirley Total:____	____	____	____	____	____	____	____
Jonathan Total:____	____	____	____	____	____	____	____

ASSESSING ATTITUDES

Recall that scientific attitudes of children are often shown by their behaviors in four broad categories: curiosity, inventiveness, critical thinking, and persistence. The sample behaviors listed under these categories are the kinds of actions you look for when you appraise growth in attitudes. Good times to assess attitudes are during hands-on activities and discussions. Remember, though, that broad attitudes cannot be developed quickly. Positive attitudes are a long-range by-product of the quality of learning activities and general atmosphere of your classroom.

Take time to sample attitudes periodically and, if necessary, develop an informal attitude inventory. It should include items like the following:

Are you curious about nature or scientific phenomena?
Do you enjoy science as much as other subjects?
Do you complete science activities outside class time?
Do you watch science-related shows at home on videotapes or television?
Have you read any science-related books lately?
Do you know a scientist in your neighborhood or community?

Visit an Inquiry Classroom
Modeling Positive Attitudes

View the *Cognitive Apprenticeship* video in the "Constructivist Pedagogy" section of the Companion CD. Mr. McKnight interacts with students as they form and test hypotheses related to earthworms and their behavior.

Review the video and ask yourself the following:
- How is Mr. McKnight modeling positive attitudes toward science?
- Which of the four broad categories, *curiosity, inventiveness, critical thinking,* and *persistence,* are modeled in the video? Explain your answer.

In *Changing and Measuring Attitudes in the Science Classroom*, Kobella (1989) asserts, "Teachers realize the importance of how students feel about science subjects and courses; nevertheless, they place little emphasis on affective objectives. The affective domain is often neglected because teachers have difficulty designing strategies to develop positive attitudes among students and documenting their development." How would you react to this statement? What strategies could you personally use to create better attitudes toward science when you become the classroom science teacher? Record your ideas and the answers to these questions in your portfolio or use the Companion Website to share your ideas.

Do you like to answer questions during science class?
Have you considered a career in a science field?

When students cannot read, try using smiling, neutral, and frowning faces on a scoring sheet. The students can respond to items as you read them. What about attitudes toward scientists?

Attitudes and Stereotypes Related to Scientists

A good way to assess attitudes toward scientists is with the Draw-a-Scientist Test (Mason, Kahle, & Gardner, 1991). In this test, children are provided a blank sheet of paper and asked to "draw a scientist." The test is scored by counting the number of stereotypical indicators, such as lab coats, pencils and pens in a shirt pocket, male gender, facial hair, and glasses. A high score on this test indicates that the student has a stereotypical or negative image of a scientist. Try this out with your students to see what their image of a scientist is like.

See the Chapter 5 Web Destinations at the Companion Website (*http:www. prenhall.com/peters*) for links related to the Draw-a-Scientist Test.

Summary

- Assessment is no longer something we do *to* students, but something we can do *with* students. Assessment should be reflective, not reflexive. With changing assessment procedures, we are no longer looking at what students do not know. Instead, we want to know what opportunities they have had to learn and what they do know or have achieved.
- Internal purpose assessments are administered to convey expectations about what is important to learn, to provide information on progress, to help

students judge their learning, to guide and improve instruction, and to classify and select students. External purpose assessments include examinations that are given to provide information for accountability, to guide policy decisions, to gather information for program evaluation, to sort and classify people for admissions, and to certify or hire.
- Essay and open-ended questions are useful in evaluating whether students are able to express

personal ideas clearly and can be designed to assess higher order thinking, the ability to solve problems, or the capability to reason about the interrelationships between concepts.

- A performance-based assessment not only will generate an answer by the student but also will indicate the process by which the student arrived at that answer.
- Project-based assessments assist students in investigating authentic questions based on scientific phenomena and allow young learners to engage in exploring important and meaningful questions through a process of investigation and collaboration.
- Peer or individual assessments allow students to creatively become involved in the assessment and learning process.

- Interviews and teacher observations are an effective way to get information directly, to identify misconceptions, and to provide the reasons for student responses.
- Journals can assist students in recording observations, outlining procedures, drafting hypotheses, developing inferences, writing the results of experiments, reflecting on what they have done, and developing a dialogue between students and teachers.
- A portfolio is a sampling of work over time that gives observable evidence of knowledge, processes, and attitudes gained by the students over one or more science units.
- Concept maps and vee maps assess conceptual knowledge through graphic representations.

Reflection

Companion CD

1. Look at the "Earthworm's Cousin—Nightcrawler" lesson linked to the *Teamwork* video on the Companion CD. How could you rewrite this lesson plan to make better use of performance-based assessment?
2. Look at the "Earthworm's Cousin—The Bearded Worm" lesson linked to the *Pacing and Time Allocation* video on the Companion CD. How could

you rewrite this lesson to focus on scientific skill development and assessment? Include a rubric for assessing the skills.

3. Look at the "Earthworm's Cousin—Planaria" lesson linked to the *Feedback* video on the Companion CD. Suppose that you were to use concept mapping as an assessment tool with this lesson. What would a sample student concept map look like for this lesson?

Portfolio Ideas

1. Next time you are at your practicum site, interview a teacher and ask what tools he uses for assessing students. Ask why he selected the particular methods for assessment and whether he thinks the procedures are effective in identifying misconceptions or skill development. Compare his views with your own and record in your portfolio.
2. Place yourself in the role of the instructor for this course. If you were to assess college students on knowledge of assessment, what form(s) of assessment would you use? Indicate sample test items or authentic procedures. Compare with those of other students in the class and record your findings in your portfolio.

3. The rapid expansion in the use of computers and the Internet has brought with it the idea of electronic portfolios. Find out what technological resources are available to assist you in developing student portfolios. Share your findings in your portfolio.
4. Using a World Wide Web search protocol, find one or two sites that include assessment information. You may want to refer to the book *Science on the Internet: A Resource for K–12 Teachers* (2nd ed) (Ebenezer & Lau, 2002). How are the sites designed? How could you adapt what you found to your classroom? Check *http://www.prenhall.com/peters* for additional links. Record findings in your portfolio.

References

Aardema, V. (1992). *Bringing the rain to Kapiti Plain*. New York: Dial Press.

American Association for the Advancement of Science (AAAS). (1993). *Benchmarks for science literacy*. New York: Oxford University Press.

American Association for the Advancement of Science (AAAS). (1998). *Blueprints for reform*. New York: Oxford University Press.

American Forest Foundation. (1996). *Project learning tree* (4th ed.). Washington, DC: Author.

Carter, G., & Berenson, S. B. (1996). Authentic assessment: Vehicle for reform. In J. Rhoton & P. Bowers (Eds.), *Issues in science education* (pp. 96–106). Arlington, VA: National Science Teachers Association and the National Science Education Leadership Association.

Collins, A. (1991). Portfolios for assessing student learning. In G. Kulm & S. M. Malcom (Eds.), *Science assessment in the service of reform* (pp. 291–300). Washington, DC: American Association for the Advancement of Science.

Ebenezer, J. V., & Lau, E. (2002). *Science on the Internet: A resource for K–12 teachers (2nd ed)*. Upper Saddle River, NJ: Merrill/Prentice Hall.

Gonzalez, V., Brusca-Vega, R., & Yawkey, T. (1997). *Assessment and instruction of culturally and linguistically diverse students with or at-risk of learning problems: From research to practice*. Boston: Allyn & Bacon.

Karlins, M. (1995). *Mendel's ladder*. New York: Simon & Schuster.

Kobella, T. R. (1989). *Research matters—to the science teacher: Changing and measuring attitudes in the science classroom*. Columbia, MO: National Association for Research in Science Teaching. Retrieved December 23, 2004, from *www.educ.sfu.ca/narstsite/publications/research/attitude.htm*

Krajcik, J., Czerniak, C., & Berger, C. (1999). *Teaching children science: A project-based approach*. New York: McGraw-Hill.

Lawrence Hall of Science. (1989). *River cutters* (Rev. ed.). Berkeley: University of California.

Locker, T. (1997). *Water dance*. Orlando, FL: Harcourt Brace.

Markle, S. (1993). *A rainy day*. New York: Orchard Books.

Mason, C. L. (1992). Concept mapping: A tool to develop reflective science instruction. *Science Education, 76*(1), 51–63.

Mason, C. L., Kahle, J. B., & Gardner, A. L. (1991). Draw-a-scientist test: Future implications. *School Science and Mathematics, 91*(5), 193–198.

McMillan, J. H. (1997). *Classroom assessment: Principles and practice for effective instruction*. Boston: Allyn & Bacon.

National Assessment of Educational Progress. (2003). *The nation's report card: Science 2000*. Washington, DC: National Center for Education Statistics. Retrieved December 23, 2004, from *http://nces.ed.gov/pubsearch/pubsinfo.asp?pubid=2003453*

National Board for Professional Teaching Standards. (1997). *What teachers should know and be able to do*. Washington, DC: Author.

National Research Council (NRC). (1996). *National science education standards*. Washington, DC: National Academy Press.

National Research Council (NRC). (2001). *Classroom assessment and the national science education standards*. Washington, DC: National Academy Press. Retrieved December 23, 2004, from *http://books.nap.edu/catalog/9847.html*

National Science Resources Center, National Academy of Sciences, Smithsonian Institution. (1997). *Science for all children: A guide to improving elementary science education in your school district*. Washington, DC: National Academy Press.

National Science Teachers Association (NSTA). (2001). *Assessment. A position statement*. Washington, DC: Author. Retrieved October 1, 2004, from *www.nsta.org/positionstatement&psid=40*

Novak, J. D., & Gowin, D. B. (1984). *Learning how to learn*. New York: Cambridge University Press.

Ochs, V. D. (1996). Assessing habits of mind through performance-based assessment in science. In J. Rhoton & P. Bowers (Eds.), *Issues in science education* (pp. 114–122). Arlington, VA: National Science Teachers Association and the National Science Education Leadership Association.

Resnick, L. B., & Resnick, D. P. (1989). Tests as standards of achievement in schools. In *Proceedings of the 1989 ETS Invitational Conference* (pp. 63–80). Princeton, NJ: Educational Testing Service.

Roth, W. M., & Bowen, M. (1993). The unfolding vee. *Science Scope, 16*(5), 28–32.

Roth, W. M., & Verechaka, G. (1993). Plotting a course with vee maps. *Science and Children, 30*(4), 24–27.

Rubba, P., Miller, E., Schmalz, R., Rosenfeld, L., & Shyamal, K. (1991). Science education in the United States: Editors' reflection. In S. Majumdar, L. Rosenfeld, P. Rubba, E. Miller, & R. Schmalz (Eds.), *Science education in the United States: Issues, crisis, and priorities* (pp. 532–537). Easton, PA: Pennsylvania Academy of Science.

Spier, P. (1997). *Peter Spier's rain*. Garden City, NY: Doubleday.

Stanley, S. (1993). *The rains are coming*. New York: Greenwillow Books.

Wick, W. (1997). *A drop of water: A book of science and wonder*. New York: Scholastic Press.

Williams, J. (2000). Implementing portfolios and student-led conferences. *enc focus, 7*(2), 21–23.

Suggested Readings

Agler, L. (1986). *Liquid explorations*. Berkeley: University of California, Lawrence Hall of Science. (a Great Explorations in Math and Science [GEMS] guide to additional water activities and assessments)

Anderson, R. D., & Pratt, H. (1995). *Local leadership for science education reform*. Dubuque, IA: Kendall/Hunt. (how changing teaching and assessment practices will assist in the reform process)

Brandt, R. S. (Ed.). (1992). Using performance assessment. *Educational Leadership, 49*(8). (special issue on performance assessment)

Brandt, R. S. (Ed.). (1994). Reporting what students are learning. *Educational Leadership, 52*(2). (special issue on assessment practices)

Hein, G., & Price, S. (1994). *Active assessment for active science: A guide for elementary school teachers*. Portsmouth, NH: Heinemann. (a practical guide on the rationale for active assessment; useful in enabling classroom teachers to develop, interpret, and score their own assessments)

Herman, J. L., Aschbacher, P. R., & Winters, L. (1992). *A practical guide to alternative assessment*. Alexandria, VA: Association for Supervision and Curriculum Development. (creation and use of alternative assessment procedures)

Linn, R. L., & Gronlund, N. E. (2000). *Measurement and assessment in teaching* (8th ed.). Upper Saddle River, NJ: Merrill/Prentice Hall. (a comprehensive text on assessment of learning)

McShane, J. B. (Ed.). (1994). Assessment issue. *Science and Children, 32*(2), 13–51. (a collection of relevant articles on assessment)

Raizen, S. A., Baron, J. B., Champagne, A. B., Mullis, I. V. S., & Oakes, J. (1989). *Assessment in elementary school science education*. Washington, DC: National Center for Improving Science Education. (a synthesis of reports and recommendations on assessment)

CHAPTER 6

SCIENCE EXPERIENCES FOR ALL STUDENTS

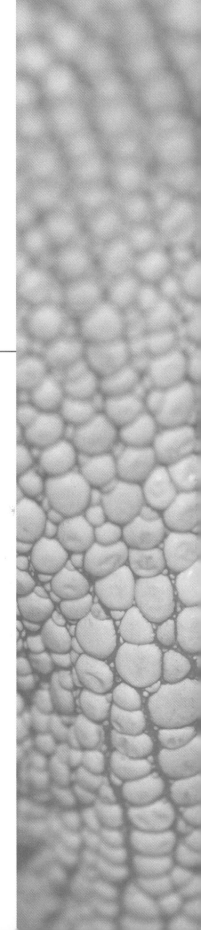

- What is meant by "science for all students"?
- What is a science learning center and how can it support your science program?
- How could a science project promote a student's construction of knowledge?
- How could you incorporate science fairs into your curriculum?
- What are some strategies for working with students who are disabled, have limited English proficiency, or are gifted?

Focus on Inquiry

Women in Science

Katherine (Kata) McCarville,
South Dakota School of Mines and Technology

My daughter is now 9 years old. She and her friends are about the same age I was when I first read about Marie Curie. Marie Curie, winner of two Nobel Prizes, is one of my personal role models. I would encourage you and your students to discover her inspiring story and those of the many other phenomenal women of science. Look in libraries and on the Web for scientists like geophysicist Inge Lehmann, astronomer Maria Mitchell, physicist Lise Meitner, computer scientist Grace Murray Hopper, and biologist Barbara McClintock.

Knowing several 9-year-olds, however, I suspect that to many elementary school students today—and perhaps even to you—these women may seem quaint and distant, even irrelevant. But on "Crazy Career Day" at her school last year, my daughter chose to dress as her mom. So instead, let me tell you about a contemporary working geoscientist.

I began my professional career in 1978 as a uranium miner in Wyoming and then became a computer programmer and analyst for an engineering firm. In 1986, I moved to a position in academic computing services at the Colorado School of Mines, a college of engineering. Next, I worked as Director of Information Technology Services at the South Dakota School of Mines and Technology, in charge of all the university's computing and networking facilities.

I am now the Associate Director of a research institute focused in the atmospheric and earth sciences. We study weather, severe storms, hydrology, greenhouse gases, and cycling of elements like carbon, using observations made from towers, balloons, and aircraft. As a research scientist, I am beginning my own research career in paleoclimatology to improve our understanding of natural climate changes. I also teach in the academic program, mentor and advise students, write grant proposals to support research projects, and manage the institute's funds of about $2 million per year.

While working in highly technical jobs and moving into management, I became active in science education through volunteer activities. I developed a personal interest in paleontology over many years through continuing education opportunities. Starting with a bachelor's degree in geology and later earning a master's degree in geology and a doctoral degree in paleontology, I am engaged in applying computing techniques, imaging technologies, and scientific visualization to the study of fossils, paleoclimatology of continental interiors, and avian paleontology.

My career path may seem odd or unusual to many people, but my story illustrates many features of today's job markets and career opportunities. The pace of change in today's workplace is accelerating. New jobs are being created that have never existed before. An increasing number of jobs, even those that have been traditionally less rigorous, now require mathematical background, experience with computer technology, and the ability to apply logical reasoning or scientific methods to investigate situations and solve problems. Nearly all positions require communications skills—speaking, reading, and writing. Added to these factors is the growing participation of women and ethnic minorities in the workforce.

What does all that have to do with geosciences and careers for women? And how can you, as a teacher, possibly be expected to prepare every one of your students for future jobs and careers that do not even exist today?

First and most important, your students need to see that you are endlessly curious about the world, always learning something new, and willing to take risks in exploring the unknown. Each student must find and develop one or more areas of interest that provide personal motivation. The earth sciences integrate all the basic sciences and mathematics, with the earth, ocean, and sky as a free laboratory available to everyone for observation, description, and explanation.

My own story illustrates how the geosciences can serve as the foundation for a varied, engaging, and successful career. Geology is my "first love"; the ongoing scientific investigation of the geologic past holds a fascination for me like nothing else. During college, that fascination gave me a reason to persevere through difficult courses in mathematics, physics, and chemistry. In the interdisciplinary breadth of geoscience, I could find a real-world example of nearly every equation and principle that was presented in the traditional disciplines. This provided a context within which I could integrate many details into a coherent body of knowledge. Geoscience gives me a unifying theme that lends stability to personal and professional relationships, while leaving ample room for career flexibility and providing a framework for lifelong learning.

Each of your students needs to meet and learn about people who are passionate about their work. It is especially meaningful if these people resemble the student in some way, so it is important to expose all students to scientists, mathematicians, and engineers, including people representing a wide diversity of backgrounds.

Invite parents and others from the community to participate in classroom or school activities. Try to arrange visits to workplaces in your area. Many professional organizations (see information elsewhere in this chapter, and use libraries and the Web to locate resources) sponsor teaching materials and teacher-education programs. Some groups provide guest speakers, science-fair judges, or sponsor mentoring programs to engage interested students with practicing professionals. Many of these programs now match partners via e-mail; the wide availability of e-mail makes this method extremely cost-effective.

Encourage all students who show an interest in science, regardless of gender. These will be the scientists of the future. The results of scientific inquiries are increasingly used in making decisions that directly affect our lives. It is important that people from a wide variety of backgrounds be involved in determining which factors are important and which are not, choosing the questions to be asked, and guiding the direction of investigations.

Geoscience encompasses everything from the purely theoretical contemplation of the origin of the cosmos to the practical application of selecting a safe site for a garbage landfill. Bring geoscience into your classroom as a cornerstone on which to build a comprehensive view of the direct relevance of mathematics and the basic sciences—with the added zing of current topics such as climate change, meteorite impacts, and dinosaurs. From the use of clay minerals in cosmetics to the exploration of the solar system, there is something for everyone in geoscience!

SCIENCE FOR ALL STUDENTS

Have you thought about promoting scientific careers for the girls you will teach as suggested in the Focus on Inquiry: Women in Science?

What are some other ways that you could motivate your students to become interested in science?

You may remember that the science standards and benchmarks have as a primary goal *science for all students*. But, should we limit scientific inquiry to activities that the entire class completes as scheduled? Do you see a need to provide a wider range of science experiences to meet the needs of all students? In this chapter, we present four ways to assist you in providing science experiences for all students: science learning centers, science projects, science fairs, and strategies for teaching students with special needs. To begin, let's visit Mrs. Snyder's classroom.

Mandy's Science Fair

Mandy is excited today. Her group will present their science fair project at the school science fair. Mandy's group developed a project in which they compared three types of grasses with respect to ability to reduce soil erosion. They planted a type of turf grass, ryegrass, and crabgrass to see which held sandy soil the best when they ran water on the grass-covered sand hills. Mandy's group developed the idea after participating in activities from the "Agent Erosion" lesson found in the AIMS book *Primarily Earth* (Hoover & Mercier, 1996).

> **Teaching Tips** For additional erosion activities, see the GEMS book *River Cutters* (Lawrence Hall of Science, 1989).

Mandy's teacher, Mrs. Snyder, also arranged for Mrs. Penton to visit her students' science fair projects. Mrs. Penton will talk to the class about a career as a sedimentologist and the importance of this type of work to protect the many farms in their area. They will also participate in the AIMS activity "What on Earth Can We Do?" from the book *Down to Earth* (Erickson, Gregg, Helling, King, & Starkweather, 1987). This activity will cause the students to think about the impact of humans' activities on the soil.

Think about the classroom in which you plan to teach. How will you promote science for all? If you are one to consider science class as "just the facts," then ask yourself the following question: Will you teach as you were taught in elementary and middle school? As you contemplate this question, consider how science education was viewed in the past.

The Chapter 6 Web Destinations on the Companion Website (*http://www.prenhall. com/peters*) lists addresses for the Association for Women Geoscientists, Women in Mining, Association for Women in Science, and other related links.

Historical Perspective

The authors of the A Program for Teaching Science: *Thirty-First Yearbook* of the National Society for the Study of Education (NSSE, 1932) recommended a continuous, integrated program for elementary science. Subsequently, the Science Education in American Schools: *Forty-Sixth Yearbook* authors advocated a similar program (NSSE, 1947). The Rethinking Science Education: *Fifty-Ninth Yearbook*, printed shortly after the launching of the Soviet *Sputnik* satellite (NSSE, 1960), was in response to the contest of the space race. This information again prompted educational professionals to look at the inadequate elementary science program. More recently, reports of research surrounding the National Research Council (NRC) *National Science Education Standards* (1996) and the American Association for the Advancement of Science (AAAS) *Benchmarks for Science Literacy* (1993) reflected the common theme of these past reports.

The general recommendation of all the above mentioned reports is a student-centered, activity-based instruction in science at every grade level and for all students. Fortunately, we find that there are teachers who see a need to complement the basic science program. They augment the standard curriculum with supplementary and individualized activities. They find that all children learn differently and adjust their teaching accordingly. One way they accommodate different learning styles is through the use of learning centers.

SCIENCE LEARNING CENTERS

A classroom learning center is a place where one or several students at a time can do activities independently, working through the materials and directions found there. A learning center is arranged so that children may choose the activities they can do or are interested in and work at a pace that is right for each child. Some teachers also permit children to select the times they go to a center and partners to work with in a cooperative manner.

An example of a science learning center on weather for an elementary class is shown in Figure 6–1. The center allows children to explore an area of high interest independently and to develop a background that they may use in a variety of ways. About four children can use this center satisfactorily at one time. Notice the activity sheets on the bulletin board. Children use these to write down data or make drawings. Completed sheets are placed in a basket on the teacher's desk for later examination.

Refer to the Chapter 6 Web Destinations on the Companion Website (*http://www.prenhall. com/peters*) for links related to the weather learning center.

Figure 6–1   **A science learning center.**

Observe other features of this center. Children's literature is available for reading either individually or in a peer-tutoring situation. A weather radio is available for listening to the weather service and noting data such as temperatures and rainfall. Individual students can listen to a tape of pertinent weather information. Notice the materials for the students' interaction at the center: alcohol-filled thermometers for measuring temperatures, a wind gauge, and a tornado simulation bottle. A "weather book" contains blank pages on which students can draw and color the weather each day.

To construct this center, the teacher considered the following matters:

- Purpose and objectives
- Activity cards and worksheets
- Materials and their resupply
- Recordkeeping and evaluation
- The physical setup

Will you use learning centers? How will you begin your own learning center?

Refer to the Chapter 6 Web Destinations on the Companion Website (*http://www.prenhall. com/peters*) for links related to the use of children's literature in science.

Deciding the Purpose of a Learning Center

The first task in making a science learning center is to decide its purpose. Do you want it for general enrichment? Although this is the most common purpose, centers may also be used to complement an instructional unit or to present an entire unit when you only have a few materials.

> **Teaching Tips**
> If materials are in short supply, then try sharing a learning center with other teachers.

One example of a learning center activity originated when Mandy's teacher, Mrs. Snyder, wanted to have students play the "Inside the Earth" game from the book *Thematic Unit: Geology* (Gosnell, 1994). Because Mrs. Snyder only made a few games, she used a center to facilitate this learning activity.

As a rule, avoid activities whose outcomes take more time to happen than the time you assign students to be at the center. Children generally want things to happen now, although activities, like the following are exceptions.

As an extension to the erosion activities, Mrs. Snyder started a "Things that Change" learning center (see Figure 6–2). Mrs. Snyder got the idea for the center from studying changes that occur with the earth's soil after reading *How to Dig a Hole to the Other Side of the World* (McNulty, 1979) and completing activities related to a story from the book *Thematic Unit: Rocks and Soil* (Hale, 1992). Mandy's classmates Paul and Billy began a "changes" jar. In the jar, they put materials that they thought would deteriorate. Over the course of a month or longer, they will view these slow changes.

Developing Activity Cards and Record Sheets

How can you communicate activities in the most understandable and appealing ways? The directions on activity cards must be simple so that independent work is possible. Use short sentences and easy words (see Figure 6–3).

Despite your best efforts, some children may not be able to read your directions. Keeping in mind the scaffolding approach, you may want to pair poor readers with good readers who will help. In some schools, the policy is to have multiage grouping for classes. In other schools, parents, a teacher aide, or a cross-age tutoring program assists students. Teachers at the primary level usually find that they must

> **Teaching Tips**
> Draw pictures beside key words if the cards are intended for less able readers.
> For future use, cover the activity cards with transparent contact paper or laminate them.

Figure 6–2 A "changes" jar begun at a center allows children to continually observe slow changes away from the center.

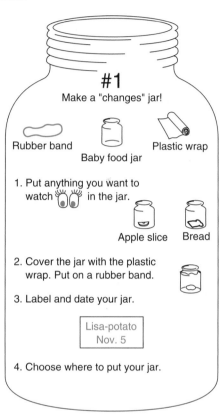

#1

Make a "changes" jar!

Rubber band   Baby food jar   Plastic wrap

1. Put anything you want to watch 👀 in the jar.

Apple slice   Bread

2. Cover the jar with the plastic wrap. Put on a rubber band.

3. Label and date your jar.

Lisa-potato
Nov. 5

4. Choose where to put your jar.

Figure 6–3 An activity card and its accompanying record sheet.

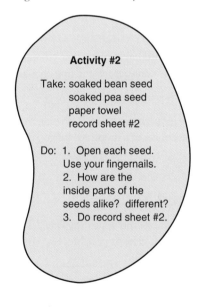

Activity #2

Take: soaked bean seed
        soaked pea seed
        paper towel
        record sheet #2

Do: 1. Open each seed.
     Use your fingernails.
     2. How are the
     inside parts of the
     seeds alike? different?
     3. Do record sheet #2.

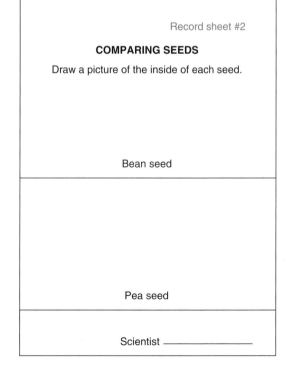

Record sheet #2

COMPARING SEEDS

Draw a picture of the inside of each seed.

Bean seed

Pea seed

Scientist _____

briefly introduce each new activity to the entire class before most children can do the activity independently.

Try to make the design of your activity cards appealing and different for each topic. To do this, you might design the cards to go with the topic. For example, with the topic "volcanoes," make each card look like a cinder cone, shield, or composite volcano. For the rocks and minerals theme, make cards in various crystal shapes. Above all, make the cards as childproof as possible. Cut them from heavy paper or tagboard. Avoid having thin, easily bendable parts. Include as many open-ended activities as you can that have possibilities for process-skill development; these make it possible for children to suggest additional activities, which they enjoy doing.

Teaching Tips: A few teachers find that recording directions on a tape recorder works satisfactorily for nonreaders.

Record sheets are a convenient way to know what the child has done, if you cannot directly observe the child at work. A record sheet may be simply a plain sheet of paper on which the child has made a drawing or recorded some data after an activity card suggestion.

Some teachers like to have a record sheet for every activity. Other teachers reserve record sheets only for activities in which data recording is necessary for the activity to make sense—graphing temperature or other changes, keeping track of results from testing different materials, or drawing a conclusion from a series of facts. Record sheets can also be called skill sheets, laboratory sheets, or data sheets. Figure 6–3 shows an activity card and its accompanying record sheet.

Materials

Kitchen science activities that can be done with common materials are perfect for science centers. The children themselves may be able to bring in most of what is needed. This is a good way to dispel the idea that science is a strange enterprise conducted with expensive and mysterious objects. You can also place in your center printed and audiovisual materials or items lent by local colleges or museums.

Teaching Tips: Many ordinary learning center materials can be obtained as donations from local retail businesses.

Recordkeeping and Evaluation

Observing children in action is the best way to learn what they need help with and what they can do. Yet, if many activities are going on, it's difficult to keep track of everything each child has tried.

One way to record progress is to have a master list of all the center's activities or objectives with the children's names written to one side. If each activity has a record sheet, the child can file these. Use a folder at the center to collect sheets. Check the record sheet against your master list. The record sheet will show what activity was performed. Develop your own code system for recording the quality of the work, indicating what is incomplete and denoting what should be done over.

Teaching Tips: Try allowing the children to develop their own assessment system for center activities.

Sometimes it may be better to have a record system in which the child refers only to her own work. To do this, some teachers give each child who uses a center a record sheet containing only activity numbers (see Figure 6–4). At the top of the sheet, the child writes the title of the center in the space provided, and draws a line under the last number that equals the center's total activities. On completing an activity, the child circles the activity number on her sheet. The child keeps the record sheet handy for the teacher to review during informal or scheduled conferences. To save time, only the more important objectives

Figure 6–4 **A record system in which each child refers only to her own work prevents all children from making critical comparisons of each other.**

```
                Record Sheet
            Science Learning Center

        on   Magnets

    Circle activity finished:

        1           8           15

        2           9           16

        3          10 LM        17

        4 LM       11           18

        5          12           19

        6          13           20

        7          14           21

            Scientist   Melinda
```

may be sampled. The record sheet remains in the child's science folder, with worksheets and other work products.

Monitor student progress to be sure that center activities are meeting your objectives and maintaining the students' interest. What about the activities appeals to the students and gets the job done? Why are the students avoiding or doing poorly with other activities? Ask the students to give their views as well. Together you can continually improve the quality of your center's learning opportunities.

To learn more about each child's accomplishments, periodically schedule individual conferences. Can the child profit from further study in the form of an independent project? Such a project can be particularly valuable with the able and older child. This may be the time to set up an education "contract" between you and the child. This is a negotiated agreement between you and the child. This is a negotiated agreement between a teacher and student that generally addresses needs, expectations, roles, and content. In some cases, the child may make a preliminary study before deciding with you on the exact topic, time, and goals for the contract.

Arranging the Physical Setup

Where is the best place to put a science learning center? How should it look? What are some ways to cut down the work in setting up new centers? These are some questions worth thinking about.

Teaching Tips
You can purchase a preconstructed backboard for your center or make one yourself with donated wood or heavy cardboard.

Can children work inside the classroom without interfering with others? Do activity outcomes happen at the center during the allotted times? Locate the center where it will not interfere with other activities and where it is visible to you at all times. Will wall space be needed? Take this into account as you locate the center in your classroom.

You can draw enlarged background pictures by making transparencies of pictures and then projecting the transparencies with an overhead projector. With these, you can enliven your center's background with familiar characters for child appeal. It's also interesting to use mystery, surprise, oddities, contrast, and drama in captions or pictures.

Managing the Science Learning Center

How can you schedule, introduce the center to children, and keep things running smoothly? It's difficult to say precisely what will be useful in every situation, because schools and individual classrooms vary so much.

If you have never worked with learning centers, start out with a familiar topic. Investigations can be made into learning centers (see Figure 6–5). Always use clear directions and check to see that the students understand the procedure. Demonstrate an activity to get their interest and model appropriate behavior with materials. Finally, keep in mind that the noise level in the classroom may increase slightly. Allow yourself plenty of time at first to ensure a successful learning experience.

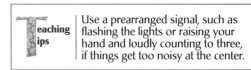 Use a prearranged signal, such as flashing the lights or raising your hand and loudly counting to three, if things get too noisy at the center.

Chances are your experience with science learning centers will be rewarding. If so, consider increasing the use of centers through a more flexible arrangement involving several subjects. Some teachers reserve mornings for the three R's and unit teaching. Afternoons are for individualized enrichment and skill-building activities at different learning centers, such as the following:

- Science
- Social studies/multicultural center

Figure 6–5 A sample learning center.

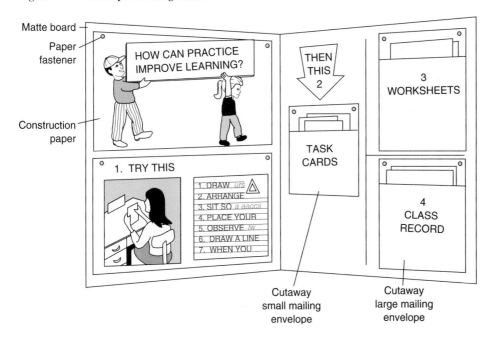

- Fine arts center
- Hobby center
- Literature center
- Writing center
- Speaking and listening center
- Math center

Work at the centers may be either assigned or optional. This choice allows you freedom to vary time and other considerations and to assist and confer with individuals. You and each child can cooperatively decide on ways to pursue interests, knowledge, and skills. The best learning usually happens when children themselves take an active part in planning their learning.

Live Animal Centers

Refer to Appendix D and *http://www. prenhall.com/peters* for animal care tips.

The use of living creatures such as mealworms, hermit crabs, lizards, fish, mice, hamsters, and rabbits is an excellent way to develop your students' observational skills and responsibility. When using animals, first refer to the school or district policy to determine which animals are acceptable for classrooms. The best policy is to have a veterinarian become your "partner in education" and ensure that the animals in your classroom are safe for student interaction.

Visit an Inquiry Classroom
The Role of Animals in the Classroom

View the *Moral Dimensions* video in the "Nature of Science" section of the Companion CD. Mr. McKnight discusses with his students the ethics of working with animals during a scientific study. They indicate that it would not be right to kill earthworms as part of scientific study.

Review the video and ask yourself the following:
- Mr. McKnight provides the following quote in his perspective on this video segment: "I think it's important to make the kids aware of their role as being sort of a guardian or steward of the earth in a way that they need to treat other living things with respect." How can having live plants and animals in the classroom support Mr. McKnight's goals provided in this statement?
- Mr. McKnight discusses the use of the Internet as an alternative to finding out specific things about earthworms. What are other ways to use the Internet to learn about animals or promote the idea of students being the "guardians or stewards of the earth"?

What is your opinion on the use of animals in the classroom? The American Society for the Prevention of Cruelty to Animals provides the website, Animals in the Classroom: Should You or Shouldn't You? at *http://www.aspca.org/site/PageServer? pagename= petsinclass*. Based on what this site provides, do you agree or disagree with the use of animals in the classroom? Explain your answer. Record your ideas and the answers to these questions in your portfolio or use the Companion Website to share your ideas.

Care for the animals should be primarily the students' responsibility; however, you should monitor the cleaning, feeding, and exercise. Help out only when the students cannot provide effective care.

Ideas for animal centers include having the students observe life cycles, compare growth rates, or observe eating patterns. It is a good idea to provide a daily observation log for the students to complete if they are observing animals.

SCIENCE PROJECTS

As professional educators, we have seen withdrawn or listless girls and boys who did not come to life until they began to create science projects. Mandy and her group partners really became involved in science when given the opportunity to complete their project for the science fair. Because they were so interested in geology, Mandy's classmates Shauna and Danielle also completed an informal project on collecting rocks and minerals. The project began at the learning center where her group read *Everybody Needs a Rock* (Baylor, 1985), *Exploring Earth's Treasures* (Olson, 1996), and *The Magic School Bus Inside the Earth* (Cole, 1987). Later, they used *Rocks and Minerals: Mind-Boggling Experiments You Can Turn into Science Fair Projects* (VanCleave, 1995) in deciding on a particular project. The group spent many hours collecting and identifying rocks and minerals.

What specifically is a project, and how does it differ from other science activities? A *project* is an organized search, construction, or task directed toward a specific purpose. One person or a small team of two or three persons ordinarily completes a project with minimal guidance from the teacher. A project is generally less formal than a "science fair project" and may clarify, extend, or apply a concept. Working on projects causes children to use science processes and develop thinking strategies. Most projects require much independent effort, so they are less appropriate for early-elementary children, who usually lack the skills and perseverance needed to operate independently.

The need for projects most often arises during a regular instructional unit; but projects may also begin with interests expressed by the students. The teacher's job is to provide some realistic project choices, give deadlines for completing the projects, tell how they will be presented, indicate the credit that will be received for projects, and check at times for progress.

Using Investigations and Activities for Projects

Investigations that you might use with the whole class or in learning centers often present one or two extra open-ended opportunities to go beyond the basic investigation. Exploration of these questions can be an enriching activity when completed as a project.

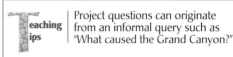

Project questions can originate from an informal query such as "What caused the Grand Canyon?"

Project activities can be short-range, straightforward demonstrations of concepts or procedures. Projects like these allow children to extend their interest by applying interviewing and reference skills to answer real needs.

Curriculum Projects

Project WILD (by the Council for Environmental Education) is a national program that promotes interdisciplinary, supplementary environmental and conservation activities for all grade levels. Teachers who attend Project WILD workshops are trained to facilitate numerous projects and activities that can be found in the guide provided to participants. The activities are grouped to take elementary or middle school students from the *awareness* of environmental concerns to the *action* of conservation and remediation.

Project WILD Aquatic (also by the Council for Environmental Education) is the companion series to Project WILD and is based on water environments. It contains many aquatic-based activities and extensions to terrestrial WILD activities.

Project Learning Tree (by the American Forest Foundation), similar to WILD, is an environmental education project that has trees as its theme. Teachers who attend these certification workshops are shown how to facilitate integrated projects and activities based on diversity, interrelationships, systems, scale, and patterns of change.

Refer to the Web Destinations for Chapter 6 on the Companion Website (*http://www.prenhall. com/peters*) for more information on Project WILD, Aquatic WILD, or Project Learning Tree.

SCIENCE FAIRS

Mandy's classmates Lucinda and Raquel are displaying the books *Volcanoes* (Branley, 1985), *The Magic School Bus Blows Its Top* (Cole, 1996), *How Mountains Are Made* (Zoehfeld, 1995), *Volcanoes: Fire from Below* (Wood, 1991), and *Discovering Earthquakes and Volcanoes* (Damon, 1990) at their science fair table. They are also exhibiting charts, graphs, and pictures related to volcanoes. Together, they prepared a science fair project that explains volcanoes. They searched the Internet for ideas and found the Volcano World site where they gathered information and developed their project.

You may want to consider having a science fair to encourage inquiry and display successful projects. The "investigatory aspect of science fairs" supports reform efforts such as the National Science Education Standards and the Benchmarks for Science Literacy (Balas, 1998, p. 1). Science fairs are also exciting for students, as you found out with Mandy's project cited earlier in the chapter. Science fairs are also good public relations tools to promote your science program at school. A well-planned science fair will involve all students because they have more options available than with regular instructional periods.

Refer to the Web Destinations for Chapter 6 on the Companion Website (*http://www.prenhall. com/peters*) for sample volcano projects and links.

General Guidelines for Science Fairs

When beginning to consider a science fair, start small. A single classroom display at an open house is a good way to begin. Then, as you develop confidence, you may want to work with a fellow teacher for a combined event or even organize a schoolwide fair. Either way, allow plenty of time for the students to complete their projects. We suggest at least 6 weeks, as follows:

- *First Week*   Hand out an information sheet and announce the science fair. Allow plenty of time for students to generate ideas and form groups if they are going to work on group projects.
- *Second Week*   Students turn in preliminary proposals for their projects by the end of the week. Remind students that you will review the proposals with them for quality of the inquiry, completeness of the proposal, and their ability to complete the project.
  - *Third Week*   Hold individual meetings with students and their teacher to discuss proposals and refine projects.
  - *Fourth Week*   Students or groups begin setting up inquiry activities, gathering data, and beginning reports.

Teaching Tips

A certificate of completion or multiple prizes can formally recognize everyone's efforts, but downplay individual comparisons, which elementary or middle school students find hard to handle.

- *Fifth Week* Students continue to work on projects and begin work on presentations and displays.
- *Sixth Week* Students refine displays and presentations, complete reports, and present projects by the end of the week. Displaying projects on Friday afternoon and Saturday morning may increase parent participation.

Invention Conventions

As part of the trend to teach science that children can apply to their lives, some science programs today recommend "invention conventions," as well as typical science fairs. Because technology is science applied to solve practical problems, the idea is to give students chances to develop solutions to their everyday problems and interests:

> How can I tell how fast the wind is blowing? (A homemade wind gauge, fashioned from cardboard and wood, could fill the bill.)
>
> I'd like to make a weird toy that rolls uphill by itself. (Try a hidden rubber band inside a coffee can.)
>
> I've heard you can make a stool from newspaper that's so strong you can sit on it safely. (Rolled-up newspaper makes surprisingly sturdy columns.)

For a variety of fun-filled ideas and ways to stimulate inventiveness in your students, see the following resources:

- Caney, S. (1985). *Steven Caney's invention book*. New York: Workman.
- Eichelberger, B., & Larson, C. (1993). *Constructions for children: Projects in design technology*. Menlo Park, CA: Dale Seymour.
- McCormack, A. J. (1981). *Inventor's workshop*. Belmont, CA: David S. Lake.

If you are interested in a competitive awards program for projects, check the National Science Teachers Association's website. There you will find listed current national and regional science competitions.

Refer to the Web Destinations for Chapter 6 on the Companion Website (http://www. prenhall.com/peters) for links to the National Science Teachers Association and other awards programs.

TEACHING STUDENTS WITH EXCEPTIONALITIES

After listening to *Caves and Caverns* (Gibbons, 1993) being read to the class, Tamika became very excited about speleology. She wanted to know more about stalactites, stalagmites, helictites, speleothems, flowstone, and dripstone. She thought that a career as a speleologist would be perfect because her physical disability would not interfere with spelunking. Fortunately, she is in an inclusive classroom where the teacher recognizes her interest as an opportunity and will support her curiosity. This situation is in keeping with McCann's (1998) statement, "Science classes provide special needs students with opportunities they may not get anywhere else" (p. 1).

Inclusive Classrooms

Inclusion is a concept that is becoming the standard in most K–12 classrooms. An inclusive classroom has a mix of physical and mental developmental levels of students, accommodating those identified as disabled in some way. According to the U.S. Department of Education (USDOE), nearly 12% of students were identified as disabled during the period 1991–1994 (USDOE, 1994). The Office of Special Education Programs reports that the number of students with disabilities served under the Individuals with Disabilities Education Act (IDEA)

Inclusion is education in the least restrictive environment and means that students would, to the extent possible, be educated with their peers.

Science experiences provide students with exceptionalities with opportunities not found in other content areas.

continues to increase at a rate higher than both the general population and school enroll-ment (USDOE, 1999). IDEA guarantees a free, appropriate education in the least restric-tive environment for students with disabilities. Obviously, science instruction is a part of this "appropriate education."

Science instruction for students with disabilities does involve some problems, how-ever. A study by Stefanich and Norman (1996) includes the following information:

- Students with mild disabilities received only 1 minute of science instruction for every 200 minutes of reading instruction.
- Elementary science teachers have little training or experience in teaching students with disabilities.
- Most teachers agree that students with disabilities benefit from hands-on instruction, yet the reality is that they are generally taught from the textbook.

Elementary and middle school teachers need to understand that the special education teacher may not take primary responsibility for science instruction, because the students will probably be in regular classrooms for science class. If you are an elementary teacher, you

Visit an Inquiry Classroom
Special Needs Adaptations

View the *Special Needs Adaptations* video in the "Planning and Management" section of the Companion CD. Mr. McKnight's students are working on an earthworm activity.

Review the video and ask yourself the following:
- Can you identify any students with special needs in the video?
- According to Mr. McKnight's perspective: "Children with learning disabilities who really struggled to gain new information by reading it in a book I think, have the best opportunity to participate and learn on an equal footing with other kids when they're able to manipulate the materials themselves and participate directly in finding that information in the same process as everybody else." Support this viewpoint with specific examples that you have seen in a classroom (your own or a field placement site).

In *The Inclusive Classroom. Mathematics and Science Instruction for Students with Learning Disabilities: It's Just Good Teaching* (1999), Jarrett states that "today's classrooms are increasingly diverse. Students can have great differences in their abilities, life experiences, cultural backgrounds, and home languages. The general education teacher will want to use instructional strategies that respect and build on these differences while helping all students to learn important concepts and skills in mathematics and science." What instructional strategies have you seen in your field experiences that help the general education teacher reach to teach the student with exceptionalities? Record your ideas and the answers to these questions in your portfolio or use the Companion Website to share your ideas.

will have to seek out opportunities during college and through in-service to gain a better understanding of children who have disabilities. Likewise, if you are a special education teacher, you will need college and in-service opportunities related to elementary or middle school science. The following sections are designed as a first step in assisting you with this.

Assisting Students with Disabilities

Mainstreaming presents both opportunities and challenges to people in schools. Children who are mainstreamed learn to live and work in settings that are more likely to develop their potentials to the fullest. The other children profit from a heightened sensitivity and a greater capacity to live and work with individual differences.

The challenges largely come from the diversity of handicaps found in special populations. As an elementary teacher, everyone who comes to your classroom has been identified as a teachable child. To help ensure this, you should share in the placement decision. Students with disabilities who probably require the most change in the science curriculum are those who are totally blind or deaf (American Foundation for the Blind, 2004). For most students with disabilities, a solid hands-on program gives the multisensory experiences they need to learn science well.

Also, realize that an individualized education plan (IEP) is developed for each child by a team of persons. Included on the team is at least one person qualified in special education. By working with a team, you are able to draw on more skills, information, and ideas than by working alone. The team shares responsibility for the child's progress. In many

Refer to the Chapter 6 Web Destinations on the Companion Website (*http://www. prenhall.com/peters*) for links related to Individuals with Disabilities Education Act (IDEA).

states, the IEP is also accompanied by whatever special instructional media and materials the team believes are essential to meet objectives. What are some characteristics of students with disabilities you are likely to teach? How can you generally help them? What resources can you draw on that apply specifically to science? The following sections review students who are visually impaired, hearing impaired, and orthopedically impaired, and those who are mentally disabled.

> **Teaching Tips**
> Reauthorization of IDEA 2004 again calls for "not less than 1 regular education teacher" to participate on an IEP team.

Visually Impaired

The problems of students who are visually impaired may range from poor eyesight to total blindness. Most mainstreamed students will have at least some functional vision, although they frequently lack firsthand experience with many objects as reflected in their language. Vocabulary and descriptive capacity, therefore, need considerable strengthening. Keep in mind the following points with students who are visually impaired:

- Use concrete, multisensory experiences to build a greater store of needed percepts.
- Give plenty of time to explore and encourage the use of descriptive language during explorations.
- Encourage communication with the students throughout activity periods.
- Use tactile cues with materials, such as a knotted string for measuring.

> **Teaching Tips**
> The American Printing House for the Blind produces several current elementary science series in large print and Braille. Illustrations and graphs are often in the form of touchable raised-line drawings.

- Walk the students through spaces to demonstrate barriers and tactile clues.
- Encourage the use of any remaining vision.
- Encourage other students to be sensitive about their use of phrases such as "over there," "like that one," or any other descriptions that require vision.
- Be tolerant of, and prepared for, spilled or scattered material.
- Use oral language or a recorder for instructions and information.
- Pair each student with a tactful sighted partner who can assist in the scaffolding process.

Hearing Impaired

Students with impaired hearing may range from mildly impaired to totally deaf. Most wear hearing aids and have partial hearing. Communication is easier when the child can read lips and certain facial movements and when sign language is used. Delayed language development is common. When teaching science to students who are hearing impaired, remember the following:

- Use concrete objects—pictures, sketches, signs, and the like—to get across ideas.
- Seat the students close to you or to the sound source.
- Give clear directions and face the students as you speak.
- Speak with usual volume and speed.
- Model, rather than correct, pronunciations for the students who are partially deaf.
- Allow longer periods of wait time.
- Make sure you have the students' attention; use direct eye contact.
- Use gestures and body language, but don't exaggerate these.
- Avoid speaking for the students or having classmates speak for the students.
- Talk with the students frequently about what they are doing.
- Maintain good lighting in the classroom.

Visit an Inquiry Classroom
Private Speech

View the *Private Speech* video in the "Constructivist Pedagogy" section of the Companion CD. Near the end of the video segment, students talk to themselves as a way to make sense of the activity in their own mind. As a teacher, this "private speech" is valuable in checking for understanding.

Review the video and ask yourself the following:
- When Mr. McKnight is interacting with the students, do you think they have a full understanding of what is being discussed? If not, how would private speech assist in understanding the concepts? If you do think they understand, what are specific things they say to show understanding?
- What are other ways that a teacher can informally check for understanding if a student is hearing impaired or has another disability that limits speech?

CW What examples of private speech have you observed in your field placements? Explain the nature and result of the private speech. Record your ideas and the answers to these questions in your portfolio or use the Companion Website to share your ideas.

Orthopedically Impaired

Students who are orthopedically impaired typically have gross- or fine-motor malfunctions that cause problems in locomotion, coordination, balance, and dexterity. One of the most common impairments is cerebral palsy. Students who are orthopedically disabled may use walkers, wheelchairs, crutches, braces, or other aids. Keep in mind the following when teaching students who are orthopedically impaired:

- Encourage participation in all possible activities.
- Modify activities as much as possible to avoid frustrations.
- Encourage the use of limbs to the fullest ability.
- Find alternative ways to manipulate objects.
- Allow alternative methods for the students to respond.
- Keep traffic lanes clear in the classroom.
- Acknowledge and deal openly with feelings of frustration.
- Have other students assist these students in moving to the next activity if needed.
- Promote the students' confidence and independence when possible.
- Use activities that foster problem solving and growth in thinking skills.
- Present materials and activities at a comfortable height for individuals in wheelchairs.

Mentally Disabled

Students who are mentally disabled are significantly below average in the abilities of cognitive tasks and often in motor development. They are likely to have problems in learning, remembering, problem solving, and life skills. Other frequent characteristics are short attention span, poor selective attention, and limited ability to make choices. Often, the child with a mental disability will require shorter work periods, more concrete tasks, more direct and structured instruction, and more frequent reinforcement, because of a short attention span. Keep in mind the following points when teaching science to students who are mentally disabled:

- Use a variety of hands-on teaching methods and materials.
- Be sure you have the students' attention before you give directions, and frequently ask them to repeat directions back to you.
- Demonstrate and model as you give simple, clear directions.
- Review new concepts and vocabulary.
- Break tasks down to simple, step-by-step parts if necessary.
- Use the least complex language possible when giving instructions.
- Outline expectations clearly for the students before work begins.
- Review and summarize ideas and procedures frequently. Have the students recapitulate experiences.
- Give positive reinforcement immediately after each small success.
  - Give responsibility within the students' limits, and let the students observe and assist in a role before giving them responsibility.
  - Apply previously constructed concepts to everyday experiences.
  - Begin instruction with what the students know and build on those concepts.

Teaching Tips

Remember that children who are victims of alcoholic or drug-abusing parents may exhibit conditions similar to those of children who are mentally disabled.

Refer to the Web Destinations for Chapter 6 on the Companion Website (*http://www.prenhall. com/peters*) for a link to documents that were developed by the ERIC Clearinghouse on Disabilities and Gifted Education.

CW

Children with Disabilities

Children who are disabled are much more likely to have a poor self-concept than other children. Many adults realize this, but they overprotect children with disabilities in order to compensate. Unfortunately, this overprotection inhibits development and confidence. Children with disabilities, in turn, often learn and accept overdependence, so a cycle develops that feeds on itself. Keep the following in mind when teaching students who are disabled:

- Consider whether help is necessary, rather than convenient.
- Except for obvious needs, get consent from the students before giving help.
- Do not persist if the students decline help; let the students discover whether help is needed.
- Provide prompts instead of answers.
- Allow peers to help or offer help matter of factly.

Children with Special Needs

Many other kinds of disabilities are found in mainstreamed classrooms, including children who are learning disabled, speech/language impaired, health impaired, and those with multiple handicaps. Be aware that entire books are devoted to each one of these and the previously described handicaps. Fortunately, you do not have to become an expert in special education to help a specific mainstreamed child. Although it is nice to have some general knowledge about a handicap, it is far more important to know how that handicap affects a particular child and what the child's individual instructional needs are. You learn this by working with the child.

Resources for Science Teaching

Several sources offer programs and information to better teach students with disabilities in the regular classroom. An excellent and well-tested program is the Full Option Science System (FOSS). Designed for students with and without disabilities in grades K–6, FOSS was developed at the Lawrence Hall of Science. It is an outgrowth of earlier projects to improve science education for students who are visually impaired and physically disabled.

Visit an Inquiry Classroom
Team Formation

View the *Team Formation* video in the "Model Inquiry Unit" section of the Companion CD. This video shows Mr. McKnight forming investigative teams first by similar topics and then later by homeroom.

Review the video and ask yourself the following:
- How will Mr. McKnight ensure that his students with exceptionalities are included on the teams?
- What are some alternative ways that Mr. McKnight could form teams that would also include students with exceptionalities?

In the "Professional Literature" tab of the *Team Formation* video segment, there is reference to forming students into cooperative learning group teams as a way to shift the burden of learning from the teacher to the student. Explain the ramifications of this on the student with a disability who would be participating as a member of a team. Record your ideas and the answers to these questions in your portfolio or use the Companion Website to share your ideas.

Several modules at each grade level include lesson plans in the earth, life, and physical sciences. Extension activities include work in language, computer, and mathematics applications. The developers worked hard to match activities with students' ability to think at different ages. Further work was done to make the program easy to instruct and manage. The commercial distributor of FOSS is

Encyclopaedia Britannica Educational Corporation

310 South Michigan Avenue

Chicago, IL 60604

Further sources that can help you plan lessons for children with different disabilities are:

Alexander Graham Bell Association for the Deaf

3417 Volta Place, N. W.

Washington, DC 20007

American Printing House for the Blind

P.O. Box 6085

Louisville, KY 40206

Center for Multisensory Learning

Lawrence Hall of Science University of California

Berkeley, CA 94720

ERIC Clearinghouse on Handicapped and Gifted Children

1920 Association Drive

Reston, VA 22091

National Center on Educational Media and Materials for the Handicapped

The Ohio State University

154 West 12th Avenue

Columbus, OH 43210

Refer to the Web Destinations for Chapter 6 on the Companion Website (*http://www.prenhall. com/peters*) for links to FOSS and other resources.

Working with Students Who Are English Learners

Not long ago, only a few cities in the United States contained significant numbers of school-children whose native language was not English. Today, they are present in nearly every school. In some schools, foreign-born students who do not speak English may be placed in bilingual classrooms and taught by someone who is proficient in both English and the foreign language. As the students acquire some English proficiency, they are mainstreamed for larger parts of the school day. In other schools, they are taught in all-English classrooms. As a regular classroom teacher, expect to have English language learners in your classroom.

Many students who are English learners experience some culture shock because what they observe now may differ radically from their earlier environment. They may be reluctant to speak because they are afraid to make mistakes. Your warm acceptance and frequent praise will boost their confidence. Whatever you can do to reduce anxiety, increase meaning of content studied, model good English, and increase chances to interact informally with English speakers will benefit them. Students who are becoming proficient in English require some extra time and attention, but they can also enrich the curriculum by bringing multicultural knowledge and perspectives to what is studied. Following are some things that may work for you:

- Use a listening–speaking–reading–writing sequence in teaching when possible. Listening lays the foundation for the other language skills. It's easier to speak what we have first heard, read what we have spoken, and write what we have read.
- Use multisensory, hands-on teaching methods when possible. Concrete materials, investigations, demonstrations, audiovisual media, graphs, and diagrams are more likely to foster meaningful learning. One great advantage of hands-on science over most other subjects is that the actual doing demands little verbal ability.
- Pair English learners with bilingual partners or in cooperative learning groups to increase the scaffolding effect.
- Speak slowly, use short sentences, and rephrase what you say if a student seems unsure, rather than repeat what you have said. Use body language, props, pictures, and sketches to clarify your words.
- Check more specifically whether a student understands by asking yes-or-no questions or by having the student do something you can observe, such as pointing to an object.
- Avoid idiomatic expressions; they can be confusing when taken literally: "It's as easy as pie."
- Make whatever you refer to as concrete as possible—what you know the students have done or observed in the past. Give observable examples in the present as well: "The handle of this pencil sharpener is also a lever."
- To help the students build schemata, write key concepts and vocabulary used during a lesson on the chalkboard. Often make a concept map to outline what is to come in a lesson or to summarize the content of a lesson.
- Emphasize and repeat key words of the lesson as you teach. This cues the students about what to remember and how the words sound.
- For the easiest and most meaningful reading, make language experience charts.

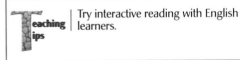
Teaching Tips | Try interactive reading with English learners.

Sixteen regional resource centers for bilingual education in the United States offer training and technical support services for schools. For the center nearest you, call or write the following:

National Clearinghouse for English Language Acquisition and Language Instruction
Educational Programs

George Washington University

2121 K Street

Washington, DC 20037

(800)321–6223 *http://www.ncela.gwu.edu*

The following references from the National Clearinghouse for Bilingual Education
can also further your work with English learners:

- Hamayan, E., & Perlman, R. (1990). *Helping language minority students after they exit
from bilingual/ESL programs: A handbook for teachers*. Washington, DC: National
Clearinghouse for English Language Acquisition and Language Instruction
Educational Programs.
- Short, D. J. (1991). *Integrating language and content instruction: Strategies and
techniques*. Washington, DC: National Clearinghouse for English Language
Acquisition and Language Instruction Educational Programs.

Working with Students Who Are Gifted

What can you expect from mainstreamed students classified as gifted by your district? Children who are gifted display many of the same developmental qualities as most other children. The difference is in the greater degree to which, and the speed with which, these qualities develop. In kindergarten, for example, students who are gifted may perform like second graders. By their senior year in high school, they typically outperform average college seniors on academic tests.

What are some of their attributes? Compared with other students, the gifted child is much more likely to do the following:

- Tolerate ambiguity and complexity
- Have a longer attention span
- Be a highly curious and sharp-eyed observer
- Be a top-notch reader who retains what is read
- Have a well-developed speaking and listening vocabulary
- Have learned the basic skills well
- Understand complex directions the first time around
- Be imaginative and receptive to new ideas
- Be interested in broad concepts and issues
- Have one or more hobbies that require thinking

Gifted students who show all or most of these attributes are often placed in a full-time special class or a pull-out program during part of the school day. But many are totally mainstreamed. How can we challenge these children?

A common problem with having gifted children in regular classrooms is that the curriculum is restrictive and unchallenging for them. They soon become bored and often will seek attention in disruptive ways. One way to keep this problem from blossoming is to use many open-ended investigations and activities. Such a program stimulates the kind of creative, divergent thinking gifted students need to grow toward their potential. Fortunately for us as teachers, our experiences described here also work well for most nongifted students.

In-depth investigations of rocks and minerals can become an extension activity for gifted students.

A second important way to help mainstreamed gifted students is to encourage them to build a large knowledge base. This is usually easy because of their broad curiosity, strong ability to locate and understand information, and ability to retain information. A wide variety of open-ended science investigations stimulates them to try multiple observations and experiments and to read for background. Gifted children readily sense how a broad array of knowledge feeds their creative and problem-solving abilities; this motivates them to learn even more.

A third way to help gifted students is to let them manage their own learning through individual and small-group projects, including those done for school science fairs. Independent study also is fostered when we show students how to locate and use references, trade books, and other instructional materials in the school library.

A fourth way to help gifted students is to expose them to persons in science and other professions who can serve as information sources and future role models. This is particularly important for students who come from economically disadvantaged backgrounds. Gifted children have the interest and quickly develop the capacity to correspond with knowledgeable adults, interview them by telephone or in person, and understand much of what they see and hear.

We can also help gifted students by attending to their social skills as they interact with other children. Some of these students may be advanced academically but be average in

Teaching Tips | Inquiry activities can be valuable in motivating gifted students.

social and personal skills. These skills are needed not only for success in many professions but also for personal happiness. A central objective for mainstreaming the gifted is to help them communicate and get along with persons of all ability levels. Remember that gifted students may not necessarily be gifted in mathematics and science. Monitor your expectations to make sure you are not expecting too much from a child who may be gifted only in language, art, music, or another area.

Refer to the Chapter 6 Web Destinations on the Companion Website (*http://www. prenhall.com/peters*) for resources you can use when working with gifted students.

Summary

- The science standards and benchmarks have as a primary goal science for all students.
- A classroom learning center is a place where one or several students at a time can conduct activities independently using materials and directions found at the center. The center may be organized so that the students can choose at least some of the activities and work at their own pace and learning level. Open-ended experiences usually serve best for these purposes.
- A science project is an organized search, construction, or task directed toward a specific purpose and ordinarily carried out by one to three students. The need for projects often arises in instructional units through interests expressed by students.
- Science fairs and invention conventions will help you encourage inquiry. They are exciting for students and can be good public relations tools to promote your science program at school.
- The Individuals with Disabilities Education Act (IDEA) guarantees a free, appropriate education in the least restrictive environment for students with disabilities. Science instruction is a part of this appropriate education.

Reflection

Companion CD

1. Look at "The Digestive System" lesson linked to the *Paradigm Shifts* video on the Companion CD. How would you modify this lesson for students with visual or hearing impairments?
2. Look at "The Circulatory System" lesson linked to the *Active Learning* video on the Companion CD.

   How would you modify this lesson for use with English learners?
3. Look at "The Respiratory System" lesson linked to the *Social Learning* video on the Companion CD. How would you enhance this lesson for use with students who are gifted?

Portfolio Ideas

1. The policy in some schools is to not allow any type of live animal. In this case, you can search the Internet for sites that have permanently mounted cameras for your students to make "live" observations. What other types of environments can you find on the Internet? What other ways can you replace the use of classroom pets? Share ideas in your portfolio.
2. If you were to arrange a science competition in your classroom, what local community resources or

   industries could help out? Try contacting one or two and see what types of resources are available to you as a classroom teacher. Record findings in your portfolio.
3. Attend an individualized education program (IEP) meeting for a student. What is expected of the parents, the regular teacher, the special education teacher, and the child? Make an entry in your portfolio on what you found out about IEPs.

References

American Association for the Advancement of Science (AAAS). (1993). *Benchmarks for science literacy*. New York: Oxford University Press.

American Forest Foundation. (1993). *Project learning tree environmental education preK–8 activity guide*. Washington: DC, Author.

American Foundation for the Blind. (2004). *Educating blind and visually impaired students: Policy guidance from OSERS*. New York: Author. Retrieved December 23, 2004, from *www.afb.org/Section.asp?SectionID=3&TopicID=138&DocumentID= 720&Mode=Print*

Balas, A. (1998). *Science fairs in the elementary school*. Columbus, OH: ERIC Digest.

Baylor, B. (1985). *Everybody needs a rock*. New York: Atheneum.

Branley, F. (1985). *Volcanoes*. New York: HarperCollins.

Cole, J. (1987). *The magic school bus inside the earth*. New York: Scholastic.

Cole, J. (1996). *The magic school bus blows its top*. New York: Scholastic.

Damon, L. (1990). *Discovering earthquakes and volcanoes*. New York: Troll Associates.

Erickson, S., Gregg, D., Helling, F., King, M., & Starkweather, J. (1987). *Down to earth*. Fresno, CA: AIMS Education Foundation.

Gibbons, G. (1993). *Caves and caverns*. New York: Voyager Books.

Gosnell, K. (1994). *Thematic unit: Geology*. Huntington Beach, CA: Teacher Created Materials.

Hale, J. (1992). *Thematic unit: Rocks and soil*. Huntington Beach, CA: Teacher Created Materials.

Hoover, E., & Mercier, S. (1996). *Primarily earth: AIMS activities grades K–3*. Fresno, CA: AIMS Education Foundation.

Jarrett, D. (1999). *The inclusive classroom. Mathematics and science instruction for students with learning disabilities: It's just good teaching*. Portland, OR: Northwest Regional Educational Laboratory. Retrieved December 23, 2004, from *www.nwrel.org/msec/images/resources/justgood/09.99.pdf*

Lawrence Hall of Science. (1989). *River cutters* (Rev. ed.). Berkeley: University of California.

McCann, W. (1998). *Science classrooms for students with special needs*. Columbus, OH: ERIC Digest. Available at *www.ericse.org/digests/dse98-5.html*

McNulty, F. (1979). *How to dig a hole to the other side of the world*. New York: Harper & Row.

National Research Council (NRC). (1996). *National science education standards*. Washington, DC: National Academy Press.

National Society for the Study of Education (NSSE). (1932). *A program for teaching science: Thirty-First Yearbook of the National Society for the Study of Education*. Chicago: University of Chicago Press.

National Society for the Study of Education (NSSE). (1947). *Science education in American schools: Forty-Sixth Yearbook of the National Society for the Study of Education*. Chicago: University of Chicago Press.

National Society for the Study of Education (NSSE). (1960). *Rethinking science education: Fifty-Ninth Yearbook of the National Society for the Study of Education*. Chicago: University of Chicago Press.

Olson, D. (1996). *Exploring earth's treasures*. Chicago: Kidsbooks.

Stefanich, G., & Norman, K. (1996). *Teaching science to students with disabilities: Experiences and perceptions of classroom teachers and science educators*. A special publication of the Association for the Education of Teachers in Science (AETS). (Available from AETS, Dr. Jon Pedersen, University of Oklahoma, 820 Van Vleet Oval, ECH 114, Norman, OK 73019)

U.S. Department of Education (USDOE). (1994). *Mini-digest of educational statistics: 1994*. Washington, DC: Author.

U.S. Department of Education (USDOE). (1999). *Twenty-first annual report to Congress on the implementation of Individuals with Disabilities Education Act*. Washington, DC: Author. Available at *www.ed.gov/offices/OSERS/OSEP/OSEP99AnlRpt/*

VanCleave, J. (1995). *Rocks and minerals: Mind-boggling experiments you can turn into science fair projects*. New York: John Wiley.

Wood, J. (1991). *Volcanoes: Fire from below*. Milwaukee, WI: Gareth Stevens.

Zoehfeld, K. (1995). *How mountains are made*. New York: HarperCollins.

Suggested Readings

Blume, S. (1991). *Science fair handbook*. New York: Macmillan/McGraw-Hill. (a resource for teachers, principals, and science fair coordinators)

Bochinski, J. (1991). *The complete handbook of science fair projects*. New York: John Wiley. (how to complete a project plus 50 award-winning examples)

Carratello, J., & Carratello, P. (1989). *All about science fairs*. Huntington Beach, CA: Teacher Created Materials. (a practical guide to help students and teachers with science fairs)

Council For Environmental Education. (2002). *Project WILD aquatic: K–12 curriculum and activity guide*. Houston, TX: Author.

DeBruin, J. (1991). *Science fairs with style*. Carthage, IL: Good Apple. (a comprehensive guide for upper-grade projects)

Fredericks, A., & Asimov, I. (1990). *The complete science fair handbook*. Glenview, IL: Good Year Books. (a good guide to conducting science fairs)

Hampton, C. H., Hampton, C. D., & Kramer, D. C. (1994). *Classroom creature culture: Algae to anoles* (Rev. ed.). Arlington, VA: National Science Teachers Association. (guidelines for setting up live animal centers in the classroom; also available as an ERIC microfiche, ERIC Document Reproduction Service No. ED 370 797)

National Science Teachers Association (NSTA). (1988). *Science fairs and projects: Grades K–8*. Washington, DC: Author. (a resource book from NSTA)

National Science Teachers Association (NSTA). (1990). *Science and math events*. Arlington, VA: Author. (a resource book on science and math events from NSTA)

Poppe, C. A., & VanMatre, N. A. (1985). *Science learning centers for the primary grades*. West Nyack, NY: Center for Applied Research in Education. (a comprehensive book for those interested in setting up centers)

Project WILD: K–12 Curriculum and Activity guide. Council for Environmental Education. (2002a). Houston, TX: Author.

Shubkagel, J. F. (1993). *Show me how to write an experimental science fair paper: A fill-in-the-blank handbook*. Independence, MO: Show Me How. (a step-by-step guide for teachers, parents, and students in upper-elementary grades)

Stone, G. K. (1981). *More science projects you can do*. Upper Saddle River, NJ: Prentice Hall. (a paperback book of many interesting projects for upper-elementary students)

Tocci, S. (1986). *How to do a science fair project*. New York: Watts. (a useful guide to science fair projects)

VanCleave, J. (1997). *Guide to the best science fair projects*. New York: John Wiley. (complete rules, display tips, and experiments on 50 topics)

Chapter 7

CONSTRUCTING
TECHNOLOGICAL
UNDERSTANDINGS

- What is the difference between educational technology and technology education?
- What are some ways to use computers in the elementary or middle school science classroom?
- What does science, technology, and society (STS) refer to as related to elementary or middle school science?
- What are some of the areas of technology education and how could you apply this information in your classroom?

Focus on Inquiry

Where the Wildflowers Are

Dr. Charlotte Boling and Dr. Pam Northrup
University of West Florida

To plan the upcoming fourth-grade unit on native wildflowers, Ms. Heubach uses STEPS (Support for Teachers Enhancing Performance in Schools), an online tool designed to assist in planning using a standards-driven model (*http://www.ibinder.uwf.edu/steps/*). The STEPS site contains a Lesson Architect that helps Ms. Heubach organize her lesson online. She will be able to store the lesson in her personal online folder and even e-mail it to her principal. Resources such as links to websites, best practices, and other model units help her in planning the lesson on wildflowers. Tutorial links are especially useful because Ms. Heubach is trying out some new technologies in her lesson. The tutorials within STEPS will guide her in how to use technology in the classroom. Using this online tool, she designed a unit that will last for several weeks.

On the first day of the unit, Ms. Heubach greets her fourth-grade students at the door and hands each a card with the words "Where the Wildflowers Are." Once everyone is seated, Ms. Heubach explains that the class will be embarking on a new unit about wildflowers. She then discusses the strategies the students will be following by using a Power-Point presentation loaded with pictures and graphics taken from the Internet. The students will be researching wildflowers, learning about where they grow, and actually growing some in their classroom. At the end of the unit, the fourth-grade students will sell their wildflowers. Ms. Heubach then poses this question: "As a scientist, how would you go about gathering information, making initial hypotheses, testing the hypotheses, and reporting?" Using Inspiration concept mapping software shown through an LCD projector, Ms. Heubach notes the students' brainstorming answers to the question. Ms. Heubach organizes students into cooperative learning groups, and they begin.

Rashid, Sherry, Xuemin, and Cherian immediately embark on a virtual field trip to the desert, to the Pitcher Plant Prairie, and to the local garden store's website. (All pertinent websites had been bookmarked earlier by Ms. Heubach to save time.) The students take notes, copy interesting pictures to their group folder on the computer, and begin comparing and contrasting types of wildflowers. Rashid finally suggests that they begin looking at

wildflowers that will grow locally. After a bit of problem solving, the students notice a link to the Global Temperature Cam and to Weather Underground. They are on their way!

Alla, Laszlo, Sharon, and Seth begin their investigation by using the CD-ROM Explorapedia. They look up wildflowers, gardening, and seeds to begin their search. They also jot down notes on their palm computers, save pictures to their computer folders, and even print some information for later use. Klaus, Zhiyong, Stuart, and Swarna's approach is to go online to the site Ask a Scientist and to study the Biomes projects. They think that the information they gain in other ways will help them better understand wildflowers. They e-mail a scientist who guarantees a 24-hour response. They also go to Global Schoolhouse to see whether other classes are studying the same topic and, they hope, to collaborate with students in other parts of the country.

After the information gathering is complete, the students create HyperStudio stacks to share with each other, with other students, and with new online partners. The stacks include projections of which types of flowers should be grown in their classroom, the soil that should be used, and the type of pot that would work best.

Kristina, Sherman, Theodore, and Barbara establish a relationship with a classroom in another part of the country. The two classrooms decide that they will plant wildflowers at the same time while predicting, observing, and recording plant data. To make the relationship as visual as possible, Ms. Heubach and Chandra create a simple website containing both classes' selection of wildflowers to grow, the type of soil selected, the HyperStudio lessons that were created, and a simple database for student groups to update weekly and monitor growth. To keep the website current, the students take digital pictures each week and load them on the website. Both classrooms download NetMeeting and begin daily conversations through their inexpensive Quick Cam camera. The students also create and share pictures of their plants with their new pen pals across the country.

While the plants mature, students establish marketing techniques. The fourth-grade students brainstorm the best approaches to marketing their wildflowers. Some engage in traditional marketing by creating posters to hang in the school. Others decide to create a bookmark by using a simple desktop publishing program and to distribute it to all they meet: *"Bookmark it! Wildflowers for Sale . . . "* along with the URL of the class website is their message. Another group believes that a video is a good approach. Using the resources that have been gathered during the past several weeks, the students go to the ITV room and create a short commercial to be played on the school's ITV network.

The plants are finally ready for sale! The students must keep track of the expenses they incurred while growing the plants (soil, pots, advertising, fertilizer) and make sure they sell the plants at a price that will allow them to make their money back and still have some left over for a class celebration. The students use a spreadsheet to keep up with the expenses and the profits.

"Step right up! This is where the wildflowers are" could be heard and seen on the school ITV system on the day of the sale!

EDUCATIONAL TECHNOLOGY, TECHNOLOGY EDUCATION, AND SCIENCE

With the possibility of exploring online resources as the students did in the Focus on Inquiry: Where the Wildflowers Are, children and their teachers have a new world of exciting possibilities open to them in today's classrooms. The students in the opening scenario constructed new knowledge about technology and science. They were excited about using their technologically enhanced learning environment and discovering new things about wildflowers as they developed inquiry skills through the use of educational technology.

What do you think of when you hear the words *technology* and *education?* If you are like most people, your response would include educational technology, or the use of computers in education. This is just one small part of technology, however. Technology education also includes the designed world (Rutherford & Ahlgren, 1990).

By including the **designed world,** we mean *technology education,* which includes areas such as the following:

> **Designed world** refers to the applications of science in the form of technology.

- Agricultural technology such as precision farming with GPS devices, grafting, and hydroponics
- Materials technology such as ceramics, plastics, and composites
- Manufacturing technology such as a continuous-production automated assembly lines, welding robots, and computer-aided manufacturing
- Energy technology such as fossil fuels, solar energy, and wind power
- Communication technology such as cell phones, laser barcode scanners, and computers
- Health technology such as biotechnology and genetics to develop new drugs, artificial limbs, and nuclear magnetic resonance
- Construction technology such as building new skyscrapers, suspension bridges, and dams
- Transportation technology such as high-speed magnetic rails, hypersonic aircraft, and hybrid electric/gas cars

In the first part of this chapter, we look at educational technology, or using computers, laser discs, CDs, DVDs, and similar tools in the classroom. We then explore the science technology society (STS) movement. In the last part of the chapter, we explore the growing field of technology education in the elementary and middle school classroom.

USING EDUCATIONAL TECHNOLOGY IN THE SCIENCE CLASSROOM

A revolution occurred in education soon after the printing press was invented. The printed book became the tool of its time and has since been noted by many groups as the greatest invention of the past millennium. Today, computer technology is the educational tool of the times. Historians tell us of the resistance to books in the 15th century. As people relied more on the printed word for educational opportunity, however, this technological advancement became commonplace. Similarly, resistance to using computers and other technology in the classroom is rapidly changing today.

Not that long ago, a single computer for a school was rare. This is no longer the case. Computers of all sizes are located in media centers, labs, and individual classrooms. Computing capacity is now at the point where the average home video game has the computing ability of the most powerful computers manufactured just a few years ago. The automobile you buy today has a greater ability to process data than any computer you may have used in school. What does this mean for you as a teacher? *You will be challenged to use the technology as a learning tool rather than learning about the tool of technology.* A recent Net-Day Survey (2004) included the following information:

- Approximately 94% of teachers said they are comfortable using computers and 87% of them are comfortable using the Internet. Geographically, urban teachers are more comfortable using computers—65% are very comfortable compared to 54% of suburban and 54% of rural teachers. The majority of teachers believe that the Internet has become important to teaching in the past 2 years—48% feel that it has become very important.

- Three fourths of teachers agree that the Internet is a tool to use to conduct research for standards-based instruction and 84% of the teachers say it improves the quality of education—nearly half say it has improved the quality a lot. Another 77% of teachers believe that their peers without Internet access are at a disadvantage and an overwhelming 64% disagree that the Internet takes away from other important educational skills.

- Despite the high comfort levels and strong positive attitudes, 67% of the teachers acknowledge that the Internet is not well integrated into their classroom.

This last point was reinforced by other studies in which researchers found that, although significant advances have been made in instructional technology, actual practice in the classroom is status quo (Kozma & Shank, 1998; Means, 1994). This is not because of unwillingness on the child's part. A recent survey found the following to be true of children ages 8 to 18 in 2003–2004:

- 96% went online
- 74% have Internet access at home
- 61% use the Internet daily (Henry J. Kaiser Family Foundation, 2004)

Similarly, the estimated $16.9 billion video game industry indicates that 92% of children and adolescents age 2 to 17 years play video games (Henry J. Kaiser Family Foundation, 2002). In sum, the uses of advanced technologies *in the classroom* have not kept pace with advances in the community. If this is still the case for you, how can you change this practice? Will your classroom look like the one in Focus on Inquiry: Where the Wildflowers Are?

See the Web Destination for Chapter 7 on the Companion Website (*http://www. prenhall.com/peters*) for links to other programs emphasizing the use of computers in the classroom.

Standards Link

Science Program Resource Standard

The K–12 science program must give students access to appropriate and sufficient resources, including quality teachers, time, materials and equipment, adequate and safe space, and the community.

- **The most important resource is professional teachers.**

- **Time is a major resource in a science program.**

- **Conducting scientific inquiry requires that students have easy, equitable, and frequent opportunities to use a wide range of equipment, materials, supplies, and other resources for experimentation and direct investigation of phenomena.**

- **Collaborative inquiry requires adequate and safe space.**

- **Good science programs require access to the world beyond the classroom.**

(Program Standard D, National Research Council, 1996, p. 218.)

The Science Program Resource Standard is included here so that you can refer to it and see the need for educational technology. As noted, inquiry requires the right equipment. Computers can provide access to data and scientists beyond the classroom. The authors of the *National Science Education Standards* (National Research Council [NRC], 1996) suggest that your students can access scientific information as well as collect, store, analyze, and display data. Think about how students in the Focus on Inquiry: Where the Wildflowers Are used technology as a learning tool. Does it seem natural for them to use computers? Do students in the chapter-opening photograph show how commonplace computers have become in the elementary and middle school classroom?

Computer Advantages, Disadvantages, and Resources

You probably already have seen some ways that computer-assisted instruction can benefit you and your students in both learning centers and larger settings. Let's look at several more advantages and then address a few concerns.

It takes only a brief experience with computers to see how much children delight in this medium. The immediate feedback to their responses prompts them to learn more quickly and confidently. Slow or fast learners may progress at their own developmentally appropriate rates. When they respond incorrectly, a good program branches them into a remedial sequence that reteaches the material in simpler steps. When they respond correctly, a good program moves them quickly into more advanced material. Computers make individualized instruction more accessible.

One of the best uses of the computer in science education is with simulations. The computer-controlled videodisc, CD-ROM, and other resources offer all kinds of opportunities for making decisions and solving problems in realistic settings. Any airline pilot can tell you that what's seen through the cockpit windshield of a flight simulator just after a right or wrong move comes uncannily close to the real thing. Now the chances for children to encounter simulated experiences are increasing.

One problem with computers is that software can be a major part of a school budget. Fortunately, a growing supply of software is available on the Internet, and much of it is available to teachers for free or for a minimal registration fee. One type of software is the web-based application software called JAVA. Accessing this type of web page sends applets, or small programs, to your computer. Once loaded, applet programs provide specific applications.

Another drawback of some elementary and middle school science software is a lack of accompanying hands-on experiences. This is more likely with older and stand-alone materials. The software integrated into today's comprehensive multimedia science programs usually provides for concrete activity.

Nearly everyone needs some extra guidance and practice to apply this remarkable tool creatively. If you are new to computing, it's easy to feel overwhelmed by the sheer quantity of unfamiliar technology and methods employed. The good news is that plenty of help is available through user groups and schoolwide or districtwide technology coordinators. Both in-service workshops and informal, person-to-person arrangements are common. Don't be surprised to meet students with considerable expertise at computing. By the sixth grade, some children have had several thousand hours of experience with computers at home and at school. They can be invaluable aides to other students and to you. Employ them in cooperative situations as much as possible.

See the Web Destinations for Chapter 7 on the Companion Website (*http://www. prenhall.com/peters*) for sample science-related JAVA applets.

| **Teaching Tips** | If you are new to a school, ask colleagues and the media specialist what devices and help are available at the school and district levels. |

Software Sources and Reviews

How can you learn what is currently available and worthwhile? The supply of usable science software continues to grow. Software publishers are producing more materials that reflect the best thinking in constructivist psychology and science education. Science textbook publishers are integrating software titles into text units and chapters. In fact, now these publishers are more accurately called multimedia science program publishers. Some also develop their own software for that purpose.

If you are unsure about a software program, keep in mind that the National Science Teachers Association (NSTA, 1992) presents the following guidelines on the use of computers in science education:

- Computers should enhance, not replace, hands-on activities.
- Tutorial software should engage students in meaningful interactive dialogue.
- Simulation software should provide opportunities to explore concepts and models not readily available.
- Computer-based labs should permit students to collect and analyze data like scientists.
- Networking should permit students to emulate the way scientists work and reduce classroom isolation.

The Uses of Computers

School computers initially served for drill and practice in mathematics and language. Now, they are also being used to teach broader applications through simulations, computer-based laboratories, project-based science, multimedia, spreadsheets, databases, and learning activities related to the Internet. With more machines available, there are improved chances for us to apply them in science activities and in whole-class teaching. You will find that some schools pool their computer resources into laboratories, some distribute their computer resources into classrooms, and some use a combination of these methods. In most cases, you will have at least one machine to allow you to create a center in your classroom.

Setting up a computer center for science raises some of the same practical questions as learning centers for other disciplines:

- What do you want to accomplish with the center?
- Are other means of instruction better?
- What kinds of compatible hardware and software are available?
- Who will use the center and when?
    - What will the users need to know?
    - How can I best scaffold the learning environment for my students?

Check the NSTA site at *http://www.nsta.org/* for other suggestions on the use of technology in the classroom.

Often, the software available to you will dictate your use of the computer. What types of software are available? Consider the kinds of software programs you are now likely to see in your school.

Multimedia Tutorials and Skill-Building Games

Tutorials and skill-building games are used to teach vocabulary, facts, topical information, or skills. Let's look at the example of CHEM4Kids. Here, students can learn about matter, elements, atoms, and related topics. These tutorials are presented in a fun and interactive manner and include accompanying activities and resources.

Another example is Butterflies 2000—On the Wings of Freedom. Children can learn about the anatomy of butterflies, the travel patterns and other behaviors, and the reproductive cycle. There is also the ability to play associated games and share butterfly-related stories.

An example of a skill-building tool is Tracking a Moving Shadow, where students investigate questions about shadows and moving bodies to make indirect observations of the earth's rotation. Students construct an 18-centimeter gnomon to answer questions as they

Visit an Inquiry Classroom
Planning to Use Computers in the Classroom

View the *Planning* video in the "Model Inquiry Unit" section of the Companion CD. Mr. McKnight explains to students how to proceed with the investigation. One aspect of the students' inquiry will be the use of the Internet.

Review the video and ask yourself the following:
- How will Mr. McKnight's students use computers as part of their investigations?
- What other ways could students use computers as part of their earthworm study?

Ann Reiff (n.d.) designed an earthworm activity that involves online data collection (*http://web.stclair.k12.il.us/splashd/wormsexp.htm*). What earthworm activities could you engage elementary or middle school students in that would involve online data collection? Record your ideas and the answers to these questions in your portfolio or use the Companion Website to share your ideas.

hypothesize and take measurements of the earth's movements. Tutorial programs can be useful in developing new concepts and skills, the language of science, or in the remediation of misconceptions.

See the Web Destinations for Chapter 7 on the Companion Website (http://www.prenhall.com/peters) for links to multimedia tutorials and skill-building sample websites.

Developing Individual Multimedia

Do you want your students to try to create their own media? HyperStudio (Roger Wagner Publishing) is an example of software that allows students to make their own multimedia presentations. With multimedia, each screen image is considered a card, and a collection of these cards is called a stack. When making stacks, students can type in text, import clip art from other disks, scan in their own pictures, record sounds, control a laser disc/CD player, or link their cards to other programs and Internet resources.

> **Teaching Tips**
> If you are considering the purchase of a computer for your classroom, you may want to include a DVD drive to be able to play the growing number of titles becoming available for classroom use.

Macromedia's Flash software provides a more advanced format for multimedia but will be too advanced for most elementary students. The advantages to using hypermedia are as follows:

- The students can research topics and make their own information stacks to share with others at their school or through the Internet.
- Classroom or school collections of hypermedia stacks provide information on a variety of topics from multiple perspectives.
- The students feel good about themselves when they are able to create a simple stack and share it with others.

You may want to try out HyperStudio or a similar program. Often, they are available free on a trial basis. How can you use such a program in your classroom? Here's an example: Have your students develop a classification of some common objects in the schoolyard, such as the rocks they can find. Use HyperStudio (Roger Wagner Publishing) to create a stack of cards based on the students' classification system.

Simulations

Simulation software is available in PC or Macintosh format and on CD-ROM or floppy disk. In simulations, students play roles in situations where they can explore scientific phenomena or approximate real events. For example, the Magic School Bus series (Scholastic/Microsoft)

See the Web Destinations for Chapter 7 on the Companion Website (*http://www. prenhall.com/peters*) for the links to sample simulation websites.

allows students to explore things like the human body, the solar system, and the ocean. Dangerous Creatures (Microsoft) allows students to explore the world of wildlife. Other programs develop early science skills through the help of an online friend such as Sammy's Science House (Edmark). Space Station Simulator (Maris) allows students to construct and view a space station. Other simulations such as PERIL (University of Guelph) allow players to decide what to do when given certain data. You can use PERIL with your upper-elementary and middle school students. They are presented information on health and safety, make appropriate choices, and identify misconceptions related to health risks.

Simulations are an excellent way to present science phenomena that are otherwise too remote, dangerous, complex, costly, or time consuming. The computer instantly feeds back information as the simulations assist students in constructing knowledge and making real-life decisions without facing real-life consequences.

One exceptional simulation is the Virtual Frog Dissection. Students can explore the frog as if they were actually dissecting it themselves. In this simulation, there is a great amount of detail without the familiar Formalin smell.

Internet Access

See Web Destinations for Chapter 7, on the Companion Website (*http://www.prenhall. com/peters*) for links to a variety of Internet resources related to zoos, science centers, and museums. You can also find the current addresses to science celebrities at this site or a variety of web search tools such a Google.

What is out there in cyberspace? A steadily growing number of people use an electronic mail address with the Internet. These are in the user@location format. Schools, Internet providers, or free services provide the mail addresses. Your students can send e-mail to people, asking for specific information related to the science topics your class is investigating. There are also millions of websites on the Internet to connect to, including zoos, science centers, museums, schools, research centers, and government agencies.

Before you explore the Internet with your students, be cautious to promote safe "surfing." Inform your students not to give out their names or personal information or assume that people they meet on the Internet are who they say they are. Monitor student browsing, check the browser's history file frequently, and complete a child/parent agreement

Visit an Inquiry Classroom
Safety

View the *Safety* video in the "Planning and Management" section of the Companion CD. Mr. McKnight's students investigate an earthworm's movement. They probe the earthworm with a pencil eraser to see its reaction and movement.

Review the video and ask yourself the following:
- Could science simulations such as the Virtual Frog Dissection offer viable alternatives to experimentation when safety is an issue? Why or why not?
- What other ways can computers be used to comply with safety issues of an elementary or middle school classroom?

The Council of State Science Supervisors provides a checklist of safety concerns in K–12 science laboratories at the *http://csss.enc.org/safety.htm* weblink. One item states, "Live animals and students are protected from one another." Explain how Mr. McKnight ensures that this guideline is being met. Record your ideas and the answers to these questions in your portfolio or use the Companion Website to share your ideas.

The use of the Internet provides powerful learning tools in the science classroom.

form (Haag, 1996). Your school or district may have specific software or regulations concerning the Internet, so make it a point to check into this.

Your students can find information or explore many science-related sites for free, once a local Internet connection to your classroom is established. Science celebrities such as Mr. Wizard, Bill Nye the Science Guy, and Beakman's World have Internet addresses.

Perhaps your school already has a *home page*, which is a globally accessible file of information on the Internet. Chances are that the college or university you are attending or your practicum site is on the web. Check with a computer support person to find out the address and how you can access these sites if you do not already know.

Can elementary or middle school students build web pages? Not only can your students access the web, but they can also become a part of the information superhighway. Students enjoy creating web pages based on science topics. Teachers also find it to be a fun activity and are delighted by the creativity of the students. The easiest way to develop a file for the web is to use a web page software tool such as FrontPage (Microsoft). This program works like a word-processing program but saves files in a format called hypertext markup language (HTML). Using HTML, any computer with browser software on the Internet can be used to access a file accurately.

Building web pages helps students develop the scientific skill of communication if they are sharing the procedure and results of an experiment. For example, Mr. McKnight's students on the Companion CD could share with other elementary and middle school classrooms the procedures and results related to the types of habitats the earthworms prefer. Other classes could repeat the activities and see if they have similar results. This models the scientific process.

Science activities are abundant on the Internet. We will begin by referring you to *Science on the Internet: A Resource for K–12 Teachers* (Ebenezer & Lau, 2003). Another good

See Web Destinations for Chapter 7, on the Companion Website (*http://www. prenhall.com/peters*) for links to creating and sharing web pages.

reference is *Internet Activities Using Scientific Data* (Froseth & Poppe, 1995), available from the National Oceanic and Atmospheric Administration (NOAA) (*http://www.noaa.gov/*).

Teaching Tips

Classroom Connect (*http://www.classroom.net/*) is another resource for well-written Internet-based activities. It produces the *lessonplan.net* series with thematic topics such as Catastrophe (Classroom Connect, 1998), which includes activities on earthquakes, hurricanes, El Niño, floods, and other disasters.

It has Internet activities involving real-time data. This guide, developed for teachers, takes you on a journey through the Internet. Your students can learn the basics of the Internet and explore possibilities for science learning.

The chapter "Science and Social Studies" in *Integrating Telecommunications into Education* (Roberts, Blakeslee, Brown, & Lenk, 1990) includes some exemplary programs, such as the National Geographic Kids Network. This project allows students to share their information with others through the Internet. Students in various schools gather data, transmit the data to a central computer, and share findings with other schools. In one unit, students in schools from around the nation measure the acidity of rain in their local area. They send the data to a scientist collaborating with the program. The data are then pooled through a central computer, organized on charts and maps, and sent back to the students. Electronic collaboration can also be a powerful way for you to improve your own classroom practice in the future (Koufman-Frederick, Lillie, Pattison-Gordon, Watt, & Carter, 1999).

Data Management Tools

Data management tools, like spreadsheets and databases, provide essential support to science activities. They are useful in collecting and analyzing data and preparing charts and graphs.

Spreadsheets

Spreadsheets allow you to arrange and automatically compute data. The use of a spreadsheet for a gradebook is a typical example. As new grades are entered, students' final grades based on the input are automatically calculated.

See Web Destinations for Chapter 7 on the Companion Website (*http://www. prenhall.com/peters*) for links to sample data-managment tool websites.

Excel (Microsoft) and ClarisWorks (Claris) are common tools for developing spreadsheets. The book *ClarisWorks 2.0 in the Classroom* (Claris, 1993) provides examples on how to use spreadsheets to determine the best factors for racing cars, to compare body measurements, or to find the best formulas for bubble mixtures. Spreadsheets can also be used to predict data. If information on plant growth is collected for a period of time, a spreadsheet can determine future trends. A spreadsheet can also be used to determine how long it would take a student to travel to another planet, given the speed of the spacecraft and the distance of the planets. Spreadsheet software such as Microsoft Excel also automatically produces charts and graphs.

Databases

A *database* is a way to create, categorize, sort, and view specific records. For example, a collection of records on Animals A–Z (Claris, 1993) may contain information like the type of animal, size, skin type, habitats, and number of legs. A database can be used to sort the information and display only records that match certain criteria. For instance, by selecting number of legs as a criterion, the database program will automatically sort the records and list those animals that have two legs.

Teaching Tips

You can use databases to categorize information on rocks and minerals, weather, and volcano records.

Trash Stats is an example of a spreadsheet to manage data. Students can use this program to monitor the number of pounds of trash they produce each day according to predetermined categories. Summary data are automatically calculated.

NASA's Planetary Photojournal database can show the advantage of a database while revealing outstanding images and information related to the solar system. Space missions, planetary satellite images and data, as well as information on people, facilities, and related technology are included.

See Web Destinations for Chapter 7 on the Companion Website (*http://www. prenhall.com/peters*) for the links to research tool–related websites.

Word Processing

Probably the most-used types of programs are the *word-processing* programs that students use to format text and correct spelling errors. This software is an excellent tool for creating science journals, writing science poetry, or creating science pal files to share over the Internet. Word processing can be promoted through selected Internet chats, instant message exchanges, and other online activities.

Research Tools

How do scientists use computers? Are children able to use computers in similar ways? Science educators and computer specialists are exploring both questions. The software and other materials coming from their efforts get children into the heart of science: gathering, organizing, and sharing real data.

Several software programs for students have accompanying hardware called *probes*. These are sensing devices connected through a cable to the computer. When used with the proper software, probes can measure temperature, light, sound, heart rate, acidity, motion, force, pressure, and other properties of matter. Several probe-type lab programs, called *computer-based labs*, have had much use in schools from about grade 3 through college.

Bank Street Laboratory (Sunburst) gives students chances to record and analyze graphs of temperature, light, and sound data. Science Toolkit (Broderbund) has rugged, easy-to-use probes for measuring light, temperature, time, and distance. Data are organized into tables, charts, and graphs. Probe labs make it easy to gather a lot of data over short or long periods and then instantly convert the data into analyzable forms.

See Web Destinations for Chapter 7 on the Companion Website (*http://www. prenhall.com/peters*) for other resources related to software examination and use.

If you do not have access to real equipment, data can be collected through numerous online sources. For example, temperature, wind speed, and other weather data are commonly found on the Internet. Tide and sea level data are another example of real-time data available through the Internet.

Software Evaluation

Finding good software for use with elementary or middle school students may be a difficult task, given the explosion of software writers and distributors. Because budgets are generally limited for software purchases, it is a good idea to complete a thorough review of the program before purchase.

See Web Destinations for Chapter 7 on the Companion Website (*http://www. prenhall.com/peters*) for links to available grants and grant assistance for purchasing items for your classroom.

A software checklist may be a helpful tool to assist you in selecting software appropriate for your students. It is important to prioritize your software purchases on the basis of the philosophy and needs of your program (Beaty, 1990). Some considerations are provided in the checklist in Figure 7–1.

Computer Accessories

If you want your students to use your classroom computer center for word processing science reports and the like, consider attaching a scanner to the computer. An inexpensive LED scanner can be purchased for under $50, and many schools and districts have small

Figure 7–1   **Software checklist.**

Y/N	Program: Distributor(s) and Price(s): Checklist:
	Is this program developmentally appropriate for children?
	Is the reading level of the program appropriate?
	Does this program meet your specific curricular needs?
	Can the child navigate through the program without adult assistance?
	Will the program hold the child's interest?
	Does the program contain positive reinforcement for children?
	Can you pilot this program to see whether it is compatible with your children?
	Does this software avoid culturally biased language or examples?
	Does this software avoid gender-biased language or examples?
	Will this program be compatible with your existing hardware?
	Will the RAM be sufficient to run the program?
	Will you have enough hard drive space for the program?
	Are any special input or input devices needed with this program?
	Will your monitor support the graphics in this program?
	Is the level of quality of this program sufficient for classroom use?
	Was this program rated by any external reviewers?
	Are there any technical problems that will make using this program difficult?
	Will other teachers be using this program, and can they help you if needed?
	Is the price of the program compatible with your budget?
	Is an educational discount available for this program?
	Are lab packs available if this program will be used on multiple machines?
	Can you make backup copies of the program for your protection?
	Is any special licensing required for this program?

grant programs to assist with this type of purchase. Like a photocopier, a scanner allows the user to incorporate photographs or drawings directly into a written report, multimedia presentation, or Internet web page.

A digital camera can be purchased for under $200 and works like a regular camera but saves the image on computer memory instead of film. The pictures can be transferred to a computer and used in other programs, like scanned pictures. The disadvantage of these cameras is that the less expensive models can only store a limited number of pictures at one time before the pictures need to be downloaded to a computer.

Computer video projectors can now be purchased for under $1,000, making them affordable for elementary and middle schools. These connect to classroom computers and project the image on a screen. The advantage of a video projector over an LCD panel is that the pictures are generally of a much better quality because they have higher resolu-

CDs and DVDs contain extensive science information and activities for children.

tions and are not subjected to the heat of an overhead projector. Most models now work in normal lighting, so students can take notes while viewing.

Other Technological Devices

The CD-ROM (compact disc, read-only memory) is a way to bring a vast amount of computer-controlled audiovisual material into your classroom. The CD-ROM is inserted into a CD-ROM drive connected to a computer. The material is accessed through the keyboard and viewed on the computer screen. The CD-ROM is simply a variation of the familiar audio compact disc. Today, almost every computer is sold with a CD-ROM drive. A CD can currently hold about 5 billion bits of information (the equivalent of 100 books), and technological advances will increase the amount to more than 50 billion bits.

DVD (digital videodisc or digital versatile disc) is a newer form of optical disk storage technology. DVD technology allows video, audio, and computer data to be encoded onto a compact disc. DVD can store greater amounts of data than a common CD. A DVD player is needed to read digital videodiscs. This player is sold as a self-contained, stand-alone device or as an accessory to a computer. Digital videodisc technology may soon replace laser disc, CD-ROM, and audio CDs.

SCIENCE TECHNOLOGY SOCIETY

The growing awareness of how *science, technology,* and *society (STS)* interrelate is evident in the STS movement in science education. The NSTA adopted the *Science-Technology-Society: Science Education for the 1980s* position statement in 1982. Ten years later, the International Council of Associations for Science Education (ICASE) developed an *STS Yearbook* (Yager, 1992). The following year, the NSTA developed another STS document for teachers (Yager, 1993), indicating the continued importance of STS in schools. NSTA continues to advocate this important topic, stating that teacher preparation programs need to cause students to consider the applications of science in society and the relationship of science to engineering (NSTA, 2004). Their shared view is that persons educated

Science and Technology Standard

As a result of the activities in grades K–4, all students should
develop

- **Abilities of technological design**

- **Understanding about science and technology**

- **Abilities to distinguish between natural objects and objects
  made by humans**

(Content Standard E, National Research Council, 1996, pp. 135, 161.)

in the ideas and processes of science and technology can solve several of the problems we face today.

Included in the National Science Education Standards is a Science and Technology Standard (see Standards Link), which shows the relationship between the two entities. Scientific and technological literacy is essential for living, working, and decision making (NSTA, 1982). STS is seen as the teaching and learning of science in the context of human experiences. The NSTA advocates that science should be real to students. An indication of this is providing scientific problems for students to solve that are based on issues of genuine interest to them.

STS in the Classroom

The Science and Technology Standard outlines ways for students to consider such issues as the need to burn coal to produce electricity against the resulting acid rain, thermal pollution, and greenhouse effect. Elementary or middle school students try to answer questions such as the energy and the environment question, follow up by testing their answers to the questions, and then take action based on their findings. Another example of an STS question is, "What is the effect on natural resources if the world's population surpasses 14 billion people in the next century versus the religious and other aspects of controlling human growth?" The STS issue investigation and action instruction model (Rubba, Wiesenmayer, Rye, & Ditty, 1996) is a good example of this teaching strategy because of its four critical factors:

- Foundations
- Awareness
- Investigations
- Action phases (p. 25)

See Web Destinations for
Chapter 7 on the
Companion Website
(*http://www.
prenhall.com/peters*) for
other resources related
to STS.

The model begins with the *foundations* phase as the teacher assists students in understanding the nature of science and technology and their interactions. In the electricity example, for instance, the teacher guides students to finding out that electricity production is a result of scientific research. Generating electricity has trade-offs, such as gaseous emissions, that are balanced against society's need for electricity.

The teacher then discusses and guides students in understanding the concepts and issues related to the topic during the *awareness* phase. The issue would be studied from every aspect, including the scientific and social science points of view. What are the gases emitted? Are other pollutants produced? What are the alternatives to coal-fired plants? What laws and other regulations relate to the topic? What processes are used in generating electricity?

Students then experiment and investigate the STS issue during the *investigations* phase. They visit a plant to see the generation process. Students experiment with making electricity on their own or investigate the effects of production.

During the *action* phase, students develop ways to take action on the issue. Can **green energy** be purchased in their community? If not, what steps can be done to change this? Can energy be conserved to help reduce any negative effects on the environment?

Green energy is energy that comes from renewable resources such as that produced by wind turbines, solar cells, and biofuels.

In keeping with current reform efforts, science educators who advocate STS agree that the overall goal for science education is to develop scientifically literate graduates who can apply science to everyday life. These citizens will be able to understand the issues, take responsibility for the issues, and make informed decisions on these issues. These goals are further reflected in the science education benchmarks and standards.

Benchmarks, Standards, and Technology

According to authors of the *Benchmarks for Science Literacy* (American Association for the Advancement of Science [AAAS], 1993) and *Blueprints for Reform* (AAAS, 1998), educational research on what students know about technology is insufficient. We need to know more about how technology relates to science, or the structures and functions of the designed world. Because of the lack of research, the author groups suggest that technology is generally ignored in schools.

Technology can, nevertheless, be useful in developing scientific inquiry skills. Authors of the standards include science and technology in the content standards for students at every grade level (see the Science and Technology Standard on page 178).

See Web Destinations for Chapter 7 on the Companion Website (*http://www.prenhall.com/peters*) for technology education standards and information.

Students and Technology

You may have witnessed a child taking apart an old appliance, nailing together some old boards, building a bridge for toy cars in a sandbox, or otherwise interacting with

Visit an Inquiry Classroom
Science Technology and Society

View the *Science Technology and Society* video in the "Nature of Science" section of the Companion CD. Mr. McKnight and his students discuss earthworm reproduction and gender.

Review the video and ask yourself the following:
- What societal implications could be associated with what is being discussed in the video segment?
- What technological implications could be associated with what is being discussed in the video segment?

In the story *Alien Earthworms Changing Ecology of Northeast Forests* (McLeish, 2003), scientists Josef Görres and José Amador's research into the possible impact earthworms may have on the environment is discussed as follows:

> The researchers are also trying to determine whether the worms are increasing the amount of carbon dioxide and methane going into the atmosphere. "The leaf litter and duff layers consist almost entirely of stored carbon, so when the worms eat and process the litter and duff, they release carbon dioxide and possibly methane in their burrows," Amador said. "We're not predicting catastrophe, of course, since the total amount of the gases they release is small. But it's a previously unaccounted potential source of greenhouse gases entering the atmosphere."

Slater (2003) also found that "earthworms appear to be stripping some North American forests of their most essential feature: the decomposing leaves and other forest litter called duff, which provides nutrients and sanctuary to new generations of trees, plants and animals." What other STS impact could there be related to native and nonnative species of earthworms invading an area? Record your ideas and the answers to these questions in your portfolio or use the Companion Website to share your ideas.

technology. You will find that children are, without a doubt, curious about technology and the designed world.

As elementry and middle school students begin explorations of technology, they understand what is human-made and what is natural. Their designs are less elaborate or functional, and they cannot easily distinguish between science and technology. By the end of the elementary years, however, students will use scientific inquiry skills to assist them in a design that will solve a problem. They will also begin to see the important relationship between science and technology. Science is the quest for answers to questions about the universe. *Science relies on technology to assist us in discovering the universe. Technology is the application of science.* Technology supports science, helps us satisfy our wants and needs, and extends our capabilities to do those things.

As you read the Focus on Inquiry: Experiencing Technology Education, determine if the children are simply playing or if there is an objective in mind with this activity. Would you consider this lesson carefully structured to promote technological literacy? Should elementary or middle school students even be involved in design activities?

Focus on Inquiry

Experiencing Technology Education

A group of six- and seven-year-olds had completed some grouping and sorting of materials (fabrics, plastics, glass, wood, paper products, and so on) and an exploration of "connectors" (glues, brass fasteners, string, clips, nails, and so forth). They had learned how to use saws, drills, and hammers. They were given a twelve- by eighteen-inch sheet of paper and asked to design something they would like and be able to build that moved in some way. They were told they could use materials from their classroom recycling center such as cartons, containers of all sorts, fabric, dowels, cardboard, wheels, and centimeter wood strips. They could also use materials brought from home. The connectors they had explored were available.

Drawing was not new to these children. They had drawn from nature in their science studies, they had illustrated stories, and drawing materials were always an option for art or classroom choice times. They had built three-dimensional constructions in the block corner and in the classroom recycling center. However, they had never been asked to draw something to be constructed in the future and then to build from their drawings. The processes of moving from two to three dimensions and of committing themselves to a plan (as opposed to planning and creating as they went along) were new experiences for these children.

Ben, a six-year-old, drew a rather conventional house with a chimney on the roof and smoke coming out of the chimney. Looking over the materials, he passed by the rectangular boxes and selected a one-liter soda bottle as the basic structure for his house. He cut out freehand a door and some windows from construction paper and taped them to the bottle. Then he chose a dowel, taped a curvy piece of black construction paper to the end and showed his teacher where he wanted the two holes for the dowel to pass through the bottle. He inserted the dowel and proceeded to push and pull it up and down, making the "smoke" extend and retreat from the chimney. He was not bothered at all by the fact that the house looked nothing at all like his drawing. What counted was that the smoke moved in and out of the chimney. With construction successfully completed, his teacher asked him to evaluate his product. Did it come out the way he had planned it? Was there something that moved? A huge smile of satisfaction spread over his face. Yes, this was exactly what he had in mind, he said; the smoke moved out of the chimney (and back in), and he wondered if he could take it home and show his parents what he had made.

Across the room, two eight-year-olds were constructing boats they wanted to move by rubber-band-powered paddle wheels. They had completed their planning and construction and were now ready to test the boats. A small plastic wading pool was filled with water, the paddle wheels were wound up, and the boats were launched. As the boats moved forward, their structures began to come apart; the children realized to their dismay that the glue must be dissolving in the water.

"We should have used a glue gun."

Their teacher watched as they reassembled the boats, connecting the wooden frames with a glue gun, a time-consuming process; they tried them again in the water, and once again watched as they fell apart. The teacher debated whether or not to suggest that they test connecting materials in the water on just a few pieces of wood rather than take the time to reassemble the entire boat. She decided to let them do it their way, and hoped they would come to this realization themselves. If not, she would bring the subject up.

"We'll have to nail them together. Can we have some small nails?"

On the third try, the boat held together and paddled across the classroom pond. Delighted and relieved that their hard work and tenacity had paid off, the boat builders were not at all ready to think about shortcuts to finding the right materials to connect wood for use in water. For these students, this lesson would have to wait for another time. For their teacher, there still remained the issue of how much to tell students ahead of time and how much to let them discover, or not discover, for themselves.

The boys' classmate Kylie eyed the recycling center, spotted a shoe box, and decided to build a car that would carry her stuffed bear. She remembered her brother once built a rubber-band-powered car. Her drawing was a rectangle with small wheels. She selected four plastic wheels and found two dowels that fit through their centers. Using a ruler, she carefully planned where to punch holes in the shoe box so the axles would be parallel to the ends of the box. She attached the wheels to the outside of the box, front and back. She then began to puzzle out how to wind up a rubber band. Once she had an idea of how it might work, she asked her teacher if there was another box she could use to try out her ideas because she "didn't want to mess up my car." Unlike the boat builders, Kylie had discovered on her own the concept of building a prototype or model. Once she worked out a rubber band system, making her mistakes somewhere other than on her car, she was ready to complete her project.

Although the entire project was ultimately successful, asking the children to draw their desired object on paper as part of the design for the project may have been too ambitious. Children this age frequently find it difficult to conceptualize three-dimensional construction through two-dimensional drawing, and they become confused by the task. They may worry about their inability to transform their drawing into the object they imagined, and shy away from the task. For example, it is unclear how Ben's drawing helped him in the design of his project, which bore no relation to the picture he drew.

From Technology Education in the Classroom *(pp. 68–69), by S. A. Raizen, P. Sellwood, R. D. Todd, & M. Vickers, 1995, San Francisco: Jossey-Bass. Copyright © 1995 by Jossey-Bass. Reprinted by permission of John Wiley & Sons, Inc.*

TECHNOLOGY EDUCATION AND SCIENCE

Children's need to explore is a concrete reminder of our need throughout history to explore, understand, and survive in our environment (Dunn & Larson, 1990). Technology has been with us since the Stone Age when humans first began to modify their environment with the tools available to them. Throughout history, technology has played a significant role in the overall societal progress of humans, their struggle for freedom, and their advances in scientific knowledge. With technology being so prominent to everyday life, why is it so neglected in our schools?

Teaching Tips   The study of technological advances is a good topic for social studies and science integration.

The term *technopeasants* refers to the common people who are left feeling that they are the victims of technology as a result of their lack of technical literacy (Pucel, 1995). Similarly, educators are viewed as *techno-ostriches* if they hide their heads in the sand when it comes to implementing technologies to create changes in schools (Papert, 1996). Either terminology insinuates that *technology education must play a larger role in the curriculum*. As suggested by some educators, society will not have future technicians if we do not integrate the curriculum and include technology education in today's classrooms (Hall & Bannatyne, 1999).

Resnick, Bruckman, and Martin (1999) question the appropriateness of children learning to play the piano versus learning to play the stereo. They cite that they would rather children become "creators" and not just "consumers" (p. 150), because this allows for a deeper understanding of music. Likewise, we want our students to design rather than just use technology.

We see technology in the schools evolving from two viewpoints. In the science curriculum, technology is used to demonstrate theories of science and to help develop inquiry skills. Technology is also a core element of the less familiar *technology education*. What specifically is technology education? It is a K–12 academic discipline designed to integrate academic and career skills with an emphasis on problem solving and decision making. In short, technology education focuses on working collaboratively through the application of technology. Whereas science seeks understanding, technology seeks solutions to problems.

To illustrate, during the elementary years, students should study such areas as "materials and their properties and how they can be used; energy in a variety of forms; control, in the form of switches, catches, valves, and mechanisms; and information used for communication" (Raizen, Sellwood, Todd, & Vickers, 1995, p. 67). Technology education should be a part of your everyday curriculum.

How can you integrate more technology into the curriculum? What are some technological areas that can be explored? The general categories to explore with your students include energy, materials, manufacturing, communication, bio-related, construction, and transportation technology.

Energy Technology

Energy comes in many forms: chemical, electrical, mechanical, radiant, thermal, and nuclear. Energy is one of the most important science and technology issues. Energy conservation awareness allows most people to realize now that we must continue to move away from exploiting the environment and toward conserving or using it wisely. Not only are energy resources of the planet limited, but also almost every year we see a greater demand on these resources from all nations. The history of progress in nations closely parallels a

A student engaged in a "mining for energy" activity.

rise in energy use. As fuels disappear, more attention will be turned to tapping into relatively inexhaustible sources such as solar, wind, tidal, and geothermal energy. Material progress and swelling populations have also increased air, water, and land pollution, along with the growing problem of managing solid waste.

Working on energy-related activities will help students construct an understanding of the importance of energy. The candle-powered steam engine and the candle-powered steamboat are two design activities that upper-elementary and middle school students could explore. The candle-powered steamboat requires an old-fashioned oilcan, a candle, and a milk carton. The steam engine uses an oilcan, a candle, wire, and an aluminum turbine blade. (See McCormack, 1981, for the full lesson on candle-powered steam engines and steamboats.)

We know that the sun is our ultimate source of energy. To demonstrate to our students the power of the sun, try cooking marshmallows. Students can design a solar cooker to capture the sun's rays in the cooker (see Miller, 1998, for an example of a solar cooker).

Materials Technology

Materials are important to technology because there would be no technical objects without materials. Materials can be the fossil fuel hydrocarbons that are mined or drilled such as coal, oil, and natural

See Web Destinations for Chapter 7 on the Companion Website (*http://www. prenhall.com/peters*) for more information on energy teaching ideas and resources.

Teaching **T**ips | See resources such as *Machine Shop* (Battcher et al., 1993), *Under Construction* (Gossett, 1997), and *Inventa Book of Mechanisms* (Catlin, n.d.) for technology project ideas.

Teaching **T**ips | Remember that safety is a consideration with this solar activity. Be sure to warn the students not to look directly at the sun or to stay out in the sunlight for prolonged periods.

gas. Materials can be genetic materials harvested from farming, forestry, or husbandry such as wheat, wood, or wool. They can be minerals that are mined such as metal ores, nonmetallic minerals, precious gems, or ceramics and clays. The study of materials helps students develop their observational skills as they interact with various materials. Students explore physical properties and determine whether materials are artificial or natural. They begin to see the need for specific materials in some designs. They also find that some materials can be used in a variety of ways.

Discussions of materials can originate with the story of *Three Little Pigs* (Feasey, 1999). Students investigate properties of the items that the pigs used for their houses, as well as several other materials. Ask your students which materials would be best if they were designing a house or a roof. Now have your students make up newspaper headlines about the materials the pigs used or should have used.

The *anoraks* activity is a primary activity during which students explore the materials of an Eskimo parka or heavy jacket. They are challenged to design an anorak for a season. This activity is a good integration with social studies if you want to develop a thematic unit (see Stringer, 1996, for the full activity).

A rough-and-smooth-surface activity is a good way for students to investigate materials (Stringer, 1998). They can even design wooden ramps of various textures and experiment on the effects of friction. Distance traveled, speed of an object down a ramp, height of the ramp, and the relation to surface friction are some beginning variables to explore. Students can also examine the use and integrity of structures and compare such variables as strength, weight, and reinforcement (Tickle, Lancaster, Devereux, & Marshall, 1990).

Upper-elementary and middle school students can design an experiment to explore bike helmet materials in relation to safety (Stringer, 1996). They can look at various helmet types and which materials are better at protection of the cranium. This activity is a good lead into the skeletal system and the protection of bones. *Designs in Science: Materials* (Morgan & Morgan, 1994) provides background information on materials and activities to extend materials investigations.

Manufacturing Technology

> **Custom production** is the making of products one at a time. Intermittent production is the making of a limited quantity of a product at one time.

> **Continuous production** is a steady, assembly-line, mass production of items.

Manufacturing involves using materials to make parts, putting parts together for a finished product that has value, and supplying the products to meet a demand. Primary manufacturing processes involve converting raw materials into industrial materials; this may include changing natural gas into plastic sheets or pellets, wood into paper stock, bauxite into rolled aluminum, or wheat into flour. Secondary manufacturing processes include forming, casting, molding, separating, conditioning, assembling, or finishing the manufactured items. Production can also be **custom** or **continuous.**

Activities that model the manufacturing process are good problem-solving tasks for students. Cooperative groups of students can be assigned to design a conveyor belt made from common materials. The conveyer belt should be able to move products effectively from one location to another. Students could also design a robot that is able to pick up and move materials (Miller, 1998). These design challenges involve all the process skills of science. Robotics kits from Lego Dacta™ are one way to integrate the use of the computer in the design (*http://www.pitsco-legodacta.com/*).

Teaching Tips

Making paper is one design activity in which elementary and middle school students enjoy learning about manufacturing. Making writing paper from toilet paper (Stringer, 1996) is generally less disappointing than making paper from recycled scrap paper.

Communication Technology

Communications include the transfer of information from one place to another. This information could be raw data from spacecraft exploring the solar system, organized data called information, or information that is used for a purpose called knowledge. Following are ways to transmit information, or communicate:

- *Printed communications,* or images printed on a material such as paper
- *Telecommunications,* or telephone, computer networks, radio, and television
- *Photographic communications,* or digital and film pictures
- *Technical communications,* or blueprints, technical illustrations, and engineering drawings

 Have your students consider communication with people from other countries who do not speak English, along with communication with alien beings. The students can brainstorm what to communicate, how to communicate, and what materials may be needed to design a communications system.

In summary, communication technology is people, their information exchange skills, and the equipment or other tools that help send and receive messages.

What if we were to communicate with space aliens? An interesting design activity for students to consider is how we would communicate with beings from other worlds (Association for Science Education [ASE], 1995).

Students may discuss or make presentations on environmental issues as a way to develop their communications skills (Miller, 1998). Technology has both positive and negative effects on our planet. For this activity, group students on both sides of such issues as the ozone layer, the greenhouse effect, vehicle emissions, and the use of landfills. Have students prepare a debate of the issues to be argued in front of an audience.

Communications is a rapidly changing area of technology. Discuss with your students any changes that they may be aware of or changes that their parents or guardians at home may have talked about. You may want to use this activity to discuss a general timeline for telecommunications (Oxlade, 1997).

Bio-Related Technology

Bio-related technology includes the disciplines of agricultural technologies, health care technologies, and technologies related to living things such as genetics. From the food you eat, the water you drink, the clothes you wear, and the health care you receive, biotechnology touches all aspects of our lives.

 Discuss how science and technology have changed current farming methods.

Technology is present in preserving and preparing foods. If the color or texture is not right, the food will not be pleasing to eat. Experimentation can be done to see the science behind food and what is appealing. Try arranging various foods for birds or other animals to eat to test which foods are most popular (Stringer, 1996). Does color make a difference? Try using M&Ms to design an experiment involving classmates. What are the variables? What are the results? Discuss genetic farming (Jefferis, 1999) and the history of past farming methods (Roden, 1996).

Designing an experiment that shows the technology used in producing hand soaps demonstrates biotechnology in action. Students can experiment with eliminating microbes by washing hands (International Council of Associations for Science Education [ICASE], 1988). Try using regular soaps versus antibacterial soaps, liquid soaps versus solid

Have students discuss whether cloned humans would have the same fingerprints on their fingers or the same DNA "fingerprint" in their cells.

soaps, or short washing periods versus longer washing periods as variables. Agar is a nutrient medium available from scientific suppliers. It is put on sterilized plates for this activity. Students touch the agar on the plates after various hand washes; the microorganism their hands left behind will then grow on the agar.

Students may also want to discuss how biotechnology is used in courtrooms. Rainis and Nassis (1998) discuss the use of DNA testing as a replacement for fingerprints. This is a good area to integrate STS issues.

Construction Technology

Construction is the process of producing structures for shelter or transportation such as houses, skyscrapers, or other buildings, stadiums, roads, tunnels, bridges, airports, or monuments. The four generally accepted types of construction are residential, commercial, public, and industrial. Technology plays a key role in helping the structures meet the personal and environmental needs of the construction project. Science is also involved in significant ways. The materials, such as plastics or alloys, used in many structures are the result of scientific research applied technologically. Geologic research on the foundations of structures is important for buildings such as skyscrapers.

A technological extension to animal and habitat study is to have students create a PowerPoint R or other slide show on the habitats of animals (Donato, 1998).

Elementary and middle school students can further develop observation and inference skills when they investigate natural structures. Looking at bird homes may result in inferences about why the birds construct the nests as they do or build them in the places they do. Adaptation to the environment is evidenced by how animals build their homes. Habitat study is a good scientific exploration for students.

Lasers are used in many construction projects. An electronic distance meter or laser transit saves time over less technical tools. Many students with access to laser pointers and mirrors can design experiments that will provide results similar to those obtained by the construction equipment.

Bridge activities are a popular technology activity. Designing a bridge that supports the most weight in relation to its own weight is a good upper-elementary or middle school activity. Bridges can be built with construction paper (Eichelberger & Larson, 1993) or toothpicks (Pollard, 1985).

Transportation Technology

Transportation technology includes air, rail, water, pipeline, space, and automobile or truck transportation. The connections between transportation and science are numerous. For instance, fuel types, the design of the vehicle to reduce friction, and alternative energy sources are examples for scientific discussion and research.

An activity that you can try with elementary and middle school students is to send e-mail to other countries and ask students there about their transportation systems. This activity provides a good contrast and comparison to different transportation systems and helps develop communication skills.

Observation and classification skills are sharpened if primary students cut transportation-related pictures from magazines and classify them in various ways. They can look at air versus water or land vehicles. Sizes of vehicles, the numbers of passengers, or energy use by the vehicle produce other classification schemes. Try to have the students develop their own classification system.

One design challenge that works with upper-elementary or middle school students is building mousetrap cars (Balmer, 1997). With the assistance of their parents, students build and race cars that are powered by mousetraps. The car that goes the farthest is the winner.

Rubber-band transportation can be explored with rubber-band-powered airplanes or vehicles (Eichelberger & Larson, 1993). Students use simple materials to design and build airplanes or other vehicles that work with the use of rubber bands. Experimentation skills are involved as students explore the effects of winding the rubber band too tight or not enough, reducing friction of the vehicle, placing weight, finding ways to make the vehicles track a straight line, or designing propellers. Balloon-powered cars (Miller, 1998) offer similar experimentation skill development for upper-elementary or middle school students.

Building model hovercraft is an interesting design activity related to transportation (ICASE, 1987). Balloons and wooden disks are all that are needed to make simple hovercraft.

Paper airplane design is another great transportation technology activity. Male pilots and astronauts are better known than female pilots and astronauts. Therefore, one way to initiate this design contest is to read about pilots in *Females First in Their Fields: Air and Space* (Buchanan, 1999). Have a challenge to see which team of girls can make the most paper airplanes fly over a 5-meter (20-foot) mark in 1 minute. Supply each team with a stack of copier paper and a marked off area to fly the planes. Holding group brainstorming and trial sessions beforehand will enhance flight distances.

As with other activities, adjust variables such as times and distances according to your students' developmental needs. It may be helpful to include the five-stage framework for technological design provided by the standards (NRC, 1996, pp. 137–138, 165–166):

1. Identify a simple problem.
2. Propose a solution.
3. Implement proposed solutions.
4. Evaluate a product or design.
5. Communicate a problem, design, and solution.

The process begins with students renaming the problem using their own words. Next, students form possible solutions—given time, costs, and materials. Then students work together to try solutions and see how their design solves the problem. Finally, students communicate how they solved the problem, including their design and evaluation.

Technology and Career Awareness

Technology is concerned with controlling or managing objects and events in improved ways. With the prevalence of technology in today's society, it is vital to prepare the future workforce for these occupations. Many career opportunities are related to technology (Schwartz & Wolfgang, 1996).

Research scientists, professional engineers, skilled technicians, and computer operators are required to have the scientific knowledge to plan and design useful inventions and creative solutions. Demand will continue to grow for workers qualified in the areas of environmental engineering, biological engineering and biotechnology, energy systems, telecommunications research and maintenance, and advanced transportation systems. Inventions and inventors are good topics to explore for promoting technology awareness and showing careers related to technology.

See *http://www.prenhall. com/peters* for references to books on invention topics.

Gender Issues and Technology

Technology topics lend themselves to opening up a new world for girls of all age levels because technology is a subject for everyone (Cross, 1998). We need to involve females in technological topics and activities when possible, not because the future workforce will rely on highly skilled, technologically literate women, but because we owe it to all our students to allow them the opportunity to be able to make good career choices later in life. These career choices will be possible because we have provided a solid scientific and technological background for males and females during the elementary and middle school years.

Look at your own practices in the classroom either now or in the future. Ask yourself these questions:

- Do my female students feel comfortable engaging in science and technology activities?
- Do my female students ask the same number of questions or provide a similar number of responses as my male students?
- Do I give equal amount of attention to both male and female students?
- Are female students embarrassed to take part in activities?

It may help to videotape yourself, or have another person observe you, and then complete a checklist to see whether you are being biased. Whether you are a male or female teacher, you may be biased toward boys when it comes to science and technology. Another tactic is to discuss careers and what future courses students should take or activities they should accomplish to be able to achieve their career goals. Also, make sure that you occasionally set up all-female learning groups, forcing girls to participate and not sit back and allow the boys to take control. Use books that focus on successful females in the sciences and technological areas. Make everyone in your class comfortable while learning or asking questions. Finally, begin now to collect resources that will assist you in your classroom.

> **Teaching Tips**
>
> One good starting point is *Girls and Technology Idea Book* and *Girls and Technology Resource Guide.* These publications are available from the National Coalition of Girls' Schools, 228 Main Street, Concord, MA 01742 or *http://www.ncgs.org.*

Technology and the Curriculum

The following notions about teaching science still exist today:

> Even a new science textbook is dated by the time it's distributed.
> I can't teach science. Who has time to keep up with it?

Contrary to these views, the basic ideas and processes taught in the science curriculum last a long time. Scientific information and vocabulary do change, but this is expected when you consider the nature of science. This changeability is all the more reason to teach about the nature of science and STS. Discussing the application of science in new technologies helps show students how science theories can be modified. Consider the shift from copper telephone wires to fiber optics, the change in the precise measurement of the speed of light from 186,198 miles per second to 186,282 miles per second, or the discovery of new subatomic particles.

Basic concepts and generalizations in effective science programs are often linked to technological applications, aeronautics, telecommunications, electric circuitry, soil conservation, and food processing. Learning about these applications can change the way children view many of the useful inventions at home and in school. Understanding how systems operate develops a realistic perspective toward the mechanisms of everyday life. A well-constructed elementary curriculum will be rooted in the basic ideas and processes of science. Technological investigations, however, will enhance science understanding by providing concrete examples of science in action.

See Web Destinations for Chapter 7 on the Companion Website (*http://www.prenhall.com/peters*) for links to current science news.

Visit an Inquiry Classroom
Technology Education in the Classroom

View the *Preparing Resources* video in the "Model Inquiry Unit" section of the Companion CD. Mr. McKnight and his students discuss some of the things that they have found out about earthworms.

Review the video and ask yourself the following:
- How is communication technology being used in the study of earthworms?
- What other forms of technology (e.g., energy, materials, manufacturing, communication, biotechnology, construction, or transportation) are being used, or could be used, in the study of earthworms?

Cornell entomologist John Losey and his colleagues sparked a worldwide controversy with the publication of a scientific paper in the journal *Nature* (1999) where he reported laboratory findings that Monarch butterfly larvae died after eating milkweed plants containing pollen from genetically modified corn. What effects could genetically modified crops have on earthworms? Research this topic and record your ideas and the answers to these questions in your portfolio or use the Companion Website to share your ideas.

CW

Summary

- A computer center can be set up and run much like a regular learning center. Computer software can include such programs as tutorials and games, multimedia, simulations, Internet access tools, spreadsheets, databases, word processing, and research tools.
- Science technology society (STS) is the teaching and learning of science in the context of human experiences. Advocates of STS think that science should be real to students and that scientific problems provided for students to solve should be based on issues that are of genuine interest to students. The STS issue investigation and action instruction model

has four crucial phases: foundations, awareness, investigations, and action phases.
- Technology use in the science classroom evolves from two viewpoints. One is from using technology to demonstrate theories of science and to help develop inquiry skills. The other is from the applied technology-based curriculum called technology education. Technology education is an academic discipline designed to integrate academic and career skills with an emphasis on problem solving and decision making.
- Areas of technology include energy, materials, manufacturing, communication, biotechnology, construction, and transportation.

Reflection

Companion CD

1. Look at the "The Nervous System" lesson linked to the *Zone of Proximal Development* video on the Companion CD. How could you modify this lesson so that students could incorporate individual multimedia projects?
2. Look at the "Environment Is Important to Living Things" lesson linked to the *Private Speech* video on the Companion CD. How could you modify this

lesson plan so that students could incorporate Internet access tools?
3. Look at "The Earthworm and Soil" lesson linked to the *Scaffolding* video on the Companion CD. How could you modify this lesson plan so that students could incorporate spreadsheets or databases into the lesson?

Portfolio Ideas

1. You can learn *from* computers, *with* computers, and *about* computers. You can also learn to think with computers or use computers to manage learning. In your portfolio, list examples of how computers and software can be used for each of these categories.

2. Check with your field placement site and college or university to see whether it celebrates National Science and Technology Week (*http://www.nsf.gov/od/lpa/nstw/geninfo/brochure.htm*). How can you become involved with your future students? Write some sample ideas in your portfolio.

3. Look at the National Science Teachers Association (NSTA) website (*http://www.nsta.org/programs/*) for technology-related competitions that would involve your future elementary or middle school students. Which competitions are especially helpful in developing technological literacy? Enter ideas in your portfolio.

4. Read *The Trouble with Dad* (Cole, 2004) and *It Could Still Be a Robot* (Fowler, 1997). In your portfolio, share with your class about the use of robots in everyday life. Also discuss society's images of scientists and inventors.

5. Look at *Standards for Technological Literacy: Content for the Study of Technology* from the International Technology Education Association (*http://www.iteawww.org/*) and National Educational Technology Standards from the International Society for Technology in Education (*http://cnets.iste.org/*). In your portfolio, compare and contrast these standards and the National Science Education Standards from the NRC (*http://stills.nap.edu/html/nses/*).

References

American Association for the Advancement of Science (AAAS). (1993). *Benchmarks for science literacy*. New York: Oxford University Press.

American Association for the Advancement of Science (AAAS). (1998). *Blueprints for reform*. New York: Oxford University Press.

Association for Science Education (ASE). (1995). *Science in space*. Hatfield, Herts., UK: Author.

Balmer, A. (1997). *Mouse-trap cars: A teacher's guide*. Austin, TX: Doc Fizzix Comix.

Battcher, D., Martini, K., Shennan, W. B., Erickson, S., Rogers, C., & Wiebe, A. (1993). *Machine shop*. Fresno, CA: AIMS Education Foundation.

Beaty, J. J. (1990). *Computer as a paintbrush: Creative use for the PC in the preschool classroom*. Upper Saddle River, NJ: Merrill/Prentice Hall.

Buchanan, D. (1999). *Female firsts in their fields: Air and space*. Philadelphia: Chelsea House.

Catlin, D. (n.d.). *Inventa book of mechanisms*. London: Valiant Technology.

Claris. (1993). *ClarisWorks 2.0 in the classroom*. Santa Clara, CA: Author.

Classroom Connect. (1998). Catastrophe! *lessonplan.net, 2*(5), 1–48.

Cole, B. (2004). *The trouble with dad*. London, UK: Egmont Books.

Cross, A. (1998). *Coordinating design and technology across the primary school*. New York: Falmer Press.

Donato, D. (1998). *Integrating technology into the science curriculum*. Westminster, CA: Teacher Created Materials.

Dunn, S., & Larson, R. (1990). *Design technology: Children's engineering*. New York: Falmer Press.

Ebenezer, J. V., & Lau, E. (2003). *Science on the Internet: A resource for K-12 teachers*. Upper Saddle River, NJ: Merrill/Prentice Hall.

Eichelberger, B., & Larson, C. (1993). *Constructions for children: Projects in design technology*. Palo Alto, CA: Dale Seymour.

Feasey, R. (1999). *Primary science & literacy links*. Hatfield, Herts., UK: Association for Science Education.

Fowler, A. (1997) *It could still be a robot*. New York: Children's Press.

Froseth, S., & Poppe, B. (1995). *Internet activities using scientific data (National Oceanic and Atmospheric Administration)*. Washington, DC: Government Printing Office.

Gossett, C. (1997). *Under construction*. Fresno, CA: AIMS Education Foundation.

Haag, T. (1996). *Internet for kids*. Huntington Beach, CA: Teacher Created Materials.

Hall, R., & Bannatyne M. (1999). Technology education and the 21st century. *Connect, 24*(4), 1–3. *www.unesco.org/education/educprog/ste/index.html*

International Council of Associations for Science Education (ICASE). (1987). *Experiments and activities on the three laws of dynamics: A teacher resource book commemorating the 300th anniversary of Newton's Principia 1687–1987*. Hong Kong: Author.

International Council of Associations for Science Education (ICASE). (1988). *Pasteur and microbes: A teacher resource guide commemorating the 100th year of the Pasteur Institute 1888–1988*. Hong Kong: Author.

Jefferis, D. (1999). *Cloning: Frontiers of genetic engineering*. New York: Crabtree.

Henry J. Kaiser Family Foundation. (2002). *Key facts: Children and video games*. Menlo Park, CA: Author. Retrieved September 27, 2004, from *www.kff.org/entmedia/loader.cfm?url=/commonspot/security/getfile.cfm&pageID=14092*

Henry J. Kaiser Family Foundation. (2004). *Survey snapshot: The digital divide*. Menlo Park, CA: Author. Retrieved September 27, 2004, from *www.kff.org/entmedia/loader.cfm?url=/commonspot/security/getfile.cfm&PageID=46366*

Koufman-Frederick, A., Lillie, M., Pattison-Gordon, L., Watt, D. L., & Carter, R. (1999). *Electronic collaboration: A practical guide for educators*. Providence, RI: LAB at Brown University.

Kozma, R., & Shank, P. (1998). Connecting with the 21st century: Technology in support of educational reform. In C. Dede (Ed.),

1998 ASCD Yearbook: Learning with technology (pp. 3–27). Alexandria, VA: ASCD.

Losey, J. E., Rayor, L. S., & Carter, M. E. (1999). Transgenic pollen harms monarch larvae. *Nature, 399,* 214.

McCormack, A. J. (1981). *Inventors workshop.* Torrance, CA: Fearon Teacher Aids.

McLeish, T. (2003, September). Alien earthworms changing ecology of Northeast forests. *The University Pacer.* Kingston, RI: University of Rhode Island. Retrieved December 23, 2004, from *http://advance.uri.edu/pacer/september2003/story12.htm*

Means, B. (1994). Introduction: Using technology to advance educational goals. In B. Means (Ed.), *Technology and education reform* (pp. 1–21). San Francisco: Jossey-Bass.

Miller, L. (1998). *KidTech: Hands-on problem solving with design technology for grades 5–8.* Menlo Park, CA: Dale Seymour.

Morgan, S., & Morgan, A. (1994). *Designs in science: Materials.* New York: Facts on File.

National Research Council (NRC). (1996). *National science education standards.* Washington, DC: National Academy Press.

National Science Teachers Association (NSTA). (1982). *Science-technology-society: Science education for the 1980s. A position statement.* Washington, DC: Author.

National Science Teachers Association (NSTA). (1992). *The use of computers in science education* (NSTA position statement). *www.nsta.org/handbook/position.asp*

National Science Teacher Association (NSTA). (2004). *Science teacher preparation. A position statement.* Washington, DC: Author. Retrieved October 1, 2004, from *www.nsta.org/positionstatement&psid=42*

NetDay. (2004). *NetDay survey 2001.* Irvine, CA: Author. Retrieved September 27, 2004, from *www.netdaycompass.org/outside_frame.cfm?thispath=instance_id=1701^category_id=5&thislink=http://www.netday.org/anniversary_survey.htm&instance_id=3123*

Oxlade, C. (1997). *20th century inventions: Telecommunications.* Austin, TX: Raintree Steck-Vaughn.

Papert, S. (1996). *The connected family: Bridging the digital generation gap.* Marietta, GA: Longstreet Press.

Pollard, J. (1985). *Building toothpick bridges.* Palo Alto, CA: Dale Seymour.

Pucel, D. J. (1995). Developing technological literacy. *The Technology Teacher, 55*(3), 35–43.

Rainis, K. G., & Nassis, G. (1998). *Biotechnology projects for young scientists.* New York: Watts.

Raizen, S. A., Sellwood, P., Todd, R. D., & Vickers, M. (1995). *Technology education in the classroom.* San Francisco: Jossey-Bass.

Resnick, M., Bruckman, A., & Martin, F. (1999). Construction design: Creating new construction kits for kids. In A. Druin (Ed.), *The design of children's technology* (pp. 149–168). San Francisco: Morgan Kaufman.

Roberts, N., Blakeslee, G., Brown, M., & Lenk, C. (1990). *Integrating telecommunications into education.* Upper Saddle River, NJ: Prentice Hall.

Roden, K. (1996). *Then & now: Farming.* Brookfield, CT: Copper Beech Books.

Rubba, P. A., Wiesenmayer, R. L., Rye, J. A., & Ditty, T. (1996). The leadership institute in STS education: A collaborative teacher enhancement, curriculum development, and research project of Penn State and West Virginia University with rural middle/junior high school science teachers. *Journal of Science Teacher Education, 7*(1), 23–40.

Rutherford, F. J., & Ahlgren, A. (1990). *Science for all Americans.* New York: Oxford University Press.

Schwartz, L., & Wolfgang, T. (1996). *Children's occupational outlook handbook.* Auburn, CA: CFKR Career Materials.

Slater, E. (2003). *Earthworms show killer instinct.* Detroit: The Detroit News *detnews.com.* Downloaded December 23, 2004, from *www.detnews.com/2003/nation/0309/24/a08d-279359.htm*

Stringer, J. (Ed.). (1996). *Science & technology ideas for the under 85.* Hatfield, Herts., UK: Association for Science Education.

Stringer, J. (Ed.). (1998). *More science & technology ideas for the under 85.* Hatfield, Herts., UK: Association for Science Education.

Tickle, L., Lancaster, M., Devereux, M., & Marshall, E. (1990). Developing practical knowledge for teaching design and technology. In L. Tickle (Ed.), *Design and technology in primary school classrooms* (pp. 29–78). New York: Falmer Press.

Yager, R. E. (Ed.). (1992). *The status of science-technology-society reform efforts around the world.* Hong Kong: International Council of Associations for Science Education.

Yager, R. E. (Ed.). (1993). *What research says to the science teacher: The science technology society movement.* Arlington, VA: National Science Teachers Association.

Suggested Readings

Cross, G., & Szostak, R. (1995). *Technology and American society: A history.* Upper Saddle River, NJ: Prentice Hall. (a text about the history of invention and the interaction of technology and society)

Eggleston, J. (1996). *Teaching design and technology* (2nd ed.). Bristol, PA: Open University Press. (a text about design and technology and its role in the national curriculum of England)

Forcier, R. C., Descy, P.E. (1999). *The computer as an educational tool: Productivity and problem solving,* 2005 (4th ed.). Upper Saddle River, NJ: Merrill/Prentice Hall. (a book on the application of computers in the curriculum to include problem solving)

Kimbell, R., Stables, K., & Green, R. (1996). *Understanding practice in design and technology.* Bristol, PA: Open University Press. (a research-based text on technology education in England)

Reynolds, K. E., & Barba, R. H. (1996). *Technology for the teaching and learning of science.* Boston: Allyn & Bacon. (a comprehensive resource on integrating technology into science education)

CHAPTER 8

SCIENCE LEARNING OPPORTUNITIES

- What types of out-of-school science learning opportunities could support your science curriculum?
- What science learning community resources are available to support your teaching?
- How can you develop individual partners in education?

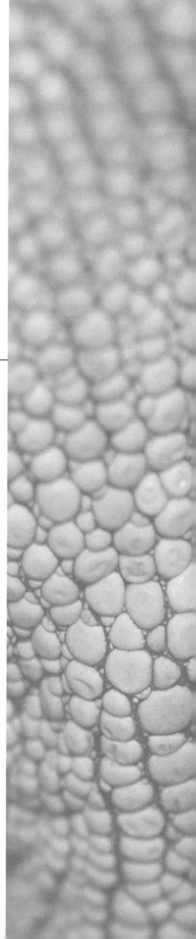

Focus on Inquiry

Zoos as Science Education Resources

Dr. Sue Dale Tunnicliffe
University of London, England, and ICASE Presecondary Science Representative

Visits to live animal collections can provide excellent opportunities for science learning. This is especially true if the teachers taking the students are familiar with the pedagogy of such visits and what opportunities are available. The knowledge that teachers need for zoo visits (and for visits to other animal collections such as natural history museums) includes the following:

- The stages of a visit in terms of the attention of students during the visit to the animals
- The features of anatomy and behaviors of the animals that the students are likely to notice spontaneously
- The colloquial or everyday names the students will use and any scientific names the teacher wants to be used
- The ability to identify and understand the concepts that the teacher wants the students to acquire

It is also very important to communicate to the chaperones who accompany your students the aims and objectives in terms of education outcomes, as well as the "housekeeping" details. If this is not done, the experience that the students within the chaperoned groups receive is different from that experienced by the students with you. It is up to us, as teachers, to ensure that each student has equal access to an effective experience.

Stages of a Visit

Students do not focus on exhibits in the same manner throughout their visit. It is important to be aware of the different phases within a school visit and to plan activities for your students accordingly.

First, groups undergo an orientation phase, when they look around and find their way. You can shorten the length of this stage by providing orientation to the site beforehand. Show slides or a video, provide the groups with a timetable, discuss opportunities for visits to the gift shop, tell when and where lunch is to be taken, and make other similar "house-keeping" arrangements.

Following orientation, the group embarks on the concentration phase: focusing on the tasks you have set, concentrating on exhibits, or participating in an educational activity provided by the zoo. It is unrealistic to expect the students to be involved in a focused task throughout the visit. After their concentration wanes, they move into the leisure-looking phase, during which their comments and observations are similar to those of "noneduca-tion" visitors. Finally, during the leave-taking phase, the attention of the group is con-cerned with gathering together for the journey home.

Spontaneous Observations

Elementary students, their accompanying adults, and family groups follow a fundamental pattern when looking at animal exhibits. It is important to be aware of this so that you can plan your activities for young students and the questions the accompanying adults or the activity sheets will ask of them; these are the starting points for science observations. Chil-dren spontaneously notice certain phenomena, such as names, anatomical features, and animal behavior, so use these as the introduction to the topic you plan.

Names

Children spontaneously use everyday or colloquial names for the animals. Primary grade students often use the term *animal* to mean only mammals, the term *bird* to mean any bird other than very memorable ones such as ostrich, eagle, penguin, vulture, and parrot. Rep-tiles are never referred to as such by children, and fish are called *fish* by children except for sharks, piranhas, eels, and any particular species about which the visitor happens to have firsthand knowledge, such as chubb or perch. Young students, those under age 7, are un-able to cope with two names for one animal; if they call a shark by that name, they deny that it is also a fish. Similarly, all insects and arachnids are "bugs" (in the everyday sense, not the zoological one) unless they know the name, such as ladybug. Spiders are just that unless they are a tarantula or black widow. You should use colloquial names but make it clear to everyone which scientific name(s) you want them to learn. This will allow you to develop zoological classification with the students during the visit or back in school.

Anatomical Features and Behavior

When looking at the structure of the animals, the students will spontaneously comment on the shape, size, color, any particularly unusual feature, such as horns, and parts that dis-rupt the body outline and/or move, such as legs and tails. If the animal is performing some behavior, the students will notice it. The position of the animal within the enclosure or display case is important to the students and school. Groups also refer in about half of all conversations to other aspects of the exhibit, such as rocks and trees or feeding bowls, of-ten in referring to the location of the animal.

If the animal is doing nothing, the students will query whether it is real, a common question posed about crocodilians in zoos. In museums, the students will be interested in the authenticity of the specimens and how they were prepared for display. Thus, the mean-ing of the word *real* depends on the context in which it is used. Often, children use the word *real* to refer to whether the animal is alive or not.

The science learning opportunities in a zoo for elementary students are content (sci-ence facts), the process (science method and inquiry), and science language and commu-nication skills.

The science content can be biological or physical. The biological content is either botanical (which highlights the role of plants in the food chain and forming the natural habitats of animals) or zoological.

Zoological studies can focus on taxonomic studies or on adaptations to the environment, including adaptations for feeding. Animal behaviors are used to establish the taxonomy of a specimen, as well as to study adaptation and forms. Behavior is thus another important area of study, in which students can make, record, and interpret their firsthand observations of the animals. Such studies require the students to observe salient features of animals, such as form, number of locomotory organs, and body covering.

Elementary students should be able to group animals into their major groups—mammals, reptiles, birds, fish, amphibians, arthropods, mollusks, and annelid worms. They should also be able to say why they make these categorizations. Students should be able to use **branching keys** and picture keys at grade 4, and by grade 6 they should be able to use and construct dichotomous keys. Students should develop an understanding of the needs of animals and the essential life processes and should be able to identify how individual specimens meet them. Natural history museums are often better equipped than zoos to provide realistic habitats, therefore providing a more satisfactory study of this feature.

Animal behavior studies can be frustrating if the students are looking for action, but action is just as important and should be used constructively. Find out before your visit which animals are likely to be active and visible within their enclosures. Ask about the pattern of the day of inactive and inaccessible animals so that the students can be given a time chart for these animals and can identify which part of their activity profile the animals are in when the students observe them. Ask the students to find the pattern of these animals' days so that the lack of activity is not a source of frustration, but an active learning experience.

Adaptation to the environment is a topic often well presented by zoo education programs. Decide which adaptations you wish your students to focus on. Very popular topics are birds' beaks (studying adaptations within this class of animals for different types of foods and, hence, different habitats), feet in mammals and birds, color of body coverings, and camouflage.

Branching key lists a common category at the top of the sheet (e.g., Fish) and then branches down into secondary categories (e.g., one top fin; two top fins). These are further branched into tertiary categories (e.g., flat or round body; long and thin; or short and round) and so on until specific species are identified (e.g., catfish, grouper).

See Chapter 8 Web Destinations on the Companion Website (*http://www.prenhall.com/peters*) for examples of picture keys available on the Internet.

Planning an Opportunity to Learn

Planning and delivering the opportunities for experiences that involve your students is essential. Instead of replying with a name when a student asks, "What is that animal?" ask the student to work out what it could be as far as she is able. Should a student identify an animal, ask him what features enabled him to make that identification.

Science is about communicating. If scientists don't communicate, no one else knows of their work. Encourage your students to share their observations and findings in a variety of ways: a science report, drama, art, journalist's report, or spoken address.

SCIENCE LEARNING OPPORTUNITIES

As you may infer from the Focus on Inquiry: Zoos as Science Education Resources, trips to the zoo are an important science education **opportunity to learn.** Together with other forms of learning opportunities in the community, trips to a zoo will round out students' science experiences and help them construct understandings of biodiversity and conservation.

Opportunity to learn refers to quality of the instruction and curricular program provided for students.

Mrs. Blackwelder's Class Trip

Mrs. Blackwelder and her third-grade class are excited today. They are planning a trip to the state park. Ranger Kellison will be discussing the wolf population and the recovery of a young wolf that was recently shot. She is glad to see the students' interest in learning about wolves.

Teaching Tips
The wolf theme is a good topic for integrated activities. Check the Companion Website (*http://www.prenhall.com/peters*) for ideas related to this topic.

The idea for this trip began 2 weeks ago as a social studies experience when the class read variations of the story of Little Red Riding Hood. Everyone became interested in comparing and contrasting accounts of this fable. Each story group read a different version. Will's group began with the traditional story *Little Red Riding Hood* (Schmidt, 1986). Erica's group read *Little Red Riding Hood: A Newfangled Prairie Tale* (Ernst, 1995), in which Grandma turns out to be the one surprising the wolf. Katelyn's group read *Red Riding Hood* (Marshall, 1987), a modern retelling of the tale. Tyler's group read a version from *Yo, Hungry Wolf!: A Nursery Rap* (Vozar, 1993), which is a retelling of three wolf-related stories in rap form.

After discussing accounts of these tales, the class investigated versions of the Three Little Pigs story. This time, Alex read the traditional *Three Little Pigs* (Gay, 1997) tale. Celeste read *The True Story of the Three Little Pigs* (Scieszka, 1989), as told by "A. Wolf." Emerald read *The Three Little Wolves and the Big Bad Pig* (Trivizas, 1993), which is a role-reversal account of the allegory. Again, the class discussed the versions.

See Chapter 8 Web Destinations on the Companion Website (*http://www.prenhall.com/peters*) for links related to wolves and the International Wolf Center.

Following up on the stories, Mrs. Blackwelder asked her students what they really knew about wolves. The students had many misconceptions about wolves, mostly from the children's stories they read and others like *It's So Nice to Have a Wolf Around the House* (Allard, 1997) and *Lon Po Po: A Red-Riding Hood Story from China* (Young, 1989). Television cartoons also provided misinformation. To provide an opportunity for her students to identify their misconceptions and develop a true understanding of the wolf, Mrs. Blackwelder encouraged the students to read more about wolves. She arranged a science center with wolves as the theme, made the Internet available, and bookmarked the International Wolf Center. Here, the students could see pictures of wolves and follow their migratory paths online.

Mrs. Blackwelder also provided a selection of other print resources on wolves. These included *Julie of the Wolves* (George, 1972), *The Call of the Wild* (London, 1993), *Baby Wolf* (Batten, 1998), *Look to the North: A Wolf Pup Diary* (George, 1998), *The Land of the Grey Wolf* (Locker, 1996), *Gray Wolf, Red Wolf* (Patent, 1990), *The Eyes of Gray Wolf* (London, 1993), *Wild, Wild Wolves* (Milton, 1992), and other reference books.

See Chapter 8 Web Destinations on the Companion Website (*http://www.prenhall.com/peters*) for links related to "Journey North."

Mrs. Blackwelder began reading the book *Wolf Stalker* (Skurzynski & Ferguson, 1997) to discuss wolf restoration projects. This, of course, led to the students wanting to visit the wolf sanctuary at the state park and Ranger Kellison.

Later, Mrs. Blackwelder encouraged other science learning opportunities with her students. Some of her students will participate in "Journey North." This Annenberg/CPB Internet-based learning activity engages students in a global study of wildlife migration. Other students will visit the local natural history museum or engage in similar out-of-class experiences to develop an understanding of wolves and their habitats.

Science Learning Opportunities and the Formal Curriculum

We are familiar with the formal learning that takes place in the school, but if you look at Mrs. Blackwelder's activities, you will notice that she strives to go beyond the traditional teacher–student classroom setting. Her curriculum planning includes endeavors to integrate other learning opportunities as part of her students' knowledge construction about wolves and their environments.

Science learning takes place outside the classroom. One viewpoint is that these learning activities are voluntary and not developed primarily for school use or an ongoing school curriculum (Crane, 1994). Others see experiences outside the classroom as supportive of the existing curriculum (Landis, 1996; Tunnicliffe, 1992).

Science learning opportunities can be in the schoolyard, at home, or in any other social setting. They can also be brought into the classroom when traditional activities are suspended. The class trip to the state park is an example of science learning in support of Mrs. Blackwelder's curricular objectives. This learning is encouraged because it can be motivating for students, can enhance social interaction, and generally provides a rich observational experience.

Teaching **T**ips	Although it takes more time for you to arrange, children generally experience meaningful learning with out-of-school science learning opportunities.

Science learning facilities outside the classroom are generally supportive and provide programs and resources for working with your students and even for your own professional development. They can be especially helpful to new teachers who are having difficulty preparing science lessons and organizing activities (Melber, 2000). Another important reason for using these learning resources is that activities can support gaps in formal education where resources are not available to the teacher. Even if learning experiences were redundant, the crucial overlap can increase the opportunity to learn important science skills and concepts (Honeyman, 1998).

The National Science Teachers Association (NSTA) "strongly supports and advocates" out-of-school science learning opportunities for children (1998, p. 1). Figure 8–1 is a summary of the association's views related to this issue.

See Chapter 8 Web Destinations on the Companion Website (*http://www. prenhall.com/peters*) for links to NSTA's position statements.

Do you think you need to go beyond the "traditional classroom" with your own science teaching? According to National Science Education Standards (National Research Council [NRC], 1996), "Good science programs require access to the world beyond the classroom" (p. 218). This idea is further reflected in the Inquiry Teaching Standard found in the Standards Link. The authors of this standard call for the identification and use of resources outside the school environment. They suggest that inquiry occurs as students engage in investigations, including those outside school. In this respect, the standards are used by teachers to bridge the gap between in-school and out-of-school experiences because they are common references for both types of learning (Hofstein, Bybee, & Legro, 1997; Katz & McGinnis, 1999).

The external resources offered generally require that you seek out community partners, parents, scientists, engineers, and business leaders in support of your goals for science education (National Research Council, 1998). This is exactly what Mrs. Blackwelder did with the wolf project and other thematic units throughout the year.

> ### Standards Link
>
> ## Inquiry Teaching Standard
>
> Teachers of science design and manage learning environments that provide students with the time, space, and resources needed for learning science. In doing this, teachers
>
> - **Structure the time available so that students are able to engage in extended investigations.**
>
> - **Create a setting for student work that is flexible and supportive of science inquiry.**
>
> - **Ensure a safe working environment.**
>
> - **Make the available science tools, materials, media, and technological resources accessible to students.**
>
> - **Identify and use resources outside the school.**
>
> - **Engage students in designing the learning environment.**
>
> (Teaching Standard D, National Research Council, 1996, p. 43.)

Figure 8–1   **NSTA declarations on informal science education.**

- Informal science education complements, supplements, deepens, and enhances classroom science studies. It increases the amount of time participants can be engaged in a project or topic. It can be the proving ground for curriculum materials.
- The impact of informal experiences extends to the affective, cognitive, and social realms by presenting the opportunity for mentors, professionals, and citizens to share time, friendship, effort, creativity, and expertise with youngsters and adult learners.
- Informal science education allows for different learning styles and multiple intelligences and offers supplementary alternatives to science study for nontraditional and second language learners. It offers unique opportunities through field trips, field studies, overnight experiences, and special programs.
- Informal science learning experiences offer teachers a powerful means to enhance both professional and personal development in science content knowledge and accessibility to unique resources.
- Informal science education institutions, through their exhibits and programs, provide an effective means for parents and other care providers to share moments of intellectual curiosity and time with their children.
- Informal science institutions give teachers and students direct access to scientists and other career role models in the sciences, as well as to opportunities for authentic science study.
- Informal science educators bring an emphasis on creativity and enrichment strategies to their teaching through the need to attract their noncompulsory audiences.
- NSTA advocates that local corporations, foundations, and institutions fund and support informal science education in their communities.
- Informal science education is often the only means for continuing science learning in the general public beyond the school years.

Source: National Science Teachers Association, 1998, Position Statements. Reprinted with permission.

When planning her activities, Mrs. Blackwelder generally begins with the selection of a theme that her students have generated an interest in learning about and that would also be supportive of her learning goals. Next, she makes a mental list of what resources may be available for that theme. As she continues to plan activities related to the theme, she incorporates out-of-class learning possibilities. Sometimes she brainstorms with a listing of possibilities such as those contained in Figure 8–2.

Keep in mind that the listing in Figure 8–2 should be considered a starting point for ideas. This guide is not meant to be comprehensive for every theme. The resources in your community will vary, depending on the topic under study. Other important considerations are student interest, available time in your own teaching schedule, time considerations of other professionals involved, general availability of community resources, and most important, the opportunity to learn that the resource will provide.

Figure 8–2   Areas of informal science education.

Museum and Science Center Resources	Museums of Science/Science Centers/Hands-on Science Centers/Equipment Lending Centers Natural History Museums Military Museums Other Types of Museums
Zoo Resources	Zoological Parks Aquariums Aviaries Specialized Zoos
Horticulture Resources	Plant Conservatories Herbariums Botanical Gardens County Extension Offices
Industrial Resources	Television/Cable Stations Radio Stations Public Utilities Malls, Stores, and Shops
Media Resources	Television Production Companies Film Production Companies Radio Broadcast Companies
Park Resources	National, State, and Local Parks Animal Refuges Geologic Sites Dendrology Exhibits Aquatic Sites Bird, Butterfly, or Insect Areas
College Resources	Biologic Displays and Groups Archeological Displays/Museums and Groups Astronomy Groups and Observatories Earth Science Displays and Groups
Community-Based Resources	Professionals in the Community Scientists High School Student Volunteers
Home-Based Resources	Parent Educators Science-Related Toys Science and Nature Magazines

SCIENCE LEARNING RESOURCES

Where can your students see science-related objects and events in their community? The many places to explore may include a zoo, wooded area, garden, nursery, greenhouse, pond, brook, bird refuge, observatory, natural history museum, road cut, construction site, waterworks, sewage treatment plant, dairy, airport, and weather bureau. Each of these places is a rewarding learning site for elementary school students to visit. Before you take a trip, however, some preparation will help make it worthwhile.

> **Teaching Tips**
> See how a zoo, museum, or related resource would fit into your curriculum before proceeding with specific arrangements.

A school district catalog of suggested places to visit in the community may be available. It can furnish the necessary details for educational trips. In general, however, you will want to keep the following points in mind:

- Be clear about the purpose for leaving the classroom.
- Check with the principal about policies such as student supervision.
- Visit the site yourself.
- Plan with the children what to look for on the trip.
- Develop behavior and safety standards to be remembered.
- At the site, make sure everyone can see and hear adequately.
- Develop a timetable of events and activities.
- Ask questions if desired.

> **Teaching Tips**
> After returning to the classroom, help your students evaluate the trip. Allow them to tell whether the trip was a meaningful educational experience.

Place special emphasis on the reason for the trip, as you consider the above points. Give your students an assignment during the trip so that they know the reason for the activity. This assignment does not have to be a written report; it should focus their observations and reduce behavioral problems. Be sure to select adults to help supervise students. These adult chaperones will need to be briefed to provide a better learning opportunity during the visit (Tunnicliffe, 1997). The following sections contain further explanation of some of the resources in Figure 8–2.

Museums and Science Centers

Mrs. Blackwelder began her investigation of wolves long before she guided her class into a unit on wolves. She read *Child of the Wolves* (Hall, 1996) and wanted to become more familiar with wolves and their travels. When she called a museum, she found out that she could work with a museum staff member to learn more about wolves. This situation is not uncommon.

In *Inquiry and the National Science Education Standards* (NRC, 2000), we find a story about a teacher named Joanna. She is participating in activities at a science museum. There, she finds that her own inquiry methods are enhanced as she participates in science as a learner. In cooperation with the museum staff, she is learning inquiry-based teaching methods such as the following:

- How both science subject matter and inquiry outcomes can be built into learning experiences
- How a deeper understanding of scientific concepts can promote discussion and the formulation of productive questions
- How the essential features of classroom inquiry can be woven into a learning experience

Wolves and children's misconceptions about wolves are good elementary and middle school science topics of study.

- What it feels like to learn this way, complete with frustrations and struggles
- The roles and behaviors instructors can use to promote and support learning (NRC, 2000, p. 101)

Joanna's experience represents a shift in the role of the museum as part of a **stakeholder** in science education as opposed to maintaining a curatorial function. Put another way, museums today are no longer static collections of human-made or natural history. Rather, they function to develop public understanding of scientific and technological concepts and provide an interface between these concepts and related societal issues. Where in the past, a staff scientist or curator provided the tour, today it is given by educational specialists or museum staff with special training in educational philosophy (Bitgood, Serrell, & Thompson, 1994). These professionals are better able to support state and national standards and science learning in general.

This philosophy provides another source of out-of-school education, such as museums, for your students as well as yourself. Another reason museums are a beneficial experience for students relates to the nature of out-of-school education itself. In-school education is a well-ordered system. Knowledge and instruction are continuous, sequential, often guided by textbooks or a specified curriculum, and explicitly assessed (Templeton, 1988). Out-of-school learning, contrarily, is often freely chosen. Exhibits at museums or similar facilities are specifically designed to attract the viewer's attention. Here, the instruction is planned to promote easy understanding. Knowledge is represented in things, not in textbooks. This representation often promotes deeper learning and can be very motivating for students and teachers alike.

Museums are also important proponents of constructive principles. A report of one such elementary-level partnership contained this quote: "If children learn best when

Stakeholders are those individuals or groups that have a "shared interest" in science education and scientific literacy.

Teaching Tips

After reading Focus on Inquiry: Zoos as Science Education Resources, you should have begun to understand the rich opportunity to learn provided by the zoo animals, the environment, and the zoo staff.

constructing their own meaning from their experiences, then indeed informal learning such as that occurring in science museums is an important model to become immersed in while learning to teach" (Nagel, Ault, & Rice, 1995, p. 34).

In sum, whether you personally take an entire class to the museum for predetermined activities in support of your curriculum, plan and encourage individual learning experiences, or provide external rewards for students who make visits on their own time, your students will certainly benefit from the experience. An analogous resource with many of the same learning benefits of the museum is the zoo.

Zoos

Teaching Tips

Mrs. Blackwelder will provide enough time for her students to draw pictures and describe the animals that they find while on the visit. This will make the experience more meaningful.

Observing animals, inquiring about their behaviors and habitats, and communicating observations provide excellent opportunities for science learning. Zoo experiences can also provide students a conservation-minded value system as they begin to appreciate the animals that are a part of the ecosystem (Harvey & Erickson, 1988).

Mrs. Blackwelder's class will arrange a visit to a zoo as a culminating activity for the wolf unit. After reading about arctic wolves in the books *To the Top of the World* (Brandenburg, 1993) and *Journey of the Red Wolf* (Smith, 1996), her students are particularly interested in looking at the physical characteristics of wolves and similar animals. They want to know what helps the wolves travel in the way that is discussed.

For a trip to a zoo to be a beneficial learning experience and not just an "entertaining outing," planning is important (Prather, 1989). You may want to try visiting only one area or ecosystem on each trip. The first step in using a zoo as a resource is to visit the zoo and contact the zoo staff to see what is available for you or your students. Today's zoos offer broader experiences than just observing animals. The zoo staff offers interactive learning experiences for children (Rennie & McClafferty, 1995). Some may even display animatronics (Tunnicliffe, 1999) so that an animated animal and its behavior can be studied in detail. Many zoos offer group tours, special programs designed just for children, career presentations, gifted or challenged student programs, or outreach programs during which the zoo staff bring animals to a class that is not able to travel to the zoo facility.

Teaching Tips

As you begin your career as a teacher, contact local zoos, museums, and other facilities to see what professional development opportunities are available there.

Keep in mind that not only is a zoo a resource for your students, but, like museums, many zoos provide professional development opportunities for teachers. Whether a curriculum development project, a summer workshop, or a paid internship, you can benefit from the experience provided by zoo educational specialists.

Horticultural Resources

See Chapter 8 Web Destinations on the Companion Website (*http://www. prenhall.com/peters*) for links related to conservatories and arboretums.

CW

Mrs. Blackwelder's class dialogue of what wolves eat from the book *Wolves* (Dudley, 1997) initiated a discussion of different types of edible mushrooms. Now, Mrs. Blackwelder is making arrangements for her class to talk with a horticulturalist. She will show interested students local varieties of mushrooms, including those that are edible and those that are poisonous.

Conservatories, herbariums, arboretums, and botanical gardens, like their animal counterparts, can be resources for indispensable science learning opportunities. These re-

Visit an Inquiry Classroom
Using Zoos, Science Centers, and Museums

View the *Scientific Method* video in the "Nature of Science" section of the Companion CD. In this video segment, Mr. McKnight works with students to develop new questions to explore about earthworms.

Review the video and ask yourself the following:

• How could Mr. McKnight use zoos, science centers, or museums to extend his students' study of earthworms?
• The students in the video engage in inquiry with earthworms. If you were using zoos, science centers, or museums local to your area, what other animals could you study? What resources could the zoos, science centers, or museums provide for your classroom?

Explore the Association of Science-Technology Centers's website (*http://www.astc.org/*). In the *ASTC Dimensions* (2004), George Hein makes the following statement:

> Effective museum education activities allow students to ask questions, interact with objects, and explore the processes that lead to a richer understanding of the world. In this era of standards-based curricula and high-stakes testing, it is worth reemphasizing the importance of keeping museum education focused in the direction of open, inquisitive use of material resources—not in the direction of the constrained, answer-driven minutiae of worksheets.

Explain what he means by this quote and describe your reaction to it. Record your ideas and the answers to these questions in your portfolio or use the Companion Website to share your ideas.

---

sources provide out-of-school learning education experiences such as schoolyard ecology programs for elementary and middle school students. Conservatories and arboretums also provide teacher education programs such as faculty development workshops. Examples of organizations that provide services or contact with experts are as follows:

• National Arbor Day Foundation
• North American Conservatories
• United States National Arboretum
• Ecological Society of America
• American Association of Botanical Gardens and Arboreta
• National Park Service
• Botanical Society of America
• National Association of State Foresters

As you can see, this is a diverse group of institutions and experts ready to assist you with your learning goals. When looking for local botanical resources, it may be helpful to begin with your county extension office. You may also want to refer to the document *Resources for Teaching Elementary School Science* (National Science Resources Center, National Academy of Sciences, Smithsonian Institution, 1996) for contacts in your area.

See Chapter 8 Web Destinations on the Companion Website (*http://www.prenhall.com/peters*) for links to county extensions.

Industrial-Based Resources

Alliances among business, industry, government, higher education, and the K–12 educational community are effective ways to supplement learning and bring the community together for science education improvement (American Association for the Advancement of Science [AAAS], 1998; International Council of Associations for Science Education [ICASE], 1990). Teachers who participate in industry-based work experiences report the following:

* Using new teaching strategies in their classrooms
* Introducing updated content into the curriculum
* Increasing the use of computers in the classrooms
* Seeking ways to work with other teachers and maintaining their connections to the businesses in which the teachers previously worked or had a summer internship
* Adding career information to the curriculum
* Gaining in self-esteem
* Affirming their decisions to become teachers

Alliances and business partners can also contribute to effective standards-based reform (Business Coalition for Education Reform, 1998; Rigden & McAdoo, 1995; Triangle Coalition for Science and Technology Education, 1996). They provide support to elementary and middle school classrooms through a variety of means such as summer internships, mini-grants to teachers or students, volunteers for tutoring, mentoring, guest lecturing, sponsoring clubs, judging contests, institutes for professional development, speaker bureaus, loans and donations of equipment, technical assistance, curriculum assistance, program development, public awareness campaigns, clearinghouses, databases, hotlines, projects for women and minorities, computer assistance, administrator training, and school restructuring (Triangle Coalition for Science and Technology Education, 1991).

To get a better perspective on which businesses in your area are supporting education, contact the Triangle Coalition for Science and Technology Education, 1201 New York Avenue, NW, Suite 700, Washington, DC, 20005. This organization provides information on the Scientific Work Experiences for Teachers (SWEPT) program. You may also want to refer to the document *A Business Guide to Support Employee and Family Involvement in Education* (Otterbourg, 1997).

To see what other resources are available in your area, your first step should be contacting your local chamber of commerce. You can begin by viewing the U.S. Chamber of Commerce Chamber Mall.

See Chapter 8 Web Destinations on the Companion Website (*http://www.prenhall.com/peters*) for links related the U.S. Chamber of Commerce.

Media Providers

See Chapter 8 Web Destinations on the Companion Website (*http://www.prenhall.com/peters*) for links to endangered species sites.

Mrs. Blackwelder encouraged her students to take a virtual tour of an endangered species site after reading the Ranger Rick book *Wolves for Kids* (Wolpert, 1990). This is one of many out-of-school learning resources available from the National Wildlife Federation. An ever-increasing supply of resources is available from media providers about wolves and many other elementary and middle school science topics. One place to begin looking for resources is with your local cable company.

The Cable in the Classroom program is a public service effort supported by the cable industry. Cable companies provide free cable connections to many classrooms in their area, as well as hundreds of hours of free programming to the schools. Videotaping of the shows is encouraged, allowing teachers flexibility in when they show the productions in their individual classrooms. Teachers can refer to Cable in the Classroom magazine, which lists the schedule and provides feature articles. The Cable in the Classroom program also provides a professional development institute that includes traveling and virtual workshops for teachers.

The Public Broadcasting System (PBS) has many science-related series, including *Nova*, *Scientific American Frontiers*, *Newton's Apple*, *Bill Nye*, and *PBS Online*. PBS includes resources such as an online *TeacherSource* guide and program listings. The *Nova* series covers a variety of science topics that are useful to teachers and students. Lesson ideas, past show resources, and online activities are available on the Internet. A printed teacher's guide is also available.

Scientific American Frontiers, produced in association with *Scientific American*, has a website that includes "Ask the Scientists," "In the Classroom," "Cool Science," and "Resource" sections.

Newton's Apple series is an excellent resource for science subjects. This is a family and classroom science show. Many "Science Try Its" are available on the related website, as are numerous activity guides for the past season's shows. New program guides are generally available a few weeks before the show, and a printed program guide is available for teachers.

Bill Nye's website is a gateway to episode guides for more than 100 shows. This site has "sounds of science" clips and home demonstrations of science phenomena.

One related but often overlooked resource for science is science fiction. It is a good beginning point for discussion of topics that are of student interest. Actual scientific principles used or misused in films and television can be better learned through the use of science fiction (Dubeck, Moshier, & Boss, 1988) because film or television series directors often use concrete ways to demonstrate abstract principles. Science fiction can be a tool for the elementary or middle school science teacher in identifying misconceptions.

> See Chapter 8 Web Destinations on the Companion Website (*http://www.prenhall.com/peters*) for Cable in the Classroom links and for Discovery Channel School links. The Discovery Channel School lists programming previews, lesson plans to accompany shows, weblinks, and discussions. *Discovery's Educator Guide* is a free reference to the educational programming on Discovery Channel, The Learning Channel, Travel Channel, and Animal Planet. There are also links to Nickelodeon, PBS, *Nova*, *Scientific American Frontiers*, *Newton's Apple*, *Bill Nye*, and *PBS Online*.

> See Chapter 8 Web Destinations on the Companion Website (*http://www.prenhall.com/peters*) for links to ICASE, NSTA, and science clubs.

Visit an Inquiry Classroom
Links Beyond Schooling

View the *Links Beyond Schooling* video in the "Constructivist Pedagogy" section of the Companion CD. This video segment displays some obvious and subtle instances of links beyond the classroom. Students engage in an Internet activity from Discovery Communications's Yuckiest Site. Mr. McKnight also has donated materials and supplies as well as posters on his classroom wall.

Review the video and ask yourself the following:
- Are there resource people or companies in your community that you could contact for classroom materials and supplies?
- Is there an agency, company, or other group close to your school that could become your partner in education?

   Look at the Education Community links on the National Science Foundation Division of Elementary, Secondary, and Informal Education's website (*http://www. ehr.nsf.gov/esie/resources/EdCommLinks.asp*). Identify resources that you could use. Record your ideas and the answers to these questions in your portfolio or use the Companion Website to share your ideas.

"Partners in education" can bring science into your classroom in special ways.

Other Resources

Resources such as state parks, local parks, colleges, community-based businesses, and home-based resources are also available to you as an elementary or middle school teacher. One specific example is the science club. Science clubs allow members to choose areas of study based on mutual interest as opposed to a specific curriculum (Tunnicliffe, 1998). For further information, see the International Association of Science Clubs, the International Council of Associations for Science Education (ICASE), or the National Science Teachers Association (NSTA) websites.

In planning to use resources, first identify your specific learning goals and then check for a local contact that will meet those needs. One way to begin is by contacting a curriculum specialist, elementary science specialist, or lead teacher within your local school or district. You can also try a general Internet search for resources in your area.

INDIVIDUAL PARTNERS IN EDUCATION

Teaching Tips

Community resource individuals can be utility-based professionals; animal care technicians; earth, space, and weather experts; botanists and agriculture specialists; social science researchers; or scientists and engineers working in general industry.

The story *The Boy Who Cried "Wolf!"* (Schecter, 1994) begins with a boy earning a living as a shepherd in his village. The villagers come to help the boy when he cries out, "Wolf!" *Peter and the Wolf* (Lemieux, 1991) is a similar story of villagers coming to the rescue when a wolf is present. Although these stories contain misinformation about wolves, they do illustrate how community members are willing to help out in difficult situations. This maxim is still true today. Parents and other community leaders are willing to help you out with your elementary or middle school science program.

Figure 8–3 Individual partner examples.

Utility-Based Partners	Engineers
	Electricians
	Environmental Scientists
	Telecommunications Specialists
	Television/Radio Technicians
	Computer Systems Designers/Operators
Animal/Human Care Partners	Veterinarians
	Zoologists
	Entomologists
	County Health Department Employees
	Hospital-Based Professionals
Earth, Space, and Weather Partners	Weather Forecasters
	Pilots/Astronauts
	Geologists
	Surveyors
	Civil Engineers/Contractors
	Paleontologists
Botanists and Agricultural Partners	Forest/Park Rangers
	Farmers and Ranchers
	Horticulturists/Landscape Workers
	County Extension Employees
Social Science Partners	Psychiatrists
	Psychologists
	Sociologists
	Anthropologists
	Geographers
General Industry Partners	Chemists
	Biologists
	Physicists
	Geologists
	Inventers
	Architects
	Engineers

When it is impossible to arrange visits away from the school, resource persons from the community may be able to visit your classroom. Many districts compile lists of informed persons who are willing to volunteer. Like the science education resources discussed in the previous section, individual partnerships can be an excellent source of assistance, ideas, and materials to support your elementary or middle school science program. Figure 8–3 lists some contacts within these categories.

The following guidelines will help in the success of developing partnerships on an individual basis. First, contact the volunteer in advance and arrange your first meeting outside the classroom. This will allow plenty of time to answer questions, explain general class procedures, determine any specific materials or equipment needed, and discuss the objectives of the visit. As the time approaches, remind the volunteer of her visit and provide the

Do not forget to offer soft drinks, water, or coffee to visitors. Also show all visitors where the restrooms are located.

school's telephone number and your home telephone number for a return call. The schedules of many professionals change often, and mistakes can occur. You do not want to have a disappointed class or have future experiences jeopardized from a poor initial experience.

When the visitor arrives, have someone there to greet her and make her comfortable with the experience. You can do this personally while another teacher or an administrator watches your class. You could also have a teacher aide or the room parent greet the visitor and bring her to the classroom. Arrange for a name tag if possible, and introduce the speaker to the class.

After the visit, follow up with a thank-you card or telephone call. Let the principal know something about the volunteer and the outcomes of the visit. The principal or you may want to alert the news media about positive experiences. If volunteers will be visiting on a continuous basis, do not forget to provide them your schedule changes. Meet with them periodically to see whether the objectives of the visits are still being met and whether they have any further suggestions.

Scientists as Professional Development Partners

A partnership with a scientist is a strategy suggested for professional development of teachers who may need to build their content knowledge or confidence in teaching science (Loucks-Horsley et al., 1999). Scientists are good partners in education, especially from a "real" science or equity standpoint. Scientists can provide real-world applications of science as they mentor teachers. Teachers, in return, allow scientists to see firsthand the condition of school science programs. Scientists also benefit by enhancing their own teaching effectiveness as they learn new strategies from educational professionals.

Following are specific goals for having a scientist make a presentation or work with your class:

- To help students understand science
- To help students gain an understanding of the work scientists do
- To help students see scientists as real people
- To help scientists develop insight into today's schools and students (Shaw & Herminghaus, 1993)

If the scientist visiting your class is new to the educational field, it may be helpful to provide some initial suggestions, such as the elements of a successful presentation or things to do in the classroom.

As a classroom teacher, you should select a topic for the scientist to present. Call the scientist and explain your needs. Be sure to provide background information and how his presentation will support your learning goals. Make sure you discuss appropriate behavior with your students beforehand.

See the article "Scientists in the Classroom" (Shaw & Herminghaus, 1993) for ideas and a reproducible checklist of things the scientist should know and "do" as part of the presentation. This resource contains information that a teaching professional will understand but that a scientist may not be aware of before the presentation. A summary developed from the list is found in Figure 8–4. The book *Science Education Partnerships: Manual for Scientists and K–12 Teachers* (Sussman, 1993) is also a good resource for use in understanding how a scientist can support science learning in your classroom and how you can develop a partnership program in your school.

Figure 8–4 Do and because list for scientists.

Do	Because
Make eye contact with students	Students love personal contact
Have presentation materials organized	Students have a hard time waiting
Use student volunteers	Students love to feel important
Require students to raise their hands	Students will all want to talk at once
Make sure they understand the task	This avoids unnecessary questions
Face the students and move about	This will help maintain interest
Ask the teacher for help with discipline	The teacher will know how to help
Use wait time	The students need time to think
Praise good behavior	This will encourage more good behavior
Enjoy the students	They have a unique perspective

Source: From Shaw & Herminghaus, 1993, p. 119.

Visit an Inquiry Classroom
Partnerships with Scientists

View the *Paradigm Shifts* video in the "Nature of Science" section of the Companion CD. Mr. McKnight's students are cleaning up after an activity where they explored earthworms. They have answered the questions that they set out to explore.

Review the video and ask yourself the following:

- If you were to bring an agronomist (scientist who specializes in soil and crops), an ethologist (scientist who studies animal behavior), or an oligochaetologist (scientist that studies earthworms), into the classroom, how might this affect how the children study earthworms?
- If a scientist was overseeing the experiments that the students just completed, what changes in your classroom routine may be needed to make the activities more successful?

 Gordon Gates is a well-known oligochaetologist. Research his work on the Internet and identify some of his findings related to earthworms. Record your ideas and the answers to these questions in your portfolio or use the Companion Website to share your ideas.

Parents as Partners

Parents are essential to their children's success in school. Out-of-school time is an important opportunity for learning (Bergstrom, 1984). According to the NSTA Board of Directors, parents can help their children by

- ***Seeing science everywhere*** Parents can help their children feel the excitement of observation and discovery. They can also promote growth in thinking, further develop problem-solving abilities, and encourage positive attitudes toward science.
- ***Doing science together*** Parents can share experiences and demonstrate that science learning is enjoyable.

- *Developing a variety of skills*   Parents can assist their children in developing science process skills and comprehending scientific information.
- *Finding the appropriate level*   Parents can assess the developmental level of their children and seek out appropriate strategies and ideas to assist their children with scientific understandings. (NSTA, 1994)

Parents can achieve the NSTA goals by simply taking the time to listen to their child, building a resource collection, and co-investigating science at home and within the community on a daily basis. Parents should also become involved in the school to make sure that science-related experiences are ongoing.

Teachers can support parents by keeping 15 to 30 kits containing activities that the students can check out and take home. These kits can be stored in small plastic containers and are easy to prepare with help from a teacher aide or parents. Begin by looking through this text and other resources that may be available to you. Look for activities and investigations that might enrich your regular science program. Select any number of these activities and make one copy of each activity.

Bring these copies to Parents' Night or similar meetings early in the school year. Start by briefly introducing your science program. Next, discuss what topics your students will study and some of the materials they will work with throughout the year. Then, show your activity sheets and example kits and give their purpose. Hand out the duplicated activity sheets, have parents examine them, and then ask for volunteers to make the kits. Encourage the parent volunteers to do the activities with their children, discuss the results together, and return the completed kits.

> **Teaching Tips**
> Do not be afraid to ask parents to assist you in the classroom. Many are afraid to take the first step to ask you, but are willing to help out in any way they can.

Some teachers like to have parents experience firsthand a few children's activities across the curriculum. This puts the parents in better touch with their children's work. Parents who are involved with your program are typically willing to supplement your science supplies with discardable items from around the home. Some will volunteer to assist at science learning centers or will share their expertise in science or technology. But for these things to happen, parents need to hear details from you about what's needed.

Parents are usually more concerned about their children's progress in reading than in other subjects. Point out to them the value of parents reading aloud with their children, sharing books, and discussing concepts that come up in the reading. Show parents several kinds of science trade books available that correlate with upcoming units. The students may check out these books from several sources, including the school, district, or public library. If your school has a newer multimedia science program, check out the science-related literature books that typically accompany these programs.

Show parents examples of useful articles from a newspaper, news magazine, *National Geographic,* or other sources they might share with their children who, in turn, might share the information at school. Explain that this material is easier to understand and remember when it relates to topics and concepts being studied at school. Stress the need to discuss the articles with the children, because these are seldom written in an age-appropriate style. Mention, too, some titles of science periodicals for children. They contain excellent current material, are more age appropriate, and will help students learn what to look for when scanning newspapers and other publications.

Some parents and children will already have visited a local natural history museum, zoo, observatory, bird refuge, or botanical garden. Ask parents about these experiences and suggest additional places recommended by seasoned colleagues and school district publications. A school catalog will have descriptions and a listing of places for families to visit at different grade levels or for certain units of instruction; and if you intend to take your

Visit an Inquiry Classroom
Family Science

View the *Team Work* video in the "Planning and Management" section of the Companion CD. Groups of students watch videos of earthworms, including a heart video.

Review the video segment and ask yourself the following:
- How could you involve parents as part of your earthworm inquiry team?
- What could the students do to showcase their earthworm explorations during a science festival or parent night?

Newton-Hair (2004) discusses having a "Compost Carnival" or "a science fair with a carnival flair." What other parent-related activities can you think of with respect to earthworms? Record your ideas and the answers to these questions in your portfolio or use the Companion Website to share your ideas.

class on study trips to these places, a parents' meeting is a good time to solicit volunteers to accompany the class.

You probably realize that we have mentioned more things to inform parents about than you will have time for in one introductory meeting, especially if you discuss other subjects. Periodic newsletters, a classroom newspaper, individual conferences, and further parent–teacher meetings all present more chances to reach them. The content of your message is far more important than its forum. When you give parents specific ways to help their children study science and support your efforts, everyone gains.

Family Science Festivals

A family science festival is a recreational community event where families participate in science activities after school (MCCPTA-EPI Hands-On Science, 1985). They are not science fairs but community events where people can have fun while they increase their awareness of science. When planning and implementing a festival, keep the following five important considerations in mind:

> **Teaching Tips**
>
> A family science festival is a time when parents can share with their children without any fears of "failure," such as a low science grade.

1. *Project Leader* The project leader is the head of the committee and is in charge of areas such as recruitment of volunteers and keeping people on task.
2. *Volunteers* Volunteers make telephone calls and make arrangements for festival day such as reminder letters, name tags, and thank-you notes.
3. *Publicity* The publicity person develops the announcements or flyers to give to the graphics team, arranges photographic support, and seeks media coverage of the event.
4. *Graphics* The graphics people print the signs or flyers for the event, as well as any necessary table decorations or instructions needed for the event.
5. *Activities/Materials* The activities crew selects and makes arrangements for the activities, including arranging to have the necessary materials on hand to complete the events. (MCCPTA-EPI Hands-On Science, 1985, p. 4)

The important thing to remember about family science festivals is that they should be fun and indicative of your school or community. They should also be a positive support for science learning.

Summary

- Science learning opportunities that take place outside the classroom can support or supplement an ongoing school curriculum. This type of learning can be in the schoolyard, at home, or in any other social setting.
- Museums and science centers, zoos, horticulture exhibits and experts, industrial resources, and various forms of media all provide learning opportunities for students and professional development opportunities for preservice and in-service teachers.

- Utility-based partners; animal/human care partners; earth, space, and weather partners; botanists and agriculture partners; social science partners; and general industry partners are all available to support your elementary or middle school science program.
- Parents can be essential learning partners for your students. One type of event that can involve parents is a family science festival, where families participate in science activities after school.

Reflection

Companion CD

1. Look at the "Earthworm Longevity: It's an Earthworm's Life" lesson associated with the *Links Beyond Schooling* video on the Companion CD. Although students do not go to zoos and natural history museums to learn about earthworms, there are many other animals available for exploration. Choose a zoo animal and develop a lesson plan on "It's an [insert your animal's name here]'s Life."
2. Look at the "Invertebrate Versus Vertebrate: Which Animals Are Which" lesson associated with the

Invitation video on the Companion CD. Develop a lesson plan that you could use at a natural history museum that would have children learn about invertebrates versus vertebrates.

3. Look at the "What Is Anatomy: What Is Earthworm Anatomy" lesson associated with the *Science as Inquiry* video on the Companion CD. Brainstorm ways that a classroom science partner could present a lesson on the anatomy of another animal.

Portfolio Ideas

1. Look at Chapter 9 of *Resources for Teaching Elementary School Science* (National Science Resources Center, 1996) or *Science Fun in Chicagoland: A Guide for Parents and Teachers* (Stills, 1995). Enter into your portfolio some out-of-school science education resources located near your community.
2. Read through *Helping Your Child Learn Science* (Paulu, 1992). Would you recommend this reading to parents? Why or why not? What does it say to you as a future teacher? Did you get any new ideas from the "Activities in the Community" section? Record ideas in your portfolio.
3. Obtain a copy of *Science Education Partnerships: Manual for Scientists and K–12 Teachers* (Sussman, 1993) and identify in your portfolio ways to develop and fund partnerships. These could be with your

students or on an individual basis as a means to further your own scientific knowledge.

4. *Learning in Living Color: Using Literature to Incorporate Multicultural Education into the Primary Classroom* (Valdez, 1999, pp. 60–79) will help you to develop lessons to integrate the wolf theme with multicultural themes such as Native American history for inclusion in your portfolio. Also show the relationship between the nature of science (skepticism) and stereotyping. What facts are related to wolves, and what fiction has skewed our understanding of wolves?
5. Review the National PTA's National Standards for Parent/Family Involvement Programs at *http://www. pta.org/parentinvolvement/standards/index.asp*. In your portfolio, develop a presentation that you can use in the future to seek parental support for your science program.

References

Allard, H. (1997). *It's so nice to have a wolf around the house*. New York: Picture Yearling Books.

American Association for the Advancement of Science (AAAS). (1998). *Blueprints for reform*. New York: Oxford University Press.

Batten, M. (1998). *Baby wolf*. New York: Grosset & Dunlap.

Bergstrom, J. (1984). *School's out—now what? Creative choices for your child*. Berkeley, CA: Ten Speed Press.

Bitgood, S., Serrell, B., & Thompson, D. (1994). The impact of informal education on visitors to museums. In V. Crane, H. Nicholson, M. Chen, & S. Bitgood (Eds.), *Informal science learning: What the research says about television, science museums, and community-based projects* (pp. 61–106). Ephrata, PA: Science Press.

Brandenburg, J. (1993). *To the top of the world: Adventures with arctic wolves*. New York: Walker.

Business Coalition for Education Reform. (1998). *The formula for success: A business leader's guide to supporting math and science achievement*. Washington, DC: U.S. Department of Education.

Crane, V. (1994). An introduction to informal science learning and research. In V. Crane, H. Nicholson, M. Chen, & S. Bitgood (Eds.), *Informal science learning: What the research says about television, science museums, and community-based projects* (pp. 1–14). Ephrata, PA: Science Press.

Dubeck, L. W., Moshier, S. E., & Boss, J. E. (1988). *Science in cinema: Teaching science fact thorough science fiction films*. New York: Teachers College Press.

Dudley, K. (1997). *Wolves*. Austin, TX: Raintree Steck-Vaughn.

Ernst, L. C. (1995). *Little red riding hood: A newfangled prairie tale*. New York: Aladdin Paperbacks.

Gay, M. L. (1997). *The 3 little pigs*. Buffalo, NY: Groundwood Books.

George, J. C. (1972). *Julie of the wolves*. New York: HarperTrophy.

George, J. C. (1998). *Look to the north: A wolf pup diary*. New York: HarperTrophy.

Hall, E. (1996). *Child of the wolves*. New York: Bantam Doubleday Dell.

Harvey, P., & Erickson, D. (1988). Making the most of the zoo. In M. Druger (Ed.), *Science for the fun of it: A guide to informal science education* (pp. 78–82). Arlington, VA: National Science Teachers Association.

Hein, G. (2004, January/February). Museum-school bridges: A legacy of progressive education. *ASTC Dimensions*. Washington, DC: The Association of Science-Technology Centers.

Hofstein, A., Bybee, R., & Legro, P. (1997). Linking formal and informal science education through science education standards. *Science Education International, 8*(3), 31–37.

Honeyman, B. (1998). Non-formal and formal learning interactions: New directions for scientific and technological literacy. *Connect, 23*(1), 1–2.

International Council of Associations for Science Education (ICASE). (1990). *Industry–education liaison*. Hong Kong: Author.

Katz, P., & McGinnis, R. (1999). An informal elementary science education program's response to the national science education reform movement. *Journal of Elementary Science Education, 11*(1), 1–11.

Landis, C. (1996). *Teaching science in the field*. ERIC/CSMEE Digest, EDO-SE-96-7. Columbus, OH: ERIC/CSMEE.

Lemieux, M. (1991). *Peter and the wolf*. New York: Mulberry Paperbacks.

Locker, T. (1996). *The land of the gray wolf*. New York: Dial Books.

London, J. (1993). *The eyes of grey wolf*. San Francisco: Chronicle Books.

London, J. G. (1993). *The call of the wild*. New York: Scholastic Paperbacks.

Loucks-Horsley, S., Hewson, P. W., Love, N., Stiles, K. E., Dyasi, H. M., Friel, S. N., Mumme, J., Sneider, C. I., & Worth, K. L. (1999). Ideas that work: Summaries of 15 strategies for professional development. In A. Thorson (Ed.), *Ideas that work: Science professional development* (pp. 10–44). Columbus, OH: Eisenhower National Clearinghouse for Mathematics and Science Education.

Marshall, J. (1987). *Red riding hood*. New York: Dial Books.

MCCPTA-EPI Hands-On Science. (1985). *Putting together a family science festival*. (Available from author at 12118 Heritage Park Circle, Silver Spring, MD 20852)

Melber, L. (2000). Tap into informal science learning. *Science Scope, 23*(6), 28–31.

Milton, J. (1992). *Wild, wild wolves*. New York: Random House.

Nagel, N., Ault, C., & Rice, M. (1995). Learning to teach and the science museum. *Science Education International, 6*(2), 31–34.

National Research Council (NRC). (1996). *National science education standards*. Washington, DC: National Academy Press. *http://books.nap.edu/html/nses/html/index.html*

National Research Council (NRC). (1998). *Every child a scientist: Achieving scientific literacy for all*. Washington, DC: National Academy Press.

National Research Council (NRC). (2000). *Inquiry and the national science education standards*. Washington, DC: National Academy Press. *http://books.nap.edu/html/inquiry_addendum/*

National Science Resources Center, National Academy of Sciences, Smithsonian Institution. (1996). *Resources for teaching elementary school science*. Washington, DC: National Academy Press. *http://stills.nap.edu/html/rtess/contents.html*

National Science Teachers Association (NSTA). (1994). *An NSTA position statement: Parent involvement in science education*. Arlington, VA: Author. *www.nsta.org/handbook/position.asp*

National Science Teachers Association (NSTA). (1998). *An NSTA position statement: Informal science education*. Arlington, VA: Author. *http://www.nsta.org/handbook/position.asp*

Newton-Hair, D. (2004). *Bin bug bingo!* Grants Pass, OR: Worm Digest. Retrieved December 23, 2004, from *www.wormdigest.org/binbugbingo.html*

Otterbourg, S. (1997). *A business guide to support employee and family involvement in education*. New York: Conference Board. *www.ed.gov/pubs/BusinessGuide/*

Patent, D. H. (1990). *Gray wolf, red wolf*. New York: Clarion Books.

Paulo, N. (1992). *Helping your child learn science*. Washington, DC: U.S. Department of Education.

Prather, J. P. (1989). Review of the value of field trips in science instruction. *Journal of Elementary Science Education, 1*(1), 10–17.

Reiff, A. (n.d.). *Coming up worms*. Belleville, IL: St. Clair County Regional Schools. Retrieved December 23, 2004, from *http://web.stclair.k12.il.us/splashd/wormsexp.htm*

Rennie, L. R., & McClafferty, T. (1995). Using visits to interactive science and technology centers, museums, aquaria, and zoos to promote learning in science. *Journal of Science Teacher Education, 6*(4), 175–185.

Rigden, D., & McAdoo, M. (1995). *Supporting the national education goals: A guide for business leaders*. New York: Council for Aid to Education.

Schecter, E. (1994). *The boy who cried "wolf!"* New York: Bantam Book.

Schmidt, K. (1986). *Little red riding hood*. New York: Scholastic.

Scieszka, J. (1989). *The true story of the 3 little pigs!* New York: Puffin Books.

Shaw, D., & Herminghaus, T. (1993). Scientists in the classroom. In G. Madrazo & L. Motz (Eds.), *Sourcebook for science supervisors* (4th ed., pp. 117–121). Arlington, VA: National Science Teachers Association.

Sills, T. W. (1995). *Science fun in Chicagoland: A guide for parents and teachers*. Chicago: Dearborn Resources.

Skurzynski, G., & Ferguson, A. (1997). *Wolf stalker*. Washington, DC: National Geographic Society.

Smith, R. (1996). *Journey of the red wolf*. New York: Cobblehill Books.

Sussman, A. (1993). *Science education partnerships: Manual for scientists and K–12 teachers*. San Francisco: University of California.

Templeton, M. (1988). The science museum: Object lessons in informal education. In M. Druger (Ed.), *Science for the fun of it: A guide to informal science education* (pp. 83–88). Arlington, VA: National Science Teachers Association.

Triangle Coalition for Science and Technology Education. (1991). *A guide for building an alliance for science, mathematics, and technology*. College Park, MD: Author.

Triangle Coalition for Science and Technology Education. (1996). *A look at industry and community commitment to educational systematic reform*. College Park, MD: Author.

Trivizas, E. (1993). *The three little wolves and the big bad pig*. New York: Aladdin Paperbacks.

Tunnicliffe, S. D. (1992). The school visit as a science learning opportunity. In *Annual proceedings of the American Association of Zoological Parks and Aquariums* (pp. 342–349). Toronto: AAZPA/American Zoo and Aquarium Association.

Tunnicliffe, S. D. (1997). The effect of the presence of two adults—chaperones or teachers—on the content of conversations of primary school groups during school visits to a natural history museum. *Journal of Elementary Science Education, 9*(1), 49–65.

Tunnicliffe, S. D. (1998). Science clubs. *Science Education International, 9*(3), 36.

Tunnicliffe, S. D. (1999). Use with care: Animatronics in museums and zoos—a new type of exhibit. *Science Education International, 10*(3), 34–37.

Valdez, A. (1999). *Learning in living color: Using literature to incorporate multicultural education*. Needham Heights, MA: Allyn & Bacon.

Vozar, D. (1993). *Yo, hungry wolf!: A nursery rap*. New York: Doubleday.

Wolpert, T. (1990). *Wolves for kids*. Minnetonka, MN: NorthWord Press.

Young, E. (1989). *Lon Po Po: A red-riding hood story from China*. Ossining, NY: Paper Star.

Suggested Readings

Committee on Biology Teacher Inservice Programs, Board on Biology Commission on Life Sciences, National Research Council. (1996). *The role of scientists in the professional development of science teachers*. Washington, DC: National Academy Press. *http://stills.nap.edu/html/role/* (a comprehensive report and reading list on the topic of the use of scientists in teacher professional development)

Kubota, C. (1993). *Education-business partnerships: Scientific work experience programs*. ERIC/CSMEE Digest, EDO-SE-93-3. Columbus, OH: ERIC/CSMEE.

National Science Resources Center, National Academy of Sciences, Smithsonian Institution. (1997). *Science for all children: A guide to improving science education in your school district*. Washington, DC: National Academy Press. (provides examples of specific partnerships in support of elementary science education)

Paulu, N., & Martin, M. (1991). *Helping your child learn science*. Washington, DC: U.S. Department of Education, Office of Educational Research and Improvement. (how parents can increase their children's science interests through home activities; available at $3.25 from OERI Outreach Office, 555 New Jersey Ave., NW, Washington, DC 20208-5570)

Pearlman, S., & Pericak-Spector, K. (1992). Helping hands from home. *Science and Children, 29*(7), 12–14. (parent volunteers make active science more manageable)

CONCEPTS AND INQUIRIES FOR TEACHING ELEMENTARY SCHOOL SCIENCE

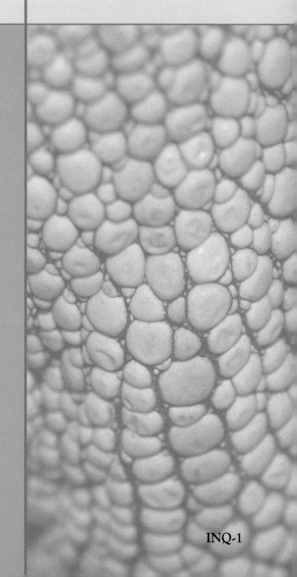

INQUIRY UNITS

The 12 inquiry units that follow help model constructivist applications for science teaching and learning. Each unit will help you reflect on the methodology and typical subject-matter areas found in children's textbooks, school district science guides, the *National Science Education Standards* (National Research Council [NRC], 1996), and the *Benchmarks for Science Literacy* (American Association for the Advancement of Science [AAAS], 1993). Each unit begins with a brief introduction, followed by sample benchmarks and standards. These are followed by inquiry activities grouped by topic. Finally, each group of activities is followed by concepts that apply to the activities provided.

As you scan through the inquiry activities, you will see that they generally follow both the constructivist learning model (Yager, 1991) and the learning cycle (Barman, 1989) model as follows:

Title

Invitation (modeled after the constructivist learning model "invitation" to inquiry)

Exploration (modeled after the constructivist learning model "exploration" part and the learning cycle "exploration" phase)

Concept Invention (modeled after the constructivist learning model "proposing explanations and solutions" part and the learning cycle "concept introduction" phase)

Concept Application (modeled after the constructivist learning model "taking action" part and the learning cycle "concept application" phase)

Specifically, the *invitation* is one or more questions or statements used to arouse children's interest and to tie in their former experiences. This sets the stage for further investigation in the next section; this section also includes the materials needed for the inquiry.

The *exploration* is the basic activity that children will use to study a scientific phenomenon or concept. This child-centered section includes teaching comments and applicable background knowledge you may need to facilitate that specific inquiry. (Note that more detailed information follows the activities in the concept invention section.)

The *concept invention* is an extension of the exploration and includes questions or extension activities or both. These will assist the children as they develop the applicable scientific concept.

Each inquiry ends with a *concept application* that challenges the children to test and apply their newly formed concepts. There is room here for the children to answer relevant questions and design extended activities.

REFERENCES

American Association for the Advancement of Science (AAAS). (1993). *Benchmarks for science literacy*. New York: Oxford University Press.

Barman, C. R. (1989). A procedure for helping prospective elementary teachers integrate the learning cycle into science textbooks. *Journal of Science Teacher Education, 1*(2), 21–26.

National Research Council (NRC). (1996). *National science education standards*. Washington, DC: National Academy Press.

Yager, R. (1991). The constructivist learning model. *The Science Teacher, 58*(6), 52–57.

LIGHT ENERGY AND COLOR

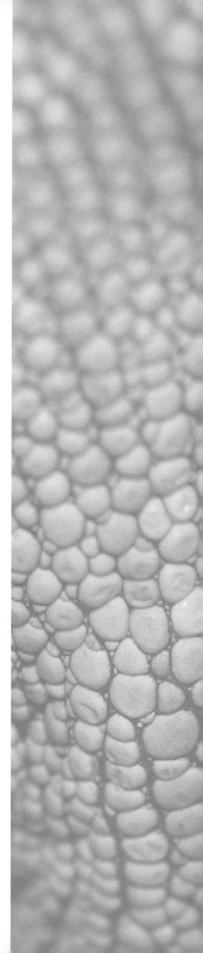

W hy does something look larger under a magnifying glass? What makes a rainbow? Why does writing appear backward in a mirror? Children want to know many things about the behavior of light. These and other phenomena become understandable when we learn how light travels, how light waves can be "bent," why light can be colored, and how we see light.

Benchmarks and Standards

Examples of standards in the area of light energy and color are guidelines related to how sunlight is made up of many colors; how light reflecting off objects allows us to see; and how light travels. Specific examples follow:

Sample Benchmarks (American Association for the Advancement of Science, 1993)

- Light from the sun is made up of a mixture of many different colors of light, even though to the eye the light looks almost white. Other things that give off or reflect light have a different mix of colors. (By Grades 6–8, p. 90)
- Something can be "seen" when light waves emitted or reflected by it enter the eye. (By Grades 6–8, p. 90)

Sample Standards (NRC 1996)

- Light travels in a straight line until it strikes an object. Light can be reflected by a mirror, refracted by a lens, or absorbed by an object. (By Grades K–4, p. 127)
- Light interacts with matter by transmission (including refraction) absorption, or scattering (including reflection). To see an object, light from that object—emitted by or scattered from it—must enter the eye. (By Grades 5–8, p. 155)

PATHWAYS OF LIGHT **Inquiry**

MATERIALS

- Salt or cereal box
- Sticky tape
- Pin
- Black paper
- Three rubber bands
- Waxed paper
- Scissors

A Camera with a Surprise Inside

Invitation

How can you make and use a pinhole camera? Have you ever used a pinhole camera like the one shown here? Light enters a tiny pinhole at one end, and travels to a waxed paper screen at the other end of the tube. You are able to observe an image of the object on the inside of the homemade camera. What you see may surprise you.

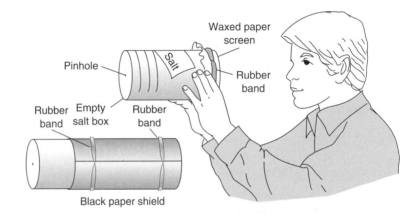

Exploration

1. Use a pin to punch a hole in the center of the box bottom.
2. Remove the box top. Put waxed paper over the box's open end to make the screen. Use a rubber band to hold it.
3. Point the camera at brightly lit objects inside or outside a dark room. What do you see on the waxed paper screen?
4. To use the camera in a lighted place, you must shield the screen from the light. Roll black paper into a large tube and fit it around the screen end of the box. Secure it with two rubber bands. Press your face against the paper shield's open end to see images on the screen.

Teaching Tips

Several kinds of boxes will serve for this activity, including milk cartons. If a black paper shield is used, it should be large. The observer's eyes will need to be about 30 centimeters (1 foot) away from the screen to see a sharp image.

Most children will be surprised to find that an upside-down image appears on the screen. You might sketch the pinhole camera on the chalkboard and invite students to think through what happens.

Scaffolding for English Learners

English learners may appear to have difficulty with concepts such as *smaller* and *larger* when, in fact, it is only due to their inability to associate the English word with the concept being taught. Teachers should be aware of the need to identify and develop key vocabulary words. (See Ovando, Collier, & Combs, 2003, for a discussion of the importance of vocabulary in science education.)

Concept Invention

1. How must you move the camera (a) to make the image move right? left? up? down? (b) to make the image get smaller? larger? What happens if the camera is still and the image moves (e.g., have a person walk from right to left)?
2. How can you make a brighter, sharper image appear on the screen? What will happen to the image if you (a) change the pinhole size? (b) line the inside of the box with black paper? white paper? (c) use a longer or larger box or a shoe box? (d) use paper other than waxed paper for the screen?
3. How can you make a pinhole camera with a larger paper cup? How can a second cup be used as a light shield?
4. What other ideas can you think of to try?

Concept Application

Describe how you will show someone else how light travels in straight lines.

Me and My Shadow ——————

Invitation

What is a shadow? How can you make a shadow? How can you change the length and direction of a shadow?

Exploration

1. Put a nail, head down, on some white paper.
2. Shine the flashlight on the nail. What kind of a shadow do you see?

MATERIALS

- White sheet of paper
- Flashlight
- Pencil
- Small nail
- Partner

Concept Invention

1. How can you make a long shadow? a short shadow?
2. How can you make a shadow that points left? right?
3. Let your partner turn off the flashlight and point it at the nail. Where will the shadow be when your partner turns on the flashlight again? (The flashlight must be held still.) Draw a line on the paper where you think the shadow will be.
4. Can you tell how long a shadow will be?

Teaching Tips

In this investigation, children discover how to predict the lengths and directions of shadows. They learn how to make shadows dark and sharp and pale or fuzzy by changing the distance between an object and the light source. They also learn that this movement affects the shadow's size.

Concept Application

Describe how you can shine the light on the nail so that there is no shadow.

Shadows in the Sun ———

Invitation

What kinds of shadows can you make and see outdoors?

Exploration

1. Go outdoors into the sunshine.
2. Make some shadows on the ground like the example shown.

Concept Invention

1. Can you and a partner make your shadows shake hands without really touching each other's hands?
2. How can you make your shadow seem to stand on the shoulders of your partner's shadow?
3. How can you make a pale, fuzzy shadow darker and sharper?
4. How should you stand so that your shadow is in front of you? in back of you? to your left? to your right?
5. Draw a line where the shadow of some object is now. Where do you think the shadow will be in 1 hour? Draw a second line and then check to see later.
6. What are some other things you can try with shadows?

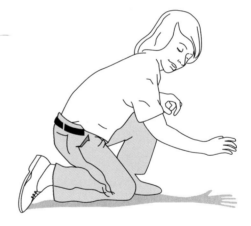

 Try determining the sizes of objects by their shadows with upper-elementary and middle grades students.

Concept Application

A shadow may be made when an object blocks some light; a shadow may be changed by moving the object or the light source in different ways. Can you think of ways to use the overhead projector to illustrate this concept?

Making Money ———

Invitation

How many pennies can you make with two mirrors?

Exploration

1. Fit two mirrors together like two walls joined to make a corner.
2. Place the penny between the mirrors. How many pennies do you see?
3. Change the mirror angle. Move the mirrors in other ways. Move the penny, too.

Concept Invention

1. What is the greatest number of pennies you can make? the fewest number?
2. Can you make more than one penny with only one mirror?

Adapting for Students with Exceptionalities

Exceptional students may have difficulty with following directions for this activity. Use classroom schedules so that students know when the activity will be taught so they can be prepared. Make sure you use a prearranged signal and have students' attention before you begin. Also make sure students are facing you when you give the directions. Use voice inflection to sustain attention and alert students to important instructions.

Concept Application

Where would the use of two or more mirrors be beneficial?

Mirror Reflections ———

Invitation

What are some things you can do with a mirror? Can you see someone else's eyes in a mirror without the other person seeing your eyes in the mirror? (Say the other person is also looking into the mirror.) How can you find out?

Exploration

1. Tape a mirror flat against a wall at your eye level.
2. Have your partner stand in back and to the right of the mirror.
3. Now you stand in back and to the left of the mirror.
4. Move around slowly until you see your partner's eyes in the mirror. Can your partner now see your eyes in the mirror?

MATERIALS
• Small mirror
• Sticky tape
• Partner

Concept Invention

1. What will happen if you or your partner moves farther to the side?
2. What will happen if you or your partner moves farther back?
3. Is there any spot where you can see your partner's eyes without your partner seeing your eyes?

Scaffolding for English Learners

Collaboration between students, as found in this mirror reflections activity, is an important strategy for assisting the English learner in constructing the content of science. (See Fathman, Quinn, & Kessler, 1992, for a discussion of the advantage of cooperative strategies with English learners.)

Concept Application

When would you want to be able to see someone without that person seeing you? Create an arrangement of mirrors you could use to make your observations.

Up Periscope

MATERIALS

- Two small mirrors
- Soft clay
- Meterstick or yardstick

Invitation

How can you use two mirrors to see over objects taller than you?

Exploration

1. Push a piece of clay into the meterstick near each end.
2. Push a mirror sideways into each lump of clay, so that the mirror surfaces face each other.
3. Fix the mirrors so that they look like those illustrated here. When done, you will have a periscope.
4. Hold the periscope upright. Look in the bottom mirror. What can you see? You may have to move the mirrors a little to see clearly.
5. Over what tall objects can you see with your periscope?

Concept Invention

1. How can you use your periscope to see around a corner?
2. How can you see around a corner with just one mirror on the stick?

Concept Application

Could you use three mirrors for your periscope? How would three mirrors need to be arranged in order to create a periscope?

Teaching Tips

When light strikes a mirror at an angle, it is reflected at the same angle in a different direction. That is why if you see someone else's image in a mirror, it is possible for that person to see yours. This also explains how periscopes work. Notice in the illustration that the two mirror angles are identical. For the same reason, a full-length mirror needs to be only about half as long as you are tall.

I Can See Myself

Invitation

Do you need a full-length mirror to see your feet and head at the same time?

Exploration

1. You can use two small mirrors instead of a large, full-length mirror. Have your partner stand at arm's length from the wall.
2. Tape one mirror flat against the wall at your partner's eye level.
3. Hold the second mirror flat against the wall below the first mirror.
4. Move the bottom mirror slowly down the wall. Have your partner say stop when she can see her shoes in the bottom mirror.
5. Tape the bottom mirror flat against the wall.
6. Now your partner should be able to see her head and feet. The top and bottom mirrors are like the top and bottom of a large, full-length mirror, as shown here.

MATERIALS

- Two small mirrors
- Meterstick or yardstick
- Sticky tape
- Partner

Teaching Tips

Check that the mirror is taped flat against the wall in the last two exploration steps. If it is not, you will likely have an error in measurement.

Concept Invention

1. How long is it from the top of one mirror to the bottom of the other mirror compared to your partner's height—half as long? three fourths as long? just as long as your partner is tall? Measure and find out.

2. Does moving back from the mirror make a difference in the size needed?
3. Does the mirror size needed depend on a person's height? How could you find out?
4. Can you predict the size of the shortest full-length mirror you'll need to see yourself? Switch with your partner and find out.

Concept Application

When light travels to a mirror at a slant, it is reflected at the same slant in another direction. Describe an everyday application of this concept.

The Real You ———————

MATERIALS
• Two mirrors

Invitation

How can two mirrors show what you really look like?

Exploration

1. Look into one mirror. Think of your image as another person facing you.
2. Wink your left eye, then your right eye. Which eye does the image blink each time?
3. Fit two mirrors together in the way that two walls are joined. Move them slightly so that half of your face is seen in each mirror as shown.
4. Wink each eye. Touch your left ear. Tilt your head to the right. What happens each time?

 Teaching Tips

Each mirror reflects half of the image onto the adjoining mirror. This puts it back to normal. A single mirror can only reflect an object backward. This is why our one-mirror image is not how we look to others.

Concept Invention

1. Study the illustration.
2. How can you explain why your right eye appears on the left, like that of a real person facing you?

Adapting for Students with Exceptionalities

Repeat directions as needed for students who are having difficulty with this activity. Try to have the students repeat the directions in their own words. (See Mercer & Mercer, 2005, for a discussion on accommodations involving interactive instruction.)

Concept Application

Why do car tires appear to be traveling "backward" in some movies?

Light Relay Races

Invitation

How can you relay light with mirrors?

Exploration

1. Hold a mirror in the light. Reflect the light onto a wall.
2. Pick a target on the wall. Reflect the light so that it shines on the target.
3. Reflect your light onto another mirror held by a partner. Have your partner try to hit the target.
4. With how many mirrors can you and some partners relay the light and hit a target?
5. Have a contest between two or more teams. Which team can hit a target fastest with light passed along from several mirrors? How can you make the contest fair?

MATERIALS

- Three or four small mirrors
- Sunshine or bright flashlight
- Partner

Teaching Tips

Caution: If using a laser, caution children not to look directly into the laser.

A fair contest will prevent one team from observing and profiting from the mistakes of the other. You can tell if every mirror in a relay is being used by shading each mirror in turn with your hand. The light shining on the target in each instance will disappear. Strong light is needed if more than two mirrors are used.

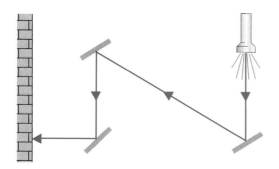

Concept Invention

How will you tell if light is being passed from every mirror?

Concept Application

Make a drawing that shows how the mirrors were held to hit the target as illustrated in this activity.

Mirror Balance

Invitation

Suppose you made a small, simple drawing. Then suppose you erased half of it. Could you hold a mirror on the drawing so that it would seem whole again? Would it depend on the drawing? In what way? Drawings that allow you to do this are said to have mirror balance, or symmetry. How can you find out what things have mirror balance?

MATERIALS

- Paper
- Pencil
- Small mirror
- Ruler

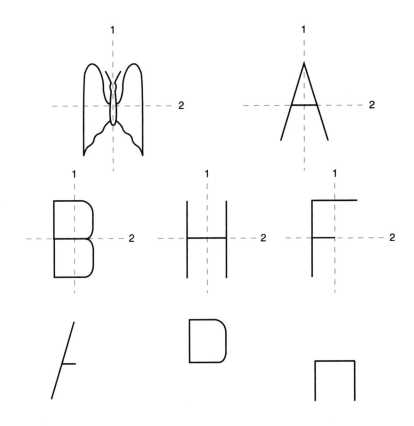

Exploration

1. Put the edge of your mirror on line 1 of the butterfly. Can you see what seems like the whole butterfly? You can because the butterfly has side-by-side balance.

2. Now put the mirror on line 2. Can you see a whole butterfly now? You cannot because a butterfly's body is balanced only one way.

3. Some letters of the alphabet have balance, too. Put your mirror on line 1 of the capital letter A. Can you see what seems like a whole letter A? You can because capital letter A has side-by-side balance.

4. Now, put the mirror on line 2. Can you see a whole letter A? You cannot because this capital letter is balanced only one way.

5. Try your mirror both ways on capital B. Notice that you cannot see a whole letter on line 1, but you can on line 2. A capital B only has up-and-down balance.

6. Try your mirror both ways on capital H. Notice that you see a whole letter both ways. A capital H has both side-by-side and up-and-down balance.

7. Try your mirror both ways on capital F. Notice that you cannot see a whole letter either way. A capital F has no balance.

Concept Invention

1. Which capital letters of the alphabet do you think have side-by-side balance? up-and-down balance? both kinds? no balance? Arrange the letters into four groups. Then check each letter with your mirror to see if you put it into the right group.
2. Some words may be made up of only letters from one group. How many words can you think of whose letters have only side-by-side balance? only up-and-down balance? only letters with both kinds of balance?
3. Use what you know to write secret code words.

Concept Application

Some objects have evenly balanced or symmetrical shapes; a mirror may be used to explore an object's symmetry. Draw some common objects and show if they have side-to-side or up-and-down symmetry.

PATHWAYS OF LIGHT CONCEPTS

Imagine reaching for something that is visible in front of you and not finding it there, or shining a flashlight in the dark and having it illuminate only something in back of you. This, of course, is not likely to happen because light travels in straight lines.

It is true that a beam of light can "bend" under certain conditions, such as when going from air into water or glass, or the reverse. Scientists also know that light passing through space is attracted and curved by the gravitational fields of massive objects in space. Other than these exceptions, though, light does appear to travel in straight lines.

This property makes many interesting things take place. For example, look at the pinhole "camera" in INQ Figure 1–1. Light enters a narrow pinhole in the cereal box end from the candle flame. At the other end, an inverted image appears on waxed paper taped over the opening. Why? The numerals in the figure suggest an answer. If light travels in straight lines, the light going from spot 1 on the left can only go to spot 1 on the right, and vice versa.

Shadows ──────

Because light travels in straight lines, it is easy to block it with objects. This is why we can identify an object from its shadow.

Only objects that we cannot see through, such as metal and wood, cast true shadows. These are called *opaque* objects. *Transparent* objects, such as clear glass and cellophane, do not cast a shadow because they block very little light. *Translucent* objects, such as frosted glass and waxed paper, allow only some light to pass through, but do not block enough light to produce a true shadow.

INQ Figure 1–1   A pinhole "camera."

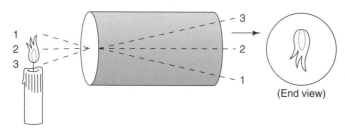

(End view)

Children can learn to make large or small shadows and clear or fuzzy shadows. They can do this by varying the distance from the light source to the opaque object and the place where the shadow falls. Shadow exploration is interesting to children of all ages. It can lay the foundation for understanding some important principles of physics in later grades.

Reflections

We can alter the pathways of light in several ways, some of them surprising. For instance, why do people powder their noses? Psychological reasons aside, they do it to scatter light reflections.

You know that a ball thrown straight down on smooth, level pavement bounces back up. Try it on rough gravel, however, and its return path is unpredictable. A smooth, shiny surface reflects light rays with very little scattering; but a rough or uneven surface may scatter the rays so thoroughly that reflections may be scarcely visible. What makes makeup powder so effective? Put some under a microscope. Greatly magnified, it resembles gravel!

Of course, even better reflections are possible with mirrors than with noses. Sprinkle some powder or chalk dust over half of the mirror and leave the remainder clear. Shine a flashlight on both sections of the mirror. Does the powder help reduce glare? Scattered light rays are called *diffused reflections*. Light rays that are not scattered are *regular reflections*.

The only time we can see something that doesn't glow by itself is when light reflects off it and travels to our eyes, such as light reflecting off the moon. Children generally do not think of light as reflecting off objects. Rather, they hold the misconception that they see all objects directly instead of the reflection of light that is cast from the objects.

Mirrors

When you deal with flat, or plane, reflectors, a special kind of regular reflection becomes possible. If you stand by a mirror and can see the eyes of another person, that person can also see your eyes. No matter from what position or angle you try it, the same results happen if you are close enough to the mirror to see a reflection. The angle at which light strikes a plane reflector (called the *angle of incidence*) always equals the angle at which it is reflected (called the *angle of reflection*).

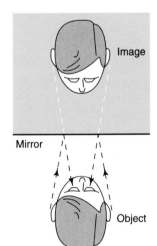

INQ Figure 1–2 **Why a mirror image is reversed.**

Some explanations of convex and concave mirrors can be discussed at the elementary level. *Convex mirrors* have a bulging center that reduces a wide field to a small area. This is way they are used for rearview mirrors on some automobiles. *Concave mirrors* have a scooped-out center that magnifies images. They are useful for cosmetic work or shaving. Observing images with flexible plastic mirrors is a way to demonstrate how bending a mirror to change its plane will change an image.

If we could not look at photographs of ourselves or at our double reflections in two mirrors, we would never know how we appear to others. A mirror always produces a reversed image of the observer.

To learn why this is so, study INQ Figure 1–2. In a sense, a mirror image is an optical illusion. Light rays reflect off the mirror into the boy's eyes. He stares outward along the lines of the incoming rays. To him, his image appears to be just as far in back of the mirror as he is in front of it.

INQ Figure 1–3   There is symmetry in letters of the alphabet. Dotted lines show how to hold a mirror to reconstruct the original letters.

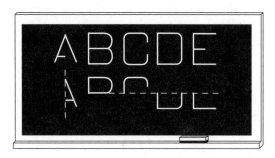

Symmetry

Working with mirrors will enable you to introduce the concept of symmetry or the idea of balanced proportions in objects and geometric forms. The concept is of value in many fields, including biology, mathematics, and the arts. A butterfly, for example, has symmetry. If you draw an imaginary line down the middle of its body, the left half is a near duplicate of its right half. A starfish has another kind of symmetry. If you turn its body around on an imaginary axis, a rotational balance is evident.

Children will be surprised at the ways a mirror can reveal balanced proportions. They can learn to predict which letter shapes will reveal the property of symmetry. Notice that each letter in INQ Figure 1–3 is symmetrical. The left and right sides of A are opposite, but alike. The remaining letters are different in that the symmetry is vertical—that is, found in the tops and bottoms, but not laterally. A few letters, such as X, O, I, and H, have both lateral and vertical balance. Some, such as L, F, and J, have none at all.

LIGHT REFRACTION **Inquiry**

Some Everyday Magnifiers

Invitation

How can you make something seem larger? That is, how can you magnify it? What everyday objects can you use to magnify things?

Exploration

1. Place a piece of waxed paper on a printed page.
2. Dip a pencil tip into some water. Let a drop run off onto the waxed paper.
3. How does the print look through the water drop?

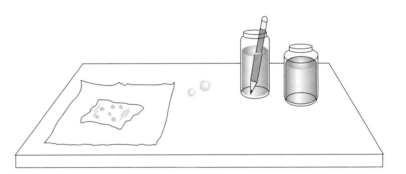

Concept Invention

1. Make water drops of different sizes. Which drops magnify the print more?
2. Put the waxed paper on a book. Make a row of drops, each drop bigger than the next. Hold up the book and paper to eye level. Look at the outline of the drops. Which are smaller and rounder? Which are larger and flatter? Which will magnify more?
3. Get two different-sized clear marbles. Which one do you think will magnify more? How much more? How will you find out?
4. Get a narrow jar of water. Put your pencil inside. Does your pencil look larger? Move your pencil to different places, inside and outside the jar. Where does it look the thickest?
5. Get another, wider jar of water. Will it magnify more or less than the narrow jar?
6. What other everyday things can you use as magnifiers?

Teaching Tips

Any clear, curved, transparent material acts like a lens; that is, light rays that pass through the material are bent. Objects viewed through the lens may appear to be magnified. Children will enjoy and learn from trials with additional examples of clear glass and plastic materials. Clear, narrow plastic pill vials become especially good magnifiers when filled with water and capped.

The magnifying power of a glass marble may be measured by placing it on narrow-lined paper. Count the number of lines seen inside the clear marble. The marble with the fewest visible lines has the greatest magnification.

Concept Application

A clear, curved object may appear to magnify things. The magnification produced by a clear, curved object increases as its diameter decreases. What type of object would be useful in making eyeglasses?

How Big Can It Get? ————

Invitation

How can you measure the magnifying power of a hand lens?

MATERIALS

• Hand lens

• Sheet of lined paper

• Ruler

• Pencil

Exploration

1. Draw two or three evenly spaced lines between each of the printed lines on your paper. A half sheet of extra lines should be enough.
2. Pencil a small **X** in the middle of the paper where you have drawn lines.
3. Center the **X** in the lens. Move the lens up and down until the **X** looks clearest.
4. Count all the lines you see inside the lens, as shown in the drawing.

Concept Invention

1. Count all the lines outside the lens that are between the first and last lines seen inside the lens.
2. Divide the number of lines you counted in step 1 by the number of lines you counted inside the lens. The answer is the power of the lens. For example, if the answer is 2, your lens makes things appear about twice as large as they are.

Teaching Tips | Thicker lenses usually magnify more than thinner lenses of the same diameter. The distance from the point of focus to the lens is the *focal length*. Because they have shorter focal lengths, thicker or curvier lenses must be held closer to the **X** to see it clearly.

Concept Application

What is the power of your lens? What is the power of other lenses you can try? How does the power of thicker lenses compare with that of thinner lenses? How far above the **X** must you hold different lenses to see it clearly?

LIGHT REFRACTION CONCEPTS

Have you ever jumped into the shallow part of a swimming pool, only to discover it was deeper than it seemed? Light travels more slowly in water than it does in air. This difference results in an optical illusion, even though we may be looking straight down into the water.

The topic of reflection and refraction lends itself to misconceptions. Illustrations in textbooks are often inadequate, and explanations are sometimes poor (Iona & Beaty, 1988). It is important to allow children plenty of time to discuss their constructions regarding these concepts.

Density and Light Speeds

The speed of light changes as it travels into or out of media of varying densities. The event is especially curious if the light beam enters or leaves a different medium at a slant. A change in speed may cause the beam to change direction of travel, or to *refract*.

Examples of refraction are all around us. A pencil placed partway into water looks bent. Distant images shimmer through unevenly heated air as we drive along a hot road. The scenery looks distorted through an inferior glass window because its thickness is uneven. Interestingly, the function of an automobile windshield wiper is to restore the rainy outside surface of a windshield to a plane surface. As water is wiped away, the light rays enter the glass at a uniform angle, rather than unevenly.

What happens when light enters or leaves water? Why does it bend? Let's look for a moment into the concept of density as it relates to this event. You know that anything in motion will slow down or stop when something is in the way. It is easy to dash across an empty room at top speed. Scatter some people around the room, and the runner will slow down, bumping head-on into some people and deflecting off others.

A similar thing happens with light as it travels through air, water, and glass. Water is denser than air. It has more matter in the same space. Therefore, glass is denser than water. When light enters a denser medium, it slows down. The reverse is also true: When light enters a less dense medium, it speeds up. What makes light bend can be understood through an analogy.

Notice INQ Figure 1–4. Part A explains why the coin in part B appears to be in front of its true location. In part A, the two wheels are rolling freely in the direction shown. But what happens when the leading wheel strikes the sand? The device moves on, but at a slightly different angle. To reverse this, if the device travels upward from the sand along the broken line, one wheel will hit the paved portion sooner. The direction will again change, but in an opposite way.

INQ Figure 1–4   **Light "bends" and changes direction (B) in the same way the wheels change direction (A) when they hit a different surface.**

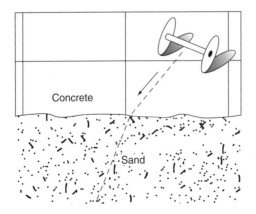

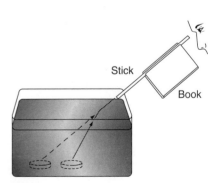

B

In part B, light bends in a similar direction. As it leaves the water, the light bends slightly toward the horizontal. The observer sights along a stick toward where the coin seems to be. The line of sight seems to be a straight line from eye to coin, but it is not. If the stick is pushed into the water at the same angle at which it is poised (sliding it in the groove formed by a closed book cover may ensure this), it will overshoot the target.

Lenses

People have learned to control light refractions with lenses. Eyeglasses can correct certain vision problems. Magnifying glasses and optical instruments extend the power of sight far beyond that available to the naked eye.

INQ Figure 1–5 shows how light refracts when passing through a convex lens. In part A, the light rays enter the eye from two opposite slants. (It may help to think of the wheels–axle analogy again.) As the eye follows these slanted rays to the lens, they seem to continue outward, and so they form an enlarged image of the object.

How can we make the object appear even larger? Compare parts B and C. Notice that the two lenses differ in thickness, although their diameters are the same. Each will bring the sun's rays to a point or focus at a different distance. The distance from the point of focus to the lens is the *focal length*. Notice that the thicker lens has the shorter focal length. By extending the slanted rays outward, you can see why it magnifies more than the lens in part C.

A curious thing may happen when we observe a moving object through a convex lens. INQ Figure 1–6 shows the focal point of a small jar of water as light passes through it. (Although the jar is really a cylindrical lens, it acts as a convex lens in this example.) If a pencil is moved to the right *inside* the focal length of the lens, its image will also move to the right; but if it is moved to the right *outside* the focal length, its image will move to the left. The reason is apparent if we notice what happens beyond the focal point. The light rays cross and go to opposite sides.

INQ Figure 1–5   **The shape of a convex lens is what determines how an image is magnified.**

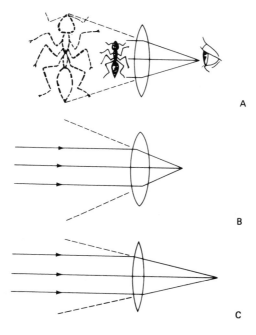

INQ Figure 1–6   When an object that is *inside* the focal length of a convex lens is moved **right, its image also moves right. But if the object is *outside* the focal length when moved right, its image moves left.**

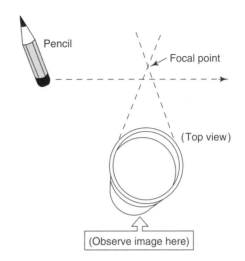

INQ Figure 1–7   A concave lens makes objects appear smaller because the light rays diverge.

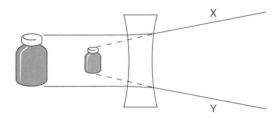

Convex lenses cause light rays to *converge*, or bring them together, as you have seen. Concave lenses cause light rays to *diverge*, or spread out; this causes objects viewed through them to appear smaller. You can see why in INQ Figure 1–7. The light from the object slants outward toward X and Y as it goes through the lens (remember the wheels–axle analogy). As the eye follows these slanted rays back to the lens, the rays seem to continue inward at a slant and form a smaller image of the object.

Thick drinking glasses and glass eye cups often have concave-shaped bases. The students can check whether images are smaller by looking through them. Perhaps the easiest concave lens to make is an air bubble in a small, capped jar of water. An object viewed through the bubble will look smaller, but if viewed through the convex part of the jar, it will appear larger.

Commercial lenses can teach a great deal. Children may learn even more, though, by fashioning their own lenses from a variety of transparent objects, containers, and fluids. A plastic soda bottle works well to bend light (Wilson, 1990). A clear-glass marble will also magnify objects, as will a water drop or drops of other fluids. A small drinking glass with vertical sides (not tapered) magnifies things well when filled with water or other fluids. Narrow olive jars make especially powerful magnifiers. However, the best possibilities for controlled study of homemade lenses will happen if you use clear, small plastic pill vials.

COLOR Inquiry

How to Mix Colors ────────

Invitation

Suppose you have two different-colored crayons. How can you use the crayons to make three different colors? How can you make more than three colors with three different crayons?

Exploration

1. Rub three short, thick lines lightly across the white paper. Make one red, one yellow, and one blue.
2. Rub three thick up-and-down lines lightly on the white paper so that they cross the first three. Use the same three colors.
3. What colors do you see where the lines cross?

Teaching Tips | Children will get the best results when combining crayon colors if they rub lightly. When red, yellow, and blue paints or dyes are paired and mixed in the right proportions, we see green, orange, and purple.

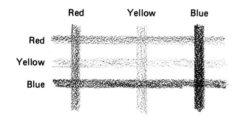

Concept Invention

1. How many colors did you make?
2. How many new colors can you make with crayons of other colors?

Concept Application

Draw pictures and color them.

Color Mix-Ups ────────

Invitation

How can you make many colors by mixing water samples of several colors?

Exploration

1. Fill three small jars half full with water.
2. Put two drops of different food coloring in each jar.
3. Put a different straw into each jar and stir the colored water.
4. Mix a little colored water from two jars into a fourth jar. Use a straw to lift out the liquid from each jar as shown in the illustration on the next page.

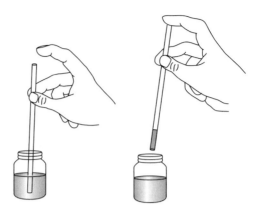

Concept Invention

1. How many new colors can you make by mixing two different colors each time? Use the same volume of each color when mixing colors. Keep a record.
2. What happens when you mix more of one color than another?
3. Mix a mystery color made from two colors. Use more of one color than another. Can someone else figure out how to match exactly your mystery color? Can you match someone else's mystery color? Try many different colors.

Adapting for Students with Exceptionalities

Students with physical impairments may have difficulty manipulating the straws in this activity. Try using eyedroppers.

Concept Application

When red, yellow, and blue dyes are paired and mixed, they produce green, orange, and purple. Mixing different proportions of the colors produces different shades. What other shades can you produce here?

Colored Comics ——————

MATERIALS

- Colored comic strips from different newspapers
- Strong hand lens

Invitation

How are the colors made in comic strips?

Exploration

1. Study different comic strip pictures with a hand lens.
2. Notice how many colors are made from only a few colors.
3. Notice that some dots may be printed side by side; or one colored dot may be printed partly over a dot of another color.
4. Observe how different shades are make by changing the distances between dots.

Teaching Tips | A dissecting microscope is ideal for analyzing colored comics.

Concept Invention

1. What side-by-side colored dots do you see?
2. What colors do they make?
3. What overprinted colors do you see?
4. What colors do they make?

Concept Application

In what ways are cartoon colors from different newspapers alike? different?

The Makeup of Colored Liquids

Invitation

You know that mixing two or more colors can make a colored liquid. Most inks and dyes are made in that way. Some of the colors that are mixed to make another color are surprising. How can you find out the colors that make up a colored dye or ink?

Exploration

1. Cut some strips from a white paper towel. Make them about 10 centimeters by 2 centimeters (4 inches by 3/4 inch).
2. Put 1 drop of red food coloring and 1 drop of blue on waxed paper. Mix them.
3. Touch a toothpick to the coloring. Make a sizable dot on the middle of one strip.
4. Hold the strip in a small jar that is about half full of water. The colored dot should be just above the water level as shown.
5. What happens to the coloring as water is soaked up past the colored dot? (This may take a minute or longer.) How many colors appear as the colored dot spreads out?

> **MATERIALS**
>
> - Food coloring (red, blue, green, and yellow)
> - Baby-food jar half full of water
> - Scissors
> - Waxed paper
> - Four toothpicks
> - White paper towel or coffee filters
> - Ruler

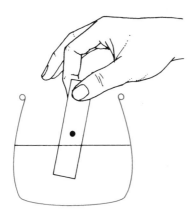

 Teaching Tips | The basic process of this investigation is called *paper chromatography*. The separate pigments that make up the color of a dye are absorbed by the paper at slightly different rates. This has the effect of spreading out the pigments, which makes them visible. Only washable (nonpermanent) dyes will work.

Concept Invention

1. What colors are in other food coloring samples? How are different brands of the same colors alike or different?
2. Try a game with a partner. Mix drops from several food colors, and then test them on strips. Keep a record. Remove the tested strips from the jar and let them

dry. Can your partner tell which food colors were mixed for each strip? Switch places with your partner. Can you tell which mixed colors were used for your partner's strips?

3. What colors make up some inks?
4. What other papers or filters can be used? How do they change the color separation?

Concept Application

The colors that make up a dye may be discovered through paper chromatography. Most dyes contain several blended colors. How do you think manufacturers produce colored cloth?

The Colors of the Sun —————

Invitation

What colors make up sunlight?

Exploration

1. Place the pan in the sun. Have the mirror face the sun.
2. Hold the mirror upright against the pan's inside rim.
3. Slowly tip back the mirror. Light must strike the mirror below the water's surface.
4. Point the mirror toward a white wall or large sheet of white paper.

MATERIALS
• Cake pan about half filled with water
• Mirror
• Sunshine
• White paper

Teaching Tips
This crude prism does an excellent job of refracting sunlight into its full spectrum of colors. Stirring the water mildly mixes the colors into white light again. The spectrum of a filmstrip projector's light will be similar but not identical to that of sunlight.

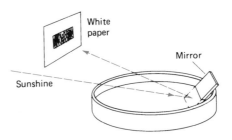

Concept Invention

1. What colors do you see on the wall?
2. What happens to the colors if you stir the water lightly?

Concept Application

Try using the light from a filmstrip projector inside the classroom. How will these colors compare with those of sunlight?

COLOR CONCEPTS

When our ancestors saw a rainbow, they were probably inclined to give a magical or supernatural explanation to account for it. Later, people thought that the colors came from the rain droplets through which sunlight passes. Not until Isaac Newton (1642–1727) per-

INQ Figure 1–8   **A prism separates white light into a spectrum of six colors.**

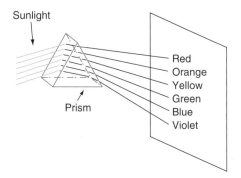

formed experiments with prisms did people realize that these colors were the parts of visible sunlight itself. The six universally recognized colors in the visible spectrum of sunlight are red, orange, yellow, green, blue, and violet.

A prism separates white light into its components because each color has a different wavelength and rate of vibration. Red light has the longest wavelength, with about 1200 waves per millimeter (30,000 waves per inch). Violet light has the shortest wavelength, with about twice that number of waves per unit. As a light beam passes through a prism, the longer waves are refracted the least and the shorter waves the most (INQ Figure 1–8).

Differences in colors are often compared to pitch differences in sound. A low-pitched sound is a result of relatively slow vibrations; its visual counterpart is the color red. A high-pitched sound is a result of fast vibrations; its counterpart is violet.

Mixing Colors

We can mix colors in two basic ways: one with colored beams of light, and the other with paints or dyes. When light beams of only three primary colors (red, blue, and green) are added together in the right proportions on a white screen, different color combinations occur. These are shown in the overlapping sections of INQ Figure 1–9. When red, blue, and green are used as colored light beams, they are called the *additive colors*. Scientists have found that three certain-colored pigments can absorb these additive colors; that is, if you shine a red, blue, or green light on the right pigment, almost no color is reflected. The pigment looks black. Blue light is absorbed by a yellow pigment, and red light by a blue–green pigment called cyan. Green light is absorbed by a purple–red pigment called magenta.

If a white light beam shines on these colored pigments, each will absorb, or "subtract," the specific color mentioned above and reflect to our eyes what is not absorbed. We can mix these pigments to get various colors, but the results we get from mixing all three are the opposite from mixing the three light beams. This is shown in INQ Figure 1–10. In summary, when viewing an object, the color we see depends on (a) the color of light shining on the object and (b) the color reflected by the object to our eyes.

Children can do some experiments with colored construction paper and colored light beams to help them understand these ideas and their practical effects. With ordinary materials, it is difficult to predict the exact hues that will result from the many possible combinations. Another interesting activity is to use colored slides, a prism, and a slide projector to experiment with color (Dalby, 1991).

Don't be surprised if you find that several boys in your class are at least partly color-blind. One male in 12 has the deficiency, contrasted with only 1 in 200 females. Most com-

INQ Figure 1–9   The additive colors. When beams of red, blue, and green light are added together in the right proportions, the overlapping colors result. Color television is produced by an additive process.

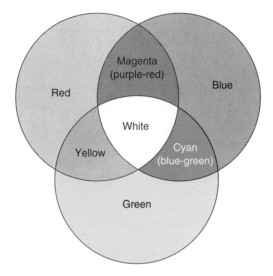

INQ Figure 1–10   The subtractive colors. Paints and dyes absorb, or "subtract," some colors from white light and reflect what is left. Note the overlapping colors when the three primary pigments are mixed in the right proportions.

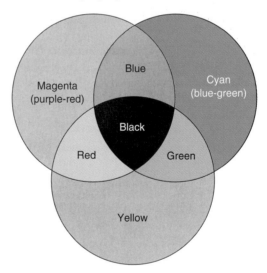

monly, reds and greens are seen in shades of gray; other colors are perceived normally. Rarely do color-blind people see all colors in black and white and shades of gray.

Color Pictures from Digital Cameras

A color digital picture begins when light, reflecting off of an image, passes through the lens of the camera. Then, instead of being focused on color photosensitive film as in a regular color camera, the image is focused on an *image sensor*. The image sensor is generally a fingernail-sized microchip called a charge-coupled device, or CCD. The CCD's surface contains an array of about 2 million or more photosensitive diodes that make up the discrete pixels of the image (*pix* for picture and *el* for elements).

Individual pixels create electrical impulses that are proportional to the intensity of the light they receive. These individual sensors are each covered with a different filter that is colored red, green, or blue (or alternatively cyan, magenta, and yellow). An analog-to-digital conversion process transforms the data for each pixel into a digital value. *Image enhancement* is then completed, as missing values are replaced through the use of software inside the camera. Using an interpolation process, the software adds information to the partially recorded image data processed by the pixels. These numbers are now used to reconstruct the image. Finally, the digital image is saved to the camera's storage.

PERCEPTION AND THE EYE **Inquiry**

How Far Is That?

Invitation

Suppose you had to see for a while with just one eye. How might this make a difference in telling how far something is from you? How can you test if two eyes let you tell distance better than one eye?

Exploration

1. Have a partner hold up a thumb at your eye level.
2. Hold a pencil upright, eraser end down, about 15 centimeters (6 inches) above the thumb. Using both eyes, try to touch the top of your partner's thumb with the eraser. Move the pencil down fairly quickly, but gently.
3. Have your partner slightly change the distance his thumb is from you.
4. Using one eye, try again to touch your partner's thumb. Move the pencil down fairly quickly, but gently.

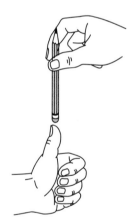

MATERIALS

- Two pencils
- Ball
- Empty soda bottle
- Partner

Teaching Tips

When we see an object with two eyes, each eye views it from a slightly different angle. So, our perception of the object's distance is usually more accurate than if only one eye is used. With distant objects, the advantage decreases. We tend to use size, background, and other clues to estimate distance.

In this investigation, it is important for an object's position to be moved for each trial. Otherwise, muscle memory alone from a preceding trial may allow the child to touch the object. For the test to be valid, the child should not benefit from experience. Also, the pencil should be moved down with some speed, although gently. If done slowly, self-correction becomes too easy.

Concept Invention

1. In which trial was it easier to touch your partner's thumb?
2. Does which eye you close make any difference? How does using two eyes compare with using one? (Be sure your partner slightly changes his thumb position for each trial.)
3. Does which hand you use make any difference?
4. How else can you test if two eyes are better than one for telling distance?

Adapting for Students with Exceptionalities

Students with visual disabilities will have difficulty with these activities. Make students comfortable in asking for assistance or pair students to complete this activity as a team.

Concept Application

How can you show that two eyes are usually better than one for judging distance?

Your Side Vision and Color —————

Invitation

Suppose you notice an object from the corner of your eye while staring straight ahead. Can you notice it is there before you can tell its color? Or can you also tell the color at the same time? How far to the side can you tell different colors?

Exploration

1. Keep your eyes on some object across the room during this experiment.
2. Have a partner stand at your right side, about a step away.
3. Ask your partner to hold up a small colored square opposite your ear. (You should not know the color.)
4. Have your partner slowly move the square forward in a big circle as illustrated.
5. Say, "Stop," when you first notice the square at your side.
6. Then tell your partner the square's color if you can.
7. If you cannot, have your partner move the square forward until you can tell.

MATERIALS

- Four small (5-centimeter, or 2-inch) paper squares of different colors

- Four larger (10-centimeter, or 4-inch) paper squares of different colors

- Partner

Teaching Tips

The eye's inside lining, or retina, contains millions of cells sensitive to light intensity and color. Most of the eye's color-sensitive cells are clustered at the back of the eyeball near the optic nerve. To see color, some colored light must reach there. When light enters the eye at an angle, this area may not be stimulated. So, we can usually detect the presence of an object at our side before we can distinguish its color.

Be sure children keep their eyes fixed on some far object as they do this investigation so that they can properly test their side (peripheral) vision.

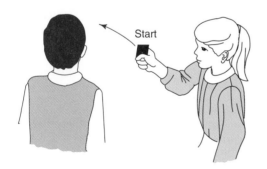

Start

Concept Invention

1. Was it as easy to notice the color as the object itself?
2. Will it make any difference if you try the test from your left side?
3. Will it make any difference if you try different colors? Can you identify some colors farther to the side than others?
4. Will it make any difference if you try the larger squares?
5. What results will you get if you test other people?

Concept Application

An object at one's side can be noticed before its color can be identified. What does this tell you about the structures in the eye?

Tired Eyes ——————

Invitation

MATERIALS

- Construction paper (blue, yellow, red, magenta, cyan, and yellow)

- Watch with second hand

- Scissors

- Pencil

- White paper

Do you get tired seeing colors?

Exploration

1. Pencil an **X** in the center of the white paper.
2. Cut out one small (5-centimeter, or 2-inch) square each of blue, yellow, and red paper.
3. Put the blue square on the **X**. Look at it steadily for 30 seconds.
4. Remove the square and look at the **X**.
5. What color appears at the **X**?

Concept Invention

1. Rest your eyes for a minute or so. Then try the yellow and red squares in the same way.
2. What color appears after the yellow square? the red square?

Concept Application

Describe what you predict will happen with magenta, cyan, or yellow paper. Try out your prediction and describe the results.

PERCEPTION AND THE EYE CONCEPTS

In this section, we examine how the eye works and apply some ideas discussed previously. Although the eye has many parts, we concentrate on three parts directly involved in sight: iris, retina, and lens (see INQ Figure 1–11).

Iris ——————

The iris contains pigment that absorbs some colors and reflects others. Because the kind and amount of this coloring matter varies in individuals, eyes appear to be brown, hazel, or

INQ Figure 1–11   **An eye illustration.**

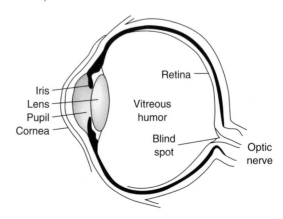

blue. Two sets of tiny muscles control the size of a small dot (pupil) in the iris. This ability regulates the amount of light entering the eye.

The pupils of cats' eyes can dilate far more than ours. This is one reason why their vision is better than humans in near darkness. A dramatic example of this capacity appears when the headlights of an automobile suddenly shine into the eyes of a cat on a dark night. The two shiny round spots we see are the headlight reflections from inside the cat's eyes.

Retina

Why is it difficult to see when we first walk into a darkened movie theater? Our eyes make a second important adjustment when light varies in brightness. The retina contains two kinds of light-sensitive cells: rods and cones. Cones are less sensitive than rods and are clustered near the back of the eyeball. They work best in strong light and enable us to see color. Rods are distributed in other parts of the retina and are sensitive to dim light.

Chemical changes sensitize either rods or cones under certain conditions. For example, when we walk into a dark theater on a sunny day, it takes several minutes before the rods work well. To achieve optimum sensitivity, up to a half hour may be required. It is thought that cones are most sensitive to three basic colors: red, green, and blue. According to this idea, we see many colors because the basic colors are seen in various combinations.

Lens

An eye lens is convex in shape and works like any other convex lens, with one important difference: A muscle permits it to change shape. If a large, nearby object appears before you, the lens thickens. This thicker lens refracts light rays entering the eye sharply enough for a focus to occur on the retina. Light rays from a small or distant object, however, enter the lens in a near parallel fashion. Only a small refraction is needed to bring the rays to a focus on the retina.

To experience this action, look at a distant object and then suddenly look at something 30 centimeters (1 foot) away. Do you feel the tug of your lens muscles pulling the lens? Do you find that the near object is fuzzy for the brief instant it takes for the muscles to adjust lens thickness? In a camera, of course, focusing is achieved by moving the lens back and forth.

Eyeglasses

The use of eyeglasses corrects two of the main vision problems in regard to image focus. In nearsightedness, the cornea or the lens may be thicker, or the eyeball longer, than normal. This causes an image to focus in front of the retina rather than on it. Notice in INQ Figure 1–12 how the problem is corrected. Part A shows a normal eyeball. Part B shows a longer-than-normal eyeball and a focal point in front of, rather than on, the retina. In part C, a concave eyeglass lens spreads out the incoming light rays. This lengthens the focal point just enough to fall on the retina.

In farsightedness, the cornea or the lens may be thinner, or the eyeball shorter, than normal. So, the focal point is at some imaginary distance beyond the retina. Part A of INQ Figure 1–13 shows this happening with a shorter-than-normal eyeball. In part B, a convex

INQ Figure 1–12   **In nearsightedness, an abnormally shaped cornea or eyeball causes an image to focus in front of the retina rather than on it. A concave lens can correct the problem.**

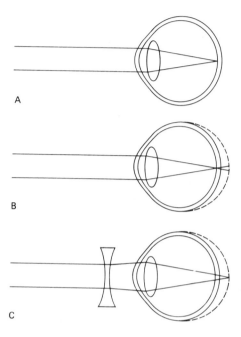

INQ Figure 1–13   **In farsightedness, the image focuses at some imaginary point beyond the retina. A convex lens can correct the problem.**

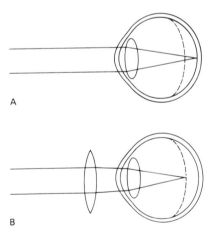

eyeglass lens corrects the defect by forcing the light rays to converge at a shorter focal point, which is on the retina.

Perception

An excellent example of how the brain and eyes work together takes place when we judge distance. Each eye sees an object from a different angle. The closer the object, the greater the difference in what each eye perceives. We actually see a tiny bit around the object. At the same time, we feel our eyes turn inward. With greater distances, the angle gets smaller. The brain interprets this accordingly.

Beyond about 46 meters (50 yards) we rely mainly on size to judge distance. A small telegraph pole looks far away mostly because we know that telephone poles are large. We also use other clues, such as increased haze and the surrounding scene.

A movie film flashes only still pictures on a screen. The apparent motion of a motion-picture projection results from persistence of vision. It takes about 1/16 of a second for an image to fade from our vision after it is withdrawn. By flashing 24 images per second on a screen, a projector creates the illusion of motion.

It took some experience before the current speed of projecting individual motion-picture frames was adopted. Early motion pictures were photographed and projected at much slower speeds. The short, unlighted pause between frames was noticeable. This is how the term *flickers* for movies originated.

It is easy to experience the persistence-of-vision effect with a pencil and a small pad of paper. For example, children can be guided to draw a cartoon with the pad of paper showing a pole that falls over. On the first page, children draw an upright pole on the bottom and center of the page. On each succeeding page, in the same spot, they draw the pole at successively lower angles, until it is horizontal. The number of pages used for this could total 20 pages, which is more than adequate. When the children rapidly flip the pad pages over, they see an animated sequence of a falling pole. Children enjoy making such flipbooks.

References

American Association for the Advancement of Science (AAAS). (1993). *Benchmarks for science literacy.* New York: Oxford University Press.

Dalby, D. K. (1991). Fine-tune your sense of color. *Science and Children, 29*(3), 24–26.

Fathman, A. K., Quinn, M. E., & Kessler, C. (1992). *Teaching science to English learners, grades 4–8.* Washington, DC: National Clearinghouse of Bilingual Education. Retrieved November 13, 2004, from *www.ncela.gwu.edu/pubs/pigs/pig11.htm*

Iona, M., & Beaty, W. (1988). Reflections on refraction. *Science and Children, 25*(8), 18–20.

Mercer, C. D., & Mercer, A. R. (2005). *Teaching students with learning problems* (7th ed.). Upper Saddle River, NJ: Merrill Prentice Hall.

National Research Council (NRC). (1996). *National science education standards.* Washington, DC: National Academy Press.

Ovando, C. J., Collier, V. P., & Combs, M. C. (2003). *Bilingual and ESL classrooms: Teaching in multicultural contexts.* Boston: McGraw-Hill.

Wilson, J. E. (1990). Bent on teaching refraction. *Science and Children, 28*(3), 28–30.

Selected Trade Books: Light Energy and Color

For Younger Children

Baines, R. (1985). *Light.* New York: Troll Associates.

Brockel, R. (1986). *Experiments with light.* New York: Childrens Press.

Carle, E. (1991). *My very first book of colors.* New York: HarperCollins.

Carle, E. (1995). *The very lonely firefly.* New York: G. P. Putnam.

Carroll, J. (1991). *The complete color book.* Parsippany, NJ: Good Apple.

Cole, J. (1997). *The magic school bus makes a rainbow: A book about color.* New York: Scholastic.

Cole, J. (1999). *The magic school bus gets a bright idea: A book about light.* New York: Scholastic.

Collins, D. (1983). *My big fun thinker book of colors and shapes.* Carson, CA: Educational Insights.

Crews, D. (1981). *Light.* New York: Greenwillow Books.

Ehlert, L. (1989). *Color zoo.* New York: HarperCollins.

Fowler, A. (1998). *All the colors of the rainbow.* Danbury, CT: Childrens Press.

Glover, D. (2002). *Sound and light.* New York: Kingfisher.

Gold-Dworkin, H. (2000). *Exploring light and color: A "hands-on" approach to learning.* New York: McGraw-Hill.

Goor, R., & Goor, N. (1981). *Shadows: Here, there, everywhere.* New York: Thomas Y. Crowell.

Hoban, T. (1995). *Colors everywhere.* New York: Greenwillow Books.

Hubbard, P. (1999). *My crayons talk.* New York: Henry Holt.

Livingston, M. (1992). *Light and shadow.* New York: Holiday House.

Macaulay, D. (1990). *Black and white.* Boston: Houghton Mifflin.

Martin, B., & Archambault, J. (1987). *Knots on a counting rope.* New York: Trumpet Club.

Moon, C., & Moon, B. (1992). *Look at a lamp*. Bothell, WA: Wright Group.

Munsch, R. (1992). *Purple, green, and yellow*. New York: Firefly Books.

Serfozo, M. (1988). *Who said red?* New York: Aladdin Picture Books.

Shepherd, D. (1995). *Light shows in the night sky: Auroras*. Danbury, CT: Watts.

Smith, K. B., & Crenson, V. (1987). *Seeing*. New York: Troll Associates.

Stinson, K. (1982). *Red is best*. Willowdale, Ontario: Annick Press.

Suess, Dr. (1996). *My many colored days*. New York: Knopf.

Taylor, B. (1990). *Bouncing and bending light*. Danbury, CT: Watts.

Taylor, B. (1991). *Color and light*. Danbury, CT: Watts.

Taylor, K. (1992). *Flying start science series: Water; light; action; structure*. New York: John Wiley.

Young, E. (1992). *Seven blind mice*. New York: Philomel Books.

For Older Children

Ardley, N. (1991). *Science book of color*. San Diego, CA: HarBrace.

Ardley, N. (1991). *Science book of light*. San Diego, CA: HarBrace.

Asimov, I. (1986). *How did we find out about the speed of light?* New York: Walker.

Berger, M. (1987). *Lights, lenses, and lasers*. New York: G. P. Putnam.

Catherall, E. (1982). *Sight*. Parsippany, NJ: Silver Burdett.

Challoner, J., & LeJars, D. (2001). *Sound and light*. United Kingdom, New York: Kingfisher.

Cooper, M. (1981). *Snap! Photography*. Parsippany, NJ: Julian Messner.

De Bruin, J. (1986). *Light and color*. Parsippany, NJ: Good Apple.

Dispezio, M., & Leary, C. (1999). *Awesome experiments in light & sound*. New York: Sterling Publications.

Dunham, M. (1987). *Colors: How do you say it?* New York: Lothrop, Lee & Shepard Books.

Farndon, J. (2000). *Light and optics (science experiments)*. New York: Benchmark Books.

Fiarotta, P., & Fiarotta, N. (1999). *Great experiments with light*. New York: Sterling Publications.

Hecht, J. (1987). *Optics: Light for a new age*. New York: Macmillan.

Hill, J., & Hill, J. (1986). *Looking at light and color*. New York: David & Charles.

Jennings, T. (1992). *Sound and light*. New York: Smithmark.

Murata, M. (1993). *Science is all around you: Water and light*. Minneapolis: Lerner.

Nankivell-Aston, S., & Jackson, D. (2000). *Science experiments with light (science experiments)*. London: Franklin Watts, Incorporated.

Searle, B., & Hewitt, S. (2002). *Light (fascinating science projects)*. Sussex, England: Copper Beech Books.

Simon, H. (1981). *The magic of color*. New York: Lothrop, Lee & Shepard Books.

Simon, S. (1985). *Shadow magic*. New York: Lothrop, Lee & Shepard Books.

Simon, S. (1991). *Mirror magic*. New York: Lothrop, Lee & Shepard Books.

Walpole, B. (1987). *Light*. New York: Garrard.

Ward, A. (1991). *Experimenting with light and illusions*. Brookmall, PA: Chelsea House.

Whyman, K. (1986). *Light and lasers*. Danbury, CT: Watts.

Whyman, K. (1989). *Rainbows to lasers*. Danbury, CT: Watts.

Wilkins, M. J. (1991). *Air, light, and water*. New York: Random House.

Resource Books

AIMS Educational Foundation. (2000). *Ray's reflections*. Fresno, CA: Author. (mirror activities)

Bartch, M. (1992). *Literature activities across the curriculum*. West Nyack, NY: Simon & Schuster. (science topics on pp. 158–194)

Butzow, C. M., & Butzow, J. W. (1989). *Science through children's literature: An integrated approach*. Englewood, CO: Teacher Ideas Press. (eye, vision, and optics topics on pp. 169–173; shadows and light topics on pp. 174–177)

Gertz, S., Portman, D., & Sraquis, M. (1996). *Teaching physical science through children's literature*. Middletown, OH: Terrific Science Press.

Hillen, J., Mercier, S., Hoover, E., & Cordel, B. (1994). *Primarily physics: Investigations in sound, light, heat, and energy*. Fresno, CA: AIMS Education Foundation.

Russell, C. (1993). *Thematic unit: Color*. Huntington Beach, CA: Teacher Created Materials.

Shaw, D. G., & Dybdahl, C. S. (1996). *Integrating science and language arts*. Boston: Allyn & Bacon. (color topics on pp. 1–52)

Sneider, C. I., Gould, A., & Hawthorne, C. (2002). *Color analyzers*. Berkeley, CA: Great Explorations in Math and Science. (light and color activities)

Tolman, M., & Morton, J. (1986). *Physical science activities for grades 2–8*. West Nyack, NY: Parker.

HEAT ENERGY

The rising cost of fuels has made more people realize that knowing about heat energy has both economic and scientific value. Energy affects many aspects of our lives. This chapter considers what happens when materials are heated and cooled, how materials change state, how heat and temperature differ, and how heat travels.

SAFETY

Some experiences require use of a lighted candle. Supervise these occasions closely. We advise that you handle any burning candle yourself; if you choose to allow children to work with fire, make sure they wear safety goggles. Never allow a child with long hair or loose, trailing apparel to work by an open flame. Always use a metal tray or other fireproof material to contain a burning or hot substance. Develop standards about not touching a hot plate or other materials at random.

Benchmarks and Standards

Students in early grades should develop an understanding that materials can exist in liquid, gas, or solid form. Experimentation with water can be effective in introducing them to the states of matter and how heat affects the movement of molecules and the state of a substance. Specific benchmarks and standards are as follows:

Sample Benchmarks (AAAS, 1993)

- Heating and cooling cause changes in the properties of materials. Many kinds of changes occur faster under hotter conditions. (By Grades 3–5, p. 77)
- Some materials conduct heat much better than others. Poor conductors can reduce heat loss. (By Grades 3–5, p. 84)

Sample Standards (NRC, 1996)

- Materials can exist in different states—solid, liquid, and gas. Some common materials, such as water, can be changed from one state to another by heating and cooling. (By Grades K–4, p. 127)
- Heat moves in predictable ways, flowing from warmer objects to cooler ones until all reach the same temperature. (By Grades 5–8, p. 155)

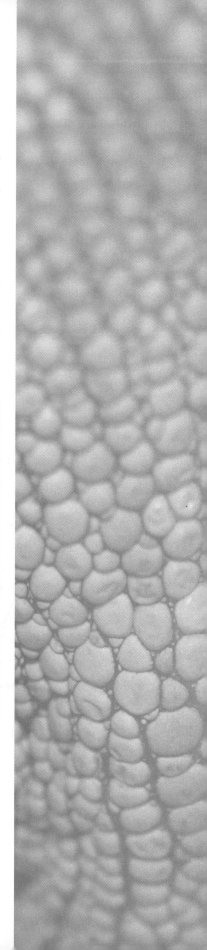

EXPANSION AND CONTRACTION Inquiry

A Hot Association ————

MATERIALS

- Brass screw and screw eye (each screwed into the eraser end of a separate pencil as shown)
- Small dish and candle
- Matches
- Safety goggles

Invitation

How does heat affect a solid?

Exploration

1. Put on safety goggles. Light the candle and fix it to the dish.
2. Try to pass the screw through the screw eye as shown. This should not be possible until heat is applied.
3. Heat the screw eye in the flame for a minute or so.
4. Try step 2 again. Does the screw head pass through the heated screw eye? If not, try step 3 again. If so, keep passing the screw head through the eye. How many seconds go by before you cannot do it?

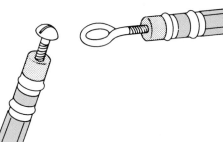

Concept Invention

What will happen if you heat the screw but not the screw eye? What will happen if you heat both screw and screw eye?

Adapting for Students with Exceptionalities

Take extra precautions to ensure the safety of exceptional students when facilitating this activity. Always stabilize equipment and maintain sufficient space for easy access and mobility.

Concept Application

Explain what happened in this activity.

MATERIALS

- Small soda bottle
- Water
- Paper towel
- Soft clay
- Refrigerator
- Small card
- Plastic straw
- Sticky tape
- Crayon
- Red food coloring
- Pencil
- Regular thermometer
- Ruler

Water Thermometer ————

Invitation

Many thermometers use mercury or red-colored alcohol in a closed tube. What happens to these liquids as they get warmer? cooler? How can you make a water thermometer that works in much the same way?

Exploration

1. Fill the bottle almost full with water.
2. Add some food coloring to the water so that it is easy to see.
3. Dry the bottle opening with a paper towel. Then put the straw about halfway into the bottle opening.
4. Use clay to stopper the bottle opening around the straw. Try to get a tight fit without getting the clay wet.
5. The water should rise about halfway up the straw beyond the clay. If it does not, move the straw up or down. Then press the clay down tightly again.
6. Put the bottle in the sun. After an hour, lightly mark the water level on the straw with crayon. Then put the bottle in a refrigerator for an hour and mark the water level.
7. Measure the distance between the two marks. On a card, mark two dots the same distance apart and draw evenly spaced lines between. Give each line a number, with the highest on top. Put the column of numbers on the right side of the card.
8. Tape the card to the straw so that the top and bottom numbers are even with the two marks on the straw as shown.
9. Use your water thermometer to take daily temperatures for a week. Record the temperatures. You might use a table like this one:

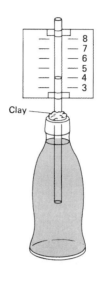

Clay

Water Thermometer Readings

Time	M	T	W	Th	F
9:30 A.M.	4	5			
Noon	6	7			
2:30 P.M.	7	7			

Concept Invention

1. At what time of day is it coolest? warmest?
2. During the week, what was the coolest morning? noon? afternoon?
3. How closely can you predict the noon temperature from the 9:30 A.M. temperature? How closely can you predict the 2:30 P.M. temperature from the noon temperature? Try this for a few days.
4. Ask a partner to make another water thermometer. Keep two separate records. How closely do your readings agree with your partner's? If they do not agree, can you figure out why?
5. Get a regular thermometer. Measure the temperature with both it and your water thermometer. Write the actual temperatures on the left side of the straw card. After a few days, use only your water thermometer to predict the real temperature. Then check the regular thermometer each time. How accurate is your water thermometer? How could you make it more accurate?

Teaching Tips — A one-hole rubber stopper and glass tube are more reliable than clay and a straw. Wet the tube and stopper before inserting the tube. Hold the tube with a thickly folded paper towel to guard against breakage, and use a twisting motion.

  Water, especially with this large volume, takes considerable time to gain and lose heat, so readings should be hours apart. Rubbing alcohol responds more quickly to heat and may be substituted.

Concept Application

How does this activity show that liquids expand when heated and contract when cooled?

Hot Air ————

Invitation

How does heat affect air?

Exploration

1. Snap the balloon opening over the bottle opening.
2. Wrap both hands around the bottle to warm it. Let a partner help, too.
3. What happens to the balloon? What seems to be happening to the air inside the bottle?
4. What will happen to the balloon when the bottle cools? Why?

Concept Invention

How else can you warm the bottle air? cool the bottle air?

Concept Application

Explain how you could use only a balloon and string to find out if heated air expands.

MATERIALS

- Empty soda bottle (cool)
- Round balloon
- Partner

 Teaching Tips | A partly filled balloon may be placed in sunlight. A string may be wrapped around it to compare before and after sizes. A round, moderately sized balloon inflates more easily than the small, tubular kind.

EXPANSION AND CONTRACTION CONCEPTS

Question: How tall is the tallest building in the United States? Answer: I don't know; its height keeps changing. Although questions and answers like this seldom come up in conversation, it is a good example of the expansion and contraction concept. The height of a tall structure may vary 15 centimeters (6 inches) or more, depending on temperature differences when the measurements are taken. Likewise, a steel bridge may change more than 30 centimeters (12 inches) in length, and a ship's captain may stride a slightly longer deck in southern waters than in northern waters.

Molecules ————

The molecular theory of matter offers an interesting explanation for these and many other events. To understand molecules, let's look for a moment at a drop of water. If we could subdivide it with an imaginary dropper, eventually we would get to a point where one more subdivision would produce two atoms of hydrogen and one of oxygen. Both are gases and, of course, look nothing like water. From this, we can say that a molecule is the smallest particle of a substance that can exist by itself and have the properties of that substance when interacting with other molecules.

Strictly speaking, only some gases are exclusively made up of molecules. Some liquids and many solids are composed of electrically charged atoms or groups of atoms called *ions*. But as nearly all ionic particles have physical properties very similar to molecules, it is convenient to treat them as such. Is there any direct proof that molecules exist? Yes, pictures of molecules have been taken through electron microscopes. It is a remarkable tribute to the brainpower of earlier scientists that they were able to forge a molecular theory from their secondhand observations.

Many early experiments may be duplicated today. A unit of alcohol added to a unit of water results in slightly less than two units of liquid. When gold and lead bars are clamped together for a long period, a slight intermingling of these elements occurs. Solid sugar crystals disappear when stirred into a liquid.

Atoms are formed from protons, neutrons, and electrons. Atoms combine to form the molecules that make up matter. Molecules have an attractive force (cohesion) between them. There is space between molecules. In a solid material, the molecules are very close together and are relatively fixed in place because their cohesion is greater than that of gases or liquids. The molecules of most liquids are slightly farther apart; their weaker cohesion permits them to slide about and take the shape of a container. Gas molecules are widest apart and have almost no cohesive attraction. Therefore, they can conform to a container's shape or escape from an uncovered container.

Molecules are always in motion, but they come almost to a standstill at absolute zero (−460°F or −273°C). Above this temperature, molecules of solids vibrate in place, whereas liquid and gas molecules move faster and more freely. With increased temperature, motion increases and the molecules move farther apart. The reverse happens when temperature is decreased. This is why most matter expands when heated and contracts when cooled.

Water

If liquids contract when cooled, why do some water pipes burst in freezing weather? Although molecular theory states that liquids contract when cooled, we note an interesting exception when water temperature drops toward freezing. Water does contract in volume with decreased temperature until about 4°C (39°F). Then its molecules begin to assemble into a crystalline form that becomes ice at 32°F (0°C). The latticelike arrangement of these crystals takes up more space, about 4% more, than an equal number of free-moving water molecules. This is why water pipes and engine blocks of water-cooled automobiles may burst in winter if the water inside them freezes.

It also explains why a lake freezes from the top down, rather than the reverse. At 4°C (39°F), water is densest and sinks to the bottom of the lake. Colder water, being less dense, floats to the surface. It freezes into surface ice and traps the heat energy in the slightly warmer water below. Unless the air temperature is extremely cold, this trapped energy is enough to keep the pond from freezing completely.

The importance of this phenomenon to living things can hardly be overestimated. Although it is clear that aquatic life is saved, consider what would happen to the world's climate if bodies of water froze from the bottom up. Because the heat trapped by ice would escape, ice formation would increase. Gradually, the earth's climate would become colder and would eventually become fatal to most life forms.

Differences in Cohesion

Different materials vary in their rates of expansion and contraction because their cohesive forces vary. It is easier to tear a paper sheet apart than an equally thin steel sheet because steel molecules attract one another with much greater force. A cohesive disparity is likewise true of alcohol and water. Notice in INQ Figure 2–1 how water bulges above the glass rim when it is overfilled.

INQ Figure 2–1   Surface tension in alcohol and water.

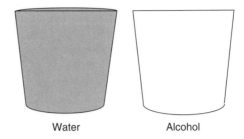

Water   Alcohol

The cohesive force of water molecules is greater than that of alcohol. This explains why equal amounts of heat energy cause alcohol to expand more than water; it is easier to overcome the weaker cohesive force. It also tells us why alcohol evaporates faster than water.

Expansion, contraction, and changes of state from solids to liquids and gases are the results of a constant tug of war between heat energy and cohesive force. Which side wins depends on which force is stronger.

Plastics and Expansion and Contraction

One way to introduce the effects of temperature on matter is to have children work with shrinkable polystyrene. Gertz, Portman, and Sraquis (1996) suggest a "Shrinky Plastic" activity incorporating the children's book *George Shrinks* (Joyce, 1998). The idea for this activity is for children to observe and compare polystyrene images of George before and after the heat source shrinks his polystyrene representation.

As an extension, children can also see which types of plastic shrink by heating a variety of plastic materials in a 325°F oven while placed on a brown paper bag inside of a disposable pie pan.

- Soda bottles (polyethylene terephthalate or PET)
- Milk jugs and detergent containers (high density polyethylene)
- Cooking oil containers (vinyl/polyvinyl chloride or PVC)
- Bread, produce, and garment bags (low density polyethylene)
- Yogurt containers and other storage containers (polypropylene)
- Foam cups, egg cartons, and meat trays (polystyrene)

When looking for shrinkable polystyrene plastic, check for recycle code 6 or the letters PS. For more information on shrinkable polystyrene, refer to *The Shrinkly Dinks Book* (Haab, 1999).

CHANGING STATES OF MATTER **Inquiry**

Melting Away ────────

Invitation

Suppose you have a glass of water. It has the same temperature as the air. Would an ice cube melt faster in the water or the air? How can you find out if water or air will melt an ice cube faster?

Exploration

1. Use a thermometer to measure the air temperature inside one glass.
2. Also measure the temperature inside a glass of water. It should be about the same as the air temperature. If not, let the water stand awhile.
3. Find two ice cubes that are the same size.
4. Put one ice cube into the empty glass. Put the other into the glass of water.
5. Compare how fast the ice cubes melt.

MATERIALS
• Thermometer
• Small plastic bag
• Water
• Salt
• Ice cubes
• Spoon
• Two matched glasses

Concept Invention

1. How can you make an ice cube melt faster in water? Will stirring the water make a difference? Will an ice cube melt faster in warmer water? Does breaking or crushing the cube make a difference? Does changing the volume of water make a difference?
2. How fast will ice cubes melt in other liquids? Will an ice cube melt faster in saltwater? Does the amount of salt make a difference? What other liquids can you try? Can you predict the melting order of ice cubes in them?

Concept Application

Design another experiment that shows the melting time of an ice cube changes with conditions.

A Cold Drink ────────

Invitation

What happens to the temperature of an iced drink as the ice melts?

MATERIALS
• Two ice cubes
• Cup of water
• Thermometer
• Clock with a second hand

Exploration

1. Put the ice cubes into the cup of water.
2. Take the water temperature once a minute throughout this activity. Stir the water a bit each time.
3. Repeat step 2 until you get the same reading twice.

Teaching Tips The ice melting process can be speeded up by heating a metal cup on a hot plate turned to low. Similar results should happen.

Concept Invention

1. What will happen to the temperature as the ice keeps melting?
2. When does the water temperature rise again?

Concept Application

Create a graph for the data in this activity.

CHANGING STATES OF MATTER CONCEPTS

Sometimes we get so used to our environment that it is difficult to imagine the things around us in new ways. Almost everyone knows that air is a mixture of gases. Yet, a favorite stunt of science demonstrators at high school assemblies is to pour liquid air grandly from one container to another. Many persons know that carbon dioxide is a gas. Yet, it is possible to trip over some or drop it on your toe when it is in the form of dry ice. Steel is certainly a durable solid, but tests conducted at high temperatures for possible spaceship uses turn the metal into vapor.

Temperature ———

The state of matter at any given moment depends on its temperature and pressure. Temperature is a measure of the average speed of molecular movements. When increased heat energy is applied to a solid, its molecules vibrate faster. If the motion is great enough to overcome the molecules' cohesive forces, the molecules move farther away, and the solid becomes a liquid. If further energy is applied, the molecules move even faster and farther apart to become a gas. With loss of heat energy, the opposite occurs. The decreased speed of molecules enables cohesive force to be reasserted, which creates a liquid, and then a solid when enough heat is lost.

Does a solid become a liquid before it becomes a gas, or does a gas become a liquid before it becomes a solid? Usually, but a mothball changes to a gas directly, as does dry ice. Frost is an example of vapor freezing directly into a solid state. These phenomena are examples of *sublimation*.

Different substances change state at different temperatures. Adding salt to fresh water lowers the water's freezing point. Seawater, for example, freezes at 28.5°F (22°C) instead of 32°F (0°C). Unless the temperature is very low, sprinkling rock salt on an icy sidewalk melts the ice. We add an antifreeze liquid to our automobile radiators to prevent freezing. A heavy salt solution would be even more effective, except for its unfortunate tendency to corrode metal.

What Pressure Does ———

Pressure also has an interesting effect on changes of state. As a liquid warms, some of its molecules move so fast that they bounce off into the air. We recognize this as evaporation.

The same thing happens with boiling, except the process is faster. To leave the surface of a liquid, though, molecules must overcome not only the cohesive pull of nearby molecules but also the pressure of air molecules immediately above.

At sea level, a 6.45 square centimeter (1-square-inch) column of air extending to outer space weighs 6.6 kilograms (14.7 pounds). At the top of a tall mountain, much less air, and therefore less weight, is pressing down. With less pressure, it is easier for liquid molecules to escape into vapor form. So, at 27,000 meters (90,000 feet), water boils at room temperature. Astronauts or pilots of high-altitude airplanes wear pressure suits, or are enclosed in a pressurized cabin, to keep their blood from boiling.

Because we usually associate boiling with a temperature of about 212°F, it is important to realize another practical effect of decreased pressure. Boiling-point temperature decreases about 1°F for each 550-foot increase in altitude. At a high location, it is difficult to cook foods satisfactorily in an open container because of the low temperature at which boiling occurs. A pressure cooker is almost a necessity.

Heat Loss and Gain

Why is it possible to skate on ice, when we cannot on other smooth surfaces? The answer is that we do not skate directly on the ice. We skate on a thin film of water that may be caused by the leading edge of a blade striking the ice and causing enough friction energy to melt a trail for the rest of the blade. This furnishes a water-lubricated surface on which we slide. As the temperature drops, however, it takes increasing pressure to melt the ice. It may be difficult to skate at all.

Does an iced drink start warming up after the ice has half melted? A change of state always results in the absorption or release of heat energy. It requires energy for the fixed, jiggling molecules of a solid, like ice, to acquire a more freely moving liquid state. Interestingly, until an ice cube melts completely in a container of water, there is no appreciable increase in water temperature. The heat energy absorbed first changes the state of the frozen water and then raises the water temperature once the cube has melted. The next time you have an iced drink, try stirring the liquid until the last bit of ice has melted. You should sense no rise in temperature until after the frozen cubes have completely changed state.

Additional energy is required for liquid molecules to move fast enough and far enough apart to become a gas. Heat is absorbed from whatever accessible substance is warmer than the changing material.

So, if you hold an ice cube in your hand, it removes heat from your body. More heat is required as the liquid evaporates. This is why evaporation has a cooling effect. As the speed of evaporation increases, so does cooling. This is why rubbing alcohol cools your skin more effectively than water. Ethyl chloride evaporates so quickly that it is used by physicians to numb flesh for painless surgery.

Conversely, heat energy is released when a gas condenses to a liquid or a liquid freezes to a solid state. The energy is released because molecular motion continually decreases with each event. It used to be common in rural homes to place tubs of water near vegetable bins in the basement. As the water froze, enough heat was given off to prevent the vegetables from freezing.

Heat is absorbed in evaporation and released through condensation. This principle is applied in electric refrigeration. A liquid refrigerant moves at low pressure into the freezing unit. There it flashes into a vaporous state, cools rapidly, and absorbs heat. As the now slightly warmed vapor leaves the unit, a motor-driven pump compresses the vapor until it has changed to a hot liquid under high pressure. The liquid next circulates in tubes attached to the back of the refrigerator that radiate the heat into the air. The cycle then repeats itself.

A heat pump is a device that warms or cools a home by transferring heat from one area to another. A heat pump works on the same principle as electric refrigeration. In its cooling cycle, it transfers hot air from inside the house to the outside. You can feel the hot air over the condenser fan motor outside the house. When the refrigerant cycle is reversed in the heating mode, the heat is transferred from outside to inside the house. The outside unit will feel cool and could even freeze in colder temperatures, if the cycle is not intermittently reversed to reheat the outside unit. If the temperature is too cool (below 40°F or 4°C), heat pumps do not work very well, and electric heat strips in the inside unit will activate to assist in heating the house.

TEMPERATURE AND HEAT ENERGY **Inquiry**

Heat Energy

Invitation

Suppose you have two iron nails, one large and one small. Both are heated to the same temperature over a candle flame. Which nail do you think would have more heat energy in it? Or, would both nails have the same heat energy? How can you compare the amount of heat energy in heated nails?

Exploration

1. Put on safety goggles. Stick the candle upright in the middle of the pan. You can melt a little wax to hold the candle in place or use clay or glue as needed to support the candle.
2. Fill both cans with enough water to cover the nails when they are dropped in later. Check to be sure the water levels and temperatures are the same in the cans.
3. Light the candle. Use tongs or pliers to hold both nails in the flame for 3 minutes.
4. Drop one nail into each can. Wait 1 minute. Then stir the water in each can lightly with a thermometer and check the temperatures.

MATERIALS
• Pie pan
• Soft clay
• Candle and match
• Safety goggles
• Large and small nail
• Two small empty juice cans
• Water
• Tongs or pliers
• Clock
• Two small thermometers

Concept Invention

1. Which can of water is warmer? Which nail had more heat energy in it?
2. Maybe one nail was just cooler than the other. Suppose you heated both nails longer to be sure they were the same temperature. Would you still get uneven results?
3. How can you give the small nail more heat energy than the larger one?
4. Suppose you heated together a large aluminum nail and a large iron nail. Which, if either, do you think would have more energy?

Teaching Tips

Supervise this investigation closely for safety.

Caution: Children should handle heated material only with tongs or pliers. Also, you might prefer to light and extinguish the candles. A hot plate can be used to heat more objects at a time than is possible with a candle. Make sure that you and the students wear safety goggles when working with fire.

> ### Adapting for Students with Exceptionalities
>
> Be flexible with the level of participation of students with behavioral difficulties or severe or multiple disabilities in activities such as this where there are safety considerations. (See Turnbull, Turnbull, Shank, & Smith, 2004, for a discussion on adapting instruction through partial participation.)

Concept Application

If the amount of heat energy in the same materials depends on their mass as well as their temperature, can you show what happens to water temperature for each minute you heat a nail? Construct a graph similar to this one to show your results.

Minutes Nail Is Heated Versus Water Temperature

Water temperature (°C)
25
20

1   2   3   4   5   6

Minutes nail is heated

The Mixing of Hot and Cold Water ————

Invitation

Have you ever added cold water to cool down hot bath water? Have you added hot water to heat up cool bath water? You can learn to predict the temperatures of a water mixture. How can you predict the temperature of two mixed samples of water?

Exploration

1. Fill one small cup with hot water. Take the temperature of the water with one thermometer and record it.
2. Fill another small cup with cold water. Take the temperature of the water with the other thermometer and record it.
3. Pour both cups of water into the large carton. Take the temperature of the mixed water and record it.
4. Study your records. Let's say your recorded temperatures are like these:

Hot Water	Cold Water	Mixture
60°C	20°C	40°C

5. Notice that the temperature of the mixture is halfway between the hot and cold temperatures (60 + 20 = 80, 40 is half of 80). Look at the temperature of your mixture. Is it about halfway between the hot and cold temperatures?

MATERIALS

- Large container of hot water
- Large container of cold water
- Two small foam cups
- Half-gallon milk carton with top cut off
- Two thermometers
- Paper and pencil

Concept Invention

1. Suppose you mix 2 cups of hot water and 2 cups of cold water. How hot do you predict the mixture will be?
2. Suppose you mix 2 cups of only hot water. How hot do you predict the mixture will be?
3. Suppose you mix 2 cups of cold water with 1 cup of hot water. Will the mixture be hotter or colder than halfway between the two temperatures? How closely can you predict the temperature of the mixture?

 Teaching Tips

The temperature of mixed water depends on the temperature and the volume of each water sample mixed. When the volumes of water samples are equal, the mixture temperature is the average of the sample temperatures; but if the volumes are different, this has to be considered when figuring the average. For example, if one water sample is twice the volume of another, it will have twice the influence on the mixture temperature.
Caution: Never heat the water beyond the point that someone can comfortably touch it.

Scaffolding for English Learners

Concepts such as heat quantity, heat capacity, thermal equilibrium, calories, and thermodynamics are especially difficult for English learners. By taking the extra time to allow students to work with materials, they begin to learn the appropriate language to explain the concepts that they are developing. Inquiry approaches are naturally inclusive and allow the English learner to use verbal interaction with peers to promote concept development. (See Hampton & Rodriguez, 2001, for a discussion of the importance of inquiry with English learners.)

Concept Application

The temperature of mixed water samples depends on the temperature and volume of each sample. The mixture temperature is always somewhere between the high and low sample temperatures. Have a classmate provide two volumes of water and corresponding temperatures. Can you determine what the resultant temperature will be when they are mixed?

TEMPERATURE AND HEAT ENERGY CONCEPTS

You have seen before that the temperature of a material depends on the speed of its molecules. So, molecules of a cold substance move more slowly than those of a hotter substance.

Heat Quantity ──────────

Although many children understand the concept of temperature, quantity of heat is a subtler idea. Consider a white-hot horseshoe just removed from a blacksmith's forge and a large bathtub of warm water. Which contains more heat? It is probably the water. The amount of heat a material contains depends on how many molecules it has, as well as on how fast they are moving. This is why the owner of a large house pays larger winter heating bills than the owner of a small house, although the same air temperature may be maintained. The concept also explains why it takes about half as long to bring 1 liter (1 quart) of water to a boil as 2 liters (2 quarts). There are half as many molecules to move.

Heat Capacity ──────────

Different materials have different capacities for heat energy. For example, it takes more heat for iron to reach a given temperature than an equal weight of lead. More energy is required to heat water to a given temperature than any other common material, liquid or solid, and water retains this heat longer.

The most important effect of water's high heat capacity is found in weather and climate. Because the earth's oceans and lakes gain and lose heat more slowly than the land, they moderate changes in air temperature throughout the world. The most noticeable effects are found in coastal regions; summers are cooler and winters warmer there than they are inland.

The Calorie and the BTU ──────────

Two measures are commonly used to tell heat capacity: the calorie and the British thermal unit (BTU). A *calorie* is the quantity of heat needed to raise the temperature of 1 gram (about 1/28 ounce) of water 1°C. The caloric value of a food is found simply by burning a dry sample of known weight in a special chamber of a carefully insulated container of pure water. The temperature rise is multiplied by the weight of water in the container. For example, suppose 50 grams of water rises 20°C. $50 \times 20 = 1000$ calories.

To make calculations less cumbersome, a "large calorie" is used in finding the heat value of foods. Equivalent to 1000 small calories, the large calorie, or kilocalorie, abbreviated C, is what you see published in diet lists.

The *British thermal unit*, or the quantity of heat needed to raise 1 pound of water 1°F, is used widely by engineers. It is found by multiplying the mass of water by the temperature increase. So, to raise the temperature of 5 pounds of water 30°F requires 150 BTU.

Of course, this information is more for you than for the students at this level. Yet, it is not too early for many children to grasp the general idea of heat quantity. For this reason, we included the inquiry activity in which children heat different-sized nails, put them in water, and measure the increases in water temperature.

Heat Conservation ──────────

Heat energy is conserved when liquids are mixed—that is, not lost but transferred in proportion to the original amount. One liter (1 quart) of warm water has half the heat energy of 2 liters (2 quarts) of water at the same temperature. Also, if two equal volumes of water at different temperatures are mixed, the resulting temperature is halfway between that of the two samples.

Thermal Equilibrium

In some elementary science curricula, the concept of equilibrium is introduced. For example, when water is brought to a boil, its temperature stays at 212°F or 100°C (at sea level) until all the water has evaporated. Because water loses heat energy as fast as it gains heat energy, we see a state of dynamic equilibrium or a stable condition that remains until the water disappears.

A second example is seen when something cools. You know that when a jar of hot water is left standing long enough, it loses heat energy to the surrounding air and surface on which it rests. Eventually, the water temperature becomes stable when it reaches thermal equilibrium with these interacting objects. The air, of course, is the chief interacting object that influences the water's final temperature.

Thermodynamics

Thermodynamics is the branch of physics that involves heat and how heat is transformed to and from other forms of energy. A thermodynamic system involves temperature, pressure, volume, and chemical composition. There are many examples of changes from one form of energy to another.

One common instance of chemical energy producing heat energy is when you eat a hot pepper. A chemical substance called *capsaicin* produces heat on your tongue. Burning a log in the fireplace is another example of chemical energy producing heat energy because the wood is combining with oxygen to make the fire.

Electrical energy can produce heat in an electric heater, hairdryer, or similar appliance. The reverse is also true. A *thermocouple* is made from two different types of wires joined together at one end. When heat is applied, a small amount of electricity is produced. The electricity can even be measured to provide an indication of temperature.

Heat energy can be produced through mechanical means as you find when you rub your hands together. A large truck needs to use lower gears going downhill because the truck's brakes would burn up if applied while descending a steep hill. Likewise, heat energy can produce mechanical energy as in the Stirling engine. These engines use a variety of fuels that provide heat used to produce mechanical energy.

CONDUCTION, CONVECTION, AND RADIATION **Inquiry**

Warm Feelings ———————

MATERIALS
• Metal object
• Newspaper
• Piece of wood

Invitation

What makes some things feel colder even when they have the same temperature?

Exploration

1. Hold the bulb of a thermometer against any metal object, such as scissors.
2. Find its temperature.
3. Do the same with a piece of wood and a folded newspaper. They should all be the same temperature. If not, keep them together and wait an hour or so.

Teaching Tips It is assumed in this activity that the temperatures of tested materials will be lower than body temperature. If your students seem capable, invite them to attempt an explanation and withhold, for a time, the explanation given.

Concept Invention

1. Touch a metal object with one hand and some wood with the other. Compare the metal and newspaper, too.
2. Which one felt coolest? warmest? Some materials conduct heat well, and some poorly. Good conductors take away heat quickly from our warm skin, so they feel cool. Poor conductors take away heat slowly; they seem warm because less heat is lost from our skin.

Concept Application

Compare other materials you find at school and home. Make a record of what you find. Share your record with others who test heat conductors.

Bottle Currents ———————

MATERIALS
• Two matched clear soda bottles
• Red food coloring
• Small card
• White paper
• Cake pan or tray
• Hot and cold tap water
• Sheet of white paper

Invitation

How do warm and cold water form a current?

Exploration

1. Fill one bottle with cold tap water and the other with hot tap water.
2. Add 3 or 4 drops of red coloring to the hot water bottle. Put this bottle on the pan.
3. Hold a card tightly over the opening of the cold water bottle. Turn the bottle upside down and place it carefully on top of the hot water bottle as illustrated.

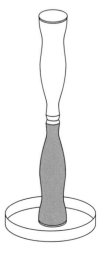

Concept Invention

What do you think will happen if you remove the card? Try it and see. Be careful not to tip over the bottle. Hold white paper behind the bottle to see the activity better.

Adapting for Students with Exceptionalities

A discrepant event is an occurrence during which things behave differently than expected. Discrepant event activities such as this may provide students with cognitive conflict because the results are unexpected. Keep in mind that situations may not be easily predictable or explainable for the students at first. Allow additional time and feedback to assist students in resolving the conflict.

Concept Application

Empty the bottles and do Exploration steps 1, 2, and 3 again, but this time put the hot water bottle on top. What do you think will happen now when you remove the card? How can you explain the results?

Warm Air

Invitation

Where does warmed air go?

Exploration

1. Stick a thumbtack into the middle of the stick near the edge. Tie string to the tack.
2. Hang the stick from the top of a wide table. Use another tack to fasten the loose string end there.
3. Fasten a string to each bag bottom with sticky tape.
4. Cut out the bottom of the bag.
5. Hang the bags from the stick ends. Use a tiny bit of clay to balance the stick if needed, as shown.
6. Place a cold, unplugged hot plate under one bag. (**Caution:** The bag should be at least 30 centimeters [1 foot] above the hot plate because it is flammable.)
7. Plug in the hot plate.

MATERIALS

- Yardstick or substitute
- String
- Scissors
- Two thumbtacks
- Two matched paper bags
- Bit of clay
- Sticky tape
- Hot plate

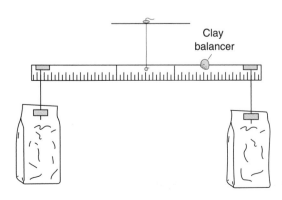

Clay balancer

Teaching Tips For safety, it's best for you to demonstrate this activity and to turn off the hot plate as soon as the bag above it rises.

Concept Invention

What do you think will happen to the bag over the hot plate when you turn on the hot plate?

Concept Application

What will happen to that bag when you turn off the hot plate?

Solar Energy and Colors

MATERIALS

- Four sheets of different-colored construction paper (such as blue, red, green, white)
- Four thermometers
- Four paper clips
- Sunshine
- Partner

Invitation

Have you ever felt extra warm when wearing a colored shirt in sunlight? When a colored shirt soaks up sunlight, it does get warmer. But how does the kind of color affect how warm it gets? How can you compare how warm different colors get in sunlight?

Exploration

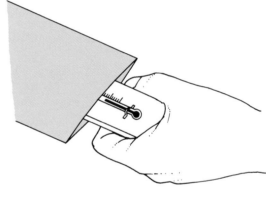

1. Fold the four colored sheets in half. Clip together the open sides.
2. Push a thermometer all the way into each folded, clipped sheet as illustrated.
3. Place the sheets in a row where it is sunny.
4. Wait 5 minutes. Then check the thermometer temperatures. (Before you check, what do you think the warmest to coolest colors will be?)

Teaching Tips It is possible on extra-bright, hot days for the temperature inside the paper folders to rise quickly. On such days, leave the thermometer tops exposed. Have someone observe and remove any thermometer before it rises near the breaking point.

Concept Invention

1. Try colored sheets such as orange, yellow, and black. What are the warmest to coolest colors?
2. How well can you feel the difference in heat among the colors? Close your eyes. Let a partner help you place your hands on the sheets. Can you feel the hottest and coolest sheets?
3. Will a large colored sheet get warmer than a small one?

Concept Application

Absorbed sunlight changes to heat energy; darker colors get warmer than lighter colors. Suppose you placed all the colored sheets in the shade. Would some colors still get warmer than others?

Staying Warm ——————

Invitation

How do greenhouses and closed automobiles get warm?

Exploration

1. Place each jar on its side. Put a piece of cloth into each jar. Place a thermometer on each cloth. Cap only one jar.
2. Place the jars in a sunny area. Turn the jars so that their tops face away from the sun.
3. Watch the thermometers. Keep a record of any changes each minute. Remove a thermometer before it gets close to its highest temperature, because it can break.

Concept Invention

In which jar does the temperature climb faster? How much faster? A graph will help you answer these questions.

Concept Application

How much, if any, difference in jar temperature will there be on a cloudy day?

MATERIALS
• Two matched glass jars
• One jar cap
• Two thermometers
• Two equal-sized pieces of dark cloth
• Sunshine
• Clock

Hot Lights ——————

Invitation

Where is it hottest around a lighted lamp?

Exploration

1. Check the room temperature with your thermometer. Then switch on the lamp.
2. Hold the bulb end of the thermometer toward the lamplight. Try the three places illustrated. Keep the thermometer the same distance from the light each time, and hold it there for the same amount of time. Wait for the thermometer to reach room temperature before trying a new place.

Concept Invention

1. How hot does the thermometer get in each place?
2. Turn the lamp upside down. Again, hold the thermometer bulb toward the light.
3. How hot does the thermometer get? How can you explain your results?

Concept Application

Set the lamp upright again. Hold a piece of transparent glass between the light and the thermometer. Hold the thermometer in all four places again. What are your findings now? How can you explain them?

MATERIALS
• Table or gooseneck lamp (shade removed)
• Ruler
• Small pane of glass
• Thermometer
• Watch

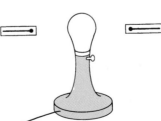

How to Keep Heat In or Out ———————

Teaching Tips

Tape the edges of the glass shield with masking tape to avoid nicked fingers. A transparent shield of plastic kitchen wrap will also work. The temperature above an unshielded bulb should be highest because both convection and radiation occur. Heat produced by convection is blocked by a transparent shield, so the temperature above a shielded bulb should be like that found in other positions around the bulb.

Invitation

Most houses have an inside and outside wall. Packed between the double walls of many houses is insulation. This is a light, fluffy material that helps keep heat in or out. You can work with cans of water and different materials to learn about insulation. What can you do to see how insulation works?

Exploration

1. Pour the same amount of hot water into each small can.
2. Cover each small can with the same size piece of foil. Use a rubber band to hold each cover tight.
3. Wrap one small can with cloth.
4. Put this can into one large can and cap it.
5. Put the other small can into the second large can and cap it.
6. After 20 minutes, remove the four can covers. Dip a finger into each small can of water. Which is warmer?

MATERIALS

- Two small tin cans
- Hot water
- Two large tin cans with lids
- Piece of cloth
- Two equal-sized pieces of aluminum foil
- Different insulation materials
- Two rubber bands
- Ice cubes
- Thermometer
- Clock

Concept Invention

1. How much warmer is one can of water than the other? How can you use a thermometer to find out?
2. How hot can you keep a small can of water? Have a contest with a friend. Try different materials, such as sawdust, cotton, wool, puffed rice, or torn paper. Or try your own secret mix of materials. Put the materials between the larger and smaller can walls. Whoever has the warmer can of water after 30 minutes (or longer) wins.
3. Can you figure out which single material is the best insulator? the worst insulator? Does how tightly it is packed make a difference?

Teaching Tips

Use matched 1-pound coffee cans with lids for the larger cans. Small, identical juice cans fit nicely into the coffee cans. Identical pieces of foil may be used to cap the small cans so that insulating materials do not fall inside. Either hot or warm water from the tap will do for this activity.

4. In summer, you want your home to stay cool. Does insulation keep heat out as well as in? Find out. How cool can you keep a small can with an ice cube inside? Have a contest with a friend. Whoever has the larger ice cube after 1 hour (or longer) wins.
5. Are the best materials for keeping the can warm also best for keeping the can cold? If not, which are best?

Scaffolding for English Learners

This activity lends itself to a cultural perspective. Discuss how homes are heated and warmed in other cultures. Which cultures use insulation? Which cultures could benefit from insulation use? What materials are natural insulators used by cultures? What natural materials could be used to insulate that are not already in use by cultures? Test the materials you discuss with this activity. (See Laplante, 1997, for the importance of cultural perspectives with English learners.)

Concept Application

Describe how insulating materials may be used to slow the movement of heat energy in your home.

CONDUCTION, CONVECTION, AND RADIATION CONCEPTS

Until, the 19th century, it was generally thought that heat was a fluidlike substance (*caloric*) that could be poured from one material to another. Scientists now realize that heat is a form of energy, with *energy* being defined as the capacity to do work.

Changing Forms of Energy

Many experiments have shown that energy can be changed from one form to another. Our practical experience also shows that this is so. Electrical energy changes to heat in toasters and hot plates; chemical energy yields heat through fires and explosives; mechanical energy (motion) provides the force needed to overcome friction, and in the process heat is released. Heat, in turn, changes to other forms of energy. Hot fuel turns a generator to produce electricity, or gasoline is burned in automobile engines to produce mechanical energy.

If you put a pan of hot water in a cool room, after a while the water cools to room temperature. Place a pan of cool water in a hot oven, however, and the water warms to oven temperature. In moving toward thermal equilibrium, as we saw before, heat energy always travels from a place of higher temperature to one of lower temperature.

A misconception of what heat is may interfere with understanding how it travels. Instead of viewing cold as a lesser degree of heat, many students think that cold is distinctly different and the opposite of heat. So, it's logical for them to think that "cold" leaves the ice cube in a drink and goes into the liquid, rather than that heat goes from the liquid into the ice cube, making it melt (Erickson, 1979).

Because heat is felt rather than seen, it may also affect children's understanding of how it travels. By about age 8, they begin to think of heat as something that travels from a source to another place. Before then, children are more likely to view a hot stove or fire, for example, as something that instantly makes them warm (Albert, 1978).

In moving from one location to another, heat energy may travel in one or more of three ways: conduction, convection, and radiation. Let's consider these ways one at a time.

Conduction

If you grasp the metal handle of a hot frying pan, you quickly let go. How is it possible for the heat energy to go from the hot stove grid to the handle? Molecular *conduction* is responsible. As heat energy enters the pan bottom, the pan's molecules begin to vibrate faster. This motion is passed along, molecule by molecule, up the pan's sides to its handle. Eventually, all the particles are vibrating faster, and you feel the heat.

Of all solids, metals are the best conductors. Their molecules are very close together and transmit heat energy quickly. But each type of metal varies somewhat in conductivity. Copper is the best common conductor, followed by aluminum, steel, and iron. Other solids are comparatively poor conductors, including ceramic materials. This is one reason for using ceramic containers for heated beverages and microwavable food.

Because molecules of liquids are farther apart than solids, it is reasonable to expect that they do not conduct heat as efficiently as molecules of solids. Our ordinary experiences with bathwater help confirm this thought. When hot water is added to cooler water, the heat takes a long time to reach all portions of the tub. For this reason, we stir the water a bit to hasten the process.

Gases are the poorest conductors of all. Their molecules are spread so far apart that they do not collide often and regularly enough to pass on increased energy to any appreciable extent. This is why it is possible for the horizontal freezers in supermarkets to be left uncovered. Very little heat energy is conducted downward from the warmer air above the freezers.

Convection

Although liquids and gases conduct heat poorly, it is easy to heat a pan of water quickly to boiling temperature or to roast a frankfurter quickly in the hot air over a campfire. These examples indicate another, more efficient method of heat transfer in liquids and gases than conduction. To identify it, examine what happens when air is warmed.

Watch the smoke from burning material. Why does it rise? Is it unaffected by gravity? A clue to its behavior is found when smoke is pumped into an airless vacuum chamber. The smoke particles fall like lead weights. Therefore, smoke does not just "rise"; something must push it up.

When the glowing part of burning material warms the adjacent air, the increased energy agitates the air molecules to increased speeds and they spread farther apart. Because fewer air molecules take up a given volume of space, the hot air is lighter than an equal volume of the surrounding air. The hotter, lighter air is pushed up with the smoke particles as it is replaced by colder, heavier air. As the mass of lighter air rises, it carries increased energy with it. This is why air near the ceiling is warmer than air near the floor.

A *convection current* is set up when a room has an opening for warm air to escape and cool air to enter. This is what happens when we open a window at both the top and bottom to freshen the air in a room. It is also the primary cause of winds in the atmosphere.

Similar convection currents are set up in heated liquids. Warmed, expanded water in a pan rises as it is continuously replaced by cooler, heavier water until the same temperature is reached in the entire container. An example is a hot water tank. Convection currents take heated water away from the heating unit and circulate the water throughout the tank. Adding color to the liquid will help children see this effect for themselves (Rubino & Duerling, 1991).

Convection also has global effects. Warm water at the equator is continuously being replaced by cold water flowing from the polar regions; this movement sets up convective ocean currents. Likewise, air convection currents, along with the earth's rotation, form winds that contribute to weather patterns.

Radiation

A common example of the third method of heat transfer, *radiation*, is found in a fireplace. This is especially noticeable when the air temperature is low. As you warm yourself in front of the fire, only the portion of your body that faces the fire feels warm. Conduction is poor because air is the conducting medium. Convection is negligible because most of the hot air escapes up the chimney. Heat reaches you primarily by radiation.

All vibrating molecules release a certain amount of energy through invisible heat rays called *infrared waves*. These waves largely pass through transparent materials like air and glass but are absorbed by opaque objects, which become warmer as a result. We are aware of radiant energy only when the emitting source is warmer than body temperature. The sun is by far our most important source of radiant energy. In its rays are found visible light, invisible infrared waves, and other forms of radiant energy.

From Solar to Heat Energy

An air traveler who goes from a cold climate to a tropical climate quickly notices many differences in the new surroundings. Among the most impressive are house colors, which are largely light pastels and dazzling white. Similar differences can be noted in clothing colors. Dark-colored materials absorb more sunlight than light-colored materials. INQ Figure 2–2 reveals why persons in tropical countries find a greater need for lighter colors than those in countries farther away from the equator. Light is most intense when it is received from directly overhead. If the same amount of light is spread out over a larger area, any part of that area receives less light and so less heat.

The changing of solar energy to heat energy is most noticeable when there is an effective way of preventing the heat from escaping.

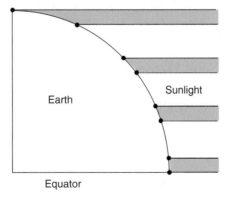

INQ Figure 2–2 When light is projected directly overhead, it is most intense. This explains why people in tropical climates find a greater need for light-colored clothing and buildings than people in other climates.

A common example is the temperature rise within a tightly closed automobile parked in sunlight. The rapidly vibrating short waves of sunlight can pass through the windows. When they strike the upholstery, they are absorbed and then reradiated as longer, slower vibrating heat waves. The longer waves are largely unable to penetrate glass, so most of the heat stays inside, building up in intensity as sunlight continues to stream in. Because the same thing happens in greenhouses, this phenomenon is aptly called the *greenhouse effect*.

INQ Figure 2–3   **A flat-plate solar energy collector.**

INQ Figure 2–3   **A flat-plate solar energy collector.**

Our atmosphere is also warmed largely by reradiated heat waves. The atmosphere is like a giant glass cover that traps the longer, reradiated heat waves. This analogy is not perfect, however. Fortunately for us, the atmosphere is far less efficient than glass. A substantial amount of reradiated heat escapes into space. Were this not so, the earth's air temperature would become so hot that it would be intolerable to life.

Because of the greenhouse effect, air temperatures get warmest in the afternoon rather than at noon. Although the sun is most nearly overhead at midday, the buildup of heat continues for several hours afterward.

Solar Heating for Homes ———————

Solar energy is becoming a popular way to heat water and even entire homes, especially in the South and Southwest. Let's examine one way this is done.

A flat-plate collector is attached to, or built into, the house roof. Its purpose is to collect as much solar energy as possible. The collector, made of metal and glass, is positioned to face the sun. The glass is mounted just over a blackened metal plate. Water pipes, also painted black, are attached to the plate. As the plate and pipes absorb sunlight, the water inside the pipes is heated by conduction. The glass cover contributes to the buildup of heat by trapping the absorbed light energy (INQ Figure 2–3).

The heated water is stored in a large tank. Pipes circulate it throughout the house as needed. Other pipes are connected to hot water faucets in the house.

Notice the three conditions that affect the efficiency of the solar collector: The collector plate and pipes are painted black to absorb sunlight; a clear glass cover admits sunlight but prevents most of the absorbed energy from escaping; and the collector is mounted on a slope that faces the sun.

Controlling Heat Loss ─────

Knowing how heat travels permits us to control it. We use insulation to prevent or retard heat energy transfer. For example, to retard conduction, we use poor conductors. Because air is a poor conductor, materials with air spaces, such as wood and wool, make excellent insulators.

In homes, using hollow walls designed to trap the air reduces convection and conduction. Because some convection takes place anyway, many homeowners fill the walls with a light, fluffy material, such as fiberglass or cellulose insulation. An excellent way to insulate for radiation is to reflect it away because it behaves like light as it travels. This is why insulating materials in the home may use a shiny foil exterior, particularly in the attic. It also explains why silver paint is used on large gasoline storage tanks.

References

Albert, E. (1978). Development of the concept of heat in children. *Science Education, 62*(3), 389–399.

American Association for the Advancement of Science (AAAS). (1993). *Benchmarks for science literacy.* New York: Oxford University Press.

Erickson, G. L. (1979). Children's conceptions of heat and temperature. *Science Education, 63*(1), 83–93.

Gertz, S., Portman, D., & Sraquis, M. (1996). *Teaching physical science through children's literature.* Middletown, OH: Terrific Science Press.

Haab, S. (1999). *The Shrinky Dinks Book.* Palo Alto, CA: Klutz, Inc.

Hampton, E., & Rodriguez, R. (2001). Inquiry science in bilingual classrooms. *Bilingual Research Journal, 25*(4), 417–434. Retrieved November 13, 2004, from *http://brj.asu.edu/content/vol25no4/pdf/ar4.pdf*

Joyce, W. (1998). *George shrinks.* New York: HarperCollins.

Laplante, B. (1997). Teaching science to language minority students in elementary classrooms. *Journal of the New York State Association for Bilingual Education, 12,* 62–83. Retrieved November 13, 2004, from *www.ncela.gwu.edu/pubs/nysabe/vol12/nysabe124.pdf*

National Research Council (NRC). (1996). *National science education standards.* Washington, DC: National Academy Press.

Rubino, A. M., & Duerling, C. K. (1991). Around the world in science class. *Science and Children, 28*(7), 37–39.

Turnbull, R., Turnbull, A., Shank, M., & Smith, S. J. (2004). *Exceptional lives: Special education in today's schools* (4th ed.). Upper Saddle River, NJ: Merrill/Prentice Hall.

Selected Trade Books: Heat Energy

For Younger Children

Ardley, N. (1983). *Hot and cold.* Danbury, CT: Watts.

Cole, J. (1998). *The magic school bus in the arctic: A book about heat.* New York: Scholastic.

Daley, M. J. (1997). *Amazing sun fun activities.* New York: McGraw-Hill Professional Publishing.

Fowler, A. (1998). *Energy from the sun.* Danbury, CT: Childrens Press.

Hillerman, A. (1983). *Done in the sun.* Santa Fe, NM: Sunstone Press.

Ketteman, H. (2000). *Heat wave.* New York: Walker & Co.

Kim, S., & Melton, L. (2000). *Transforming energy: All about heat, work and energy (the activity learning books).* New York: Science Kids.

Llewellyn, C. (1991). *First look at keeping warm.* Milwaukee, WI: Gareth Stevens.

Maestro, B., & Maestro, G. (1990). *Temperature and you.* New York: Lodestar Books.

Oleksy, W. (1986). *Experiments with heat.* Danbury, CT: Childrens Press.

Petersen, D. (1985). *Solar energy at work.* Danbury, CT: Childrens Press.

Santrey, L. (1985). *Heat.* New York: Troll Associates.

Stille, D. R. (1990). *The greenhouse effect.* Danbury, CT: Childrens Press.

Wade, H. (1979). *Heat.* Austin, TX: Raintree.

For Older Children

Bendick, J. (1974). *Heat and temperature.* Danbury, CT: Watts.

Cobb, V. (1973). *Heat.* Danbury, CT: Watts.

George, J. C. (1983). *One day in the desert.* New York: Thomas Y. Crowell.

Kaplan, S. (1983). *Solar energy.* Austin, TX: Raintree.

Knapp, B. (1990). *Fire.* Austin, TX: Steck-Vaughn.

Langley, A. (1986). *Energy.* Danbury, CT: Watts.

Mebane, R. C., & Rybolt, T. R. (1987). *Adventures with atoms and molecules*. Springfield, NJ: Enslow.

Scott, J. M. (1973). *Heat and fire*. Springfield, NJ: Enslow.

Searle, B. (2001). *Heat and energy (fascinating science projects)*. Brookfield, CT: Copper Beech Books.

Whyman, K. (1987). *Heat and energy*. Danbury, CT: Watts.

Wood, R. (1996). *Heat fundamentals: Funtastic science experiments for kids*. New York: McGraw-Hill.

Yount, L. (1981). *Too hot, too cold, or just right*. New York: Walker.

Resource Books

Bartch, M. (1992). *Literature activities across the curriculum*. West Nyack, NY: Simon & Schuster. (science topics, pp. 158–194)

Butzow, C. M., & Butzow, J. W. (1989). *Science through children's literature: An integrated approach*. Englewood, CO: Teacher Ideas Press. (states of matter topics, pp. 200–205)

Gertz, S., Portman, D., & Sraquis, M. (1996). *Teaching physical science through children's literature*. Middletown, OH: Terrific Science Press.

Hillen, J., Mercier, S., Hoover, E., & Cordel, B. (1994). *Primarily physics: Investigations in sound, light, heat, and energy*. Fresno, CA: AIMS Education Foundation.

Tolman, M., & Morton, J. (1986). *Physical science activities for grades 2–8*. West Nyack, NY: Parker.

SOUND ENERGY

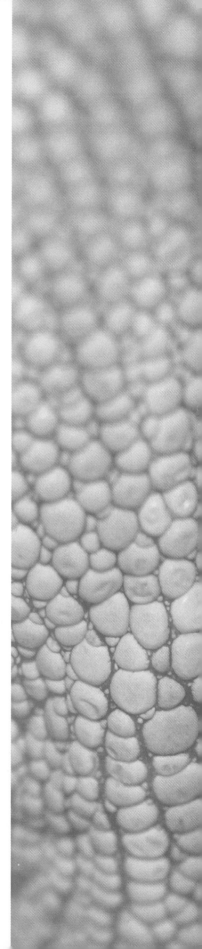

Play a radio loudly, and the windows rattle. Watch a parade at a distance, and the marchers seem to be out of time with the music. Sing in the shower, and suddenly your voice takes on new dimensions. Hold a seashell to your ear and the soft, ambient sounds are resonated and amplified by the shape of the seashell's cavity. Blow a dog whistle and you cannot hear it, but your pet comes running to you. The sound of a passing train changes as it approaches and retreats. Bats and dolphins use echolocation, or reflections of their own sounds, to move about. Caterpillars hear with hairs all over their body, and you use the hairs in your cochlea to hear.

Few topics present so many accessible materials and interesting things to explore as sound energy. Sound is produced by mechanical radiation, or the movement of energy from one place to another through a medium such as air or water (sound cannot be produced in a vacuum). Vibrations from an object moving back and forth cause molecules in the surrounding medium to begin vibrating and radiating waves of sound energy. We hear these regular, pleasant sounds as music and the irregular vibrations, or unpleasant sounds, as noise.

In this chapter, we consider how sound vibrations are made; how sounds travel in air, water, and solids; how sounds are reflected and absorbed; how the pitch of sounds may change; and how we hear.

Benchmarks and Standards

Children in the early grades have trouble associating the characteristics of sounds with the properties of the sound's source. Experiences with activities involving the making and hearing of sounds will provide students opportunities to make these associations. Additionally, children will begin to understand that sounds are vibrations and travel in waves. Some specific benchmarks and standards are as follows:

Sample Benchmarks (AAAS, 1993)

- Things that make sound vibrate. (By Grades K–2, p. 89)
- Vibrations in materials set up wavelike disturbances that spread away from the source. Sound and earthquake waves are examples. These and other waves move at different speeds in different materials. (By Grades 6–8, p. 90)

Sample Standards (NRC, 1996)

- Sound is produced by vibrating objects. The pitch of the sound can be varied by changing the rate of vibration. (By Grades K–4, p. 127)

SOUND VIBRATIONS Inquiry

A Vocal Activity

MATERIALS
• No materials are needed

Invitation

What makes your vocal cords work?

Exploration

1. Hum softly and feel your throat. Feel your voice box vibrate.
2. Hum with tightly closed lips. Then pinch your nose.
3. What happens? Why?

Teaching Tips

Air is needed in all these cases to make the vocal cords vibrate. It is difficult to speak while breathing in because the normal way humans make sounds is by breathing out.

Concept Invention

1. Breathe out as much air as you can from your lungs. Try to say something without taking in air.
2. What happens? Why?

Concept Application

Try to say your name the way a cat or cow makes sounds—while breathing air in. What happens? Why is this hard to do?

MATERIALS
• Tuning fork
• Two matched large soda bottles
• One small soda bottle

Good Vibrations

Invitation

How can one vibrating object make another vibrate?

Exploration

Teaching Tips

The first part of the exploration is an example of forced vibrations. If a tuning fork is unavailable, a sturdy, stiff rubber comb may be used instead. Run a finger down the teeth ends while holding the comb against a surface. The second part of the exploration is an example of sympathetic vibrations. If you vibrate one object, a second object may also vibrate if it has the same natural rate of vibrations as the first. No actual touching is necessary. The transfer of energy occurs in the air.

Caution: If the bottles are used by more than one student, sterilize the bottle openings between uses. Dampen a paper towel with rubbing alcohol, wipe the bottle openings well, and then rinse the alcohol off well with running water. Dry with a clean paper towel.

1. Strike a tuning fork against a rubber heel (never against something hard).
2. As the sound dies, place the handle end against a tabletop. Notice how the sound gets louder as the tabletop is also made to vibrate.
3. Try holding the vibrating tuning fork against many different objects.
4. From which object can you get the loudest sound?
5. Which object allows you to hear the tuning fork when it has almost stopped vibrating?
6. Blow over the top of one large bottle to make a sound. Blow short, strong tones.
7. Hold the opening of a second large bottle close to your ear, but not touching. Blow short sounds again with the first large bottle.
8. Do you hear the same note from the second bottle? If you are not sure, have someone else blow short notes on one bottle while you listen with the second bottle.

Concept Invention

Repeat Exploration steps 6 and 7, but this time listen with the small bottle.

Concept Application

Do you hear the same note from the small bottle? Do you hear any note?

Mystery Sounds ———

Invitation

Can you hear something make a sound and tell what it is without looking? How can you find out if you can identify something by sound?

Exploration

1. Place one object from each pair of rolling objects on your desk.
2. Give the other rolling objects to your partner. He should put these where you cannot see them.
3. Have your partner put one of his objects in the shoe box. You should not know which one it is. Have your partner put the lid on the shoe box.
4. Slowly tip the covered shoe box back and forth. Listen to the sound.
5. Look at the objects on your desk. Which one may be the same as the one in the box? Point to a desk object so that your partner knows which one you picked.
6. Look inside the shoe box. Does the object inside match the desk object you picked?

Concept Invention

1. How many of the rolling objects can you identify? Which object is easiest to tell? the hardest to tell?
2. Suppose your partner holds and tips the box. Can you tell each rolling object just as easily?
3. How many of the sliding objects can you identify? Which object is easiest to tell? the hardest to tell?

MATERIALS

- Pairs of small objects that roll (crayons, table tennis balls, marbles, pencils, BBs, small pill vials)

- Pairs of small objects that slide (buttons, paper clips, checkers, dominoes, bottle caps, safety pins)

- Shoe box with lid

- Partner

Teaching Tips

This investigation mainly calls for children to make inferences by interpreting data. Try to use objects of about the same weight. This will eliminate weight as a clue. Children will focus on the sounds they hear or the vibrations they feel in their fingers as they handle the shoe box.

Older students can be challenged by increasing the number and similarity of paired objects to select from.

Adapting for Students with Exceptionalities
When working with students with hearing impairments, try prerecording sounds and playing them back at a higher than normal volume.

Concept Application

Describe how an object may be identified by the sounds it makes when interacting with another object.

SOUND VIBRATIONS CONCEPTS

Every so often in science fiction, a scientist will invent a machine that can collect and play back all the sounds that have ever been made. Plots usually reveal that at first the scientist uses the machine to help historians, but that soon after he offers the enemy military secrets discussed at the Pentagon.

Molecules and Sounds ──────────

Of course, all signs show that such a machine could never be invented. Sounds are simply waves of compressed molecules pulsating outward in all directions and planes from a vibrating source.

Consider the air around you. It is composed of tiny, individual molecules of different gases mixed similarly throughout the lower atmosphere. These molecules are rapidly and randomly moving about. A fast-vibrating source, such as a hummingbird's beating wings, a struck bell, a plucked guitar string, or a "twanged" ruler held on the edge of a desk, compresses billions of these molecules with each back-and-forth movement because the molecules are in the way. Because air molecules are elastic, they quickly assume their original shape after moving out of the vibrating object's path. Before this happens, however, they transfer energy to other molecules over a distance.

Note that it is the wave of energy, rather than the molecules, that may travel a great distance. Each molecule may move less than a millionth of a hair's width, but this is enough to bump the next randomly moving molecule and pass on the outward movement. INQ Figure 3–1 shows a wave motion resulting from a compression and rarefaction effect on molecules pushed by a vibrating ruler.

A sound fades away when energy behind the original vibrations is used in the transmitting process. As one molecule bumps another, it uses a tiny amount of energy. As more molecules are bumped, less energy is available. The sound stops when energy of the randomly moving molecules exceeds the wave's energy. The molecules simply resume their normal helter-skelter movements.

Loudness ──────────

How is loudness explained? First, for the moment, let's call it *intensity*; "loudness" is what we actually hear. If our ears are working poorly, a very intense sound may be barely heard. So, loudness is a matter of individual perception. Intensity, in contrast, can be consistently and accu-

INQ Figure 3–1   These frames illustrate a vibrating ruler producing sound waves. In part 1, the ruler pushes the air molecules together (compression). Notice the thinned-out space below it (rarefaction). Part 2 shows the opposite happening, with the first part of the sound wave now moving away. Parts 3 and 4 show other sound waves being produced. The wave moves outward as the molecules push others in the way, which in turn squeeze other molecules.

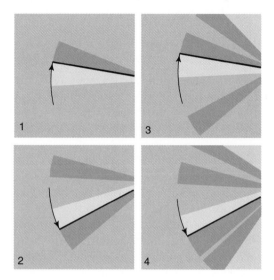

rately recorded by a sensitive sound detector in terms of the *decibel*, a unit of measurement in sound. The distinction between loudness and intensity may be too subtle for most children.

You know that shouting requires more energy than whispering. A boost in energy forces any vibrating medium to vibrate to and fro more widely than usual, but in the same amount of time. This movement compresses molecules more forcefully, so the greater energy is able to move more molecules.

Of course, distance is also a factor in sound intensity. The farther away we are from the source, the weaker the sound that gets to us. Molecules are pushed less because progressively less energy is available.

Interestingly, the same mathematical relationship is found in sound loss as in other forms of energy, such as light, magnetism, and electricity. Intensity fades as the distance between any sound source and the listener increases. In fact, the mathematical relationship used to compare sound intensity for two listeners standing at different distances from the sound source is the ratio of the square of the shorter distance to the square of the longer distance. For example, at 6 meters (20 feet), a sound has only one fourth of the intensity it exhibits at 3 meters (10 feet) from the source ($3^2 = 9$; $6^2 = 36$; $9/36 = 1/4$).

Waves ————

Sometimes the analogy of a water wave is used to teach how sound travels. A pebble is dropped into water, and a circular series of ripples spreads out on the water's surface. This example may be useful to show to your class, but it contains two main defects. First, water waves are up-and-down motions that travel at right angles to the line of the waves. These are called *transverse waves*. Sound waves come from back-and-forth motions that make *longitudinal waves*. This is the kind of wave you see when a row of dominoes falls, each one striking the next in order. Second, water waves move only horizontally, whereas sound waves travel outward in all planes. Many science teachers ask their students to imagine sound waves as they would a series of rapidly blown soap bubbles, each enveloped within another that is slightly larger, all quickly expanding.

The wave idea is useful to distinguish between sounds and noises. A *sound* consists of regularly pulsating vibrations; the time interval between each compression and rarefaction is the same. *Noise* is heard when irregular vibrations are passed on.

Forced Vibrations ───────────

If you place the handle of a vibrating tuning fork against a tabletop; the sound suddenly gets louder. The vibrating fork forces the tabletop to vibrate with equal speed. This sets in motion many more air molecules than would the fork alone. Try putting a vibrating tuning fork against other objects. Almost any hard object can be forced to vibrate at the fork's natural frequency.

A peculiar example of forced vibrations can occur when a group of soldiers marches over a bridge. If enough persons are marching in step, the entire structure can be forced to vibrate in time to the step, and the bridge may weaken or collapse. For this reason, soldiers do not stay in step when crossing a bridge.

Thomas Edison used his knowledge of forced vibrations when inventing the phonograph. He attached a sharp needle to a thin diaphragm that vibrated when sound waves struck it. The needle was placed against a cylinder wrapped with soft metal foil. As he spoke, he slowly cranked the cylinder around and around. The vibrating needle cut a series of impressions into the metal. To play back his sounds, he placed the needle in the impression first scratched and cranked the cylinder. As it followed the impressions, the needle was forced to vibrate, thus causing the diaphragm to vibrate. Edison could hear his recorded voice!

Sympathetic Vibrations ───────────

Have you ever heard windows vibrate in their frames as a low-flying airplane passes overhead? Or noticed dishes faintly rattle occasionally as a loud radio is played? To see why this happens, consider two identical tuning forks. If one vibrates and is held near the other, the second one also begins to vibrate; but with two tuning forks of different pitches, only the struck one vibrates.

When tuning forks are of identical pitch, sound waves arrive at the proper time to set the still fork in motion. Each additional air compression pushes a prong as it starts to bend in from a previous one. Each rarefaction arrives as the prong starts to bend back out. The steady, timed, push-pause-push-pause rhythm sets the fork vibrating in almost the same way as you would push someone on a swing.

When tuning forks are of different pitch, the timing is wrong for this process to happen. For example, a prong may bend inward properly with a compression, but as it starts to bend back, another air compression may strike it prematurely and slow or stop it. The same thing would happen with a moving swing that is pushed while only partway back on a downswing.

Every solid object has a natural frequency of vibration. If sound waves of that frequency push against an object, it may start resonating—vibrating sympathetically.

Remember that objects vibrate sympathetically only when they have the same natural pitch as the initial sound maker. In contrast, objects forced to vibrate always do so at the frequency of the vibrating object placed against them, regardless of their own natural frequency.

You may have learned that a very loud note sung or played into a thin drinking glass can shatter it through violent sympathetic vibrations; such vibrations have the natural pitch of the glass. It is not true, however, that seashore sounds may be detected in shell souvenirs. This is only true when listening through them at the beach. Otherwise, only sympathetic reflections of nearby sounds are heard through the shell.

Properties of Objects and Vibrations

Suppose someone hands you two closed shoe boxes. Inside one is a marble. Inside the other is a small ruler. Could you tell which box contains which object by tipping them back and forth and listening to the sounds? Of course, you may say. But what allows you to do this?

Every object has certain physical properties that produce "appropriate" vibrations. We expect a round (cylindrical) pencil to roll smoothly and a six-sided pencil to roll roughly. We assume that a short pencil lying crosswise in a box takes longer to slide and bump against the side than a longer pencil, if the box is tipped from side to side.

HOW SOUNDS TRAVEL **Inquiry**

It Sounds Fast ———————

MATERIALS
• Large outdoor space
• Partner
• Hammer
• Thick piece of wood

Invitation

How fast does sound travel?

Exploration

1. Go outdoors to a large, open space.
2. Place a thick piece of wood on the ground. Walk a few steps away.
3. Watch a partner sharply hit the wood once with a hammer.
4. Do you hear the sound at about the same time the hammer hits?

Concept Invention

1. Move farther away. Have your partner hit the wood again. Repeat this moving-and-listening pattern several times until you are far away.
2. When do you hear each sound now—at the same time the hammer hits? Or does each sound appear later and later, after each hit?

> **Teaching Tips**
> To ensure enough space for this activity, we suggest two widely separated, familiar reference points at least the length of a football field apart.

Concept Application

Why do you think that thunder and lightning occur at the same time when they are near but you hear thunder a few seconds later if it is farther away?

Sound Travels ———————

MATERIALS
• Meterstick or yardstick
• Partner
• Wristwatch (one that ticks; used watches can often be found at yard sales or donation centers; other sound sources can be used)

Invitation

Does sound travel farther in air or in wood?

Exploration

1. Hold a ticking wristwatch or other sound source tightly against the end of a meterstick.
2. Touch the other end of the stick to your partner's ear. Only you should hold the stick, as shown.
3. Can your partner hear the ticking through the wood? If not, move the watch forward on the stick until the ticking is heard.
4. Measure the distance between the watch and the ear when the ticking is heard.

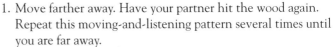

Concept Invention

1. Next, do not use the meterstick. Hold the watch in the air at ear level the same distance you found in the Exploration.

2. Can your partner hear the ticking now? (If you think your partner is just guessing, remove and then return the watch a few times. Each time, ask if the watch can be heard.)
3. From how far away can you hear a ticking watch through wood? Try a broomstick, a window pole, a long narrow board, and other wooden objects around you.

Adapting for Students with Exceptionalities

For students who have hearing disabilities, substitute a device that makes a louder noise when facilitating this activity. Also try to eliminate all other sounds in the classroom. (See Mastropieri & Scruggs, 2004, chapter on science and social studies for a discussion on adapting science activities involving sound.)

Concept Application

Predict how sound will travel through other materials, such as metals or water. Design an experiment to test your predictions.

The Vibrations of Metal Objects ———

Invitation

Many everyday objects made of metal make beautiful sounds when they vibrate. A metal coat hanger is one example. These objects sound much better when you hear them through a solid material than through the air. String is one such solid material. How can you hear the sounds of a metal hanger through a string?

Exploration

1. Cut a piece of string about 60 centimeters (2 feet) long.
2. Loop the middle of the string once around the hanger hook.
3. Wrap several turns of string end around the tip of each forefinger.
4. Gently put the tip of each wrapped finger into an ear, as illustrated on page INQ-76.
5. Bend from the waist so that the hanger hangs free. Ask your partner to strike a pencil and other objects gently against the metal. You can also make the hanger vibrate by yourself. Sway back and forth until the hanger swings. Then have it hit something that is hard, such as a table leg.

Concept Invention

1. How can you describe the sounds you hear?
2. What happens to the sound if your partner holds one of the strings? holds both strings?
3. What kind of string will give the clearest, loudest sound? Cut off equal lengths of different kinds of string and yarn. Test them in pairs. Tie one string end to the hook of one hanger. Tie another to a second matched hanger. Put one string end

MATERIALS
• Two matched metal hangers
• Scissors
• Yarn
• Different metal objects
• Several kinds of string
• Partner

 Teaching Tips Oven cooling racks, barbecue grills, and other gridlike objects of metal make particularly strange, even eerie, sounds. These sounds come from the overtones produced when the many parts of the object vibrate differently.

into each ear. Have a partner first strike one hanger, then the other. When you find the best string, try it with both ears.

4. Does the length of a string affect the loudness? If so, in which kind of string do you notice it most? (You can test pairs of strings.)

5. What sounds do other metal objects make? Test such objects as old spoons, forks, cooling racks, oven racks, and different-sized cans.

Adapting for Students with Exceptionalities

This will be an excellent activity for students with severe hearing loss because they should feel the vibrations.

Concept Application

The sounds of a vibrating object may be heard more loudly and clearly through a solid than through air because solid materials help to channel the sounds. How many everyday applications of this concept can you find (for example, a mechanic would put her ear to a metal rod held against a running engine to hear sounds that the engine is making)?

A String Telephone

Invitation

Have you ever used a "string telephone"? It's a handy way to talk to someone far across a large room without shouting. How can you make a string telephone?

Exploration

1. Use a nail to punch a hole into the bottom center of each cup.
2. Put one end of a string into each hole.

MATERIALS

- Two sturdy paper cups
- Two paper clips
- Strong string (about 8 meters, or 26 feet, long)
- Partner
- Nail

3. Tie each string end to a paper clip. This will keep the string from slipping out of each hole.
4. Stretch the string tightly between you and your partner.
5. You speak into one cup while your partner listens with the other cup.

Concept Invention

1. Can you hear better through the string telephone than through the air? Whisper softly through the phone. Do it a little louder until your partner hears you. Then whisper to her at the same loudness without the telephone.
2. How can you stop a sound from reaching you on the string telephone?
3. Suppose two other children have a string telephone. How can you make a "party line"?
4. What can you do to make your phone work better? Try containers of different sizes and materials. Try different kinds of string and waxing the string with candle wax.

Teaching Tips

Holding the string or letting it sag will dampen or stop sounds, as will touching the vibrating cup bottom. For a party line, cross and loop around once the lines of two sets of phones.

Cylindrical cereal boxes (e.g., oatmeal containers) and table salt containers work well for string telephones. Metal can bottoms are too thick and rigid to vibrate well. Hard string or waxed string is superior to softly woven string.

Concept Application

Sound vibrations can travel through string and other solid materials. Can you describe some materials that sound will travel through?

Underwater Sounds ———

Invitation

What are underwater sounds like?

Exploration

1. Press an ear against the tank above the water level. Listen.
2. Have your partner repeatedly hit two spoons together inside the tank, but above the water.

MATERIALS

- Half-filled aquarium tank or large glass bowl
- Partner
- Two spoons

3. Again, press your ear against the tank but below the water level. Listen.
4. Now have your partner hit the spoons together below the water level, as shown here.

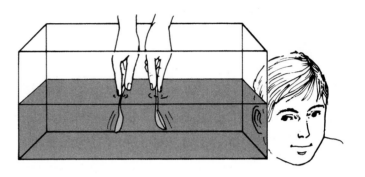

Concept Invention

How can you describe the difference between the two sets of sounds?

Concept Application

Does sound seem to travel better in water or in air?

HOW SOUNDS TRAVEL CONCEPTS

Watch a parade from afar, and band members seem to be out of step with the music they are playing. See a carpenter hammering a nail on a distant rooftop, and you hear the sound as the hammer is lifted instead of when the nail is struck.

Speeds of Sound

The speed at which sound waves travel lies behind each of the events mentioned. Light travels so fast (about 297,000 kilometers [186,000 miles] per second) that it seems instantaneous to our eyes. But sound is another matter. At sea level and 6.5°C (42°F), sound waves move about 330 meters (1100 feet) per second in the air, only as fast as a low-power rifle bullet. Sound also travels in liquids and solids. It moves about 5 times faster in water than it does in air; in steel, sound may travel 15 times faster than it does in air.

Three conditions affect the speed of sound: density, the elasticity or "springiness" of the molecules conducting the sound, and temperature. Density by itself does not increase the speed of sound. In fact, the speed of sound may decrease with density; but often associated with density is greatly increased elasticity of molecules. When highly elastic, close-together molecules of a solid transmit sound, the sound travels much faster than in either air or water.

Sounds travel faster when the temperature goes up. In fact, it is about 1 foot per second faster in air for every 1 degree Fahrenheit. Have you ever wondered why sounds carry such large distances on certain days? On a cold winter day with snow on the ground, for example, air next to the ground is often colder than the air far above the ground. Instead of a sound wave spreading out uniformly and then rapidly dying out, the temperature difference causes parts of the wave to travel at different speeds.

Given the same medium and temperature, all sounds travel at the same speed. If this were not so, it would be difficult or impossible to conduct concerts in large auditoriums. The reedy sound of an oboe and the brassy timbre of a trombone always reach your ears at the same time, if they are begun at the same time.

Sonic Booms

When children live where sonic booms often occur, one of the children may ask what happens when an airplane "breaks the sound barrier." We know that a sound-producing object sends out sound waves in all directions. When the object is set in motion, it continues to send out waves in all directions. But let's continue to increase this object's speed. As it goes faster, it is more difficult for waves to travel outward in front of it. When an airplane reaches a certain speed (about 1200 kilometers [750 miles], per hour, but varies greatly with altitude and temperature), air compressions of these sound waves pile up into a dense area of compressed air. This can subject the airplane to severe stresses.

A powerful engine and proper design enable an airplane to wedge through the dense air; but what happens to the compressed air? The tremendous energy is passed on, molecule to molecule, until it hits the earth as a booming shock wave. The shock wave continues on the ground in a wide strip that traces the airplane's flight path. It stops only when the pilot slows the aircraft to less than the speed of sound. Sonic booms that cause the least damage start at very high altitudes. By the time energy in the original area of compressed air is passed on to the ground, much of it has dissipated.

An explosion forms similar shock waves, except they may move out equidistantly in all directions. Very rapid expansion of gases in an explosion compresses the surrounding air. As the shock wave of compressed air moves outward, it may flatten almost anything in its path until the pressure finally dissipates over a distance.

REFLECTED AND ABSORBED SOUNDS **Inquiry**

Sounds and Megaphones

MATERIALS

- One sheet of heavy paper
- Sticky tape
- Two partners
- Windup clock
- Meterstick or yardstick

Invitation

What do you do when you want your voice to project farther? Do you cup your hands to your mouth? Doing this helps to keep the sound from spreading out, so it travels farther. There's another way to do this. You can make a megaphone. How can you make and use a megaphone?

Exploration

1. Roll up one sheet of heavy paper from one corner to make a cone. The small opening should be large enough to speak into.
2. Fasten the two ends and middle with sticky tape as illustrated.
3. Have a partner stand across the room from you.
4. Point the megaphone toward your partner. Whisper some numbers.
5. Have your partner walk toward you until he hears you and then stop walking.

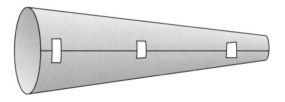

Concept Invention

1. Can your partner hear you without the megaphone? Have him stay where he stopped. Whisper numbers just as before. How can you tell if your partner hears you?
2. Can you send a message to someone without another person hearing? Have a second partner stand to one side of you. She should be as far from you as your first partner. Point the megaphone toward your first partner and whisper numbers. How can you tell if only your first partner hears you?
3. How close must someone be to your first partner to hear you whisper?

Teaching Tips

A megaphone tends to conserve sound energy by reflecting it in a specific direction. This allows sound to travel farther than when it spreads out in all directions. The effect also happens in reverse. The large end of a megaphone can gather sound and reflect it inward, like the old ear trumpets that were used before electronic hearing aids were invented. If we listen at the small end, the sound is louder than without the megaphone. More sound energy reaches the ear.

Concept Application

How can a megaphone help us to hear something better? Put the clock on a table. Stand where you cannot hear the clock. Put the megaphone to your ear. Point it toward the clock. Slowly move toward the clock until you hear it. Then stop. Can you hear the clock without the megaphone at that distance? How much closer will you need to be to hear it? Will different-sized megaphones make a difference in how far the sound travels? How can you find out? How does this activity show that a megaphone reflects sounds in one direction or that a megaphone may be used to increase our speaking or hearing range?

Echoes

Invitation

You probably know that smooth, hard walls reflect sounds well. A reflected sound that you hear is called an *echo*. Sound vibrations take time to travel to a wall and then back to you. When you are at the right distance, you hear the returning sound as a separate sound. How can you make an echo happen?

Exploration

1. Find a big wall outdoors in a large area. Try to locate a wall that has no buildings opposite it.
2. Measure a distance of about 25 meters (82 feet) from the wall. (You might cut a 5-meter string to speed up measuring.)
3. Hit a piece of wood once sharply with a hammer. Listen for an echo. If you hear more than one echo, try to find another place.

MATERIALS
• Meterstick or yardstick
• Scissors
• String
• Piece of wood
• Large outdoor wall
• Hammer

Teaching Tips

A trundle wheel is even more efficient than a 5-meter string for quick measurements. This device is a wheel with an attached broomlike handle. The wheel's size is such that, when rolled once around on a surface, it travels 1 meter (or 1 yard, as the case may be).

When listening for an echo, children will probably run out of space before they can fully answer the question. They should become aware, however, that increasing the distance also increases the time it takes to hear an echo. With the reflecting wall echo problem in the Concept Application, the clearest results should occur with two widely separated, opposing walls.

Concept Invention

1. How close can you be to the wall and still hear an echo?
2. How far away from the wall can you hear an echo? As you move farther away, does it take less or more time to hear the echo?
3. Try another wall. How do the results compare with the wall you already used?

Concept Application

How many echoes will there be with two reflecting walls? Try to find two facing, widely separated walls. Stand at different distances between them and bang the hammer. How do these results compare with those from a single wall? How does doing this illustrate that sounds are reflected over a distance?

MATERIALS

- Shoe box with lid
- Newspaper
- Pencil and paper
- Aluminum foil
- Windup alarm clock
- Different kinds of cloth
- Meterstick or yardstick
- Insulation materials of your choice

Materials That Quiet Sound ———

Invitation

Many people today are trying to cut down unwanted noise. They are putting materials around them that soak up sounds. These materials are called *sound insulators*. Some materials are better insulators than others. How can you find out which materials are good sound insulators?

Exploration

1. Wind up an alarm clock. Set the clock to ring within a few minutes.
2. Put the clock inside a shoe box and put on the lid.
3. Wait until the alarm rings. Measure how far away you can hear the ringing.
4. Record the distance.

Concept Invention

1. Suppose you wrap a sheet of newspaper around the clock. From how far away can you hear the sound now? Record and compare this distance with the first one.
2. What will happen if you wrap the clock in cloth? Record and compare this distance with the other distances.
3. What insulation materials will work best? Is it possible not to hear any ringing at all? Arrange your materials any way you want. All should fit inside the shoe box. How will you know whether the alarm has gone off?

 Teaching Tips

Loosely woven, soft, fluffy materials absorb sounds well. Hard surfaces reflect sounds. This is why a formerly empty room seems quieter after carpeting, drapes, and upholstered furniture are put in. Many younger children will be unable to measure the hearing distance with a meterstick. Let them measure with different lengths of string or the number of footsteps between them and the clock.

Scaffolding for English Learners

One method of increasing the scientific literacy of English learners is to increase the relevancy of the science lesson to the student's everyday life. In this lesson, take the time to expand on the concept of *unwanted sounds*. Most likely, there will be cultural differences that can be integrated into this lesson as students brainstorm possible sound insulators. Think about what other items could be placed in the shoe box instead of an alarm clock. (See Fathman, Quinn, & Kessler, 1992, for a discussion of relevancy and science.)

Concept Application

What is another way to show that loosely woven, fluffy materials are good sound insulators?

REFLECTED AND ABSORBED SOUNDS CONCEPTS

Sound Reflection ───────

One reason why singing in the shower is so popular has to do with the nature of sound reflections. As a sound hits the smooth shower walls, it bounces back and forth, seeming louder and prolonging the notes a little. This is pleasing to the ear. The smoother the reflecting surface, the better sound reflects. On a very smooth wall, sound reflections bounce off like light reflections from a mirror. The angle of reflection equals the angle of incidence.

Because sound can be reflected, we can direct or channel it in certain directions by using different devices. Open-air theaters often have large shell-like structures surrounding

INQ Figure 3–2   Open-air theaters often have shell-like structures to reflect sounds to the audience.

the stages (see INQ Figure 3–2). This shape enables sounds to be directed toward an audience with reduced energy loss. The same principle is used with cheerleaders' megaphones.

An even more efficient way to conserve sound energy is to enclose it within a tube. Because the sound is kept from spreading out by continual reflections within the encircling wall, such concentrated sound loses energy slowly and may travel a long way. Sometimes children use garden hoses as speaking tubes because these work well at surprising distances.

A reverse application of this reflection principle is found in the old-fashioned ear trumpet and in the ears of animals such as rabbits and donkeys. In these cases, sounds are "gathered," or reflected inward. Besides large ears, many animals have the additional advantage of being able to cock them separately in different directions.

Echoes

Because sound takes time to travel and can be reflected, it stands to reason that at a certain distance you should be able to hear a distinctly separate reflection of an original sound, an echo. Most persons need an interval of at least 0.10 second to distinguish between two sounds. If the interval is shorter than this, they hear one sound, much like the way the brain interprets separate frames of a motion picture as continuous motion.

If we assume that a sound wave travels at a speed of 330 meters (1100 feet) per second, in 0.10 second it travels 33 meters (110 feet). To hear an echo, or a distinguishable, separate sound, we must stand far enough away from a reflecting surface for the sound wave to travel a total distance of 33 meters (110 feet). Because the sound travels to the reflecting surface and back to our ears, a distance of 16.5 meters (55 feet) from the surface is adequate to hear an echo. Remember, this distance varies a bit with temperature variations.

INQ Figure 3–3 **A bat's ears are well suited for echolocation.**

Sometimes the combination of a loud sound and many distant reflecting surfaces produces multiple echoes, or *reverberations*. A common example is thunder, which may reverberate back and forth from cloud to earth and among air layers of varying densities.

An interesting application of echo detection is found in a U.S. Navy device called *sonar*. (The term is an acronym for SOund NAvigation and Ranging.) This apparatus sends a sound wave through the water and detects reflections from any direction. The time between an initial sound and its received echo enables a sonar operator to know the distance of a reflector, whether a submarine or an underwater obstruction. Similar devices are used on fishing vessels to detect schools of fish.

The use of sound reflections is found in nature in bats, dolphins, and porpoises. By listening to reflections of its cries, for example, a bat flying in total darkness avoids collisions and catches insects in midair. This ability to use sound reflections is referred to as *echolocation* (see INQ Figure 3–3).

Absorbed Sounds

Have you ever noticed how different the sounds seem in a room before and after furnishings are installed? Rugs, draperies, and cloth-covered furniture absorb more sound waves than we commonly realize. But even a furnished room may have a "hollow" sound if the walls and ceilings are hard and smooth. Porous acoustical tile on ceilings and rough, porous plaster blown on with a compressed-air applicator can reduce sound reflections. Besides absorbing some sound waves, a rough surface interferes with the wave reflection, just as light is diffused when it hits an irregular surface.

Sometimes older children ask, "What happens to a sound when it goes into a porous material?" It appears that sound energy is changed to heat energy. The regular pulsating movements of a wave are broken up into the normal, irregular motions of individual molecules. As this happens, any energy passed into the porous substance is transmitted to other air molecules, slightly raising the temperature.

Reverberation and Reflected and Absorbed Sounds

A reverberation was defined earlier as a multiple echo. After being produced, sound waves travel through the air in all directions. In a room, the various surfaces and materials absorb sound. The sound waves slowly lose a small amount of energy that is absorbed with each reflection until the waves gradually diminish and become inaudible.

The *reverberation time* is the number of seconds that a sound's average loudness can be heard, before it becomes completely inaudible under quiet conditions. This time depends on the ability of the room to reflect sound and may vary from about 1 second in a so-called dead room to 10 seconds in a highly reverberant room. Classrooms are designed to reverberate for less than 1 second, since the maximum reverberation time for understanding speech is about 2 seconds. Music halls are designed for reverberation times between 1.5 and 2 seconds, the ideal reverberation time for orchestral music.

HOW PITCH CHANGES Inquiry

Changing Pitches

Invitation

What happens to pitch as the speed of vibrations changes?

Exploration

1. Hold a comb in one hand and a card in the other.
2. Pull the card tip across the teeth of the comb slowly and steadily. Listen to the pitch of the sound (how high or low it is).
3. Repeat step 2, but faster this time. Listen again.
4. Try many different speeds. Listen each time.

Concept Invention

1. What is the pitch like when the vibrations are slow?
2. What happens to the pitch as the vibrations move faster?

Concept Application

Turn a bicycle upside down. Crank a pedal around slowly to move the rear wheel. Hold the tip of a card against the spokes as the wheel slowly turns. Listen to the pitch as the card vibrates. Crank the wheel faster and faster. Listen again to the pitch as the card vibrates faster and faster. What is the pitch like when the vibrations are slow? What happens to the pitch as the vibrations move faster?

> **MATERIALS**
> - Comb
> - Small card
> - Bicycle

 Teaching Tips | **Caution:** For safety, be sure that fingers holding the card are well away from the spinning bicycle wheel in the Concept Application.

How to Make a Rubber-Band Banjo

Invitation

What kinds of stringed instruments have you seen? How are they played? How can you make a rubber-band banjo?

Exploration

1. Write the numbers 1 through 8 on the inside of the lid. Use a ruler to space them evenly across the whole lid.
2. Put four thick rubber bands around half of the lid. Space them from numbers 1 through 4.
3. Put four thinner bands around the other half of the lid. Space them from numbers 5 through 8.

> **MATERIALS**
> - Stiff shoe box lid or topless cigar box
> - Ruler
> - Eight rubber bands (four thick, four thinner)
> - Pencil and paper

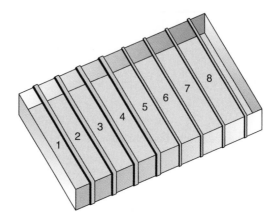

The tightness, thickness, and length of a rubber band (or string) all affect its pitch. Sounds are higher with taut, thin, short strings; they are lower with looser, thicker, or longer strings on any stringed instrument.

The tension of each rubber band may be adjusted by pulling up or down at the side of the lid. Friction between the band and the lid will hold the band in place for a while. However, the band will need to be strummed or plucked gently. A sturdy lid is preferable to a flimsy one that bows in the middle.

Concept Invention

1. Pluck one of the rubber bands. How can you make a soft sound? How can you make a loud sound?
2. Which bands—thick or thin—make the higher sounds? (The highness or lowness of a sound is its pitch.)
3. What happens to the pitch when a band is shortened? Press down a rubber band halfway across the lid. Pluck the band half nearest you.

Can you design another musical instrument that shows that length, tension, and thickness affect the pitch of a vibrating string?

A Soda-Straw Oboe ————

MATERIALS

- Paper or plastic straws (one should be smaller to fit inside a larger one)
- Straight pin
- Cellophane tape
- Scissors
- Small paper cup

Invitation

Have you ever seen an oboe? It is a reed instrument. When the player blows on the mouthpiece, two flat, thin reeds vibrate. This makes the air inside the oboe vibrate. By opening and closing holes, the player makes different amounts of air vibrate. The different amounts change the pitch of the notes played. You can make an instrument like this from a soda straw. How can you make a soda-straw oboe?

Exploration

1. Pinch the end of one straw between your thumb and forefinger to flatten it.
2. Snip off the flattened corners with scissors, as illustrated. If you have a plastic straw, cut to make a point.
3. Put about 3 centimeters (1 inch) of the cut straw end into your mouth. Keep your lips closed but a little loose. Blow hard into the straw. If no sound is made, blow less hard until a sound is made.

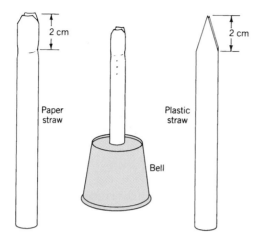

Concept Invention

1. What happens if you change the length of the straw? Join another straw of the same size to the first straw. To do so, slightly pinch the end of the second straw. Then gently push the pinched end into the first straw. Try adding a third straw in the same way.

2. What happens if you change the length another way? Try to fit a smaller straw into the larger one. If it is too loose, wrap some cellophane tape around the end of the smaller straw. Slide the second straw up and down as you blow.

3. What do you think will happen if you snip off pieces of a single straw while blowing? Try it and see.

Concept Application

How can eight people with different-sized straws play a song?
Does this demonstrate that changing the length of the vibrating air column inside changes the pitch of a wind instrument?

Teaching Tips

Paper straws typically work more easily than plastic straws in this activity. If students find it difficult or impossible to produce a sound, often the cut "reed" is to blame. It may help to press down gently with the lips on the straw just below the flattened part. This will open up the reed slightly and let it vibrate more easily when blown. A plastic-straw reed should be pointed for best results.

A "bell" for the instrument can be made by punching a small hole in the bottom of a paper cup and inserting the straw end into it. It should noticeably increase the loudness of the instrument.

A Bottle Xylophone

Invitation

Do you know what a xylophone looks like? This instrument has a row of different-sized blocks of wood. The player makes sounds by striking the blocks with two special sticks. You can easily make an instrument that works like a xylophone, but instead of wood, you can use bottles of water. How can you make a bottle xylophone?

Exploration

1. Put different levels of water in each bottle.
2. Line the bottles in a row in any order.
3. Tap each of the bottles lightly with a pencil. Notice how high or low each sound is. This highness or lowness is called *pitch*.

MATERIALS

- Eight matched soda bottles
- Pencil and paper
- Water

Bottles made of plain glass make clearer, purer sounds than those made of rippled glass. If you or one of your students can play the piano, the class may enjoy playing this eight-note xylophone either as an accompanying or as a leading instrument. The students may also enjoy singing with the instrument.

Caution: If the bottles are used by more than one student in the Concept Application, sterilize the bottle openings between uses. Dampen a paper towel with rubbing alcohol, wipe the bottle openings well, and then rinse the alcohol off well with running water. Dry with a clean paper towel.

Concept Invention

1. How much water is in the bottle of highest pitch? lowest pitch?
2. Can you put the bottles in order from lowest to highest pitch?
3. What must you do with the bottles to make an eight-note scale?
4. Can you play a simple song? Put paper slips in front of the bottles. Number them from 1 to 8 for an eight-note scale. Notice the numbers of the notes you play.
5. Can you write a song so that someone else can play it correctly? Write on paper the numbers of the notes to be played. Use your own made-up song or a known song. Observe how well the song is played.
6. How can you improve the way you wrote your song?

Concept Application

An instrument's pitch depends on how much mass vibrates. As mass increases, pitch lowers. With less mass, the pitch gets higher. Suppose you blew over each bottle top. Now the air inside would vibrate rather than the water. How do you think that would affect each pitch? Try it and see and then record the results.

HOW PITCH CHANGES CONCEPTS

Many pilots of crop-dusting airplanes actually rely on sound to gauge the safeness of their air speed. While flying low, it is difficult to watch both an air-speed indicator in the cockpit and ground obstructions. Flying speed is therefore estimated by listening to the pitch of sound made by the vibration of the airplane's struts and wires as the wind rushes past. Some seasoned pilots can judge their margin of safety to within narrow limits by this method.

Sometimes children fasten small cards against the spokes of their bicycle wheels to simulate a motor sound while riding. As the spokes go around and hit the card, it vibrates and makes a sound. The pitch rises with increased speed of vibrations and lowers with decreased speed of vibrations.

Stringed Instruments

In a stringed instrument, pitch depends on the length, tightness, and thickness of the strings. Shortening a string causes faster vibrations, raising the pitch. Lengthening a string has the opposite effect. Tightening a string also increases pitch, whereas loosening a string decreases pitch. A thick string vibrates more slowly than a thin one and so produces a lower-pitched sound.

Why do different instruments—a violin and a cello, for instance—play a note at the same pitch and yet sound different? The quality of tone (*timbre*) produced by these instruments is different. Most vibrations include more than just simple, back-and-forth movements along a string's entire length. Although a fundamental vibration governs the basic pitch, other parts of the string vibrate at faster frequencies. The combinations of vibrations are different with each string and with various stringed instruments. Together they produce tones of distinctly recognizable qualities.

Wind Instruments ———————

In wind instruments, a vibrating column of air makes the sound. The vibrations may be started by a player's lips, as with trumpets and tubas, or by blowing past a reed, as with the saxophone and clarinet.

Pitch is regulated by changing the length of the air column vibrating within the instrument. In a wind instrument such as the saxophone, opening and closing valves with the fingers changes air-column length. In a trombone, air-column length is changed by pulling or pushing a long, closed double tube called the *slide*.

The property of timbre is also present in wind instruments. In this case, it is caused by the combinations of additional air vibrations set up within each instrument. Quality of voices is produced in much the same way. This is regulated by the size and shape of air cavities in the mouth and nose.

Homemade Instruments ———————

An interesting way for children to learn about pitch and tonal quality is for them to make their own stringed and wind instruments. Rubber bands of different sizes make pleasant sounds when placed around topless cigar boxes or sturdy shoe box lids. Strong nylon fishing line fastened on pieces of wood with nails and screw eyes also works well (see INQ Figure 3–4).

INQ Figure 3–4 **Children can experiment with pitch and tone by making their own instruments.**

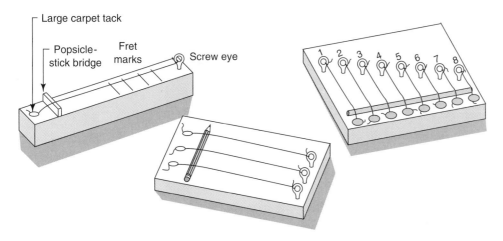

When the line is fastened to a screw eye, its tension can be adjusted by turning the eye in the appropriate direction. Tuned properly, nylon fishing line sounds somewhat like the string on a regular instrument. Simple tunes can be composed and played on the stringed instruments that children fashion.

Soda straws and bottles make acceptable wind instruments. Interestingly, opposite results in pitch occur with partly filled soda bottles, depending on whether they are used as wind or percussion instruments. That is, if you blow over the tops of soda bottles containing varying volumes of water, the scale may go from low to high, left to right. If you strike those same bottles sharply with a pencil, however, the opposite happens; the scale will go from high to low, left to right. With blowing, the bottle's air mainly vibrates; when striking the bottle, the water and glass mainly vibrate.

Mass and Noise ————————

When a noise is made, the amount of mass in the vibrating object usually determines the pitch. A large, dropped wooden block sounds lower than a dropped smaller one. When thick paper is torn, it sounds lower than a torn thin paper. A dropped nickel sounds lower than a dropped dime. Both young and older children show interest in this phenomenon.

HEARING AND LOCATING SOUNDS **Inquiry**

Do You Hear What I Hear? —————

Invitation

How do you locate sounds with your ears?

Exploration

1. Have your partners sit in a large circle about half the width of the classroom.
2. Sit in the center of the circle. Keep your eyes tightly closed. Listen with both ears.
3. Let each partner, in random order, lightly tap two pencils together once.
4. Can you tell from which direction the sound comes? Point to the spot each time. Have someone record how often you are right or wrong.

Concept Invention

1. Now try Exploration steps 2 and 3 again, but this time listen with only one ear. Hold a hand tightly over the other ear.
2. Can you locate the sounds as well as before?

Concept Application

Will you get the same results with your other ear?

> ### MATERIALS
> - Eight partners
> - Quiet room
> - 16 pencils

HEARING AND LOCATING SOUNDS CONCEPTS

The ear must be ranked among the body's most remarkable organs. In our hearing, sound waves are channeled into the ear canal by the outer ear, which acts as a megaphone in reverse. As sound waves collide with the eardrum, this thin membrane of stretched skin begins vibrating at the same frequency as the waves.

Just inside the eardrum are three tiny connected bones: the hammer, anvil, and stirrup (see INQ Figure 3–5). A vibrating eardrum starts the attached hammer shaking, and this movement is transmitted through the connected bones to the cochlea, or inner ear.

INQ Figure 3 –5 **The human ear.**

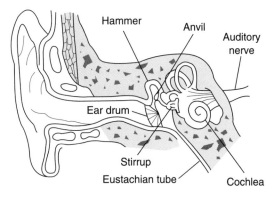

This snail-shaped apparatus is filled with a watery fluid and lined with sensitive nerve endings that trail off to the auditory nerve and brain. The transmitted vibrations pass through the fluid and excite the nerve endings. These excitations are converted into electrical impulses that zip to the brain.

Children should learn some reasonable rules for ear care and safety. A sharp object jabbed into the ear may cause a punctured eardrum. A puncture greatly impairs or prevents eardrum vibrations and results in hearing loss in the affected ear. Children should also beware of a sharp blow against the outer ear. This compresses air within the air canal and may cause a ruptured eardrum. Blowing the nose forces air up through the eustachian tube. If a person is suffering from a cold, hard blowing may force germs up the tube and infect the middle ear.

Hearing Ranges

Although our ears are sensitive to a wide range of pitches, there are limits to what we can hear. Almost no one can detect a sound that vibrates less than about 16 times per second or one that vibrates more than 20,000 times per second. As we grow older, this range is gradually narrowed.

Hearing ranges in animals often exceed those of humans. A bat may detect sounds that vary between 10 vibrations to 100,000 vibrations per second. A dog's hearing begins at only several vibrations per second and goes to 40,000 vibrations per second; this is why it is possible to use a "silent" whistle for calling a dog: The pitch is simply too high for humans to hear. A cat's hearing is even more remarkable; it can detect sounds up to 50,000 vibrations per second. Elephants can communicate with each other by producing rumblings too low pitched for us to hear; the elephants' huge outer ears act as giant funnels for channeling these rumblings to the ear canals. Sounds that are inaudible to us are called *infrasonic* when they vibrate too slowly and *ultrasonic* when they vibrate too quickly.

Locating Sounds

Most people can tell the direction from which a sound comes, even when blindfolded. With two ears, a sound usually reaches one ear just before the other. The slight difference is enough to let the brain interpret the information.

A person with only one functioning ear can receive similar signals by quickly turning the head slightly on hearing the first sound. When the sound is very short, this may not be possible.

References

American Association for the Advancement of Science (AAAS). (1993). *Benchmarks for science literacy.* New York: Oxford University Press.

Fathman, A. K., Quinn, M. E., & Kessler, C. (1992). *Teaching science to English learners, grades 4–8.* Washington, DC: National Clearinghouse of Bilingual Education. Retrieved November 13, 2004, from www.ncela.gwu.edu/pubs/pigs/pig11.htm

Laplante, B. (1997). Teaching science to language minority students in elementary classrooms. *Journal of the New York State Association for Bilingual Education, 12,* 62–83. Retrieved November 13, 2004, from www.ncela.gwu.edu/pubs/nysabe/vol12/ nysable124.pdf

Mastropieri, M., & Scruggs, T. E. (2004). *The inclusive classroom: Strategies for effective instruction* (4th ed.). Upper Saddle River, NJ: Merrill/Prentice Hall.

National Research Council (NRC). (1996). *National science education standards.* Washington, DC: National Academy Press.

Ovando, C. J., Collier, V. P., & Combs, M. C. (2003). *Bilingual and ESL classrooms: Teaching in multicultural contexts.* Boston: McGraw-Hill.

Selected Trade Books: Sound Energy

For Younger Children

Allington, R. L., & Cowles, K. (1980). *Hearing*. Austin, TX: Raintree.

Ardley, N. (1991). *The science book of sound*. Chicago: Harcourt Brace Jovanovich.

Barrett, S. (1980). *The sound of the week*. New York: Good Apple.

Berger, M. (1992). *Sound, heat & light: Energy at work*. New York: Scholastic.

Broekel, R. (1983). *Sound experiments*. Danbury, CT: Childrens Press.

Carle, E. (1997). *The very quiet cricket*. New York: G. P. Putnam.

Cole, J. (1995). *The magic school bus in the haunted museum: A book about sound*. New York: Scholastic.

Davis, K. (2000). *Who hoots?* Orlando: Harcourt.

Diller, H. (1996). *Big band sound*. Honesdale, PA: Boyds Mills Press.

Friedman, J. T. (1981). *Sounds all around*. New York: G. P. Putnam.

Gibson, G. (1995). *Hearing sounds (science for fun)*. Providence, RI: Copper Beech Books.

Hughes, A. E. (1979). *A book of sounds*. Austin, TX: Raintree.

Jennings, T. (1990). *Making sounds*. Danbury, CT: Watts.

Kaner, E. (1991). *Sound science*. Reading, MA: Addison-Wesley Publishing Company.

Lee, J. D. (1985). *Sounds!* Milwaukee, WI: Gareth Stevens.

Moncure, J. B. (1982). *Sounds all around*. Danbury, CT: Childrens Press.

Oliver, S. (1991). *Noises*. New York: Random House.

Parnall, P. (1989). *Quiet*. New York: Morrow Junior Books.

Pfeiffer, W. (1999). *Sounds all around*. New York: HarperCollins.

Ramsay, H. (1998). *Sound*. Danbury, CT: Childrens Press.

Richardson, J. (1986). *What happens when we listen?* Milwaukee, WI: Gareth Stevens.

Rowan, J., & Perham, M. (1993). *Making sounds*. Chicago: Childrens Press.

Spier, P. (1990). *Crash! Bang! Boom!* New York: Doubleday.

Wade, H. (1979). *Sound*. Austin, TX: Raintree.

Webb, A. (1988). *Sound*. Danbury, CT: Watts.

Wood, N., & Rye, J. (1991). *Listen: What do you hear*. New York: Troll Associates.

Wyler, R. (1987). *Science fun with drums, bells, and whistles*. Parsippany, NJ: Julian Messner.

For Older Children

Ardley, N. (1991). *Sound waves to music: Projects with sound*. Danbury, CT: Watts.

Birch, B., & Corfield, B. (1995). *Marconi's battle for radio*. Hauppauge, NY: Barron's.

Brandt, K. (1985). *Sounds*. New York: Troll Associates.

Catherall, E. (1982). *Hearing*. Parsippany, NJ: Silver Burdett.

Cobb, V. (2000). *Bangs and twangs: Science fun with sound*. Brookfield, CT: Millbrook Press.

Fleischman, P. (1988). *Joyful noise: Poems for two voices*. New York: HarperTrophy.

Grimshaw, C. (1999). *Invisible journeys: Sound*. Chicago: World Book.

Guthridge, S. (1986). *Thomas A. Edison: Young inventor*. New York: Aladdin Paperbacks.

Kettlekamp, L. (1982). *The magic of sound*. New York: Morrow.

Knight, D. C. (1980). *Silent sound: The world of ultrasonics*. New York: Morrow.

Knight, D. C. (1983). *All about sound*. New York: Troll Associates.

Kohn, B. (1979). *Echoes*. New York: Dandelion.

Mathers, D. (1992). *Ears*. Mahwah: NJ: Troll Associates.

Morgan, S., & Morgan, A. (1994). *Using sound*. New York: Facts on File.

Newman, F. R. (1983). *Zounds! The kid's guide to sound making*. New York: Random House.

Pettigrew, M. (1987). *Music and sound*. Danbury, CT: Watts.

Riley, P. (1987). *Light and sound*. New York: David & Charles.

Simon, S. (2003). *Eyes and ears*. New York: HarperCollins.

Taylor, B. (1991). *Sound and music*. Danbury, CT: Watts.

Ward, A. (1991). *Experimenting with sound*. Brookmall, PA: Chelsea House.

Ward, B. (1981). *The ear and hearing*. Danbury, CT: Watts.

Wood, R. W. (1997). *Sound fundamentals: Funtastic science activities for kids*. Philadelphia Chelsea House Publishers.

Resource Books

Butzow, C. M., & Butzow, J. W. (1989). *Science through children's literature: An integrated approach*. Englewood, CO: Teacher Ideas Press. (sound and hearing topics, pp. 112–118)

Cordel, B., & Hillen, J. (Eds.). (1994). *Sense-able science: Exploring and discovering our five senses*. Fresno, CA: AIMS Education Foundation. (hearing topics, pp. 120–137)

Hillen, J., Mercier, S., Hoover, E., & Cordel, B. (1994). *Primarily physics: Investigations in sound, light, heat, and energy*. Fresno, CA: AIMS Education Foundation. (sound activities pp. 2–39)

LeCroy, B., & Holder, B. (1994). *Bookwebs: A brainstorm of ideas for the primary classroom*. Englewood, CO: Teacher Ideas Press. (sound activities, pp. 57–63)

Sullivan, E. P. (1990). *Starting with books: An activities approach to children's literature*. Englewood, CO: Teacher Ideas Press. (hearing impairment topics, pp. 23–25)

Tolman, M., & Morton, J. (1986). *Physical science activities for grades 2–8*. West Nyack, NY: Parker. (over 180 hands-on activities including sound activities)

MAGNETIC INTERACTIONS

The use of magnets dates back more than 3000 years. Ancient Greeks, Romans, and Chinese discovered that the type of rock we now know as magnetite attracted bits of iron. This finding later became very important to sailors when they discovered that a floating piece of magnetite, or lodestone (meaning "lead" stone), would align with north–south direction. Sailors no longer had to rely on land sightings or star-filled skies to navigate their ships. Children today can magnetize a steel needle and float the needle on a small bit of cork, or suspend a bar magnet from a string, to repeat this discovery. One question often asked with this activity is, "Why isn't the steel needle already magnetized like the magnetite?" The answer is in how the steel and magnetite were formed.

Magnetite is a mineral containing a large amount of iron. The magnetite we find today was formed during the slow hardening of the earth's crust. As it cooled, the magnetite was either magnetized by the earth's magnetic field or possibly subjected to lightning strikes. Because of this, the magnetite developed a north-seeking and a south-seeking pole. The iron and steel we make today do not develop poles because these materials harden too fast to be affected by the earth's magnetism.

At the primary level, magnets may be studied more than any other science topic. It is common for young children to have their own magnets and magnetic toys. Let's consider several kinds of magnets and what they attract, how to make magnets, the field of force that surrounds a magnet, magnetic poles, and the theory and care of magnets.

Benchmarks and Standards

Magnets are commonly studied in the primary grades. Children should complete activities designed to observe and classify magnetic and nonmagnetic objects. Early activities will also lay the groundwork for future study of forces. Specific examples of benchmarks and standards are as follows:

Sample Benchmarks (AAAS, 1993)

- Magnets can be used to make some things move without being touched. (By Grades K–2, p. 94)
- Without touching them, a magnet pulls on all things made of iron and either pushes or pulls on other magnets. (By Grades 3–5, p. 94)

Sample Standard (NRC, 1996)

- Magnets attract and repel each other and certain kinds of other materials. (By Grades K–4, p. 127)

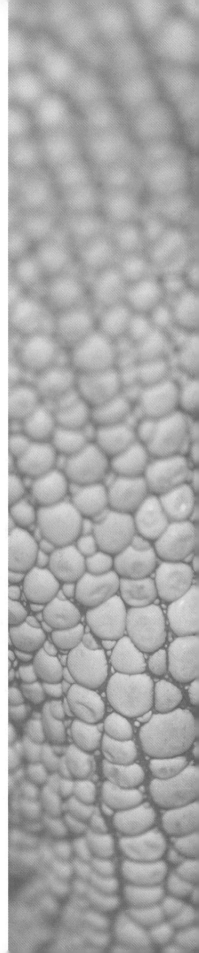

MAGNETS AND WHAT THEY ATTRACT Inquiry

Objects Magnets Can Pull

MATERIALS

- Two bags of small objects
- Magnet

Invitation

Have you ever played with a magnet? If so, what were you able to do with it? How can you find out which objects magnets can pull?

Exploration

1. Take out the objects from only one bag now.
2. Touch your magnet to each object.
3. Which objects are pulled by the magnet? Put these in a group.
4. Which objects are not pulled by the magnet? Put those in another group.

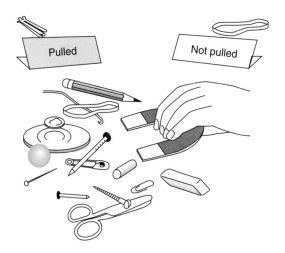

 Teaching Tips

Try to get a variety of attractable and nonattractable small objects for both bags of test materials. Following are common objects and their chief metals or metal alloys.

Object	Metal
Nail	Iron
Wire	Copper (if reddish color; wires of other colors are other metals)
Safety pin	Steel (or brass)
Screw	Brass (or iron or aluminum)
Hair curler	Aluminum
Penny	Bronze

Give children the names of metals as needed to help them generalize about their experience.

Concept Invention

1. How are the objects in the pulled group alike?
2. Can you make a rule about which objects your magnet pulls? Put the objects back into the bag. Put the bag away.
3. Take out the objects from the second bag. Which do you think your magnet will pull? Which will it not pull? Put the objects into two groups. Now use your magnet on the objects in each group. Was every object in the correct group?
4. Which objects around the room will your magnet pull? Record your prediction and verify.

Concept Application

What other magnets can you try? Will they pull the same objects your first magnet pulled? How does this show that a magnet pulls objects made of iron or steel?

Magnetic Separations ———

Invitation

How can a magnet separate mixed materials?

Exploration

1. Put two spoonfuls each of filings and salt into the jar.
2. Cap the jar and shake it to mix the two materials.
3. Pour the mixture onto a white paper "tray."
4. Try using the spoon to separate the filings and salt.

Concept Invention

1. Cover the magnet's poles with kitchen plastic wrap. Now try using the covered magnet to separate the filings and salt.
2. To remove the filings from the magnet, remove the kitchen wrap.
3. Which was an easier way to separate the filings and salt, using the spoon or using the magnet?

Concept Application

Many bits of iron may be found in sands and soils. Cover the magnet's poles again with wrap. Poke the magnet around in a sandbox or loose soil. How many iron bits do you find?

MATERIALS
• Magnet
• Plastic spoon
• Salt
• Small jar with lid
• Kitchen plastic wrap
• White paper with turned-up edges
• Iron filings
• Sandbox or loose soil

The Power of Magnets ———

Invitation

Some people say they can tell how strong a magnet is just by looking at it. What do you think? How can you find out the power of a magnet?

Exploration

1. Put a paper clip on two pieces of soda straw, placed on a sheet of lined paper.
2. Make a pencil mark at the front of the clip.
3. Line up an end (pole) of a magnet with the clip as shown.
4. Slowly bring the magnet near the paper clip.
5. Stop moving the magnet when the clip moves.
6. Count the lines between the pencil mark and magnet.

MATERIALS
• Several different kinds of magnets
• Two small pieces cut from a straw
• Pencil
• Sheet of lined paper
• Paper clips

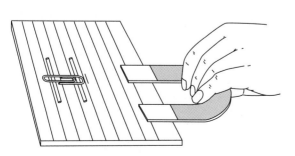

A magnet attracts objects most strongly at the ends, or poles. The attractive power gradually weakens toward the center of the magnet. The center has very little or no magnetic attraction.

Concept Invention

1. Test several magnets. Which is the most powerful? Can you put them in order from weakest to strongest?
2. Are both ends (poles) of a magnet equally powerful? How can you find out?
3. Do all parts of a magnet pull the clip? Which part of a magnet is strongest? Which is the weakest?

Concept Application

Magnets vary in power; magnets attract objects most strongly at their poles. What are some other ways to test a magnet's power? Do you get the same results?

MAGNETS AND WHAT THEY ATTRACT CONCEPTS

There are many magnets around the home and classroom for us to use as examples in teaching. In kitchens, cloth potholders containing magnets are placed on the sides of stoves. Automatic can openers have magnets to hold opened can lids. Cabinet doors remain closed because of magnets. Some people wear magnetic earrings. Toy stores have many toys that in some way use magnetism. At school, speakers, magnetic paper holders, and some games also have magnets.

What Magnets Attract

In nearly all these cases, the metals attracted to a magnet are iron and steel. Less well-known magnetic metals are cobalt and nickel. Among the more common metals not attracted by magnets are brass, aluminum, tin, silver, stainless steel, copper, bronze, and gold.

It will help you to know several facts that can clear up some common misunderstandings your students may have. For example, a question may arise about the attractable property of so-called tin cans. These are made of thin sheet steel and coated lightly with tin. Although tin is not attractable, steel is. Confusion may also result if some straight pins are attracted by a magnet and other identical-appearing pins are not because they are made of brass. Also, the U.S. 5¢ piece is largely composed of copper and so should not be used as an example.

Lodestones

Natural magnets are sometimes called lodestones, or "leading stones," because ancient mariners used them as crude compasses to point to the lodestar or leading star (the North Star), which is how they acquired their name. The lodestar is also known as the pole star, or North Star, presently Polaris. Lodestones are made of magnetite, an iron ore found in different locations on the earth's crust.

Only some of these ore deposits are magnetized, and scientists have developed theories to explain this phenomenon. One such theory holds that lightning may have been responsible. It is thought that electricity discharged into the ore may have arranged many atoms within the ore in a manner like that found in magnets.

INQ Figure 4–1   **Magnets (A) bar; (B) V; (C) U; (D) horseshoe; (E) cylindrical; and (F) lodestone.**

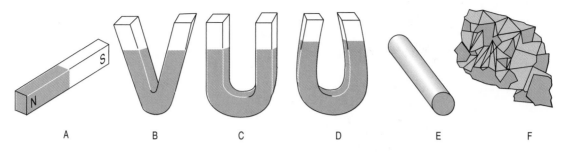

Traces of magnetite are common in soils. A magnet dragged along the ground or in a playground sandbox may attract many particles. These particles can be an effective substitute in activities in which iron filings are used.

Manufactured Magnets

Artificial magnets are often made of steel and magnetized by electricity. Named for their shapes, there are bar, **V**, **U**, horseshoe, and cylindrical magnets, to name the more familiar varieties (INQ Figure 4–1). Each of these magnets attracts substances most strongly at the ends, or poles. The **U**, **V**, and horseshoe magnets are more powerful than the others when all other factors except shape are equal; they are bent, so two poles attract instead of one.

Powerful alnico magnets are available from scientific supply houses and in commercial kits. These are made from aluminum, cobalt, nickel, and iron. Alnico magnets are used for home and commercial purposes.

MAKING MAGNETS Inquiry

How to Make Magnets

MATERIALS

- Strong magnet
- Two large matched iron nails
- Steel straight pins
- Two screwdrivers (large and small)

Invitation

Suppose you have an iron nail and a magnet. With these materials, you can make another magnet. How can you make a magnet?

Exploration

1. Get a large iron nail. Touch it to some steel pins to see if it attracts them.
2. Put one end of the magnet on the nail near the head.
3. Stroke the whole nail with the magnet 20 times. Stroke in one direction only, as illustrated.
4. Touch the nail again to some pins. How many pins does the nail attract? Record this number.

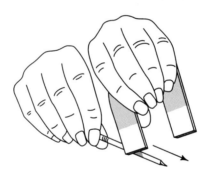

Teaching Tips

An iron or steel object may be magnetized by stroking it with a magnet. A soft iron object that is magnetized, such as a nail, weakens after several minutes. A steel object, such as the shank of a screwdriver, retains its magnetism. However, steel is more difficult to magnetize. Only a strong magnet is likely to produce significant results. Stroking an object both ways with a magnet is less effective than stroking it in one direction. Use steel straight pins to test the strength of whatever magnets are made.

Concept Invention

1. How much stronger can you make your nail magnet? How many pins does it attract after 30 strokes? 40 strokes? Record how many pins are attracted each time you test it.
2. How strong is the nail magnet after 10 minutes? Compare.
3. Test the other nail to see if it attracts pins. If it does not, stroke this nail back and forth, instead of just one way. How strong is the magnet after 20 strokes? 30 strokes? 40 strokes?
4. Suppose you stroke a small steel screwdriver one way with a magnet. How many pins will it attract after 20 strokes? 30 strokes? 40 strokes? Record and compare your findings with those for the nail.
5. Suppose you stroke a large steel screwdriver one way with a magnet. Will you get the same results?
6. How strong do you think both screwdrivers will be after 10 minutes?

Adapting for Students with Exceptionalities

For students experiencing difficulty with the directions, try highlighting the significant parts (e.g., the number of strokes). (See Mercer & Mercer, 2005, for a discussion on accommodations involving instructional materials.)

Concept Application

Iron and steel may be magnetized by a magnet; steel holds its magnetism longer than iron. What other objects can you make into magnets? How strong can you make each one?

Long-Lasting Magnets

Invitation

How can you make long-lasting magnets with electricity?

Exploration

1. Tightly roll a small file card around a pencil. Fasten it with sticky tape.
2. Tightly wind about 80 turns of thin copper wire in one direction around the tube. Leave 30 centimeters (1 foot) of wire free at each end. Tape the coil ends so that the wires stay tightly wound.
3. Use scissors to strip the insulation from the wire ends.
4. Remove the pencil from the tube. Put a straightened bobby pin inside.
5. Put three flashlight batteries together as pictured.
6. Touch the stripped ends of the wire to opposite ends of the batteries. Do this for no more than 5 seconds.
7. Remove the bobby pin and touch it to some tacks.
8. How many tacks does the bobby pin pick up?

> ### MATERIALS
> - Thin (number 26 or 28) insulated copper wire
> - Magnet
> - Three D-size batteries
> - Pencil
> - 3-by-5-inch file card
> - Scissors
> - Two steel bobby pins
> - Tacks
> - Sticky tape

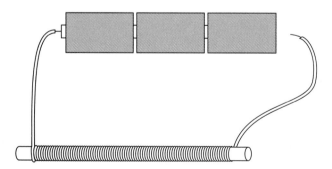

Concept Invention

1. Suppose you made a second bobby-pin magnet by stroking it with a regular magnet. Could you make it as strong as or stronger than the "electrocuted" bobby pin?
2. If you think you can, how many times would the bobby pin need to be stroked? Find out.

> ## Adapting for Students with Exceptionalities
> This activity can result in overheating of the wires if students are not careful. Be sure to warn students to let go of the wires or batteries if they get warm. Also, as with any activity involving a safety issue, be sure to list rules, explain them, and enforce them during the experiment. Be sure to employ behavior management techniques to keep students safe and on task.

Concept Application

Magnetize with electricity other things that will fit into the tube. Which objects can be magnetized? Which will hold most of their magnetism over a week or more? Which will not?

MAKING MAGNETS CONCEPTS

Magnets made from a relatively soft material, such as iron, usually hold their magnetism only a short time, so they are called *temporary magnets*. Those made from a harder material, such as steel, retain their magnetism far longer, so they are called *permanent magnets*. You can make either kind from common materials. Let's see how.

Temporary Magnets ————

A magnet can be made from an iron nail by stroking the nail in one direction with one pole of a permanent magnet. The nail's magnetic power increases with the number of strokes you apply. Be sure to lift the magnet clear at the end of each stroke before beginning another. Merely rubbing it back and forth will usually bring poor results. Within a few minutes after making this magnet, you will notice a marked loss in its power, regardless of how many strokes it has received.

A second way to make a temporary magnet is by holding a permanent magnet very close to any attractable object. For example, if you hold a magnet near the head of a small nail, you may be able to pick up a few tacks or a paper clip with the nail. Move the magnet farther away from the nail head, and the objects typically will fall off the nail. This kind of magnetism is called *induced magnetism*.

You can also make a temporary magnet by wrapping an insulated wire around a nail and connecting the two wire ends to a battery. This is an *electromagnet*. Any wire that carries an electric current generates a weak magnetic field around it. Wrapping the wire around the nail core concentrates the field into the core. Disconnect the wire from the battery, and the nail is no longer an effective magnet.

Permanent Magnets ————

It takes longer to magnetize a steel object by stroking it with a magnet than it does an iron one. However, steel may hold its magnetism for years.

A more efficient way to make permanent magnets is by electricity. The steel object is placed into a tube wrapped in wire and attached to a battery or other electrical source. Current is applied for a few seconds to magnetize the object.

Making Superconducting Magnets

Superconducting magnets are electromagnets made from special alloys such as niobium-tin or niobium-titanium. A coil of superconducting wire is wrapped around a bobbin to make the magnet. These magnets are then cooled with liquid helium to reach a very low temperature while they are being used. At this very low temperature, almost all resistance to the flow of electricity has been eliminated. This lack of resistance prevents the electrons that are traveling through the magnet from burning the wires up due to friction.

Superconducting magnets can be very large, as in the case of the 6.7 meters (22 feet) long, 181 ton (200 short ton) superconducting dipole magnet built by Argonne National Laboratory. Superconducting magnets are also very powerful. The Superconducting Magnet Group at the Lawrence Berkeley National Laboratory developed a 1 meter (3.3 feet) long superconducting electromagnet that has coils made of 22.5 kilometers (14 miles) of niobium-tin wire. This magnet reached the field strength of 13.5 tesla. Tesla is the SI unit of flux density, or field intensity, for magnetic fields and is also called magnetic induction. One tesla is defined as the field intensity generating one newton of force per ampere of current per meter of conductor. The cost to build this prototype magnet was about $1 million.

The superconducting magnets built today will be used in future particle accelerators, devices that can accelerate electrons or other particles to high energies. The highest-energy particle accelerator in use today is the Tevatron. It is 6.4 kilometers (4 miles) in circumference and has 1000 superconducting magnets that are cooled by liquid helium to $-450°F$ ($-268°C$).

For more information on superconducting magnets, check the Superconducting Magnet Group at the Lawrence Berkeley National Laboratory (http://supercon.lbl.gov/), the Argonne National Laboratory (http://www.anl.gov/), or the Superconducting Magnets site of the National High Magnetic Field Laboratory in Tallahassee, Florida (http://www.magnet.fsu.edu/). To find out more about accelerators, check the Fermi National Accelerator Laboratory (http://www.fnal.gov/).

FIELDS OF FORCE Inquiry

Magnetic Fields

MATERIALS

- Container of iron filings
- Four matched bar magnets
- Four matched horseshoe or **U** magnets
- Two sheets of stiff white paper with turned-up edges
- Partner

Invitation

Have you found that some objects can be attracted to a magnet even when the magnet does not touch them? That is because around every magnet is an invisible field of force. The magnet pulls on any attractable object within its field. Although the field is invisible, there are ways to tell where it is. How can you find out about a magnet's field of force?

Exploration

1. Place a bar magnet on a table. Lay a sheet of white paper with turned-up edges over it.
2. Sprinkle some iron filings on this paper tray. Do this over and around where you think the magnet is.
3. Observe closely how the filings line up and where they are thick and thin.

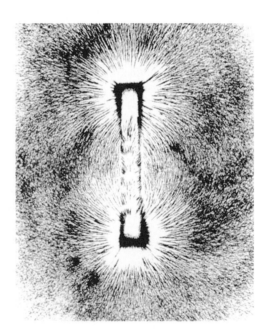

 Teaching Tips

Students should learn that iron filings only crudely show a magnet's field of force. The field extends much beyond where the filings stop. Permanent inference sheets of magnetic fields can be made easily. These will allow individual students to do the activity by trying to match the sheets. To make a permanent record of a field, use plastic spray to fix the filings on a stiff sheet of paper. Hold the spray can far enough away from the sheet that the filings are not blown away. For best results, use fine, powderlike filings and sprinkle lightly. Let the spray dry before removing the sheet from the underlying magnets.

You may also use a magnetic field detector available from scientific supply companies. These show the lines of force more accurately and work very well with refrigerator magnets.

Concept Invention

1. Ask your partner to observe your magnetic field, but do not reveal how you arranged your magnet or what kind it is. Can your partner make one just like it?
2. Have your partner make a magnetic field for you. Can you match it?

Concept Application

Here are more fields for you and your partner to try: How will two bar magnets look with like poles close together? How will they look with unlike poles close together? How will horseshoe or **U** magnets look with like and unlike poles close together? First, draw what you predict. What fields can you make with different combinations of magnets, positions, and distances apart? A field of force surrounds a magnet; it is most powerful near the ends or poles. What were the easiest fields of force for you and your partner to figure out? What were the hardest fields to figure out?

Does Magnetism Go Through Objects? ————

Invitation

Do you think magnetism can be blocked by some materials? If so, which ones? Do you think it can pass through other materials? If so, which ones? How can you find out if magnetism can go through materials?

MATERIALS

- Ruler
- Strong **U** or horseshoe magnet
- Books
- Small paper clip
- Thread
- Small thin materials to test

Exploration

1. Set up your objects as illustrated. Be sure that the clip does not touch the magnet.
2. Make the space between the clip and magnet as big as possible, but do not let the clip fall. Slowly pull the thread end to widen the space.
3. Test one of your thin, flat materials. Put it in the space between the clip and the magnet without touching them.
4. Does the clip stay up? Then magnetism can go through the material. Does the clip fall? Then magnetism cannot go through the material.

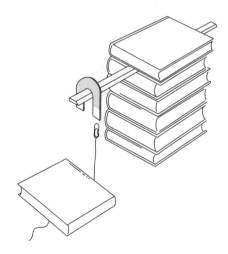

Concept Invention

1. Which of your materials do you think magnetism will go through? Which will magnetism not go through? Put the materials in two piles, and then test them to find out.

In the exploration, try to provide materials thin enough to pass between the paper clip and magnet.

2. Will magnetism go through two materials put together? Test the materials to find out. (Be sure the two materials can fit between the magnet and the paper clip.)

Concept Application

Magnetism goes through many objects, but not those made from iron or steel. Do you think magnetism will go through water? How can you find out? What are other ways to test if magnetism can go through your objects?

FIELDS OF FORCE CONCEPTS

As children explore with magnets, they can observe that a magnet can attract from a distance. For example, a small nail or paper clip will "jump" to a nearby magnet. They will also see that the attractive force is strongest at the poles. This gives us the chance to introduce the field of force surrounding a magnet.

Inferring the Field

Although we cannot see a magnet's field directly, its presence may be inferred. Sprinkle iron filings on a sheet of stiff white paper placed over a magnet, and you will see the filings distribute in an orderly way. Their greatest concentration will be at the poles. Theoretically, a magnetic field extends outward to an indefinite distance. For practical purposes, the field ends when we can no longer detect it.

Magnetic Transparency

If you hold a powerful magnet against the back of your hand, it can attract through your hand and move a paper clip in the palm of your hand. A magnetic field can also go through many other materials without any apparent loss of power. It seems as if these materials are "transparent" to the field's lines of force. This property makes it possible for people to wear magnetic earrings and for plumbers to locate iron pipes in closed walls.

Note that computer disks and other media, televisions, and wristwatches may be affected by magnets. Materials of iron or steel are considered "opaque" to this force. When a magnet touches them, the force passes inside them and back into the magnet.

MAGNETIC POLE **Inquiry**

Make Your Own Compass

Invitation

How can you make a needle compass?

Exploration

1. Place a glass on a paper towel. Fill it to the brim with water.
2. Magnetize a sewing needle. To do this, stroke it 10 times, from thick end to point, with the magnet's S pole.
3. Scratch a narrow groove in the sliced cork top. Lay the needle in the groove. (This will keep it from rolling off.)
4. Carefully float the cork and needle on the water surface, as shown.
5. In what direction does the needle point?

MATERIALS
• Two sewing needles
• Magnet
• Cork top (thin slice or Styrofoam chip)
• Water
• Drinking glass
• Paper towel

Concept Invention

1. Move the needle gently so that it points somewhere else. Wait a few seconds. What happens?
2. Use your magnet. How can you push away either end of the needle with it?
3. How can you pull either end of the needle with the magnet?

Teaching **T**ips | A glass filled to the brim with water keeps a floating cork centered. With less water, the cork will drift against the sides of the glass.

Scaffolding for English Learners

Students often construct different views as to what causes the needle compass to work, yet compasses have been used by various cultures for many years. Discuss how explorers in other cultures used compasses. Would they have constructed the same concept for how the needle compass works? Explain your views. (See Laplante, 1997, for a discussion on English learners and constructivism.)

Concept Application

Replace the magnetized needle with one that has not been magnetized. Float the cork and needle on the water as before. What do you think will happen if you repeat Concept Invention steps 1 through 3? Find out.

Finding Directions —————

MATERIALS

• Topless cardboard box (large)

• Partner

• Large open area outdoors

• Magnetic compass

Invitation

How can you use a compass to tell directions?

Exploration

1. Go to a large, open space outdoors. Study the compass. Notice how the needle points. Turn the compass so that the part marked "north" is under the pointing needle.
2. Walk 20 steps toward the north and observe the needle. While walking, try to keep the needle exactly on north.
3. Stop and then turn completely around. Look at the compass. Now "north" is behind you and "south" is straight ahead. The other end of the needle should point south. Walk 20 steps toward the south while watching the needle. Keep it exactly on south. If you do so, you should return to where you started.

 Teaching Tips "North" as shown on a compass may vary slightly from true north because of regional magnetic variation. For the purpose of this activity, such variation may be ignored.

Concept Invention

1. Can you use your compass well enough to walk somewhere and find your way back? How close will you get? Mark the spot where you are. Put something over your head so that you cannot see around you. Looking at only your compass, walk 300 steps north and then 300 steps south. Have a partner watch out for you.
2. How well can you do in step 1 without a compass?

Adapting for Students with Exceptionalities

It may be difficult for students who are mentally challenged to use a compass. Alter the content to allow these students to learn relevant skills. You may want to avoid tracking the number of steps. Have the students look at a GPS device that will display the direction of travel as they walk in nonspecified directions in the open space. (See Turnbull, Turnbull, Shank, & Smith, 2004, for a discussion on altering the curriculum.)

Concept Application

How can you use your compass to walk east or west? Practice these directions as you did in the Concept Invention.

MAGNETIC POLE CONCEPTS

Suspend a bar magnet from a string anywhere in North America, and a curious thing happens: It points toward the north magnetic pole. Do the same in South America, and the magnet points toward the south magnetic pole. (This result assumes no interference from nearby metals.) A magnetized needle placed horizontally on a floating slice of cork or foam plastic chip also points toward a magnetic pole.

To see why this is so, consider the poles of a magnet. When another magnet or magnetized object is held near a suspended or floating magnet, the like poles (north–north or south–south) repel each other. The opposite poles (north–south or south–north) attract each other.

The Earth's Magnetism

The earth itself acts like a giant magnet. No one knows why, but scientists have proposed some theories. One explanation holds that several parts of the earth's interior rotate at different speeds. The resulting friction strips electric particles from atoms, causing an electric current to be generated that creates a magnetic field. Because the earth's core is supposedly made of nickel-iron, the effect is that of a huge electromagnet buried within the earth.

Recall the earlier discussion about magnetic fields of force. When iron filings are sprinkled on paper placed over a bar magnet, they reveal lines of force looping from one pole to another and concentrating at both poles. On a gigantic scale, a similar kind of magnetic field happens with the earth's magnetism (see INQ Figure 4–2).

Lines of force from the earth's magnetism run roughly north and south far into space and then loop down to concentrate at the north and south magnetic poles. Therefore, a freely swinging magnet—bar, horseshoe, or any other type with dominant poles—aligns itself parallel to these lines of force. Because lines of force end at the magnetic poles, properly following a compass in the Northern Hemisphere eventually results in your arrival at the north magnetic pole. This is located above the upper Hudson Bay region of Canada. If you follow a compass south, your trip will end near Wilkes Land, a part of Antarctica.

Geographic Poles

The north and south magnetic poles should not be confused with the north and south geographic poles. The geographic and magnetic poles are about 1600 kilometers (1000 miles) apart in the north and 2400 kilometers (1500 miles) apart in the south. In other words, when a compass points north, it does not point true north, or toward the North Star.

INQ Figure 4–2   **The earth has a magnetic field that is concentrated at both poles.**

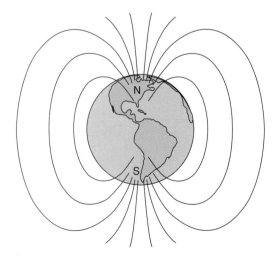

INQ Figure 4–3   Note in A, B, and C an angle between the meridian on which the compass is located and the direction toward which the needle points. These differences must be added to or subtracted from a compass heading to determine true north. For example, true headings for A, B, and C should all be 0°, or north. Actual readings are 35°, 5°, and 315°. A chart would show the need to subtract 35° from A, 5° from B, and the need to add 45° to C.

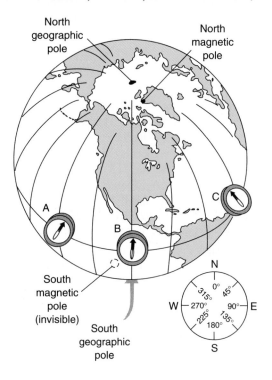

Charts made for navigators must show the angular variation between true north and the direction toward which a compass points. These charts must be periodically updated, as the magnetic poles are slowly but continually shifting (see INQ Figure 4–3).

MAGNETIC THEORY AND CARE OF MAGNETS **Inquiry**

Lost Magnetism? ————

Invitation

What are some ways a magnet can lose its magnetism?

Exploration

1. Test to see how dropping a magnet affects its magnetism. (Use magnetized nails so that regular magnets will not be destroyed.) To do this, follow these steps.
2. Magnetize two nails. Stroke the length of each nail 30 times with one pole of a magnet.
3. Test to see if each of the nail magnets attracts the same number of tacks. If they do not, stroke the weaker magnet until it is equally strong.
4. Hold one nail high and drop it on a hard surface, such as a concrete sidewalk. Do this 20 times.
5. Test each nail again. You might record what you find in this way:

	Dropped Magnet	Other Magnet
Before	6 tacks	6 tacks
After	2 tacks	5 tacks

6. How did dropping the nail magnet affect it?
7. What will happen if you drop the second nail magnet?

Concept Invention

1. Test to see how heating affects magnetism. Repeat the steps above to magnetize two nails.
2. Put on safety goggles. Light the candle in the dish. Use tongs or pliers to hold one magnetized nail upright in the candle flame for 3 minutes.
3. Before testing, dip the nail in water to cool it.
4. Test the two nails. Record your findings.
5. How did heating the nail magnet affect it? What will happen if you heat the second nail magnet?

MATERIALS

- Magnet
- Concrete sidewalk
- Two large matched nails
- Tacks or paper clips
- Small dish and candle
- Match
- Safety goggles
- Glass of water
- Tongs or pliers
- Clock

 Teaching Tips

Iron nails do not retain magnetism very long. So, it is possible that the second magnet, too, will be weaker during the posttest; but this change should be slight.
Caution: Supervise the candle activity closely for safety.

Scaffolding for English Learners

One way to assist English learners in this activity is to write their questions on the chalkboard or markerboard with small illustrations when appropriate. Key vocabulary are also identified, and written and illustrated if possible. This assists the English learners with visual and linguistic cues so that they can share their knowledge constructions with others in the class. (See Amaral, Garrison, & Klentschy, 2002, for a discussion of the importance of visual and linguistic cues.)

Concept Application

What are other ways to lose magnetism? Test your theories and record the results.

MAGNETIC THEORY AND CARE OF MAGNETS CONCEPTS

Although magnetism has been known and used for many centuries, science cannot fully explain it. One theory, when simply explained, can be understood by children. It is based on observations they can make for themselves: Heating or repeatedly dropping a magnet will cause it to lose its magnetic properties. And, although a magnet may be broken into smaller and smaller pieces, each fragment continues to have a north and south pole. To find out why, you need to understand domains.

Magnetic Domains

Scientists believe that many tiny clusters of atoms, called *domains*, are contained within potentially magnetic objects. The clusters are usually randomly arranged; but when an object is stroked in one direction, or otherwise magnetized, the domains line up in a single direction. Notice that in part A of INQ Figure 4–4, the bar magnet could be broken into many pieces, yet each piece would continue to have opposite poles. Heating a magnet forces the domains into violent motion, and so they are likely to be disarranged, as in part B. As a magnet is repeatedly dropped, the tiny clusters of atoms or domains are jarred out of line, therefore causing the same result as if the magnet was heated.

Caring for Magnets

Magnets can keep much of their power for years when properly cared for and stored. Storing magnets improperly in the classroom is probably the chief reason why they quickly become weak. A small metal bar, called a keeper, should be placed across the poles of a magnet before it is stored. If the regular keeper has been lost, a nail can be substituted. Placing opposite poles of magnets together is another effective way to store them. Children can also learn not to drop magnets, which is another common reason why magnets become weaker.

INQ Figure 4–4   A magnetized steel bar (A) with the domains aligned and an unmagnetized steel bar. (B) with randomly arranged domains due to heat or violent action.

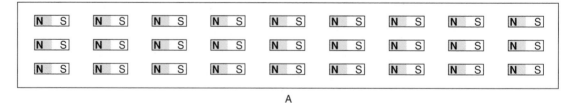

A

B

INQ Figure 4–5 **Sample charts to help children remember how to handle magnets.**

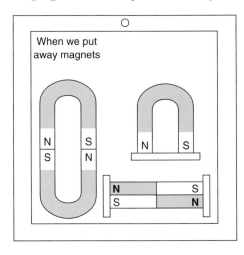

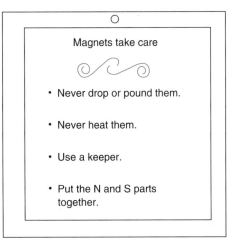

A   B

INQ Figure 4–5 shows two charts that provide guidance to help children remember some rules when handling magnets. Chart A is for primary children; chart B is suitable for older children.

References

Amaral, O. M., Garrison, L., & Klentschy, M. (2002). Helping English learners increase achievement through inquiry-based science instruction. *Bilingual Research Journal*, 26(2), 213–239. Retrieved November 13, 2004, from http://brj.asu.edu/content/vol26 no2/pdf/ART2.PDF

American Association for the Advancement of Science (AAAS). (1993). *Benchmarks for science literacy*. New York: Oxford University Press.

Laplante, B. (1997). Teaching science to language minority students in elementary classrooms. *Journal of the New York State Association for Bilingual Education, 12*, 62–83. Retrieved November 13, 2004, from www.ncela.gwu.edu/pubs/nysabe/vol12/nysabe124.pdf

Mercer, C. D., & Mercer, A. R. (2005). *Teaching students with learning problems* (7th ed.). Upper Saddle River, NJ: Merrill/Prentice Hall.

National Research Council (NRC). (1996). *National science education standards*. Washington, DC: National Academy Press.

Turnbull, R., Turnbull, A., Shank, M., & Smith, S. J. (2004). *Exceptional lives: Special education in today's schools* (4th ed.). Upper Saddle River, NJ: Merrill/Prentice Hall.

Selected Trade Books: Magnetic Interactions

For Younger Children

Borton, P., & Cave, V. (1994). *The Usborne book of batteries and magnets.* London, England: Usborne Publishing Ltd.

Branley, F. (1999). *What makes a magnet?* Topeka, KS: Econo-Clad Books.

Challand, H. J. (1996). *Experiments with magnets: A new true book.* Chicago: Childrens Press.

Fowler, A. (1995). *What magnets can do.* Danbury, CT: Childrens Press.

Freeman, M. (1980). *The real magnet books.* New York: Scholastic.

Gibson, G. (1995). *Playing with magnets.* Brookfield, CT: Copper Beech Books.

Glover, D. (1993). *Batteries, bulbs, and wires.* New York: Kingfisher Books.

Jennings, T. (1990). *Magnets.* Danbury, CT: Watts.

Kirkpatrick, R. K. (1985). *Look at magnets.* Austin, TX: Raintree.

Knight, D. C. (1967). *Let's find out about magnets.* Danbury, CT: Watts.

Podendorf, I. (1971). *Magnets.* Danbury, CT: Childrens Press.

Schneider, H., & Schneider, N. (1979). *Secret magnets.* New York: Scholastic.

Wade, H. (1979). *The magnet.* Austin, TX: Raintree.

Ward, A. (1992). *Magnets and electricity.* New York: Franklin Watts.

Whalley, M. (1993). *Experiment with magnets and electricity.* Minneapolis: Lerner.

Wood, R. W. (1990). *Physics for kids: 49 easy experiments with electricity and magnetism.* Blue Ridge Summit, PA: Tab Books.

For Older Children

Adamsczyk, P., & Frances-Law, P. (1993). *Electricity and magnetism*. London, England: Usborne Publishing Ltd.

Adler, D. (1983). *Amazing magnets*. New York: Troll Associates.

Adler, I., & Adler, R. (1966). *Magnets*. New York: Day.

Catherall, E. A., & Holt, P. N. (1969). *Working with magnets*. Lebanon, NH: Whitman.

Fitzpatrick, J. (1987). *Magnets*. Parsippany, NJ: Silver Burdett.

Freeman, M. B. (1968). *The book of magnets*. Portland, OR: Four Winds.

Friedhoffer, R. (1992). *Magnetism and electricity*. Chicago: Franklin Watts.

Levine, S., & Johnstone, L. (1997). *The magnet book*. New York: Sterling.

Santrey, L. (1985). *Magnets*. New York: Troll Associates.

Sootin, H. (1968). *Experiments with magnetism*. New York: Norton.

Victor, E. (1967). *Exploring and understanding magnets and electromagnets*. New York: Benefic.

Ward, A. (1991). *Experimenting with magnetism*. Broomall, PA: Chelsea House.

Wood, R. W. (1997). *Electricity and magnetism fundamentals*. New York: McGraw-Hill.

Woodruff, J. (1998). *Magetism*. London, England: Hodder Wayland.

Resource Books

Shaw, D. G., & Dybdahl, C. S. (1996). *Integrating science and language arts: A sourcebook for K–6 teachers*. Boston: Allyn & Bacon. (physical cycles including magnetism, pp. 93–110)

Tolman, M., & Morton, J. (1986). *Physical science activities for grades 2–8*. West Nyack, NY: Parker. (magnetism activities pp. 189–209)

Winkleman, G. (Ed.). (1994). *Mostly magnets*. Fresno, CA: AIMS Education Foundation. (27 complete magnetism activities and a resource section)

ELECTRICAL ENERGY

Can children learn to appreciate the advantages of a ready source of electricity? One good beginning is for them to count the number of electrical devices we use and then try to devise nonelectrical substitutes for them. By doing such activities in this chapter, children should also begin to appreciate some things that make electrical energy available and the principles that make them work.

We consider how electrical circuits are closed and opened, conditions that affect the flow of electricity, electromagnets, and ways to produce electricity.

Benchmarks and Standards

The idea of a complete circuit is complex for most students. They have difficulty conceptualizing not only that the electrons flow from the source but also that the circuit back to the source must be complete. It is important to use hands-on activities to develop this understanding. Further recommendations for electrical principles are as follows:

Sample Benchmarks (AAAS, 1993)

- Electric currents and magnets can exert a force on each other. (By Grades 6–8, p. 95)
- Make safe electrical connections with various plugs, sockets, and terminals. (By Grades 3–5, p. 293)

Sample Standards (NRC, 1996)

- Electricity in circuits can produce light, heat, sound, and magnetic effects. Electrical circuits require a complete loop through which an electric current can pass. (By Grades K–4, p. 127)
- Electrical circuits provide a means of transferring electrical energy when heat, light, sound, and chemical changes are produced. (By Grades 5–8, p. 155)

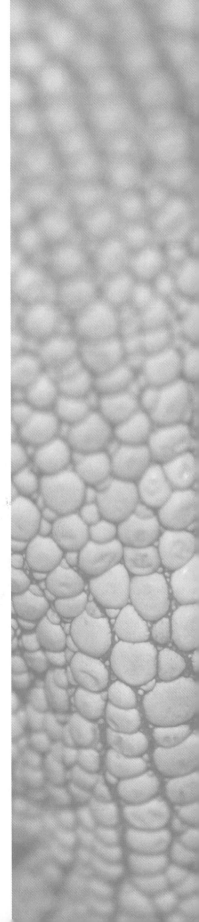

CLOSED AND OPEN CIRCUIT **Inquiry**

How to Make a Bulb Light

Invitation

Have you ever used a flashlight? The electricity to light the bulb comes from one or more batteries. You don't need a flashlight to make the bulb light. You can do it with a single wire and a battery. How can you light a flashlight bulb with a wire and a battery?

Exploration

1. Use scissors or wire strippers to remove the insulation from the wire ends.
2. Put the bulb bottom on the raised button end of the battery as shown.
3. Touch one wire end to the metal part of the bulb.
4. Touch the other end of that wire to the battery bottom.

 Teaching Tips Use number 22 or 24 bell wire, available at Radio Shack or most hardware or electrical supply stores. Be sure the students strip the insulation from both ends of the wires to ensure good contact.
  Caution: Advise students to notice quickly, and to discontinue trying a connection, if the wire they use to connect the bulb and battery begins to get warm. Heating occurs when the bulb (resistor) is bypassed and the wire ends touch only the battery terminals—a type of short circuit.

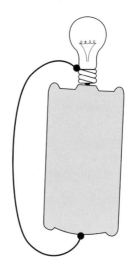

Concept Invention

1. How many other ways can you light the bulb? Keep a record of what you do. Make drawings of the circuits.
2. Study each of the drawings shown. Which ways will light the bulb? Which will not? Record your predictions and then test them.

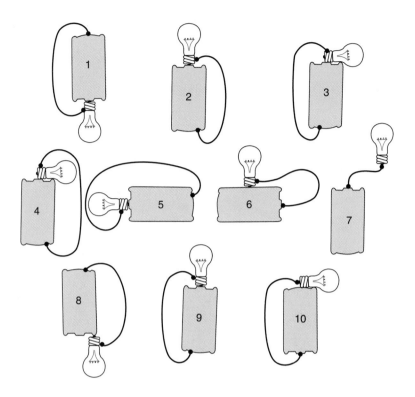

Scaffolding for English Learners

This activity is one that often surprises even preservice teachers as they discover how electricity must flow in order to light the bulb. Often, the teacher must provide verbal clues to assist students. This *linguistic scaffolding* helps the students light the bulb. It is especially important to use an array of verbal gestural, written, and graphic forms of communication to facilitate success with English learners. (See Hart & Lee, 2003, for a discussion of linguistic scaffolding.)

Concept Application

Electricity flows when a circuit is complete; there are several ways to light a bulb. How many ways can you light a bulb with two wires? (Use one battery.) Record your observations. How many ways can you light two bulbs with two wires? (Use one battery.) Record your observations.

Switches ———

Invitation

How can you make some paper clip switches?

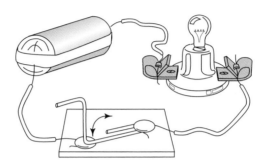

MATERIALS

- Flashlight bulb
- Two paper clips
- Sticky tape
- Cardboard
- Bulb holder
- Six paper fasteners
- Scissors
- Five small wires
- D–size battery

Teaching Tips

For the light to work properly, all connections need to be tight. Be sure the paper fasteners are securely seated and the wires are stripped of insulation where contact is made.

Exploration

1. Cut a small piece of cardboard. Punch two holes in it and put in two paper fasteners as shown in the illustration.
2. Use scissors to strip the insulation off the wire ends. Assemble the rest of the materials as shown. Bend a paper clip for the switch.
3. What happens when you move the switch on and off the paper fastener? How does this switch work in the circuit?

Concept Invention

1. Suppose you have a stairway light. You need to control it from both upstairs and downstairs. Make a pair of switches to control a single light (a "three-way" switch). Do it as illustrated here.
2. What happens when you move each switch from one paper fastener head to another? What would happen if only a single wire was between the two switches? How do these switches work?

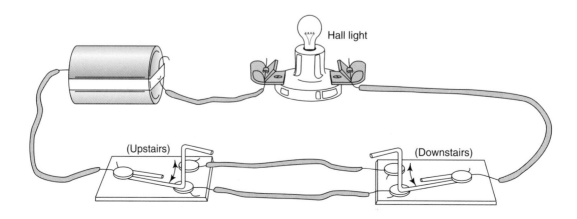

Hall light

(Upstairs)   (Downstairs)

Adapting for Students with Exceptionalities

Some students with exceptionalities are impulsive, not reflective. Monitor activities involving electricity to be sure students do not try to plug wires or paper clips into outlets. Keep them away from classroom wiring, outlets, lights, switches, and devices.

Concept Application

Would it be possible to control a light from three different locations (a "four-way" switch)?

CLOSED AND OPEN CIRCUIT CONCEPTS

Each time we push a button or flip a switch that "turns on" electricity, there is a continuous flow of electrical energy in wires connected from the generating plant to our appliance and back again to the plant. On a smaller scale, much the same thing happens when a battery is connected to a miniature bulb. If the connection between the source of electricity and the appliance or device using it is continuous, lights go on, bells ring, or motors spin. This continuous connection is called a *closed circuit*. Anytime a break or gap occurs in the circuit, the flow of electricity stops. This incomplete connection is called an *open circuit*.

Switches

Regardless of their shape, size, or method of operation, electric switches serve only to open or close circuits. They offer a safe and convenient way of supplying the flow of electricity when we want it by providing a linkage through which the energy can flow to the connecting wires.

Batteries

Much of the work in this chapter calls for the use of dry cells (children are more familiar with the term *batteries*), copper wire, and flashlight bulbs. D-size dry cells or number 6 dry cells should be used because they are safe, fairly long lasting, and relatively inexpensive. When fresh, they deliver 1 1/2 volts of electricity, as contrasted with 110 to 120 volts or so supplied in the home. **Caution:** House current is dangerous for electrical investigations, and children should be reminded never to use household electric current for investigations.

Bulbs

It will be helpful to be familiar with using miniature bulbs properly, since they are a requirement for many of the experiments in this chapter. Miniature bulbs are designed to be used with a loosely specified number of 1 1/2-volt dry cells. Therefore, there are one-cell, two-cell, or multicell bulbs. One-cell bulbs are sometimes marked "1.2V," two-cell bulbs "2.5V," and so forth.

INQ Figure 5–1   A number 6 dry cell (center) and two D-size cells connected in complete circuits.

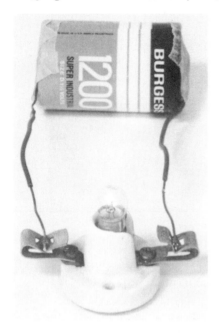
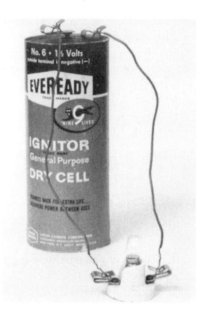

If three dry cells are connected to a one-cell bulb, it is likely that the thin tungsten filament inside will burn out quickly. Be careful to match the bulb with the number of cells used. Too many cells will cause the bulb to burn out quickly; too few will cause it to glow feebly, if at all.

Fahnestock (Wire) Clips

Many unit activities call for the use of commercial-type miniature bulbs and sockets. Several substitutes are possible, but most of these are cumbersome and less useful. For maximum ease in using miniature sockets, a Fahnestock clip should be fastened to each side of the socket with the screw found there (see INQ Figure 5–1 for an example). To connect a wire, simply press down on the springy, open end of the clip and insert the wire end into the exposed half loop. The wire stays in place when you release the pressure on the clip.

Wire

The wire you use should also be selected with an eye to convenience. Number 22 wire is excellent for almost every activity. Get plastic-covered solid copper wire, rather than cotton-covered wire consisting of many small, twisted strands. These strands become unraveled at the ends, and cotton insulation is harder to strip off than a plastic covering.

Insulation can be removed quickly with a wire stripper (INQ Figure 5–2). This device also cuts wires efficiently. With the wire suggested here, scissors may serve almost as well. In fact, the activities call for students to use scissors to strip off the insulation from the wire ends.

INQ Figure 5–2   **A wire stripper.**

Connections ————————

There are several easy ways to connect cells and bulbs, depending on the kinds of materials you have. INQ Figure 5–1 shows how a D-size cell and a number 6 dry cell can be connected to form a closed or complete circuit. Tape or a wide rubber band will hold the stripped wire ends snugly against the D-cell terminals. The center terminal (positive), recognizable by the bump, corresponds to the center terminal on a large cell. The opposite terminal (negative) is equivalent to the rim-mounted terminal on the large cell. The third arrangement needs only a single wire, with one end touching the negative terminal and the other wrapped around the bulb base. The base touches the positive terminal to complete the circuit. Notice that the wire end wrapped around the bulb base also serves as a bulb holder.

Two-, Three-, and Four-Way Switches ————————

Students are challenged to explore three-way switches in the Concept Invention section of the Switches inquiry on page INQ-122. The term *three-way switch* may be confusing, since there are only two switches pictured. Historically, the term *three way* evolved because electricians had to make three "drops," or installations. Electricians installed two switches and one "load," which was often a light fixture. Therefore, a "two-way" switch would be one switch and one load, and a "four-way" switch would be three switches and one load.

A three-way switch works because it can be on in either the up or down position, depending on the position of the other switch. A three-way switch requires an extra wire between the two switches as compared to a two-way switch. In other words, a two-way switch only switches the black "power" or "hot" wire on and off. A three-way switch has an additional red traveler, or switch wire, between the two switches, as well as a load connection on one switch and a power connection on the other. For more information, you may want to refer to the How Things Work website (http://www.howthingswork.com/three-way1.htm).

SERIES AND PARALLEL CIRCUIT **Inquiry**

Series Circuits

MATERIALS
• Three flashlight bulbs
• Four wires
• Three bulb holders
• Two D-size batteries

Invitation

What does the word *series* mean to you? Here, it means placing electric bulbs in order, with one ahead or behind the next one. How can you set up a series circuit?

Exploration

1. Use scissors to remove the insulation from the wire ends.
2. Use two bulbs and bulb holders, two batteries, and three wires. Set up the circuit as shown.
3. Suppose you remove light A. What will happen to light B? If you remove light B, what will happen to light A?

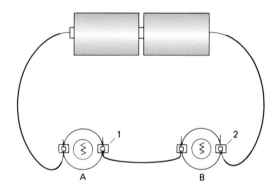

Concept Invention

In a series circuit, if any wire or bulb is disconnected, all the bulbs go out. This occurs because all the electricity flows through each connected part. For the same reason, adding more bulbs to the circuit causes all the lighted bulbs to dim. Each resistor cuts down the available flow of electricity.

1. Suppose you disconnect the wire at place 1. What do you think will happen to light A? light B?
2. Suppose you disconnect the wire at place 2. What will happen to light A? light B?
3. Add another bulb to the series. Use one more wire, bulb, and bulb holder. What, if anything, happens to the lights?

Adapting for Students with Exceptionalities

Encourage students with exceptionalities to work with other students in small groups to develop graphic organizers to assist in organizing the conceptual material such as series and parallel circuits. (See Mercer & Mercer, 2005, for a discussion on accommodations involving student performance.)

Concept Application

Does the fact that in a series circuit all the electricity flows through each connected part explain the results you found above? How does electricity seem to flow in a series circuit?

Parallel Circuits ——————

Invitation

What does the word *parallel* mean to you? Here, it means placing electric wires side by side in a parallel circuit. How can you set up a parallel circuit?

Exploration

1. Use scissors to remove the insulation from the wire ends.
2. Use two batteries, two bulbs and bulb holders, and four wires. Set up the circuit as shown.

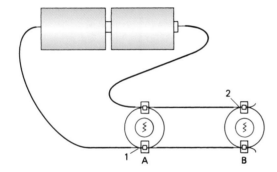

Concept Invention

1. Suppose you remove light A. What will happen to light B? If you remove light B, what will happen to light A?
2. Suppose you disconnect the wire at place 1. What do you think will happen to light A? light B?
3. Suppose you disconnect the wire at place 2. What will happen to light A? light B?
4. Add another bulb to the circuit. Use two more wires and another bulb and bulb holder. What, if anything, happens to the brightness of the lights?

Teaching Tips

In a parallel circuit, the wires are arranged to bypass a burned-out or missing bulb. Therefore, adding more bulbs to the circuit does not noticeably affect bulb brightness. Each bulb beyond receives the same flow of electricity (but all bulbs must have the same resistance in order to burn with equal brightness).

Concept Application

Does the fact that in a parallel circuit the electricity flows both to and around each connected bulb explain the results you found above? How does electricity seem to flow in a parallel circuit?

Hidden Parts of Electrical Circuits ———

MATERIALS

- Paper punch
- Ruler
- D-size battery
- Pencil
- Manila folder
- Scissors
- Aluminum foil
- Two wires
  (30 centimeters, or
  12 inches, long)
- Sticky tape
- Flashlight bulb

Invitation

Suppose you have a folder like the one shown. Notice the four holes on the front cover. Each hole has aluminum foil underneath, so each looks the same. Now, look at the back of the front cover. A foil strip goes from hole 1 to hole 3. It conducts electricity like a wire. However, only small pieces cover holes 2 and 4. Suppose you do not know where the strip is and you cannot open the folder. How can you test for and find the hidden strip?

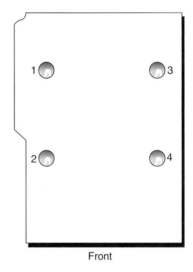

Front

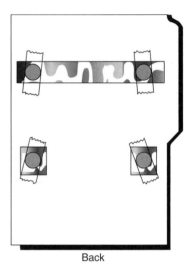

Back

Exploration

1. First, prepare your own folder. Cut a regular-size manila folder in half the short way. (Save the other half for later use.)

2. Use a paper punch to punch four holes. Cover them with foil as shown in the first illustration. Fasten the foil with sticky tape. Number the holes on the cover.

3. Now prepare your tester as shown next. Use scissors to bare the ends of two wires. Tape the ends to a D-size battery. Bend one of the opposite wire ends into a loop. Wrap the other end around the bulb base and twist it to hold it fast.

4. Touch the bulb bottom to the looped end of the other wire. If the bulb lights, you are ready to test your folder.

5. Press the bulb bottom into one hole. Press the wire loop into another hole. Test these pairs of holes; see which completes the circuit and lights the bulb:

1—2	2—3	3—4
1—3	2—4	
1—4		

> **Teaching Tips**
>
> In this case, the foil strip conductor is hidden and stretches between two holes. Touching the bulb bottom and the free wire end to the strip completes the circuit, allowing electricity to flow. The free wire end is bent into a loop to avoid gouging the foil.

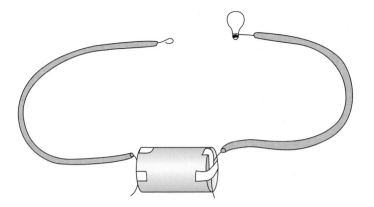

Concept Invention

1. Suppose you tested another folder with the following results:

Paired Holes	Bulb Lights
1—2	Yes
1—3	No
1—4	Yes
2—3	No
2—4	Yes
3—4	No

2. Let's say there are two strips connecting holes. How do you think they are arranged? Is more than one way possible? Make drawings of your ideas. Then prepare a folder and test your ideas.

Scaffolding for English Learners

An extension of this activity would be to have groups of students pair English and Spanish words with the foil. Students who choose correct English and Spanish pairs will light the tester.

Concept Application

Parts of an electrical circuit may be inferred from tests if the wires are hidden. Can you test and find out how different folders are "wired"? Have others prepare hidden circuits for you. (You can do the same for them.) Keep a record of your results and what you observe. Then open each folder to check your observations.

Test Your Nerves

Invitation

How can you make an electric "nerve tester" game?

MATERIALS

- Bare copper bell wire (60 centimeters, or 2 feet, long)
- Sticky tape
- Number 22 or 24 insulated wire
- Bulb holder
- Clay
- Pencil
- Heavy cardboard
- D-size battery
- Flashlight bulb
- Scissors

Exploration

1. Put two lumps of clay on some cardboard, as shown.

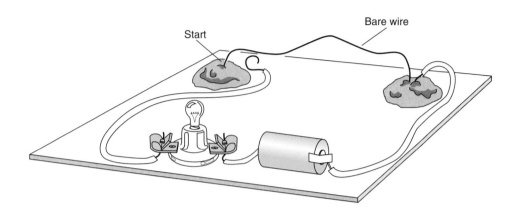

 Teaching Tips

Any single-strand, somewhat stiff wire will serve for the heavier bare wire. Even a piece cut from a wire coat hanger will work if the paint is sanded off. To make the bulb light more brightly when the wire is touched, use two D-size batteries in series.

2. Bend the heavy bare copper wire as shown and stick each end into a clay lump.
3. Cut three pieces of the lighter, insulated wire as shown. Use scissors to bare the ends.
4. Put the bulb in the bulb holder. Attach the three wires to the bulb holder and the D-size battery. Attach the free end of the battery wire to the end of the heavy bare wire. Twist it around and push the twisted wires slightly into the clay.
5. Bend the free end of the bulb-holder wire around a pencil to make a slightly open loop. Touch the loop end to the heavy bare wire. See if the light goes on.
6. To play the game, carefully place the open loop over the heavy bare wire so that the wire is inside the loop. Move the loop from one end to the other and back without touching the heavy bare wire. If it touches, the light will go on. The person who lights the bulb least often wins.

MATERIALS

- Two flashlight bulbs and holders
- Scissors
- Ruler
- Four large tacks
- Sticky tape
- Two small wooden blocks
- Wire (6 meters, or 7 yards)
- Hammer
- D-size battery
- Thin aluminum pie pan
- Partner

Concept Invention

1. Predict and observe the following:
   - Who has the steadiest nerves in the class?
   - How does practice help?
2. Is your left hand shakier than your right hand?

Concept Application

How could you test if people's hands are shakier before or after lunch? What else might affect how shaky people's hands are? How is this "nerve tester" different from a "lie detector" used by police?

Blinking Signals

Invitation

How can you make a two-way blinker system?

Exploration

1. Cut three short pieces of wire and two equally long wires, as shown. Use scissors to bare the ends of all five wires.
2. Cut two strips 10 centimeters (4 inches) long from the pie pan. Attach the strips, wires, and battery. Use tape to fasten wires to the battery. Use a hammer to pound the tacks into the wooden blocks.
3. Test your signal blinker.

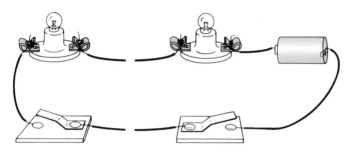

Concept Invention

1. Could you use this device to send dot–dash signals?
2. Press the "key" (the pie pan strip) a short or longer time. Your partner must hold down the second key while you are sending a message. Both bulbs will flash on and off as signals are sent.

Teaching Tips	If both bulbs are dim, add a second battery in series; if only one bulb is dim, replace it with another that matches the bright bulb.

Adapting for Students with Exceptionalities

Substituting a doorbell or buzzer for the light bulb in this activity makes it readily adaptable for students who are visually impaired or blind.

Concept Application

Try using the International Morse Code to send signals, as follows:

A	B	C	D
. —	— . . .	— . — .	— . .
E	F	G	H
.	. . — .	— — .	. . . .
I	J	K	L
. .	. — — —	— . —	. — . .
M	N	O	P
— —	— .	— — —	. — — .
Q	R	S	T
— — . —	. — .	. . .	—
U	V	W	X
. . —	. . . —	. — —	— . . —
Y	Z		
— . — —	— — . .		

What messages can you send and receive? How can you send clearer messages?

SERIES AND PARALLEL CIRCUIT CONCEPTS

Electrical devices in a circuit can be connected in only two basic ways: series or parallel wiring (INQ Figure 5–3).

Connecting Wires

In series wiring (INQ Figure 5–3A), all the usable electricity flows through each bulb or appliance. A chief disadvantage of this circuit is obvious to anyone who has had a bulb burn out in an old-fashioned, series-type string of Christmas-tree lights. When one bulb burns out, the circuit is broken and all the lights go out. All the bulbs must then be tested to discover which one needs to be replaced.

To avoid the troubles of series circuits, most wiring for home and commercial use is parallel wiring. In this kind, electricity flows through a main wire and through branching wires connected to it as well, as shown in INQ Figure 5–3B. (In this figure, the Fahne-stock clips represent the branching wires.) If a bulb or other fixture should burn out, no other bulb or fixture is affected. Bulbs receive electricity regardless if the others are in use. When children make parallel circuits, they will notice no change in bulb brightness as bulbs are added.

Connecting Cells

Cells can also be arranged in series and parallel as shown in INQ Figure 5–4. A wide rubber band can serve to affix wires to flashlight batteries, but the lined-up batteries will buckle where they join unless they are enclosed in a plastic sheath or other holder. A sheet of rolled, stiff paper can be used for this purpose. Pairing students up will preclude the use of holders, since four hands will be able to hold everything together.

INQ Figure 5–3   **Two contrasting circuits: (A) lights in series and (B) lights in parallel.**

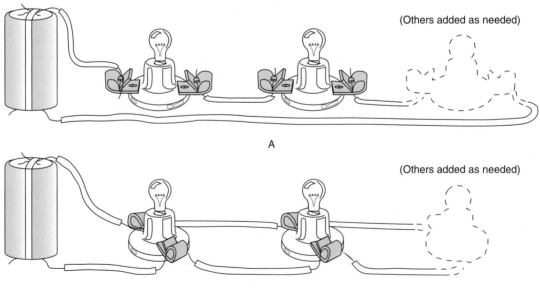

(Others added as needed)

A

(Others added as needed)

B

Note that in the series examples, negative terminals (−) join to positive (+) terminals. In the parallel examples, positives are joined to positives and negatives are joined to negatives.

Voltage

Hooking up cells in series increases the voltage, or pressure, behind the flow of electricity. In contrast, arranging several or more cells in parallel makes available a longer lasting supply of current without increasing the voltage. For example, a bulb connected to two cells in series will burn about twice as brightly as when the cells are connected in parallel. However, the bulb will burn about two times longer with the parallel arrangement.

An analogy, as shown in INQ Figure 5–5, can clarify why these differences take place. Cells in series are like connected tanks of water, one mounted higher than the other. The force of the water flow is directly related to how many higher tanks are used. In contrast, cells in parallel are like water tanks mounted on the same level. The water flows at about the same rate as it would with one tank. So, in this case, the water supply lasts about twice as long as in the other setup (see Fife, 1996).

Voltage is an electromotive force. It can be thought of as the energy source in a circuit that produces the force that causes electrons to flow. Voltage is measured in volts. Current is the actual flow of the electrons, and it is measured in amps (amperes). Resistance, measured in ohms, is the opposition to the flow of electrons in a circuit or the ability to resist, or slow down, the flow of electric current. To again use the water analogy, consider a garden

INQ Figure 5–4   **Cells arranged in series (A) and parallel (B).**

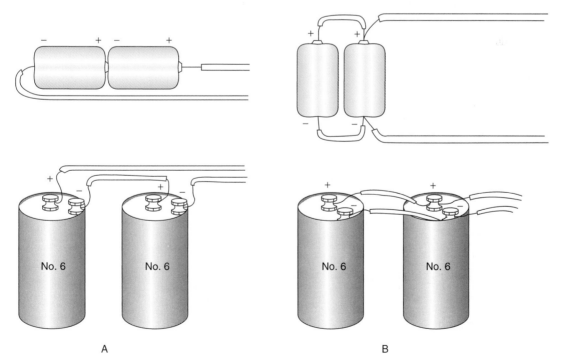

A   B

INQ Figure 5–5   **A is twice as forceful as B, but B will flow twice as long.**

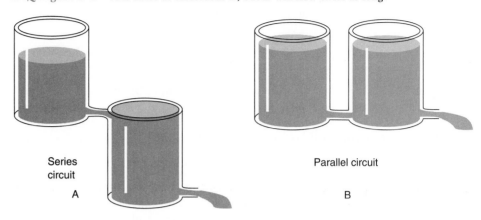

hose. Water pressure is the voltage, the diameter of the hose sets the resistance, and the amount of water actually coming out of the hose is the current.

Voltage, current, and resistance are related through Ohm's law. This law states that the voltage needed to force a given amount of current through a circuit is equal to the product of the current and the resistance of the circuit. Another way to state this is that the amount of current in a circuit is equal to the voltage applied to the circuit divided by the resistance of the circuit. Finally, the resistance of a circuit is equal to the voltage applied to the circuit divided by the amount of current in the circuit. Symbolically, we could state this as follows: Voltage = E, Current = I, and Resistance = R; then $E = IR$, $I = E/R$, $R = E/I$.

In studying circuits, children have many interesting chances to make predictions about which bulbs will light and to make inferences about hidden wires.

ELECTRICAL FLOW Inquiry

Materials That Conduct Electricity

Invitation

You know that electricity can travel through a wire, but how about other materials? How can you find out which materials conduct electricity?

Exploration

1. Arrange your materials as shown, except for the key. Use scissors to bare both ends of each wire. Be sure the wire is wrapped tightly around the bulb base by twisting the end.
2. Touch the bulb bottom to the end of the other wire. If the bulb lights, you are ready to test materials.
3. Get some objects to test, such as a key. Touch the bulb bottom to one part. Touch the end of the other wire to another part. If the bulb lights, the object is a conductor of electricity. If it does not light, the object is a nonconductor of electricity.

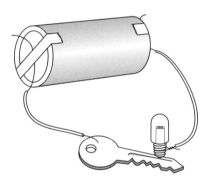

MATERIALS
• Small wooden objects
• Small rubber objects
• Small metal objects
• Sticky tape
• Pencil
• Small plastic objects
• Small glass objects
• Flashlight bulb
• D-size battery
• Scissors
• Two wires (30 centimeters, or 12 inches, long)

Concept Invention

1. What, if any, rubber objects are conductors? plastic objects? metal objects? wooden objects? glass objects? Make a chart like the following to record your findings.

 Teaching Tips — If the bulb is to operate properly, the wire wrapped around the bulb base should be twisted tightly for good contact.

Object	Made From	Conductor	Nonconductor
Key	Metal	X	
Others			

2. Some objects are made of several materials. With a pencil, you can test wood, paint, metal, rubber, and graphite. Which of these will conduct electricity?

Concept Application

Metals are usually good conductors of electricity. Most other solid materials are nonconductors or poor conductors. Look around the room. What other objects can you test? Make your conductor tester more powerful. Use two batteries end to end. Test some materials again. How do these results compare with your first results?

How to Measure Bulb Brightness —————

MATERIALS

- Two sheets of paper
- Partner
- Flashlight bulbs
- D-size battery
- Scissors
- Sticky tape
- Several batteries of the same size
- Wire (30 centimeters, or 12 inches, long)
- Pencil

Invitation

Have you noticed that a bulb burns less brightly as a battery wears down? A bulb's brightness can help you know how fresh a battery is. How can you measure the brightness of a lit flashlight bulb?

Exploration

1. Have a partner light a bulb with one battery and wire (make sure the wire ends are bare).
2. Tear a small piece from a sheet of paper.
3. Hold it tightly against the bulb. Can you see the glow through the paper, as illustrated?
4. Tear off another piece of paper. Hold both pieces together tightly against the bulb. Can you still see the glow through the double thickness?
5. Keep adding pieces until you cannot see the bulb's glow.
6. Record the largest number of pieces through which you saw the bulb glow.

 Teaching Tips Most fresh D-size batteries can be interchanged and a given bulb will glow with no noticeable difference in brightness. As batteries wear down unevenly, however, the brightness is affected.

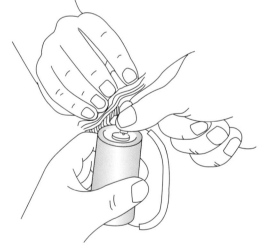

Concept Invention

1. Get some batteries of the same size. How can you compare how strong each is? Can you put them in order from weakest to strongest? Record your findings.
2. How many times brighter will the bulb be with two batteries? with three batteries? Add batteries end to end. (The raised button end of each battery should face the same way.) Record your findings.

Concept Application

The brightness of a flashlight bulb may vary because of its resistance to electricity and the power of the battery. Try different flashlight bulbs. How can you compare how brightly each burns? Can you put them in order from dimmest to brightest? Record your findings. Will someone else get the same results?

Dimmer Switches ──────

Invitation

How can you make a dimmer switch?

Exploration

1. Tape each end of the graphite to a tabletop.
2. Touch the bulb base of the tester to the graphite. Touch the wire end just next to it. The bulb should light.
3. Slowly, move the wire end of the tester along the graphite. Move it first away from the bulb, then back again, as shown.

> ### MATERIALS
> - Graphite (pencil "lead" about 7 centimeters, or 3 inches, long)
> - Circuit tester
> - Sticky tape
> - Tabletop

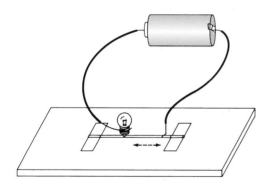

Concept Invention

1. What happens to the bulb brightness as the graphite connection gets longer?
2. What happens to the bulb brightness as the graphite connection gets shorter?

> **Teaching Tips**
> Graphite from either a mechanical or cut-apart wooden pencil may be used. Graphite is resistant to electricity. If the tester bulb does not light, try adding one or two more batteries in series.

Concept Application

Where have you used dimmer switches at home or elsewhere?

Fuses ————

Invitation

How does a fuse work?

Exploration

1. Prepare the fuse. Cut a piece from the gum wrapper about 4 centimeters (1 and 6/10 inches) long and 0.5 centimeter (2/10 inch) wide. Leave the paper attached to the foil. Cut a V-shaped nick in the middle of the piece so that barely any foil is left.
2. Use scissors to bare the ends of the three wires. Also bare a small section in the middle of two of those wires.
3. Set up the materials as shown.
4. Holding the insulated part of the wire, touch one bare wire part with the other. This makes a short circuit.

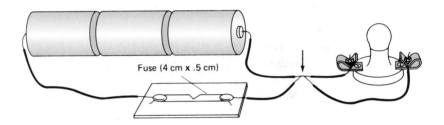

Fuse (4 cm x .5 cm)

MATERIALS

- Three D-size batteries
- Small piece of heavy cardboard
- Three short insulated wires
- Two all-metal tacks
- Flashlight bulb and holder
- Foil from a gum wrapper
- Scissors
- Ruler

Concept Invention

1. What happens to the fuse?
2. What happens to the wires?
3. What happens to the bulb?

Concept Application

Why do you think it is important to have a fuse in a house current?

ELECTRICAL FLOW CONCEPTS

Conductors ————

The term *conductor* is usually given to any substance that permits an easy flow of electricity. Metals are by far the best conductors of electricity, and so they are commonly used for wires. Although several of the precious metals are better conductors, copper is most often used, as it is comparable in efficiency and yet inexpensive enough to use in quantity. We often hear the term *nonconductor* for materials such as rubber, glass, plastic, cloth, and other nonmetallic substances. This term is misleading, as almost anything will conduct electricity if given enough voltage. These materials are better called *poor conductors* or *insulators*.

The concept of insulators is the reason electricians may wear rubber gloves, and electric wires are covered with cloth, plastic, or rubber. It also explains why appliance plugs are covered with rubber or plastic, and glass separators are used on power line poles to keep apart high-voltage lines.

Some poor conductors become good conductors when wet. Pure, or distilled, water is a poor electrical conductor, but when dissolved minerals are added to it, the resultant mixture becomes a fairly good one. Wet human skin is a far better electrical conductor than dry skin. For this reason, it is safer to turn appliances on and off with dry hands.

Resistance

Although metals are better electrical conductors than nonmetals, metal wire still has some resistance to the flow of electrons. The length of the wire has a direct relationship to the amount of resistance; the longer the wire, the greater the resistance.

You may have experienced the gradual dimming of lights in a theater or adjusted the brightness of dashboard lights in an automobile. In both cases, the change may have been caused by a *rheostat,* or dimmer switch. One kind of rheostat increases or decreases the length of wire through which electric current flows, thereby increasing or decreasing the wire's resistance. A simple model is shown in INQ Figure 5–6. Some metals have so much resistance to the flow of electricity that they glow brightly when enough electrical pressure, or voltage, forces a relatively large quantity of electricity to flow in them. Unfortunately, most metals melt or evaporate within a short period of time when hot enough to give off light.

This unfortunate property of most metals necessitated a long search by Thomas Edison for materials to use as bulb filaments before he found reasonable success. Some of the materials he tried reveal the exhaustive character of the search: Bamboo slivers, sewing thread, and even human hair were carbonized and then tested.

Tungsten, sometimes called wolfram, is the metal used in incandescent bulbs today. (Any bulb that gives light from a very hot filament is called an incandescent bulb.) With a melting point of almost 3400°C (6200°F), tungsten is well able to withstand the temperature caused by the movement of electricity through its highly resistant structure. An inactive gas, such as argon, is pumped into the bulbs to help prevent the burning away of the filament. Still, some of the tungsten evaporates eventually, and the filament separates, breaking the circuit. The ever-darkening appearance of the portion of the bulb next to the filament shows the deposition of the evaporating tungsten. Electric heaters also have wires of highly resistant metal. Most heaters today use Nichrome wire, a combination of nickel and chromium.

So far, you have seen that length and composition of wire affect resistance to the flow of electricity. Another factor is the diameter of the wire. An analogy here will help explain why wire size affects resistance. Imagine part of a large crowd in a sports stadium converging into a narrow passageway. As some of the people begin to enter the passageway, the

INQ Figure 5–6 **A simple rheostat, or dimmer switch.**

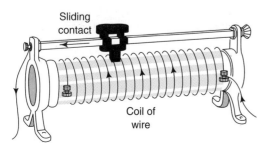

Sliding contact

Coil of wire

forward speed of the crowd slackens. At the end of the passageway, the forward pace again picks up.

A thick wire presents a broad pathway for the flow of electricity. A narrow wire constricts the flow. In the "effort" of electrons to crowd through the narrow pathway, much friction is created, and the wire gets hot. If the wire is thin enough and made of material like tungsten, it can also produce much light as it heats.

Circuit Hazards ——————

You have seen that when bulbs or appliances are wired into a circuit, they show resistance to the flow of electrical energy. At the place where the energy enters these resistors, a change of energy takes place. Some of the electrical energy changes into heat (as in a heater), or light (as in a bulb), or sound (as in a radio), or motion (as in a motor). In other words, a significant amount of electrical energy is "used up," or changed.

Suppose, though, there is no resistor connected within the circuit. Because the copper wire has relatively low resistance, a great surge of electricity flows through the wire. The wire now heats up rapidly even though it usually offers little resistance to a current.

Short Circuits ——————

In residential and commercial circuits, intense heating of the wires may come from a "short circuit." This may happen when two bare wires touch each other, preventing the main supply of current from flowing through the resistor. Because the resistor is largely bypassed, a huge amount of electricity flows.

A common cause of short circuits is an appliance cord placed under a heavily traveled rug. If the insulation between the two internal wires wears away, they may touch and a short may develop. A circuit is not necessarily shortened in length for a "short" circuit to occur. The essential thing is that the resistor is bypassed.

Overloaded Circuits ——————

Overloading a circuit is perhaps an even more frequent cause of wires overheating. Many older houses, for example, were wired when only a few of today's common appliances were widely used. Small-diameter, lightly insulated wires were adequate then; but as more and more of today's appliances are added to circuits, intense heating occurs and poses a potential threat of fire.

Fuses and Circuit Breakers ——————

Fuses and circuit breakers protect us from electrical fire hazard. In some older houses, a screw-in type of fuse contains a narrow metal strip that melts at a fairly low temperature. When a fuse is placed in a circuit, the electricity must travel through the strip. If the wire heats up to a dangerously high temperature, then the strip melts and the circuit opens, thereby shutting off the current.

A bimetallic strip circuit breaker is used instead of a fuse in many houses. It consists of two thin metal ribbons fused together. The ribbons are made of two different metals. When placed in a circuit and heated, the bimetallic strip bends away from one of the contact points, opening the circuit. The bending is the result of different expansion rates of the metals. Another modern type of circuit breaker works because any wire containing electric current generates some magnetism. Increasing the supply of current has the effect of increasing the magnetism. When a movable steel rod is enclosed in a coil of wire placed in a circuit, it may be pulled upward as the current (and so magnetism) increases. If the rod is connected to a contact point, its upward movement will result in the circuit being opened. A spring catch that can be reset by hand prevents the rod from dropping down again. An electromagnetic device that operates in this way is called a *solenoid*.

ELECTROMAGNET Inquiry

MATERIALS

- Pencil
- Partner
- Box of paper clips
- Large iron nail
- Aluminum rod
- Wire (one piece should be 2 meters, or about 6 feet, long)
- Scissors
- Two D-size batteries

Electromagnets

Invitation

Suppose you have some wire, a large nail, and a flashlight battery. With these materials you can make a magnet or an electromagnet. How can you make an electromagnet?

Exploration

1. Get a large nail. Touch it to a paper clip to test the nail for magnetism. The nail should be free of magnetism at the start.
2. Use scissors to bare the wire ends. Wrap the 2-meter-long wire tightly around the nail. Leave about 0.5 meter (1.5 feet) of wire free at both ends.
3. Have your partner touch the bare wire ends to a battery. Touch the nail end to some paper clips. How many paper clips does your electromagnet pick up?
4. Have your partner move one wire away from the battery. What happens? *Note:* Do not leave the battery connected for more than 10 seconds each time.

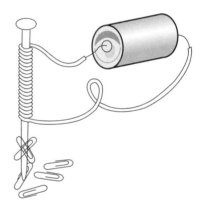

 Teaching Tips Use number 22 or 24 bell wire insulated with plastic. Strip off some insulation at both ends so that good contact can be made with the battery. A regular D-size battery works well. Be sure to advise children that the wires should be held to the battery no more than about 10 seconds without interruption. Otherwise, its power will be drained quickly. A 3- to 4-inch iron nail should be adequate for the core of the electromagnet. If possible, get a similar-sized rod of aluminum. It will present an interesting contrast if used in place of the nail.

Most of the materials attracted to an electromagnet fall when the electromagnet is disconnected from the battery. One paper clip or other light item may remain. This shows that some magnetism is left in the nail.

Concept Invention

1. Which end of your electromagnet will pick up more clips?
2. How can you change the strength of your electromagnet? Make a record of what you try and the results.
3. What will happen if you wrap more wire around the nail?
4. What will happen if you take away the iron nail?
5. What will happen if you switch a pencil for the nail?
6. What will happen if you use an aluminum rod instead of the nail?

Concept Application

Electricity flowing through a wire acts like a magnet; its magnetic power can be increased in several ways. Can an electromagnet attract anything a regular magnet cannot attract? What will happen if you use two batteries end to end?

ELECTROMAGNET CONCEPTS

In 1820, a professor of physics in Copenhagen made a discovery that opened for development one of the most useful devices ever conceived: the electromagnet. Hans Christian Oersted had believed for years that a relationship existed between magnetism and electricity. Despite much research, Oersted had not succeeded in discovering a useful connection between these two phenomena. One day, while lecturing to a class, he noticed that a wire carrying electric current was deflecting a nearby compass needle. Oersted realized immediately that the wire was generating a magnetic field. His later experiments, writings, and lectures helped spread the new concept of electromagnetism to the world.

The telephone, the electric motor, and many other tools of modern living had their origin in Oersted's work and related discoveries. We consider some of these devices here.

Electric Bell ───────────

An electric bell or a buzzer operates because its electric current is "interrupted," or continually turned off and on. INQ Figure 5–7 shows how this happens. Follow the current as it moves from the battery into the bell. When the current flows around into the two electromagnets, they pull the metal clapper, which rings the bell. The act of moving the clapper breaks the circuit at the contact point, and the electricity stops flowing. The clapper then springs back into place and current flows again to repeat the cycle.

The Telephone ───────────

INQ Figure 5–8 shows how the telephone works. Notice the complete, or closed, circuit between the transmitter and the receiver. When we speak into the transmitter, a very thin metal diaphragm vibrates from the sounds we make. The diaphragm variably squeezes the

INQ Figure 5–7 **An electric bell or buzzer.**

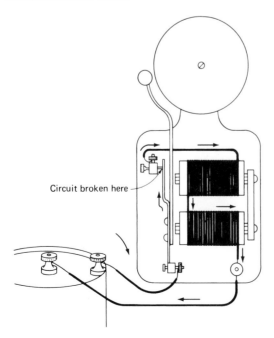

Circuit broken here

INQ Figure 5–8   **A telephone circuit.**

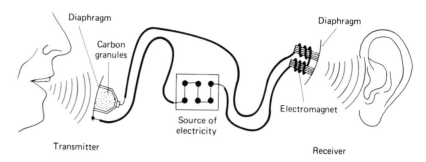

carbon granules behind it. Loud sounds, for example, squeeze the granules more tightly than soft sounds. This makes the granules conduct variable electrical pulses rather than a steady current.

The electrical impulses, rather than the voice itself, are transmitted in the wire. So, they are able to travel to the other telephone's receiver almost instantly, rather than at the much slower speed of sound. As the variable electric current reaches the receiver, it also causes the electromagnets to pull the diaphragm in a variable way. This pulling sets the diaphragm vibrating in the same manner as the first one, and sounds are created.

To summarize, sound energy is used to vary electrical energy at one end, which is then used to make sound energy at the other end. Students can experiment with old telephones and batteries to see how this works.

Electric Motor

You may know that it is possible to rotate a suspended bar magnet with a second bar magnet. You can do this because unlike poles attract each other, and like poles repel each other. The suspended magnet is rotated by alternately attracting and repelling each pole. To do this, you twist the bar magnet you are holding so that the poles are attracted at first and then repelled. If timed properly, the suspended magnet will rotate smoothly.

You can demonstrate a similar technique with an electromagnet; however, you will not need to twist it to make the suspended magnet rotate. INQ Figure 5–9 shows how to proceed. First, find the pole on the electromagnet that is the opposite of the bar magnet's nearer pole. It will attract the bar magnet. Next, reverse the way you touch the terminals on the battery. This will also reverse the poles on the electromagnet. The nearer pole of the bar magnet will now be repelled. Rotate the suspended magnet smoothly by touching the battery terminals first one way and then the opposite way. A child can hold the electromagnet in one fixed position while you do this.

In an electric motor, the electromagnet spins. A device reverses the current automatically, which continually reverses the poles of the electromagnet. The electromagnet spins because it is first attracted to, and then repelled by, another magnet inside. An electric motor is really a spinning electromagnet.

Relays

Another example of the use of an electromagnet is a relay. A relay is a simple electromechanical switch that is activated by an electrical signal. A relay consists of an electromagnet, an armature (moveable "arm") that can be attracted by the electromagnet, a

INQ Figure 5–9   You can get a bar magnet to spin by alternately reversing the way you touch the wire ends of an electromagnet to a battery's terminals.

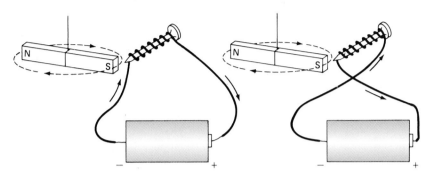

spring (to return the armature back when no longer attracted by the electromagnet), and a set of contact points (to connect the armature to the main circuit). The electromagnet functions to open or close the contact between main terminals. This allows one circuit to control another completely independent circuit.

A relay uses a small amount of power, consisting of a few volts at extremely low milliamperage, to turn an electromagnet on and off. The electromagnet, in turn, will allow the armature and contacts to switch on and off a much larger current such as the 120 volts or 240 volts of current that you might need to run a large appliance in your house. For example, a relay might control the compressor of a refrigerator, a dehumidifier, or an air conditioner. Another place a relay is found is in your car's engine. A relay uses a small amount of current to control the starter motor, since this motor uses a large amount of current that would shock you if you made the contact directly. Relays are used so extensively that challenging students to find relay examples is a good extension activity to the electromagnetic inquiry.

GENERATING ELECTRICITY **Inquiry**

Static Electricity

Invitation

When you comb your hair on a dry day, does it crackle and stick to the comb? Have you felt a shock when you touched something after crossing a carpet? These are examples of static electricity. You can get static electricity by rubbing different objects together. What objects can you rub together to produce static electricity?

Exploration

1. Use sticky tape to attach string to the spoon. Attach it where the spoon balances. Hang the spoon from a table edge. Tape the string end to the table.
2. Hold the fork backward. Bring the fork handle near the hanging spoon handle, but do not touch it, as illustrated. Notice that probably nothing happens. So far, there is no static electricity.

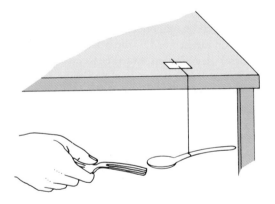

MATERIALS
• Plastic spoon and fork
• Piece of wool and piece of nylon
• Paper and pencil
• Sticky tape
• Heavy string
• Plastic bag
• Rubber comb

 Teaching Tips   Almost any plastic items may be substituted for the fork and spoon. The use of a heavy string will keep the suspended object from spinning too freely. Students will find that using an unlike material in the Exploration will change their findings. Postpone this activity on rainy or especially humid days, as results will be less noticeable.

3. Rub each handle with wool. Bring the fork handle near the spoon again. Watch what happens.
4. Rub one handle again with wool but the other with nylon. Watch what happens. (Static electricity may have either a positive [+] or a negative [−] charge. When two objects have the same charge, positive or negative, they repel, or push each other away. When each has a different charge, they attract each other.)

Concept Invention

1. Did the objects in Exploration step 3 have the same charge, or did they have different charges? How about in Exploration step 4?
2. What happens when you rub the handles with different materials?
3. Which combinations make the handles repel?

4. Which combinations make the handles attract? Keep a careful record. To do so, you might set up a chart like this:

	Spoon Rubbed with Wool	Spoon Rubbed with Plastic Bag	Spoon Rubbed with Nylon
Fork Rubbed with Wool	Repel		
Fork Rubbed with Plastic Bag			
Fork Rubbed with Nylon			

5. After you complete the first column, can you predict the remaining results?

Concept Application

Rubbing different materials together may produce static electricity. Like charges repel each other, and unlike charges attract each other. What results will you get if you substitute other objects for the plastic fork? For example, what happens if you rub a rubber comb with each material?

A Way to Generate Electricity ——————

Invitation

Have you ever seen an electric generator in a power plant? Usually, a magnetic field produces an electric current in a coil of wire. You can even produce a current by moving a small magnet in and out of a small coil of wire. But the current will not be enough to light a bulb. To tell that a current is present, you need a current detector, or galvanometer. How can you generate electricity and tell it is being produced?

Exploration

1. Use scissors to bare the wire ends.
2. Coil 50 turns of wire around your hand. Slip off the coil and fasten it in three places with sticky tape. This will keep the coil tight.
3. Wrap 20 turns of wire narrowly around the compass. This will be your galvanometer.
4. Twist the bare ends of the wire together to close the circuit.
5. Push a magnet end into the coil. See how the compass needle moves. Pull the magnet out of the coil. Watch again how the needle moves. The needle moving shows you have generated a current each time. The farther the needle moves, the stronger the current. (However, be sure the magnet is far enough from the compass so that it does not directly affect it. You want the electricity in the wires to move the needle.)

MATERIALS

- Insulated wire (12 meters, or 13 yards, long)
- Magnetic compass
- Two strong magnets (one stronger)
- Scissors
- Sticky tape

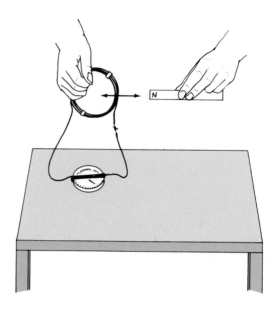

Teaching Tips

By moving the magnet alternately in two directions, the current that is produced also alternates directions. This is shown by the compass needle moving first one way and then the other. The mechanical energy used to move the magnet comes, in this case, from the students. The teaching strategy of the discovery sequence is to provide the type of experience that encourages students to experiment on their own.

Concept Invention

1. Does it make any difference if the coil or the magnet moves?
2. What happens to the needle if you move the magnet more quickly?
3. What happens to the needle if you move the magnet more slowly?
4. What difference does it make if you move the magnet's other end?
5. How does using a stronger or weaker magnet affect the compass needle?
6. How does changing the number of turns in the coil affect the needle?

Concept Application

An electric current may be generated when a magnet and a wire coil interact. A galvanometer may be used to detect the current. What is the strongest current you can generate? That is, how far can you make the compass needle move? Describe how you made the strongest current.

GENERATING ELECTRICITY CONCEPTS

Electricity can be generated in several ways. First we consider how to produce static electricity, then current electricity, and last, electromagnetic waves that can be sent to various places without wires.

Static Electricity

Not all electricity is useful. Almost everyone has experienced some form of static electricity. You may have heard the crackling sound of hair when it is combed after having been washed and dried, or you may have felt a slight shock from a metal doorknob when you touch it after you've scuffed across a rug. You may also have heard the flash of lightning that briefly illuminates a darkened sky. In each case, an electric charge appears to build up on an object and then stay there (hence, the name *static*) until a conductor provides a route through which the charge can escape. Although forms of static electricity vary considerably, their causes are similar. To understand these causes, it will be helpful for us to peer briefly into the makeup of molecules and atoms.

We know that most matter is made up of molecules. A *molecule* is the smallest bit of any substance that retains the chemical properties of that substance. If we subdivide the molecule further, it no longer resembles the original substance. In this case, we have arrived at the atomic level.

Only two of the particles that make up an atom need concern us here: electrons and protons. Each of these particles has a tiny electric charge. The electron has a negative charge; the proton has a positive charge.

In their "normal" state, atoms have as many electrons as protons. Because these charged particles attract each other with equal force, they balance, or neutralize, each other. The atom is said to be neutral, or uncharged. But electrons are easily dislodged or torn away from atoms by rubbing and other means. When two neutral, unlike materials are rubbed together, one of the materials has a tendency to lose electrons to the other. For example, when a hard rubber rod is rubbed with a wool material, the wool loses some of its electrons to the rod. This gives the wool a positive charge and the rod a negative charge. When a glass rod is rubbed with silk, however, some electrons leave the glass and go onto the silk. This gives the silk a negative charge and the glass a positive charge.

The basic law of static electricity is "like charges repel each other and unlike charges attract each other." Children may discover that identical objects rubbed with the same material will repel each other. If the objects are rubbed with different materials, they will usually attract each other. What causes lightning? It is produced by friction. A cloud contains varying amounts of dust particles, raindrops, air (gas) molecules, and sometimes ice crystals. When violent currents occur in clouds, these substances rub together in various combinations. If a huge electric charge builds up, an oppositely charged cloud or the ground may attract it. When this happens, we see lightning. (Thunder results when the air through which lightning passes quickly heats up and cools. The rapid expansion and contraction of the air forces air molecules to smash together, which causes loud sounds.)

Current Electricity

Static electricity is both unreliable and difficult to manage, so we use current electricity to meet our needs. This electricity generally comes from two sources: batteries (both wet cells and dry cells) and power plants.

Batteries

Children are curious about how a battery can "make" electricity. Some think it is stored, as water is stored in a tank. What really happens is that chemical energy changes into electrical energy.

Here is how an automobile battery (a wet cell) works. When strips of two different metals (e.g., zinc and copper) are placed into an acid, both strips begin to dissolve slowly. However, the zinc dissolves more quickly than the copper. A surplus of electrons from the dissolving parts of the zinc strip builds up on the rest of the strip, giving it a strong negative charge. Some electrons are also released at the slower-dissolving copper strip, but these go into the acid, leaving the copper strip with a positive charge. If we connect the end of the zinc strip to the end of the copper strip with a wire, a continuous circuit is set up. Electrons flow from the zinc strip through the wire to the copper strip. If we connect a bulb in this circuit, it lights; if we connect a starter in this circuit, it starts an automobile engine. Many pairs of dissimilar metal strips, or *electrodes*, can be used to get this effect, and other liquids besides acid can work to release and hold electrons. Such liquids are called *electrolytes*.

A dry cell or flashlight battery works in a way similar to the wet cell as described. A moist, pastelike electrolyte is used in place of a liquid. The electrodes are most commonly a carbon rod (found in the center of the cell) and a zinc cylinder (which surrounds the paste and rod).

Dry cells are convenient, but they are too weak and expensive for widespread residential or commercial use. Mechanical energy, the energy of motion, is by far the main method for generating electricity. Today, most electricity is produced by changing the energy in fuels and falling water.

Power Plants

In hydroelectric power plants, water falls on the blades of huge wheels, causing them to revolve. Other power plants may use oil, coal, natural gas, or atomic energy to heat water into steam. The steam or falling water forces giant turbines to whirl. A wire coil is spun inside an electromagnetic field, causing electrons to flow into the wire.

Producing Electromagnetic Waves

You know that a steady electric current produces a weak magnetic field around a wire. This is why we can make an electromagnet. Long ago, scientists learned that by rapidly varying the electric current in a wire they could change the magnetic field. Instead of a steady field, rapidly vibrating energy waves were given off by the wire. These are called *radio waves*.

At a radio station, music or voice vibrations are changed into a variable electric current. The method is like that used in a telephone transmitter. The vibrating current is strengthened until strong radio waves are given off by the wire carrying the current. The waves are beamed off in all directions from a tall tower. Some of the waves strike a radio antenna. A weak current begins vibrating in the antenna, and the current is picked up and strengthened in the radio. A connected loudspeaker vibrates and produces sound energy much like a telephone receiver.

References

American Association for the Advancement of Science (AAAS). (1993). *Benchmarks for science literacy.* New York: Oxford University Press.

Fife, J. (1996). *Watered-down electricity: Using water to explain electricity.* Huntington, WV: University Editions.

Hart, J. E., & Lee, O. (2003). Teacher professional development to improve the science and literacy achievement of English language learners. *Bilingual Research Journal, 27*(3), 475–501. Retrieved November 13, 2004, from http://brj.asu.edu/content/vol27 no3/art6.pdf

Mercer, C. D., & Mercer, A. R. (2005). *Teaching students with learning problems* (7th ed.). Upper Saddle River, NJ: Merrill/Prentice Hall.

National Research Council (NRC). (1996). *National science education standards.* Washington, DC: National Academy Press.

Selected Trade Books: Electrical Energy

For Younger Children

Bailey, M. W. (1978). *Electricity*. Austin, TX: Raintree.
Bains, R. (1981). *Discovering electricity*. New York: Troll Associates.
Berger, M. (1990). *Switch on, switch off*. New York: HarperCollins.
Challand, H. (1986). *Experiments with electricity*. New York: Childrens Press.
Cole, J. (1997). *The magic school bus and the electric field trip*. New York: Scholastic.
Curren, P. (1977). *I know an electrician*. New York: G. P. Putnam.

Lawson, R. (1988). *Ben and me: An astonishing life of Benjamin Franklin*. Boston: Little, Brown.
Lillegard, D., & Stoker, W. (1986). *I can be an electrician*. Danbury, CT: Childrens Press.
Taylor, B. (1991). *Batteries and magnets*. Danbury, CT: Watts.
Wade, H. (1979). *Electricity*. Austin, TX: Raintree.
Wood, Robert W. (1990). *Physics for kids: 49 easy experiments with electricity and magnetism*. Blue Ridge Summit, PA: Tab Books.

For Older Children

Adamsczyk, P., & Frances-Law, P. (1993). *Electricity and magnetism*. London, England: Usborne Publishing Ltd.
Ardley, N. (1984). *Discovering electricity*. Danbury, CT: Watts.
Bains, R. (1982). *Discovering electricity*. New Jersey: Troll Associates.
Birch, B., & Corfield, R. B. (1995). *Benjamin Franklin's adventures with electricity*. New York: Barron's Juveniles.
Brandt, K. (1985). *Electricity*. New York: Troll Associates.
Clemence, J., & Clemence J. (1991). *Electricity*. Ada, OK: Garrett Educational Corp.
Cobb, V. (1986). *More power to you!* Boston: Little, Brown.
De Bruin, J. (1985). *Young scientist explores electricity and magnetism*. Torrance, CA: Good Apple.
Friedhoffer, R. (1992). *Magnetism and electricity*. Chicago: Franklin Watts.
Fritz, J. (1982). *What's the big idea, Ben Franklin?* New York: Coward-McCann.
Glover, D. (1993). *Batteries, bulbs, and wires*. New York: Kingfisher Books.
Gutnik, M. J. (1986). *Electricity: From Faraday to solar generators*. Danbury, CT: Watts.

Mackie, D. (1986). *Electricity*. Cincinnati: Penworthy.
Math, I. (1981). *Wires and watts*. New York: Scribner.
Parker, S. (1992). *Electricity*. New York: Dorling Kindersly.
Seifer, M. (1991). *Nikola Tesla: The man that harnessed Niagara Falls*. Kingston, RI: MetaScience.
Taylor, B. (1990). *Electricity and magnets*. Danbury, CT: Watts.
Vogt, G. (1985). *Electricity and magnetism*. Danbury, CT: Watts.
Vogt, G. (1986). *Generating electricity*. Danbury, CT: Watts.
Ward, A. (1986). *Experimenting with batteries, bulbs, and wires*. New York: David & Charles.
Ward, Alan. (1992). *Magnets and electricity*. New York: Franklin Watts.
Whyman, K. (1986). *Electricity and magnetism*. Danbury, CT: Watts.
Wilcox, C. (1996). *Powerhouse: Inside a nuclear power plant*. Minneapolis: Carolrhoda Books.
Wood, R. W. (1997). *Electricity and magnetism fundamentals*. New York: McGraw Hill.
Zubrowski, B. (1991). *Blinkers and buzzers*. New York: Morrow.

Resource Books

Butzow, C. M., & Butzow, J. W. (1989). *Science through children's literature: An integrated approach*. Englewood, CO: Teacher Ideas Press. (batteries and electrical circuit topics, pp. 226–231)
Erickson, J., & Beals, K. (2002). *Electric circuits: Inventive physical science activities*. Berkeley, CA: Great Explorations in Math and Science. (electical activities)
Gosnell, K. (1994). *Thematic unit: Electricity*. Huntington Beach, CA: Teacher Created Materials. (thematic electrical activities)
Shaw, D. G., & Dybdahl, C. S. (1996). *Integrating science and language arts: A sourcebook for K–6 teachers*. Boston: Allyn & Bacon. (electrical circuit topics, pp. 102–103)

Summers, M., Kruger, C., & Mant, J. (1997). *Teaching electricity effectively: A research-based guide for primary science*. Hatfield, Herts., UK: Association for Science Education. (research-base electrical activities)
Tolman, M., & Morton, J. (1986). *Physical science activities for grades 2–8*. West Nyack, NY: Parker. (static and current electricity activities pp. 211–259)
Winkleman, G., & Youngs, D. (Eds.). (1991). *Electrical connections*. Fresno, CA: AIMS Education Foundation. (30 electrical activities)

SIMPLE MACHINES

Imagine a parade of the world's machines including airplanes, tweezers, bulldozers, baby carriages, computers, and egg beaters—an almost endless line of inventions without which we would fare far less well. But perhaps the most remarkable thing about these inventions lies in their construction. All machines, no matter how complex, are variations of just six simple machines: inclined plane (ramp), wedge, screw, lever, wheel and axle (windlass), and pulley. Let's take a closer look at these machines and the effects of motion and friction on them.

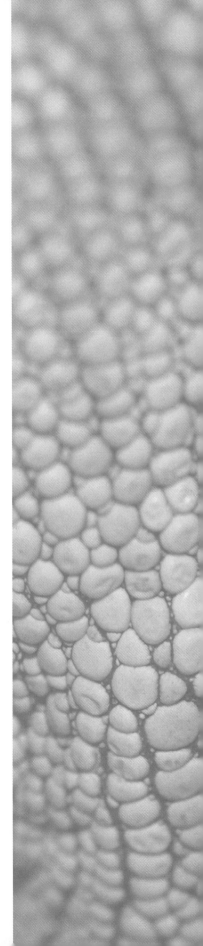

SCREWS AND INCLINED PLANES **Inquiry**

Inclined Planes ———————

MATERIALS

- Flat board
  (60 centimeters,
  or 2 feet, long)

- Seven same-sized
  books

- Paper clip

- Rubber band (or
  spring scale)

- Roller skate

- Ruler

Invitation

Is it easier to walk up a steep hill or a low hill? Suppose both hills were the same height, but one was twice as long. Which would be easier then? A hill is a kind of inclined plane. How can you measure the force needed to use an inclined plane?

Exploration

1. Lay an end of the smaller board on one book as shown.
2. Place a roller skate on the board. Hook a bent paper clip around the tied shoelace. Attach a rubber band.
3. Pull the skate slowly up the board. Measure with a ruler how much the rubber band stretches (or measure the pull with a spring scale).

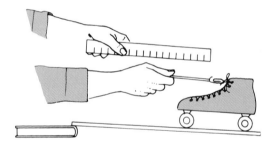

4. Now make the inclined plane or "hill" three books high. Do steps 2 and 3 again.

Concept Invention

1. What was the difference in rubber band stretch in the two trials?
2. How much stretch will there be with "hills" of different heights? Measure also a height of two books, then five and six books. (Do not measure four books now.) Record what you find on a graph such as this:

Number of Books High Versus Amount of Stretch in Inches

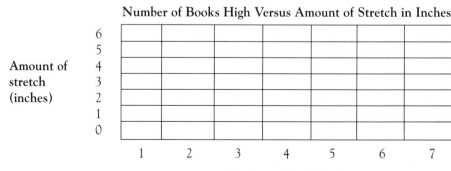

Amount of stretch (inches)

Number of books high

3. Examine your graph data for heights of one, two, three, five, and six books. Can you predict the stretch for four books? Write this down and then test your prediction.
4. Examine your data again. Can you predict the stretch for seven books?
5. What pictures of different inclined planes can you bring to school?

Concept Application

The force needed to go up an inclined plane increases with height and decreases with distance. Switch this board for one twice as long. Suppose you used one through seven books again. What do you think your results would be? Write down your ideas and then test them.

Teaching Tips

One long board, rather than two different-sized boards, can be used to demonstrate how differing board lengths affect the force needed to go up a given height. The books may first be placed under the midpoint of the board, and the board tilted. The tilted part beyond the books may be ignored; this may confuse some students, however, especially the younger ones. Pairs of boards of almost any lengths may be used, but the larger one should be twice as long as the smaller one.

A spring scale is likely to yield more accurate measurements than a rubber band. A rubber band may not stretch uniformly and, of course, does not indicate force in standard units. Try several rubber bands; select one that stretches easily for heights of one to seven books. If needed, snip and use a single strand.

Two kinds of predicting occur in this inquiry. The child predicts within the data (interpolating) and beyond the data (extrapolating).

Adapting for Students with Exceptionalities

When working with exceptional students, use predetermined and explicit teaching procedures before, during, and after instruction. Take the time to review directions and accurately record data. (See Mercer & Mercer, 2005, for a discussion on accommodations involving instruction.)

SCREWS AND INCLINED PLANES CONCEPTS

For any machine to do work, force must overcome gravity, inertia, molecular cohesion (the binding force that holds materials together), and friction. Machines may be used to reduce the force needed to do work, speed up work, or change the direction of a force.

Inclined Planes

Although they may not have thought about it, even small children have had experiences with inclined planes, such as climbing stairs, walking up a hill, or coasting down a slanted driveway on roller skates. They know from these experiences that it is harder to climb a steep hill than a gradual hill. Children may even unknowingly use the idea that distance may be increased to decrease force, as when a bicycle rider rides diagonally back and forth up a hill. This background of common experiences lets us focus on force–distance relationships fairly quickly when working with inclined planes.

INQ Figure 6–1   **An inclined plane.**

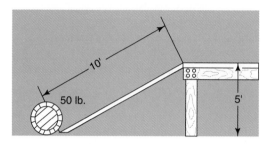

Does an inclined plane or other simple machine make work "easier"? No, if we mean that some part of the total effort is saved. In terms of work, or force moving a resistance over a distance, it is impossible to get out of a machine any more than is put into a machine. Another way of saying this is:

Effort times distance equals resistance times distance, or ED = RD

Let's apply this idea to the inclined plane in INQ Figure 6–1. Suppose we want to push a 50-pound barrel to a height of 5 feet and the inclined plane is 10 feet long. If we were to push the barrel up the incline, it would take less force (25 pounds of force) than if we were to pick it straight up (50 pounds of force). The total amount of force to move the barrel up the incline would be the distance of the incline, which is 10 feet, times the effort required, which is 25 pounds. This is a total of 250 foot-pounds. Notice that this equals the 250 foot-pounds of work that would be required to lift the barrel straight up a distance of 5 feet times an effort of 50 pounds.

In both cases, we assume that we are physically able to do the work. Yet, it is easier for us to apply less force for a longer distance and time. Muscles get tired quickly from concentrated, heavy work. In that sense, then, a simple machine makes work "easier."

The reduction of force provided by a simple machine is called its mechanical advantage. This is a number found by dividing the force of the resistance by the force of the effort. In the foregoing example, the *mechanical advantage* is

R (50 pounds)/E (25 pounds) = 2

In other words, it is twice as easy to lift the barrel with the inclined plane as without it. Or, we can say it takes half as much effort.

Children can make crude measurements to grasp the force–distance relationship. For instance, a string can be used to compare the length of an inclined plane with the height to which it rises. A rubber band attached to an object may have a ruler held beside it to measure different degrees of applied force in terms of "stretch." A spring scale, if available, is even more effective than a rubber band.

Wedges

A *wedge* can be thought of as a combination of two inclined planes. Although the classic use of this machine has waned, along with professional rail-splitters and woodchoppers, the wedge principle is utilized in many other ways. For example, streamlining is a way of better enabling objects to pierce air and water. More speed can be achieved with the same amount of applied force. Paper cutters, knives, pencil sharpeners, nails, and needles are all wedges we use every day for cutting or piercing functions.

INQ Figure 6–2   **The pitch of a screw is the distance between its threads.**

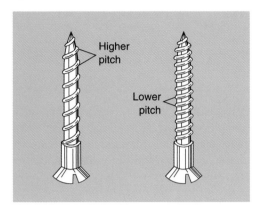

Screws

"The screw is just an inclined plane wrapped around a nail." This is what one child said, and it is a fairly accurate description. We usually think of the screw as a nail-like object with a spiral thread that holds together pieces of wood or metal. But other applications of this machine are all around us: spiral staircases, roads that wind around steep hills or mountains, vises for workbenches, clamps to hold things together, adjustable piano stools, and the adjustable parts of wrenches, to name just a few. Sometimes a screw is not so obvious, like propellers for ships and airplanes.

When a screw is used to lift objects, its mechanical advantage is the greatest of any simple machine. It is relatively easy for a small person to lift the front of an automobile with a screw-type jack, and jackscrews employed by house movers actually lift entire houses off their foundations. As with an inclined plane, though, the price paid for such a gain in force is increased distance.

Each time a screw is given a complete turn, it advances into a piece of wood or lifts an object only as far as the distance between its threads. This distance is called pitch and is illustrated in INQ Figure 6–2. The paired drawings show that two screws of similar size but different pitches would vary in the number of times turned if screwed into some wood or used to lift an object. We expect a steep spiral staircase to take more effort to climb than a longer, gradual one when walking up to the same height. Likewise, the steeper (or higher) the pitch of a screw, the more force needed to make it rotate. However, it advances farther and faster than one with a narrower (or lower), more gradual pitch.

The mathematical relationships here are identical to those of other simple machines. Mechanical advantage is again found by dividing resistance by effort.

LEVER **Inquiry**

Common Levers ————————

MATERIALS

- Real or picture examples of levers in everyday things (canoe paddle, crowbar, paper cutter, baseball bat, seesaw, post puller, house broom, can opener, wheelbarrow, tennis racket, golf club, boat oar).

Invitation

Have you ever used a baseball bat, a seesaw, or a house broom? These and many other objects we use are examples of levers. How levers work can be surprising. Some that are similar in appearance may actually work differently. Some that are different in appearance may work the same way. How can you tell in which ways levers are alike and different?

Exploration

1. The illustration shows a fishing pole in action. Notice how this lever is used. The tip carries the load, or resistance (R). The opposite end, which is held, moves very little. This is the fulcrum (F). To pull up the resistance takes effort (E). This happens between the fulcrum and the resistance.
2. Study the three smaller drawings in the illustration. Levers can be grouped into three classes, depending on how they are used. Each group has a place for the fulcrum, resistance, and effort. But notice that, in each group, the placement of these points is different. This is a good way to tell them apart.

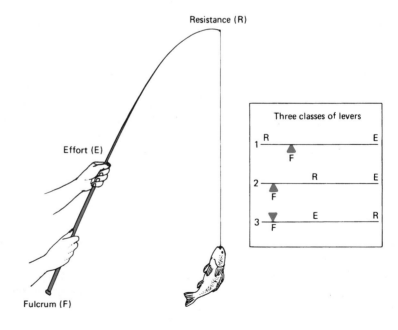

Concept Invention

1. In which group does the fishing pole belong?
2. Examine real or picture examples of many levers. Use them, or think of how they are used. In which group does each belong? Following is a way to record what you find.

Lever	1. RFE	2. FRE	3. FER
Fishing pole			
Paper cutter			
Others			

3. Which of these levers are really alike?
4. Examine your forearm. It is a lever, too. In which group does it belong?
5. Play a game with some friends. Think of a common lever. Can they find out what it is by asking questions? You can answer only yes or no. If they get stuck, act out the way it is used. A good way for them to begin is to find out the resistance (load)–fulcrum–effort order.

Teaching Tips

It is the internal order of resistance–fulcrum–effort that counts in classifying levers. So, there is no difference between R–F–E and E–F–R, for example. (This may be a difficult concept for a few students.) It is not important for children to memorize the internal order of each class, but it is worthwhile for them to develop skill in observing and classifying likenesses and differences in objects.

In step 4 of Concept Invention, the part played by the upper arm muscle (bicep) in moving the forearm may be confusing. The actual pull on the forearm is just below and opposite the elbow on the inside.

Adapting for Students with Exceptionalities

Some students may experience difficulty with the vocabulary of this activity. Provide a glossary of the key terms with illustrations of the sample lever classes and the associated resistance, effort, and fulcrum points. (See Mercer & Mercer, 2005, for a discussion on accommodations involving instructional materials.)

Concept Application

Levers may be grouped by where places on each are used for the resistance, fulcrum, and effort. What other real or picture examples can you find? In which group does each belong? Illustrate and label some levers of your choice.

Common Double Levers

Invitation

Scissors are an example of a double lever that has cutting parts. We use many tools that are double levers. How many can you name or describe? Some that are similar in appearance may work differently. Some that are different in appearance may work about the same way. How can you tell in which ways double levers are alike and different?

MATERIALS

- Scissors
- Pliers
- Tweezers
- Lemon squeezer
- Nutcracker
- Sugar tongs
- Tin snips

In classifying double levers, it is the internal order of the resistance–fulcrum–effort that counts, just as it did with single levers. There is no difference between R–F–E and E–F–R, for example.

Exploration

1. In the pair of scissors, notice how the parts are used, especially the cutting parts. When you cut something, it resists being cut. So, each part that does this work is called the *resistance* (R).
2. Notice where the two parts of the scissors join and pivot. This is the *fulcrum* (F).
3. Observe the handles in action. To cut something requires force, or effort, so each of these parts is called the *effort* (E).

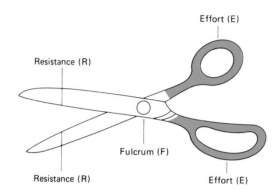

Concept Invention

1. All tools that are double levers have parts for the resistance (R), fulcrum (F), and effort (E). But they are not always in that order. Examine some real or picture examples of double-lever tools. Which tools are arranged differently? How many different arrangements do you find?
2. You can classify these and other double levers by how the three parts are arranged. In which group will each fit?

   Following is a way to record what you find.

Double Lever	1. RFE	2. FRE	3. FER
Scissors			
Pliers			
Others			

3. Can you name parts of your body that work like a double lever?

Concept Application

Double levers may be grouped by how places on each are used for the resistance, fulcrum, and effort. What other real or picture examples of double levers can you find? In which group does each belong? Illustrate and label some double levers of your choice.

The Making of a Mobile

Invitation

Notice the balanced group of objects shown. This is a *mobile*. The word means "something that moves." Even a tiny breeze can move the objects. They may almost seem to be alive! What kinds of mobile objects would you like to make? Fish, birds, butterflies, balloons, and airplanes are all fun to do. You can even use cutout letters of your name. How can you make a mobile?

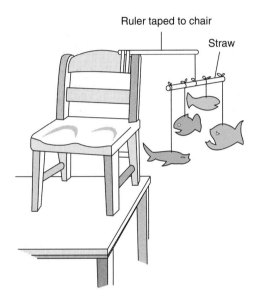
Ruler taped to chair
Straw

MATERIALS

- Plastic soda straws
- Tagboard
- Thin knitting yarn
- Sticky tape
- Paper clips
- Ruler
- Scissors
- Crayons or paints and brushes

Exploration

1. Cut some strings of yarn 20 to 30 centimeters (8 to 12 inches) long.
2. Tie one end of each string to a paper clip.
3. Decide what shapes of objects to hang. Then cut three or four object shapes from tagboard.
4. Set up a place to hang your mobile. Tape a ruler to a chair. Put the chair on a table.
5. Hang the shapes from a straw with yarn. Loop the yarn once around the straw. Make half a knot. Then, pull the yarn tight. Clip the paper clip to each shape in the usual way.
6. Try to balance the shapes. Slide the yarn on the straw. Change where each shape is clipped if necessary.

Scaffolding for English Learners

As students are learning the concepts related to levers, they could use shapes of objects labeled with the English word on them to reinforce English vocabulary. (See Ovando, Collier, & Combs, 2003, for a discussion of the use of integrated content and language development with English learners.)

Concept Invention

1. How can you make a mobile with more straws and shapes? It will help to draw your mobile on paper first. Start with a few materials and then add more as you are building your mobile.

2. What can you do to balance your shapes?
3. How can you keep the shapes from touching?
4. How big should each shape be?
5. Where should each shape be placed?
6. How long should each string be?
7. Where is it best to clip the string on each shape?

8. How can you color your shapes with crayons or paints?

> **Teaching Tips** Making mobiles is an interesting way to combine artwork with valuable concepts about balance.

Concept Application

For mobile shapes to balance, we consider such variables as size and shape, weight, string length, best positions for the shapes, and where to fasten them. Design a mobile below. Use a combination of shapes from heavy and light materials.

LEVER CONCEPTS

No one knows who actually first contrived the lever, but it has been known and used for a very long time. The ancient Greek scientist Archimedes is purported to have said to King Hiero that he could move the world if given a long enough lever, a fulcrum, and a place to stand. It is widely assumed that primitive people also had knowledge of levers in a practical way.

The principles of this simple machine are used in so many ways that a moment's reflection produces surprising examples: The ancient Japanese sport of judo is based on knowledge that the human skeleton is comprised of lever systems. Also, a golfer with long arms may swing the club head faster than a golfer with shorter arms.

Three Parts

The seesaw is a lever familiar to most children. It has three parts: (a) *fulcrum*, the point on which it pivots; (b) *effort arm*, the part on which the force is exerted; and (c) *resistance*, or load, *arm*, the part that bears the load to be raised. When the seesaw is perfectly balanced on the fulcrum, the resistance and effort arms will alternate if two equally heavy riders alternately push against the ground to make the seesaw go up and down.

As in other machines, effort multiplied by the distance (from the fulcrum) equals resistance times distance (from the fulcrum). This is shown in INQ Figure 6–3. The me-

INQ Figure 6–3   **To find the mechanical advantage of a lever, divide the effort-arm length by the resistance-arm length.**

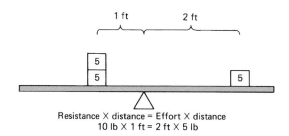

Resistance × distance = Effort × distance
10 lb × 1 ft = 2 ft × 5 lb

chanical advantage in this example is 2. Another way to calculate the mechanical advantage is simply to divide the effort-arm length by the resistance-arm length. Friction is usually so minor in the lever that it does not need to be taken into account.

Primary students can arrive at an intuitive understanding of the "law of levers" if they are given experience with balancing objects.

Three Classes

Levers are found with parts arranged in three different combinations called classes. Children do not need to memorize these combinations or even their examples; but analyzing how everyday levers work can sharpen their observation and classification skills. Notice the three arrangements in INQ Figure 6–4.

Seesaws, crowbars, and can openers are first-class levers. Two levers of this kind are placed together in tools such as scissors and pliers. By varying the effort-arm length, you change the amount of required force or gain in speed and distance. This type also changes direction of movement. You exert force in a direction opposite to which the load moves. With both effort and resistance arms equal in length, however, a first-class lever will only be able to change the direction of a force. Neither reduced force nor gain in speed and distance takes place.

The wheelbarrow and post puller illustrate second-class levers. A nutcracker illustrates joined, double levers of this type. Speed or distances are not as likely to be considerations when using a second-class lever as in the first-class lever.

A very basic and tangible example of a third-class lever is your arm. Your elbow is the fulcrum, your bicep provides the effort at a point just below and opposite the elbow, and your fist represents the load or resistance. Other common applications are found in the broom, baseball bat, fly swatter, and fishing pole, to name just a few. Sugar tongs or ice cube tongs represent double levers of the class. Analysis of this lever reveals that force is traded to get added speed or distance. With a fishing pole, for example, you want to increase the speed of your hands to hook a nibbling fish securely before it can react and get away.

INQ Figure 6–4   **Three classes of levers; R is resistance, E is effort.**

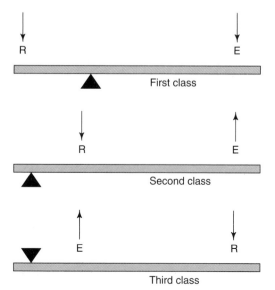

Mobiles

A mobile is a combination of several suspended levers with attached figures. In some mobiles, even the figures may function as levers (INQ Figure 6–5).

When children work on mobiles, they may have problems balancing the figures and keeping them from touching. For solutions, they need to think about variables such as figure size and shape, string length, best position for figures, and where to fasten them. This task sharpens their thinking skills. Mobiles are also an interesting way to combine artwork with science.

Archimedes and the Application of Levers

We began the lever concepts section with the bold statement to King Hiero that Archimedes could move the earth if he had a big enough lever. Even today, it would be an impossible engineering feat considering you would need a lever that was 88,000,000,000,000,000,000,000 miles long (Berquist, 1995).

Archimedes did show, however, that the principles behind the lever could be applied in useful ways even back in 215 B.C.E. In addition to designing a block-and-tackle system to move a huge ship and the Archimedean screw that is used to pump water even today, Archimedes was called upon to develop war machines to protect Syracuse from the battle between Rome and Carthage. Responding to King Hiero's challenge, Archimedes designed a massive catapult that could hurl enormous masses of stone against an enemy. The historian Plutarch (as cited in Downs, 1982) noted that just the noise and violence that Archimedes' catapults produced sent soliders running away. Archimedes also developed immense cranes that could lift enemy ships right out of the water if they came too close to Syracuse.

Archimedes' practical applications of his geometric ideas are found everywhere. Even the mobiles discussed in the previous section relate back to Archimedes. His experiments with equilibrium and the center of gravity showed that the balancing point of an object is not always at its center. He experimented with finding the centers of gravity of triangles, parallelograms, and other plane figures. Could you design an "Archimedean" mobile to find the centers of gravity for geometric shapes?

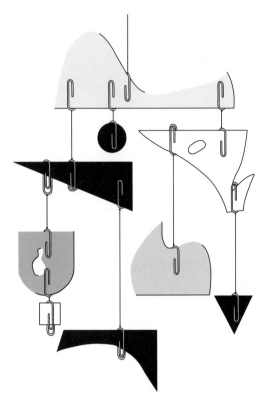

INQ Figure 6–5   **A tagboard and paper clip mobile.**

WHEEL AND AXLE Inquiry

Easier Work ———————

Invitation

How does a screwdriver handle make work easier?

Exploration

1. Use a hammer to tap in the screw so that it sticks into the wood.
2. Hold the screwdriver below the handle at the steel shank. Try to turn the screw.
3. Now hold the handle. Again, try to turn the screw.

Concept Invention

1. Which was easier?
2. Maybe your hand slipped on the smooth steel shank. Probably it did not slip on the handle. What will happen if you wrap masking tape around both parts and try again?
3. Which is easier this time?

Concept Application

Look at the screwdriver on end from the steel tip toward the handle. Notice the difference in width between the steel shank and the handle. Why do you think it is easier to turn a screw by using the handle rather than by using the shank?

> **MATERIALS**
> - Screwdriver with round handle
> - Masking tape
> - Piece of soft wood
> - Screw
> - Hammer

Wheel–Belt Systems ———————

Invitation

Have you ever noticed how bicycle gears turn? A chain connects the two gears. As one gear rotates, the other gear moves, too. A *gear* is just a wheel with teeth. There are many ways to connect wheels. Often, they are connected with belts. Several connected wheels are called a *wheel–belt system*. You can make your own wheel–belt system with spools and rubber bands. How can you make a wheel–belt system?

Exploration

1. Pound four nails into the board as shown.

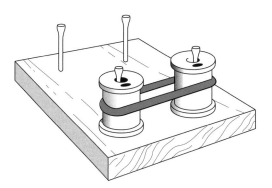

> **MATERIALS**
> - Four empty sewing spools
> - Board (about the size of this page)
> - Four finishing nails
> - Four rubber bands
> - Crayon
> - Hammer

2. Make one crayon dot on the rim of each spool.
3. Put a spool on each of two nails.
4. Place a rubber band around the two spools.
5. Turn one spool. Watch the other spool turn too.

Part of an end piece from a discarded vegetable crate is ideal for the wheel–belt system base. Be sure that only finishing nails are pounded into the wood. These nails have small heads, allowing the spools to slip easily over them.

This investigation deals only with the direction the spools turn. By using different-sized spools, children can also study how size governs the speed of turning. Because much slipping will happen with the rubber bands, the size–speed relationship cannot be determined accurately. Children can get the idea better by inverting a bicycle and studying the relative turnings of the large gear and the small gear.

Concept Invention

1. How will the spools turn when connected in different ways? Notice the eight drawings in the first illustration. Each set of spools starts with the left spool. An arrow shows how each is turning. Another spool in the set has a question mark. It is next to a dot on the spool rim. See how the spools are connected.

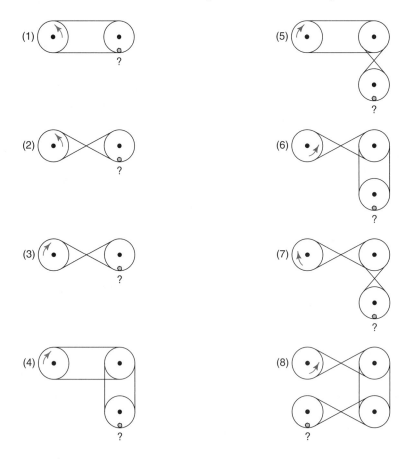

2. Will the dot on the rim turn left or right? Make a record of what you think. Then use your wheel–belt board to find out.

3. Notice the four drawings in the second illustration. How should the spools be connected to turn in these ways? How many different connections can you think of? Make drawings of what you think. Then, use your wheel–belt board to find out if they work.

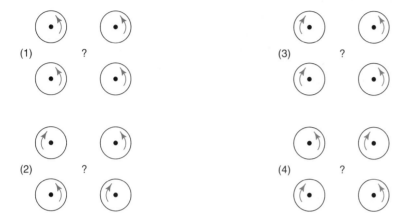

Concept Application

A wheel–belt system can be used to change the direction of a force. What wheel–belt systems can you invent? Record them below. Make up and trade some problems with friends. Fix your board so that you can use more spools.

Gearing Up for Speed ——————

Invitation

How do bicycle gears affect speed?

Exploration

1. Observe the different-sized gears or sprockets on the rear wheel of the bicycle. Notice that all are smaller than the large pedal sprocket. See how a chain connects the large sprocket with a smaller one.
2. Adjust the chain so that it is on the largest of the small gears.
3. Turn the bicycle upside down. Face the chain side.
4. Move the near pedal around. Notice how the rear wheel turns.
5. How many times will the wheel turn, in comparison to the pedal?
6. Chalk a spot on the rear tire. Crank the pedal around one full turn. Count the turns made by the chalked wheel.
7. Adjust the chain so that it is on the smallest rear gear. (You may have to set the bicycle upright to do so.)
8. Crank the pedal one full turn. How many times does the rear wheel turn now?

MATERIALS

- Ten-speed bicycle
- Chalk

Teaching Tips | Ten-speed bicycles have two different-sized front sprockets. When the smaller one is used, it causes the pedals to revolve faster. This decreases the forward speed but allows less force to be used. For simplicity, use only one front sprocket in this activity.

Concept Invention

1. How does changing the rear gear size affect how fast you can go?
2. Try several gear combinations to see if your theory is correct.

Adapting for Students with Exceptionalities

Activities involving force and motion concepts are especially difficult for exceptional students. Incorporate examples from the students' experiences to help reinforce new concepts. (See Mastropieri & Scruggs, 2004, chapter on science and social studies for a discussion on activities related to force and motion.)

Concept Application

Where else are there gears that may help change speed?

WHEEL AND AXLE CONCEPTS

The *windlass,* or wheel and axle, is a commonly misunderstood simple machine. Although a windlass looks like a wagon wheel and axle, it is different. We put wheels on a wagon to reduce friction by lessening the surface area that comes in contact with the road. The axles are stationary. Greater "leverage" is indeed present in a large wheel, compared with a small wheel. This is why a large wheel can roll over uneven ground more easily than a small wheel. Still, a wagon wheel and axle combination is not regarded as a simple machine.

In a windlass, the axle and wheel are firmly fixed together. Spinning the axle causes the wheel to rotate; force at the axle is traded off to gain an advantage in speed and distance on the outside of the wheel. By turning the wheel, though, an advantage in force can be gained; speed and distance are then reduced or sacrificed at the axle.

A windlass is really a continuous lever on a continuous fulcrum. Therefore, when a handle is placed anywhere on the wheel, it becomes the end of the force arm. The axle's radius is the load arm. INQ Figure 6–6 illustrates this idea. The theoretical mechanical ad-

INQ Figure 6–6   **A windlass is a lever.**

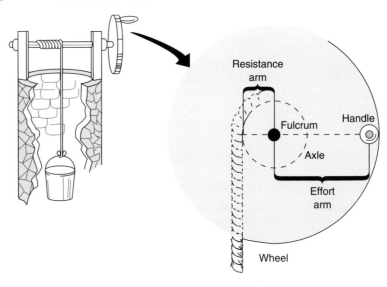

INQ Figure 6–7   **A pencil sharpener can be used as a wheel and axle.**

vantage in a windlass is calculated like that of a lever. If the effort-arm length is 45 centimeters (18 inches) and the resistance-arm length is 5 centimeters (2 inches), the mechanical advantage equals 9. Because friction is so great with a windlass, however, actual mechanical advantage is found only through dividing resistance by effort.

Placing the windlass handle (effort) ever farther away from the axle (fulcrum) decreases needed effort, just as it did with the lever. At the same time, it increases the distance through which the effort is applied.

Understanding the force–distance relationship makes it easy for children to see why a pencil sharpener with a normal size handle (INQ Figure 6–7) works better than one with a short, broken handle. Children may also realize that a large steering wheel is easier to turn than a smaller one.

Gears, Chains, and Belts ──────────────

Wheel-and-axle combinations may be modified to interact with one another by using belts, chains, and wheels with toothlike projections (gears). The bicycle is a common example of two modified wheels and axles joined by a chain. Because the front gear, or sprocket, is larger than the rear sprocket, one turn of the larger sprocket forces several or more turns of the smaller rear one. Older students can find the theoretical mechanical advantage of the larger sprocket by counting and comparing the number of teeth on each sprocket.

PULLEY **Inquiry**

How Pulleys Work ——————

Invitation

Many people use pulleys to help them work. Have you used a pulley to raise and lower a flag on a flagpole? Painters and roofers use pulleys to haul supplies up and down. Sometimes people work with only a single pulley, but often two or more are used together. How can you set up one or more pulleys to lift a load?

Exploration

1. Make a place to hang the pulley. Lay a stick over the backs of two separated chairs. Use tape to keep it from sliding. Loop and tie cord around the stick. Hang a single-wheel pulley from the loop. Hook a rubber band at the free end to act as a handle.
2. Set up a single pulley as illustrated in part A. This is a fixed pulley. Use a book for the load. Pull the cord down to lift the load. Practice a few times.
3. Now set up the pulley differently, as shown in part B. This is a movable pulley. Pull the cord up to lift the load. Practice a few times.

MATERIALS

- Two single-wheel pulleys
- Sticky tape
- Rubber band or spring scale
- Book
- Strong cord
- Ruler
- Broom handle or stick
- Scissors
- Paper clip
- Two chairs

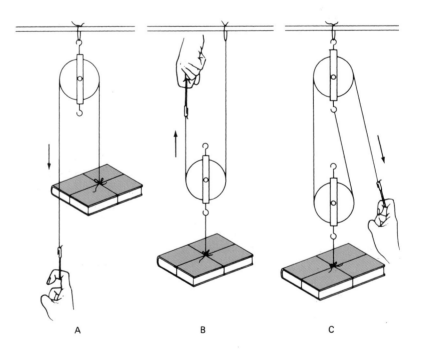

A   B   C

Concept Invention

1. What differences do you notice in using both pulleys?
2. Which takes less force to lift the load—the fixed pulley or the movable pulley? How much less? To measure, hook a rubber band to the pull cord with a paper clip. Measure the stretch with a ruler, or use a spring scale.
3. How far must you pull the cord to lift the load 1 meter (3 feet) with each pulley? Measure length of pull from where the cord leaves the pulley.
4. Refer to part C in the illustration. It shows a fixed and a movable pulley working together. This is a *block and tackle*. Which do you think takes less force to lift a load—a single fixed pulley or a block and tackle? How far must you pull the cord with each to lift the book 1 meter (3 feet)? Predict and then measure to answer each question.
5. Compare the block and tackle with the single movable pulley. Which do you think takes less force to lift a load? How far must you pull the cord with each to lift the book 1 meter (3 feet)? Predict and then measure to answer each question.
6. What examples of pulleys can you find in the classroom? What examples of pulleys can you find in the school? How do they work?

Teaching Tips

If a spring scale is used, be sure the load does not exceed its capacity. If you plan to do this investigation in a whole-group setting, consider placing the broomstick holder and supporting chairs on a table. This will allow students a clearer view.

Concept Application

A fixed pulley changes the direction of a force. A movable pulley reduces the force needed to lift a load. What other pulleys can you collect and try? How do they compare with the three pulleys of this investigation?

PULLEY CONCEPTS

Pulleys for teaching can be bought through science supply houses. Yet, in elementary school activities, two clothesline pulleys or two smaller single pulleys, found in most hardware stores, should work just as well. A single pulley has one grooved wheel or sheave. Some pulleys have two or more sheaves for combined use with other pulleys in heavy lifting.

Fixed and Movable Pulleys ———————

As its name implies, a fixed pulley is securely fastened to some object. A movable pulley moves vertically—or laterally, as the case may be—with the load (INQ Figure 6–8). The pulley's similarity to a lever and windlass is diagrammed in INQ Figure 6–8. As with a windlass, the wheel-like arrangement is really a continuous lever.

Observe why a fixed pulley can do no more than change the direction of a force. Like a seesaw whose fulcrum is centered, the effort arm and the resistance arm are of equal length. There is no useful mechanical advantage. If 30 centimeters (1 foot) of rope is pulled downward, the resistance moves upward 1 foot. This happens, for example, when a flag is raised on a flagpole.

Note that a movable pulley offers a theoretical mechanical advantage of 2. The resistance arm is only half the effort-arm length. Like a wheelbarrow, this is a variation of a second-class lever. Distance is traded for decreased effort. We must pull the rope 2 feet for each 1 foot the load is lifted.

INQ Figure 6–8   **A fixed pulley offers no mechanical advantage because its effort and resistance arms are equally long. A movable pulley, however, does make work easier because its resistance arm is only half the length of its effort arm.**

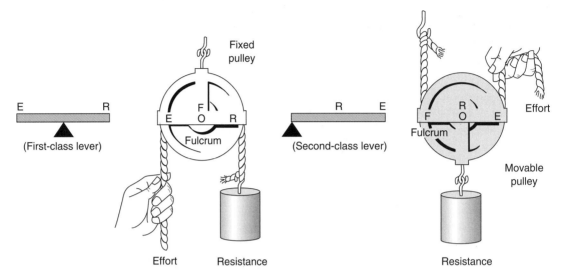

INQ Figure 6–9   **Block and tackle.**

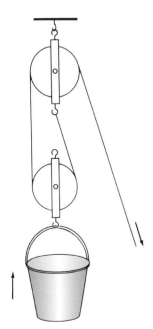

Block and Tackle

By placing a fixed and a movable pulley in combination, we are able not only to change the direction of a force but also to decrease the force necessary to lift a load. Such an arrangement is called a *block and tackle* (INQ Figure 6–9). By adding more movable pulleys (or pulleys with two or more sheaves), effort can be reduced even further.

Friction limits how far we can go in adding pulleys to reduce effort. It can be partly overcome by greasing or oiling the axle. Because each rope in a block-and-tackle setup supports an equal fraction of a load, it is easy to know the theoretical mechanical advantage. Two supporting ropes have a mechanical advantage of 2, three ropes 3, and so on. Because of friction, though, actual mechanical advantage must be calculated by dividing resistance by effort, as with all simple machines.

Children may use a rubber band (or spring scale) in the activities to measure differences in the force needed to lift objects by using pulleys. To attach a rubber band, first fashion a paper clip hook. Simply pierce or loop the pulley cord at the place where you wish to measure needed force, insert the hook, and then attach a rubber band to it. As before, a ruler can measure the amount of stretch.

Power Pulleys

The use of a pulley is not limited to lifting an object. Pulleys can be used in a system to deliver power. A smaller pulley can turn a larger pulley that goes slower, but provides more torque. One example of the use of a pulley system is in an automobile. A fan belt, powered by a pulley connected to the engine, is used to rotate the water pump (to circulate water to the radiator), the fan (to blow cooler air across the radiator), and the alternator (used to recharge the battery). In the home, pulleys are used to rotate the drum of the clothes dryer or to move the wheels attached to a computer hard disk or VCR head, to mention just a few examples.

Power pulley systems were used extensively in early factories. A water wheel, and later a steam engine, was used to supply energy to the layshaft, a long, cylindrical bar with small pulley wheels that rotated and transmitted power down the center of the workspace. Various machines such as power looms (used in weaving fabrics), lathes (machines for shaping a piece of material), or magnets (in generators to produce electricity) were connected to the layshaft by large belts and pulleys.

MOTION AND FRICTION Inquiry

Moving Parts ———————

MATERIALS

- Magazine pictures of different machines
- Toy machines

Invitation

How do machines and their parts move?

Exploration

1. Some machines move mostly in a straight line when they work, such as a locomotive and roller skates. Some machines or their parts go back and forth, such as a swing and the pendulum in a grandfather clock. Some machines or their parts go around, such as a merry-go-round and a bicycle wheel. Find pictures of machines and machine parts in magazines.
2. Cut out and group the pictures by how the machines or their parts seem to move.
3. Which machines or parts move mostly in a straight line?
4. Which machines or parts go back and forth?
5. Which machines or parts spin or go around as they work?
6. Which machines or parts do all of these things?
7. Which machines or parts do some of these things?
8. How do some toy machines and their parts move?

Concept Invention

1. Look for real examples of machines working.
2. Watch how they and their parts move.
3. Make a record of what you find out.

Scaffolding for English Learners

Look for opportunities to apply science concepts into the community. What machines are representative of your student's cultures? How do the parts on these specific machines move? Using community resources will assist in concept development of your English learners. (See Ovando, Collier, & Combs, 2003, for a discussion of the importance of community resources in science education for English learners.)

Concept Application

What machine can you make up and draw below? How will your machine or its parts move? What work will it do?

Pendulums ————

Invitation

Have you ever seen an old-fashioned grandfather clock? One kind has a long, weighted rod underneath that swings back and forth. The swinging part is called a *pendulum*. You can keep time with your own pendulum made with a string. How can you make a string pendulum?

Exploration

1. Tape a pencil to a table edge so that it sticks out.
2. Bend a paper clip into a hook shape. Tie one string end to the hook.
3. Loop the free end of the string once around the pencil. Tape the string end to the tabletop.
4. Put two washers on the hook, as shown.
5. Move the washers to one side and then let go. Each time the washers swing back to that side, count one swing. Be sure the string does not rub against the table edge.

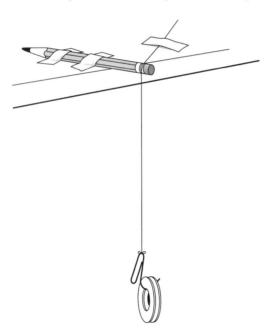

> ### MATERIALS
>
> - Thin string (about 1 meter, or 1 yard, long)
> - Meterstick or yardstick
> - Pencil
> - Three heavy washers
> - Paper clip
> - Clock or watch with second hand
> - Sticky tape
> - Graph paper
> - Table

Concept Invention

1. How many swings does the pendulum make in 1 minute? Have someone help by observing the second hand on a clock. Then you can count the swings.
2. Do wide swings take more time than narrow swings? Suppose you let go of your pendulum far to one side. What difference might that make in the number of swings it takes in 1 minute?

The timing of events is possible with a pendulum because its to-and-fro motion recurs with near-perfect regularity. Through manipulating variables, children can discover that the length of the weighted string affects the swing rate, or *period,* of a pendulum. Be sure children realize that one complete swing consists of the swing out and return movement.

An easy way for younger children to see the effect of manipulating a variable is to set up two identical pendulums. When both are set to swinging, they should perform in the same way. Thereafter, change only one variable at a time with one pendulum—weight or width of swing or length—so that its performance may be contrasted with the unchanged pendulum.

3. Does the amount of weight used change the swing time? What might happen if you use a one-washer weight? What might happen if you use a three-washer weight?

4. Does the length of string used make a difference in swing time? (Measure length from the pencil to the end of the washers.) What might happen if you use a shorter string? What might happen if you use a longer string?

5. How can you get your pendulum to swing 60 times in 1 minute?

6. How well can you predict with your pendulum? Make a graph such as the one shown. Try several string lengths for your pendulum. Count the swings for each length. Let's say you find that a 20-centimeter (8-inch) string swings 65 times in 1 minute. Make a mark on your graph where lines running from these two numbers meet, as shown in the graph. Make marks for three or four other string lengths and their swings. Then draw a straight line between the marks. Suppose you know the length of a pendulum but you have not yet tried it. How can you use your graph to predict its number of swings? Suppose you know the number of swings of a pendulum but you have not yet measured its length. How can you use your graph to predict the pendulum's length? How can you make your predictions more accurate?

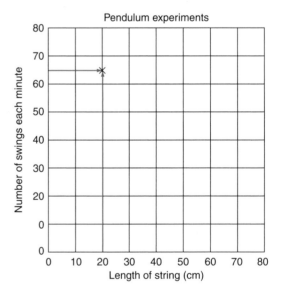

Concept Application

A pendulum is any object that swings regularly back and forth; its length affects its swing rate. Suppose you had a grandfather clock that was running slow. What could you do to its pendulum to correct it? What if it was running fast?

Friction

Invitation

Suppose someone asks you to slide a wooden box across the floor. On what kind of floor surface would it be easiest to start the box sliding? What kind would be the hardest? When an object catches or drags on a surface, we say much friction is present. If it slides or moves easily, little friction is present. How can you find out about the friction of different surfaces?

Exploration

1. Place a wooden block on a wooden table. Fasten a rubber band to it with a thumbtack.
2. Hook a thin rubber band with an opened paper clip. Hold the rubber band end over the end of a ruler as illustrated here.
3. Pull the rubber band very slowly. Observe where the rubber band end is over the ruler. How far does the band stretch before the block moves? Read the ruler to the nearest whole number. Always make the reading before the block starts to slide.

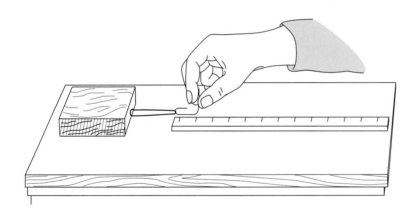

MATERIALS

- Two same-sized wooden blocks
- Paper clip
- Ruler
- Two round pencils
- Thumbtack
- Sheets of sandpaper
- Sticky tape
- Waxed paper
- Thin rubber band
- Three wide rubber bands
- Kitchen foil
- Construction paper
- Table

Concept Invention

1. How much will the rubber band stretch if you pull the block a second time?
2. How much will the rubber band stretch if you pull the block a third time? Record the results and the average for the three trials as shown below:

Surface Tested	Predicted Stretch	Stretch for Each Trial (cm)	Average Stretch (cm)
Wood	10	11, 15, 13	13
Others			

3. How much will the band stretch if the block is placed on other surfaces? Tape a small piece of kitchen foil to the table, and place the block on it. Test this and other surfaces such as sandpaper, waxed paper, or construction paper. (To prepare

a rubber surface, wrap three wide rubber bands around the block.) Try to predict first how far the band will stretch each time. Record the results.

4. How much will the band stretch if the block is placed on its side? How much will the band stretch if a second block is put on top?
5. How much will the band stretch if two round pencils are placed under the block?

Concept Application

Friction between two surfaces depends on the force that presses the surfaces together and the materials that make up the surfaces. Some surfaces have more friction than others. How can you make the most friction between the block and surface? How can you make the least friction between the block and surface? (Use more materials if necessary.)

MOTION AND FRICTION CONCEPTS

Most machines we use are complex; that is, they are combinations of simple machines. It is interesting to see how these machines and their parts move and interact.

Three Basic Motions

Some machines have mainly a *straight-line motion*. A few examples are toy or real trains, a bicycle (turning requires some leaning), roller skates, and steamrollers. Some machines or their parts make a repeated forward and backward movement called *periodic motion*. The pendulum in a grandfather clock is one example. Others are a swing, a mechanical walking doll, a metronome, and some lawn sprinklers.

Some machines or their parts make a continuous spinning motion in one direction as they work. This is *rotary motion*. A few examples are the merry-go-round, the turntable on a record player, a rotary lawn sprinkler, and clock hands. It can be fascinating to examine mechanical toys and other machines; their parts are designed to produce a particular motion and, in some cases, to change it.

Any moving machine or part continues to produce its designed motion unless another force is applied to alter, reverse, or stop it. When we rotate a telephone dial, for instance, a metal stop prevents us from going beyond one rotation. A spring then returns the dial to its original position. Also, the front wheel of a moving bicycle may be turned by applying a force to the handlebars. But what happens if the force is applied too strongly? Perhaps painful experience has taught you that bicycle and rider will continue in a straight line until road friction finally stops both.

Friction ———————

Accompanying all motion is *friction*, the resistance produced when two surfaces rub together. No surface is perfectly smooth. The tiny ridges in a "smooth" surface, or the larger bumps and hollows in a rough one, catch and resist when surfaces rub together. The mutual attraction of molecules on the opposing surfaces also adds to the resistance we call friction. Surface pressure is another condition that affects friction. A heavy object has more friction than a lighter one.

Lubricating a surface is effective because the oil or grease fills in the spaces between the ridges and bumps. Opposing surfaces mostly slide against the lubricant, rather than rub against each other.

In many machines, ball bearings or roller bearings are used to change sliding friction to rolling friction. Rolling friction is less than sliding friction because a load-bearing rolling object rolls over tiny surface ridges or bumps, rather than catches against them.

Friction reduces a machine's efficiency by robbing some of its power (and so its energy). It also creates heat as surfaces rub and wears out parts. But not all its effects are bad. Friction also allows us to brake a car or bicycle, walk or run, or write on paper. A frictionless world would create far more problems than it would solve.

References

American Association for the Advancement of Science (AAAS). (1993). *Benchmarks for science literacy*. New York: Oxford University Press.

Berquist, L. (1995). *Archimedes and the door of science*. Warsaw, ND: Bethlehem Books.

Downs, R. (1982). *Landmarks in science: Hippocrates to Carson*. Littleton, CO: Libraries Unlimited.

Mastropieri, M., & Scruggs, T. E. (2004). *The inclusive classroom: Strategies for effective instruction* (4th ed.). Upper Saddle River, NJ: Merrill/Prentice Hall.

Mercer, C. D., & Mercer, A. R. (2005). *Teaching students with learning problems* (7th ed.). Upper Saddle River, NJ: Merrill/Prentice Hall.

National Research Council (NRC). (1996). *National science education standards*. Washington, DC: National Academy Press.

Ovando, C. J., Collier, V. P., & Combs, M. C. (2003). *Bilingual and ESL classrooms: Teaching in multicultural contexts*. Boston, MA: McGraw-Hill.

Selected Trade Books: Simple Machines

For Younger Children

Barton, B. (1987). *Machines at work*. New York: Harper & Row.

Gibbons, G. (1982). *Tool book*. New York: Holiday House.

Hodge, D. (1998). *Simple machines* (Starting with science series). Toronto, Ontario: Kids Can Press.

Kiley, D. (1980). *Biggest machines*. Austin, TX: Raintree.

Lampton, C. (1991). *Marbles, roller skates, doorknobs: Simple machines that are really wheels*. Brookfield, CT: Millbrook Press.

Lampton, C. (1991). *Sailboats, flag poles, cranes: Using pulleys as simple machines*. Brookfield, CT: Millbrook Press.

Lampton, C. (1991). *Seesaws, nutcrackers, brooms: Simple machines that are really levers*. Brookfield, CT: Millbrook Press.

Lauber, P. (1987). *Get ready for robots*. New York: Scholastic.

Pipe, J. (2002). *What does a wheel do?* Brookfield, CT: Copper Beech Books/Millbrook.

Robbins, K. (1983). *Tools*. New York: Macmillan.

Rockwell, A., & Rockwell, H. (1985). *Machines*. New York: Harper & Row.

Tompert, A. (1993). *Just a little bit*. Boston: Houghton Mifflin.

Wade, H. (1979). *Gears*. Austin, TX: Raintree.

Wade, H. (1979). *The lever*. Austin, TX: Raintree.

Weiss, H. (1983). *The world of machines*. Austin, TX: Raintree.

Wells, R. (1996). *How do you lift a lion?* Morton Grove, IL: Albert Whitman.

Wilkin, F. (1986). *Machines*. Danbury, CT: Childrens Press.

Wyler, R. (1988). *Science fun with toy cars and trucks*. Parsippany, NJ: Julian Messner.

For Older Children

Adkins, J. (1980). *Moving heavy things*. Boston: Houghton Mifflin.

Baines, R. (1985). *Simple machines*. New York: Troll Associates.

Barrett, N. S. (1985). *Robots*. Danbury, CT: Watts.

Brown, W. F., & Brown, M. G. (1984). *Experiments with common wood and tools*. New York: Macmillan.

Busby, P. (2003). *First to fly: How Wilbur and Orville Wright invented the airplane*. New York: Crown Books for Young Readers.

Catlin, D. (n.d.) *The inventa book of mechanisms*. London, UK: Valiant Technology.

DeWeese, B. (1994). *Playground physics: Simple machines*. Monterey, CA: Evan-Moor.

Fleisher, P., & Keeler, P. (1991). *Looking inside: Machines and constructions*. New York: Macmillan.

Friedhoffer, B. (1997). *Physics lab in a hardware store*. Danbury, CT: Watts.

Gardner, R. (1980). *This is the way it works*. New York: Doubleday.

Glass, A. (2003). *The wondrous whirligig: The Wright Brothers first flying machine*. New York: Holiday House.

Hellman, H. (1971). *The lever and the pulley*. Philadelphia: J. B. Lippincott.

Hewitt, P. G. (1998). *Conceptual physics for parents and teachers— Mechanics*. Newburyport, MA: Focus.

Hulls, J. (2003). *Rider in the sky: How an American cowboy built England's first airplane*. New York: Crown Books for Young Readers.

James, E., & Barkin, C. (1975). *The simple facts of simple machines*. New York: Lothrop, Lee & Shepard Books.

Jupo, F. (1972). *The story of things (tools)*. Upper Saddle River, NJ: Prentice Hall.

Lasky, K. (2003). *The man who made time travel*. New York: Farrar, Straus, and Giroux.

Rockwell, A. (1985). *Planes*. New York: Dutton's Children's Books.

Sauvain, P. A. (1992). *Motion*. New York: Macmillan.

Taylor, B. (1990). *Force and movement*. Danbury, CT: Watts.

VanCleave, J. P. (1993). *Janice VanCleave's machines*. Hoboken, NJ: John Wiley.

Weiss, H. (1983). *Machines and how they work*. New York: Harper & Row.

Resource Books

Butzow, C. M., & Butzow, J. W. (1989). *Science through children's literature: An integrated approach*. Englewood, CO: Teacher Ideas Press. (force and movement topics, pp. 197–199)

Cordel, B., Erickson, S., Hillen, J., & Winkelman, G. (Eds.). (1993). *Machine shop*. Fresno, CA: AIMS Education Foundation. (lever, pulley, inclined plane, wheel, and friction activities)

Goldfluss, K., & Sima, P. (1993). *Thematic unit: Inventions*. Huntington Beach, CA: Teacher Created Materials. (thematic invention activities)

Merrell, J. (1994). *Thematic unit: Simple machines*. Huntington Beach, CA: Teacher Created Materials. (thematic simple machine activities)

Shaw, D. G., & Dybdahl, C. S. (1996). *Integrating science and language arts. A sourcebook for K–6 teachers*. Boston: Allyn & Bacon. (wheel and gear topics, pp. 96–100)

Tolman, M., & Morton, J. (1986). *Physical science activities for grades 2–8*. West Nyack, NY: Parker. (simple machine activities, pp. 137–187)

PLANT LIFE

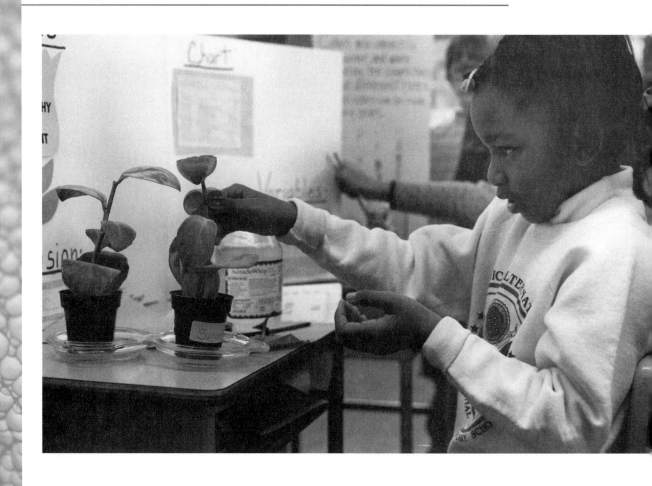

"Chances for open-ended experiments are greater with plants than with any other area of elementary school science." That is what one longtime teacher said, and we agree. At the same time, there is more need for planning ahead and keeping track of activities so that they may be interrelated. Living things take time to grow, and growth rates can seldom be predicted exactly. The most complex and familiar plants we see are those that produce seeds, of which there are two basic groups. One group is the *gymnosperms*. These plants are flowerless; they develop seeds attached to open scales or cones. Evergreens such as pine, hemlock, spruce, juniper, fir, and redwood are examples of gymnosperms. There are about 600 species.

The second and far larger group (about 250,000 species) is the *angiosperms*, or flowering plants. These form their seeds in closed compartments or cases within the flowers.

In this section, we consider seeds and how they grow, how new plants can be started from plant parts, how environmental conditions affect plants, how plant parts work, and how plants respond to their environment. A brief, final section takes up the tiny plantlike organisms called *molds*.

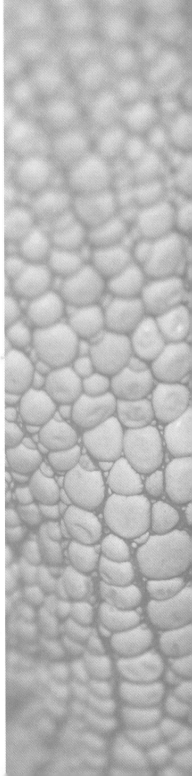

Benchmarks and Standards

Throughout the elementary years, it is important that children build an understanding of biological concepts through direct experiences with living things. Plants are excellent sources for observational activities, classification tasks, and experimentation. A sampling of benchmarks and standards related to the study of plants in the elementary classroom follows:

Sample Benchmarks (AAAS, 1993)

- Plants and animals have features that help them live in different environments. (By Grades K–2, p. 102)
- Plants and animals both need to take in water, and animals need to take in food. In addition, plants need light. (By Grades K–2, p. 119)

Sample Standards (NRC, 1996)

- Each plant or animal has different structures that serve different functions in growth, survival, and reproduction. (By Grades K–4, p. 129)
- Plants and some microorganisms are producers; they make their own food. (By Grades 5–8, pp. 157–158)

SEED-RELATED Inquiry

Seed Parts ───────

MATERIALS

- Bean seeds
- Paper towel
- Corn seeds
- Glass of water
- Variety of other kinds of seeds

Invitation

What is inside a bean seed? Can you draw a picture of how it might look inside? How can you find out about the parts of seeds?

Exploration

1. Soak some bean and corn seeds in water overnight.
2. Use your thumbnail to open a soaked bean seed.

 Teaching Tips Seeds from flowering plants have three things in common: a protective seed cover, a baby plant (embryo), and a food supply. The food nourishes the sprouted embryo as it pushes up through the soil and grows into a young plant. When its food supply is gone, a green plant can make (photosynthesize) its own food from substances in air, water, and soil if light shines on it. In the seeds of some plants, such as the bean and sweet pea, the food supply is located in two seed halves, or *cotyledons*. In the seeds of other plants, such as corn and rice, there is only a single cotyledon; the food supply is located there.

If possible, let older children gather and examine some seeds from evergreen plants such as the pine, hemlock, spruce, fir, juniper, and redwood. They may observe how the seeds are attached to open scales or cones. Have them look up information about the reproductive process of such plants.

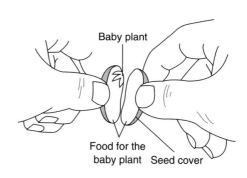

Baby plant

Food for the baby plant   Seed cover

Concept Invention

1. What do you notice about your seed?
2. How many different parts do you find?
3. How does the seed feel to you without its cover?
4. What does the seed smell like?
5. Open the corn seed. How is it like the bean seed? How is it different?

Concept Application

Most seeds have a baby plant, a food supply, and a cover. Soak and open other kinds of seeds. In what ways are they alike and different? How well can you describe a seed? Put a seed among three different kinds of seeds. Describe it. Will someone be able to pick it out?

The Growth of Seeds ———

Invitation

Where do green plants originate? Have you planted seeds? What did you do? How can you plant seeds so they may grow?

Exploration

1. Use a pencil or large nail to poke holes into the carton or cup bottom.
2. Put the carton on a pie pan.
3. Fill the carton almost full with soil.
4. Water the soil slowly until water leaks into the pie pan.
5. Poke a hole in the soil. Make it about as deep as the seed you plant is long.

MATERIALS

- Soil
- Bean seeds soaked overnight in water
- Water
- Paper towel
- Pencil or large nail
- Topless milk carton or paper cup
- Pie pan
- Glass or watering container
- Paper strips
- Paste
- Large sheet of paper
- Sand, sawdust, or different soils for planting seeds
- Salt
- Freezer
- Boiling water
- Seeds (bean, pea, and flower)

6. Put the bean seed into the hole. Cover it with wet soil. Tap the soil down lightly.
7. Water the soil when it feels dry to your touch, but not more than once a day.
8. Measure your growing plant three times a week. Put a strip of paper alongside. Tear off some to match the plant's height. Date the strips and paste them on a large sheet of paper. What can you tell from this plant record?

 Teaching Tips | A seed that is soaked before it is planted will sprout faster than one planted dry. But don't leave a seed in water longer than overnight; it may die from insufficient air.

Concept Invention

1. Experiment with more materials. In what kind of soil will a seed grow best? Try sand, sawdust, or soil from different places; or mix your own soil from some of these.
2. Will a seed live and grow if you water it with saltwater? How much salt can you use? What else might you use to "water" a growing seed?

3. Will a broken or damaged seed grow? Will a seed that was frozen or boiled grow? Will a seed grow if the seed cover is taken off?
4. Does the position of a seed make a difference? For example, what will happen if you plant a seed upside down?

Adapting for Students with Exceptionalities

Avoid excessive watering when growing plants. Set up a detailed schedule with students' names, amounts of water, and how the water is to be measured (predetermined mark on a measuring cup). (See Mastropieri & Scruggs, 2004, for a discussion on activities related to plants in the chapter on science and social studies.)

Concept Application

Some plants grow from seeds; proper conditions are needed for seeds to sprout and grow. Design an activity to see if the same conditions work well for different types of seeds. For example, do pea seeds and bean seeds like the same conditions? How about flower seeds? Do not forget to use a control group with this experiment.

Deep Down Seeds

MATERIALS

- Six sprouted bean seeds
- Soil
- Sticky tape
- Tall, clear jar with straight sides
- Black paper
- Radish seeds

Invitation

How deep can you plant a seed and still have it grow?

Exploration

1. Plant two seeds in soil at the bottom of the jar. Place the seeds next to the sides of the jar so that they can be seen.
2. Add more soil. Plant two seeds in the middle of the jar the same way.
3. Add more soil. Plant two seeds near the top of the jar.
4. Tape black paper around the jar. Remove the paper for a short time each day to observe the seeds. Water the seeds as needed.

Concept Invention

1. Which seeds will have enough food energy to grow to the surface?
2. What happens to the seeds that do not reach the surface?

Adapting for Students with Exceptionalities

Slow-growing plants may lose students' interest. Try substituting Fast Plants® (*http://www.fastplants.org/*) for the bean seeds. (See Mastropieri & Scruggs, 2004, for a discussion on activities related to plants in the chapter on science and social studies.)

Concept Application

What would happen if you planted smaller seeds, like radish seeds? Why are some seeds larger than others?

Where Are the Seeds?

Invitation

In what places are seeds in the soil?

Exploration

1. Line some shoe boxes with plastic bags.
2. Half-fill each shoe box with bare soil from a different place. Try garden soil, soil where weeds grow, and other bare soils.
3. Use a marker to label where each place is on the box.
4. Water the soils so that they are damp.
5. Cover each box with clear kitchen wrap.
6. Leave each box in a warm, well-lighted place for several weeks or more.

Concept Invention

1. In which box do you expect seeds to grow?
2. In which box, if any, did seeds grow?

Concept Application

Would wild plants grow in the exact places from which you took soil? Observe these places from time to time and record your observations.

> ### MATERIALS
> - Shoe boxes
> - Bare soil from outdoor places
> - Clear kitchen wrap
> - Small shovel
> - Plastic bags
> - Marker
> - Water
> - Glass or watering container

SEED-RELATED CONCEPTS

"Where do seeds come from?" is a question curious children may ask when they study flowering plants. Seeds are produced in the *ovary*, in the central part of the flower. As the ovary ripens, its seeds become enveloped either by a fruity pulp, a pod, or a shell, depending on the kind of plant.

Pears and peaches are fruits whose pulp we eat. Beans, peas, and peanuts are examples of seeds enclosed in pods. When we "shell" string beans, lima beans, peas, or peanuts, we are removing these seeds from their pods. Walnuts, pecans, and coconuts have hard outer shells.

Seed Parts

Seeds come in many shapes, colors, and sizes. Still, they have three things in common: a protective seed cover, a baby plant (embryo), and a food supply that nourishes the seed as it pushes up through the soil and grows into a young plant. In the seeds of some plants, such as the bean and sweet pea, the baby plant's food supply is in two seed "leaves," or *cotyledons* (INQ Figure 7–1). In the seeds of other plants, such as corn and rice, there is a single cotyledon; the baby plant's food supply is in there.

INQ Figure 7–1 **Parts of a bean seed.**

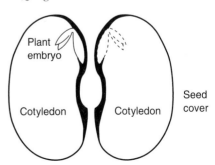

Growth Stages

What happens when a seed grows into a young plant, or *seedling?* INQ Figure 7–2 is an illustration of the growth stages. In A, the seed swells from absorbing

INQ Figure 7–2   **Growth stages: from seed to seedling.**

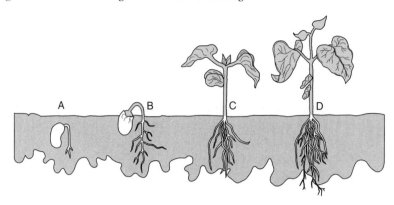

moisture from the soil. The coat softens and splits. A tiny root and stem emerge. In B, the upper part of the stem penetrates the soil surface and lifts the folded cotyledons out of the seed cover. In C, the cotyledons and tiny plant leaves unfold. Roots deepen and spread. In D, roots become more extensive. The cotyledons are smaller and shriveled. Nearly all the food supply has been consumed. The plant begins to make its own food through photosynthesis within its maturing leaves. In a short while, the shriveled cotyledons, now useless, will drop off the growing plant. This growth process, from seed to seedling, is called *germination*.

Survival Conditions

Some flowering plants produce thousands of seeds a year. If they all grew into plants, before long there would scarcely be room on the earth for anything else. Fortunately, a variety of factors enable only a small percentage of wild seeds to grow. Birds, insects, bacteria, and other organisms destroy seeds, and unless proper conditions of moisture, temperature, and oxygen are present, seeds remain dormant. After several years in a dormant state, all but a few kinds of seeds lose their potential ability to germinate. These few, however, may not lose this ability for hundreds or even thousands of years.

Weeds are everywhere about us. What makes them so prolific? Perhaps you have noticed that weeds appear at different times during a growing season. They grow in different seasons because the growth requirements of moisture, temperature, and oxygen vary greatly among different kinds of seeds. Of course, this diversity has great survival value.

How Seeds Travel

We know that people plant seeds in gardens. But they do not plant weeds in fields and vacant lots. Nor do they plant seeds in many other places where plants grow. Where do these seeds originate?

Children can learn that seeds travel in several ways. Some are scattered through the actions of animals and people. For example, the sharp hooks or barbs on the cocklebur, burdock, and beggar tick cling to clothing or animal fur (INQ Figure 7–3). Birds eat fleshy fruits but may not digest the hard seeds; the seeds pass out of their bodies some distance away. People throw away fruit pits or watermelon seeds. The wind blows many seeds. Some, such as the goldenrod, milkweed, and dandelion, have "parachutes"; maple tree seeds have "wings." Water can carry seeds from place to place because many seeds float. The capacity of seeds to disperse widely and in different ways is another survival feature.

INQ Figure 7–3   **Some common seeds.**

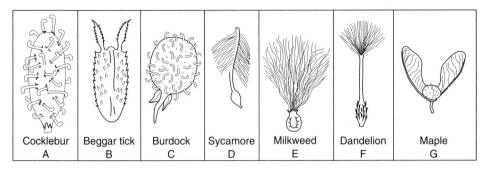

| Cocklebur A | Beggar tick B | Burdock C | Sycamore D | Milkweed E | Dandelion F | Maple G |

Sprouting Seeds

It is much less expensive to buy seeds (the kind you eat) at a grocery store than at a seed store even though a smaller percentage will grow. Some easy-to-grow seeds are kidney beans, lima beans, pinto beans, whole green peas, and yellow peas. To ensure that only live, healthy seeds are planted, treat them as follows:

- Soak the seeds in water for several hours to soften them.
- Remove the seeds from the water and drop them into a mixture of one part liquid bleach to eight parts water.
- Take out the seeds immediately after immersing them.

To sprout the treated seeds, first soak several paper towels in water. Fold and place them in an aluminum pie pan or dish. Place the treated seeds on top of the wet towels. Then cover the pan with clear plastic wrap to prevent the water from evaporating.

Inspect the seeds every day. Within several days to a week, many bean or pea seeds will have parts sticking out of their seed covers. These sprouted seeds are alive. They are likely to grow into plants, if planted while moist and cared for properly.

Soil

All containers may be filled with garden soil, sand, sawdust, or vermiculite, an inexpensive insulating material of fluffy bits of mica. Only the garden soil will have minerals needed for healthy growth of plants beyond the seedling stage.

Other "soil" materials allow air to circulate around the seed cover and plant roots. They are also more porous in order to protect the plant from excess water. Plants rooted in these materials may be more easily removed, examined, and replanted without serious root damage.

Small holes punched in containers will aid good drainage. Any water runoff can be caught in a saucer placed below. If holes cannot easily be made, as with a glass jar, include 2.5 centimeters (1 inch) of gravel in the jar bottom before adding soil. Water only when the soil surface feels slightly dry.

Instruct students to plant seeds only slightly deeper than the seed length; but always follow instructions on the seed package for seed store varieties. Because it takes energy to push through the soil, a small seed planted too deeply runs out of food before it reaches the surface. Also, keep the soil somewhat loose so that air can get to the roots.

VEGETATIVE REPRODUCTION **Inquiry**

New Plants from Old Plants

MATERIALS

- Three clear plastic drinking glasses
- Soil
- Sand
- Water
- Knife
- Healthy geranium plant
- Ruler

Invitation

How can you grow new plants from cut stems?

Exploration

1. Cut a strong stem about 13 centimeters (5 inches) long from the plant. Cut just below where leaves join the stem. Trim away all but two or three leaves from the top of the plant.
2. Stick the cutting into a glass half-filled with water. Watch every day for roots to appear.

Concept Invention

1. Some cuttings grow roots faster when placed in sand or soil. Make two more cuttings. Plant one at a slant in a glass containing sand. Plant the other the same way in soil. The stem end should be against the glass. In this way, you will be able to see roots start.
2. Keep the soil or sand damp.
3. In which container does the cutting grow roots fastest?

Teaching **T**ips | **Caution:** Handle the knife yourself or closely supervise its use.

Concept Application

Does the thickness of a cutting affect root growth? Does the length of a cutting affect root growth? Record your findings from what is observed.

Sweet Potatoes

MATERIALS

- Sweet potato
- Wide-mouthed plastic drinking glass
- Three toothpicks
- Water

Invitation

How can you grow sweet potato vines?

Exploration

1. Sweet potatoes are the swollen root ends of the sweet potato plant. You can grow beautiful, trailing vines from them indoors.
2. Place the sweet potato into a glass of water, stem end up. (This end has a small scar where it was attached to the plant.) Stick toothpicks in the sides to support it, if needed. Only about one third of the sweet potato should be in the water. Keep the water level the same during this activity.
3. Leave the glass in a warm, dark place until buds and roots grow. Then put it in a sunny or well-lighted place.

Concept Invention

1. How long does it take before you see the first growth?
2. What changes do you notice as the buds and roots grow?
3. What happens to the sweet potato as vines grow?

Concept Application

What are similar plants that will grow vines? Experiment with different types of plants and write your conclusions.

Tapping into New Growth ——————

Invitation

How can you get new growth from taproots?

Exploration

1. Cut off the top 5 centimeters (2 inches) of each carrot. (You may eat the rest.) Trim away any stems and leaves growing from the top.
2. Put gravel into each tumbler. Stick each carrot top about halfway into the gravel.
3. Fill each jar with just enough water to cover the bottom. Leave each tumbler in a warm, well-lighted place. Observe each day.

Concept Invention

1. How long does it take for stems and leaves to grow?
2. What happens to the taproot part as stems and leaves grow?
3. Which, if either, carrot top shows more growth?
4. What will happen if you plant the carrot tops in soil?

Concept Application

Can you get new growth from other taproots? Try a beet, turnip, and parsnip and describe the results.

> **MATERIALS**
>
> - Two fresh carrots (one small and one large)
> - Knife
> - Ruler
> - Three small tumblers (preferably clear plastic)
> - Gravel
> - Soil
> - Other taproots (beet, turnip, parsnip)

 Teaching Tips | **Caution:** For safety, you may wish to cut the carrots for the children.

VEGETATIVE REPRODUCTION CONCEPTS

Many people think that only seeds produce new flowering plants. Yet, some of the most useful and interesting ways to grow new plants are through the propagation of roots, stems, and even leaves. This technique is called *vegetative reproduction*.

Roots ——————

Consider the orange taproot of the carrot plant (the part we eat). A carrot plant is usually grown from seed in the spring and harvested some months later. If left in the ground, however, all parts above the soil surface die as the weather becomes cold. No growth occurs during this time. As warmer weather approaches, tender shoots grow from the taproot and emerge into the sunlight. These grow into stems and leaves. Some time thereafter, flowers and seeds are produced. Like a seed, a taproot provides the food energy needed for shoots to emerge and grow. Parsnips and beets are other examples of taproots that grow in this way (INQ Figure 7–4).

New plants may be grown from taproots in the classroom by embedding them in moist sand or garden soil. A favorite method of many teachers is to cut off all but the top quarter of a taproot and embed it in a small bowl containing a layer of pebbles and some water. At least half of the root cutting is above water to ensure a sufficient oxygen supply. When sufficient foliage and roots have emerged, cuttings are planted in garden soil for full growth.

Stems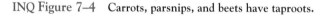

Most ground-cover plants, such as grass, strawberry, and ivy, spread quickly after planting. These plants send out stems or runners that take root, push up shoots, and develop into new plants. These lateral stems may spread above ground, as the strawberry plant and Bermuda grass do, or below ground, as quack grass does. The most persistent weed grasses are of the underground-stem variety, as frustrated lawn growers will testify.

New geranium and begonia plants may be propagated from stem cuttings. Other common plants whose stems grow independently are the coleus, oleander, philodendron, and English ivy. Dipping the ends of stem cuttings in a commercial hormone preparation may start root growth in half the usual time.

Sometimes, on opening a bag of white potatoes, we find some of them beginning to sprout. Usually, this happens when the potatoes have been left undisturbed for a time in a dark, warm place. White potatoes are swollen parts of underground stems, called *tubers*. The dark spots, or "eyes," are buds from which shoots may grow.

Farmers today seldom, if ever, use potato seeds in growing potato crops. Instead, they cut potatoes into several bud-bearing parts and plant these. Each bud grows into a new plant that produces more potatoes.

Occasionally, we see shoots growing from onion bulbs stored in the home pantry. Bulbs, too, are modified stems. All contain thick, fleshy leaves wrapped tightly around a

INQ Figure 7–4   Carrots, parsnips, and beets have taproots.

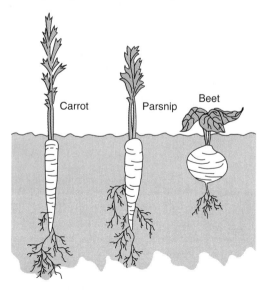

small, immature stem. Tulips and gladioli are typical flowers that may be grown from both bulbs and seeds.

Leaves

Even some leaves may develop into whole plants. Suggestions follow for using an African violet, echeveria, and bryophyllum plant.

Use a fresh African violet leaf with attached *petiole* (leaf stalk). Put the stalk into 2.5 centimeters (1 inch) of water in a drinking glass. For better support of the leaf, use an index card with a hole punched in it placed across the glass rim. Insert the leaf petiole through the hole and into the water. After roots begin to grow, plant the leaf in rich soil. The bryophyllum leaf is sometimes sold in variety stores under the name "magic leaf." To propagate, pin it down flat on damp sand with several toothpicks or straight pins. Tiny plants should grow from several of the notches around the leaf rim.

Why Vegetative Reproduction?

Sometimes children ask, "If plants can grow from seeds, why are the other ways used?" There are several reasons: All of these methods result in whole plants in far less time. Also, some plants cannot be grown from seed (e.g., seedless oranges). In this case, branches of seedless oranges are grafted onto an orange tree grown from seed. But the most important reason for growing plants in other ways besides seeds is quality control. We can never be sure of the results when we plant seeds of some plants. Vegetative reproduction ensures that the new plants will be very much like the parent plant. If large, healthy potatoes are cut up and planted, for instance, we probably can harvest near-identical specimens.

Today, as the demand for plants to feed us and provide energy is on the rise and farmable land is becoming scarcer, vegetative propagation techniques are being used in conjunction with genetic engineering to provide new plants. These *transgenic* plants carry new genes from other species of plants or animals in order to grow better fruit, vegetables, and grains; change flavors; resist disease and insects; or better tolerate herbicides used to kill weeds growing around new plants. For example, an antifreeze protein from a cold-water fish is being used to develop strawberries that can be grown in cold climates (Jefferis, 1999). This growing body of research will provide many new plants to help us meet our energy needs, become healthier, and enjoy tastier foods.

All the foregoing methods of vegetative reproduction are *asexual*. In other words, reproduction does not require involvement of plant sex organs. Certain lower animal-like forms also can reproduce themselves asexually. In another section, we discuss sexual reproduction in flowering plants—that is, how fertile seeds are produced.

ENVIRONMENTAL CONDITIONS **Inquiry**

How Colored Light Affects Plant Growth

MATERIALS

- Four cellophane or plastic sheets (red, green, blue, and clear)
- Four topless shoe boxes
- Scissors
- Ruler
- Lawn area
- Sticky tape
- Water
- Watering container
- Variety of plants

Invitation

Plants need light to grow. But must it be white sunlight? Perhaps plants will grow just as well or better in colored light. What can you do to find out how plants grow in colored light?

Exploration

1. Cut out the bottoms of four shoe boxes. Leave a 2.5-centimeter (1-inch) border on all sides.
2. Cover each cutout bottom with a different color of cellophane. Fasten the sheets with sticky tape.
3. Place the shoe boxes close together, with cellophane sheets facing up, on a healthy patch of lawn, as illustrated. Lift the boxes once each day for 2 weeks to observe the grass. Water the grass as needed but do not mow it.

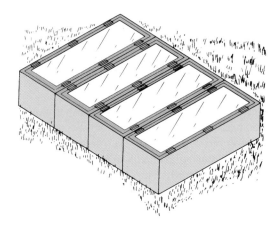

 Teaching Tips

As illustrated, other kinds of plants may be tested with shoe boxes as well. Punch holes in the sides of the boxes for adequate air circulation. The boxes may be slipped off quickly for observing, measuring, and watering the plants.

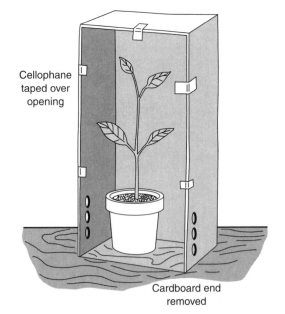

Cellophane taped over opening

Cardboard end removed

Concept Invention

1. What differences, if any, do you notice each day in the grass under the boxes?
2. How do the grass samples compare in height and color?
3. What kind of a record can you make to keep track of what happens?
4. What color seems best for grass growth?
5. What color seems worst for grass growth?
6. What other colors can you test?
7. How will the grass be affected?

Some children may also like to try growing plants under artificial light. A gooseneck lamp with a 50-watt bulb works well as a light source. If the bulb is left on 24 hours a day, the children may discover that plant growth slows down.

Adapting for Students with Exceptionalities

Use instructional conversations with rich dialogue as opposed to question-and-answer formats when working with students who have hearing impairments, especially on activities that may involve difficult concepts. Be sure to focus on the concepts and content (e.g., why light is needed for plant growth, why colored light may make a difference in plant growth, the "colors" that white light contains). (See Turnbull, Turnbull, Shank, & Smith, 2004, for a discussion on augmenting instruction of students who have hearing impairments through instructional conversations.)

Concept Application

Plants grow better in natural light than in colored light. How can you test other plants? How will they be affected? Try out your ideas and record the results.

How Saltwater and Other Liquids Affect Plants ——————

Invitation

Many places have too little freshwater to grow plants. So, some people want to use ocean water, which is salty. How do you think saltwater would affect land plants? How can you find out what saltwater does to plants?

Exploration

1. Mix 1 teaspoonful of salt into 0.5 liter (1 pint, or 2 cups) of water.
2. Water one container of plants with only this saltwater.
3. Water a matched container of plants with only freshwater.
4. Observe both sets of plants each day.

MATERIALS

- Two matched containers of healthy young radish plants
- Matched containers of other land plants
- Two measuring cups
- Water
- Iodine-free salt
- Other liquids
- Teaspoon

Teaching Tips

If ocean water is available, it may be used in place of the saltwater mixture. If needed, ocean water may be diluted with freshwater. Steps in the Exploration require two containers with three radish plants each. Steps in the Concept Application require similar containers of different kinds of plants.

Younger children will be able to do the activities if given help in matching plants and otherwise controlling variables.

Concept Invention

1. What changes do you notice from day to day?
2. Keep a record of what you observe.
3. Will the plants live if any salt is in the water?
4. How much can you use?

Concept Application

When watered with saltwater, land plants die or grow poorly. How will other plants be affected by saltwater? What other liquids can be used to water plants? How do you think the plants will be affected?

ENVIRONMENTAL CONDITIONS CONCEPTS

Plants grow and flourish only when the environment provides proper amounts of minerals, water, light, temperature, and—more indirectly—space. Because the classroom is an artificial habitat, or home, for plants, children will need to furnish the conditions the plants need for survival.

Growth Conditions

Children will find that soil-watering requirements for plants are like those for germinating seeds. Excess watering causes plants to die of oxygen deprivation or disease. Not enough watering usually results in droopy, malnourished plants. The absence of vital soil minerals and extremes in temperature also has a weakening, or even fatal, effect on plants.

Crowding of plants is harmful to growth largely because competition deprives individual plants of enough of what they need for good growth. Even the hardiest plants develop to less-than-normal size under crowded conditions.

Green plants need light energy, but not necessarily sunshine, to manufacture their own food. Electric lights may be substituted. Many commercial flower growers take advantage of this fact to regulate the growth rates or blooming times of their flowers to coincide with different holidays. Plants generally grow faster when exposed to light for increased time periods, but overexposure retards growth and delays normal blooming times.

Three Habitats

Even the casual observer can notice that different kinds of plants live in different habitats. Cacti are unlikely to be found in woodlands, and ferns do not ordinarily live in deserts. It may be difficult for us to take children directly to different habitats. It is possible, though, to bring several habitats to the classroom in miniature form.

The terrarium is a managed habitat for small land plants and, if desired, small animals likely to be found with the plants. Three basic kinds are the woodland, marsh, and desert terrariums. Almost any clear, large, glass or plastic container will do for the basic structure. An old aquarium tank is usually best, but a large jar turned on its side will also do. The container should be thoroughly cleaned before use. To make a woodland terrarium, cover the bottom of the container with a 2.5-centimeter (1-inch) layer of pebbles, sand, and bits of charcoal mixed together. This layer will allow drainage, and the charcoal will absorb gases and keep the soil from turning sour. Add to the bottom layer a second layer, about twice as thick, consisting of equal parts of rich garden soil and sand mixed together with a bit of charcoal. Sprinkle water on the ground until moist, but do not leave it wet, as molds may develop.

Dwarf ivy, ferns, liverworts, and lichens are ideal plants. Partridgeberry and mosses provide a nice ground cover, if desired.

After a week or so, the plants should take hold, and a few small animals may be introduced. A land snail, earthworms, a small land turtle, a salamander, or a small frog are suitable for a miniature woodland habitat. A little lettuce will feed the snail or turtle; earthworms get nutrition from the soil. Appropriate foods for frogs and salamanders include small live insects, such as mealworms, flies, sow bugs, and ants. A small, shallow dish pressed into the soil can serve as a water source.

Keep the terrarium covered and out of the sunlight to avoid the buildup of heat. A glass sheet loosely fitted to permit air circulation will help keep high humidity inside, reducing the need to water the soil. Here, too, water will evaporate from the soil, condense on the underside of the glass cover, and fall as "rain" in a miniature water cycle.

To make a marsh terrarium, the soil must be more acidic and damper than in the previous terrarium. Cover the container bottom with pebbles. Add to that a 6-centimeter (2.5-inch) layer of acid soil and peat moss mixed in about equal parts. These materials can be bought at a plant nursery. Suitable plants are the Venus flytrap, sundew, pitcher plant, mosses, and sedges. Appropriate animals include frogs, toads, small turtles, and salamanders. Again, press a small, shallow dish of water flush with the soil surface for the animals. Keep this terrarium covered and in a cool part of the room.

To make a desert terrarium, cover the container bottom with about 3 centimeters (1 inch) of coarse sand. Sprinkle this lightly with water and an equally thick layer of fine sand on top. Get a few small potted cacti or other desert succulents. Bury these so that the pot tops are flush with the sand surface. Sprinkle the plants lightly with water about once a week. Suitable animals are lizards, including the horned toad. Push a partly buried dish of water into the sand for their water source. Mealworms and live insects will do for their food. Place a stick and a few stones in the sand on which the animals may climb or rest. This terrarium may be left uncovered and in the sun.

Terrarium Investigations ———————

A woodland terrarium can be a good source of further investigation for your students. Many terrarium-related activities are suggested in the GEMS *Terrarium Habitats* book (Hosoume & Barber, 1994). For example, investigating and then later adding earthworms to the terrarium will help to introduce the concept of a *decomposer*. A decomposer feeds on and, in turn, breaks down dead plant and animal matter. This action is essential to the terrarium because it recycles the organic nutrients, making them available for the remaining plants to grow in the terrarium or any other ecosystem. You will want to have a hand lens available for the students to look at the earthworms, both inside and outside of the terrarium. It will be surprising to see how students will respond to the chance to investigate earthworms up close.

Another animal that you may introduce to a moist woodland terrarium is the pillbug, a small terrestrial crustacean in the isopod subgroup. Pillbugs breathe through gill-like structures and acquired their name because they roll up in the shape of a pill when agitated or in danger of dehydrating. Students can investigate the anatomy of pillbugs, where they hide out, where they walk, how they move, and other characteristics. A good source of activities for these investigations is *The Pillbug Project* (Burnett, 1992).

A desert terrarium provides a good environment to observe how plants and animals adapt to harsh conditions. Students can investigate where the animals go during the heat of the day or how they eat and drink in the desert environment. In addition to investigations of the cacti, lizards, and other plants and animals that you have in your desert terrarium, you may want to use the AIMS book *Exploring Environments* (Mercier & Hoover, 1999) to study other species of plants and animals that have adapted to desert conditions.

PLANT PART AND FUNCTION Inquiry

Plant Roots

Invitation

What do plant roots look like? What are some of the characteristics?

Exploration

1. Dig up some small weeds from both dry and wet places if possible. Try not to damage the roots. Dig deeply and loosen the soil around each weed. Then slip the shovel under it.
2. Soak the roots in water to remove the soil.
3. Carefully place each plant inside a folded sheet of newspaper. Observe the plant roots in class.

Concept Invention

1. Which plants have a single, large taproot with smaller branching roots?
2. Which plants have branching roots?
3. Can you see tiny root hairs with a hand lens?
4. On what parts of the roots do most appear?

> **Scaffolding for English Learners**
>
> Cultures vary on their use of plants for medicinal purposes. Some parents are very knowledgeable on the effects of various roots, stems, leaves, and flowers of plants. Invite select parents into the classroom to discuss plant parts and functions.

Concept Application

What other differences among the roots do you notice? What similarities have you observed? Where would you most likely find a lot of plants in the environment?

How Water Rises in Plant Stems

Invitation

We usually water the roots of a plant. How, then, does water in the roots get to the leaves? How can you use a celery stalk to study how water travels in plant stems?

Exploration

1. Put a few drops of red coloring into a glass of water. This will help you see how the water moves through the stalk.
2. Use a knife to cut off the lower end of the stalk at a slant.

MATERIALS

- Places where weeds grow
- Newspaper
- Small shovel
- Hand lens
- Pail of water

MATERIALS

- White celery stalk (fresh, with many leaves)
- Other celery stalks
- Red food coloring or water-soluble ink
- Other food colorings
- Two glasses of water
- Liquids other than water
- Knife
- Ruler
- White flower with long stem (such as a carnation)

3. Put the stalk into the colored water right away.
4. Leave the stalk where it will get bright light.

Concept Invention

1. Check the stalk every hour. How far does water rise in 1 hour? How far does water rise in more than 1 hour? Make a record of what you see each time.
2. After a few hours, or the next day, remove the stalk. Cut the stalk across near the bottom. What do you notice about this cutoff part?
3. Cut the stalk the long way. What do you notice? Can you find any long colored tubes?
4. Use other celery stalks for experiments. What can you do to change how fast the water rises? For example: Does the number of leaves on the stalk make a difference? Does the amount of light make a difference? Does wind make a difference? Will using liquids other than water make a difference? Have a race with someone to see whose celery stalk wins.
5. How can you prevent water from rising in the stalk if it stands in water?

Sometimes the water-conducting tubes in a celery stalk or flower stem become clogged. To open the tubes, make a fresh diagonal cut across the stalk or stem base. Immerse it quickly to keep air bubbles from forming in the tubes.

Concept Application

Stems conduct liquids from one part of a plant to another. Light, wind, and the condition and number of attached leaves affect the conduction rate. Get a white carnation with a long stem, or some other white flower. How can you make it a colored flower? Suppose you split the flower stem partway up and stand each half in a different color of water. What do you think will happen to the flower?

The Properties of Leaves

Invitation

Have you ever collected different kinds of leaves? There are more than 300,000 different kinds! How can you tell one leaf from another? What do you look for? How can you describe the properties of leaves?

Exploration

1. Size: How large is the leaf? Compare their sizes with the sizes of other things in the classroom.
2. Shape: What is the shape of the leaf? Some are oval; some are almost round. Others are shaped like a heart, a star, or another figure.
3. Color: What is the color of the leaf? Most fresh leaves are green, but some are darker or lighter than others. Some leaves have other colors.
4. Veins: Veins are the small tubes that carry liquids throughout the leaf. How do the veins look? In some leaves, they are side by side. In others, the veins look like many Vs in a row with a main center vein. Some leaves have several long veins with Vs. In a few leaves, veins cannot be seen.
5. Edges: What do the leaf edges look like? Some are smooth. Some edges look like saw teeth. Others are wavy. An example of each is shown in the drawings.
6. Feel: How does the leaf feel to you? Is it rough? Is it smooth? Is it waxy? Is it hairy? Is it slippery? Is it sticky?
7. Smell: What does the leaf smell like? Some leaves may not have a noticeable smell.

MATERIALS
• Six or more different kinds of leaves
• Partner
• Pencil and paper

Important: To further the processes of careful observation and communication, use only leaves that are roughly similar in this investigation. You want different kinds of leaves, but leaves that are grossly and obviously different from others will defeat the purpose of the investigation. It is best to do this investigation with fresh, unblemished leaves, such as weed leaves. Copy leaves on a copy machine and have children cut them out to use in class if needed.

Concept Invention

1. Play a game with a partner. Sort your leaves into two groups according to one property (shape, veins, etc.). Let your partner study your groups. Can your partner tell which property you used to sort your leaves? Try other properties. Take turns with your partner in this sorting game.
2. How well can you describe your leaves? Can you make a chart that someone else can use to identify them? Make a chart of all the properties you observe about your leaves. Label your leaves in A, B, C order. Try to remember which is which.

Leaf	Size	Shape	Color	Veins	Edges	Feel	Smell
A							
B							
C							
D							

3. Give your completed chart and your leaves to your partner. They should be out of order, so your partner must study your chart to tell which leaf is A, B, C, and so on. Which chart descriptions were helpful? Which confused your partner? How could you make these descriptions clearer?

Concept Application

Leaves vary in size, shape, color, texture, vein pattern, and other properties; no two leaves are identical. Describe how you think scientists may classify leaves.

How Leaves Lose Water ———

Invitation

A plant usually takes in more water than it can use. What do you think happens to the extra water? How can you find out if water is lost from leaves?

Exploration

1. Fill one glass almost full with water.
2. Use scissors to make a small hole in the center of a piece of cardboard.
3. Cover the glass with the cardboard.
4. Take a fresh leaf. Use a knife to cut off at a slant the tip of its stalk.
5. Quickly put the stalk into the hole in the cardboard.
6. Seal around the hole with petroleum jelly.
7. Put another glass upside down on top of the cardboard.
8. Leave the glass in sunlight for several hours.

MATERIALS
- Fresh leaf with stalk
- Water
- Four matched plastic water glasses
- Petroleum jelly
- Knife
- Paper towel
- Two cardboard squares
- Scissors

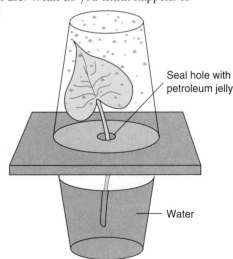

Seal hole with petroleum jelly

Water

Concept Invention

1. Do water drops form inside the top glass? Where do you think they originate?
2. Maybe water drops would appear in the glass without the leaf. How could you find out?
3. What affects how many water drops appear—leaf size? the kind of leaf? the freshness of the leaf? Does the amount of light affect how many drops appear? How can you find out?

Concept Application

Plants lose water through tiny openings in their leaves; the amount of water lost depends on several conditions. From which side does the leaf give off water—the top? the bottom? both sides? Describe how you could use petroleum jelly to find out. Try out your idea and keep a record of your results. Compare your record with the records of others.

Teaching Tips

Many tiny openings, called *stomata* (singular, *stoma*), are found in a green leaf, where gases enter and exit during the leaf's food-making process. Water, in the form of water vapor, also releases through the stomata. In this activity, the released water vapor is trapped by the plastic cover. It then condenses into visible water drops on the plastic. In land plants, stomata are usually found in the bottom leaf surface. Water loss varies with weather conditions and the size and kind of leaf.

Leaf Rubbings

Invitation

How can you make leaf rubbings?

Exploration

1. Place tissue paper over a fresh leaf.
2. Rub a crayon back and forth on it. A beautiful vein pattern will appear.
3. Try different colors and leaves.

Concept Invention

1. Play a matching game with someone.
2. Can your partner match each of your patterns with the right leaf? Can you match your partner's patterns and leaves?

Concept Application

What does your leaf rubbing tell you about your leaf? How can you use your patterns to make holiday or greeting cards?

MATERIALS

- Different leaves with thick veins
- Tissue paper
- Crayons
- Construction paper
- Partner

A Budding Activity

Invitation

How can you learn about plant buds?

Exploration

1. Find a low tree or bush with fallen leaves.
2. Look for small branches or twigs that have buds.
3. Observe just above where each leaf was attached to the twig or stem.
4. Cut off a few twigs that have buds. (Ask permission first.)

MATERIALS

- Small branches and twigs from plants
- Thin nail
- Pruning shears or knife
- Jar of water

The beginning of spring is a good time to collect twigs for budding.

Concept Invention

1. How are the buds arranged on the twigs?
2. What patterns, if any, do you notice?

Concept Application

Pick apart one or two buds with a thin nail. How can you describe the buds? Which of the remaining buds will grow leaves? To see, stick the twig into a jar of water. Change the water every 2 or 3 days and record your findings.

Inside a Flower ———

MATERIALS

- Several flowers
- Straight pin
- Newspaper
- Hand lens

Invitation

What is inside flowers?

Exploration

1. Bend back a few petals to see inside the flower, as shown.
2. Remove one of the stamens. Pick apart the anther, the part on the end. Can you see any dustlike pollen?
3. What color is it?
4. How does the pollen look under a hand lens?
5. Examine the pistil end.
6. What does it look like? Is it sticky when touched?
7. Carefully use a pin to slit open the pistil's thicker end.
8. Can you see any baby seeds inside? What do they look like?

 Florists are usually willing to donate to schools flowers that are unable to be sold.

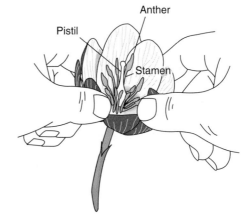

Concept Invention

1. Examine other flowers in the same way.
2. How are other flowers alike?
3. How are other flowers different?

Concept Application

Draw a diagram of the inside of one of the flowers you explored. How does it compare to the flower illustrated?

PLANT PART AND FUNCTION CONCEPTS

Children are usually surprised to learn that, besides fruits and vegetables, all the meat they eat has originally been derived from green plants. Flesh-eating animals depend on plant-eating animals. This is true in the ocean as well as on land. Everything alive basically depends on food synthesized from raw materials in the leaves of green plants.

A plant itself depends on the proper working of its several parts to produce this food. In this section, we examine how these parts work. Let's begin with plant roots.

Roots ————

The experience of weeding a garden makes us very conscious of one function of roots: They anchor plants. We also know that food storage in roots enables plants to survive when food making cannot occur. Another function of roots is the absorption of soil water.

Plants that are transplanted sometimes grow poorly for a while, or even die. This is usually the result of damage done to the tiny, very delicate root hairs that grow from the older root tissue (INQ Figure 7–5). It is the root hairs, not the older fibrous material, that absorbs all of the water for the plant.

A single plant may have billions of root hairs, enough to stretch hundreds of kilometers if laid end to end. If laid side by side in rows, they would take up the floor area of an average-size home. Root hairs are so small that they are able to grow in the tiny spaces between soil particles and make direct contact with water and air trapped within the soil. Root growth takes place largely at the tip of a root. A tough root cap protects the sensitive growing portion as it punches through the soil. Because soil is abrasive, the root cap tissue is continually worn off and replaced by new tissue.

Stems ————

Water absorbed by the roots goes into the stems, through which it is transported by narrow tubes to all parts of the plant. Dissolved minerals in the water are deposited within the cells of these parts. When water reaches the leaves, some of it evaporates into the air.

Exactly how does this continual movement of water happen in the plant? This process was a mystery until recent times. Modern molecular theory gives an answer. As you know, molecules that are alike have an attractive force that binds them together (cohesion). These molecules may also be attracted to unlike molecules (adhesion). The thin tubes that transport water in a plant run from root to stem to leaf. Adhesion of water molecules to the tube walls helps support the narrow water column. Cohesion causes the water molecules to stick together. As water molecules evaporate into the air, they "tug" slightly at the molecules below because of cohesive attraction. Because of cohesion, all the other molecules rise in a kind of chain reaction unless an air bubble separates some molecules to a distance beyond their effective cohesive attraction.

INQ Figure 7–5   A seedling has many root hairs.

Leaves ——————

A leaf seems thin and simple in structure from the outside. Yet, the intricate mechanisms within it, which produce the world's food supply, have never been fully duplicated by scientists.

Inside the leaf cells is a green-pigmented chemical, chlorophyll. Chlorophyll enables a leaf to chemically combine carbon dioxide from air with water to form a simple sugar. The energy needed to power this chemical synthesis in the leaf comes from sunlight, which is absorbed by the chlorophyll. *Photosynthesis,* as the process is called, literally means "to put together with light."

From the sugar that the leaves manufacture, the plant's cells make starch, which may be stored in all parts of the plant. With additional compounds received from the soil and through soil bacteria, plant cells can manufacture proteins and vitamins.

Carbon dioxide is taken up in photosynthesis, and oxygen is released as a waste product. But when a plant consumes the food stored in its cells, it takes up oxygen and gives off

INQ Figure 7–6   **Guard cells regulate the stomata in a leaf.**

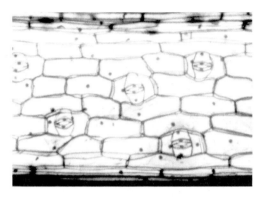

carbon dioxide as a waste product. Fortunately for us, much more oxygen is released to the air through photosynthesis than is used by plants in oxidizing their stored food. In fact, green plants are the chief source of the world's current oxygen supply.

How do these gases enter and leave the leaf? Thousands of microscopic openings, called *stomata,* may be found in a green leaf. In land plants, these are largely, but not exclusively, located in the leaf's underside. Each stoma is surrounded by two special cells that regulate the size of the opening (INQ Figure 7–6). As water moves into and out of the guard cells, their shape changes slightly, opening and closing the opening (stoma) between them. Water in the leaf evaporates into the air through the stomata, a process called *transpiration.* Regulation of these openings has great survival value. In dry spells and at night, the stomata stay closed, thereby preventing any appreciable loss of water.

Interestingly, most photosynthesis on the earth happens in the ocean within uncountable numbers of microscopic algae that float on and near the water's surface. We have not yet learned how to use the tremendous food supply this source potentially affords to a hungry world.

Flowers

Many people value flowers because of their beauty. But for flowering plants, flowers have a more vital function. They are the only means by which species can naturally survive. The flower is the reproductive system of a flowering plant. Its two principal organs are the *pistil,* which contains unfertilized egg cells, and *stamens,* which produce dustlike pollen cells (see INQ Figure 7–7).

When a pollen grain lands on the sticky end of a pistil, a tube begins to grow that "eats" its way down to the pistil base, or ovary. There, it joins onto an egg cell, or *ovule.* A sperm cell released from the pollen grain travels down the tube and unites with the ovule. Other ovules in the ovary may be fertilized by additional pollen in the same way.

The ovules, now fertilized, begin growing into seeds. The entire ovary begins to swell as a fleshy fruit begins to grow around the seeds. As the ovary becomes larger, parts of the flower drop off. Finally, a whole fruit forms. In the apple, for example, the ovary is enveloped by a stem part that swells up around it. The next time you eat an apple, look at the core end opposite the fruit stem. Quite likely, the tiny dried-up remains of the pistil and stamens will be visible.

It is best to examine single flowers, such as tulips and sweet peas, with children rather than composite flowers, such as daisies and sunflowers. The centers of composite types con-

INQ Figure 7–7   **Parts of a flower.**

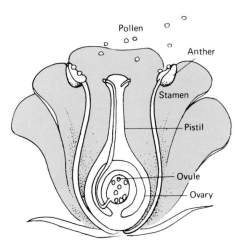

sist of many tiny flowers, each complete with pistil and stamens that are very minute. With these parts not readily observable, a description of the parts of a flower may be confusing to younger children.

Pollination ⸻

Self-pollination happens when pollen from a flower's own stamens fertilizes its ovules. *Cross-pollination* occurs when pollen from another flower performs this function. Pollen must be from the same type of flower, however, for fertilization to take place.

Much pollination depends on gravity, as when pollen simply falls from tall stamens onto a shorter pistil; or pollen may fall from a flower high up on a stem to one lower down. Insects are also primary distributors of pollen. As they sip nectar from flowers, pollen grains rub off onto their bodies. When the insects visit other flowers, these grains may become dislodged. It is interesting to note that brightly colored and fragrant flowers are visited by the most insects. Wind is also an important distributor of pollen. In spring, the air contains billions of pollen grains, bringing pollination to plants and hay fever to many people.

Life Cycles ⸻

Many garden flowers and vegetables grow from seeds, then blossom, produce seeds, and die in one growing season. These are known as *annuals*. Examples are petunias, zinnias, beans, and tomatoes. Those that live two seasons are *biennials*. Examples are hollyhocks, forget-me-nots, carrots, and turnips. Plants that live more than two growing seasons are *perennials*. Trees and most shrubs fit into this classification.

ADAPTATION AND SURVIVAL **Inquiry**

Plants and Gravity ———————

Invitation

How does gravity affect a growing plant?

Exploration

1. Line the inside of a glass with a wet, folded paper towel.
2. Crumple and stuff some towels inside the lined glass. These will hold the first towel in place.
3. Put a soaked radish seed between the glass and the first towel. The seed should be in the middle of the glass.
4. Pour about 2.5 centimeters (1 inch) of water into the glass.
5. Observe the seed in the glass every day.
6. Wait until the seed sprouts, grows leaves, and roots. Then pour out what water is left. Cover the glass with plastic wrap to keep the towel lining moist.
7. Tip over the glass onto one side.

Concept Invention

1. What happens to the upper stem of the plant over the next few days?
2. What happens to the roots?
3. What will happen if you tip over the glass onto the opposite side?

MATERIALS
• Paper towels
• Water
• Soaked radish seed
• Plastic drinking glass
• Plastic kitchen wrap

Scaffolding for English Learners

The English as a Second Language (ESL) Standards of the Teachers of English to Speakers of Other Languages (TESOL) organization recognize that upon entry to school, English learners must acquire an additional language and culture and learn the English language competencies that are characteristic of native English speakers. As you complete the geotropic and phototropic activities, think about how you are addressing these standards. We know that language acquisition takes place "during activities that are of a cognitive or intellectual nature where learners have opportunities to become skilled in using language for reasoning and mastery of challenging new information" (ESL Standards Introduction, TESOL, 1997). Are you providing students opportunities to use English as they interact with these activities? Do you provide feedback on their language use? (See the *http://www.tesol.org* weblink for the text of the standards.)

Concept Application

Predict what would happen if you again turned the glass after a few more days. Record your prediction. Try tipping the glass to check your prediction. Was your prediction correct?

Growing to the Light ———

Invitation

How can you make a plant grow toward the light?

Exploration

1. Plant one or two bean seeds in a small paper cup of soil. Water the plant as needed.
2. Wait until leaves appear.
3. Use a pencil to punch a hole into the side of the large paper cup.
4. Cover the small cup with the large cup. Uncover it briefly when you need to water the plant.
5. Leave the cups in a well-lighted place. Be sure the cup hole faces the light.

Concept Invention

1. What do you notice after a few days?
2. What do you think would happen if you turned the plant around? Try it. (Be sure the cup hole faces the light.)

Concept Application

Can you grow a plant in total darkness? Record your prediction. Try to grow a plant in a dark closet. Describe what happens.

MATERIALS
• Small and large paper cups
• Bean seeds
• Soil
• Water
• Pencil

ADAPTATION AND SURVIVAL CONCEPTS

Adaptation ———

If you were asked to invent a plant, what adaptive features would you want it to have for survival value? Whatever your design, it would be wise to have your plant regulate itself to some extent according to its needs.

Assume that it has the same needs as other plants. Because it requires water, and because water soaks down into the soil, you would want your plant's roots to grow downward. But what if the soil below the roots contained no water? You would want your plant to have roots that could overcome the pull of gravity and grow toward a water source, even if the source were to one side or above the roots.

Because your plant would need light, you would want the stem to have the ability to grow toward a light source. At the same time, it would be desirable to design the leaf stalk to give the leaf maximum exposure to sunlight. An efficient stalk should be able to grow longer if another leaf blocks its light. The stalk might also turn its leaf perpendicular to the sun's rays as the sun appears at different positions in the sky. Most green plants respond to gravity, water, light, and touch. These responses to environmental stimuli are called plant *tropisms*. Let's see why they happen.

Tropisms ———

INQ Figure 7–8 shows a radish seedling growing on wet blotting paper inside a glass. The glass has been placed on its side for 24 hours. Notice that the seedling shoot, or stem, is beginning to curve upward although the root is starting to grow downward. Both reactions are responses to gravity.

INQ Figure 7–8   Seedling shoots curve upward and roots grown downward almost as soon as sprouting occurs.

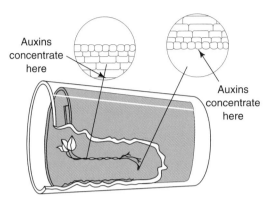

Auxins concentrate here

Auxins concentrate here

Why the opposite directions? Check the magnified sections of the seedling. Gravity concentrates plant hormones (auxins) all along the bottom cells from the beginning of the stem to the root tip. The cells along the bottom of the stem are stimulated by the hormones to grow faster than cells above. Growth of these cells is fastest by the stem tip (see INQ figure 7-8, left inset). As these bottom cells elongate, the stem begins to curve upward. Root cells, however, are much more sensitive than stem cells. So, the concentration of hormones along the bottom root cells has the opposite effect; it inhibits cell growth. Top cells are least affected and elongate faster, so the root tip begins to curve downward. Cell growth is fastest by the tip.

Geotropism, or the plant's response to gravity, is only one of many reactions of a plant to its environment. Hydrotropism is the plant's response to water. Generally it is the increased growth of roots in soil as a response to increased moisture. Scientists have observed that roots that happen to grow into an area of moist soil will grow more and branch more than roots that happen to grow into a dry area. Chemotropism, or a plant's ability to grow roots toward needed nutrients in the environment, is a subject of controversy in the scientific community.

Phototropism can be defined as a plant's movement to (positive tropism) or away from (negative tropism) a light source. When the light source is sunlight, the plant's response is called heliotropism. Plants that require sunlight will turn leaves around to grow toward the light. As with the case of geotropism, this response is driven by the hormone auxin. On the side of a plant facing the light, the auxin is inactivated and only the side away from the light elongates and continues to grow. The result is the plant tends to bend toward the light. Alternatively, shade plants will use this mechanism to turn their leaves away from bright light.

Charles Darwin (1989) is credited with demonstrating that the growing tips of plants bend toward a light source. Related to phototropism, scientists have also observed that vine tips will move slowly along the ground toward vertical objects by responding to the stimulus of the darkest sector of the nearby horizon. This response is called skototropism, or growing toward darkness. This response is widely used in vines of the tropical rain forests. Vines must grow away from the dim light and into darkness until they reach a tree trunk where they can grow upward to reach full sunlight.

Thigmotropism is another tropism in which contact with a solid or a rigid surface is the orienting factor for the plant. Haptotropism is a response of an organism to stimulation by touch or contact. Since vines depend on other plants or surfaces for support, there is a tendency of the vine to respond to touch or contact with such supports. In this case, vines such as the sweet pea or Boston ivy will attach specialized tips of leaves known as *tendrils* to continue their growth. Another example of the response to touch is found in the sticky hairs of a sundew plant, which bend around an insect when it comes into contact with them.

Tropistic responses seem to be the result of plant hormones that concentrate in various parts of the plant. As we have seen, this difference causes some cells to grow faster than others. Such responses can happen only in growing tissue.

Survival and Environment

The survival of plant (and animal) species is more than a matter of properties the organism inherits by chance. The environment also plays a part because it is continually changing.

For example, a long dry spell will favor plants with small, bad-tasting leaves and deep roots. Why? Large-leafed plants will lose too much water to survive. Shallow-rooted plants will not be able to tap moisture deep down. Plants with tasty leaves will be eaten first by hungry, thirsty animals.

MOLDS AND FUNGI Inquiry

How Molds Grow

Invitation

On what things have you seen molds? How did the molds look? How can you make a mold garden?

Exploration

1. Fill a large glass jar about one-third full with sand.
2. Put the jar down on its side. Shake the jar so that the sand settles evenly.
3. Place a flattened piece of clay under the jar to keep it from rolling.
4. Use a spoon to sprinkle some water on the sand to make it damp.
5. Put different objects that might mold on the sand.
6. Screw the lid on the jar. Do not remove it.
7. Leave the jar where you can observe it each day.

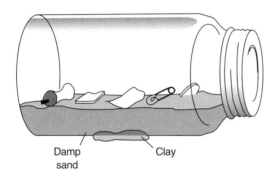

Damp sand   Clay

Concept Invention

1. On which objects do you think molds will grow?
2. Which objects will not mold?
3. Which do you think will be covered by molds first?
4. Which do you think will be covered by molds last? Keep a record of your results.

Concept Application

Some molds grow well under dark, moist, and warm conditions. Try some experiments. How can you get a fresh piece of bread to mold? Keep the bread inside a baby food jar (or plastic bag). Keep the lid on each jar after starting each experiment. Is water needed for molds to grow on bread? If so, how much water is needed? Fresh bread may contain some moisture. How can you start with dry bread? Will bread molds grow better in the dark or the light? How about dim light? How can you prevent mold from growing on a piece of bread? What other experiments would you like to try?

Teaching Tips

For bread experiments, try to get the white home-baked kind or store bread without preservatives. Commercial bread often contains a mold-inhibiting chemical called sodium propionate.

Caution: The molds or other organisms in this investigation are typically harmless. Play it safe, however, by having children (a) keep all moldy materials covered, (b) wash their hands if they touch a mold, (c) avoid sniffing molds, (d) avoid growing molds in soil samples, and (e) dispose of all used, still-closed containers in a tightly sealed bag.

MOLDS AND FUNGI CONCEPTS

In recent years, growing molds has become popular in elementary science programs. It offers students many chances to experiment with variables at several levels.

Molds are a subgroup of a broader group of organisms called *fungi*. Some common examples of other fungi are mushrooms, mildews, puffballs, and yeasts. Molds will grow on a wide variety of animal and plant materials and some synthetic materials.

Tiny, seedlike spores from molds are found in the air almost anywhere. When the spores settle on a substance, they may grow. Molds get the nutrients they need to live from the materials on which they grow. Unlike the green plants, molds and other fungi cannot manufacture their own food.

Molds grow under a wide variety of conditions. But those found commonly in classrooms are most likely to thrive when their environment is dark, moist, and warm.

References

American Association for the Advancement of Science (AAAS). (1993). *Benchmarks for science literacy*. New York: Oxford University Press.

Burnett, R. (1992). *The pillbug project: A guide to investigation*. Arlington, VA: National Science Teachers Association.

Darwin, C. (1989). *The power of movement in plants* (Reprint ed.). New York: New York University Press.

Hosoume, K., & Barber, J. (1994). *Terrarium habitats*. Berkeley, CA: Great Explorations in Math and Science.

Jefferis, D. (1999). *Cloning: Frontiers of genetic engineering*. New York: Crabtree.

Mastropieri, M., & Scruggs, T. E. (2004). *The inclusive classroom: Strategies for effective instruction* (4th ed.). Upper Saddle River, NJ: Merrill/Prentice Hall.

Mercier, S., & Hoover, E. (1999). *Exploring environments*. Fresno, CA: AIMS Educational Foundation.

National Research Council (NRC). (1996). *National science education standards*. Washington, DC: National Academy Press.

Turnbull, R., Turnbull, A., Shank, M., & Smith, S. J. (2004). *Exceptional lives: Special education in today's schools* (4th ed.). Upper Saddle River, NJ: Merrill/Prentice Hall.

Selected Trade Books: Plant Life

For Younger Children

Brown, R. (2001). *Ten seeds*. New York: Knopf/Random House Children's Books.

Busch, P. (1979). *Cactus in the desert*. New York: Thomas Y. Crowell.

Challand, H. (1986). *Plants without seeds*. Danbury, CT: Childrens Press.

Cole, J. (1995). *The magic school bus meets the rot squad: A book about decomposition*. New York: Scholastic.

Cole, J. (1995). *The magic school bus plants seeds: A book about how living things grow*. New York: Scholastic.

Cole, J. (1996). *The magic school bus gets eaten: A book about food chains*. New York: Scholastic.

Gibbins, G. (1991). *From seed to plant*. New York: Holiday House.

Gibbins, G. (1998). *Marshes and swamps*. New York: Holiday House.

Goodman, S. E. (2001). *Seeds, stems, and stamens: The ways plants fit into their world*. Brookfield, CT: Millbrook Press.

Heller, R. (1999). *The reasons for a flower*. Ossining, NY: Paper Star.

Kirkpatrick, R. K. (1985). *Look at seeds and weeds*. Austin, TX: Raintree.

Kuchalla, S. (1982). *All about seeds*. New York: Troll Associates.

Lauber, P. (1981). *Seeds: Pop, stick, glide*. New York: Crown.

Miner, O. I. (1981). *Plants we know*. Danbury, CT: Childrens Press.

Moncure, J. B. (1990). *What plants need*. Plymouth, MN: Child's World.

Moss, M. (2000). *This is the tree*. Lajolla, CA: Kane/Miller Book Publishers.

Orr, R. (1995). *Nature cross-sections*. New York: Dorling Kindersley.

Penn, L. (1986). *Wild plants and animals*. Torrance, CA: Good Apple.

Pfeffer, W. (1997). *A log's life*. New York: Simon & Schuster.

Posada, M. (2000). *Dandelions: Stars in the grass*. Minneapolis, MN: Carolrhoda Books/Lerner.

Schories, P. (1996). *Over under in the garden: An alphabet book*. New York: Farrar, Straus & Giroux.

Selsam, M. E., & Hunt, J. (1977). *A first look at flowers*. New York: Walker.

Silverstein, S. (1964). *The giving tree*. New York: Harper & Row.

Taylor, B. (1991). *Growing plants*. Danbury, CT: Watts.

Tresselt, A. (1992). *The gift of a tree*. New York: Lothrop, Lee & Shepard Books.

Webster, V. (1982). *Plant experiments*. Danbury, CT: Childrens Press.

For Older Children

Bates, J. (1991). *Seeds to plants: Projects with botany*. Danbury, CT: Watts.

Cochrane, J. (1987). *Plant ecology*. Danbury, CT: Watts.

Coldrey, J. (1987). *Discovering flowering plants*. Danbury, CT: Watts.

Conway, L. (1980). *Plants*. Torrance, CA: Good Apple.

Conway, L. (1986). *Plants and animals in nature*. Torrance, CA: Good Apple.

Gallant, R. A. (1991). *Earth's vanishing forests*. New York: Macmillan.

Hogner, D. C. (1977). *Endangered plants*. New York: Thomas Y. Crowell.

Holley, B. (1986). *Plants and flowers*. Cincinnati: Penworthy.

Lambert, M. (1983). *Plant life*. Danbury, CT: Watts.

Leutscher, A. (1984). *Flowering plants*. Danbury, CT: Watts.

Marcus, E. (1984). *Amazing world of plants*. New York: Troll Associates.

Patent, D. H. (2003). *Plants on the trail with Lewis and Clark*. New York: Clarion Books.

Penn, L. (1987). *Plant ecology*. Danbury, CT: Watts.

Pratt, K. (1992). *A walk in the rainforest*. Nevada City, CA: Dawn.

Ryden, H. (2001). *Wildflowers around the year*. New York: Clarion Books.

Sabin, L. (1985). *Plants, seeds, and flowers*. New York: Troll Associates.

Taylor, K., & Burton, J. (1993). *Forest life*. New York: Dorling Kindersley.

Resource Books

American Forest Foundation, & Western Regional Environmental Education Council. (1995). *Project learning tree*. Washington, DC: Author.

Butzow, C. M., & Butzow, J. W. (1989). *Science through children's literature: An integrated approach*. Englewood, CO: Teacher Ideas Press. (tree topics on pp. 49–54; seed topics on pp. 55–60)

Butzow, C., & Butzow, J. (1999). *Exploring the environment through children's literature: An integrated approach (through children's literature)*. Englewood, CO: Teacher Ideas Press. (hands-on environment activities)

Echols, J. C., & Kopp, J. (1993). *Tree homes*. Berkeley, CA: Great Explorations in Math and Science. (appreciation for trees)

Fredericks, A. D., Meinbach, A. M., & Rothlein, L. (1993). *Thematic units: An integrated approach to teaching science and social studies*. New York: HarperCollins. (plant topics on pp. 123–131)

Hillen, J., & Hoover, E. (Eds.). (1990). *Primarily plants*. Fresno, CA: AIMS Education Foundation.

LeCroy, B., & Holder, B. (1994). *Bookwebs: A brainstorm of ideas for the primary classroom*. Englewood, CO: Teacher Ideas Press. (seed activity on p. 69)

Malnor, B., & Malnor, C. (1998). *A teacher's guide to a walk in the rainforest*. Nevada City, CA: Dawn.

Mercier, S., Richmond, B., Mitchell, D., Hoover, E., & Wagner, B. V. (1999). *Exploring environments*. Fresno, CA: AIMS Education Foundation. (plant interactions with the environment)

Shaw, D. G., & Dybdahl, C. S. (1996). *Integrating science and language arts. A sourcebook for K–6 teachers*. Boston: Allyn & Bacon. (plant topics on pp. 60–62)

Wilson, J., Cordel, B., & Hillen, J. (Eds.). (1995). *Magnificent microworld adventures*. Fresno, CA: AIMS Education Foundation.

Winkleman, G., & Hillen, J. (Eds.). (1995). *The budding botanist*. Fresno, CA: AIMS Education Foundation.

ANIMAL LIFE

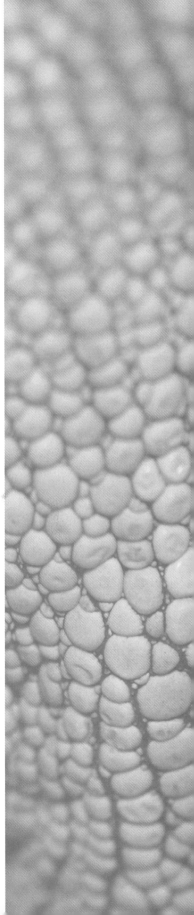

Can a gnat have anything in common with an elephant? Despite their enormous diversity, all animals share certain common needs and physical properties. By carefully observing how animals are formed, we can place them into groups with common properties. These groups enable us to learn many of the interesting adaptations of animals without having to study each group member.

This section discusses animals with backbones, animals without backbones, and interactions of living things with each other and their environment, or ecology. But right now, let's briefly consider some ways to classify animals.

Benchmarks and Standards

Elementary students place animals high on their list of topics they are most curious about and want to explore further. Animals provide basic understandings of interrelationships, habitats, cycles, structures, and functions. Many concepts are related to animals, the following of which are provided as examples of basic benchmarks and standards:

Sample Benchmarks (AAAS, 1993)

- A lot can be learned about plants and animals by observing them closely, but care must be taken to know the needs of living things and how to provide for them in the classroom. (By Grades K–2, p. 15)
- All living things are composed of cells, from just one to many millions, whose details usually are visible only through a microscope. Different body tissues and organs are made up of different kinds of cells. (By Grades 6–8, p. 112)

Sample Standards (NRC, 1996)

- Organisms have basic needs. For example, animals need air, water, and food. (By Grades K–4, p. 129)
- Millions of species of animals, plants, and microorganisms are alive today. (By Grades 5–8, p. 158)

CLASSIFICATION OF ANIMALS **Inquiry**

Animal Classification ————

MATERIALS
• Computer with Internet access and a printer • Scissors • Tape • Newsprint end rolls (available from newspaper publishers)

Invitation

How can you classify animals?

Exploration

1. Search the Internet for pictures of animals. Print out pictures of various animals.
2. Cut out the pictures and arrange them on the newsprint according to your own classification system.
3. Compare your classification system with those of other students.

Adapting for Students with Exceptionalities

Using the Internet may be difficult for students with visual impairments. Allow classmates to print large pictures for students with visual impairments to use with this activity. (See Turnbull, Turnbull, Shank, & Smith, 2004, for a discussion on adapting instruction for students who have visual difficulties.)

Teaching Tips | Older children can look up scientific classifications of the animals and compare systems after they have developed their own classification system. Pictures from magazines may also be substituted for Internet pictures. As an extension activity, children can search the Internet for sites that show live animals, such as viewable Ant Farms®.

Concept Invention

1. How are your systems the same?
2. How are your systems different?

Concept Application

How do you think your system would compare with the scientific system?

CLASSIFICATION OF ANIMALS CONCEPTS

Of some 1,250,000 different forms of living things, animals make up almost 1,000,000. They run, walk, crawl, fly, slither, and swim. They range in size from microscopic organisms to the blue whale, which may be up to about 30 meters (100 feet) long. Their colors embrace all shades of the spectrum. The diversity of animals is truly amazing.

How do scientists keep track of them? A system developed by the Swedish naturalist Carolus Linnaeus (1707–1778) provided the foundation for modern classification. Its basis is the physical structure of the living thing. His six main categories range from the general to the particular description of group properties. For example, a dog is classified in INQ Table 8–1.

Most children think of living things as either animals or plants. Scientists, however, classify living things into five kingdoms:

- *Animalia:* multicellular animals that are heterotrophic (cannot make their own food), are eukaryotic (have a membrane-bound nucleus), and reproduce sexually.
- *Plantae:* multicellular plants that are generally autotrophic (make their own food through photosynthesis), are eukaryotic, and reproduce sexually.

Table 8–1

Classification of the Common Dog

Category	Name	General Meaning of Each Category
Kingdom	Animalia	The subject belongs to the animal, not any other, kingdom.
Phylum	Chordata	It has a backbone or a notochord.
Class	Mammalia	It is a mammal.
Order	Carnivora	It eats meat.
Family	Canidae	It belongs to a group with doglike characteristics.
Genus	Canis	It is a coyote, wolf, or dog.
Species	familiaris	It is a common dog.

- *Protista:* single-celled or multicelled plantlike and animal-like organisms that are autotrophic or heterotrophic, are eukaryotic, and reproduce either sexually or asexually (no male and female).
- *Monera:* single-celled bacteria that are autotrophic or heterotrophic, are prokaryotic (no membrane-bound nucleus), and reproduce asexually (some also reproduce sexually).
- *Fungi:* single-celled or multicelled organisms that are eukaryotic, are heterotrophic, and generally reproduce asexually (some also reproduce sexually through conjugation).

Such a classification system has important advantages to biologists. It is possible to pinpoint most living things and to note relationships that otherwise might be easy to miss. Scientists throughout the world use this system.

For elementary school science, however, you will want to work with a simpler classification scheme. The following one should be useful and will fit into the more formal structure a child will develop later in high school and college. Although we do not study all of the subgroups described, the overall classification scheme should be helpful to you.

We can divide the entire animal kingdom into two huge groups, each with a manageably small number of subgroups.

Animals with Backbones (Vertebrates)

Mammals (e.g., human, dog)

Birds (e.g., sparrow, penguin)

Reptiles (e.g., turtle, lizard)

Amphibians (e.g., frog, toad)

Fishes (e.g., carp, bass)

Animals without Backbones (Invertebrates)

Echinoderms Animals with spiny skins (e.g., sand dollar, starfish)

Arthropods Animals with jointed legs: insects (e.g., fly, moth); arachnids (e.g., spider, scorpion); crustaceans (e.g., crab, lobster); myriapods (e.g., millipede, centipede)

Mollusks Animals with soft bodies (e.g., clam, snail)

Worms (e.g., flatworm, segmented worm, ribbon worm, round worm)

Corals and relatives (e.g., sea anemone, coral)

Sponges (The natural sponges we use are the fibrous skeletons of these animals.)

When young children use the term *animal*, they are inclined to mean mammal or, at best, another animal with a backbone. Yet, the five classes of vertebrates—mammals, birds, reptiles, amphibians, and fishes—make up a scant 5% of the known animal species. Animals without backbones make up the rest. Insects, which make up 70% of all animals, represent by far the largest class of invertebrates—more than 800,000 species. (A *species* is a group in which the members can only reproduce among themselves.)

Animal Classification Extensions ────────

One way to extend classification activities is to challenge your students to see how male, female, juvenile, or animal groups are classified. For example, when classifying a gerbil, the baby is a pup, the male is a buck, the female is a doe, and the family is called a horde. Peafowl include peacocks, peahens, and peachicks with the family name of muster, ostentation, or pride. Crocodiles are bulls, cows, and crocklets and the families are basks or congregations. Sharks are bulls, females, pups, or cubs and the families are schools or shivers (University of Alberta, 2001).

Classifying male, female, juveniles, or groups of animals can be a fun way to lead into other activities such as a "Find It" activity (Carratello & Carratello, 1994). This activity involves finding animals in the schoolyard and then completing a chart with the name and type of animal, a hand-drawn picture of the animal, and descriptive words related to the animal. Once charts are complete, topics such as *diversity* and *animal traits* can be discussed. Later, as students discuss what an animal is, they will better understand how diverse the animal kingdom is.

ANIMALS WITH BACKBONES **Inquiry**

Bones

Invitation

What bones make up a chicken skeleton?

Exploration

1. See the drawing of a chicken skeleton. Notice the different kinds of bones for each of its parts.
2. Examine the chicken bones brought from home.
3. Can you find the leg bones?
4. Which are the large back and breast bones?
5. Which are the rib bones?
6. Which are the wing bones?
7. What other bones can you find? Can you tell what they are?

The head bones and feet are usually not provided with store-bought chickens.

Concept Invention

1. Why do the bones differ in structure?
2. Do you think turkey bones are similar?

Concept Application

Without referring to the drawing, sketch how the bones you have may be put together. Which bones seem to be missing?

Tadpoles

Invitation

How can you raise and observe tadpoles?

It is likely that the school semester will end before the tadpoles grow into adult frogs or toads. If this is the case, you may release them where the eggs were found or with the parents' permission, allow children to take them home.

Exploration

1. Put the frog or toad eggs and pond water into the tank. The water should have a few plants and algae for the tadpoles to eat.
2. Place a large, sloping rock into the tank. It should rise out of the water at one end. When the tadpoles grow legs, they can crawl onto the rock.
3. When the tadpoles grow legs, sprinkle some dry fish food into the tank twice a week.
4. Every 2 weeks, replace the old pond water with fresh pond water. Use a small dip net to transfer the tadpoles.
5. Use a hand lens to observe the tadpoles.

Concept Invention

When can you see the following things happening?

- Tiny tadpoles with gills hatching from the eggs
- Tiny tadpoles sticking closely to the water plants
- Bodies and tails getting longer
- Hind legs starting to grow
- Gills disappearing
- Front legs developing
- Tails shrinking

Concept Application

What else can you notice about tadpoles?

How to Train Goldfish ─────────

MATERIALS

- Two goldfish in tank
- Fish food
- Flashlight
- Guppies

Invitation

Have you trained a dog or other pet to do something? Many animals can learn to respond to some signal. You can even train goldfish. How can you get goldfish to respond to the light from a flashlight?

Exploration

1. Shine the flashlight into a corner of the tank. The goldfish should not swim toward the light.
2. Each day, sprinkle a little food near the same corner of the tank. At the same time, shine the flashlight on the food, as illustrated. Watch the fish swim toward the lighted food.
3. Do this for at least 4 days in a row.
4. At the next feeding time, just shine the light.

Concept Invention

1. How do the fish act now when only the light, but no food, is used?
2. How many times will the fish respond if only the light is used? (Do not skip more than 2 feeding days.)
3. How can you train the goldfish to respond to an unlit flashlight?
4. How can you train the goldfish to respond to a sound?
5. What differences, if any, do you notice in the behavior of the two goldfish?
6. How will other fish, such as guppies, respond to training?

 Teaching Tips If the fish do not respond, try extending the training period. Also, make sure the fish are fed only sparingly. Should more fish and containers be available (plastic containers can be used), small groups can pursue different discovery problems.

Children enjoy telling others about training animals. Reporting their attempts and successes allows many chances for verbal and written language development (science journals).

Adapting for Students with Exceptionalities

Make sure to avoid overfeeding. Set up a detailed schedule with students' names, amounts of food, and how the water is to be placed for the animal to eat. When using animals in the classroom, be sure to follow school rules and restrictions. (See Mastropieri & Scruggs, 2004, for a discussion on adapting activities related to animals in the chapter on science and social studies.)

Concept Application

Animals can be conditioned to respond to signals. Are some fish "smarter" (more quickly trained) than others? How could you find out?

Changing Temperatures ———————

Invitation

How do temperature changes affect a fish?

Exploration

1. Notice how the fish's gills open and close. This is called a *gill beat*.
2. How many gill beats does it make in 1 minute? Take the water temperature and record it.
3. Slowly pour ice water into the bowl. Do not lower the temperature more than about 10°C (15°F) below the starting temperature. Observe the gill beats again.
4. How many beats does the fish make in 1 minute now?
5. Wait long enough for the water temperature to rise again to the first reading.

Concept Invention

About how many gill beats per minute do you think the fish will make? Watch and find out.

Concept Application

What do you think happens if fish go from cool winter waters to hot waters that are discharged from industrial sources?

MATERIALS

- Goldfish in small bowl of water
- Pitcher of ice water
- Watch with second hand
- Thermometer

Making Casts of Animal Tracks ———————

Invitation

When animals walk in mud or on damp ground, they leave tracks. By examining these tracks closely, we may be able to tell many things about an animal. A large, heavy animal may leave deep, large tracks. A track of a running animal may be pushed up a little at one end. Each kind of animal leaves a different track. Animal tracks are interesting to study and keep, but rain can wash them away. There is a way you can save them. You can make a cast of an animal track. How can you make a cast of an animal track?

Exploration

1. Have someone in your class make a shoe print in the damp ground. (It will be more fun if you don't know who that person is.)
2. Make a low wall around the shoe track with cardboard. Tape it closed.
3. Spread petroleum jelly thinly on the inside surface of the wall. This will keep the plaster from sticking to it.
4. Mix plaster of paris and water in a bowl. Go easy on the water. Make the mixture like a thick milkshake. Pour about 2.5 centimeters (1 inch) of the mixture into the wall, as illustrated.
5. Wait about 1 hour for it to harden. Remove the cast from the shoe print and take off the cardboard. Notice that the cast is an opposite, or raised model, of the shoe print. To make a model that looks like the real shoe print, you must make a second cast, or mold.

MATERIALS

- Place with damp dirt
- Paper towel
- Thin cardboard
- Scissors
- Old plastic bowl
- Sticky tape
- Plaster of paris
- Newspaper
- Stick for mixing
- Water
- Petroleum jelly
- Flat-bladed, dull knife

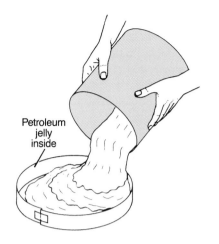

Petroleum
jelly
inside

Teaching Tips

Check the local school policy about the use of plaster of paris. Some districts or schools discourage or ban its use.

If plaster is in short supply, you might have students begin with a small animal track rather than a human footprint. Caution children not to spill plaster on their clothing. Small spills, however, may be brushed off after drying. Almost any large discardable container will serve to mix the plaster and water. A flexible plastic container can be bent to pour the mixture more neatly into a narrow form.

6. Spread petroleum jelly thinly over the top of the first cast. Place it on newspaper. Put a cardboard wall, also coated thinly on the inside with petroleum jelly, around the cast. Tape it closed.
7. Pour about 2.5 centimeters (1 inch) of plaster mix into the wall. Wait again 1 hour for it to set.
8. Remove the wall. Carefully slip a knife between the two casts to separate them. Clean off the petroleum jelly with a paper towel. The second cast should now look like the original shoe print.

Concept Invention

1. What can you tell from the cast of the shoe print?
2. Do you think a girl or a boy made the print?
3. How large or heavy might the person be?
4. What kind of shoe was worn?
5. Does anyone's shoe fit the mold?

Concept Application

We can infer some things about an animal from its tracks. Make a cast of a track from an animal that does not wear shoes. What bird or other animal do you think it might be? How large or heavy might it be? Was it walking or running? Where can you find the most animal tracks around your school? Where can you find the most animal tracks around your home? What kind of collection of animal track casts can you make?

ANIMALS WITH BACKBONES CONCEPTS

Despite their fewer numbers, the five classes of vertebrates represent the highest forms of life on this planet. We begin here with the most advanced form, mammals.

Mammals

Look around long enough, and you will find animals everywhere: below the ground (e.g., mole, gopher, woodchuck); on the ground (e.g., human, giraffe, elephant); in trees (e.g., monkey, sloth, tree squirrel); in the air (e.g., bat); and in the water (e.g., whale, seal, dolphin). What can such a diverse collection of creatures have in common? All of them are *mammals*; that is, all have some fur or hair, and all have milk glands. To be sure, you will not find much hair on a whale, only a few bristles on the snout; and sometimes fur or hair is greatly modified, as with the porcupine's quills. But look closely enough, and if it is a mammal, it has hair.

Both male and female mammals have *mammary*, or milk, *glands*. (You can see how the term *mammals* originated.) Ordinarily, of course, only the female produces the milk used in suckling the young.

Another distinction of mammals is their intelligence, the highest of all animal groups. But other unique properties are few and subtle.

Internal Development

Mammals are born wholly formed, and then continue to grow to the adult stage of the life cycle. The embryo develops within the mother from a tiny egg fertilized by a sperm cell from a male of the same species.

During its development, the embryo is attached to the mother by a placenta, or membranous tissue. Water, oxygen, and food pass from mother to embryo through this tissue. In turn, liquefied waste materials flow the other way. These are absorbed into the mother's bloodstream, sent to the kidneys, and eliminated. The navel pit in the abdomen of humans, or "belly button," is a reminder of this early state of our development. The two known exceptions to this developmental pattern are the spiny anteater and duck-billed platypus, both of Australia. Each lays eggs. The hatched young, though, are cared for and suckled by the mother just like other mammals.

Warm-Blooded

Mammals are warm-blooded and have efficient hearts with four definite chambers. Their blood temperatures stay at relatively the same level, whether the air warms or cools. Animals of lesser complexity are cold-blooded; that is, their blood temperature changes as their environmental temperature changes.

It is both an advantage and a disadvantage to be warm-blooded. Vigorous activity is possible within most air temperature ranges. But the body heat of mammals must be conserved or else death occurs.

In cold climates, thick blubber or fur performs this function, as do hibernation and, in some cases, migration. In warm climates, humans perspire. Some animals *estivate*, or become relatively inactive for a period in whatever suitably cool refuge can be found.

Some cold-blooded animals can withstand great cold or heat, but most depend on a narrow temperature range for normal activity or survival. We go into more detail later with several specific animals.

Although the terms are still relative, it is more accurate to say "constant-temperatured" and "variable-temperatured" rather than "warm-blooded" and "cold-blooded" when we refer to animals. In hot weather, for example, a cold-blooded animal might have a higher body temperature than a warm-blooded one.

Teeth

The teeth of mammals are particularly interesting to observe because they seem adapted to specific uses. We can see the four main kinds of teeth by examining our own in a mirror. In front are the chisel-like *incisors*. On both sides of these teeth are the conelike *canines*. Farther back are the *front molars*, and last, the *back molars*. Now note how these teeth are used by several kinds of mammals.

Prominent, sharp incisors are characteristic of gnawing mammals such as rats, mice, gerbils, guinea pigs, hamsters, muskrats, beavers, and rabbits. The incisors of these rodents grow continuously at the root and are worn down at the opposite end by gnawing. When such an animal is prevented from gnawing, its incisors may grow so long that the animal cannot close its mouth, and so starves to death.

The flesh eaters have small incisors and prominent canines, sometimes called "fangs." Their molars have curved, sharp edges. The canines are useful for tearing meat. The molars are suited for chopping it into parts small enough to swallow.

Plant eaters have wide, closely spaced incisors and large, flat-surfaced molars. Canines do not appear. The incisors work well in clipping off grasses and plant stems. The molars grind this material before it is swallowed.

You and I are omnivores; in other words, we are capable of eating both plants and animals. Human teeth include all four types.

Classroom Mammals

The classroom is likely to be a restrictive place for mammals, so it is wise to select those that can be reasonably taken care of and live well in that type of environment. It is also important to get an animal that can be used to fulfill some lasting educational purposes. (Most school districts have policies on what animals, if any, are permitted in classrooms.)

Experienced teachers often recommend use of white rats and gerbils (INQ Figure 8–1) over common classroom animals such as white mice, hamsters, and guinea pigs. Although

INQ Figure 8–1 **A gerbil.**

INQ Figure 8–2   **A commercially produced cage such as this is well suited for housing white rats.**

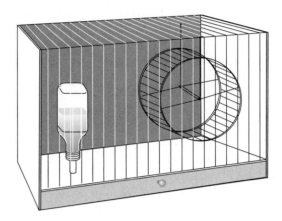

simple cages for rodents can be homemade from strong screening material, a commercial cage is usually more secure and better suited to the animals' needs. A commercial cage, like that shown in INQ Figure 8–2, should serve well and last indefinitely.

Following are some suggestions for housing and caring for a female and male white rat or gerbil.

Cage

Use a commercially produced cage with exercise wheel and inverted water bottle as recommended. Cover the floor with a four-page thickness of newspaper. Scatter a generous covering of sawdust, wood shavings, peat moss, or shredded newspaper over the paper. Remove the floor covering and replace with fresh materials twice a week or more often if odor develops.

The cage should be in a draft-free location, as rodents are quite susceptible to colds. Ideally, the temperature should not fall below 15°C (60°F). A deep floor covering, however, usually provides some insulation against the loss of heat energy, because the animals will burrow into it.

Food

Dry food pellets for small laboratory animals, including rats, are sold at most pet and feed stores. In addition, provide bits of carrot, lettuce, cheese, and bread for the animal to eat. A constant supply of pellets and other nonperishable food may be left in a small, flat container in the cage. However, remove any perishable food within an hour after it has been offered. A fresh bottle of water and tray of pellets should last over weekends, but provisions for feeding will need to be made for longer periods.

Handling

White rats are typically very gentle, likable creatures. They should be handled daily for a short period. This tames them and accustoms them to being around children. Although there is little chance that a white rat will bite if treated gently, remind children to keep their fingers away from the animal's mouth when handling it. Notify the school nurse immediately if any classroom animal bites a child. Although the bite itself is usually minor, germs the animal may harbor in its mouth may cause infection unless the wound is promptly treated.

Breeding

Rats will usually breed within a few days. Provide some loose cotton or shredded newspaper for the female to use in preparing a nest. Remove the male from the cage after it appears obvious that the female is pregnant. Return the male to the pet store, or give it to the Humane Society.

About 3 to 4 weeks after mating, the female will give birth to eight or more young in the nest. Do not disturb the female for 10 days after this event. The newborn young will be blind and hairless. They may be weaned gradually to a regular diet after they are about 2 weeks old. Feed them milk that contains soft bread crumbs for a week and adult food thereafter.

All rats should be given to a responsible party after completion of this activity. Abandoned rodents become wild and add quickly to the local pest population.

During the 8 weeks or so of working with these animals, try to have time for frequent, short class discussions about the behavior and habits of the caged rats. Emphasize the birth, appearance, care, feeding, and physical development of the young. You may note rapid day-to-day improvement in children's verbal reporting skills as they tell the latest news about their rats. It is also an excellent journal-writing activity.

Use a chart with rotating names for assigning such tasks as replacement of water, paper, and food. Most children are delighted to serve. This may be an excellent opportunity to motivate children and help them achieve a greater sense of responsibility.

Birds

"A bird is an animal with feathers." This is a primary child's definition, but it really cannot be much improved. Almost all other properties we see in birds may be found here and there among other animal groups, although not in the same combinations. The coloring and construction of birds' feathers vary tremendously, from the luxuriant plumage of a peacock to the scruffy covering of a New Zealand kiwi.

Although we ordinarily think of birds as fliers, chickens and roadrunners seldom fly, and some birds, like the ostrich, penguin, and kiwi, cannot fly at all.

Food and Heat Loss

"He eats like a bird." How often we have heard a person who eats sparingly described this way. It is hardly fitting. Few other animals possess such voracious appetites for their size. Many birds must eat their weight in food each day just to stay alive.

To see why this is so, examine a small, flying bird closely. Notice that its body volume is relatively small when compared to the large surface area of its skin. As body volume decreases, the relative size of skin surface increases. If this seems unclear, inspect a pint and a quart milk carton. The small carton holds only half as much but clearly has more than half the surface area of the larger carton.

A large skin surface area causes heat energy to radiate rapidly away from the body. This is bad when the body volume is small, because the heat-generating capacity is also small. To generate enough heat energy for normal functioning when heat energy is being radiated away quickly, a high *metabolic rate* (the rate at which food is oxidized and assimilated) must be maintained. The rapid burning of fuel causes body temperatures in birds of 39° to 43°C (102° to 110°F), the highest of any animal group.

The same principle of volume relative to surface area applies to mammals. Smaller mammals usually eat more for their size than larger ones. As we travel toward the earth's polar regions, we can observe a general increase in mammals' body size. As body volume increases, the relative size of skin surface decreases. Comparatively less heat energy is radiated away. This has great survival value.

Flight Adaptations

The bodies of most birds are well suited for flight. Inside are several air sacs connected to the lungs. Many bones are hollow, or nearly so, and further reduce body weight. Even a chicken has relatively little marrow in its longer bones. It is said that the evolutionist Charles Darwin had a pipe stem made from a wing bone of an albatross.

The body of a bird is streamlined and closely fitted with three kinds of feathers. Next to the skin are fluffy, soft *down feathers*. These contain numerous "dead air" pockets that help conserve body heat. *Contour feathers* hug the body closely, and large *flight feathers* help propel and steer the bird as it flies.

Most birds continually preen their feathers. This is done by using the bill to press a drop of oil from a gland located just above the tail and then spreading the oil over the feathers. A shiny, waterproof coating results. It is so effective that a duck can float for many hours without becoming waterlogged. If the oil were suddenly removed, a swimming duck would disappear into the water like a slowly submerging submarine.

If you can locate a large, recently molted feather, dip it in water before and after washing it in soap or detergent. Notice how water soaks in after the washing.

The thick white meat or breast section on poultry is partly the result of selective breeding by humans. However, nearly all birds have their largest and strongest muscles in this section because these muscles control the major wing movements.

Senses

The remarkably keen eyesight of birds has been well known. Less acknowledged is the fact that they have three eyelids. Two shut the eye, and the third, which is transparent, sweeps back and forth, cleaning away dust or other foreign matter without the need for blinking. The eyes of most birds are located on the sides of the head. So, birds must continually cock the head to one side to see directly forward. Their hearing is also acute despite the lack of outer ears. Two small ear holes suffice. Birds do not appear to discriminate well, however, among various odors or tastes.

Beaks and Feet

Most birds have horny beaks; their various shapes show great diversity of function. Although all known modern birds are toothless, fossil records indicate that a variety of toothed birds lived in ancient times. The feet of birds are equally diverse in form. On the legs we find scales, which reveal their evolutionary connection to the reptiles.

INQ Figure 8–3 shows some common structures and functions of birds' bills and feet. The duck's bill is useful for scooping up small fish and plants in water because it is shaped like a shovel. The scooped-up water spills out through the uneven sides of the bill, but the food remains inside. The duck's webbed feet are useful for paddling in water.

The woodpecker's bill is like a large, pointed nail, useful for digging insects out of tough tree bark. (The bills of most other insect catchers are more slender.) Its feet can dig securely into a vertical tree trunk.

The sparrow's bill is small but strong enough to crack open seeds and some nuts, similar to a pet canary. Its feet are useful for perching because they automatically close around a tree limb. It requires no effort, and the bird may sleep in this position without danger of falling.

The hawk's bill is like a sharp hook, useful for tearing the flesh from bones of field mice and other small animals of preys. Its feet are useful for grasping and holding prey.

INQ Figure 8–3   (A) Duck, (B) woodpecker, (C) sparrow, (D) hawk.

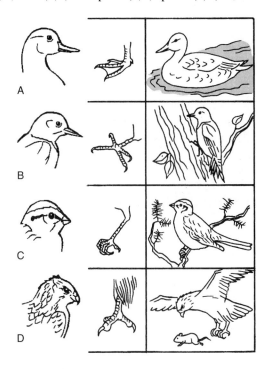

Reproduction

As in mammals, sexual reproduction begins with an egg cell fertilized within the female by a sperm cell. However, fertilization is not necessary for an egg to be laid. Many chickens lay an egg every day. We eat these unfertilized eggs. An egg acquires its hard shell in the lower part of the hen's *oviduct,* or egg-conducting tube. Glands produce a limy secretion that gradually hardens over a period of hours before the egg is laid. The shell is porous and permits oxygen to enter and carbon dioxide to leave. In a fertilized egg, this gas exchange is essential for life in the developing chick embryo.

Chick Hatching

It is fairly easy to hatch chicks in the classroom. To do so, you will need fertilized eggs and an incubator. Get the eggs from a hatchery or farmer. Buy a small incubator from a pet shop or scientific supply house. It is essential to success that a near-constant temperature of 38° to 39°C (101° to 103°F) be maintained for the 21-day incubation period. Fertilized eggs should be turned over twice a day. This change in position keeps the growing embryo from sticking to the shell. A mark placed on the egg will allow you to keep track of egg positions.

In 21 days, or sooner if the eggs have not been freshly laid, the hatching will take place. This process may take several or more hours. Because some hatching may happen at night, it is good to have several eggs. This will increase the chance that a few chicks will hatch during school hours.

Children can observe how a chick breaks out of its shell by using a tiny "egg tooth" on top of its beak. This projection drops off shortly after the chick emerges (see INQ Figure 8–4). The chick will look wet and scraggly until its downy feathers dry. No food is necessary for at least 24 hours, as it will have digested the egg yolk and some egg white before breaking out

INQ Figure 8–4   **A chick starts to peck itself out of the egg. Notice the egg tooth.**

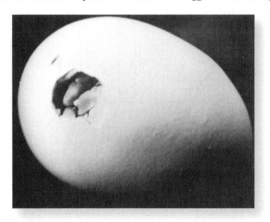

of the shell. (It is a common misconception that an egg yolk is the undeveloped embryo, rather than the chick's principal food.)

Caring for Chicks

Chicks need constant warmth furnished by a brooder or warm box. An incubator can be used temporarily if the lid is raised, but it may be too confining after a few days. If the chicks are to be kept for more than several days, use a cardboard box with a shielded, gooseneck lamp shining into it.

Chick feed may be bought at a pet store. Leave some feed and clean water in dishes within the brooder at all times. A fresh newspaper floor cover each day will keep the brooder clean.

Reptiles

Many children know that snakes are reptiles but are unaware that the group also includes turtles, lizards, alligators, and crocodiles. What do these animals have in common? Typically, they have dry, scaly skin. Those with feet have five clawed toes on each foot. They all have lungs in order to breathe, or are lung breathers, which means that even an aquatic turtle will drown if placed underwater for an extended time period.

Cold-Blooded

Reptiles have well-developed hearts with three chambers (some have almost four). Unlike mammals and birds, reptiles are cold-blooded. In winter, reptiles in relatively cold climates hibernate below ground; they become unable to move when the temperature drops very low. It is no accident that reptiles are rare in regions beyond the temperate zones and proliferate in the tropics.

Reproduction

In reptiles, reproduction begins with the internal fertilization of an egg, similar to mammals and birds. But the process thereafter is different enough to warrant our attention. All turtles and most lizards and snakes lay eggs in secluded areas on land. The eggs have tough, leathery covers and for the most part depend on the sun's warmth for incubation.

Some snakes and lizards retain the fertilized eggs internally until the incubation period is complete. The young are then born alive. However, the process differs from the development of mammalian young.

INQ Figure 8–5   **A typical small lizard, the Eastern fence swift.**

In mammals, as was noted, the embryo is attached to the female and nourished directly through a placental membrane. In reptiles, there is no internal attachment. The egg incubates until the growing embryo inside is sufficiently developed to hatch and so leave the female.

Eyes

Turtles and most lizards have three eyelids on each eye, as do birds. Snakes have no eyelids. A transparent, horny cover over the eye protects it from injury as the animal moves among sticks and vegetation. Just before a snake sheds its skin, up to several times a year, the transparent eye cover becomes milky in color. Interestingly, the only easy way to tell the several species of legless lizards from snakes is to note whether the eyes blink.

Common Lizards

Children may bring lizards, often swifts, to class (see INQ Figure 8–5). In the southwestern United States, it is common for children to bring in the gentle and easily tamed horned toad. Nearly all lizards may be housed satisfactorily in a terrarium containing some sand and placed where it is sunny. The anole (American chameleon), the kind often bought at fairs and pet shops, is more suited to a woodland terrarium.

Chameleons (anoles) are interesting for children to observe. Like many lizards, they change body color under different conditions of light, temperature, and excitation. However, the color change is greater in chameleons than in most other lizards. It is brought about by dilation and contraction of blood vessels in the skin.

Many lizards have fragile tails that break off easily when seized. In some species, the broken-off tail wriggles about animatedly, thereby often distracting the attention of a would-be captor until the lizard escapes. Lizards can *regenerate*, or grow back, new tails.

Classroom Snake

If possible, try to get a small, tame snake for the children to examine. Let the children touch it and learn that it has dry, cool skin, rather than a slimy coating. Children can learn that nearly all snakes in this country are highly beneficial to humans and that snakes consume many thousands of destructive rodent and insect pests each year.

At the same time, children should learn an intelligent respect for snakes. If poisonous snakes are found locally, show pictures of them. Instruct children never to hunt for snakes unless accompanied by a responsible and informed older person. In the continental United States, the rattlesnake, copperhead, water moccasin, and coral snake are dangerous to humans.

Amphibians

Amphibians are animals that typically spend part of their lives in water and part on land. The main kinds are frogs, toads, and salamanders. Amphibians represent an interesting evolutionary link between fishes and reptiles and have many properties of both groups. If animal life originally began and evolved in the sea, as is generally hypothesized, it is probable that early amphibians were the first vertebrates to emerge from the water and live successfully on land.

Cold-Blooded

Amphibians are cold-blooded and have hearts with three chambers. Like other cold-blooded animals, they hibernate in cold weather, usually by burrowing in the ground or mud. The adults breathe through lungs but are also able to absorb some oxygen through the skin. The latter method of breathing is especially useful in hibernation. Still, skin breathing is inadequate for sustained activity, and even a frog will drown eventually if forced to remain underwater.

Frogs and salamanders usually have moist, smooth skins that must remain moist if they are to survive. For this reason, a bowl of water is needed in a terrarium that houses these creatures.

Frogs and Toads

One day, a child may show you a small amphibian and ask, "Is this a toad or a frog?" Although it is difficult to distinguish between them all the time, a toad usually has dry, rough skin and a broad, fat body. In addition, its eyelids are more prominent than those of frogs. Another indicator is where it was caught. Frogs are more likely to live by water, whereas toads are mostly land dwellers (INQ Figure 8–6).

INQ Figure 8–6   Toad (left) and frog (right). Notice the external eardrum, just behind and below the eye.

Can toads cause warts? Many children think they can. The toad's warty-looking tubercles are glands that secrete a fluid that can sicken attacking animals, but the substance cannot cause warts. It may irritate the eyes, though, if they are rubbed after the person has handled a toad. Advise children to wash their hands after playing with a toad.

Salamanders

Less common than frogs and toads are salamanders; chances are that few children will have these as pets. Typically, a salamander has four legs of the same size and a long, tubular body with a tail. Superficially, they resemble lizards and are often mistaken for them. They differ from lizards in several ways: Each foreleg of a salamander has four toes instead of five and no claws; typically, the skin is smooth rather than rough. A salamander's skin may secrete a mild poison, so hands should be thoroughly washed after handling it.

Reproduction

Perhaps the most striking difference between amphibians and the other groups we have examined is in their means of reproduction. Female amphibians lay their eggs in water or in very moist places on land. Immediately after the eggs are laid, the males fertilize them by shedding sperm over them. Therefore, fertilization is external, unlike that in higher order animals. A single female frog or toad may lay several thousand eggs at one time. The eggs are coated with a thick, jellylike substance that quickly absorbs water and swells in size. This substance protects the developing embryos and serves as a first source of food. Eggs may often be found in ponds in spring. Look for gelatinous clumps (frog) or strings (toad) near grassy edges or where cattails grow.

After 1 to 2 weeks, the embryos hatch as tadpoles, or "polliwogs," which look completely unlike the adults. Only after several months to several years, depending on the species, do tadpoles acquire the adult body form (see INQ Figure 8–7). This process of

INQ Figure 8–7   **Metamorphosis of the frog.**

changing forms, called *metamorphosis*, is another distinct departure from the growth and development pattern of higher animals.

In their initial growth stages, tadpoles breathe like fishes; that is, they obtain oxygen from water through gills. Thus, be sure to "age" tap water for at least 24 hours to rid it of chlorine before adding it to the container in which the tadpoles are kept. Use tap water only if pond water is not available.

Fishes

Next to mammals, fishes are the vertebrates that present the greatest diversity in appearance, adaptations, and habits. Certainly, fishes are most numerous, both as individuals and in numbers of species. (When only one species is referred to, *fish* is both singular and plural. *Fishes* means those of several species.) Fossil records show that these creatures were the first animals with true backbones.

Breathing

Fishes are cold-blooded and have hearts with only two chambers. They breathe through gills instead of lungs. Their gills are composed of thousands of blood vessels contained in hairlike filaments located in back of the head on both sides. We cannot easily see these filaments on a live fish, as gill covers conceal them.

A fish breathes by opening and closing its mouth. In the process, water is taken into the mouth and then is forced out the gill openings. As water passes over the gills, oxygen dissolved in the water enters the filaments and blood vessels and then circulates throughout the body. At the same time, carbon dioxide leaves the filaments and is swept away. One advantage of carefully classifying living things by structure is that it enables us to see relationships we might otherwise miss. In fishes, for example, an organ called the *air bladder* appears to be a forerunner of the lung. The air bladder is an air-filled sac usually located in the middle of a fish between its kidney and stomach. By compressing and expanding its air bladder, a fish can rise and descend in the water.

In the lungfish, this organ has been modified into a crude lung, enabling it to breathe air directly in addition to breathing through the gills. A lungfish typically lives in a muddy pond or marsh, which may dry up in summer. It survives by burrowing into the mud and breathing air supplied through a hole in the mud cover. When its pond fills again with seasonal rainfall, the lungfish resumes the normal gill-breathing behavior of fishes. The lungfish appears to be a clear link between fishes and amphibians in the long evolutionary march of vertebrates from the sea.

Body

The body of a fish is well suited for its environment. Its streamlined contours offer a minimum of resistance to the water. A slimy, mucouslike secretion that exudes between the overlapping body scales further reduces friction and insulates the skin from attack by microorganisms. A large tail fin, wagged from side to side, propels it through the water. Vertical fins on top and bottom keep the fish on an even keel while it is moving. Two pairs of side fins, one pair near the gills (pectoral fins) and the other pair farther back (pelvic fins), balance the fish when it is stationary. These fins are also used to assist turning, in the manner of oars, and for swimming backward. When held out laterally, they brake the swimming fish to a stop. Pectoral fins correspond to forelegs, and pelvic fins correlate to hind legs, in other animals.

Senses

The eyes of a fish are always open because it has no eyelids. Focusing is done by shifting the pupil forward and back, rather than by changing the lens shape, as in humans. So-called flatfish, such as the flounder and halibut, lie on one side. Both eyes are arranged on one side of the head. Because these fish are typically bottom dwellers, this eye arrangement permits greater vision.

Although fishes have no external ears, they hear with *auditory capsules* deep within the head. In many fishes, a *lateral line* of sensory scales extends along both sides of the body from head to tail. These scales are particularly sensitive to sounds of low pitch. Some expert anglers claim that a fish can hear heavy footsteps (always of other, inexpert anglers, of course) on a nearby bank.

The taste sense appears to be mostly lacking, but a fish is sensitive to smells. Nostril pits on the snout lead to organs of smell just below. The whole body, and especially the lips, seems to be sensitive to touch. In species like the catfish, extra touch organs are found in the form of "whiskers."

Reproduction

In fishes, reproduction is accomplished by either external or internal fertilization of the egg, depending on the species. The female goldfish, for example, lays eggs on aquatic plants. The male fertilizes the eggs by shedding sperm cells over them. Goldfish usually reproduce only in large tanks or ponds. Guppies and many other tropical varieties use internal fertilization. The male has a modified anal fin that carries sperm. The fin is inserted into a small opening below the female's abdomen, and sperm cells are released. Fertilized eggs remain in the female's body until the embryos hatch and are "born." Many of the young guppies are eaten by the adult fish unless sufficient plant growth makes it difficult to detect them.

To raise as many guppies as possible, place the pregnant female (its underside will look swollen) and some plants in a separate container. After the young are born, remove the mother. The young may join the adult guppies safely in about 1 month. Try not to be too efficient at breeding guppies, however. Someone good at arithmetic has calculated that a single pair will become 3 million guppies in a year, assuming that all generations and off-spring stay alive. A female guppy may produce several dozen young every 4 to 6 weeks at a water temperature of 21° to 27°C (70° to 80°F).

Male guppies differ from the females in several ways. They are about half the size (exclusive of the tails), much narrower in body, and more brilliantly colored (INQ Figure 8–8).

Setting Up an Aquarium

An aquarium is an excellent source to observe ecological principles firsthand. In this watery habitat, plants and animals interact with each other and their environment, and reproduction takes place in several ways. It is possible to see a near balance of nature through the interactions, and the consequences when there is an imbalance.

It is easy for children to set up small aquariums for short-range observations of a week or two. For the containers, they may use large, wide-mouthed jars or plastic shoe boxes. One or two goldfish and a few sprigs of water plants per container should do nicely. Tap water can be put into the containers and aged for at least 24 hours before the fish are introduced. A tiny amount of fish food, no more than the fish can eat in a few minutes, should be sprinkled on the water once a day. A more elaborate, long-range habitat for aquatic animals and plants is described next.

INQ Figure 8–8   **Female (left) and male (right) guppy.**

Tank

The materials needed are a tank, some clean sand (not the seashore variety), a few aquatic snails and plants, and several small fish. A rectangular tank of 19- to 23-liter (5- to 6-gallon) capacity serves best for a classroom aquarium. The rectangular shape has less viewing distortion than a bowl. It also permits more oxygen from the air to dissolve in the water because of the relatively greater surface area exposed at the top.

The tank must be clean. Dirt, grease, or caked lime can be removed by scrubbing thoroughly with salt and water. The salt is abrasive enough to have a scouring effect. Should detergent or soaps be needed, repeated rinsing of the tank is essential. Any residue may be harmful to future inhabitants. About 5 centimeters (2 inches) of clean sand may then be placed and spread evenly on the bottom of the tank.

Plants

A pet store can supply several varieties of inexpensive plants, any of which will serve well. Sagittaria and vallisneria will produce more oxygen than others and are rooted plants. Anchor the plants firmly in the sand. If necessary, also anchor them with several clean stones. Placing the plants toward the back of the tank will permit easier viewing of the fish.

Water

Put a large piece of paper or cardboard over the plants before pouring or siphoning water into the tank. This prevents the plants from becoming dislodged and helps keep the sand in place. The paper should be removed immediately thereafter. Should tap water be used, it must stand for at least 24 hours to permit the chlorine to escape and the water to reach room temperature. The water level should be about 2.5 centimeters (1 inch) lower than the tank top.

Moving the tank after it is filled may warp the tank seams and start a leak. (If a leak does occur, apply epoxy glue to the inside joints and seams after thoroughly drying out the tank.)

Animals

Goldfish and guppies are among the best fishes to use, as they can withstand a broad temperature change. But do not mix the two, because goldfish prey on guppies.

Freshwater angelfish are also a popular aquarium fish. Angelfish have many variations such as silver, gold, black, and marble. The juveniles and adults are colored differently in many species. Most species of angelfish are a few centimeters long, but some may reach lengths of 60 centimeters (2 feet). Angelfish will breed on broadleaf plants and will care for their young if not frightened. If angelfish do become threatened, they might eat their young. Angelfish are sometimes aggressive and will fight with each other or eat small fish of other species.

The neon tetra is another freshwater fish that is often kept in aquariums. Tetras have blue and red markings and, like the angelfish, originate in the Amazon waters of South America. Tetras are a good community fish and often move throughout the aquarium in groups. They should not be kept with larger fish since they are easy prey.

The black molly is a hybrid tropical fish that does not have a native counterpart living in the wild. Black molly fish are very hardy so it is easy to breed them in an aquarium. The females are livebearers and produce a large number of fry.

"Chinese" algae eaters that come from Northern India and Thailand are useful to remove unwanted algae. As juveniles, they are peaceful and stay to themselves. As adults, however, they tend to be very aggressive and territorial. An alternative to the Chinese algae eater is the plecostomus catfish that is notoriously good at keeping an aquarium free of algae. The fish has an elongated, brown body and a large head. It cleans the tank by sucking at the aquarium glass or tank decorations with its strong mouth. Small catfish, sunfish, minnows, zebras, and bullheads are also easy to keep and are interesting to observe.

If several water snails are bought at the pet store along with the plants and fish, they will add interest and value. Snails keep the aquarium clean by scavenging excess fish food and eating the green slime (algae) that may form on the glass. Only a few are needed, as they multiply rapidly and can become a problem. Children delight in examining snails' eggs, laid on the glass sides, and seeing the snails scrape off and eat the algae. A few hand lenses placed around the aquarium make the viewing easier.

A properly set-up aquarium needs little attention. Plants give off some of the oxygen needed by the animals and absorb some of their waste materials. The animals also provide carbon dioxide needed by the plants for photosynthesis. What if the aquarium is not properly set up? Here, we can look for clues that may indicate improper light, temperature, oxygen, and feeding.

Light

If algae grow rapidly on the sides, the tank is getting too much light. A northeast corner location or other place of good but indirect light will work best. Adding more snails and wrapping black paper around the tank for a while can retard growth of algae, but it may also be necessary to clean the tank. Algae will not hurt the fish unless they are so abundant that some decay; however, visibility into the tank may be obscured.

Temperature

If the temperature is too low, reproduction will slow noticeably or stop. Some fish may die. The best temperature range for fish recommended here is 10° to 21°C (50° to 70°F). An exception is the guppy, which requires 21° to 29.5°C (70° to 85°F) water to reproduce.

When most kinds of tropical fishes are used, a heater is a necessity. This can be in the form of a light mounted in the cover of the tank, although an immersible heater works better.

Oxygen Supply

Insufficient oxygen is indicated when fish stay very close to the surface. This is where the greatest amount of oxygen dissolved directly from the air is located. Occasionally, some fish might be seen to break the surface and gulp air directly. Insufficient surface area or overcrowding can cause this condition.

One small, approximately inch-long, goldfish (not including the tail) per gallon of water is proper. If guppies are used, about six fish per gallon are satisfactory. Having too many snails will also add to an oxygen-poor condition. Increase the number of sagittaria and vallisneria for more oxygen.

Cloudy Water

A cloudy water condition occurs from excess feeding or from not removing dead plants and animals. Bacterial action on uneaten food and other organic matter poisons the water and promotes the growth of other microorganisms. The most practical solution is to discard everything but the fish, filter, and gravel, carefully clean the tank, and begin again.

Feeding

Only a small sprinkling of packaged fish food every other day (enough to be completely eaten in 5 minutes) is required for feeding. Tiny bits of chopped beef and earthworm may also be used. Feeding is not needed over weekends, but some means for feeding during vacations is necessary.

Cover

A glass top or piece of kitchen plastic wrap may be used to cover the aquarium. For better air circulation, leave some space open or punch a few holes in the plastic-wrap cover.

A top helps keep the water clean and cuts down on loss of water through evaporation or loss of an overly athletic fish. It also shows condensation and precipitation in a small water cycle, because water droplets form on the bottom surface and fall back into the tank.

ANIMALS WITHOUT BACKBONES Inquiry

Mealworms and What They Do

Invitation

Have you ever seen a mealworm? You can buy mealworms at a pet store to feed to lizards and fish. It's fun to observe mealworms and what they do. How can you find out about mealworms and what they do?

Exploration

1. Take a mealworm out of the jar of bran. Put one in an upturned shoe box lid.
2. Use a spoon and card to move it to where you want.
3. Use a hand lens to see it more clearly.

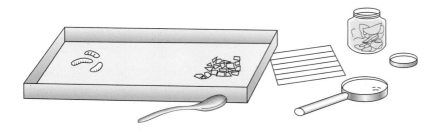

MATERIALS

- Mealworms
- Spoon
- Three rulers
- Small card
- Shoe box lid
- Small jar of bran
- Hand lens
- Cotton swab
- Rough paper towel
- Water
- Clock with second hand
- Samples of foods (cornflakes, flour, bread, crackers, and others)
- Ice cube
- Drinking straw
- Sheet of black paper

Concept Invention

1. What do you notice about the mealworm? How many legs does it have? How many feelers on its head? What is on its tail end? How many body segments, or parts, does it have?
2. Put the mealworm on a rough paper towel, and then on a smooth surface. On which does it seem to travel more easily?
3. Put a few more mealworms in the shoe box lid. Observe how they look and act. In what ways can you tell different mealworms apart?
4. In what ways can you get a mealworm to back up? Which way is best?
5. Suppose you place the mealworms on a slant. Will they go up or down? Does the amount of slant make a difference?
6. How far can a mealworm go in half a minute?
7. Which food do mealworms seem to like best? Try cornflakes, flour, bread, crackers, and other foods.
8. Suppose you put two mealworms into a narrow straw, one at each end. What do you think will happen when they meet?
9. Do mealworms like moisture? How could a cotton swab be used to find out? How else might you find out?
10. Will a mealworm move toward or away from a cold place? How could an ice cube be used to find out?
11. Will a mealworm move to a dark or light place? How can black paper be used to find out?

Teaching Tips

Mealworms are the larval stage of the grain beetle, an insect often found in rotting grain or flour supplies. They may be bought inexpensively at pet stores and are fed to a variety of small animals, including some fishes. Mealworms can be kept in closed glass jars containing bran or other cereal flakes. Punch small holes in the jar lids for air. A potato or apple slice can be added to provide extra moisture. When the old bran looks powdery, dump out everything and then wash and dry the jar. Put fresh bran and the live, healthy-looking mealworms back into the jar.

12. In each of the four illustrations, which way will a mealworm go?
13. How can you get a mealworm to go in a straight line for at least 10 centimeters (4 inches)? No fair touching it!

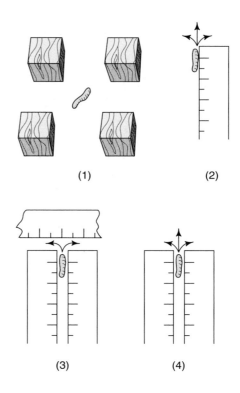

(1)   (2)

(3)   (4)

Scaffolding for English Learners

Teachers of English to Speakers of Other Languages (TESOL) suggest that assessment should be reliable, valid, and ongoing for English learners. In the concept application section of the mealworm activity, students are challenged to watch a mealworm go through its life cycle. How could you make this an assessment activity for English learners' conceptual understanding of life cycles? (See TESOL, 2001, for a discussion of assessment practices and English learners.)

Concept Application

Some behaviors of an animal are inborn, and some are influenced by its environment. What are some other questions about the mealworm's behavior that you would like to investigate? Watch the mealworm go through its life cycle. What do you notice at the different stages of life?

Crickets

Invitation

How can you raise crickets?

Exploration

1. Put about 5 centimeters (2 inches) of dry soil into the container.
2. Fill the custard cup with soil. Sprinkle water on it until it is all damp. Bury it in the dry soil so that the damp soil is even with the dry soil. (This is where the female can lay eggs.)
3. Scatter some pieces of torn paper towel around the container. (The crickets can hide underneath when needed.)
4. Scatter some dry oatmeal and a few raisins at one end.
5. Put no more than three or four crickets inside the container. Cover it with a screen large enough to bend down at the sides.

Concept Invention

1. How do the crickets act?
2. How do they use the pieces of toweling?
3. How do the females lay eggs?
4. How do the crickets eat?
5. How do the crickets move about?
6. What happens when cricket eggs hatch?
7. What do the young (nymphs) look like?
8. What do they look like as they get older? (Use a hand lens to help you see.)

Concept Application

What else can you observe about the crickets?

MATERIALS

- Several male and female crickets
- Plastic shoe box
- Custard cup or small dish
- Screen top for shoe box
- Paper towel
- Ruler
- Water
- Dry soil
- Dry oatmeal or bran
- Raisins
- Hand lens

Teaching Tips

If children are unable to catch crickets in fields, they may often be bought at fish-bait stores. The female may be recognized by a long slender "tail," or ovipositor, through which it deposits eggs in damp soil. Development from egg to adult takes about 6 months, and adults live about 3 months.

MATERIALS

- Vial of brine shrimp eggs
- Tap water
- Noniodized salt
- Hand lens
- Plastic teaspoon
- Small baby food jars with lids
- Measuring cup
- Crayon or marker
- Baking soda
- Small package of brewer's yeast

Brine Shrimp ———

Invitation

Have you ever visited a salt lake? If so, maybe you have seen brine shrimp. These small animals lay tiny eggs. You can find out many interesting things about brine shrimp, but first you will need to hatch the eggs. How can you hatch brine shrimp eggs?

Exploration

1. Let a cup of tap water stand overnight. Then mix 4 teaspoons of salt into it.
2. Pour the water into several baby food jars.
3. Use one jar now. Cap and save the other jars for later use.
4. Take just a tiny pinch of eggs from the vial. Sprinkle them on top of the water.
5. Observe the eggs closely a few times each day. Use a hand magnifier to see the eggs more clearly.

Teaching Tips

Brine shrimp are sold at pet stores for fish food. The eggs may be hatched in saltwater. You can use about 4 teaspoons of salt per cup of water for both hatching and growth; but the shrimp may hatch within a wide range of salt concentrations. Be sure to use either noniodized or marine salt.

About 6 weeks are needed for the shrimp to reach maturity under the best conditions. A water temperature of about 27°C (80°F) is ideal. Children will be able to distinguish female from male adults most easily by the females' egg pouches. It is harder to keep brine shrimp alive for a lengthy period than it is to hatch them. Some precautions will help. Have children use a crayon to mark the beginning water level on each jar. Be sure that any evaporated water is replaced by aged tap water containing the proper salt concentration.

The water should stand for at least 24 hours to allow the chlorine to escape. Put a tiny pinch of baking soda into each shrimp container once a week to neutralize the acid that builds up. Above all, do not overfeed the shrimp. A tiny pinch of brewer's yeast once a week is adequate to grow the bacteria on which the shrimp feed. As with other long-range observational activities, this one is ideal for motivating artwork and language experiences.

Concept Invention

1. When do you first notice changes in the eggs? What changes do you see?
2. When do you first notice tiny brine shrimp? How do they look to you? Can you describe what they are doing?
3. What changes do you notice as the brine shrimp grow? Observe them each day.
4. Do brine shrimp ever seem to rest or sleep? How can you find out?
5. How long does it take for a shrimp to start growing?
6. How long can you keep a brine shrimp alive?
7. Do newly hatched shrimp go where it is light or dark? How about month-old shrimp? How can you find out?
8. How can you tell which brine shrimp are female?
9. Will brine shrimp eggs hatch in freshwater?
10. Will brine shrimp eggs hatch in water with twice as much or more salt than you first used?

Concept Application

Brine shrimp will hatch and grow from eggs, stay alive, and reproduce when conditions are like those of their natural habitat. Suppose you hatch many shrimp eggs in one jar and only a few in another. What do you think will happen as the shrimp grow? What else would you like to investigate about brine shrimp?

Snails and What They Do

Invitation

Have you ever seen a snail? If so, where? Many water snails live in and around the edges of ponds. Land snails can be found in gardens, lawns, and around damp soil. They are easiest to find early in the morning or at night. Land snails are usually larger than water snails, so they are easier to observe. What they do is surprising. How can you find out about land snails and what they do?

Exploration

1. Put a snail on a pie plate.
2. Use a spoon and card to move it where you want.
3. Use a hand lens to see it more clearly.

Concept Invention

1. What do you notice about the snail? How does it move? How can you describe its head? How can you describe its shell? How can you describe its other parts?
2. How many stalks (feelers) do you observe on its head? Which seem to have eyes? Which seem to be used for feeling?

MATERIALS

- Live land snail
- Small stiff card
- Wide-mouthed glass jar, with lid, containing some damp soil
- Hand lens
- Spoon
- Aluminum pie plate
- Ruler
- Sheet of black paper
- Piece of lettuce
- Paper towel
- Small paper cup of water
- Clock with second hand
- Paper and pencil
- Samples of different foods

Teaching Tips

Land snails can be found where there is plenty of vegetation and moisture. They seem to prefer cool, shady places, especially under leaves, logs, and rocks. Early morning is probably the easiest time to collect snails, when leaves are heavy with dew. If you collect them in a dry "resting" condition, place them on a water-soaked paper towel to reactivate them. Several collected snails may be kept in one glass jar covered with a lid that has holes punched into it for air. Place 2.5 to 5 centimeters (1 to 2 inches) of soil inside and keep it damp. For extra moisture, sink a bottle cap flush with the soil surface and fill it with water. Leave a small piece of lettuce inside for food. Keep the jar in a shady place. After several days, the jar will need to be cleaned. Try to have several snails available for observation and experiments; even when treated gently, this animal needs a rest period between activities.

3. What happens when you gently touch the two longer stalks? What happens when you gently touch the two shorter stalks? How close can you get before the stalks move?

4. How can you get the two longer stalks to move in different directions?

5. What happens when you tap the snail's shell gently?

6. Try to put the snail upside down on its shell. Can the snail right itself? If so, how?

7. Put the snail on black paper. Observe the silver trail it makes. How far does the snail go in 1 minute?

8. How well can you draw an animal? Make a drawing of your snail. Show it to someone who does not know you are studying snails. Can that person tell it is a snail?

9. How well can you describe an animal? Write a description of your snail without saying what it is. Show the description to someone who does not know you are studying snails. Can that person tell that you described a snail?

10. Give the snail some lettuce to eat. Use a hand lens to observe its mouthparts. How does it eat?

11. What foods does your snail seem to like best? Circle your snail with bits of different foods. Which does the snail go to first? What happens when you try this several times? How long should you wait between each trial? Why?

12. Will a snail go to the dark or the light? Put your snail into the pie pan. How can you use a sheet of black paper to find out?

13. Will a snail go where it is dry or wet? How can you use a paper towel to find out?

Adapting for Students with Exceptionalities

To assist students with exceptionalities, when doing this activity, try using a concept diagram that includes the "concept name" (snail behavior), "overall concept" (animal behavior), "key words" (snail, head, stalks, shell, trail, and mouthparts), "characteristics" (responds to touch and light, eats, leaves a trail, body parts), "exploration of examples" (likes lettuce, likes cucumbers, does not like carrots), "practice with a new example" (similarities with an earthworm), and "definition" (snails are soft-bodied mollusks that have a single shell and secrete mucus). (See Mastropieri & Scruggs, 2004, chapter on science and social studies for a discussion on concept diagrams.)

Concept Application

Some behaviors of an animal are inborn, and some are influenced by its environment. What other experiments would you like to try with snails? What other kinds of snails can you find to try?

ANIMALS WITHOUT BACKBONES CONCEPTS

The invertebrates make up most of the animals on earth. Of these, insects are by far the largest group. We begin this section with insects and why they have done so well and then consider four more animals you might have for many classroom activities: crayfish, brine shrimp, snails, and earthworms.

Insects and Life Cycles ────────

If we were to eliminate all insects, some very undesirable consequences would result. Here are only a few: Probably half of all the flowering plants on the earth would disappear, because bees, flies, moths, and butterflies help pollinate them. Most land birds would vanish because their main source of food is insects. Biological research would be hampered because the short life cycles of insects are ideal for quick results in medical and hereditary studies.

As mentioned, insects make up an astounding 70% of all animal species. Hundreds of new species are discovered each year. They are found almost everywhere on the earth. What makes them so successful?

Legs and Skeleton

The first things we might note about insects is that they have jointed legs and segmented bodies. Instead of an internal skeleton, such as we find in vertebrates, they have an external skeleton made of a crusty substance called *chitin*. Muscles and other body parts are attached inside to this semirigid exterior. To continue growing, an immature insect must *molt*, or shed its outside covering from time to time. We can see that the need for molting greatly limits insect size. A heavy body would collapse before the soft, new covering hardened. Jointed legs and an external skeleton are also typical of the several other classes that make up the phylum of arthropods.

The Adult Insect

The easiest way to recognize an adult insect is to look for three pairs of legs and three body parts: head, thorax (chest), and abdomen (INQ Figure 8–9). Notice that these two characteristics leave out spiders, which have four pairs of legs, and many other arthropods, such as sow bugs, centipedes, or scorpions.

The *head* contains a primitive "brain" and mouthparts that vary considerably among insect orders. Most insects have one pair of compound eyes, which are aggregates of many lenses, and several simple eyes as well, each of which has only one lens. The eyes are always open because they lack eyelids. Two hairlike feelers, or *antennae*, sensitive to touch and sometimes smell, are also found on most insect heads.

The middle section, or thorax, is where the legs and wings are attached. Some insects have one pair of wings, and others have two pairs; a few have none.

The *abdomen* contains the organs of digestion, excretion, and reproduction. Tiny holes (*spiracles*) in the thorax and abdomen furnish air for breathing. The air is piped into the internal organs by a network of connected tubes.

INQ Figure 8–9   **Insects have three distinct body parts and three pairs of legs.**

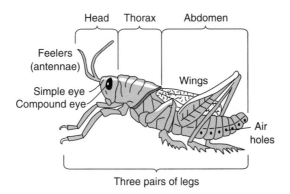

Crickets and katydids hear through a tiny eardrum located on each foreleg just below the "knee" joint. Look for an oval spot of slightly different color. Grasshoppers also have visible eardrums. These are located on each side of the abdomen's first section. Lift up the insect's wings and look for a disklike membrane just above where the rear legs are attached.

Survival Features

Insects have survived so successfully for several reasons. Most can fly; this provides a great range for potential food. Insects typically have very sensitive nervous systems; they are particularly sensitive to odors related to their food. The thorax may be packed with striated muscles that can contract immediately on signal; this makes many insects difficult to catch. The compound eyes increase this advantage because they cover a wide-angle view.

Although insects are cold-blooded, as are all known invertebrates, their small size often permits them to secure adequate shelter when the weather becomes cold. Many pass through the winter months in a resting or inactive stage. Perhaps most important for their survival as a group is how quickly they produce new generations.

Life Cycles

The life cycles of insects are most interesting. Eggs are fertilized internally and hatched externally. In most species, the insect goes through a complete metamorphosis of four stages as it matures: egg, larva, pupa, and adult. The fertilized *egg* hatches a *larva* (caterpillar), which eats continually and sheds its skin several times as it grows. Then it either spins a cocoon (e.g., moth larva) or encases itself in a chrysalis (e.g., butterfly larva) and enters the *pupa* stage. The body tissues change during this "resting" period. Sometime later an *adult* insect emerges.

Some insects, such as the grasshopper, cricket, termite, and aphid, go through an incomplete metamorphosis of three stages: egg, nymph, and adult. The fertilized *egg* hatches a young, or *nymph*, which resembles the *adult* except that it appears out of proportion and lacks wings. As it grows, molting takes place several times. There is no pupa stage (see INQ Figure 8–10).

Students will enjoy observing some insects go through several stages of their life cycles, and they will learn from this procedure. Suggestions for doing so with crickets and mealworms are included in upcoming activities.

INQ Figure 8–10   **Grasshopper and butterfly metamorphoses.**

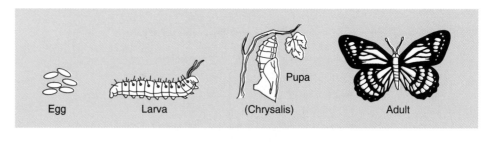

Butterflies and Moths

Insects are distributed throughout the world, from the polar regions to the tropics. They range in size from microscopic to more than 60 centimeters (2 feet). With 800,000 species already found, scientists believe more than 800,000 insect species could be on the earth. Common insects are the butterfly, moth, and mealworm.

Some teachers like to show stages in the life cycles of butterflies and moths. Children will not be able to locate eggs, as these are usually too small to see. Even so, they should be able to find and bring in caterpillars, cocoons, and chrysalises. Remind them to take several leaves from the plant on which the caterpillar was feeding when captured. A fresh supply may be needed every few days.

Use a glass jar or similar container to house each of these specimens (INQ Figure 8–11). Place inside some soil and an upright twig from which the larva might suspend its chrysalis. Either a cheesecloth lid secured with an elastic band or a perforated jar top should provide enough air. Moisten the soil occasionally for cocoons and chrysalises, as they may dry up without sufficient humidity.

For a larger, more elaborate insect terrarium, see INQ Figure 8–12. You will need two cake pans, a section of wire screen, paper fasteners, an upturned jar lid (for water), several twigs and leaves, and some soil. Roll the screen into a cylinder to fit inside the cake pans. Secure the screen seam with several paper fasteners. Put soil in the base. To make the base heavier and firmly implant a small branch, you may want to pour some mixed plaster of paris into the bottom cake pan before adding the soil.

To show the entire life cycle of an insect from egg to adult, raise some silkworm moths in class. Within about 8 weeks, children will see larvae hatch from the eggs, feed busily for a time, spin cocoons and pupate, emerge from the cocoons as adult moths, mate, lay eggs, and die. Eggs and specific instructions can be purchased inexpensively from a biological supply house. The mulberry leaves on which the larvae feed are found in most parts of the continental United States.

Another insect with a short (6–8 weeks) life cycle is the greater wax moth. It also may be bought from several biological supply companies.

INQ Figure 8–11 **A transparent jar may permit children to observe the life cycles of some insects.**

INQ Figure 8–12   **A homemade terrarium for butterflies and moths.**

Cake pan

Paper
fastener

Mealworms

The grain beetle (*Tenebrio molitor*) is one of the easiest insects to keep and observe. It, too, undergoes a complete four-stage metamorphosis. This insect has a particularly interesting larval stage, during which time it is called a *mealworm*. Mealworms shed their skin from 10 to 20 times during the 4 to 5 months they remain in the larval stage. The entire metamorphosis takes 6 to 9 months. Cultures of this insect can be bought inexpensively at pet stores.

Crayfish and Brine Shrimp

Crayfish, shrimp, lobsters, crabs, water fleas, barnacles, and sow bugs are in a class of animals called *crustaceans*. Like insects and other animals with jointed legs, most crustaceans have external skeletons made of chitin. Muscles and other body parts are attached inside to this semirigid exterior. Like insects, crustaceans need to shed their outside covering, or molt, several times in order to grow.

Unlike insects, which have three body parts, crustaceans have only two: a fused-together head and thorax, and an abdomen. All crustaceans but the sow bug and its relatives live in water. All breathe through gills and have two main pairs of feelers, or antennae.

Crayfish

With its hard shell and five pairs of legs, the crayfish looks much like a lobster (INQ Figure 8–13). Crayfish are widely found in the United States, living in and along the banks of muddy freshwater streams, marshes, and ponds.

Crayfish are caught with minnow traps, scooped up with small nets, or simply pulled up when they grasp a chunk of fish dangling at the end of a string. Biological supply houses (see Appendix C) also furnish them.

Crayfish are found more easily at night, when they emerge from burrows or from between stones to prey on small fish and insects. During the day or night, they may also be caught by flipping over flat stones and quickly grasping them by hand from the rear. They

INQ Figure 8–13 **A crayfish.**

INQ Figure 8–14 **Brine shrimp.**

can be safely brought back to the classroom in a plastic bucket loosely filled with wet grass and pond weeds and just enough water to cover the bucket bottom.

Crayfish need a roomy, shallow water habitat. A child's plastic wading pool is suitable for keeping them in a classroom. Their behaviors there give many chances for observing, reporting, and other language activities. Their interactions are particularly interesting to observe, as a recognizable "pecking order" soon emerges.

Brine Shrimp

Adult brine shrimp are no more than 12 millimeters (0.5 inch) long (INQ Figure 8–14). However, these animals are crustaceans, just like their distant cousins, the shrimp, which we eat. Their tiny eggs are found around the shores of salt lakes and salt flats.

Brine shrimp eggs may be hatched in saltwater within a wide range of salt concentrations. The eggs are produced in a curious way. The first group of eggs produced by the female hatch inside her body. What emerges are tiny, almost transparent brine shrimp. Any further eggs produced by the same female are released directly into the water. These eggs will hatch only if they are first dried. They may survive for years in a dry condition before being hatched.

Snails

Snails belong to one of the largest animal phyla, the soft-bodied *mollusks*. Most live in the ocean; they include the squid, octopus, oyster, clam, and many other less familiar animals. Mollusks are divided into three subgroups according to how the foot is attached.

Snails are among the belly-footed mollusks (*gastropods*). A snail has a single shell and travels on what seems to be its abdomen, but what is really a soft, muscular *foot*. The foot secretes a *mucus*, or slime, that reduces friction and protects it from being irritated as the snail moves over different surfaces. The mucus is so effective that a snail may travel over a row of upturned razor blades without injury (although children should not try this).

Water, or pond, snails have one pair of stalks, or tentacles, each with a tiny eye at the base. Most are smaller than the land snails, and many breathe through gills. Land, or garden, snails are lung breathers and have two pairs of tentacles. The upper pair has primitive eyes at the tips. The lower pair carries organs of smell. When threatened, land snails retract their tentacles; water snails do not.

Like the water snail, each land snail has both male and female sex organs. It lays tiny, single eggs, up to about 100 at a time. These may be found in small depressions in the soil, often by the base of a plant. The tiny snails that hatch from the eggs eat leaves, as do the adults. The adults live for about 5 years.

Land snails need a humid environment to be active. When its habitat begins to dry out, a land snail usually attaches itself to some object. A mucous secretion forms and dries over its shell opening. This seal greatly reduces water loss. The snail may remain in this inactive state for months, until its habitat becomes humid again.

Snails have filelike tongues that shred vegetation into bits small enough to be swallowed. In an aquarium, the tongue of a snail may be observed with a hand lens as it scrapes green algae off the sides of the tank.

Earthworms

The earthworm is a *segmented worm*, the most developed of three broad groups of worms. Its body may have more than 100 segments. The earthworm's peculiar way of eating makes it valuable to farmers and gardeners: It literally eats its way through the soil. The decaying plant and animal matter in the soil is digested as it passes through the earthworm's body. The soil that the earthworm eliminates from its body is improved in fertility, but the side effects are even more important: The soil is loosened and aerated. Also, mineral-rich soil below the surface is brought up and mixed with mineral-depleted surface soil. The earthworm moves through and on the soil by alternately stretching and contracting its body.

Earthworms are skin breathers; that is, they take in oxygen and release carbon dioxide directly through the skin. For this to happen, the skin must be moist. It is important to have wet hands or use a wet file card and spoon when handling them since this dries out their skin.

ECOLOGICAL **Inquiry**

Food Chains

Invitation

What is a food chain? Plants need the sun to grow. Many insects eat plants, many toads eat insects, many snakes eat toads, and many hawks eat snakes. This is one example of a food chain. What do you think happens when a food chain is broken?

MATERIALS

- Six cards with one of these words or pictures on each (*sun, plant, insect, toad, snake, hawk*)

- Six persons

- Six pins

Exploration

1. Each person should pin a card to his or her clothes.
2. Stand in line and hold hands in this order: sun, plant, insect, toad, snake, and hawk.
3. What animals would die if they had no snakes to eat? (The snake person should drop hands now.)
4. What animals would die if they had no toads to eat? (The toad person drops hands.)
5. What animals would die if they had no insects to eat? (Insect person drops hands.)
6. What animals would die if they had no plants to eat? (Plant person drops hands.)
7. What would happen if there were no sun to help plants grow? (Sun person drops hands.)

Concept Invention

1. What would happen if there were no hawks?
2. Do hawks belong to other food chains?
3. Do we belong to any food chains?

Teaching Tips

Be sure to point out that these animals might eat a wider variety of food than is shown in this simple chain, but the basic idea of interdependence is valid. This idea can be clarified further by making more food chains. Older children can connect two or more food chains to make a more complicated *food web*. Run strings between and among individuals in the web to show the intricate interrelationships involved.

Scaffolding for English Learners

One way to make this activity easier and more meaningful for English learners is to use computer drawing or animation software in the development of a sample food chain. (See Buxton, 1999, for a discussion of the value of using software with English learners.)

Concept Application

Can you think of other animals and plants that might comprise a food chain? List them, and draw lines and arrows showing who eats what in your food chain.

How Color Protects Animals ————

Invitation

If you were an insect that lived in the grass, what enemies might you have? How might having the right color protect you from being eaten by birds and other animals? How can you test whether color affects the chances to survive?

Exploration

1. Cut out 100 same-sized pieces of green paper and 100 of brown paper. Make each piece about the size of your thumbnail.
2. Have someone scatter 50 pieces of each color on a lawn area.
3. Pretend the paper pieces are insects and you are a bird. Try to find as many pieces as you can in 1 minute. As shown, let some partners help you.

MATERIALS

- Brown and green construction paper
- Lawn area
- Scissors
- Bare dirt area
- 1/2 cup of birdseed
- Set of food colorings
- Jar
- Stopwatch or nonelectric clock with second hand

Teaching Tips

Try to have the colors of the construction paper match as closely as possible the lawn and bare dirt areas. For the birdseed activity, allow several hours between scattering the seeds and locating the surviving seeds. Make sure students realize that they may not be able to locate all the surviving seeds. How can they increase their chances of locating survivors? They may decide to enclose groups of seeds with string or to try other methods.

Concept Invention

1. How many pieces of each color of paper did you find? Which color would be better if you were a lawn insect?
2. Suppose you were an insect that lived in a bare dirt area. Which color would be better? What could you do to find out?
3. How could colored seeds be tested with real birds? Mix a few drops of food coloring with water in a jar. Drop in the seeds to color them.
4. Observe closely the insects on different plants. How are their colors like those of the plant? How are their colors different from those of the plant?

Concept Application

Survival chances increase when an animal's color matches its surroundings. How are other animals protected by their skin colors? Look in books and magazines for colored pictures of animals in their natural habitats. Describe what you find.

Ant Responses to Sweeteners ———

Invitation

Some people do not use regular sugar because it has a high energy value. Instead, they may use an artificial sweetener, which has a low energy value. Many people cannot tell the difference between the tastes of the two. You probably know that ants and some other insects are attracted to sugar. But what attracts them? Is it the taste or something else? How can you test ant responses to real and artificial sugar?

Exploration

1. Mix about one bottle cap each of sugar and water in a cup. Use a spoon to stir. Pour the mixture into one cap until it is full.
2. Do the same with sweetener and water. Use a second cap and cup. Remember to rinse the spoon clean before you stir again.
3. Place both caps close together where there are ants. Mark which cap contains the sugar. Watch what happens.

MATERIALS

- One or more artificial sweeteners
- Sugar
- Two small matched bottle caps
- Water
- Two paper cups
- Teaspoon
- Outdoor area with ants

Teaching Tips | You may want to check where children put the caps. They should be equally accessible to the ants.

Concept Invention

1. What do you notice? Which mixture attracts more ants?
2. What will happen if you test the sweetener by itself?
3. What will happen if you test it with different kinds of ants?
4. What will happen if you test different sweeteners?

Concept Application

The ability to respond to a high-energy food can help an animal survive. How can you find out how other insects will act toward artificial sweeteners? Keep a record of your findings. Look it over. How do the responses of these animals help them stay alive?

The Fright Distances of Wild Animals ———

Invitation

One difference between wild and tame animals is how easily they are frightened. How close have you come to a wild bird before it flew off? How about other wild animals? What are the fright distances of some wild birds?

MATERIALS

- Wild birds
- Different kinds of bird food (bread crumbs, seeds, bacon bits)
- Handkerchief
- Meterstick or yardstick

Teaching Tips

Children can usually notice differences in bird species, but they often have trouble communicating what they see. A simple bird identification book can help. If possible, let children repeat this activity over several days. They will discover that birds and other wild animals typically decrease their fright distances if the same harmless stimulus is presented each time. Remember that children should never touch wild animals that approach humans and never feed them by hand. Such animals are abnormal and may be ill.

Exploration

1. Go where there are some wild birds.
2. Sprinkle some breadcrumbs on the ground at different distances from you.
3. Watch where the birds pick up the crumbs each time. Measure the closest distance the birds dare to come near you.

Concept Invention

1. What is the fright distance of these birds? Is every bird in this group frightened at the same distance? Are other kinds of birds frightened at another distance?
2. What would be the fright distance if you tried other foods?
3. Suppose you go to the same place and drop crumbs each day for a week. What do you think the fright distance of the same birds would be then?
4. How close can you get to different birds without food? Slowly walk toward each perched bird until it flies away. Measure the distance between you and the perch place each time.
5. How do different sounds and noises affect fright distance? different movements?

Concept Application

Fright behavior is an inborn property of wild animals that helps them survive. Fright distance may decrease when animals become familiar with objects or events. What are the fright distances of other wild animals? Find squirrels, chipmunks, and other animals. Make a record of what happens with other animals.

MATERIALS

- Several abandoned bird nests
- Pencil
- Tweezers
- 60-centimeter (2-foot) cardboard square
- Aluminum foil
- Large nail
- Different kinds of string
- Scissors
- Different kinds of cloth
- Different colors of yarn
- Different kinds of paper
- Tack or nail
- Hammer

Bird Nests

Invitation

Have you ever seen a bird nest close up? Birds do not have to learn how to make nests. This is an inborn behavior. Birds use the nest to lay and hatch eggs. The hatched chicks stay there until they grow up enough to go out on their own. The materials used for the nest may come from many different things. Sometimes the materials birds use are quite surprising. How can you find out more about how some birds make nests? Given choices, what materials will some birds pick to make nests?

Exploration

1. Look for abandoned bird nests in trees and large bushes. Collect several nests. Ask a responsible adult to help you. Bring the nests to class.
2. Punch many holes in the cardboard with a large nail. Wiggle the nail in each hole to make it larger. Cut narrow pieces of cloth, paper, and foil. Cut small pieces of string and yarn. Thread these materials partway through the cardboard's holes. Label under each hole what is there. Tack the cardboard to a tree where other trees and bushes grow. Check the board each day to see what is missing.

Concept Invention

1. What is the size and shape of each nest that was collected? How is each made? How are the nests alike? How are the nests different? What materials were used to make these nests? Use tweezers and a pencil to help you pick apart the nests.
2. Make a list of the materials. Which seem to come from where the birds live? Which, if any, seem to come from far away? What kind of bird probably made each kind of nest? Get some bird books from the library. See if they can help you find out.
3. Which of your materials were taken first when birds were making new nests? Replace these materials right away. Will they be taken again before other materials? Check again to see.
4. How can you change the picked materials to make them less attractive? You might cut longer pieces of yarn, for example, or cut wider cloth strips. How can you make the unpicked materials more attractive?
5. What will happen if you move the board to another place? How will your findings compare with those before?

Teaching Tips

Bird nests are usually abandoned by winter and are rarely used again. So, winter is a good time to collect nests. In the unlikely event that eggs are found, the nest should be left undisturbed. The materials-selection board is best placed off the ground on a tree trunk or low limb away from traffic, but visible and accessible to the children.

Concept Application

Birds use materials from the environment to build their nests; the ability to build nests has survival value. Make a list of the materials selected by the birds to make new nests. How does it compare with the list of nest materials in the nests that you found?

ECOLOGICAL CONCEPTS

In previous sections, you have seen some ways that animal bodies are adapted to the requirements of their physical environments. In this section, we take up some factors that influence the numbers and quality of animal populations. To do so, we first need to examine some concepts from *ecology*, or the study of interactions of living things with each other and their physical environment.

Habitats and Their Dwellers

A *habitat* is the specific environment or place where an animal or plant lives. There are many different kinds of habitats. On land, we see desert, woodland, frozen tundra, farm, vacant lot, and garden habitats, to name just a few. Each contains animals and plants equipped to live in these locations. The many freshwater and saltwater habitats contain diverse living things, too. Some habitats fluctuate between a semidry and a watery condition, like seashores. Here, too, we see creatures equipped to live and continue their kind.

Populations

Within a habitat, we usually can find any number of organisms of the same kind that live and reproduce there. This is a *population*. A habitat is likely to have more than one population. For example, a "vacant" lot may contain a half-dozen different animal populations: worms, snails, mice, spiders, or various insects. It most likely will contain different plant populations as well: dandelions, alfalfa, clover, or various grasses or weeds.

Communities

A human community is made up of people with different skills and needs. When groups of these persons interact properly, the community sustains itself. Likewise, a natural *community* is made up of interacting plant and animal populations. Plants grow when their needs for raw materials are met. Plant eaters eat some of the plants, and animal eaters eat some of the plant eaters.

Food Chains and Webs

The connection between plants, plant eaters, and animal eaters is called a *food chain*. For example, in a freshwater habitat, tiny fish called minnows eat water plants, and the minnows in turn are eaten by frogs. We can diagram the relationship like this:

Water plants → minnows → frogs

The arrows show the direction of food transfer.

Real-life food chains and food webs are seldom so simple. Usually, more animals are involved, and they eat more than one kind of plant or other animal. For example, we may see something like INQ Figure 8–15.

We can classify the organisms in this food web into three groups: *producers* (plants), *consumers* (animals), and *decomposers* (bacteria and molds). All three types are usually present in a food web. Consumers are further grouped as *predators* (animal eaters) and *prey* (animals eaten by the animal eaters). Most preyed-upon animals are plant eaters.

A large percentage of plants and animals do not complete their life cycles because they are consumed. Those that do complete their cycles finally become food for the decomposers. These organisms are essential to new life because, through decay, they break down animal and plant matter into minerals, water, and gases. The minerals become part of the soil. The water and gases go back into the air. These elements are used again by growing plants.

An Ecosystem and Its Energy

To survive, animal and plant communities depend on interactions with the physical environment and with each other. Air, water, soil, temperature, and light all play a part in sustaining life. This web of relationships between a community and its physical environment is called an *ecosystem*. There is no strict agreement about its size. Some scientists regard the whole earth as one ecosystem. Others regard the term as referring to the interactions within a small habitat.

All life in any ecosystem depends on the transfer of energy. You saw how this happens with food webs. But some source must start the energy transfer. That source is the sun. The process that makes the energy usable, of course, is photosynthesis. Even our fossil fuels hold the sun's energy, locked up millions of years ago in buried plant and animal forms.

INQ Figure 8–15   **Food web.**

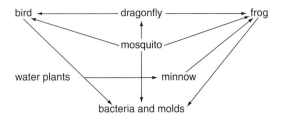

Biotic Potential

Earlier, we jokingly suggested that you not be too efficient at breeding guppies. A single pair might result in 3 million guppies in a year. A huge reproductive capacity is found in many other living things as well. The greatest increase possible in a population without deaths is called its *biotic potential*. For many reasons, no population achieves this potential. Let's look at some of these reasons.

Limiting Factors

Every known organism needs certain environmental conditions to survive. Without certain supplies of air, chemicals, water, light, or proper temperature, for example, living things typically die. If only a certain amount of these factors is present, organisms may barely survive but not reproduce. Every organism seems to have an optimum range of conditions in which it flourishes. Knowing these conditions is the key to success at cultivating plants and raising animals.

Physical barriers, disease, and predators also limit populations. Sea plant growth stops at the shores, animals suffer from diseases just as humans do, and predators must eat to stay alive.

Adaptations

Both animals and plants have some adaptations that allow many to survive when limiting factors come into play. When winter comes, some birds migrate and some mammals hibernate or grow thicker coats of fur. At other times, many insects go undetected by predators because their body colors blend into their surroundings. Grasshoppers may literally fly on to greener pastures when they run low on food. In a huge population, the sheer number allows some members to survive even with a combination of bad conditions.

With less prolific animals, such as birds and mammals, fewer offspring would seem to pose a greater risk to population survival. But these animals compensate for the lack of numbers by an increased capacity to care for their young.

For example, a bird may build a nest for its eggs and feed its young until they are ready to fly. It has the capacity to pick the proper materials from its environment and assemble them in a way that suits the function. The bird does not have to learn this task from older birds; it does the intricate job properly the first time.

So-called instinctive behavior is a common property of animals. A spider does not have to learn how to make its complex web. Nor does an ant have to learn to choose between a solution of high-energy sugar water and an artificial sweetener of little caloric value. Nature abounds with many such examples.

Such adaptations bring about a dynamic balance in population sizes. Limiting factors reduce populations, but adaptive behaviors counter these factors enough so that population sizes stabilize.

The significant exception to the rule, of course, is the human animal. By eradicating most diseases and predators, the human population has grown at a fantastic pace. In the long run, however, limiting factors will exact their toll unless we, too, live in ways that make ecological sense.

Pollution

The problem of environmental pollution is that it introduces another limiting factor into ecosystems. Pollution usually happens faster than organisms can adapt to the changes introduced. The result is a decline in at least some of the populations subjected to the pollution. The populations most likely to decline are the more complex forms of plant and animal life, incluidng humans. Those less likely to decline are the primitive plants and animals, the decomposers, and their kin.

INQ Figure 8–16   **Carbon dioxide–oxygen cycle.**

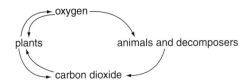

INQ Figure 8–17   **Nitrogen cycle.**

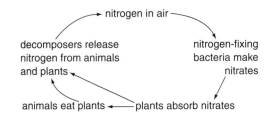

Material Cycles ———————

Scientists refer to the earth as a *closed ecosystem*; that is, almost no new raw materials enter or leave the system. Because an ecosystem ultimately depends on its raw materials, it is essential to life that these materials are never used up. Fortunately, they never are. The materials basic to life are used over and over in a kind of cycle. Next, we consider three important cycles.

Carbon Dioxide–Oxygen Cycle

Living things need oxygen to convert stored food into energy. As a by-product, they give off carbon dioxide. This is true of plants as well as animals. Decomposers also release carbon dioxide as they work. Fortunately, plants need carbon dioxide to carry on photosynthesis. During this process, plants take in carbon dioxide and give off much oxygen.

Decomposers and animals give plants carbon dioxide, and plants give all living things oxygen. The process is continual and may be diagrammed like INQ Figure 8–16.

Another side to this gas exchange is important to realize. An essential part of living cells is the element carbon. Plants get the carbon they need from the food they make during photosynthesis. Animals get carbon from the plants they eat or from animals that eat plants.

Nitrogen Cycle

Another cycle occurs with the element nitrogen. It, too, is an essential part of living cells. The air contains plenty of nitrogen, but neither plants nor animals can use it in a gaseous form. How can it be converted into a form living things can use? The basic way this is done in nature is through bacteria attached to the roots of such plants as clover, beans, alfalfa, and peas. The bacteria combine nitrogen with other elements to make chemical compounds called *nitrates*. Plants absorb the nitrates as they grow. Animals eat the plants and therefore get the nitrogen they need. When the animals die, decomposers convert the nitrogen into a gaseous form again as part of the decay process. This process is continual and may be diagrammed as illustrated in INQ Figure 8–17.

Water Cycle

As you may know, water on the earth's surface continually evaporates, condenses at some altitude in the sky, and falls again as rain, hail, or snow. Living things need water to transport chemicals to cells and remove waste materials from cells. Plants release water through *transpiration*, a process whereby water vapor passes out mainly through holes in the leaves into the air. Animals release water through exhalation, through perspiration, and in waste products. The released water goes into the air and becomes part of the water cycle.

Seen in this way, it is possible that a trace of the water that sustains you today may once have fallen on a dinosaur or on Julius Caesar's Rome.

References

American Association for the Advancement of Science (AAAS). (1993). *Benchmarks for science literacy*. New York: Oxford University Press.

Buxton, C. (1999). Designing a model-based methodology for science instruction: Lessons from a bilingual classroom. *Bilingual Research Journal, 32*(2, 3). Retrieved November 13, 2004, from http://brj.asu.edu/v2323/articles/art4.html

Carratello, P., & Carratello, J. (1994). *Animals (hands-on minds-on science series)*. Huntington Beach, CA: Teacher Created Materials.

Mastropieri, M., & Scruggs, T. E. (2004). *The inclusive classroom: Strategies for effective instruction* (4th ed.). Upper Saddle River, NJ: Merrill/Prentice Hall.

National Research Council (NRC). (1996). *National science education standards*. Washington, DC: National Academy Press.

Teachers of English to Speakers of Other Languages (TESOL). (2001). *Position statement on language and literacy development for young English language learners*. Alexandria, VA: Author. Retrieved November 13, 2004, from www.tesol.org/s$$$tesol/bin.asp? CID532&DID5371&DOC5FILE.PDF

Turnbull, R., Turnbull, A., Shank, M., & Smith, S. J. (2004). *Exceptional lives: Special education in today's schools* (4th ed.). Upper Saddle River, NJ: Merrill/Prentice Hall.

University of Alberta. (2001). *Animal terms or what do you call a . . . ?* Retrieved April 1, 2001, from www.biology.ualberta.ca/uamz.hp/name.html

Selected Trade Books: Animal Life

For Younger Children

Aaseng, N. (1987). *Meat-eating animals*. Minneapolis: Lerner.

Aaseng, N. (1987). *Prey animals*. Minneapolis: Lerner.

Berger, M. (2003). *Let's-read-and-find-out science books—Spinning spiders*. New York: HarperTrophy.

Breeden, R. (Ed.). (1974). *Creepy crawly things*. Washington, DC: National Geographic Society.

Bruchac, J. (1992). *Native American animal stories*. Golden, CO: Fulcrum.

Carle, E. (1987). *The very hungry caterpillar*. New York: Philomel.

Carle, E. (1995). *The very lonely firefly*. New York: Philomel.

Cousins, L. (1991). *Country animals*. New York: Morrow.

Crump, D. (1983). *Creatures small and furry*. Washington, DC: National Geographic Society.

Day, J. (1986). *What is a mammal?* New York: Golden Books.

Dewey, J. O. (2002). *Once I knew a spider*. New York: Walker and Company.

Dreyer, E. (1991). *Wild animals*. New York: Troll Associates.

Fleming, D. (1993). *In the small, small pond*. New York: Henry Holt.

Fowler, A. (1992). *It's best to leave a snake alone*. Danbury, CT: Childrens Press.

Freedman, R. (1980). *Tooth and claw: A look at animal weapons*. New York: Holiday House.

George, T. C. (2001). *Jellies: The life of jellyfish*. Brookfield, CT: Millbrook Press.

Glaser, L. (2003). *Brilliant bees*. Brookfield, CT: Millbrook Press.

Greenway, S. (1992). *Can you see me?* Nashville, TN: Ideals Children's Books.

Heiligman, D. (1996). *From caterpillar to butterfly*. New York: HarperCollins.

Lauber, P. (1965). *Who eats what? Food chains and food webs*. New York: HarperCollins.

Llewellyn. C. (2003). *Starting life butterfly*. Chanhassen, MN: Northword Press.

Markle, S. (2002). *Growing up wild: Penguins*. New York: Antheneum.

Mastro, J., & Wu, N. (2003). *Antarctic ice*. New York: Henry Holt & Co.

Miller, D. S. (2000). *River of Life*. New York: Clarion Books.

Oppenheim, J. (1986). *Have you seen birds?* New York: Scholastic.

Palotta, J. (1992). *The icky bug counting book*. Watertown, MA: Charlesbridge.

Pandell, K. (1996). *Animal action ABC*. New York: Dutton Children's Books.

Patent, D. H. (2003). *Fabulous fluttering tropical butterflies*. New York: Walker and Company.

Patent, D. H. (2003). *Slinky scaly slithery snakes*. New York: Walker and Company.

Penn, L. (1983). *Young scientists explore animal friends*. Torrance, CA: Good Apple.

Penny, M. (2000). *Giant panda: Habitats, life cycles, food chains, threats (natural world)*. Austin, TX: Raintree Steck-Vaughn Publishers.

Pfloog, J. (1987). *Wild animals and their babies*. Cambridge, Ontario: Western.

Posada, M. (2002). *Ladybugs: Red, fiery, and bright*. Minneapolis: Carolrhoda Books/Lerner.

Priestly, A. (1987). *Big animals*. New York: Random House.

Rockwell, A. (2001). *Let's-read-and-find-out science 1—Bugs are insects*. New York: HarperCollins.

Savage, S. (1992). *Making tracks*. New York: Lodestar Books.

Sayer, A. P. (2002). *Army ant parade*. New York: Henry Holt.

Sill, C., & Sill J. (2003). *About arachnids: A guide for children*. Atlanta: Peachtree Publishers.

Stone, L. M. (1983). *Marshes and swamps*. Danbury, CT: Childrens Press.

Sutton, F. (1983). *The big book of wild animals*. New York: G. P. Putman.

Tagholm, S. (2000). *Animal lives: The rabbit*. New York: Kingfisher.

Tatham, B. (2001). *Let's-read-and-find-out science series—Penguin chick*. New York: HarperCollins.

Urquhart, J. C. (1982). *Animals that travel*. Washington, DC: National Geographic Society.

Walker, S. M. (1998). *Sea horses (early bird nature)*. Minneapolis: Carolrhoda Books/Lerner.

Walker, S. M. (2001). *Fireflies*. Minneapolis: Lerner Publications.

Wildsmith, B. (1991). *Animal homes*. Norway, ME: Oxford Group.

Winer, Y. (2002). *Birds build nests*. Watertown, MA: Charlesbridge Publishing.

Wozmek, F. (1982). *The ABC of ecology*. Los Altos Hills, CA: May Davenport.

Zemlicka, S. (2002). *From egg to butterfly*. Minneapolis: Lerner Publications.

Zuchora-Walske, C. (2000). *Leaping grasshoppers*. New York: Kingfisher.

For Older Children

Branzei, S. (1996). *Animal grossology*. Reading, MA: Planet Dexter/Addison-Wesley.

Bright, M. (1987). *Pollution and wildlife*. Danbury, CT: Watts.

Crenson, V. (2003). *Horseshoe crabs and shorebirds: The story of a food web*. New York: Marshall Cavendish Corporation.

Crump, M. (2002). *Amphibians, reptiles, and their conservation*. North Haven, CT: Linnet Books.

Dean, A. (1977). *How animals communicate*. Parsippany, NJ: Julian Messner.

Dean, A. (1978). *Animal defenses*. Parsippany, NJ: Julian Messner.

Earle, S. A. (2000). *Sea critters*. Washington, DC: National Geographic Society.

Earthbooks Staff. (1991). *National Wildlife Federation's book of endangered species*. Winchester, VA: Author.

Fichter, G. S. (1991). *Poisonous animals*. Danbury, CT: Watts.

Galan, M. (1997). *There's still time: The success of the Endangered Species Act*. Washington, DC: National Geographic Society.

Gallant, R. A. (1986). *The rise of mammals*. Danbury, CT: Watts.

Hansard, P., & Silver, B. (1991). *What bird did that? A driver's guide to some common birds of North America*. Berkeley, CA: Ten Speed Press.

Heinz, B. J. (2000). *Butternut hollow pond*. Brookfield, CT: Milbrook Press.

Hickman, P. (1998). *Animal senses: How animals see, hear, taste, smell, and feel*. Toronto, Ontario: Kids Can Press.

Horowitz, R. (2000). *Crab moon*. Cambridge, MA: Candlewick Press.

Hostetler, M. (1996). *That gunk on your car: A unique guide to insects of North America*. Berkeley, CA: Ten Speed Press.

Imes, R. (1992). *The practical entomologist: An introductory guide to observing and understanding the world of insects*. New York: Simon & Schuster/Fireside.

Jenkins, S. (1997). *What do you do when something wants to eat you?* Boston: Houghton Mifflin.

Johnson, J. (2000). *National Geographic animal encyclopedia*. Washington, DC: National Geographic Society.

Kaufman, K. (2000). *Focus guide to the birds of North America*. Boston: Houghton Mifflin.

Leon, D. (1982). *The secret world of underground creatures*. Parsippany, NJ: Julian Messner.

Lerner, C. (1998). *Butterflies in the garden*. New York: HarperCollins.

Mason, C. (1998). *Everybody's somebody's lunch*. Gardiner, ME: Tilbury House.

Maynard, T. (1991). *Animal inventors*. Danbury, CT: Watts.

Patent, D. H. (2002). *Animals on the trail with Lewis and Clark*. New York: Clarion Books.

Penny, M. (1987). *Animal evolution*. Danbury, CT: Watts.

Pringle, L. (1987). *Home: How animals find comfort and safety*. New York: Macmillan.

Reed-Jones, C. (2001). *Salmon stream*. Sierra Nevadas, CA: Dawn Publications.

Ross, M. E. (2000). *Pond watching with Ann Morgan*. Minneapolis: Carolrhoda Books/Lerner.

Sabin, F. (1985). *Ecosystems and food chains*. New York: Troll Associates.

Sanders, J. (1984). *All about animal migrations*. New York: Troll Associates.

Swinburne, S. R. (2002). *The woods scientist*. Boston: Houghton Mifflin.

Thomas, P. (2000). *Marine mammal preservation*. Brookfield, CT: Twenty-First Century Books/Millbrook Press.

Witmer, L. (1995). *The search for the origin of birds*. Danbury, CT: Watts.

Yamashita, K. (1993). *Paws, wings, and hooves*. Minneapolis: Lerner.

Resource Books

Barrett, K. (1986). *Animals in action*. Berkeley, CA: Great Explorations in Math and Science.

Beals, K., Parizeau, N., & MacPherson, R. (2003). *Life through time*. Berkeley, CA: Great Explorations in Math and Science. (evolution activities)

Berg, C. (1994). *Chameleon condos: Critters and critical thinking*. Arlington, VA: National Science Teachers Association.

Burnett, R. (1992). *The pillbug project: A guide to investigation*. Arlington, VA: National Science Teachers Association.

Butzow, C. M., & Butzow, J. W. (1989). *Science through children's literature: An integrated approach*. Englewood, CO: Teacher Ideas Press. (animal reproduction and development topics on pp. 61–65; ducks, ants, spiders, ladybugs, and fish topics on pp. 66–94; animal adaptation topics on pp. 102–106)

Cordel, B. (Ed.). (1998). *Cycles of knowing and growing*. Fresno, CA: AIMS Education Foundation.

Cordel, B. (Ed.). (1998). *Field detectives*. Fresno, CA: AIMS Education Foundation.

Council for Environmental Education. (1992). *Project WILD*. Bethesda, MD: Author.

Echols, J. C. (1987). *Animal defenses*. Berkeley, CA: Great Explorations in Math and Science. (predator–prey relationships)

Echols, J. C. (1999). *Buzzing a hive*. Berkeley, CA: Great Explorations in Math and Science. (bee social behavior and habitat)

Echols, J. C. (1999). *Ladybugs*. Berkeley, CA: Great Explorations in Math and Science. (ladybugs and animal adaptation)

Echols, J. C. (2000). *Penguins and their young*. Berkeley, CA: Great Explorations in Math and Science. (penguin characteristics and social behavior)

Echols, J. C., Blinderman, E., & Kopp, J. (2001). *Elephants and their young*. Berkeley, CA: Great Explorations in Math and Science. (elephant characteristics and social behavior)

Echols, J. C., Hosoume, K., & Kopp, J. (1996). *Ant homes under the ground*. Berkeley, CA: Great Explorations in Math and Science.

Echols, J. C., Kopp, J., Blinderman, E., & Hosoume, K. (1999). *Mother opossum and her babies*. Berkeley, CA: Great Explorations in Math and Science. (opossum adaptations)

Fredericks, A. D., Meinbach, A. M., & Rothlein, L. (1993). *Thematic units: An integrated approach to teaching science and social studies*.

New York: HarperCollins. (animals and how they grow topics on pp. 111–122)

Hillen, J., Wiebe, A., & Youngs, D. (Eds.). (1992). *Critters*. Fresno, CA: AIMS Education Foundation.

Hoover, E., & Cordel, B. (Eds.). (1999). *Exploring environments*. Fresno, CA: AIMS Education Foundation.

Hosoume, K., & Barber, J. (1994). *Terrarium habitats*. Berkeley, CA: Great Explorations in Math and Science.

LeCroy, B., & Holder, B. (1994). *Bookwebs: A brainstorm of ideas for the primary classroom*. Englewood, CO: Teacher Ideas Press. (animal activities on pp. 30–31)

Mason, C., & Markowsky, J. (1998). *Everybody's somebody's lunch teachers' guide: The roles of predators in nature*. Gardiner, ME: Tilbury House.

Shaw, D. G., & Dybdahl, C. S. (1996). *Integrating science and language arts: A sourcebook for K–6 teachers*. Boston: Allyn & Bacon. (animal life topics on pp. 57–59)

THE HUMAN BODY AND NUTRITION

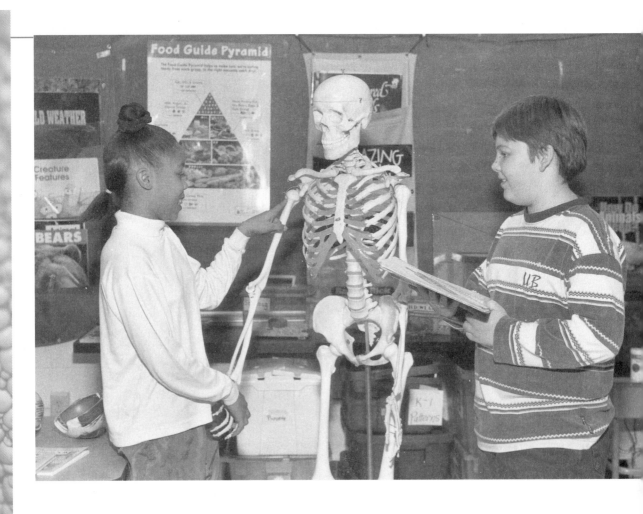

By any measure, the human body is a masterpiece of organization. It is composed of millions of tiny cells, many of them differing in shape, size, and internal makeup according to the work they do. Groups of cells that work together are called *tissues*. Examples are the connective tissue that holds the body together, muscle tissue, nerve tissue, blood tissue, and epithelial (skin) tissue. Tissues that work together are called *organs*. Examples are the lungs, heart, stomach, and eyes. Organs that work together are *systems*.

We now consider several body systems, including the skeletal and muscle systems, which support and move the body; the nervous system, which controls the body; the circulatory and respiratory systems, which move the blood and permit breathing; and the digestive system, which fuels the body by breaking down foods into simpler forms. A final section examines nutrition: the makeup of foods and how they affect the body.

Benchmarks and Standards

As students progress through the elementary years, they gain a more comprehensive understanding of the complexity of the human body and the need to care for it through proper nutrition and exercise. Examples of specific standards related to the human organism are as follows:

Sample Benchmarks (AAAS, 1993)

- People need water, food, air, and waste removal, and a particular range of temperatures in their environment. (By Grades K–2, p. 128)
- Food provides energy and materials for growth and repair of body parts. Vitamins and minerals, present in small amounts in foods, are essential to keep everything working well. (By Grades 3–5, p. 144)

Sample Standards (NRC, 1996)

- Humans have distinct body structures for walking, holding, seeing, and talking. (By Grades K–4, p. 129)
- The human organism has systems for digestion, respiration, reproduction, circulation, excretion, movement, control, and coordination, and for protection from disease. These systems interact with one another. (By Grades 5–8, pp. 156–175)

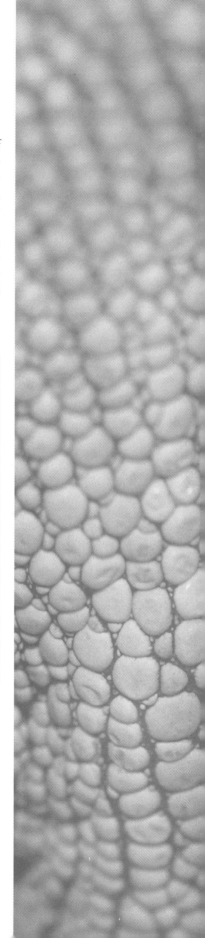

SKELETAL AND MUSCLE SYSTEMS **Inquiry**

Soft Bones

MATERIALS

- Narrow jar and cap
- Vinegar
- Safety goggles
- Two clean matched chicken bones
- Water

Invitation

What happens when minerals are removed from a bone?

Exploration

1. Put one bone in the jar. Leave the other one outside.
2. Put on safety goggles. Fill the jar with enough vinegar to cover the bone.
3. Cap the jar and remove your safety goggles. Wait 5 days.
4. Remove the bone from the jar and rinse it with water.

Concept Invention

1. Compare the bones. In what ways are the two bones different?
2. How easily does each bone bend?
3. How are the bones still alike?

Concept Application

What difference would it make if your bones had no hard minerals? What foods are rich in minerals?

All Thumbs

MATERIALS

- Paper clip
- Pencil and paper
- Tape

Invitation

How useful are your thumbs?

Exploration

1. Make a list of some things you can do now with one or two hands. Which do you think you cannot do without thumbs? Which might you do less well? Which might you do as well?
2. You might record what you think on a chart. You can make a check mark first for what you think, and then an X for what you find out.

Can Do With Thumbs	Can't Do Without Thumbs	Do Less Well	Do as Well
Pick up paper clip	✓		
Tie shoelace	✓		
Write my name		X	
Shake hands			
Button a shirt			
(Other)			

3. Ask someone to tape your thumbs to your hands.
4. Try doing the things on the list without using your thumbs.

Concept Invention

1. What surprises, if any, did you find?
2. How do your thumbs help you?

Concept Application

What would it be like if other mammals had thumbs like ours? How would this change their ways of doing things or survival?

Tired Muscles ————

Invitation

What happens when you overwork your muscles?

MATERIALS

- Pencil and paper
- Watch with second hand

Exploration

1. Open one hand all the way and then quickly close it to make a tight fist.
2. Open and close it just like that for 1 minute without stopping. Do it as fast as you can.
3. Count and record what you are able to do during the first and last 30 seconds.

Concept Invention

1. How do the first half and the last half figures compare?
2. What difference might it make if you change hands?

Scaffolding for English Learners

When identifying the muscles or bones of the body, try to use no more than 12 new vocabulary words in a lesson. (See Fathman, Quinn, & Kessler, 1992, for more information on language principles for English learners.)

Concept Application

If you went more slowly, would you be able to make more fists in 1 minute? Can you make as many fists in a second trial? If not, how long must you rest in between to do so?

SKELETAL AND MUSCLE SYSTEMS CONCEPTS

It is difficult to imagine how the human body would look without bones. It has more than 200 bones joined into a skeletal framework that gives the body its overall shape and support. The bones are not all individual, unique pieces that fit together. Rather, the bones are in groups, all well fitted for their specialized work.

Groups of Bones ————————

The main part of the skull consists of eight relatively flat bones joined into the characteristic helmetlike shape. In children, the joints between the bones are movable. This allows the bones to grow as children get older. In adults, the skull bones will have grown together into a solid, curved surface with immovable joints. The only head bone we can ever move voluntarily is the jawbone. Chewing and normal conversation depend on this movement.

The skull is joined to a stack of oval and irregular small bones called the *vertebrae*, or spine. The vertebrae permit bending and twisting motions. Between each small bone is a pad of tough, elastic tissue called *cartilage*. The cartilage pads keep the spinal bones from grinding or hitting together during movement. As we age during adulthood, the pads continue to compress, making us shorter. Between ages 40 and 70, for example, we may lose 2.5 centimeters (1 inch) or more in height.

Each spinal bone also has a hole in its middle. The holes in the bones are lined up, making the vertebrae into a kind of hollow tube. The bundle of nerves that make up the spinal cord runs through the length of this protective tube of vertebrae. Side holes in the vertebrae permit nerve branches from the spinal cord to go out to other parts of the body.

Many children think that "standing up straight" means having a straight backbone. This is not so. Although the vertebrae are stacked in a column, the column is curved in a shallow S form. This shape permits better balance than a vertical backbone.

Attached to the backbone are 12 pairs of *ribs*. The top 10 pairs curve around and join the *breastbone* in front. But if you feel your two pairs of bottom ribs, you may notice that they are not joined in front. For this reason, they are called "floating ribs."

The ribs form a flexible cage that protects the heart, lungs, and other organs in the chest area. The cartilage that fastens the ribs is somewhat elastic, and the ribs are bendable. This is why the chest can expand and contract during breathing. The hipbones are fastened at the other end of the backbone. With the bottom of the backbone, they form a large and open shallow bowl in front, called the *pelvis*. The bowl helps support the body and protects some of the organs below the waist. The lowest parts of the hipbones are used for sitting.

The long bones of the arms and legs are the levers that allow us to walk, run, and throw. These bones are strong but also light for their size, because they are mostly hollow inside. If they were solid, the increased weight would slow us down considerably. Long bones are thicker at the ends than in the center section and fit the ends of adjoining bones.

Composition of Bones ————————

A soft material called *marrow* is found inside many bones, particularly the long bones. There are two kinds of marrow. Red marrow is found at the ends of the bones, where red blood cells are manufactured. Yellow marrow is stored inside the middle of the bones and is mainly composed of fat.

A newborn baby's skeleton is composed mostly of soft cartilage. As the baby grows, its body continually replaces the cartilage with calcium and other minerals from digested food, so the skeleton continually hardens. Children's bones typically are softer than those of adults because they contain more cartilage. This makes their bones less likely to break under stress. Some cartilage never changes to bone, like the ears and the tip of the nose.

Movable Joints

A rigid skeletal framework would be of little use to us. We can move because many bones are held together by movable joints. Tough, thick cords of elastic tissue, called *ligaments*, join bone to bone. We have several kinds of movable joints, and each allows different movements. *Hinged joints* allow us to bend the elbow, knee, and fingers. Notice that the movement is in only one direction.

The thumb is particularly interesting. It has only two hinged joints, yet we can move the thumb so that it opposes any finger. A third joint up near the wrist makes this movement possible.

A *ball-and-socket joint* at the shoulder allows rotary motion of the arm. A similar socket connects the upper leg bone at the hip, but movement in this case is more restricted. Other kinds of joints allow wrist, head, foot, and other motions. In all, we have six kinds of movable joints.

Muscles

Under the skin and inside the body are about 600 muscles, two thirds of which are *voluntary muscles*. These muscles are connected to bones, and we can move them on command. Some muscles, such as those that move food through the intestines and those that make the heart beat, cannot ordinarily be controlled. These are *involuntary muscles*.

Muscles can only pull, not push. In other words, they work in opposite pairs. This is easiest to see with the jointed leg bones. If you swing a leg forward, muscles in the front part of the thigh and hip contract and pull the leg forward. If you swing the leg back, muscles in the back part of the thigh and hip contract and pull the leg back.

Tendons

Muscles are attached to bone and cartilage by *tendons*. These are tough, white, twisted fibers of different lengths. Some are cordlike; others are wider and flat. Tendons are enclosed in sleeves of thin tissue that contain a slippery liquid. This lubricating liquid permits them to slide back and forth without rubbing.

Tendons are strong and unstretchable. Some that are easy to observe are found inside the elbow and at the back of the knee. One of the strongest and thickest tendons in the body is the Achilles tendon, located just above the heel of the foot. Also easy to observe are the tendons that pull the finger bones as you wiggle your fingers. If you try this and touch the forearm with the opposite hand, you will notice that muscles in the forearm, not muscles in the hand, mainly move the fingers. Children are usually surprised by this.

Makeup of Muscles

How do muscles work? Why do they get tired? Why does exercise make us warm? A microscope reveals that voluntary muscles are made up of bundles of fibers, each about the size of a human hair but far stronger. Like the entire muscle, each fiber shortens as it pulls and lengthens as it relaxes. The number of fibers that work depends on how heavily the muscle is strained. Also, not all the fibers work simultaneously. Each is rapidly and continually switched on and off by the nervous system as the muscle works. This allows each fiber some rest and greater overall endurance for the muscle.

The energy to move a muscle comes from a form of sugar called *glycogen*. It is found inside the muscles' cells. About one fourth of the energy released by this sugar goes into moving the muscle; the rest is released as heat. The faster a muscle is used, the more heat is produced. This is why heavy exercise makes us warm.

Sooner or later, heavy exercise fatigues the muscle. Not only is the supply of glycogen consumed, but waste products also build up in the cell faster than they can be removed. As the waste products build up, the muscle fibers work more and more slowly.

NERVOUS SYSTEM **Inquiry**

Eye Blinking

Invitation

When do your eyes blink? Do they blink when something suddenly comes near them? Eye blinking can protect your eyes. Have you also found that your eyes blink at other times? Regular eye blinking wipes your eyes clean and keeps your eyes soft and moist. How much can you control your protective eye blinking?

Exploration

1. You will need to make an eye shield. Cut out the center of a large file card. Leave at least a 2-centimeter (1-inch) border.
2. Stick a double layer of clear kitchen plastic wrap to the border with tape.
3. Hold up the shield to your eyes. Look at your partner through the clear wrap, as illustrated. Let him gently toss a tiny wad of tissue toward it.

MATERIALS

- Clear kitchen plastic wrap
- Sticky tape
- Tissue paper
- Scissors
- Large file card
- Partner
- Ruler
- Clock with a second hand

Teaching Tips

Closely monitor this activity. Blinking is an automatic reflex that children like to investigate. Many children find it hard to prevent the protective blinking reaction when the wad is tossed at the shield. This is good because the reaction has survival value. Regular blinking, of course, is easily controllable when we are conscious of the act. The rate varies widely among persons and is influenced by a variety of factors.

Concept Invention

1. Do your eyes blink each time the wad hits the shield? Can you stop your eyes from blinking?
2. Are you able to control your eye blinking with practice? If so, how much practice? Keep a record.
3. Trade places with some other people. How does their protective eye blinking compare with yours?
4. How often do a person's eyes blink the regular way? Secretly observe the number of times someone blinks for 1 minute. Compare the blinking rates of different people. Do their blinking rates change when they know you are observing them?

Adapting for Students with Exceptionalities

It may be hard for some students with physical handicaps to complete this activity. Allow them to work in groups of three so that they can have an extra partner for assistance or observation.

Concept Application

Eye blinking is a protective reflex action that is partly controllable. The rate of blinking varies among different people. How often do some animals blink their eyes? Which animals can you observe?

Your Reaction Time ————

Invitation

Have you ever had to stop fast when riding your bike? The time between when we sense something and when we act is called our *reaction time*. What people would you expect to have fast reaction times? What people would you expect to have slowed reaction times? How can you find out about your reaction time?

Exploration

1. Have your partner hold up a ruler just above your open thumb and forefinger. The ruler's lowest marked number should be facing down. Keep your eye on this ruler end.
2. Have your partner drop the ruler without warning. When you see it drop, close your fingers quickly and catch the ruler.
3. At what number did you catch the ruler? Read the closest whole number just above your two closed fingers. This is your reaction time number.

> **Teaching Tips**
>
> For meaningful comparisons, it is important that students do the test in the same way. It is also important that the ruler be turned before it is dropped. You want the flat part of the ruler, not the ruler edges, to be pinched by the two fingers.

Concept Invention

1. What persons in your class may have faster reaction times than yours? What persons in your class may have slower reaction times? Test these persons and your partner. Keep a record.
2. Will you react to a sound you hear faster than to what you see? Have your partner make a sound just as she drops the ruler. Your eyes should be closed. Catch the

ruler when you hear the sound. Compare this reaction time number with the one made when you saw the ruler drop.

3. Will you react to a touch faster than to sound or sight? Your eyes should be closed. Your partner can touch your head lightly when she drops the ruler. Catch the ruler when you feel her touch. Compare this reaction time with the other times.

Concept Application

People have different reaction times. The sense signal people react to also makes a difference in their reaction times. Does the time of day affect your reaction time? Does practice make a difference? Does which hand you use make a difference? How can you find out? What other ideas would you like to try?

How Practice Improves Learning

Invitation

Suppose you learn to do something one way, and then someone says you must learn to do it another way. Why might this be hard to do? How might learning to draw or write backward be a problem? How might practice help? How can you learn to do mirror drawing or writing?

Exploration

1. Draw a triangle on paper, no larger than the one pictured here.

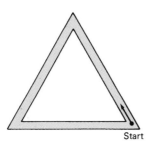

Start

2. Arrange the paper, a mirror, and a book as shown. Use two pieces of clay to hold up the mirror.

MATERIALS
• Small mirror
• Paper
• Clay
• Pencil
• Book
• Ruler
• Watch or clock that indicates seconds
• Graph paper

3. Sit so that you must look into the mirror to see the triangle.

4. Place your pencil point on the triangle corner at "start."

5. Observe a watch and notice the time.

6. Draw a line inside and around the whole triangle. Look at the mirror to see what you are doing. Keep the line between the inside and outside border of the triangle. If you go beyond the borders, stop drawing. Start again from the place where you left the border.

7. When you complete the drawing, check the time again. Record in seconds how long it took for this first trial.

Teaching Tips

You may have to help some children with the line graphs if they lack experience. Also, expect some children to have trouble deciding how many seconds it takes to draw completely around each figure.

Number of Trials	Time to Finish (Seconds)
1	160
2	140
3	100
4	70

Concept Invention

1. How will practice affect the time needed to draw around the triangle? How much faster will your second trial be? How much faster will your third trial be? How much faster will your fourth trial be? Make a record like this of what you find out.

2. Make a graph of your findings. Notice how to do this on the graph shown here. Suppose it took 160 seconds to finish the first trial.

3. Put your finger on 1 at the bottom. Follow the line up to and opposite 160. Place a dot where the two lines cross. Check to see how the other figures are recorded. See how a line has been drawn from one dot to the next. This line is called a *curve*. The graph tells about learning, so the line may be called a *learning curve*.

4. Study your own learning curve. How fast do you think you can draw the triangle after 6 trials? after 7 trials? after 8 trials? after 9 trials? after 10 trials? Record your findings on your graph and complete your learning curve.

5. How does your learning curve compare with those of others? Do some people learn mirror drawing faster than others?

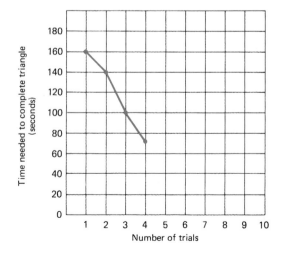

Concept Application

An earlier learning may interfere with a later learning. Proper practice can improve one's performance. Try a mirror drawing of another figure, such as a large 8 like the one shown here. What shape will your learning curve be for this figure? Will people who learned fast before learn fast again? What other problems about learning mirror drawing can you investigate?

Start

Your Sense of Touch —————

Invitation

What can you tell about an object by touch? What are some small objects you might know just by touching them? What objects can you match just by touch?

Exploration

1. Blindfold your partner or ask him to close his eyes. He should not see what you are doing.
2. Put two small, unlike objects inside the box, which should be upside down.
3. Place another small object outside the box. It should match one of the objects inside. Let your blindfolded partner feel it.
4. Next, have your partner feel the objects inside the box. Can he tell which one matches the outside object?
5. Take turns with your partner in playing this game. Use different objects each time. Later, use as many objects each time as you can.

Concept Invention

1. Which objects are hard to tell apart? Which are easy? What makes them easy or hard to tell apart?
2. Can you use touch to put objects in order by size? Can you use touch to put objects in order by roughness? Which objects?
3. Is it easier to tell what an inside object is if you can see the outside objects? How can you find out?
4. Is it easier to tell what an inside object is with two hands than with one? How can you find out?

Concept Application

Several properties of an object can be discovered by touch. Try a challenging variation that stresses communication skills. One child holds an object behind her and describes its properties to a partner. The partner touches several objects inside the box and selects one that matches the description. The described and selected objects are then compared to see if they are identical. To make the task harder, make the differences among the objects less obvious. Also, put more objects inside the box. Describe your experiences.

MATERIALS

- Cloth blindfold
- Open cardboard box (with a hand-sized hole cut in each side)
- Matched pairs of small objects
- Partner

Teaching Tips

Many small objects around the classroom and home may be used in this activity. Among objects easily paired are chalk, pencils, leaves, erasers, crayons, nails, coins, washers, rubber bands, cloth of various sizes and textures, paper, foil, and toy figures. Size, texture, shape, hardness, and, to a minor extent, weight will be the properties used by children to identify objects by touch.

The Sensitivity of Your Skin ───────

MATERIALS

- Ruler
- Paper and pencil
- Partner
- Paper clip

Invitation

Suppose you could not tell if something was touching your skin. How might this change your life? How can you find out how sensitive your skin is to touch?

Exploration

1. Open up and then bend a paper clip into a U shape.
2. Push the two points together so that they meet.
3. Touch the points lightly to the palm of your partner's hand. His eyes should be closed.
4. Ask your partner if he feels two points or one.
5. Separate the two points a short distance, as shown. Ask again if he feels two points or one.
6. Keep repeating this action. Each time, move the two points farther apart until your partner feels two points. Then measure the distance between the two points with a ruler.
7. Switch with your partner so that you can have your skin tested.

Teaching Tips

Many of our nerve ends are found near the skin surface and are distributed unevenly. Typically, our fingertips are more sensitive to touch than other body parts, because a high concentration of nerve endings is located there. It is important that children who are being tested keep their eyes closed. Otherwise, their perception of touch may be altered by what they see. Supervise this activity closely to ensure that the paper clip points are touched lightly to the skin.

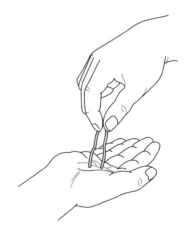

Concept Invention

1. Where on your skin can you feel the two points soonest? Let your partner measure and make a record like the one shown.

Body Part	Distance Between the Points
Fingertip	
Palm of hand	
Back of hand	
Back of neck	
Lips	

2. Look carefully at your completed record. Which seems to be the most sensitive place measured?
3. In what order should the places go if arranged from least to most sensitive?

Concept Application

Some places on the skin are more sensitive to touch than other places; also, some people are more sensitive to touch than others. How does your record compare with those of other people? Are some people more sensitive than others? If so, which people? Are certain places on people's skin more sensitive than others? If so, which places?

Your Sensitivity to Temperature

Invitation

Suppose you have two containers of water. One is slightly warmer than another. Could you tell by touch a temperature difference in the water? Does it depend on how much the difference is? How can you find out the smallest temperature difference you can feel?

MATERIALS

- Two cups half-filled with water (one water sample should be warm)
- Paper and pencil
- Partner
- Thermometer (waterproof type)
- Clock with second hand

Exploration

1. Dip a finger into each cup, as illustrated. It is probably easy now for you to tell which cup of water is cooler and which is warmer.

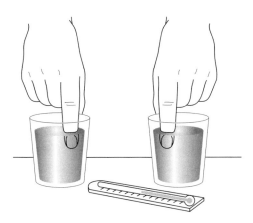

The beginning temperature difference between the two water samples should be obvious, but it need not be a wide one. If you do not have access to a hot-water tap, warm some water on a hot plate. Or, draw two half-cups of tap water and slip an ice cube into one for several minutes. Children will need the ability to read thermometers to do this investigation. The average child can detect a temperature difference as little as 1.5°C (3°F). Some children will detect an even smaller difference. The tester's eyes should be closed for each test.

2. Let your partner pour a little of the cooler water into the warmer water. You can probably still easily feel the temperature difference.
3. Have your partner continue to reduce the temperature difference between the two cups. She can do this by pouring a little water back and forth between the cups. Keep feeling the water in both cups each time.
4. Stop when you can just barely tell there is a temperature difference. Make sure you are not just imagining this. Close your eyes and let your partner switch around the cups a few times. Tell your partner which cup is cooler or warmer each time. Always keep your eyes closed when the cups are switched.
5. Put the thermometer into each cup for at least half a minute. What is the difference between the two readings?

Concept Invention

1. What is the smallest temperature difference your partner can feel?
2. Get some more warm and cool water and find out.

Concept Application

People differ in their sensitivity to temperature. Are some people more sensitive than others? Are people with thin fingers more sensitive than those with thicker fingers? Are toes more sensitive than fingers?

NERVOUS SYSTEM CONCEPTS

The Nerves ───────

What happens inside the nervous system when we sense an object and react to it? The central part of the nervous system is composed of the brain and spinal cord. Nerves connected to the brain and spinal cord branch out in ever smaller tendrils to all parts of the body.

When nerve endings are stimulated in some sense organs, ordinarily an electrical message is zipped through *sensory nerves* from the receptors to the spinal cord and then to the brain. In turn, the brain flashes back a message along *motor nerves,* which control muscles. The time between when the brain receives a signal and when it returns a command to the muscles is called one's *reaction time*.

Quick Reflexes ───────

A curious thing happens, however, when a quick reflexive action is required. The brain is bypassed until the *reflex* action happens. For example, if you should touch a finger to a hot stove, the electrical impulses travel from the finger to the spinal cord. But instead of the signal going on to the brain, the spinal cord itself flashes a signal along the motor nerves, which immediately activate muscles to jerk the hand away. Meanwhile, the spinal cord also sends impulses to the brain that cause you to feel pain. The sensation, though, is felt after you have already reacted to the danger. This process, of course, has survival value.

The Brain ───────

The brain is the control center of the body. Instead of a single mass, it consists of three parts: the cerebrum, the cerebellum, and the medulla. Each has a different job.

The *cerebrum* is the brain's largest part. It consists of two halves that occupy the top portion of the skull. This is the part that governs the conscious, rational processes and that receives signals from the senses. The cerebrum also controls the body's voluntary muscles.

The *cerebellum* is a far smaller part and is located below and behind the cerebrum. It governs perception of balance and coordinates the voluntary muscles.

The *medulla* adjoins the top of the spinal column at the base of the skull. It governs the involuntary muscles used for digesting food, coughing or sneezing, breathing, pumping blood, and the like.

Learning

How successfully we adapt to the environment often depends on our ability to learn. We learn in several ways. At the lowest level is trial-and-error learning. This is how we learn to do handwriting or hit a golf ball. The brain works in combination with the senses and muscles to provide corrective feedback.

Learning increases when we organize our data. Recognizing patterns, outlining, and drawing diagrams are some ways we improve learning. Learning also increases when we associate something we do not know with something we do know. Using memory devices to learn names or to remember spelling words are examples. Reasoning and problem solving are at the highest levels of learning.

The Senses

We receive most of the sensations that our brains turn into perceptions through five organs: the eye, ear, nose, tongue, and skin. How do they work? Let's look at each in turn.

The Eye

In the eye, as in the other sense organs, are the tiny nerve endings of neurons, or nerve cells. The *retina,* or back section of the eyeball, contains two kinds of light-sensitive neurons: rods and cones. The *cones* are clustered in and around the center of the retina and are sensitive to color. The *rods* are distributed outside the cones and are sensitive to light but not to color. The nerve endings of both rods and cones join into a bundle called the *optic nerve,* which leads to the brain. Electrical impulses from our eyes travel along this nerve to the brain. At that point, we see.

The Ear

The ear has three parts: outer, middle, and inner. The first two parts pass on sound vibrations to the inner ear, located deep inside the skull. The inner ear contains the *cochlea,* a spiral passage shaped like a snail's shell. Inside are sound-sensitive nerve endings and a liquid. When vibrations move into the inner ear, the cochlea's liquid vibrates and stimulates the nerve endings. This movement instantly transmits electrical impulses to the *auditory nerve,* which then zips them to the brain. At that point, we hear.

If you have ever been seasick, you can probably blame your inner ear. It has an intricate part that controls our sense of balance. The part consists of three tubes, formed in half circles, called the *semicircular canals.* The tubes contain a thin liquid and are arranged in three different positions relative to each other. These positions correspond to the three ways we move our head: up and down, sideways tilt, and the turning motion. Each motion of the head sloshes the liquid in one of the canals, stimulating nerve endings inside. The impulses are flashed along a branch of the auditory nerve that leads to the cerebellum rather than to the large cerebrum.

One seasickness theory states that the several motions felt in the inner ear conflict with what we see. This is especially so below deck. The sensory conflict triggers the body reaction we know as seasickness.

The Nose

The nose has nerve endings in the nasal cavity that are sensitive to chemicals. When breathed into the nose, the chemicals dissolve in the moist film of mucus that covers a membrane in the nasal cavity. There, nerve endings are stimulated to send signals to the sensory nerves and brain. Continual exposure to one odor causes the nerve cells to become insensitive to that odor. Yet, other odors may be detected very well at the same time.

Nerve cells of the nose seem to sense only four primary odors: burnt, rancid, acid, and fragrant odors. Some scientists think that every other odor may simply be some combination of two or more of the four primary odors.

The Tongue

Exactly what we taste is an individual matter, even though our tongues are similarly constructed. The tongue contains clusters of nerve cells in the tiny bumps we call *taste buds*. Taste buds are sensitive to four flavors: sweet, sour, salty, and bitter. Most buds are clustered in the tip, on the edges, and in the back of the tongue. The tip tends to be sensitive to sweet and salty flavors, the sides to sour flavors, and the back to bitter flavors. However, the exact places vary with people. The taste buds clump into small mounds called *papillae*. These are connected to a sensory nerve that leads to the brain.

Do you remember how tasteless food is when a head cold causes a stuffy nose? It is easy to confuse the sense of taste with that of smell. As we eat, the odors given off by the food stimulate the sense of smell. So, the organs of taste and smell work together.

Sometimes the sense of smell dominates. For example, if you chew a tiny piece of radish while you hold a small fresh piece of apple or onion under your nose, you will believe that you are eating the apple or onion.

The Skin

Our skin contains no fewer than five kinds of nerve endings, which are sensitive to pressure, touch, pain, heat, and cold. These nerve endings are positioned at various depths in the skin. Pressure, for example, is felt much deeper in the skin than touch.

Our nerve endings are also scattered unevenly. The lips and fingertips have many more endings clustered together than other places such as the back of the neck or arm. This is why they are so sensitive.

CIRCULATORY AND RESPIRATORY SYSTEMS **Inquiry**

People's Pulse Beats

Invitation

Your heart pumps blood through long tubes in your body called *arteries*. Your arteries are very elastic. They stretch and then shrink slightly each time the heart pumps more blood through them. These tiny movements are called *pulse beats*. You can tell how fast your heart pumps by feeling your pulse beats. How can you feel and measure how fast your pulse beats are?

MATERIALS

• Watch or clock with second hand

• Paper and pencil

Exploration

1. Press on the inside part of your wrist with four fingers as shown.

2. Find where you can best feel your pulse.
3. Count how often your pulse beats in 1 minute while sitting. The number of pulse beats in 1 minute is your "resting" pulse rate (this would differ when exercising).
4. Record your pulse rate on paper.

Concept Invention

1. How does what you do change your pulse rate? For example, how does standing affect your pulse rate? How does lying down affect your pulse rate? How does exercise affect your pulse rate?
2. How do your pulse rates compare before and after eating?
3. Where else on your body can you feel your pulse? Is the pulse rate there the same as at the wrist?

 Teaching Tips

The pulse may also be felt quite easily on each side of the throat just under the chin. The pulse rate usually slows with age and size. Also, boys have slightly slower rates than girls. Seven-year-olds average around 90 beats per minute, which is almost twice the rate for the very aged. Athletic training also reduces the rate because it helps to develop a stronger heart. These factors similarly influence animal pulse rates, particularly size. An elephant, for example, has a very slow pulse rate. This investigation provides several opportunities to make useful graphs. For example, how long does it take for the pulse to return to a resting rate after exercise? What is the effect of eating on the rate? Also, watch for chances to control variables and make operational definitions: What is a tall, young, old, heavy, or tired person? If we are testing for age, how can we control height and weight?

Scaffolding for English Learners

When working on activities involving the human body, ensure that activities are culturally acceptable for all students. (See Laplante, 1997, for a discussion of approaches to teaching that are sensitive to culture.)

Adapting for Students with Exceptionalities

For students with a hearing impairment, use a stethoscope when listening to the heart. (See Mastropieri & Scruggs, 2004, for a discussion on activities involving anatomy in the chapter on science and social studies.)

Concept Application

One's pulse rate is a measure of how fast the heart beats in 1 minute. A variety of conditions may affect it. How do the pulse rates of different people compare? For example, how do the pulse rates of boys and girls compare? How do adults and children compare? How do young and old adults compare? Does tallness make a difference in a person's pulse rate? Does weight make a difference in a person's pulse rate? What else do you notice about people or what they do that might affect pulse rates? How do you think the pulse rates of dogs, cats, and other animals compare with those of humans? How can you find out?

The Volume of Air You Breathe ———

MATERIALS

- Large bowl or pail, placed in a sink
- Masking tape
- Plastic or glass bottle with cap (1 gallon, or 4 liter)
- String
- Rubber tube
- Ruler
- Paper strips
- Partner
- Pencil
- Water
- Graph paper

Invitation

How much air do you breathe in a single breath? How big a container do you think you would need to hold it? How can you find out how much air you breathe?

Exploration

1. Stick a strip of tape down the side of the bottle.
2. Mark the strip into 10 equal parts.
3. Partly fill a large bowl or pail with water.
4. Fill the bottle with water and cap it.
5. Put the bottle, upside down, into the bowl.
6. Remove the cap while the bottleneck is underwater.
7. Put one end of the tube into the bottle. (You may have to tip the bottle a little. Have someone hold the bottle so it does not go far over.)
8. Wrap a paper strip around the other end of the tube.
9. Take a regular breath. Then blow out the air through the tube. Quickly pinch the tube shut when you finish blowing. Observe how much water was forced out of the bottle. This tells you how much air you blew out.

10. Refill the bottle each time you try a breath test.

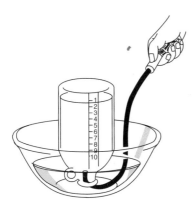

Teaching **T**ips

A child can measure chest sizes with string.

For good hygiene, a fresh strip of paper should be wrapped around the tube end each time it is used. Or, you may want to snip 5-centimeter (2-inch) pieces of plastic drinking straw and have each child stick one piece into the end of the tubing to act as a mouthpiece to blow into. After each blow, the straw piece should be discarded and a fresh one used.

A typical plastic 1-gallon container has curved sides and some space for the bottle neck. Therefore, to divide it accurately into 10 parts requires more mathematics than is currently suggested. Children can use a measuring cup to calculate the total number of ounces (or milliliters) in the bottle, and divide by 10. Then they can fill the bottle one tenth at a time to make each mark.

The jug could also be calibrated in 200-ml increments (or 500 ml or whatever calibration you prefer) by pouring 200 ml of water into the jug, marking the level with a wax pencil, adding 200 ml more, and so on.

Concept Invention

1. By what tape mark is the water level for a regular breath? Make a record, so that you can compare it with other marks.
2. How much more air can you hold when you breathe deeply? Take a deep breath. Blow out all the air you can. Compare the new and old marks.
3. How much air can other persons blow out in one breath? (Wrap a fresh piece of paper around the tube end each time a new person blows through it.)
4. Make a graph of your findings. Use each person's chest size, or height, or weight for one part of your graph. Use each person's water level mark for the other part, as shown.

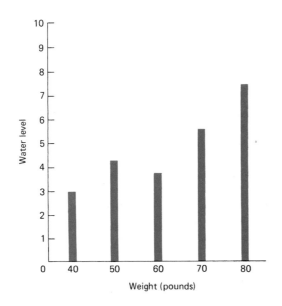

Concept Application

The volume of water displaced by "lung" air is a rough measure of lung capacity. People's lungs vary greatly in air capacity. Can you use your graph to predict more findings? For example, will two persons who weigh the same get the same results? Will two persons with the same height or chest size get the same results? What else do you notice about people that might affect how much air they can hold? For example, do athletes have more lung space than others? What is an "athlete"?

How Fast People Breathe ──────

MATERIALS

- Watch or clock with second hand
- Pencil and paper

Invitation

How many breaths do you take each minute? Does everyone breathe equally fast? What conditions may affect how fast people breathe? How can you find out how many breaths you take each minute?

Exploration

1. Count one breath each time you breathe out while sitting.
2. Observe the time on a clock. Count the number of times you breathe out in 1 minute.
3. Record the number on a piece of paper.

Teaching Tips The main purpose of this investigation is to help children record and think about data. Children will discover a variety of breathing rates, but reasons for these differences will be inconclusive at their level of understanding. You might mention that there is no single proper breathing rate for everyone. What is natural for one person may not be for another.

Concept Invention

1. How fast do you breathe after exercise? Bend and touch your toes or do some other easy exercise for 1 minute. Then count your breaths for 1 minute.
2. How fast do other people breathe while sitting? Compare people who are different in weight, height, and sex. Tell them how to count their breaths. Keep time for 1 minute. Record each person's name and how fast each breathes.
3. How fast do other people breathe after exercise? Record your findings.
4. Can you predict how fast some people will breathe? Study your records and observe the people. What are the people like who are slow breathers? What are

the people like who are faster breathers? Perhaps other people who are like them will also be fast or slow. Pick a few people you have not tested before and find out.

Concept Application

People have different breathing rates. Exercise affects one's breathing rate. What else about people or about what they do might affect how fast they breathe?

CIRCULATORY AND RESPIRATORY SYSTEMS CONCEPTS

Circulatory System ————

It would be difficult to design a better system than the human blood system for the same function. *Blood* is the vehicle that transports food, chemicals, and oxygen to all parts of the body. It picks up wastes from the cells and moves them through organs whose job is to remove them. Blood also protects the body.

The liquid part of blood is a clear, yellowish substance called *plasma*. In the plasma are three kinds of solid materials: red blood cells, white blood cells, and platelets. The *red blood cells* are most numerous and give the blood its characteristic color. They carry oxygen from the lungs to the body's cells and carbon dioxide from the cells back to the lungs. *White blood cells* are larger and move about freely among the body's cells, attacking and consuming disease germs. *Platelets* also have an important function; they help make the blood clot wherever the body is injured and bleeding.

Blood moves throughout the body because the *heart*, a powerful muscle about the size of one's fist, pumps it by alternately contracting and relaxing. Oxygen-poor blood flows into one side of the heart. Squeezing motions pump this blood to the lungs, where it picks up oxygen and gets rid of carbon dioxide. The oxygen-rich blood then flows back into the opposite side of the heart, from where it is pumped to the rest of the body.

In a sense, the circulatory system is really a combination of two interconnected networks of tubes of various sizes. One network sends the blood from the heart to the lungs and back again to the heart. The other sends the blood from the heart to the rest of the body and returns it to the heart.

Oxygen-rich blood flows from the heart to the body through thick tubes called *arteries*. Arteries branch out all over the body, getting progressively narrower until they become extremely fine *capillaries*. Capillaries may be as narrow as one fiftieth the diameter of a human hair and are threaded throughout the cells. Digested food and oxygen pass out of the blood in the capillaries and into the adjacent cells. Blood in the capillaries also takes up carbon dioxide and other waste products from the cells. The waste-carrying capillaries join into progressively larger tubes called *veins*, which carry blood back to the heart. The entire trip takes about 15 seconds. Note that the veins do not carry "blue" blood, as most children's science text illustrations would indicate. Those of us who have donated blood realize that it is a dark red, as opposed to the bright red of oxygenated blood found in arteries.

Respiratory System ————

The body's cells use oxygen to *oxidize*, or "burn," food. This process releases energy. Carbon dioxide and water vapor are by-products of this process, just as they are when a candle burns inside an inverted jar. A candle goes out when the oxygen supply is diminished. Likewise, oxidation of food requires a steady supply of enough oxygen. The job of the respiratory system is to replace the carbon dioxide and water vapor in the blood with oxygen. Let's see how this is done.

As we breathe in air through the nose, it passes through hollow nasal passages above the mouth where it is warmed and filtered. Hairlike, moving cilia inside the passages catch dust and airborne particles. These particles are swept to the mouth and coughed up or swallowed. The membrane lining the passages is coated with mucus, which also traps airborne materials.

The air then moves through the voice box, or *larynx*, and down into the throat. Two tubes are found there. One tube channels food into the stomach and is called the gullet, or *esophagus*. A second tube, the windpipe, or *trachea*, is located in front of the esophagus. It goes to the lungs. A flap of tissue, the *epiglottis*, covers the windpipe automatically when we eat or drink. This action usually prevents food or liquids from entering the windpipe.

The windpipe shortly divides into two tubes called *bronchi*. One bronchus is attached to each *lung*. In the lungs, the bronchi split into progressively smaller branches of tubes. Each of the tiniest tubes ends in a tiny air sac. Because of the many thousands of these sacs, the lungs have a soft, spongy appearance.

Each sac swells like a tiny balloon when we breathe air into our lungs. Surrounding each sac are many capillaries. Oxygen from breathed-in air in the sac passes through the sac's thin wall into the blood in the capillaries. Carbon dioxide and water vapor in the capillaries pass the opposite way into the air sacs; these gases then move up through the branched tubes and are exhaled.

Your students may read that body cells use oxygen to "burn" digested food and that carbon dioxide is one by-product of the process. But don't be surprised if most still assume that the air they breathe out is the same as the air they breathe in (Mintzes, 1984).

To show them the difference, you might get some limewater (calcium oxide in water; an indicator for carbon dioxide) from a drugstore, two identical balloons and small glass jars, and a bicycle tire pump. Pour the clear limewater into each of the two jars until half full. Have a child fill one balloon with the pump and the other using lung power. Release the air from one balloon under the limewater surface of one jar, and then do this with the second balloon and jar. The limewater exposed to the lung air should turn milky, an indication that carbon dioxide is present; the other should stay about the same.

Breathing ————————

Children typically believe that the act of breathing in forces the lungs to draw in air and expand. This is not what happens. Breathing in occurs because of unequal air pressure. Examine the process yourself.

Notice what happens when you take a deep breath: The chest cavity enlarges. It enlarges because rib muscles contract and pull the ribs up and outward. At the same time, the *diaphragm*, a thin sheet of muscle between the chest and the abdomen, pulls downward. This further enlarges the chest cavity. Enlarging the chest cavity lowers the air pressure inside the lungs. So, the higher outside air pressure forces air into the air passages and lungs.

When we breathe out, the diaphragm relaxes and moves upward. At the same time, the rib muscles relax, and the ribs move down and inward. This reduces the size of the chest cavity, which forces air out of the lungs.

The Cardiopulmonary System and Vital Signs ————————

Your temperature, pulse rate, respiratory rate, and blood pressure are indications of your health, called *vital signs*. Temperature is measured with a glass or electronic thermometer orally, axillary, rectally, or aurally. The normal oral temperature is 37°C (98.6°F) and is slightly less when taken axillary, within the armpit, and slightly more when measured rectally or aurally.

The rhythmical throbbing in the arteries that is produced by the heart's regular contractions causes your pulse. A pulse rate is generally found by compressing your radial artery with an index and middle finger and then feeling the throb for 1 minute. Pulse rates vary from 150 beats per minute in an embryo to about 60 in the elderly. The respiration rate is taken immediately after a pulse, so that you do not know the measurement is being taken. In an adult, the normal resting respiratory rate is between 14 to 20 breaths per minute.

Blood pressure is the force exerted by circulating blood against the walls of the blood vessels. It is greatest when the heart contracts (systole) and lowest when it relaxes (diastole). The pressure is measured with a sphygmomanometer, or blood pressure cuff. To take a blood pressure reading, wrap the cuff around the upper arm and inflate the bladder by pumping a rubber bulb. The health professional listens to a stethoscope that is placed against an artery lower on the arm. As the cuff expands, it compresses the artery and stops the blood circulation. Systolic pressure is measured when no pulsations can be heard. As the cuff is slowly deflated, a spurting, or Korotkoff, sound occurs as the heart contraction forces blood through the compressed artery. Diastolic pressure is measured when the blood is flowing smoothly again and the spurting sound is no longer heard. The blood pressure measurements are given as a ratio of maximum over minimum; normal blood pressure is in the range of 110/60 to 140/90 millimeters of mercury. Blood pressure varies with factors such as a person's age, level of physical fitness, weight, general heath, strength of the heartbeat, and elasticity of the arterial walls.

DIGESTIVE SYSTEM **Inquiry**

Sweet Crackers

MATERIALS

- Two small jars or glasses
- Two teaspoons
- Starch
- Sugarless soda cracker
- Sugar
- Water

Teaching Tips In the Concept Invention, children will need to know that when a material dissolves it is no longer visible. The solution looks clear.

Invitation

How does changing starch into sugar help the body?

Exploration

1. Bite off a piece of sugarless cracker and chew it for at least 1 minute.
2. How does the taste of the cracker change as you chew it?
3. A soda cracker is made up mostly of starch. The saliva in your mouth starts changing the starch into a sugar. It is changed the rest of the way in your small intestine. Before food can be used by your body cells, it must be in a dissolved form.

Concept Invention

1. Does changing a starch into a sugar help it dissolve? Find out for yourself.
2. Half-fill two small jars with water.
3. Put 1 teaspoon of sugar in one jar. Use a second teaspoon to put 1 teaspoon of starch in the other. Mix each for 1 minute with its correct spoon.
4. Which food dissolves? Will stirring help to dissolve the food even more?

Concept Application

What other starches can you turn into sugars by chewing? Try out some starchy foods and record your results.

DIGESTIVE SYSTEM CONCEPTS

We can eat food, but when is it inside the body? The answer to this seemingly simple question depends on whose point of view we take.

Most people would say that food is inside the body once it is swallowed. To biochemists, however, any food still within the 9-meter (30-foot) digestive tube they call the *alimentary canal* is considered outside the body. This definition underlines the uselessness of foods we eat until they are *digested,* or chemically broken down and dissolved into a form that can be used in the cells. The digestive system (INQ Figure 9–1) is marvelously suited to this function. Let's see how it works.

The Mouth

The digestive process begins when we start chewing food. Our front teeth (*incisors* and *canines*) cut and tear the food. Back teeth (*molars*) crush it into small particles. At the same time, saliva pours into the food from six salivary glands in and near the mouth. *Saliva* softens the food and begins the chemical breakdown of starches. A gradual, sweetening flavor is experienced when we chew starchy foods such as cooked potato, soda cracker, or bread. The saliva contains an enzyme called *ptyalin* that reduces large starch molecules into simple sugar molecules. (An enzyme is a *catalyst*, or chemical that brings about or speeds up chemical reactions without itself becoming altered.) Besides ptyalin, several other enzymes in the body's digestive system help break down food into usable form.

The Food Tube

Swallowed food passes into the *esophagus*, or food tube. It is squeezed down into the stomach by regular, wavelike contractions of smooth muscles that surround the esophagus. Similar muscles are located all along the alimentary canal. Because muscle action (*peristalsis*), not gravity, moves the food inside the canal, it is possible to eat and swallow while standing on our heads.

The Stomach

Peristaltic motions continue in the *stomach*. The food is churned slowly in gastric juices secreted from the stomach lining. Several enzymes and diluted hydrochloric acid break down most of the proteins. Digestion of starch stops because acid prevents ptyalin from working. Some fats are broken down, but for the most part, fats go through the stomach undigested.

If the stomach's hydrochloric acid is so powerful, why doesn't this corrosive liquid digest the stomach itself? Only in recent years have researchers pinpointed the reason. A small amount of ammonia (this is an alkali or base) is secreted in the lining of the stomach. It effectively neutralizes acid next to the lining without interfering with the acid's digestive action elsewhere in the stomach. We use the same principle of neutralizing an acid when we drink seltzer or soda water to settle a "sour" stomach.

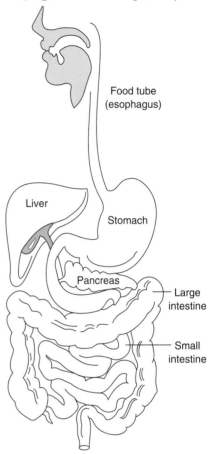

INQ Figure 9–1   **The digestive system.**

The Intestines

After about 2 to 6 hours in the stomach, depending on what and how much has been eaten, the partially digested food materials are pushed into the *small intestine*. Here, glands within intestinal walls produce digestive juices with enzymes that begin working on the food. Additional digestive juices are secreted into the small intestine from small tubes connected to the liver and pancreas.

Throughout the small intestine, peristaltic motion continues as digestive juices complete the breakdown of carbohydrates into simple sugars, proteins into amino acids, and fats into fatty acids and glycerin. At various portions of the small intestine, the sugars and amino acids are absorbed into blood vessels within its lining. Digested fats are first absorbed into the lymph system and then later are transported into the bloodstream.

Nondigestible material, or waste, composed chiefly of cellulose, passes into the large intestine. Much of the water contained in waste material is absorbed into the intestinal walls. The remaining substance is eliminated from the body.

Food products dissolved in the blood are distributed to the body cells after the liver processes them. In the cells, these products are oxidized, changed into protoplasm, or stored as fat.

FOOD AND NUTRITION Inquiry

Starchy Foods ———————

MATERIALS

- Iodine
- Safety goggles
- Piece of white chalk
- Medicine dropper
- Cornstarch
- Tiny pieces of foods (such as white bread, rice, macaroni, cheese, potato, cereals)
- Teaspoon
- Waxed paper
- Piece of very ripe banana
- Piece of unripe banana

Invitation

Which foods have starch?

Exploration

1. Place a bit of cornstarch on waxed paper. Crush a small piece of white chalk next to it with a spoon.
2. Put on safety goggles. Place a drop of iodine on each goggle. Notice how the cornstarch turns purple-black. The chalk should look red-brown. When a food turns purple-black, it has starch.
3. Test your food samples with the iodine. Crush each sample first with the spoon. Wash the spoon off each time.

Concept Invention

1. Which samples seem to have starch? Which do not?
2. Taste a little piece of unripe banana and a little piece of very ripe banana. Now try the starch test on part of an unripe banana. Now try the starch test on part of an unripe banana. Then test part of a very ripe banana.
3. What difference do you notice? When does a banana seem to have more starch? When does it seem to have more sugar?

Concept Application

Make a list of predictions of starchy foods to test with the iodine. Test the foods and make a chart of your correct and incorrect predictions.

Fatty Foods ———————

MATERIALS

- Brown paper bag
- Drop of oil
- Small pieces of different foods (such as bacon, olive, margarine, bread, apple, cheese)
- Drop of water

Invitation

Which foods have fats?

Exploration

1. Spread a drop of oil on the brown paper. Fat is mostly oil.
2. Spread a drop of water alongside it. Allow it to dry.

Concept Invention

1. Hold up the paper to the light.
2. Notice the difference in the two spots. Fat shows as a shiny, oily spot.

Concept Application

Which foods do you think have fat? Make a list and then test the foods you can. Rub each small piece into the brown paper. Record which made an oily stain. How do your findings compare with what you thought?

Some Properties of Powdered Foods

MATERIALS

• White powders
  (such as baking
  powder, baking
  soda, white flour,
  powdered sugar,
  cornstarch,
  powdered milk)

• Small jar of water

• Three medicine
  droppers

• Two teaspoons

• Small jar of iodine
  solution

• Safety goggles

• Paper towel

• Small jar of white
  vinegar

• Hand lens

Invitation

You eat many different white powders. Cake is made with baking powder. White bread is made with white flour. Cornstarch helps make gravy. You can even make milk by mixing powdered milk with water. If you take a quick look at any white powder, they seem alike. But each is really different in several ways. How can you tell one white powder from another? (Do not use the sense of taste for this investigation.)

Exploration

1. Put less than a quarter-teaspoon of one powder on a paper towel. Only a little is needed, as shown.
2. Observe it carefully through a hand lens. How does it look?
3. Feel the powder with your fingers. How does it feel?
4. Put a drop of water on the powder. What happens?
5. Put on safety goggles. Put a drop of iodine solution on the powder. What happens?
6. Put a drop of vinegar on the powder. What happens?

Concept Invention

1. How does this powder compare with other powders? Test a few more powders (make sure to wear safety goggles). Record what you observe on a chart such as this:

Powder Tested	How It Looks Magnified	How It Feels	Reaction to Water	Reaction to Iodine	Reaction to Vinegar
Cornstarch					
Flour					
Baking Soda					
(Others)					

2. Which test(s) seem most useful to tell the powders apart? Which test(s) seem least useful to tell the powders apart?

Any material has certain physical properties that may be used to identify it. By performing certain tests, children may learn some different properties of similar-looking powdered foods, as well as other powders. Small baby-food jars make excellent containers for the powders and test liquids. For the iodine solution, mix two full medicine droppers of iodine in a half-full baby-food jar of water. Children may try additional tests, such as heating the powders and mixing them with water. A small cup can be formed from kitchen foil and held over a candle flame with a spring clothespin.

Caution: Supervise closely for safety. Only a tiny amount of powder needs to be heated. A powder may also be mixed in water in a clear glass jar and then compared with other water–powder mixtures. Students should not taste powders. Explain that some powders they should not eat may get mixed with some powdered foods in this investigation. For example, some nonfoods they may want to test are powdered detergent, white tempera paint powder, crushed white chalk, talcum powder, alum, scouring powder, tooth powder, and plaster of paris.

3. Can you identify an unknown powder? Ask someone to put a quarter-teaspoon of powder on a fresh paper towel. You should not know what powder it is, but it should be one recorded on your chart. Make some tests and use your chart to identify it.

4. Can you identify two unknown powders mixed together? Have someone choose two chart powders and mix them. Then you test the mixture.

Adapting for Students with Exceptionalities

For students who have difficulty reading the directions or following the steps of these activities, record the directions on tape. (See Mercer & Mercer, 2005, for a discussion on accommodations involving instructional materials.)

Concept Application

A material may be identified by tests to reveal its physical properties. What other ways can you test white powders? What other powders can you test?

FOOD AND NUTRITION CONCEPTS

We may eat hundreds of foods combined in thousands of ways. But nutritionally speaking, there are four kinds of foods: sugars, starches, fats, and proteins. Some persons would add three more: vitamins, minerals, and water. These seven nutrients may be combined into three groups:

1. Foods for energy: sugars, starches, and fats
2. Foods for growth and repair of cells: proteins
3. Foods for regulation of body processes: vitamins, minerals, and water

Carbohydrates

If we heat table sugar in a test tube, the sugar will gradually turn black, and water vapor will be given off. The black material is carbon. The water is formed as hydrogen and oxygen atoms given off by individual sugar molecules combine. Heat some starch, and again carbon and water appear. Both sugar and starch are *carbohydrates*, a name that means "carbon and water."

Although sugars and starches are composed of the same elements, these elements may appear in various combinations and form relatively small or large molecules. *Simple sugar* molecules, for example, are the smallest carbohydrate molecules. They may be found in grapes and many other fruits. When two simple sugar molecules become attached, a *complex sugar*, such as table sugar, is formed. A starch molecule is nothing more than a long chain of sugar molecules tightly attached to one another.

In digestion, carbohydrates are broken down into simple sugars. Only in this form are these molecules small enough to pass through cell membranes into the cells, where they "burn" and release energy. The burning is a result of *oxidation*, a process in which oxygen chemically combines with fuel—in this case, sugar—and releases heat energy. (Rusting is a form of slow oxidation; fire is very fast oxidation.) The oxygen comes from the air we breathe.

Fats

Analysis shows that fats are also composed of carbon, hydrogen, and oxygen. However, fat molecules have relatively fewer oxygen atoms than carbohydrates. Because they are oxygen "poor," fat molecules can combine with more oxygen atoms and yield about twice as much energy as carbohydrates.

Foods rich in carbohydrates and fats provide our principal source of energy. But when we eat more than we need of these materials, the cells store any excess in the form of fat. Fat storage does not occur uniformly throughout all body cells, as every figure-conscious person knows.

Proteins

Proteins are extremely complex, large molecules. A single protein molecule may contain thousands of atoms. Like the preceding nutrients, proteins are made up of carbon, hydrogen, and oxygen; but proteins also contain nitrogen and, typically, sulfur. Proteins are the main source of materials (amino acids) needed for growth and repair of body cells. Excess proteins can be oxidized in cells and so provide energy.

Although all animal and some plant foods (mainly beans, peas, and nuts) are rich in proteins, no single plant source contains sufficient amino acids for complete growth and repair of body cells. A combination of legumes and grains (beans and rich), however, can furnish all the needed amino acids.

Vitamins

Vitamins are essential to health because they regulate cell activities. These substances permit biochemical processes to take place. Without proper vitamins, the body may suffer from several deficiency diseases, such as scurvy, rickets, and anemia. A balanced diet is usually all that is needed to prevent the disease. Particularly in the last decade, however, scientists have found clues that vitamins may play a larger role than previously thought in achieving optimal health and in preventing some chronic diseases such as cancer, decline of the immune system in the aged, heart disease, and eye degeneration. This is why some nutritionists recommend a daily multivitamin as "insurance." Most researchers, however, see the need for more evidence before they can recommend large doses of vitamins aimed at specific diseases or conditions.

Minerals

Several minerals are essential because they help regulate cell activities. In addition, some minerals are incorporated into body tissue. Calcium and phosphorus form the hard portions of our bones and teeth. Milk is especially rich in these two minerals. Iron and copper help form red blood cells. A proper amount of iodine is needed in the thyroid gland for normal oxidation to take place in cells. Salt is often iodized to prevent goiter, an iodine deficiency. Some minerals cannot be used by cells unless specific vitamins are present. Most fruits and vegetables are rich in vitamins and minerals.

Water

For many reasons, water is essential to life and good nutrition. It changes chemically to form part of protoplasm. Water is the chief part of blood. It cools the body and carries away accumulated poisons. It is important to digestion and excretion. About two thirds of the body itself is composed of water.

Besides drinking water directly, we take in much water in the food we eat. For example, celery is about 95% water, and fresh bread is about 35% water.

Choosing a Healthful Diet

Years ago, many Americans suffered from malnutrition. Today, the problem is often the opposite. Most of us eat too much, particularly of foods rich in fat, such as meat and dairy products. This food consumption increases the risk of heart disease, stroke, and diabetes and may also increase the incidence of certain types of cancer. Nutritionists today recommend that we eat far more grains, fruits, and vegetables than has been customary in the American diet.

Most children and adults realize that they must eat a variety of foods to have a proper, or "balanced," diet but are unsure of what to eat or what are proper serving sizes. To help us select healthful combinations of nutrients, the U.S. Department of Agriculture publishes "MyPyramid." This food pyramid helps children and adults choose foods and serving sizes that are right for them by taking into account individual differences in activity levels, age, and gender.

To determine your appropriate number of calories, including serving sizes of grains, vegetables, fruits, discretionary calories, milk, meat and beans, log on to the http://www.mypyramid.gov/mypyramid/index.aspx website. The intent of MyPyramid is to promote variety in the foods we eat as well as stressing proportionality and moderation by eating more foods that are healthy and less foods that are high in trans fats, sugar, salt, and cholesterol.

INQ Figure 9–2   **Food guide pyramid.**

Source: U.S. Department of Agriculture, Washington, DC, 2005.

References

American Association for the Advancement of Science (AAAS). (1993). *Benchmarks for science literacy.* New York: Oxford University Press.

Fathman, A. K., Quinn, M. E., & Kessler, C. (1992). *Teaching science to English learners, grades 4–8.* Washington, DC: National Clearinghouse of Bilingual Education. Retrieved November 13, 2004, from *www.ncela.gwu.edu/pubs/pigs/pig11.htm*

Laplante, B. (1997). Teaching science to language minority students in elementary classrooms. *Journal of the New York State Association for Bilingual Education, 12,* 62–83. Retrieved November 13, 2004, from *www.ncela.gwu.edu/pubs/nysabe/vol12/nysabe124.pdf*

Mastropieri, M., & Scruggs, T. E. (2004). *The inclusive classroom: Strategies for effective instruction* (4th ed.). Upper Saddle River, NJ: Merrill/Prentice Hall.

Mercer, C. D., & Mercer, A. R. (2005). *Teaching students with learning problems* (7th ed.). Upper Saddle River, NJ: Merrill/Prentice Hall.

Mintzes, J. J. (1984). Naive theories in biology: Children's concepts of the human body. *School Science and Mathematics, 84*(7), 548–555.

National Research Council (NRC). (1996). *National science education standards.* Washington, DC: National Academy Press.

Selected Trade Books: The Human Body and Nutrition

For Younger Children

Adler, D. A. (1991). *You breathe in, you breathe out.* Danbury, CT: Watts.

Berger, M. (1983). *Why I cough, sneeze, shiver, hiccup, and yawn.* New York: Harper & Row.

Bishop, P. R. (1991). *Exploring your skeleton.* Danbury, CT: Watts.

Carle, E. (1997). *From head to toe.* New York: HarperCollins.

Cole, J. (1989). *The magic school bus inside the human body.* New York: Scholastic.

Cole, J. (1999). *The magic school bus explores the senses.* New York: Scholastic.

Hawcock, D. (1997). *Amazing pull-out pop-up body in a book.* Hillsdale, NJ: DK Publishing.

Hoover, R., & Murphy, B. (1981). *Learning about our five senses.* Torrance, CA: Good Apple.

Hvass, U. (1986). *How my body moves.* New York: Viking.

Janulewicz, M. (1997). *Yikes! Your body up close.* New York: Simon & Schuster.

Kindersley, D. (1991). *What's inside my body?* Hillsdale, NJ: DK Publishing.

Mayer, G. (1998). *This is my body (Little Critter).* New York: Golden Books.

Parker, S. (1991). *Eating a meal: How you eat, drink, and digest.* Danbury, CT: Watts.

Penn, L. (1986). *The human body.* Torrance, CA: Good Apple.

Sattler, H. R. (1982). *Noses are special.* Nashville, TN: Abingdon Press.

Showers, P. (1982). *You can't make a move without your muscles.* New York: Thomas Y. Crowell.

Simon, S. (1999). *The Heart.* New York: HarperTrophy.

Simon, S. (2000). *Muscles.* New York: HarperTrophy.

Simon, S. (2003). *Eyes and ears.* New York: HarperCollins.

Sproule, A. (1987). *Body watch: Know your insides.* New York: Facts on File.

For Older Children

Allison, L. (1976). *Blood and guts: A working guide to your own little insides.* Boston: Little, Brown.

Arnold, N. (1998). *Horrible science: Blood, bones, and body bits.* New York: Scholastic.

Behm, B. (1987). *Ask about my body.* Austin, TX: Raintree.

Berger, M., & Berger, G. (1998). *Why don't haircuts hurt? Questions and answers about the human body.* New York: Scholastic.

Brynie, F. H. (2003). *101 Questions about sex and sexuality: With answers for the curios, and cautious, and confused.* Minnepolis: Lerner Publishing Group.

Davidson, S., & Morgan, B. (2002). *Human body revealed.* New York: Dorling Kindersley Publishing.

De Bruin, J. (1983). *Young scientists explore the five senses.* Torrance, CA: Good Apple.

Gabb, M. (1991). *The human body.* Danbury, CT: Watts.

Galperin, A. (1991). *Nutrition.* Broomall, PA: Chelsea House.

Harlow, R., & Morgan, G. (1991). *Energy and growth.* Danbury, CT: Watts.

Hausherr, R. (1989). *Children and the AIDS virus: A book for children, parents, and teachers.* New York: Clarion Books.

Klein, A. E. (1977). *You and your body.* New York: Doubleday.

Knutson, R. (1999). *Fearsome fauna: A field guide to the creatures that live in you.* New York: Freeman.

Mayle, P. (1997). *What's happening to me?* Secaucus, NJ: Carol.

Parker, S. (1991). *Nerves to senses: Projects with biology.* Danbury, CT: Watts.

Patent, D. (1992). *Nutrition: What's in the food we eat.* New York: Holiday House.

Rayner, C. (1980). *The body book.* Hauppauge, NY: Barron's.

Rutland, J. (1977). *Human body.* Danbury, CT: Watts.

Simon, S. (1979). *About the foods you eat.* New York: McGraw-Hill.

Suzuki, D. (1991). *Looking at the body.* New York: John Wiley.

Taylor, R. (1982). *How the body works.* St. Paul, MN: EMC.

Walker, R. (2004). *Guide to the human body.* Buffalo, NY: Firefly Publishing

Walpole, B. (1987). *The human body.* Parsippany, NJ: Julian Messner.

Ward, B. R. (1991). *Diet and health.* Danbury, CT: Watts.

Wilson, R. (1979). *How the body works.* New York: Larousse.

Wolf, D., & Wolf, M. L. (Eds.). (1982). *The human body.* New York: G. P. Putnam.

Wong, O. (1986). *Your body and how it works.* Danbury, CT: Childrens Press.

Wyatt, V. (1999). *Earthlings inside and out: A space alien studies the human body.* Toronto, Ontario: Kids Can Press.

Zim, H. S. (1979). *Your skin.* New York: Morrow.

Resource Books

Butzow, C. M., & Butzow, J. W. (1989). *Science through children's literature: An integrated approach*. Englewood, CO: Teacher Ideas Press. (nutrition topics on pp. 107–111)

Cordel, B., & Hillen, J. (1994). *Sense-able science*. Fresno, CA: AIMS Education Foundation.

Fredricks, A. D., Meinbach, A. M., & Rothlein, L. (1993). *Thematic units: An integrated approach to teaching science and social studies*. New York: HarperCollins. (health topics on pp. 140–145; body system topics on pp. 189–194)

Harris, R. (1994). *It's perfectly normal*. Cambridge, MA: Candlewick Press.

Jasmine, G. (1995). *Thematic unit: My body*. Huntington Beach, CA: Teacher Created Materials.

Jefferies, D. (1993). *Thematic unit: The human body*. Huntington Beach, CA: Teacher Created Materials.

Shaw, D. G., & Dybdahl, C. S. (1996). *Integrating science and language arts: A sourcebook for K–6 teachers*. Boston: Allyn & Bacon. (circulatory system topic on pp. 65–67)

VanCleave, J. (1995). *The human body for every kid*. New York: John Wiley.

Wiebe, A. (Ed.). (1986). *Jaw breakers and heart thumpers*. Fresno, CA: AIMS Education Foundation.

Wiebe, A., Ecklund, L., & Mercier, S. (Eds.). (1986). *From head to toe*. Fresno, CA: AIMS Education Foundation.

THE EARTH'S CHANGING SURFACE

Shifting sand dunes, eroding hillsides, weeds growing on an asphalt playground, and muddy water running in gutters are all evidence that the earth's surface is changing. This section of the book examines forces that wear down and build up the earth and their rock and soil products. The four parts are weathering and erosion, soil and its makeup, the building up of the land, and the formation of rocks.

Benchmarks and Standards

Most children have explored with soil, rocks, and play sand or seen pictures or movies that include volcanoes and earthquakes. Activities in elementary school should further refine these explorations and allow children to discover additional properties about the earth. Sample benchmarks and standards include the following:

Sample Benchmarks (AAAS, 1993)

- Chunks of rocks come in many sizes and shapes, from boulders to grains of sand and even smaller. (By Grades K–2, p. 72)
- Waves, wind, water, and ice shape and reshape the earth's land surface by eroding rock and soil in some areas and depositing them in other areas, sometimes in seasonal layers. (By Grades 3–5, p. 72)

Sample Standards (NRC, 1996)

- Soils have properties of color and texture, capacity to retain water, and ability to support the growth of many kinds of plants, including those in our food supply. (By Grades K–4, p. 134)
- Some changes in the solid earth can be described as the "rock cycle." (By Grades 5–8, p. 160)

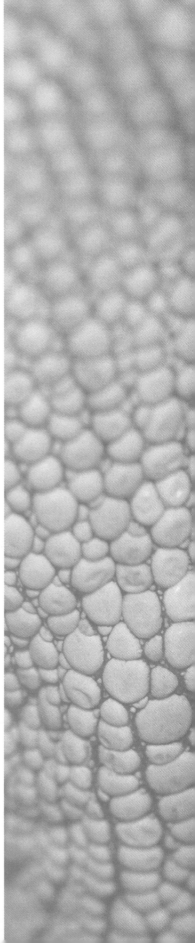

WEATHERING AND EROSION **Inquiry**

Breaking Rocks ———

Invitation

How can seeds break up rocks?

Exploration

1. Soak some bean seeds in a jar of water overnight.
2. Plant them in a small carton half-filled with moist soil.
3. Use a stick to mix some plaster of paris and water in a second carton. Make the mixture like a thick milkshake.
4. Pour the plaster mixture lightly over the soil. Make the cover about 0.5 centimeter (0.25 inch) thick.

Concept Invention

1. Will the growing seeds be strong enough to break through the hard cover? If so, how long do you think it will take?
2. If the seeds do break through, how thick a plaster cover will beans go through?

Concept Application

What examples can you find of plants breaking up rocks and other hard materials? Look for plants growing in cracks in rocks, sidewalks, asphalt, and other paved surfaces. Record what you find.

MATERIALS

- Two small topless milk or juice cartons
- Moist soil
- Plaster of paris
- Stick
- Bean seeds
- Jar of water
- Ruler

How Weathering Breaks Down Minerals ———

Invitation

Over time, gases in the air can cause a chemical change in many different minerals in rocks. The process is called *chemical weathering*. A rock that is chemically weathered becomes loose and easily crumbled. Something like this happens when iron or steel breaks down as it rusts. You can learn more about chemical weathering by making things rust. How can you make an iron nail rust?

Exploration

1. Rub a nail with steel wool for a few seconds. This will take off any chemical that may have been put on to prevent rusting.
2. Get a container of wet soil. Bury the nail just under the surface. Dig up the nail each day to see if, or how much, it is rusting. Put the nail back in the same way each time. Keep the soil damp.

MATERIALS

- Plain iron nails
- Container of dry soil
- Container of wet soil
- Container of water
- Steel wool

Concept Invention

1. When does rust first appear?
2. How quickly is the whole nail covered with rust?
3. Will a nail rust more quickly on the wet soil's surface than below it? What do you think?
4. What would happen if you put a nail in water?
5. What would happen if you buried a nail in dry soil?
6. Will a piece of steel wool rust faster than a nail?

Concept Application

Gases in the air may cause chemical weathering in rocks. Rust is an example of chemical weathering. What are some other materials that might rust? In what other ways can you get them to rust? How can you prevent materials from rusting? Record your ideas.

Teaching Tips

Make sure that any steel wool used is the variety without soap. Plastic margarine or cottage cheese containers are handy to hold soil for this activity. Soil may be dried, if needed, by spreading it on a newspaper and exposing it to sunlight.

Oxygen chemically combines directly with many minerals, as in the rusting process. Carbon dioxide also produces chemical weathering, but indirectly. It dissolves in rainwater to form a weak acid called *carbonic acid*. This acid attacks limestone and cementing materials that hold minerals together in some rocks.

Cave Deposits ———————

Invitation

How do mineral deposits form in caves?

Exploration

1. Fill a large paper cup three-fourths full with water. Dissolve as much Epsom salt in it as you can.
2. Pour the solution into the two small paper cups.
3. Tie a small stone to each end of the string to weigh them down. Put one string end into each small paper cup. Have the string sag between cups.
4. Place the cups on top of the washcloth. Leave at least 4 centimeters (1 3/4 inches) between the cloth and the string. Allow a few days for mineral deposits to form on the string and cloth, as illustrated.

MATERIALS

- Epsom salt
- Two small paper cups
- Thick, soft string
- Large paper cup
- Spoon
- Two small stones
- Thick washcloth or piece of towel
- Water
- Ruler

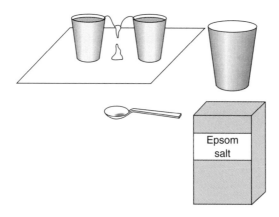

Concept Invention

1. In a real cave, water with dissolved minerals in it drips from the cave ceiling to the floor. The water leaves minerals behind as it evaporates at both places. Little by little, the mineral deposits build up to look like "icicles" of stone. Those that hang down are called *stalactites*. Those that point up are called *stalagmites*. (To remember them, think of C for "ceiling" and G for "ground.") In your model, where is the stalactite?
2. Where is the stalagmite in your model?

Concept Application

Describe how your model compares with real stalactite and stalagmite formations. Research related terms such as *speleothems*, *speleologist*, *spelunking*, *columns*, *helictites*, and *flowstone*.

Freezing Water and Rocks ————

MATERIALS
• Several porous or cracked rocks
• Freezer bag
• Container of water
• Freezer

Invitation

How does freezing water break up rocks?

Exploration

1. Leave some rocks in a container of water for several hours. Use cracked rocks and those that soak up water. Sandstone and limestone are good to use.
2. Put the rocks into a bag. Place the bag in a freezer overnight. Examine the rocks the next day.

Concept Invention

1. What, if anything, happened to the rocks?
2. How can you explain your results?

Concept Application

If some rocks broke, maybe the cold in the freezer alone did it. How can you experiment to make sure it was the freezing water that actually broke the rocks in this case? Try placing similar soaked and unsoaked rocks in the freezer. What happens? Could you use porous and nonporous rocks (porous rocks may be detected by placing some rocks in water and looking for those on which bubbles form) to test your theory?

MATERIALS
• Several different weathered rocks
• Thick paper bag
• Soft paper towel or facial tissue
• Hand lens
• Empty egg carton
• Hammer

Changing Rocks ————

Invitation

How does weathering change a rock?

Exploration

1. For safety, to break open a rock, put it into a thick paper bag. Hold the bag against a cement curb or sidewalk. Hit the rock a few times with a hammer through the bag.
2. Look at the weathered and fresh rock surfaces through a hand lens.

Concept Invention

1. How are they different?
2. How are they alike?

Adapting for Students with Exceptionalities

Instead of standard science supply samples, try to find local large specimens of rocks when working with students who are visually impaired. (See Mastropieri & Scruggs, 2004, chapter on science and social studies for a discussion on activities involving rocks and minerals.)

Concept Application

Make a weathered rock display. Take two of the larger pieces of a rock. Wrap one piece in tissue or a soft towel so that only the weathered part shows. Wrap the other so that only the fresh surface shows. Place them in opposite spaces in an egg carton. Do this with other broken rocks, too, until you fill the carton. What will happen if you shift the rocks around so that the samples are not opposite one another? How many of the rocks will your friends be able to match? If someone shifts them for you, how many will you be able to match?

Soil Erosion ————

MATERIALS

- Two throwaway pie pans
- Soil
- Two matched plastic saucers
- Two small matched juice cans
- Measuring cups
- Meterstick or yardstick
- A small- and a medium-sized nail
- Hammer
- Water
- Several leaves

Invitation

After a rain, have you noticed how water has carried away, or eroded, soil? Splashing raindrops and running water are responsible for much soil erosion. But not all places with soil erode, and some places erode much more than others. How can you test to see what affects soil erosion?

Exploration

1. Use a hammer and small nail to punch 10 holes in the bottom of one juice can. Use the hammer and a medium-sized nail to punch 10 holes in the second can. Both cans should be open at the top.
2. Fill a saucer level and to the brim with soil. Put the dish into a pie pan to catch any spilled material.
3. Place a meterstick or yardstick upright behind the dish. Hold the small-holed can 60 centimeters (2 feet) above the dish.
4. Have someone pour a half-cup of water into the juice can. When the can stops "raining," observe the soil and pie pan.

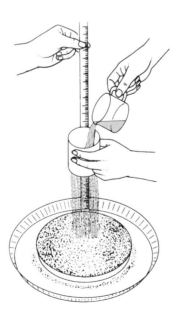

Teaching Tips

Finding actual samples of erosion is important to achieving full understanding.

Concept Invention

1. What, if any, signs of erosion can you observe?
2. How will a heavier "rain" affect erosion? Fill a second saucer with soil. Use the medium-hole can for rain and compare the results with the first trial.
3. How does loose soil erode, compared with tightly packed soil? Prepare two saucers and find out.
4. How will tilted soil erode, compared with level soil?
5. How will covered soil erode, compared with bare soil? Cover the soil in one dish with several leaves.

Scaffolding for English Learners

The soil erosion activity provides a good opportunity to learn. Teachers of English learners see opportunity to learn as a key to English language acquisition. (See TESOL, 1992, for a discussion of the opportunity to learn for English learners.)

Concept Application

What conditions seem to reduce soil erosion? What conditions seem to increase soil erosion? If rainfall, soil cover, degree of incline, and compactness of the soil affect soil erosion, what examples can you find outdoors that show some or all of these conditions?

Wind Erosion

Invitation

What happens to loose soil on a windy day? The moving of soil or rocks from one place to another is called *erosion*. Soil erosion by wind is a big problem in some places. How can you find out about wind erosion in your area?

Exploration

1. Make a wind erosion recorder. Cut two narrow slots on top of a small milk carton.
2. Stick two rulers through the slots.
3. Fill the carton with sand or soil to make it heavy.
4. Cut two 45-centimeter (18-inch) strips of sticky tape.
5. Put one strip evenly over the top of each ruler, sticky side out. Use tape to fasten the strip ends to each ruler.
6. With crayon, draw an arrow on the carton top.
7. Place your recorder where the wind is blowing loose soil. Point the arrow north. Leave the recorder for 30 minutes. Notice how bits of windblown soil collect on the sticky tape.

MATERIALS

- Two rulers
- Sticky tape
- Crayon
- Scissors
- Small empty milk carton
- Open, unpaved area outdoors
- Sand or soil
- Large sprinkling can
- Directional compass

Teaching Tips

Some children may not realize at first that some variables need to be controlled in this investigation. If two areas are to be tested, two identical recorders must be exposed to wind within equal areas at the same time. When possible, let the children discover this for themselves.

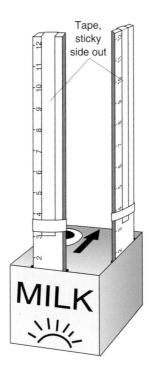

Tape, sticky side out

Concept Invention

1. Examine the sticky tape on all four sides. Which side has the most soil? From which direction did the wind blow most?
2. Where do you think is the most wind erosion around the school? Where do you think is the least wind erosion? Make more recorders. Put one in each place and find out. What reasons can you give for what you find?
3. What difference in wind erosion is there between grass-covered and bare soil? How can you find out?
4. What difference in wind erosion is there between dry and damp soil? How can you find out?
5. Collect windblown soil bits each day for a week with your recorder. Change the sticky tape each day. Can you arrange the strips in order from most to fewest soil bits? On what day did the most wind erosion occur? On what day did the least wind erosion occur? Can you tell from which main direction the wind blew each day?

Concept Application

Soil erosion by wind depends on how hard the wind blows and how the soil is protected from the wind. When during the day does the most wind erosion occur where you live? How can you find out? What else can you discover with your recorder? Record your ideas.

Glaciers ————

Invitation

How do glaciers change the land?

MATERIALS
• Aluminum pie pan
• Freezer
• Rocks and pebbles
• Place with bare soil
• Water
• Meterstick or yardstick

Exploration

1. Put some rocks and pebbles into a pie pan. Spread them about halfway around the inside edge of the pan as shown.
2. Put some water into the pan, but let the tops of the rocks stick out of the water.
3. Leave the pan in a freezer overnight.
4. Remove your frozen glacier model from the pan. Turn it over so that the rocks sticking out are underneath.
5. Place the model flat on some bare dirt. Push it so that the stones are forward. Press down at the same time. Push it in a straight line for about 60 centimeters (2 feet).

6. Let your model stay and melt at the end of that distance. Come back to this place several hours later after the model has melted. Observe carefully everything that has been left behind.

Concept Invention

1. How can you tell the direction in which the "glacier" moved?
2. How can you tell how wide it was?
3. How can you tell where the forward part of the glacier stopped and melted?

Concept Application

What geological features show that glaciers were once in the United States? Describe these features and their locations.

WEATHERING AND EROSION CONCEPTS

Perhaps the only permanent feature of the earth's surface is the continuous process of change it reveals. The forces that weather and erode the land are powerful and ceaseless.

Weathering refers to the breaking down of rocks into smaller parts through the action of such agents as plants, chemicals, frost, and changes of temperature. *Erosion* includes weathering plus the process of transporting weathered material from one location to another, as in the action of running water, wind, and glaciers.

Plant Actions ─────────

It is difficult for some children to realize at first that plants break down rocks. After all, rocks are "hard" and plants are "soft," they reason. But plants weather rocks in several ways.

Growing roots may wedge deeply into a cracked rock and force it apart. As dry plant seeds absorb water, they swell with surprising force and may perform a similar wedging

INQ Figure 10–1   Lichens play a part in weathering rock.

function. Tiny flat plants called *lichens* grow on bare rock (INQ Figure 10–1). Acids released by these plants decompose and soften the rock. Larger plants may then follow in a long succession, each contributing to the rock's destruction.

Chemical Weathering

Oxygen and water in the air combine with rock surfaces to produce "rust." Reddish soils, for example, usually contain oxidized iron compounds.

Falling rain picks up a small amount of carbon dioxide in the air and forms carbonic acid. Although it is well diluted, this substance slowly wears down limestone. Older limestone buildings and statuary have a soft, worn look from the dissolving effect of acidic rainwater. This is especially noticeable in England and in several areas in the northeastern United States, where coal burning has been prevalent. Abnormal quantities of sulfur dioxide released into the air increase the acidic content of rain and hasten weathering.

Rainwater that percolates into the ground may encounter a limestone formation and dissolve some of it, thus forming a cave. This is how Carlsbad Caverns of New Mexico, Luray Caverns of Virginia, and Mammoth Caves of Kentucky were formed. Because the surface appearance of a rock is somewhat altered by chemical weathering, we must often chip or break it to note its natural color.

Expansion and Contraction

Frozen water also contributes to weathering. Many rocks are relatively porous. Water, you may remember, is one of the few substances that expands as it freezes. As absorbed water in a rock expands, bits of rock are broken off. In addition, ice may wedge apart cracked rocks.

Stones placed around campfires are sometimes cracked because rocks conduct heat poorly. The difference between a hot surface and the cooler interior may produce strains that cause parts to flake off. But some of this *exfoliation*, as it is called, may be from expansion that results from release of pressure. Rocks formed underground are subjected to great pressures. When they finally appear on the surface because of erosion or other means, these rocks may have a tendency to "unsqueeze" slightly, thus starting some cracks.

Running Water

Moving water is no doubt the most erosive force on the earth. Abrasive, waterborne rocks and particles have gradually formed the Grand Canyon over millions of years. Millions of tons of soil daily wash from banks and hills over the world into streams and are eventually carried into the ocean. Ocean waves ceaselessly pound huge cliffs and boulders into sand.

Water running down hills usually forms gullies. As the slope angle increases, water moves more swiftly, so hastening erosion. Rain splashing on near-level fields has a different erosive effect. Broad sheets of soil wash off into lower places without obvious gullying.

Wind Erosion

The effect of wind erosion became dramatically apparent to millions of Americans in the Dust Bowl years of 1934–1935. Prairie lands originally covered by a grassy sod had been broken up for agriculture. A combination of dry weather and marginal farming practices resulted in the most destructive dust storms ever seen in the United States.

Glacial Erosion

Glaciers also contribute to land erosion. Huge snow deposits build up when snowfall exceeds the melting rate. Gradually, some of the underlying snow compacts into ice and the glacier flows slowly downhill, as in the case of mountain valley glaciers.

Continental glaciers are much larger, ranging to thousands of square kilometers in size. At one time, a large part of North America was buried under snow and ice. Today, such glaciers cover much of Greenland and Antarctica. Gravity forces these glaciers to spread out as more and more snow piles on top. When glaciers move, they scour the land under their tremendous weight, scooping out basins and leveling hills. As they melt, huge deposits of soil and rocks are left at the sides and leading edge. Effects of glaciation may be seen in many parts of our country, particularly in New England and the north central states (INQ Figure 10–2).

Interplanetary Weathering

How does the interplanetary space environment change the rocky and icy surfaces of planetary bodies? How can this information help us better understand the weathering processes here on earth or the formation of the solar system? Finding answers to these questions is an ongoing research emphasis of planetary geologists.

An important step in understanding interplanetary weathering involves the study of the samples of soils and rocks that the *Apollo* astronauts retrieved from the surface of the moon. Along with other observations, scientists have been able to begin to understand the effect of impacts and solar wind on the moon. *Galileo* spacecraft images of asteroids

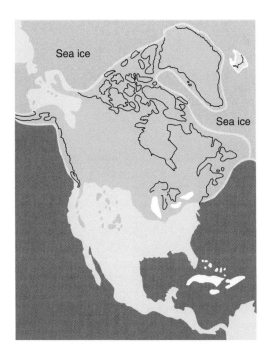

INQ Figure 10–2 About 11,000 years ago, glaciers advanced deeply into what is now the northern United States.

951 Gaspra and 243 Ida revealed to planetary geologists that the surfaces of these asteroids undergo space weathering. NASA's Near-Earth Asteroid Rendezvous mission that touched down on the asteroid 433 Eros on February 12, 2001, also confirmed this information. Similarly, the *Galileo* and *Cassini* spacecraft may provide results for space weathering questions about surfaces such as the icy moons of Jupiter and Saturn. The Spitzer Space Telescope was launched in August of 2003 to study infrared radiation and the effect of heat. In 2005, the Deep Impact spacecraft was launched to study comets and their weatering patterns.

SOIL AND ITS MAKEUP Inquiry

The Makeup of Soils ─────────

MATERIALS

- Bags of two different types of fresh soil
- Spoon
- Three glass jars with caps
- Newspaper
- Water
- Four sheets of white paper
- Hand lens
- Paper cup
- Partner

Invitation

What are some things you eat that grow in soil? How is soil important in your life? What do you think makes up soil? How can you find out what makes up soil?

Exploration

1. Spread newspaper on a table or desk. Put a sheet of white paper on top.
2. Pour some soil from one bag onto the white paper, as shown. What is the color of the soil?
3. Spread out the soil with a spoon. Use a hand lens to better observe the soil. What animals or animal parts do you see? (Put live animals into a paper cup.) What plant or plant parts do you see? Animal and plant materials in soil are called *humus*.
4. Feel the soil between your fingers. Rough soil has more large rock bits or particles than smooth soil. Use a hand lens. Can you find three sizes of rock particles? Which size makes up most rock particles in your sample?
5. Sort the different humus and rock materials into layers, as follows: Fill a glass jar half full with the soil you are observing. Fill the rest of the jar with water. Cap the jar and shake it. Then let it settle for an hour. Where does the humus settle? How much is there? In what order do the different-sized rock particles settle? How much is there of each size?

Concept Invention

1. How good a soil detective are you? Can you tell which two soil samples are from the same place? Have a partner pour some soil onto three white sheets. Two soil samples should come from one bag and one soil sample from the other bag. (Do not look while this is done.)
2. Try to identify the two soil samples from the same bag. Observe color, humus, and rock particles. Try the shake test.

Teaching Tips   The two bags of soil in the Exploration should come from two very different locations. Make sure the materials in each bag of soil are fairly evenly distributed. Otherwise, it will be difficult to match soil samples that come from the same bag.

Adapting for Students with Exceptionalities

Be sure to review the key questions before students begin this activity so that they understand what they are looking for in the soil. Use a video camera and laptop or closed circuit television system to enlarge images for students with visual impairments.

Concept Application

Soil consists of humus and rock particles. The kinds and amounts of these materials may identify different soils. What is the makeup of soil from different places? Get samples of different soils around school and home. How are the soil samples alike and different? How does deeper soil compare with surface soil from the same place? How many soil samples can you match?

How Water Sinks into Different Soils

Invitation

Some rain that falls on soil runs off it into streams. Some rain also soaks into the ground. This water can help crops grow. If water sinks deep below the surface, it may be pumped to the surface for many uses. How fast water soaks into soil depends on several conditions. You can find out some for yourself. What can you do to test how fast water sinks into soils?

Exploration

1. Get a can that is open at both ends. Scratch a mark sideways on the can's side 2.5 centimeters (1 inch) from one end.
2. Go to a place with soil outdoors. Use your foot to press the can into the soil up to the mark.
3. Fill the second can with water. Pour the water into the first can without spilling any, as illustrated. With a watch, check how long it takes for all the water to sink in.

> **MATERIALS**
>
> - Two matched cans (one with both ends removed)
> - Watch with second hand
> - Water
> - Different outdoor places with soil

> **Teaching Tips**
> A steel can is likely to hold up better than an aluminum can for this activity. Some hard soils may require an adult's weight to push the can down to the mark.

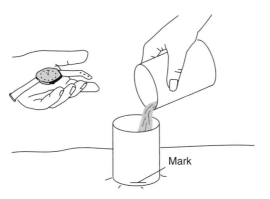

Mark

Concept Invention

1. How much time is needed for the water to sink into the soil?
2. Compare the sink times of different soils. How will soil with grass compare with the same kind of soil without grass?

3. How will sandy soil compare with sticky soil?
4. How will hard-packed soil compare with loose soil?
5. How will soil that is usually in the sun compare with soil that is usually in the shade?
6. How will soil on a hill compare with soil that is on a flat surface?

Concept Application

Permeable soils tend to be loosely packed and consist of coarse mineral particles with little or no humus. What are some things about soil that seem to make water sink in quickly or slowly?

SOIL AND ITS MAKEUP CONCEPTS

Many children understand that weathering and erosion can wear underlying rock into small particles; but they often do not realize that productive soil is more than just rock particles. Not until decomposed plant and animal matter is added (or manufactured chemicals applied) does the soil become productive enough to support agriculture (INQ Figure 10–3).

Humus, as this organic matter is called, supplies plants with essential elements such as nitrogen, phosphorus, and potassium. The decomposition of organic material is done by soil bacteria. Acids released in decomposition also dissolve other minerals in the soil particles. Humus retains water well and so keeps soil from drying out rapidly. The darkish color of humus-laden soil absorbs sunlight efficiently, and so it is warmer than light-colored soil. This warmth speeds up plant growth and reduces seed failure.

Earthworms, you may recall, are important to soil for several reasons. They help break up the soil and so allow air, as well as water, to reach the plant roots. (Root cells die unless they absorb sufficient oxygen.) As earthworms eat through soil, they mix it and leave castings that contain rich fertilizing ingredients.

Soil Makeup

The composition of soil is easily studied if you mix some earth in a water-filled jar and allow the jar to stand several hours. Gravity causes the various materials to settle in order. Heavier, coarser particles like pebbles settle first, followed by sand, silt, and clay. Any humus present floats on the water's surface.

The best soil for most plants is loam, composed of sand (30% to 50%), silt (30% to 50%), clay (up to 20%), and abundant humus. Silt and clay have small particles that retain water well. Having been eroded from rocks rich in certain minerals, they contain elements that plants need for healthy growth. Coarser sand particles make soil porous, enabling air and water to reach plant roots. A soil composed of sand or clay alone lacks the moderate degree of porosity that seems best for watering plant roots.

Soils differ greatly in their degree of acidity and alkalinity. Strawberry plants thrive in acidic soil. Many grasses grow well in alkaline or basic soils. Clover does best in soil that is neither basic nor acidic, but neutral.

INQ Figure 10–3   A soil profile, or cross section, 3 feet (0.9 meter) deep. Subsoil becomes coarser and contains less humus with depth.

Soil Conservation

One reason why erosion is a fearsome enemy of the farmer is the time required for good soil to form. It may take up to 500 years for a single inch of good topsoil to be produced by natural means. With a rapidly multiplying world population, topsoil conservation is a serious concern.

Methods that farmers can use to preserve topsoil are shown in INQ Figure 10–4. Each is directed toward a specific problem. *Contour plowing,* for example, is used when plowing hilly land. Plowing straight up or down a hill will cause gullies to form during rain or irrigation; plowing around the hill reduces gully erosion. *Strip cropping* alternates a row crop that has much bare soil exposed, such as corn, with a ground cover crop, such as clover. This method reduces wind erosion. A *tree windbreak* will also help if the field is located where a strong wind usually blows from one direction. *Terracing* may be used to prepare relatively flat areas for growing crops on steep slopes. *Check dams* of stones or logs may be used to slow water in a stream or to prevent a gully from widening.

Another good farming practice for conserving farm topsoil is called *residue management.* This method does away with the plow, because even the best plowing practices bare soil to water and wind erosion. Now, many farmers leave the residue or stubble from harvested crops in place to hold soil and moisture. Tractor-pulled machines gouge places for seeds, which then sprout and grow through the decomposing residue. Besides minimizing erosion, the method actually rebuilds the precious topsoil.

INQ Figure 10–4 **Ways of preventing erosion: (A) contour plowing, (B) strip crops, (C) terraces, (D) check dams, and (E) tree windbreak.**

BUILDING UP OF THE LAND Inquiry

The Earth's Changing Crust

MATERIALS

- Box lid or tray
- Round balloon (large, deflated)
- Sand or dry soil
- Three chocolate sheet cakes (unfrosted)
- Ruler
- Relief globe

Invitation

What are some forces acting on the earth's crust? When rocks melt underground, they form a thick, fiery-hot liquid called *magma*. Hot gases and steam that are released when the rocks melt mix with the magma and build up great pressure. This pressure forces the magma to squeeze into cracks or weak places under the earth's crust. Magma may push up and bend rock layers above without coming to the surface. This can make a dome mountain. Can you make a model of one? Earthquakes may also change the earth's surface. In the three types of earthquakes, the crust moves horizontally, diagonally, or vertically. How can you demonstrate the three types of earthquakes?

Exploration

1. Spread a thin layer of sand or soil in a box lid or tray.
2. Lay a balloon on the sand. Let its neck stick out over the lid's side. Cover the balloon with about 5 centimeters (2 inches) of sand or soil. Make the "land" surface level.
3. Slowly blow air into the balloon so that it is partly filled.
4. Now, holding the first of the three cakes with one hand on each side, push the cake together until a crack develops in the cake. This is a *fault*.
5. Hold the second cake on its side with both hands and gently pull the cake apart until a "fault" forms a *trench*.
6. Hold the final cake as above, but with your left hand pull toward your body and with your right hand pull away from your body, producing a *strike slip fault*.

 Teaching Tips

A large, round balloon is recommended. Small balloons are hard to inflate, and the weight of the soil will make this even harder to do. A small plastic bag may also be easily inflated if its opening is tightly wrapped around the end of a drinking straw and fastened with sticky tape.

Thin layers of alternating chocolate and vanilla cake simulate rock layers when performing the earthquake activity.

Concept Invention

1. What happened to the land surface when you blew up the balloon? What in the model is like the magma? What is like the layers of rock above the magma?
2. Compare and contrast each of the three faults made with the cakes.

Scaffolding for English Learners

Be sure to include your students' countries of origin when discussing the earth's changing surface. Have them chart the patterns of volcanic and earthquake activity from their native region onto a classroom world map. Many online data sources provide information on volcanic and seismic activity.

Concept Application

Look on a raised surface (relief) globe for examples of volcanoes and faults similar to those you made here. Where do you find volcanoes occurring? Where are examples of each type of fault found?

BUILDING UP OF THE LAND CONCEPTS

Careful geological studies show that the powerful forces of weathering and erosion should have long ago worn down the earth's surface to a low-lying plain. Then why does the earth have mountains? Part of the answer is seen in volcanic activity.

Magma

Fiery molten rock from deep underground, called *magma*, thrusts up through weak spots and cracks in the earth's crust. When this material reaches the surface, it is called *lava*.

Sometimes the accumulation of magma and high-pressure gases is so great that the molten rock shoots up to the surface in a spectacular eruption. This can happen under the ocean, as well as on land. The Hawaiian Islands are the eroded tops of volcanoes, as are the Azores in the Atlantic Ocean.

Sometimes magma may quietly ooze up through great cracks in the crust and spread out over the ground. Large parts of the Pacific Northwest are covered with hardened lava beds to depths of thousands of meters. Similar lava flows have occurred in Iceland.

Several types of magmatic activity are not directly visible until erosion has worn away parts of the crust. Magma may stop flowing and cool before it reaches the surface, or it may push up part of the crust, forming a dome, or *laccolith*. Erosion of the surrounding crust uncovers the dome and makes the dome more prominent (INQ Figure 10–5).

Where does heat energy for volcanoes originate? Several theories have been developed. Some scientists think that radioactive rocks are responsible in some places. One radioactive element is uranium, which continually shoots off helium atoms and changes to

INQ Figure 10–5   **A volcano and a laccolith.**

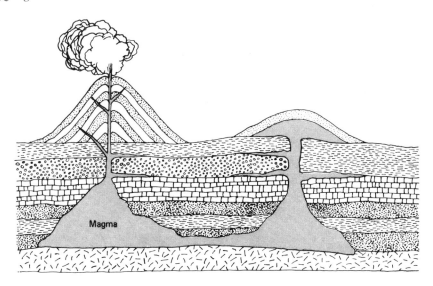

Magma

lead, and in the process, generates a tiny amount of heat energy. If many rocks of this type become concentrated, it is conceivable that they could bring about enough heat energy to melt rocks, thus forming magma.

Earthquakes and Faults

There has been a lot of attention given to earthquakes and earthquake monitoring since the December 26, 2004 earthquake off the coast of Northern Sumatra, but what causes earthquakes? Earthquakes happen when the earth's crust breaks under the strain of its deforming forces. Parts of the crust may move horizontally, diagonally, or vertically along a huge crack, or *fault*. Over a long time, *block mountains* may develop through tilted or vertical movements along a fault line. This seems to be how the Sierra Nevada range was formed.

Other mountains seem to be made through *folding*. Immense forces push parts of the crust into giant wrinkles. The Appalachians are an example.

Plate Theory

How do scientists explain such major changes in the earth's crust? When we look at a world map, certain land masses of the earth, though far apart, seem to fit together like pieces of a jigsaw puzzle. The east coast of South America and the west coast of Africa are examples. Could it be that these and other continents were once joined?

Many earth scientists infer this. They think the earth's thin crust was once solid, but now is fragmented into six to eight immense "plates" and several smaller ones that fit in between. The plates drift on the earth's fiery mantle of molten rock some 100 kilometers (60 miles) or so below. The continents float on the plates like passengers on rafts. Plate edges do not necessarily coincide with the edges of continents. According to *plate tectonics* theory, the plates continually pull apart, collide, grind edges, or partially slide under each other.

Ocean floors, for example, form when two plates drift apart. Magma pushes up from the mantle and fills the ever-widening gap between the plates. When one plate pushes into or under another, folded mountains and block mountains may be formed. A plate edge that thrusts downward under another melts into the fiery mantle below. Some of the magma resulting from this thrusts up through weak spots in the solid crust to form volcanoes. Earthquakes may happen as plates slide past each other in opposite directions. The great friction between the two massive plates may cause the movements to stop temporarily. However, stresses build up until the crust suddenly fractures and the plates grind onward.

Plate movements are surprisingly fast, up to 20 centimeters (8 inches) a year in some locations, given the approximate age of the earth at 5 billion years. Apparently, the force needed to move the rigid plates comes from convection currents in the molten mantle below.

Note the correlation between regions of earthquake and volcanic activity in INQ Figure 10–6. Many scientists infer that these active regions reveal some boundaries of the huge, drifting plates. The "Cakequake" (Hardy & Tolman, 1991) is a fun way to introduce plate tectonics through types of plate movements.

INQ Figure 10–6   Earthquake (A) and volcanic (B) regions of the world.

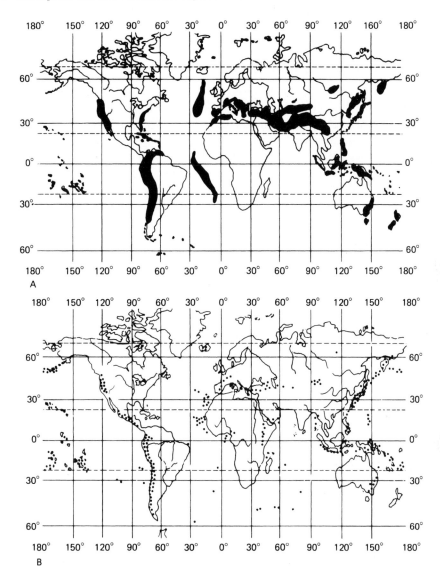

HOW ROCKS ARE FORMED Inquiry

The Properties of Rocks ———

MATERIALS

- Penny
- Six different rocks
- Large iron nail
- Partner
- Glass baby-food jar
- Pencil and paper
- Vinegar
- Safety goggles
- Piece of white tile
- Paper cup
- Hand lens

Invitation

Have you ever heard the saying, "It's as hard as a rock"? Does this mean all rocks are equally hard? What do you think? How can you find out the hardness of different rocks? What other properties of rocks can you observe and describe?

Exploration

1. Study the following hardness scale for help in grouping your rocks.

Hardness Scale	Rock Test
Very soft	Can be scratched with your fingernail.
Soft	A new penny will scratch it. A fingernail will not.
Medium	A nail will scratch it. A penny will not.
Hard	It will scratch glass. A nail will not scratch it.

2. Test each rock according to this scale. Record the hardness of each rock. One way is to label each rock with a different letter. Write the letter on a slip of paper. Then put the rock on the slip, as illustrated. Record each rock's letter and hardness on a sheet of paper.

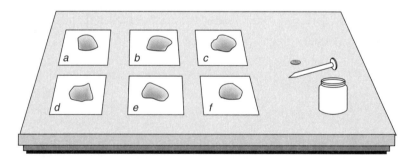

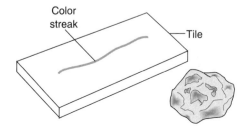

Color streak — Tile

3. What is the color of each rock? Note that some rocks have several mixed colors.
4. What is the color of the streak left by rubbing the rock on a tile? Rub the rock on the rough side of some tile, as shown. What color is the streak?

5. How does the rock feel to you? Is the rock's texture rough? Is it smooth? Is it soapy?
6. Does the rock seem to be made up of flat layers pressed together? Use a hand lens to get a closer look.
7. Does the rock have many small holes in it?
8. Put on safety goggles. Place the rock into a small cup of vinegar. Do many tiny bubbles appear?
9. Can you see tiny parts of seashells or other such materials? Use a hand lens to get a closer look.
10. How heavy or light does the rock seem for its size?
11. What other properties of your rocks can you observe?

 Only about 30 minerals make up most common rocks. So, you will observe some of the same minerals many times in different rocks.

Concept Invention

1. Will someone else who tests your rocks' hardness agree with you? Let your partner test your rocks. They should be on the lettered paper slips. Have her record each rock's letter and hardness. How much is this record like yours? Are there differences? Why? How can you put your six rocks in order from softest to hardest? (*Hint:* How can scratching one rock with another help?) What other rocks can you test for hardness? How much will someone else agree with you if they test the same rocks?
2. Try comparing color, streak, texture, or other properties of your rocks. How can these properties be used to classify rocks?

Concept Application

Rocks vary in hardness, color, texture, and other properties. To understand these properties better, play a game with a partner. Sort some of your rocks into two groups according to one property (use hardness, color, feel, or other properties). Can your partner tell which property you used to sort them? Also play the "I'm-Thinking-of-a-Rock" game with a partner. Place four or more rocks in a row. Think of just one rock and some of its properties. Can your partner find out which rock you have in mind? He must ask you only questions that can be answered by *yes* or *no*. Example: "Is it a rough rock?" (Yes) "Does it have holes?" (No) How well can you describe your rocks? Can you make a chart that your partner can use to identify them (see following example)? Make a chart of all the properties you observe about your rocks. Label your rocks and try to remember which rock is which. Show your completed chart and rocks to your partner. The rocks should be out of order, so he must study your chart to tell which rock is A, B, C, and so on. Which chart descriptions were helpful? Which confused your partner? How could these be made clearer?

Rock	Hardness	Color	Feel	Layers	Holes
A	Medium	Gray	Smooth	No	Yes
B					
C					

Growing Crystals —————

Invitation

It is interesting to see the crystals that make up some rocks. Most crystals are formed underground when melted minerals collect and grow in size as they cool. You can learn more about crystals and how they "grow" by making some yourself. How can you grow crystals?

Exploration

1. Wear safety goggles for steps 1 and 2. Stir as much salt into a half-cup of hot water as will dissolve.
2. Pour the salt solution into a saucer. Put a short string in the solution. Leave part of it out of the liquid so that you can pick up the string later. Put the saucer where it will not be disturbed.
3. Wait several days until most of the salt solution has evaporated. Carefully pour off what is left. Then give the crystals forming on the saucer bottom and string a day to dry.
4. Examine the dry crystals with a hand lens.

MATERIALS

- Glass or ceramic saucers
- String
- Scissors
- Hand lens
- Hot water
- Table salt
- Cup
- Alum (potash)
- Spoon
- Borax
- Safety goggles
- Refrigerator

 Teaching Tips

Alum (potash) is sold in drugstores, rather than in grocery stores. Sugar is another substance from which a solution may be prepared for crystal growing. All solutions should be very heavy or saturated for good crystals to form. A solution that cools quickly forms small crystals; this is like molten rock that cools relatively quickly at or near the earth's surface. A solution that cools more slowly has time to form larger, coarser crystals; this is like molten rock that cools slowly deep underground.

Concept Invention

1. How do the salt crystals look? Study their shape, size, and cohesiveness.
2. What do alum and borax crystals look like? Prepare crystals from these materials as you did from salt. Remember to wear safety goggles. Study the crystals carefully with a hand lens.
3. Have someone show you strings of crystals prepared from salt, alum, and borax. Can you tell which is which without being told?
4. How, if at all, does quickness of cooling affect crystal size?

Adapting for Students with Exceptionalities

Some students may become impatient with this activity because of the time involved. Set up a classroom observation schedule (wall chart) with names, dates, and observation times. Have students fill in what they see each day to help maintain interest.

Concept Application

Crystals may form from molten rock or may be grown from mineral solutions. The size of crystals depends on how fast the molten rock and solutions cool. Prepare two solutions of alum in separate saucers. Refrigerate one so that it will cool fast. Put the other where it will cool slowly. Examine each solution the next day. Record your results.

HOW ROCKS ARE FORMED CONCEPTS

"What are rocks made of?" children often ask. Rocks are made of minerals, natural inorganic materials that constitute most of the earth's crust. Some minerals are a single element, such as copper or carbon. A beautiful diamond is an example of almost pure carbon formed under enormous pressure underground. Other minerals are compounds of two or more minerals, such as mica or quartz. The chemical makeup of a mineral is the same anywhere it is found on the earth. A pure copper or quartz sample is as recognizable in Asia as in North America.

Geologists have developed many ways of identifying a mineral. These include observing its color, hardness, luster, crystal structure, and density, and how it splits along a plane, breaks, and reacts to chemicals.

Just as a word may be made up of one or more letters of the alphabet, rocks may be composed of one or more minerals. But there are far more known minerals than letters of the alphabet (about 2000). Most are seldom seen. Fewer than 100 minerals make up the bulk of the earth's crust.

Usually, rocks are given the same name when they contain essentially the same minerals, like granite. Some samples, though, may contain a greater proportion of one or more of the minerals than other samples. So, not all granite samples look alike, nor do many other rock samples that are given a certain name. Although there are many minerals, rocks are formed in just three ways.

Sedimentary Rocks ───────

Sediments from eroded rocks are the raw materials for new *sedimentary rocks*. The sediments are usually moved and deposited by rivers into coastal trenches and basins. Some rivers deposit sediments into large lakes. Sand, clay, silt, pebbles, and stones are common sedimentary materials. Sediments gradually collect layer upon layer where they are deposited, which makes the layers press harder and harder on the lower sediments. The enormous pressure, plus chemicals dissolved in the water, act to cement the sediments together. Sand particles become sandstone, mud or clay becomes shale, and pebbles and rocks and sand combine to form conglomerate.

Not all sediments come from eroded materials. Limestone and chalk are examples of rock formed on the ocean floor from the compressed skeletons and shells of billions of ocean animals, including clams, mussels, and corals. Some sedimentary rock may also form from previously dissolved chemicals that deposit out of solution when the water can no longer hold them.

Igneous Rocks ————

A second way rocks are formed is through the cooling of magma or lava, creating *igneous rocks* (the word *igneous* means "formed from fire"). A common example of igneous formation happens in volcanic domes, or *laccoliths*. Magma squeezes under a surface rock layer, slowly cools, and becomes solid. When the surface rocks erode away, the underlying hardened magma rock is exposed. Granite is the most frequently found rock of this kind. Its large crystals reveal that it cooled slowly.

Lava that is blown from a volcano or that flows out of cracks in the crust cools quickly. So, it has small crystals or no visible crystals. The light, spongy rock called *pumice* and the black, glassy rock called *obsidian* are examples.

Metamorphic Rocks ————

Sedimentary and igneous rocks may be subject to severe pressure and heat as parts of the crust move, fold, thrust deeper under the ground, or are buried under lava flows. This may cause physical and chemical changes in the rocks, making them *metamorphic rocks* (the word *metamorphic* means "changed in form"). Sedimentary rock such as limestone becomes the metamorphic rock marble, sandstone may become quartzite, and shale becomes slate. Igneous rock, such as granite, changes to gneiss (pronounced "nice"), or soft coal changes to hard coal.

Metamorphic rocks are harder than the original rock material. They often have compression bands of different colors. Usually, crystals are small. Still, it is easy to confuse metamorphic rocks with igneous rocks.

INQ Table 10–1 shows 12 kinds of rocks that children can use to become acquainted with the three basic rock types. They are fairly distinctive and easy to obtain. Some, and perhaps all, of these rocks may be included in specimens children bring to school. If not, they may be acquired from local rock collectors, museums, and science supply companies.

Fossils ————

The remains or signs of animals or plants in rock are called *fossils*. The most likely rocks in which fossils are found are sedimentary. Occasionally, fossils are found in partly metamorphosed sedimentary rocks, but pressure and heat usually destroy fossils.

Fossils are formed in different ways. When some animals died, sediments covered them. The soft body parts decomposed, but teeth and skeletons remained, preserved by hardened layers of sediment. In other cases, even the skeletons disintegrated, but before they did, mineral-laden water infiltrated into the bones and replaced bone with minerals. This process left a perfect cast replica of the skeleton in many cases. Some trees have left casts in a similar way. This is how specimens of the Petrified Forest in Arizona were formed. Additional fossils have been discovered frozen in ice, found in tar pits, and other places.

The so-called fossil fuels—coal, oil, and natural gas—were formed from the remains of plants and animals that died millions of years ago. Mud, silt, and other sediments covered

Igneous, Sedimentary, and Metamorphic Rocks

Igneous Rocks	Description	How Formed
Pumice	Grayish, fine pores, glassy, frothy, light, floats on water.	From rapid cooling of frothy, surface lava containing gases.
Volcanic Breccia	Consolidated fragments of volcanic ash, such as glass, pumice, quartz.	From being exploded high into the air from a volcano and settling.
Obsidian	Black, glassy, no crystals.	From very rapid surface cooling of lava.
Basalt	Dark, greenish-gray, very small crystals, may have some holes.	From very rapid cooling of lava close to the surface. Escaping gases form holes.

(continued)

Igneous, Sedimentary, and Metamorphic Rocks—Continued

Igneous Rocks	Description	How Formed
Granite	Coarse crystals, white to gray, sometimes pinkish.	From slow, below-surface cooling of molten rock (magma), as when domes are formed.

Sedimentary Rocks	Description	How Formed
Conglomerate	Rounded pebbles, stones, and sand cemented together.	From loose materials compacted by pressure of overlying sediments and bound by natural cement.
Sandstone	Sand grains clearly visible, gray, yellow, red.	From sand compacted by pressure of sediment, bound by natural cement.
Shale	Soft, smells like clay, fine particles, green, black, yellow, red, gray.	From compacted mud bound by natural cement.

Sedimentary Rocks	Description	How Formed
Limestone	Fairly soft, white, gray, red, forms carbon dioxide gas bubbles when touched with acids.	From dead organisms that used calcium carbonate in seawater in making body parts; from evaporation of seawater containing calcium carbonate.

Metamorphic Rocks	Description	How Formed
Marble	Different, mixed colors, may have colored bands, medium to coarse crystals, fizzes if touched with acids.	Formed when pure limestone is subjected to intense heat and pressure.
Slate	Greenish-gray, black, red, splits in thin layers, harder than shale.	Formed when shale is subjected to intense heat and pressure.
Quartzite	Very hard, white, gray, pink, indistinct grains, somewhat glassy.	Formed when sandstone is subjected to intense heat and pressure.

huge masses of organic matter in swampy forests. Gradually, the sediments formed into stony layers. Pressure and heat from immense crustal movements caused physical and chemical changes in the buried organic matter. Some formed into seams of coal trapped between shale and slate. Some deposits changed into thick, black oil and natural gas, often trapped between layers of folded rock.

Rock Cycle

The same processes that formed rocks in the past continue today. Over many thousands of years, rocks change their forms. Even so, much evidence indicates that the same mineral materials are used over and over in a kind of rock cycle. INQ Figure 10–7 shows what seems to happen.

All three kinds of rocks erode when exposed on the earth's surface. The resulting sediments, under pressure, form into rock cemented with water-borne chemicals. When these rocks undergo further pressure, torsion, and heat, they metamorphose. The metamorphic rocks turn into magma when heated further. When the magma cools and hardens, it becomes igneous rock. Some of the magma may metamorphose if folded, twisted, or heated again. Some of the magma may also erode, and the cycle continues.

INQ Figure 10–7 **The rock cycle.**

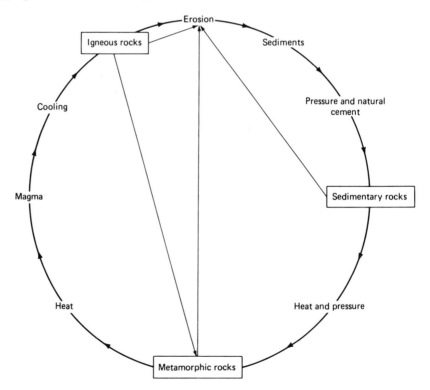

References

American Association for the Advancement of Science (AAAS). (1993). *Benchmarks for science literacy.* New York: Oxford University Press.

Hardy, G. R., & Tolman, M. N. (1991). Cakequake! An earthshaking experience. *Science and Children, 29*(1), 18–21.

Mastropieri, M., & Scruggs, T. E. (2004). *The inclusive classroom: Strategies for effective instruction* (4th ed.). Upper Saddle River, NJ: Merrill/Prentice Hall.

National Research Council (NRC). (1996). *National science education standards.* Washington, DC: National Academy Press.

TESOL (Teachers of English to Speakers of Other Languages). (1992). *TESOL Statement on the education of K-12 language-minority students in the United States.* Alexandria, VA: Author.

Selected Trade Books: The Earth's Changing Surface

For Younger Children

Baylor, B. (1974). *Everybody needs a rock.* New York: Aladdin Paperbacks.

Booth, E. (1985). *Under the ground.* Austin, TX: Raintree.

Branley, F. (1986). *Volcanoes.* New York: HarperTrophy.

Branley, F. M. (1994). *Earthquakes.* New York: HarperTrophy.

Butler, D. (1991). *First look under the ground.* Milwaukee, WI: Gareth Stevens.

Cole, J. (1988). *The magic school bus inside the earth.* New York: Scholastic.

Cole, J. (1996). *The magic school bus blows its top: A book about volcanoes.* New York: Scholastic.

Dorros, A. (1990). *Feel the wind.* New York: HarperTrophy.

Harris, S. (1979). *Volcanoes.* Danbury, CT: Watts.

Hiscock, B. (1988). *The big rock.* New York: Aladdin Paperbacks.

Ingoglia, G. (1991). *Look inside the earth.* New York: G. P. Putnam.

Leutscher, A. (1983). *Earth.* New York: Dial.

Lewis, T. (1971). *Hill of fire.* New York: HarperTrophy.

Lindop, L. (2003). *Probing volcanoes (science on the edge).* Brookfield, CT: Twenty-First Century Books/Millbrook.

McNulty, F. (1979). *How to dig a hole to the other side of the world.* New York: HarperCollins.

Merrians, D. (1996). *I can read about earthquakes and volcanoes.* New York: Troll Associates.

Pellant, C. (2000). *The best book of fossils, rocks, and minerals.* New York: Larousse Kingfisher Chambers.

Podendorf, I. (1982). *Rocks and minerals.* Danbury, CT: Childrens Press.

Roberts, A. (1983). *Fossils.* Danbury, CT: Childrens Press.

Rosenblum, R. (1994). *Earthquakes: Let's read and find out about science.* New York: HarperTrophy.

Ross, M. E., & Smith, W. (2000). *Exploring the earth with John Wesley Powell (Naturalist's Apprentice).* Minneapolis, MN: Carolrhoda Books/Lerner.

Schwartz, L. (1991). *My earth book.* Santa Barbara, CA: Learning Works.

Simon, S. (1999). *Mountains.* Topeka, KS: Econo-Clad Books.

Sipier, P. (1986). *I can be a geologist.* Danbury, CT: Childrens Press.

Williams, L. (1986). *The changing earth.* Bothell, WA: Wright Group.

Wyler, R. (1987). *Science fun with dirt and mud.* Parsippany, NJ: Julian Messner.

Zoehfeld, K. (1995). *How mountains are made.* New York: HarperTrophy.

For Older Children

Aulenbach, N. H., & Barton, H. A. (2001). *Exploring caves: Journeys into the earth.* Washington, DC: National Geographic Society.

Blobaum, C. (1999). *Geology rocks: 50 hands-on activities to explore the earth.* Charlotte, VT: Williamson.

Bramwell, M. (1987). *Planet earth.* Danbury, CT: Watts.

Challand, H. (1983). *Volcanoes.* Danbury, CT: Childrens Press.

Downs, S. F. (2000). *Earth's fiery fury.* Brookfield, CT: Twenty-First Century Books/Millbrook Press.

Fordor, R. V. (1978). *Earth in motion: The concept of plate tectonics.* New York: Morrow.

Fordor, R. V. (1983). *Chiseling the earth: How erosion shapes the land.* Springfield, NJ: Enslow.

Gallant, R. A. (1986). *Our restless earth.* Danbury, CT: Watts.

Hooper, M. (1996). *The pebble in my pocket: A history of our earth.* New York: Viking.

Lampton, C. (1994). *Earthquake (a disaster book).* Brookfield, CT: Millbrook Press.

Lauber, P. (1991). *Volcanoes and earthquakes.* New York: Scholastic.

Levine, E. (1992). *If you lived at the time of the great San Francisco earthquake.* New York: Scholastic.

Levine, S., & Grafton, A. (1992). *Projects for a healthy planet.* New York: John Wiley.

Levy, M. (1997). *Earthquake games: Earthquakes and volcanoes explained by games and experiments.* New York: Margaret McElderry.

Lye, K. (1991). *The earth.* Brookfield, CT: Millbrook Press.

Marcus, E. (1984). *All about mountains and volcanoes.* New York: Troll Associates.

Nixon, H. H., & Nixon, J. L. (1980). *Glaciers: Nature's frozen rivers.* New York: Dodd.

Rickard, G. (1991). *Geothermal energy.* Milwaukee, WI: Gareth Stevens.

Ruthland, J. (1987). *The violent earth.* New York: Random House.

Rydell, W. (1984). *Discovering fossils.* New York: Troll Associates.

Selden, P. (1982). *Face of the earth.* Danbury, CT: Childrens Press.

Sussman, A. (2000). *Dr. Art's guide to planet earth: For earthlings ages 12 to 120.* Chelsea, VT: Chelsea Green Publishing Company.

VanCleave, J. (1996). *Rocks and minerals: Mind-boggling experiments you can turn into science fair projects.* New York: John Wiley.

Williamson, T. (1985). *Understanding the earth.* Parsippany, NJ: Silver Burdett.

Winner, P. (1986). *Earthquakes.* Parsippany, NJ: Silver Burdett.

Resource Books

Butzow, C. M., & Butzow, J. W. (1989). *Science through children's literature: An integrated approach*. Englewood, CO: Teacher Ideas Press. (volcano, rock, and soil topics on pp. 123–138)

Butzow, C. M., & Butzow, J. W. (1994). *Intermediate science through children's literature: Over land and sea*. Englewood, CO: Teacher Ideas Press. (geological topics on pp. 62–88)

Cordel, B., & Hillen, J. (1996). *Primarily earth*. Fresno, CA: AIMS Education Foundation.

Cuff, K., Sneider, C., Bergman, L., Gould, A., & Seltzer, J. (1996). *Stories in stone*. Berkeley, CA: Great Explorations in Math and Science.

Ecklund, L., Mercier, S., & Wiebe, A. (Eds.). (1987). *Down to earth*. Fresno, CA: AIMS Education Foundation.

Fredericks, A. D., Meinbach, A. M., & Rothlein, L. (1993). *Thematic units: An integrated approach to teaching science and social studies*. New York: HarperCollins. (the changing earth topics on pp. 202–209)

Gosnell, K. (1994). *Geology: Thematic unit*. Huntington Beach, CA: Teacher Created Materials.

Hale, J. (1992). *Rocks and soil: Thematic unit*. Huntington Beach, CA: Teacher Created Materials.

Shaw, D. G., & Dybdahl, C. S. (1996). *Integrating science and language arts: A sourcebook for K–6 teachers*. Boston: Allyn & Bacon. (rock cycle topic on pp. 78–82; rock topics on pp. 111–130)

Sneider, C., & Barrett, K. (1989). *River cutters*. Berkeley, CA: Great Explorations in Math and Science.

WATER, AIR, AND WEATHER

It's easy to take clean air and water for granted, and why not? For many of us, all we need do is breathe easily and turn on a faucet. But experiences of recent years with pollution and water shortages are making people lose their complacency. Let's examine some properties of water and air, the importance of a clean supply of both, and some concepts basic to understanding weather, organized under three headings: water, air and its properties, and weather.

Benchmarks and Standards

Weather, air, and water are popular topics in the elementary grades. Students frequently complete daily weather logs and journal descriptions of the changing weather patterns, often including pictures of what they see. Representative benchmarks and standards related to water, air, and weather include the following:

Sample Benchmarks (AAAS, 1993)

- Water left in an open container disappears, but water in a closed container does not disappear. (By Grades K–2, p. 67)
- Some events in nature have a repeating pattern. The weather changes day to day, but things such as temperature and rain (or snow) tend to be high, low, or medium in the same months every year. (By Grades K–2, p. 67)

Sample Standards (NRC, 1996)

- Weather changes from day to day and over the seasons. Weather can be described in measurable quantities such as temperature, wind direction and speed, and precipitation. (By Grades K–4, p. 134)
- The atmosphere is a mixture of nitrogen, oxygen, and trace gases that include water vapor. (By Grades 5–8, p. 160)

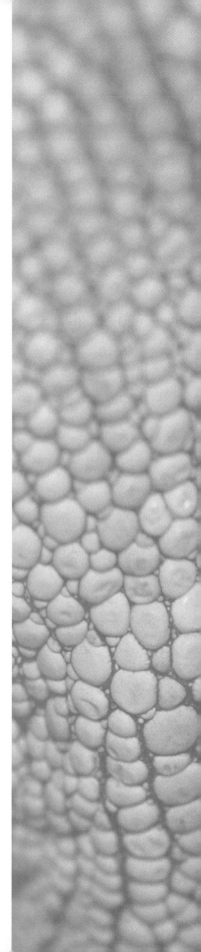

WATER Inquiry

How Water and Other Liquids Stick Together ————————

Invitation

Suppose you fill a glass with water to the very top. What do you think will happen if you add more water? How high can you fill a container of water before it spills?

Exploration

1. Fill a small container to the top with water.
2. Gently drop paper clips into the container one at a time as shown.
3. Watch how the water "heaps" higher in the container. Count the number of clips it takes for the water to spill. Make a record.

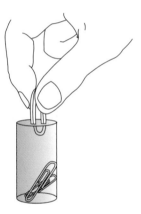

MATERIALS
• Three small plastic vials
• Spoon
• Three matched medicine droppers
• Newspaper
• Water
• Liquid soap or detergent
• Paper clips
• Rubbing alcohol
• Safety goggles
• Paper cup
• Meterstick or yardstick
• Partner

Teaching Tips

Any liquid has the property of cohesion, which is the tendency for its molecules to stick together. The cohesion of water is strong, compared with that of some other liquids. This is why water forms a bulge that rises above the rim of an overly full glass. Soap weakens the cohesive power of water, so the bulge of slightly soapy water is noticeably lower. That of alcohol is lower still; its cohesion is relatively weak. This is one reason why it evaporates so quickly.

Caution: Wear safety goggles while you are doing the steps in the Concept Invention and Concept Application.

Concept Invention

1. How high can you heap other liquids? Try soapy water and alcohol. How do these liquids compare with water? Put the three containers side by side and see. How many paper clips does it take for soapy water and alcohol to spill?
2. How large are the drops of different liquids? Take up plain water in one medicine dropper and alcohol in another. Hold up the droppers side by side. Slowly squeeze each bulb until a drop forms at each open end. How do the drop sizes compare? Try soapy water, too.
3. Which liquid—plain water, soapy water, or alcohol—has the largest drops? Which liquid has the smallest drops? Here is another way to find out. Put 100 drops of each liquid into separate, matched, small containers. Compare how high each liquid is inside.
4. What kinds of drop prints do different liquids make on newspaper? Hold a meterstick or yardstick upright over newspaper. Squeeze a drop of water from a medicine dropper held near and about halfway up the stick. What does the drop

print look like on the newspaper? How large is it? Let a drop fall from the top of the stick. How does the print look now? Try drops of soapy water and alcohol, too.

5. Can you match up a liquid with its drop print? Can you tell from how high each drop fell? Ask a partner to make drop prints as you did. Do not watch as the prints are made.

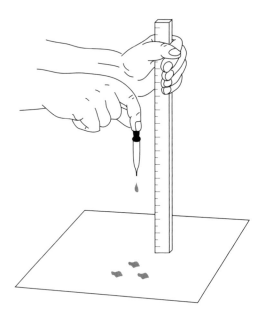

Adapting for Students with Exceptionalities

Make sure to have a lot of paper towels on hand to clean up spills. Also consider students wearing lab coats. Used lab coats can be donated by a local hospital or hospital laundry supply company. (See Mastropieri & Scruggs, 2004, chapter on science and social studies for a discussion on adapting science activities, including preparing for skills.)

Concept Application

Some liquids seem to stick together more strongly than others. What other liquids can you test? How do you think they will compare with your first liquids? Record your hypothesis and observations. Was your hypothesis correct?

How to Measure Volume with Water ⎯⎯⎯⎯⎯⎯

Invitation

Rocks and other solid objects have many different shapes. Sometimes it is hard to tell which of two different-shaped objects is larger—that is, takes up more space. (The amount of space an object takes up is its *volume*.) How can you compare the volumes of small solid objects?

MATERIALS

- Five small different-shaped rocks
- Ruler
- Oil-based modeling clay
- Large clear jar with straight sides
- Small lead fishing sinker
- Water
- Masking tape and pencil
- Fork or spoon
- Variety of small objects

Exploration

1. Fasten a strip of masking tape on a jar the long way.
2. Half-fill the jar with water.
3. Put one rock into the jar. Mark the water level on the tape with a pencil.
4. Remove the rock with a fork or spoon.
5. Put a second rock into the jar. Compare the new water level with the pencil mark. Remove the rock.

This investigation may help some children learn to conserve volume as measured by displaced water; that is, the space an object takes up is determined by its overall surface, rather than shape, weight, or number of parts.

Concept Invention

1. How can you put the rocks in order from smallest to largest?
2. Make a clay ball the size of some rock. Where will the water level be if you put it into the jar? Mark the tape to show your estimate, and then test your hypothesis.
3. Suppose you form the same clay ball into another shape. Where do you think the water level will be? Try many different shapes.
4. Suppose you break the same clay piece into two parts. Where do you think the water level will be? What happens to the water level when you break the clay into more than two parts?
5. Will a heavy clay ball make the water level rise higher than a lighter one? Make two clay balls the same size, but have a lead weight in the middle of one ball. Try each ball and find out.
6. How much larger is one rock compared with another? With a ruler and pencil, make evenly spaced marks on the jar's tape strip. Call each pencil mark 1 "unit." Compare the difference in water-level units before and after a rock is put into the jar. How much difference in units is there between your smallest and largest rock?

Concept Application

The volumes of different-shaped solid objects may be compared by the water each displaces. Get other small objects and record them. How well can you predict the volume of each in units? Experiment and check your predictions.

Things That Float in Water

Invitation

Can you tell, just by looking at an object, if it will float in water? What kinds of objects float? What kinds of objects sink? How can you find out which small objects will float?

Exploration

1. Half-fill a plastic bowl with water.
2. Empty the bag of small objects onto your desk. Put those you think will float into one group. Put those you think will sink into another group.
3. Place all the objects from one group into the water. Observe what happens, and then remove the objects. Do the same thing with the other group of objects.

Concept Invention

1. How many objects did what you thought? What are the objects like that floated? What are the objects like that sank?
2. What can you do to sink the objects that floated?
3. What can you do to float the objects that sank?
4. In what ways can you get a piece of foil to float? In what ways can you get a piece of foil to sink? Can you make a foil boat? How many washers can your foil boat carry? What can you do to make it carry more washers?
5. How can you get a piece of clay to float? Can you make a clay boat the same size as your foil boat? Which do you think will carry more washers?
6. Can you make two foil boats that will carry, from the first try, exactly the same weight? Can you make two clay boats that will carry the same weight from the first try?

Teaching Tips

Children can develop some understanding in this investigation about the buoyancy of different objects in water and how the density of water affects buoyancy. You might also want children to explore liquids other than water. A bag of small objects to test for floating might include a wooden checker, pencil, key, marble, plastic objects, pieces of leather, rubber eraser, and small toy figures. The children can bring in many more. Uniform objects other than large washers may be used to measure the weight-carrying capacity of children's boats. Identical marbles, pennies, or small pieces of ceramic tile work well. To avoid rust, be sure all steel washers are dried before they are stored.

MATERIALS

- Plastic bowl
- Water
- Salt
- Bag of small objects to test
- Ruler
- Oil-based modeling clay
- Spoon
- Large washers
- Paper towels
- Aluminum foil (15 centimeters, or 6 inches, square)

Scaffolding for English Learners

The floating and sinking activity is a common elementary science activity that is not language/vocabulary intensive. It presents an opportunity for English learners to show that they understand a science concept despite language problems. Activities such as this help differentiate true learning disabilities from language disabilities. Many English learners are inappropriately identified as students with special needs due to language difficulties. (See Baca, Baca, & deValenzuela, 2004, for a discussion of the current status of bilingual special education.)

Concept Application

Objects that are light for their size float and adding salt to the water makes floating easier. How do your boats work in saltwater? Can they carry more weight? What can you get to float in saltwater that cannot float in freshwater? List the items. Can you find anything that will float in freshwater and sink in saltwater? List these items, too.

Water Pressure ————

Invitation

What happens to water pressure with depth?

Exploration

1. Punch a nail hole in the carton's side, halfway up, from the inside out.
2. Punch another hole above it and a third hole below it, from the inside out.
3. Place the carton in a sink. Cover all three holes tightly with three fingers. Fill the carton with water. Keep it in the sink.
4. If you take away your fingers, what do you think will happen?
5. Remove your fingers quickly from the three holes.

Concept Invention

1. Explain what happened.
2. In what part of the carton was the water pressure the greatest?

Concept Application

Do you think that water pressure will be greater in the bottom of the Pacific or Atlantic Ocean or in one of the Great Lakes? Explain your answer.

MATERIALS

- Tall, empty milk carton
- Nail or sharp pencil
- Sink
- Water

Teaching Tips Sometimes the torn edges of the holes will impede the flow of water. Punching the holes from the inside out makes this less likely.

High Water ————

Invitation

How high can water flow, compared to its origin?

Exploration

1. Stick the funnel end tightly into a tube end. Do this activity in a sink.
2. Hold up the funnel. Have someone pour water into it.
3. When water comes out of the tube, pinch it off.
4. Have someone fill the funnel with water. Keep the tube end pinched off. How high will you be able to hold the tube end and still have water come out? Can you hold it higher than the funnel? What if you hold the tube end the same level or lower than the funnel?
5. Let go of the tube end.

MATERIALS

- Rubber tube (1 meter, or 1 yard, long)
- Container of water
- Funnel that fits the tube
- Sink

Concept Invention

1. Try holding it at different heights.
2. What did you find?

Concept Application

Do you think that water flow will be greater from a hillside reservoir or from a water tower high above a city? In a tall building, would the water faucets in the sinks on the first floor work differently from the faucets on the top floor, if plumbers did not compensate for the height of the building? How would plumbers make this compensation? What if the building was higher than the water reservoir? Explain your ideas.

The Filtering of Polluted Water

Invitation

Most cities have water treatment plants to clean, or purify, their drinking water. The unclean water is first pumped to a large settling tank, where it stays for a while. Some of the dirt and other polluting particles in the water settle to the bottom. The cleaner water on top then goes into a filtering tank, which has thick layers of sand and gravel. Sometimes a layer of charcoal is put between these layers. As the water filters through, still more polluting materials are left behind. It's not easy to clean polluted water, even by filtering. How can you clean polluted water by filtering?

Exploration

1. Punch some holes with a nail in the bottom of a cut-off milk carton.
2. Spread some cotton inside on the carton bottom. Add some clean sand.
3. Put crushed charcoal on top of the sand. (To crush charcoal, put a briquette into a small bag and pound it with a rock.) Then add another layer of sand.
4. Place the filter on top of a small glass jar.
5. Pour some clean tap water into your filter. (This will pack the materials more tightly together.)
6. Prepare a jar of soil water. To do this, put a handful of soil into a jar of water and mix. Let the water settle for a half hour.
7. Pour some soil water from the top of the jar into the filter. Watch the filtered water trickle into the small jar, as illustrated.

MATERIALS
• Cut-off pint milk carton
• Clean sand
• Charcoal briquette
• Cotton
• Small glass jar
• Nail
• Jar of soil water
• Small paper bag
• Rock
• Clean tap water

 Teaching Tips Caution the children not to drink their filtered water. They should know that a chemical is added to filtered water in city water plants to kill germs that survive filtering. Try having a contest to determine the best filter. Children may need to be reminded that everyone should filter samples of the same polluted water.

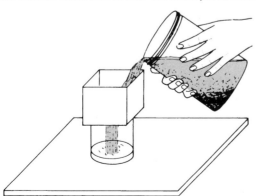

Concept Invention

1. How clean is the filtered water compared to the soil water?
2. How clean would the water get with fewer filtering materials? How clean would the water get with just one filtering material?
3. Will your filter remove ink or food coloring?
4. Does the order in which you place your filter materials matter?

Concept Application

Some water pollutants may be removed by filtering the water through layers of different permeable materials. Would more or other materials work better? How else could you improve your filter? Record your experiments.

WATER CONCEPTS

Our need for water commands our attention in both direct and indirect ways. Water is vital to life. Water transports chemicals to body cells, removes waste materials, and performs other vital bodily functions. Although humans may survive for weeks without food, they need water within a few days. Bathing, cooking, and recreational activities also require water.

Agriculture consumes enormous volumes of water for irrigating plants in rain-poor regions. Industry, too, is a huge user of water. The manufacture of paper, steel, rubber, chemicals, and other products continually requires more water. Even our future energy resources depend, in part, on having adequate water. For example, coal in the western United States would be most efficiently transported if crushed and sent through pipes after being mixed with water. The extraction of oil from shale rock also requires much water. But there is not enough water in the right places to meet all such needs. Because water has so many uses, it is important to understand its properties. Let's look at some now.

Water Properties ——————

Water is an excellent solvent. In fact, more substances dissolve in water than in any other common liquid. Some other properties of water basic to our discussion are its molecular attraction, how it exerts pressure, and how it flows.

Molecules and Water

You may recall that the attractive force between molecules is called *cohesion*. In a solid, the spaces between molecules are relatively small, so a solid material sticks together, or coheres, well enough to maintain its own shape. Molecules of a liquid are farther apart; their weaker cohesion causes them to slide about and assume the shape of their container. The cohesion of gas molecules is weaker still because these molecules are even farther apart.

Cohesion of water molecules is central to the process of evaporation. Heat energy must overcome water's cohesive force, as well as the force of air pressing down. If this could not happen, evaporation could not take place. The sun, of course, is the earth's chief source of heat energy. When we spread out a water puddle to make it dry faster, the sun's energy overcomes the cohesive force of more water molecules at one time. So, the rate of evaporation increases.

Pressure

The weight of water gives it pressure. That is to say, as water depth is greater so is its pressure. This is one reason why a dam is built with a thicker base than top. At any depth, the pressure is exerted in all directions and planes.

Pressure is also involved when something floats. For an object to float, opposing balanced forces work against each other. Gravity pulls down on the object, and the water pushes up on it. The key to floating is the object's size relative to its weight or density. If it is light for its size, it has relatively high volume; in other words, it presents a large surface area for the water to push against. This is why a ship made of steel floats. The water displaced by an object that is light for its size pushes up as forcefully as gravity pulls down.

An object floats higher in the ocean than in freshwater because ocean water has more minerals dissolved in it, especially salt. Therefore, a cup of ocean water weighs more than a cup of freshwater. Having more weight, it pushes back with greater force on any object that displaces it. This pushing force allows a ship to carry a heavier cargo in saltwater than in freshwater.

Water Flow

Gravity is the force that moves water in nature. Water cannot flow higher than its source unless some other force is more powerful. To store their water supplies, some towns and small cities pump water into large tanks mounted on towers. Water then flows by gravity through all pipes connected to the towns' tanks.

In some places, buildings are constructed that are taller than the tower. Pumps are installed in the buildings so that water can reach the higher floors. Sometimes a tank is located on the roof of a tall building so that water is available above the normal water source levels. Special plumbing is also required so that water pressure is not extreme at the lower floors, compared with the upper floors.

Clean, Adequate Water

Will there be enough water for enough people in enough places in the foreseeable future? A dependable answer to this question seems impossible now. But we can survey what it takes to get a clean and adequate supply of water, beginning with some sources of water.

Sources

A look at a globe tells us the earth has no shortage of water. About 71% of the earth's crust is covered with it. Most, though, is in the oceans and is too salty for either land plants or animals to drink. So, our immediate sources of freshwater are found elsewhere, such as in lakes, rivers, reservoirs, and beneath the land surface as groundwater.

Groundwater comes from rainwater that is absorbed into the soil and porous rock. It continues to sink until it reaches a layer of solid, nonporous rock. As more rainwater soaks into the ground, more of the below-surface section becomes saturated. The upper limit of the saturated section is called the *water table*. The water table profile often corresponds roughly to that of the earth's surface. Where the earth's surface dips below the water table, we see a lake or spring. Groundwater does not always come from rainwater sinking from directly above. Groundwater may percolate through ground and porous rock diagonally or horizontally for some distance before it stops.

To construct a water well, a hole is drilled or dug to some depth below the water table. This depth helps ensure a steady supply of water should the water table lower during dry spells. Ocean water is the main source of evaporating water on the earth. So, the oceans are the basic source for freshwater. When ocean water evaporates, the salt is left behind. Air currents carry the water vapor far inland. There it condenses and falls as rain, hail, or snow.

Over the long run, the water cycle gives what should be a steady supply of groundwater and other water. But several factors today make finding usable freshwater difficult in many places. Increased uses for water, as mentioned earlier, are one reason; another reason is pollution.

Pollution

Many cities continue to dump partly treated or raw sewage into nearby rivers or lakes, from which drinking water is often drawn. As a result, purification of water is getting more difficult and more expensive. Factories, too, often discharge wastes into accessible waters. Another major source of pollution is agriculture. Chemical fertilizers and pesticides wash off the land into streams and bays.

An overload of fertilizers or sewage in a lake or other body of water causes an abnormally large population of algae to grow. The algae block sunlight from reaching aquatic plants under the water's surface; so, the plants, as well as the animals that feed on them, die. Dead material piles up on the lake bottom. The overcrowded algae also die in time, and the decomposers take over. Eventually, the oxygen supply in the water is largely depleted, and the decomposers die, too. They are replaced by bacteria that can live without oxygen. What was once a source of clean water and a complex community of living things is a silted, near-dead, putrescent swamp. A reversal can occur through natural changes of the land surface and a gradual succession of ever higher forms of life, but this may take centuries or longer.

In recent years, much publicity has been given to a particularly ominous threat to the nation's water supply: hazardous waste dumps. At such sites, poisonous chemicals may leak from storage containers and percolate down through the ground, contaminating groundwater, nearby streams, and lakes. Drinking or swimming in the water, and eating fish whose organs have accumulated the poisons, have been linked to severe health problems, including brain damage, cancer, and birth defects.

Acid Rain

Many waste products are discharged into the air, as well as on the ground and into bodies of water. These, too, may end up polluting our water and other natural resources. The burning of fossil fuels in factories, power plants, and automobiles releases sulfur and nitrogen oxides into the atmosphere. When water vapor is also present, these gases are converted into sulfuric acid and nitric acid. The rain that falls from a polluted region can be as acidic as vinegar.

Acid rain, including acid sleet, hail, and snow, is contaminating water supplies, killing trees and fish stocks, and corroding water systems. Its effects are easily noticeable in areas that have large concentrations of coal-burning power plants, heavy industry, and automobiles. But even more damage may result far beyond these places. Winds aloft, especially the prevailing westerlies in the United States, sweep the pollutants into large, distant regions. The northeastern United States and adjacent Canadian areas have been most affected.

Some progress has been made in reducing pollutants through the use of chemical filters in industry and pollution control devices for automobile exhaust systems. But large-scale improvements in industrial pollution bear a daunting price tag. Especially nettlesome is the answer to the question: Who pays? When suspected sources of pollution are hundreds of kilometers away and thousands of jobs or millions of utility bills are affected, an acceptable answer becomes highly complicated.

Conservation

It seems inevitable that people will need to change certain water-use habits. Many habits were fostered when regional populations were small, pollution was less severe, water uses were fewer, and resources were more abundant. Conservation, or the wise use, of water resources is becoming more common because more people are aware of the consequences if it is not practiced.

Stricter laws to protect water supplies are continually enacted. More attention is being given to the recycling of industrial wastes and the safe storage of long-lasting, harmful chemicals. Bare slopes are being planted to protect watersheds. Fertilizers and pesticides are being used under more controlled conditions in agriculture. People are learning to use less water in more situations without wasting it. An important by-product of water conservation is energy conservation. A significant amount of the nation's energy is used in pumping water and heating it.

Future Water Supply

It's possible that even increased conservation measures will fail to save enough water to meet our future water needs. Where will we get more usable water? Just as some scientists are looking for ways to directly tap the sun's energy, others are investigating methods for directly converting ocean water to freshwater.

One way to remove salt from ocean water is to distill it. The water is heated, changed to a vapor, and condensed, much like in the water cycle. Another method freezes ocean water. The ice that forms at the surface is mostly freshwater. It is removed and melted. Many other methods are now being used and explored, such as reverse osmosis. At present, all are too expensive for widespread use. If more economical means can be found, the direct conversion of ocean water to freshwater could bring major changes in many dry regions of the world and in the world's food supply.

AIR AND ITS PROPERTIES **Inquiry**

Where Air Can Be

Invitation

Air is found everywhere on the earth. Air can go into tiny places. But can air get inside everything? What things do you think have some air inside? What things do not have air inside? How can you find out what things have some air inside?

Exploration

1. Put a piece of brick into a bowl of water.
2. Watch for tiny bubbles on the brick. These are air bubbles. This shows some air was inside the brick.
3. Put a coin into the water. You will probably see no bubbles. This shows the coin probably had no air inside.

MATERIALS

- Plastic bowl half-filled with water
- Orange peel
- Sand
- Coin
- Several kinds of stones
- Cracker
- Piece of brick
- Leather
- Soft wood
- Several kinds of fabrics

 Teaching Tips Some soft materials show dramatically that they contain air if squeezed under water. Soft pine, balsa wood, and leather are examples. Pliers or tongs may serve as squeezers, if needed. The spaces between sand or soil particles commonly contain much air. Surface air bubbles may easily be seen if water is poured into a small jar with sand inside. (Although water also usually contains air, the volume is small compared with that found in the spaces between sand particles.)

Concept Invention

1. Does a piece of cloth have air in it? Do some kinds of cloth have more air in them than others?
2. Does leather have air in it?
3. Can a soft piece of wood have air in it?
4. Does a cracker have air in it?
5. Does an orange peel have air in it?
6. Can a stone have air in it? Try several different kinds.
7. Does sand have air in it? How can you find out?

Concept Application

Air can be found almost everywhere. Most porous materials contain some air. What else do you think might have air in it? What else might not have air in it? Record your predictions and check for accuracy.

Soap Bubbles ———————

Invitation

Have you ever blown soap bubbles? If so, how big was your biggest bubble? How small was your smallest bubble? How can you blow soap bubbles? What is it like inside a bubble?

Exploration

1. Cut the straw end into four parts. Use the end that bends.
2. Push back the four parts as shown in the drawing.
3. Bend the straw into a J shape.
4. Dip the cut end into the bubble liquid.
5. Put the other straw end into your mouth and blow gently.
6. Place a mixture of dish soap (32–64 ounces), glycerin (10 tablespoons), and water in a child's plastic pool. Place a Hula-Hoop on the center of the bottom of the pool. Set a small wooden box or stool inside the Hula-Hoop (above the water line).
7. Place a student on the stool and then quickly pick the Hula-Hoop straight up from the bottom of the pool to above the student's head. A bubble will form and surround the student. Larger amounts of glycerin or dish soap or both will make longer lasting bubbles.

MATERIALS

- Paper cup of bubble liquid
- Soda can with ends removed
- Bendable plastic straw
- Paper cup half-full of water
- Small piece of cardboard
- Liquid detergent or soap
- Scissors
- Glycerin
- Thin wire (15 centimeters, or 6 inches, long)
- Spoon
- Child's plastic swimming pool
- Hula-Hoop
- Small wooden box or stool
- Water

Concept Invention

1. What different kinds of bubbles can you blow? How big a bubble can you make? How small a bubble can you make?
2. How many bubbles can you blow with one dip of your pipe? How few?

Use either a commercial bubble-blowing liquid or prepare your own from liquid detergent. Many teachers have gotten excellent results from Dawn® or Joy® liquid dish detergent. Both products contain a high glycerin content. A water mix of 1 part detergent to 16 parts water works well. Add some glycerin (sold at drugstores) for even bigger bubbles. Mix the solution thoroughly.

This investigation is done best outdoors. However, when students try to steer their bubbles in a certain direction by waving a piece of cardboard (Concept Invention step 5), a near-windless condition is needed. On a windy day, this activity can be done indoors in a more limited way. Children can discover that a bubble stays up best if the cardboard or hand is waved rapidly from side to side over the bubble. This movement decreases the air pressure over the bubble and so the surrounding air rushes in, holding up the bubble. Likewise, for lateral motion, a bubble will "follow" a waved cardboard.

3. What do you see when you look at a bubble? What do you see when you look through the large bubble around you?
4. What will happen if you catch a bubble in your hand? What will happen if your hand is soapy?
5. How can you make a bubble floating in air stay up? Move to your left or right? (*Hint:* How might a piece of cardboard help you?)
6. Bend pieces of wire into loops and other shapes. Dip them into the liquid and blow. What kinds of bubbles do they make?
7. Make extra-large bubbles. Take a soda can that has no top or bottom. Dip one end into bubble liquid. How big a bubble can you make?

Concept Application

A soap bubble is made up of air inside and soap outside. Big bubbles have more air inside than small ones. Moving air can make soap bubbles move. Test the relative effectiveness of several commercial preparations or your own bubble preparations. Which one makes the biggest bubbles? Which one makes bubbles that last the longest? Can you make a better bubble liquid? Mix a capful of liquid detergent or soap in a half-cup of water. How does it work? Will adding some glycerin make bigger bubbles? How much works best? Record your ideas and results.

Adapting for Students with Exceptionalities

Be sure students do not taste the soap mixture or inhale on the straws. To make larger bubbles, use a bent coat hanger or length of string. Some students may want to explore bubbles from the inside through the use of a small plastic swimming pool with bubble solution and a milk crate inside and a Hula-Hoop to make the bubbles (see *http://bubbles.org/*).

Parachutes

Invitation

How does a parachute help someone who jumps from an airplane? What makes a parachute fall slowly? You can learn more about real parachutes by making small ones. How can you make a small parachute?

Exploration

1. Cut a square the size of a handkerchief from thin plastic.
2. Cut a small hole in the center of the plastic.
3. Cut four strings the same length.
4. Tie one string end to each corner of the plastic.
5. Tie the other string ends together in a knot.
6. Shape a small ball of clay around the knot as illustrated.

MATERIALS

- Thin plastic (dry cleaners bag)
- Sticky tape
- Thin cotton cloth
- Scissors
- String
- Modeling clay

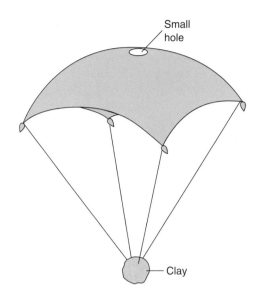

Small hole

Clay

Teaching **T**ips

Learning about parachutes allows children to manipulate several variables thoughtfully. In doing so, they learn to think of air as a tangible, material substance. The thin plastic clothes bags that dry cleaners use are excellent material for chutes. (Remind children that a plastic bag should never be placed over the head.)

Concept Invention

1. Try out your parachute on the playground. Drop it from the top of the play slide. Then roll it up loosely and throw it into the air. Does rolling make it work better?
2. Suppose you cover the hole with sticky tape. What difference might this make?
3. Suppose you make the hole larger. What difference might this make?
4. Suppose you add more clay to the ball. What difference might this make?
5. How can you make a parachute that will fall more slowly than the one you have now?
6. How can you get a small and a large parachute to fall equally fast?
7. What is the smallest parachute you can make that will work correctly?
8. What other materials can you use to make parachutes?

Concept Application

A parachute is built to catch the air as it falls. It can be changed to fall faster or slower. Can you construct a parachute with improved performance? Can you predict the effect of wind drift on your parachute? Describe your improved parachute and how it performed.

Air and Space

Invitation

How can you show that air takes up space?

Exploration

1. Fill the bowl three-fourths full with water.
2. Hold a glass with the open end down. Push it straight down into the water.
3. Put a second glass in the water sideways so that it fills with water.
4. Now tip the first glass. Try to "pour" the air up from the first glass into the second glass, as illustrated.

MATERIALS

- Deep, large clear bowl
- Water
- Two small clear glasses
- Paper towels

Concept Invention

1. What happens to the water in the higher glass?
2. What happens in the lower glass?
3. How can you get the air back into the first glass?

Concept Application

Suppose you put a crushed paper towel in the bottom of a glass. How could you put the open glass underwater without getting the towel wet? Explain your answer.

Balloon Buoyancy

MATERIALS

- Two matched balloons
- Meterstick or yardstick
- Scissors
- Sticky tape
- String
- Paper clip

Invitation

If you have two balanced balloons, will adding air to one balloon cause a change in the balance?

Exploration

1. Hang a meterstick evenly from a doorway or other place. Use a string and tape.
2. Attach a string loosely to each of the two deflated balloons.
3. Tape each string to an end of the stick. Be sure the stick is level after the balloons are hung. If not, place a partly open paper clip on the stick where needed to balance it.

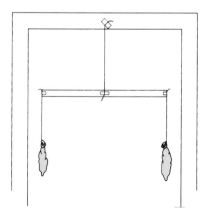

Concept Invention

1. What will happen if you blow up one balloon and rehang it?
2. What will happen if the balloon is later deflated and rehung?

Concept Application

In what ways can you make the stick level again? (The strings must stay at the ends of the stick.) Describe your experiment.

Air Needed for Burning

Invitation

What are some ways you can stop a candle from burning? How important is air for a candle to keep burning? How long do you think a candle will burn inside a closed jar?

Exploration

1. Stick some clay to the middle of a pie pan.
2. Stand a candle upright in the clay.
3. Put on safety goggles. Light the candle. Put the used match in the pan.
4. Pick up your next-to-smallest jar. Put it upside down over the candle as shown.
5. Look at a clock that has a second hand. How long does it take for the candle to go out? Record this time.
6. Remove the jar. Move a wad of several paper towels in and out of the jar a few times. This will clear out the bad air inside.

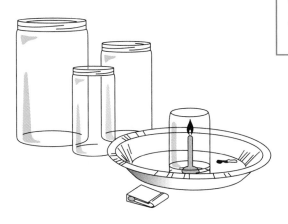

MATERIALS

- Small candles of different sizes
- Matches
- Safety goggles
- Modeling clay
- Four different-sized, wide-mouthed glass jars
- Clock or watch with second hand
- Metal pie pan
- Pencil and paper
- Paper towels
- Graph paper
- Measuring cup
- Pairs of matched jars of different shapes

Concept Invention

1. How long will the candle burn a second time? How long will the candle burn a third time? Be sure to remove the bad air after each trial. Record the trial times and the average time in a chart such as the following:

Jar Size	Time for Each			Average Time	Predicted Time
Smallest					
Next Smallest	30	34	32	32	
Next to Largest					
Largest					

Children should wear safety goggles when working with lighted candles. Also check that all children have long hair tied back and loose sleeves pushed up and out of the way. Note that some schools restrict the use of matches or an open flame to responsible adults.

A candle flame dies out in a closed container after it uses a certain percentage of the oxygen in the air. The flame burns longer in a large jar than in a small one because of the larger oxygen supply. Provide at least four different sizes of wide-mouthed glass jars with straight sides for the investigation. You might try half-pint, pint, quart, and half-gallon sizes, or 200-, 400-, 800-, and 1600-milliliter sizes. The exact capacities are not critical.

If you wish to stress the graphing activity, you might begin with it and continue through the sequence. If you think your students are not ready for it, omit this activity. If many points are plotted on this graph, the line drawn between them will resemble a curve rather than a straight line. Use this finding to demonstrate that using more data allows more accurate predictions.

2. How long do you think the candle will burn in the smallest jar? How long do you think the candle will burn in the next-to-largest jar? Write your predicted times on the chart. Use three trials for each jar. Record the trial times and the average times on your chart. Compare the average and predicted times.

3. How much larger than the other jars is your largest jar? Compare your jars and then study your chart. How long do you think the candle will burn in the largest jar?

4. You can make better predictions. Get different jars. Use a measuring cup to discover how much water each jar holds. Find out burning times for the smallest and largest jars. Then make a graph. Mark the average burning times of the smallest and largest jars. Draw a light line in between.

5. How closely can you predict the burning times for other jars? Find the jar size column on the bottom of the graph. Follow the column up until you reach the drawn line. Then, look straight across to the left at the burning time. How will recording more jar times make it easier to predict more accurately?

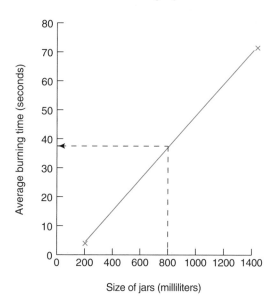

Candle burning experiments

6. What difference will it make in burning times if you change the candle? For example, does candle size make a difference? Does the flame's closeness to the jar top make a difference? Will two candles die out twice as fast as one?

Concept Application

A flame needs air to burn. The time that a flame burns depends, in part, on how much air it has. Does the shape of the jar make a difference in burning times?

Compare pairs of matched jars with different shapes and find out. How can you make a candle burn longer in a small jar than in a larger jar? Can you think of several ways?

AIR AND ITS PROPERTIES CONCEPTS

Air has many of the properties of water and may contain much water in gaseous form. However, air also has some unique properties. To better understand some of its specific features, let's first take an overall look at where our immediate air supply comes from: the atmosphere.

The Atmosphere

Space exploration has made us more aware of how dependent we are on our atmospheric environment. Without an air supply, humans cannot survive for more than minutes. Although we may travel in comfort thousands of kilometers across the earth's surface, an ascent of only 5 kilometers (3 miles) into the sky may require special oxygen apparatus.

How far out does the atmosphere extend? No one knows exactly, but meteorologists have identified four roughly separable layers of differing properties: troposphere, stratosphere, ionosphere, and exosphere (INQ Figure 11–1).

Troposphere

The *troposphere* extends to a height ranging from 8 kilometers (5 miles) at the poles to about 16 kilometers (10 miles) at the equator. This is the region where practically all weather takes place.

Why the difference in altitudes? Tropospheric air is coldest at the poles and so weighs more per unit than warmer, equatorial air. Also, the earth spins on its axis. The fastest speed of rotation, about 1600 kilometers (1000 miles) per hour, is at the equator. This offsets the earth's gravitational pull to some extent. The speed of rotation decreases as distance to the poles decreases, just as a person who runs on an inside track can slowly jog along, while someone on an outside track must run swiftly just to keep abreast. As the rotational speed slows, gravity has an increasing effect. In the troposphere, stable air temperature steadily decreases with altitude.

INQ Figure 11–1 **The atmosphere has several layers.**

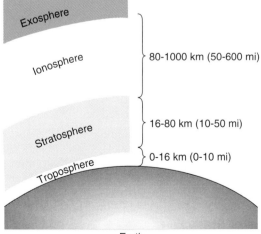

Exosphere

Ionosphere   80-1000 km (50-600 mi)

Stratosphere   16-80 km (10-50 mi)

Troposphere   0-16 km (0-10 mi)

Earth

Stratosphere

Just above the troposphere is the *stratosphere*, which reaches to about 80 kilometers (50 miles). This is the layer airlines use on some routes for long-range cruising. The cold, thin air is remarkably clear and turbulence free because vertical movements of warmed air and atmospheric dust particles are largely confined to the layer below. Air travelers may note some pale clouds of ice crystals above cruising altitude, but these are infrequent.

Between the lower reaches of the stratosphere and the troposphere are found winds that vary greatly in force and direction. Most interesting are the *jet streams*, rivers of high-velocity air several kilometers high and more than 150 kilometers wide. They range to thousands of kilometers in length and tend to flow from west to east. A pilot may increase the speed of a plane several hundred kilometers per hour by locating and staying within a jet stream.

In the stratosphere, at an altitude of 16 to 48 kilometers (10 to 30 miles), is a layer of ozone that absorbs much of the sun's harmful ultraviolet radiation. The layer is largely composed of molecules that have three atoms of oxygen, rather than the usual two. Certain chemicals released into the atmosphere, called *chlorofluorocarbons (CFCs)*, collect unevenly in the ozone layer and destroy the ozone molecules. This destruction greatly reduces the layer's capacity to block ultraviolet rays, and so more get through to the earth's surface at various places.

Excess ultraviolet radiation increases the risk of skin cancer, eye damage, and immune system impairment. It can also reduce crop yields and disrupt ocean food chains. International agreements in force require the phasing out of CFCs that were once widely used in refrigerants, air conditioners, industrial cleaning solvents, and the manufacture of some plastics. Less harmful but more expensive chemicals have generally replaced CFCs.

Ionosphere

Beyond a height of about 80 kilometers (50 miles), the stratosphere gradually blends into the *ionosphere*. In this region are *ions*, or electrically charged particles formed when high-energy solar and cosmic rays hit air molecules. These harmful rays are largely absorbed at and below this level. Auroras are sometimes visible. Meteors burn to ashes from friction as they strike scattered air molecules.

The ionosphere is an invaluable aid to radio communication on the earth. The earth's surface is curved, but radio waves travel in straight lines. How can straight radio waves be made to travel from city to city on the curved earth? One way of overcoming this problem has been to transmit radio waves to the ionosphere, where they are reflected downward to other points on the earth. Because solar "storms" frequently disturb the ionosphere and disrupt communication, this reflection has not proved to be a completely satisfactory solution. Radio and television signals reflected from communications satellites are turning out to be a better solution to this problem.

Exosphere

The *exosphere* begins at about 1000 kilometers (600 miles) up and extends to an undetermined distance. A few air molecules have been detected beyond where the ionosphere adjoins the exosphere, and it is probable that others are scattered thousands of kilometers beyond. For practical purposes, this region may be considered the beginning of interplanetary space.

Although scientists estimate the entire weight of our atmosphere at an enormous 4.5 quadrillion metric tons, more than half of all air molecules are concentrated below a height of 5.6 kilometers (3.5 miles). The combination of this enormous pressure and the unimaginably small size of air molecules results in the presence of air in practically everything on or near the earth's surface. Air is found in most soils, water, and even in some rocks. Consider now more effects of this pressure.

Air Pressure

Because the average weight of air is about 1 kilogram per square centimeter (14.7 pounds per square inch) at sea level, tons of air press against us right now. Why, then, are we not crushed? There are two basic reasons. Like water pressure, air at a given level presses with equal force in all directions. Because every force has a counteractive force, the pressure is neutralized. Counteractive pressure also takes place in our bodies. Air molecules are so tiny that they dissolve in our bloodstreams, besides occupying space in our lungs and other body cavities.

Unlike free air, the air in our bodies lags somewhat in building up or reducing counteractive back pressure as atmospheric pressure changes. Have you noticed that your ears "pop" while rising quickly in an elevator of a tall building? This happens because air pressure in the inner ear tends to remain the same while the outside air pressure decreases with increased altitude. The result is an uncomfortable outward pushing sensation behind the eardrums. A slow elevator gives more opportunity for inner ear pressure to be adjusted through the eustachian tube, which connects the inner ear to the nasal passages and mouth.

A similar but much more dangerous situation is faced by deep-sea divers. As they descend into the water, air is pumped under increasing pressure into the diving helmet and suit to counteract increasing water pressure. After working for 20 to 30 minutes, a diver's circulatory system contains an abnormal amount of air. If the diver ascends rapidly to the surface, a region of much lower air pressure, air in the blood may expand and form bubbles. The presence of bubbles in the blood causes a very painful and possibly fatal condition known as "the bends."

The lag in adjusting to outside atmospheric pressure may also help explain why some persons complain of aches and pains just before rainy weather. Outside air pressure usually lessens before a storm. If the body's blood pressure remains the same, the blood will now press outward a little more forcibly than usual against body joints and tissues. It is possible that the slight extra pressure may cause discomfort.

Makeup of Air

So many references are made to the earth's "ocean of air" that it is easy for us to get the impression that pure air is a uniform compound, such as pure water. Actually, the air we breathe is a mixture of several separate and distinct gases; the three most important to survival are oxygen, nitrogen, and carbon dioxide.

Oxygen makes up about 21% of the air, and nitrogen 78%. Oxygen is essential to us because it combines readily with sugars in our body cells and releases heat energy. Oxygen is also essential to burning.

Nitrogen is essential to survival because it is necessary for plant growth. It also dilutes the oxygen we breathe. Continual breathing of pure oxygen speeds up metabolic processes to the point where the body cannot get rid of waste products fast enough to survive. The small amount of carbon dioxide in the air, about 3/100 of 1%, is needed for photosynthesis in green plants. Besides these gases, the air contains less than 1% of such gases as argon, krypton, helium, neon, radon, and xenon. All these atmospheric gases are remarkably well mixed by winds up to a height of 8 to 10 kilometers (5 to 6 miles).

But this is not all we breathe. As hay fever sufferers know, other substances are mixed in the air. Besides the troublesome pollens are dust, smoke, salt particles, water vapor, chemicals, spores, bacteria, and viruses.

The Reality of Air

Because pure air has no taste, color, or odor, its study for children, especially primary students, has an elusive quality not present in many other areas. So, it is usually good to begin with activities that bring out the tangibility of air. Like other material objects such as automobiles, houses, books, and people, air is a real thing. Children can feel it and see it move things in the form of wind. A blown-up balloon or a soap bubble shows that air takes up space. A slowly falling parachute demonstrates that air resists motion. A can that is crushed when some inside air is removed shows that air has weight. Sipping liquid through a straw shows this, too. Because many children are confused about how a straw works, consider it for a moment.

When we sip some air out of a straw, the air pressure in the straw is reduced. Because the atmosphere now has more relative pressure, it presses down on the liquid's surface and pushes it up inside the straw's space once occupied by the air.

If you are skeptical, try the following experiments. Place two straws in your mouth, but leave one outside a full soda bottle or water glass. You will find it now practically impossible to drink the liquid. Why? Air traveling inward through the outside straw restores the pressure in your mouth and drinking straw to normal. The pressure of the surrounding air is no longer greater than that in the straw and so cannot push down on the liquid and force it up into the straw; air in the straw is pushing back equally hard. For the second experiment, fill a flask with water and seal it tightly with a one-hole stopper containing a glass tube. No matter how hard you sip, no water goes up the tube. No air is pressing down on the water. With a two-hole stopper, though, normal drinking is possible. Air pressure is exerted through the second hole.

As with drinking straws, the events we associate with "suction" are really a result of removing or reducing air pressure from one part of a device. Air pressure on all other parts then pushes and performs the work. In vacuum cleaners, for example, the motor whirls a reversed fan that reduces air pressure at the cleaning nozzle. The surrounding air then pushes dirt particles into the nozzle. A suction cup works in a similar way. By pressing down on the pliable rubber cup, you force out most of the air that is inside. Air from all other sides pushes against the cup's exterior and holds it fast to whatever surface it has been pressed.

Origins of Our Atmosphere

Most scientists agree that the earth formed about 5 billion years ago. By about 4.4 billion years ago, the earth had an atmosphere that could hold a thin layer of gas known as the earth's primeval atmosphere. Outgassing, or the release of embedded gases from rocks through volcanic activity, allowed gases such as carbon dioxide, nitrogen, water vapor, and smaller amounts of ammonia, methane, and sulfur dioxide to accumulate in the atmosphere.

As the earth cooled for the next half billion years, the water vapor condensed into clouds. These clouds soon provided the first rains, streams, rivers, and seas, thus beginning the water cycle here on earth. The accumulation of water caused a reduction of carbon dioxide in the atmosphere as it dissolved into newly created ocean waters.

Almost 2 billion years ago, oxygen, produced through photosynthetic action in the oceans, began to significantly accumulate in the atmosphere, reaching its current level of almost 1% by volume. Carbon dioxide was reduced to less than 1% as we currently find in the layers of air that we call the troposphere and stratosphere—from the earth's surface to 80 kilometers (50 miles) above the earth.

WEATHER **Inquiry**

Heating Soil and Water

Invitation

How fast does soil heat and cool, compared to water?

Exploration

1. Fill one jar with soil and the other with water.
2. Leave the jars in a shady place for 1 hour.
3. Touch the soil and water surfaces to see if both are about the same temperature. If not, wait a while. If they are, then put both jars in the sun for 1 hour.
4. Touch both surfaces again.

Concept Invention

1. Which feels warmer, the soil or water surface?
2. Which will cool faster if you put both back in the shade?

Concept Application

How does this activity help you understand the unequal heating of the earth's surface as the cause of winds?

MATERIALS

- Two matched glass jars
- Sunny and shady areas
- Soil
- Water

Evaporation

Invitation

Many persons hang their wet laundry on a clothesline. After a while, the laundry is dry. What do you think happens to the water? When water disappears into the air, we say it evaporated. You can find out more about evaporation by drying wet paper towels. How can you get a paper towel to dry? How long will it take?

Exploration

1. Put a paper towel underwater to soak it.
2. Bunch the wet towel in your fist. Squeeze out all the water you can.
3. Open the towel and lay it on a pie plate, as illustrated.

MATERIALS

- Plastic bowl of water
- Piece of cardboard
- Paper towels
- Two aluminum pie plates
- Sunny and shady areas
- Paper clips

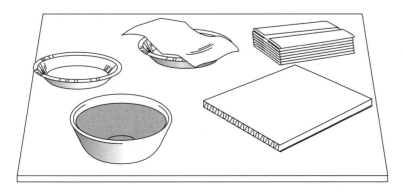

This inquiry gives children several chances to manipulate conditions that affect the evaporation rate of water. The Concept Invention activities encourage them to manipulate these conditions creatively. Step 3 calls for fanning one wet towel with cardboard to simulate a windy condition. Clipping the towel to the pie plate with several paper clips will keep it from blowing off the plate.

4. Leave the plate on your desk. Check the time.
5. Every so often, feel the towel to see if it is dry. Check the time again when it is all dry.

Concept Invention

1. Suppose you put one wet towel where it is shady and cool, and another where it is sunny and warmer. Which wet towel do you think will dry first?
2. What can you do to show that a dried-out towel is completely "dry"? How many of your classmates agree with you?
3. Suppose, to make it windy, you fan one wet towel with cardboard. You do not fan a second wet towel. Which towel do you think will dry first?
4. Suppose you spread out one wet towel and leave another bunched like a ball. Which towel do you think will dry first?
5. Suppose you leave one wet towel on top of a plate. You leave a second wet towel under another plate. Which towel do you think will dry first?
6. Play a game with a friend. Who can dry a wet paper towel faster? How can you make the game fair?
7. What is the longest you can keep a wet paper towel from drying?

Concept Application

Wind, heat, and an uncovered and spread-out condition all help a wet paper towel dry faster. Could you find a way to predict the drying times in each of the activities? Could you calculate the drying rate of a wet towel or sponge by using a beam balance? Will half of a wet towel have half the evaporation rate of a whole towel? Try to answer these questions by designing appropriate experiments.

Relative Humidity ——————

Invitation

Can you remember times when the air has felt very dry or very humid? The amount of moisture, or water vapor, in the air often changes. Warm air can hold more moisture without raining than cold air. The percent of moisture now in the air compared with the percent it can hold at the current temperature is the *relative humidity*. You can make an instrument to measure the relative humidity. It is called a *hygrometer*. How can you make a hygrometer?

Exploration

1. Fasten two thermometers to the sides of an empty milk carton. Use rubber bands to hold them in place.
2. Use a pencil to punch a hole in the carton under one thermometer.
3. Put about 2.5 centimeters (1 inch) of water into the carton. Close the top with a paper clip. This will keep the water from evaporating quickly.
4. Wet a strip of cotton cloth with water.
5. Stick one end of the strip through the punched hole into the water inside. Fasten the other end to the bulb of the thermometer above, as shown.

MATERIALS

- Two matched Fahrenheit thermometers
- Cardboard
- Narrow cotton cloth strip or thick cotton shoelace
- Two rubber bands
- Empty quart milk carton with top still on
- Paper clip
- Pencil
- Water
- Ruler
- Clock
- Shady area

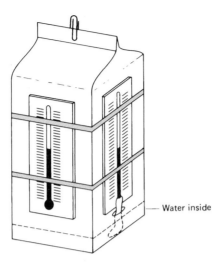

— Water inside

6. To use your hygrometer, fan the thermometers with a piece of cardboard for 3 minutes in a shady place. Read the temperatures of each thermometer.
7. Use the relative humidity table to find the percent of moisture in the air. At the left, mark the wet bulb temperature lightly with pencil. At the top, lightly mark the dry bulb temperature. Move one finger across the row and another down the column from the marked spots. Notice the percent of relative humidity where your two fingers meet.

Teaching Tips

When no difference appears between the wet and dry bulb temperatures, the relative humidity is 100%. This condition is unlikely to be recorded outdoors unless there is dense fog or rain. Children may notice a marked difference between indoor and outdoor readings. This is most likely in winter. As the room is heated, the air in it is able to hold more moisture, so the relative humidity goes down.

Dry bulb temperature (°F)

Wet bulb temperature (°F)	56	58	60	62	64	66	68	70	71	72	73	74	75	76	77	78	79	80	82	84
38	7	2																		
40	15	11	7																	
42	25	19	14	9	7															
44	34	29	22	17	13	8	4													
46	45	38	30	24	18	14	10	6	4	3	1									
48	55	47	40	33	26	21	16	12	10	9	7	5	4	3	1					
50	66	56	48	41	34	29	23	19	17	15	13	11	9	8	6	5	4	3		
52	77	67	57	50	43	36	31	25	23	21	19	17	15	13	12	10	9	7	5	3
54	88	78	68	59	51	44	38	33	30	28	25	23	21	19	17	16	14	12	10	7
56		89	79	68	60	53	46	40	37	34	32	29	27	25	23	21	19	18	14	12
58			89	79	70	61	54	48	45	42	39	36	34	31	29	27	25	23	20	16
60				90	79	71	62	55	52	49	46	43	40	38	35	33	31	29	25	21
62					90	80	71	64	60	57	53	50	47	44	42	39	37	35	30	26
64						90	80	72	68	65	61	58	54	51	48	46	43	41	36	32
66							90	81	77	73	69	65	62	59	56	53	50	47	42	37
68								90	86	82	78	74	70	66	63	60	57	54	48	43
70									95	91	86	82	78	74	71	67	64	61	55	49
72											95	91	86	82	79	75	71	68	61	56
74													96	91	87	83	79	75	69	62
76															96	91	87	83	76	69
78																	96	91	84	76
80																			92	84
82																				92

Percent of relative humidity

Concept Invention

1. What is the relative humidity now?
2. How, if at all, might relative humidity change from day to day? How, if at all, does it change?
3. How well can you use your senses to tell if the air is drier or moister from day to day? Use your hygrometer to check how well you do.
4. How does the relative humidity outdoors compare with that indoors?
5. What would you expect the relative humidity to be outdoors on a rainy day? Measure it in some partly sheltered place and see.

Scaffolding for English Learners

Having a teacher-learner alongside of English learners will assist in student development of a difficult concept such as relative humidity. Following this procedure helps maintain the balance between teacher direction and student initiative during the activity. (See Fradd, Lee, Sutman, & Saxton, 2001, for a discussion of teachers and students learning together and the effect of this approach on English language learners.)

Concept Application

A hygrometer can be used to measure the relative humidity. This is the percent of moisture that air holds, compared with the percent it can hold at a given temperature. How do your relative humidity measurements compare with those of the local weather bureau? Develop a chart and compare readings for a 2-week period.

Water Vapor ————

MATERIALS

- Clean, shiny can
- Water
- Thermometer
- Ice cubes

Invitation

How can you collect and see water vapor in the air?

Exploration

1. Half-fill the can with water. Add five or six ice cubes.
2. Put a thermometer inside the can of ice and water.
3. Watch for tiny drops on the can's sides. When they first appear, record the water temperature. (This is called the *dew point*. It tells the temperature at which water vapor changes from a gas to a liquid and forms drops, or *condenses*, on objects.)

Concept Invention

1. At what temperature was the dew point?
2. Will the dew-point temperature be different in a smaller or larger container?
3. Can an ice-water mixture get colder than the dew point?

Concept Application

How, if at all, will the dew-point temperature change from day to day? Explain your answer.

Air Pressure Changes

Invitation

How can you measure changes in air pressure?

Exploration

1. Make a barometer. Cut out a large part of a balloon. Stretch it tightly over the jar opening. Use a rubber band to hold it fast.
2. Pinch one straw end flat. Cut a point with scissors at this end.
3. Glue the straw's other end to the center of the stretched balloon.
4. Use two thumbtacks to fasten a file card to a wall. Place the barometer by it. Have the straw pointer centered on the card and almost touching.
5. Make a mark on the card where the straw points each day for 1 week.

MATERIALS

- Glass jar
- Balloon
- Rubber band
- Scissors
- Straw
- File card
- Glue
- Two thumbtacks

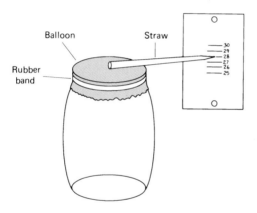

Concept Invention

1. On what day was the air pressure the highest? On what day was the air pressure the lowest?
2. When, if at all, was there no change in air pressure?

Adapting for Students with Exceptionalities

Comprehending air pressure and other weather concepts will be especially difficult for students with exceptionalities. Expand on students' prior knowledge to assist with concept development. (See Mastropieri & Scruggs, 2004, chapter on science and social studies for a discussion on activities related to weather.)

Concept Application

Do you notice any weather changes associated with your barometric pressure readings? Chart the current weather and readings for a 1-month period. Note any associations between the pressure and weather.

Teaching Tips

As air pressure outside the jar increases, it pushes down harder on the balloon diaphragm; this makes the straw pointer go up. As air pressure outside the jar decreases, the higher air pressure inside the jar pushes up on the diaphragm; this makes the straw pointer go down. The movement can be increased a bit by gluing a piece of matchstick under the straw at the jar rim. You might challenge students to calibrate their barometers. They can note the daily barometric pressure in the newspaper or call the weather bureau. After a week or so of recording the official pressure next to their own recordings, they may be able to predict roughly the official pressure from their own barometers. Place this kind of barometer where it will have the least change of temperature. Otherwise, the air in the jar may expand and contract so much that the effects of changing air pressure will be obscured.

WEATHER CONCEPTS

Weather is the condition of the lower atmosphere at a given time and place. If you have been rained on while expecting a sunny afternoon, you know how quickly weather can change. Weather changes happen because changes in temperature, moisture, pressure, and other variables alter the way air "behaves." We examine some of these variables in this section.

Causes of Winds

At early morning off an African coast, hundreds of fishing boats point out to sea as a fresh land breeze fills their colorful lateen sails. The boats return in the afternoon with sails taut from a sea breeze blowing in the opposite direction. You have probably experienced a similar shift of winds at the seashore or by a large lake. How does this happen? (See INQ Figure 11–2.)

Temperature Differences

You may recall from Inquiry Unit 2 on heat energy that warmed air expands and is pushed up by denser, colder air that rushes in and replaces it. The unequal heating and cooling of the earth's surface cause winds. During the day, solar radiation is absorbed by the sea and the land. The land heats up much faster. One reason is that sunlight penetrates only a short distance below the land's surface, but penetrates more deeply into water. Another reason is that water has a higher heat capacity.

After a short period of sunlight, air immediately above the earth is heated by the ground and begins expanding. Cooler, heavier air from the sea rushes in and pushes the lighter air upward. The reverse occurs at night and until the following morning. During this period, the land cools quickly and stays cool while the sea remains relatively warmer. As air warmed by contact with the water expands, it is pushed upward by cooler air rushing in from the cooler land.

INQ Figure 11–2   **Winds are caused by the unequal heating and cooling of the earth's surface.**

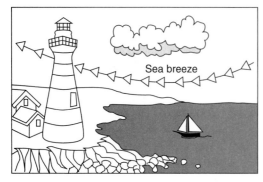

Day

Night

These air movements are not confined to land and sea settings. The same basic air movements take place between any surfaces that have a temperature difference. As temperature differences increase, the resulting wind force increases. This is one reason why a large fire is so destructive; it creates a powerful, localized wind that fans and spreads the flames.

Prevailing Winds

The world's prevailing winds are caused by the same unequal heating of the earth's surface on a grand scale. But the earth's rotation adds a factor. If the earth did not rotate, heavy, cold air at the poles would simply flow due south and north, and push up warmed, expanding equatorial air. The rotation results in a wind deflection (named the *Coriolis effect*) to the right in the Northern Hemisphere and to the left in the Southern Hemisphere. With a globe and some chalk, you can see why this happens. Rotate the globe from west to east. While it is moving, draw a line from the North Pole due south toward the equator. Notice that the line curves to the right. Draw a line from the South Pole, and the curve is reversed.

Winds Aloft

Detailed understanding of wind patterns requires much more background than can be given here. For example, we have briefly discussed jet streams. Other winds, however, are also aloft. It is possible for an airplane pilot to meet a wind blowing from one direction at one altitude and another blowing from another direction higher up. You will not want to explore this subject in detail at the elementary level. Still, it will be worthwhile to help children learn that wind direction aloft may differ from surface wind direction.

To calculate winds aloft, meteorologists use measuring instruments to observe small, helium-filled balloons as they rise to various altitudes. A cruder method is to observe cloud movements with a *nephoscope*, a circular mirror marked with the points of a compass. Properly aligned, this instrument can show children the direction of cloud movement as the cloud reflection moves across the mirror.

Air Temperature

In parts of southern California and in Mexico, it is sometimes possible in winter to observe snowy mountain peaks while lying on a warm, sunny beach. Children are curious about conditions like this (e.g., "Aren't the mountain peaks closer to the sun?"). Most adults know that air is colder at higher altitudes. But why does this occur?

Temperature and Altitude

One reason why air is colder at higher altitudes is the varying distance of air molecules from the earth's surface. Air molecules closest to the earth are warmed more easily by conduction and heat waves radiated from the earth's surface than those farther away.

Second, as we get closer to sea level, more and more molecules are piled up. This increased weight compresses the air. With reduced space for movement, more energy is exchanged among molecules as they collide. So, the heat energy in the denser molecule "population" is concentrated into a relatively low, dense layer.

Third, as warmed air is pushed up, it expands and cools when it meets lower air pressure with the increased altitude. Whatever heat energy is contained in the original air parcel is dissipated throughout an ever-larger volume.

The combined effect of these causes makes pushed-up air cool about 2°C for each 300 meters (3.5°F for each 1000 feet). As pushed-down air is compressed, the opposite happens.

Temperature and Pollution

The atmosphere is a gigantic greenhouse that slows the loss of heat received from solar radiation. Fortunately, the earth loses and gains about the same amount of heat each day. A narrow temperature range enables life as we know it to continue. Since the Industrial Revolution, though, conditions have been developing that may upset this delicate balance.

Most scientists think the lower atmosphere is gradually becoming slightly warmer because of increased levels of carbon dioxide from the burning of fuels such as coal and oil. As light waves from the sun warm the earth's surface, heat waves going from the surface into the atmosphere are partly blocked by carbon dioxide. Some of the heat energy cannot escape into space. This causes the atmosphere to lose slightly less heat than it gains from solar radiation. Recent data seem to support a global warming trend.

Yet, a few scientists say it is also possible that the trend may be reversing. To them, data suggest that the earth's atmosphere is cooling very gradually. In recent years, there has been a large increase in air pollution throughout the world. The greater number of suspended pollutants in the air may be causing more and more sunlight to be reflected away from the earth before it reaches the earth's surface. If true, this could overcome the effect of the increased carbon dioxide.

Although not everyone agrees about what is happening to the air temperature, a definite trend in either direction could bring trouble. An average increase of a few degrees could turn huge, fertile land areas into semideserts, and an average temperature drop of 4° to 5°C could launch another Ice Age.

Evaporation and Humidity ————

Many children understand in a limited way the concepts of evaporation and humidity but may not understand how the two are related. This section can help deal with these concepts.

Evaporation

In an earlier inquiry, you saw that heat and atmospheric pressure affect an evaporating liquid. Increased heat energy increases the speed of molecules. Additional speed enables molecules to overcome the cohesive forces of nearby molecules, and greater numbers leave the liquid's surface than before. Any decrease of atmospheric pressure also affects evaporation because it tends to "take the lid off." The counterforce of air molecules pressing down on the surface of an evaporating liquid becomes weaker, and more evaporation takes place. This is a reason why mountain climbers must be so careful with dehydration.

It is easy to see why increasing a liquid's surface area increases the rate of evaporation. There is greater exposure to the air above and a higher probability of more molecules escaping. This is why you have to add water more often to an open rectangular aquarium than to an open fish bowl of equal volume.

The wind, too, speeds up evaporation. When air just above the surface of an evaporating fluid becomes saturated, the wind blows it away and replaces it with drier air.

Humidity

Another factor influencing evaporation is *humidity*, which is the amount of moisture already present in the air. On humid days, we feel sticky and uncomfortable because our perspiration evaporates very slowly. We may use a fan to feel more comfortable. Moving air from a fan cools us because it speeds up evaporation of perspiration from the skin.

Without an evaporating liquid, a fan has no cooling effect at all. You can see this by putting a thermometer in front of a whirling electric fan. There is no difference in the before and after readings. But dampen some cotton and stick it to the thermometer bulb, and the rapidly evaporating water will cause a noticeable drop in temperature.

The moisture content of air changes considerably from time to time. The capacity of air to hold moisture depends on its temperature, so warm air holds more moisture than cooler air. The percentage of moisture in air at a certain temperature, compared with all it could hold at that temperature, is called its *relative humidity*. During a period of low relative humidity, our skin moisture evaporates more quickly than it can be effectively replaced. This results in dry, chapped skin.

One reason why we have more colds in winter may be directly related to the relative humidity of the air in our homes. The cool air of winter holds comparatively little moisture. As heaters warm it, the air expands and becomes even drier. Unless the home heating system is equipped to give additional moisture, the air becomes increasingly dry. The protective mucous film that coats the delicate nasal membrane evaporates, and we become more open to infections that begin in the nasal cavities.

Relative humidity is often measured with a wet-and-dry bulb thermometer apparatus called a *hygrometer*. Two identical thermometers are placed next to each other. The bulb of one instrument is enclosed in a wet cotton wick that is immersed in water. The wet-bulb thermometer is fanned rapidly until its reading steadies at some lower point. As water evaporates from the wick, it is continually replaced by water traveling upward through the wick by capillary action. Any difference in thermometer readings can be translated into the percentage of relative humidity by consulting a reference table.

Condensation

Dew

Many mornings, we see dewdrops glistening on lawns, parked automobiles, spider webs, and other surfaces. When the ground cools during the night, its temperature may fall below that of the surrounding air. As the surrounding air loses heat energy, the air's molecules slow down. Water molecules in the air slow enough to be attracted to, and condense on, cool nearby surfaces. The same thing happens when water droplets form on a cold soda bottle or cold water pipe.

Remember, relative humidity varies with air temperature. Any parcel of air containing some water vapor becomes saturated if cooled enough. The loss of heat energy slows molecular speed and reduces the range of molecular movement. The attractions of water molecules for one another now draw them together into visible drops.

Dew Point

The temperature at which condensation takes place is called the *dew point*. In very humid air, as in a steamy shower room, water vapor condenses on walls and mirrors although they may be only several degrees cooler than the air. Comparatively dry desert air may have to be cooled much more before reaching its dew point.

Fog

We may see fog when the surface temperature is low enough to cool air that is a short distance above the ground to its dew point. In this case, water vapor condenses on tiny specks of airborne dust and this water remains suspended.

Sometimes fog results from the unequal cooling of land and water. Such fog is common over a lake in summer. Cool air from the land flows over warm, moist air just above the lake. As the warmer air cools to its dew point, condensation occurs and we see fog. Fog can be considered a low cloud.

Clouds and Cloud Types

Clouds at higher altitudes are formed in several ways, but all involve a parcel of air that is cooled to its saturation, or dew, point. In one method, wind may blow moist air up a mountain slope. As the air rises, it expands because of decreasing air pressure, cools, and condenses on airborne dust particles. If the dew point is below freezing, tiny ice crystals may form.

Sometimes air is pushed aloft when two huge air masses merge. The cooler, heavier air mass will push under the warmer, lighter mass. Again, expansion, cooling, and condensation take place.

A third method of cloud formation happens when heat from the ground develops convection currents. The affected air near the ground is heated and is pushed up by heavier, cooler surrounding air. The rising air finally cools and its moisture condenses.

When enough moisture is present, the tiny, constantly moving droplets within a cloud collide from time to time and combine to form larger drops. These large drops may fall as rain. In freezing temperatures, ice crystals collect and fall as snow.

Knowing the air temperature and its dew point can enable you or upper-grade students to roughly calculate cloud heights in the following manner. Suppose the outdoor air temperature is now 88°F. Stir a thermometer around in a metal can of ice and water. At the exact instant water droplets occur on the can, read the temperature of the immersed thermometer. This is the dew point. Say it reads 74°F, which makes a difference of 14°F between the two figures. Rising air cools at about 3.5°F for each 1000 feet of altitude. Fourteen (14) divided by 3.5 results in a quotient of 4. Multiply this figure by 1000. The bases of nearby clouds should be about 4000 feet above you. (With metric measures, use 2°C for 3.5°F and 300 meters for 1000 feet.)

Although experts have invented more than 200 cloud classifications, young children can be taught to recognize three basic cloud forms. *Cirrus clouds* are high, wispy formations of ice crystals. *Cumulus clouds* are white, fluffy, and usually associated with clear visibility and fair weather. *Stratus clouds* are lower, darker formations that appear as a dense layer. These clouds may blanket the entire sky and precipitate rain within a short time (see INQ Figure 11–3).

Water Cycle

You can see that condensation is the opposite of evaporation. Together, they form the water cycle. Powered by the sun, an immense but finite volume of water over the earth constantly evaporates, condenses, and falls without apparent end.

Air Masses and Cyclones ———————

At one time, it was thought that air pressure over any one certain point was always the same. We now know otherwise. Huge masses of air continually move over the earth, bringing changes in pressure and weather.

Air Masses

An *air mass* is a huge volume of air that picks up distinctive temperature and humidity conditions from the surface underneath. These conditions are fairly uniform throughout the mass, which may cover thousands of square kilometers.

INQ Figure 11–3   Three basic cloud forms: (A) cirrus, (B) cumulus, and (C) stratus.

A

B

C

An ocean air mass is typically moist. Air over land is drier. Air near the polar regions is cold, whereas that near the equator is warm. So, four kinds of air masses are possible: cold and dry, cold and moist, warm and dry, and warm and moist. INQ Figure 11–4 shows the origins of four kinds of air masses that often move into the continental United States.

Cold air is heavier than the same volume of warm air. Dry air is heavier than the same volume of moist air. Just as water flows from a high point to a lower one, air flows from a region of relatively high pressure to one of lower pressure. But because of the earth's rotation, the flow is not in a straight line.

Cyclones and Anticyclones

The Coriolis effect causes air masses and the general circulation of air to move in gigantic spirals called cyclones and anticyclones. (Cyclones should not be confused with *tornadoes*, which are small, violent, twisting air currents that come from a mixture of superheated and cold air.) A *cyclone* is a large area of relative lower pressure with the point of lowest pressure in the center; it is also called a low. An *anticyclone* is a large area of relatively high pressure with the highest pressure in the center; it is also called a high.

In the Northern Hemisphere, air movements spiral counterclockwise toward the center of a low. In a high, they spiral clockwise, away from the center of highest pressure. These movements are reversed in the Southern Hemisphere. Highs and lows may move hundreds of kilometers a day. A typical pattern of movement in the United States is from west to east. Lows often bring bad weather. This is so because cold or dry heavier air moves in and

INQ Figure 11–4   **Four common kinds of air masses.**

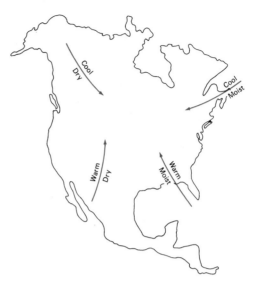

pushes up warm or moist lighter air. The moisture condenses when the air rises to its dew-point altitude and falls as rain or snow.

Highs usually bring more pleasant weather. As cool or dry heavier air spirals downward from the center of a high, it warms about 2°C for each 300 meters (3.5°F for each 1000 feet) loss of altitude. As it warms, the mass of air is able to hold more and more moisture without it condensing. The result is usually clear, sunny weather.

Measuring Pressure

Highs and lows are detected by noting changes in cloud, temperature, and wind patterns. The most important changes observed, however, are those in air pressure. An instrument used for measuring air pressure is the *barometer*. There are two kinds.

In a *mercurial barometer*, a glass tube about 90 centimeters (36 inches) long and closed at one end is filled with mercury and inverted into a dish of mercury. While some of the liquid runs out, a column of about 76 centimeters (30 inches) remains. This height tells the force of air pressing on the liquid's surface. As air pressure increases, the column rises higher into the vacuum above. The reverse takes place with reduced pressure. Because mercurial barometers are easily broken and cumbersome, most weather observers use an *aneroid barometer* (INQ Figure 11–5). It consists of a thin, flexible, metal box from which almost all air has been removed. As air presses on it with varying degrees of force, the box moves in and out accordingly. A cleverly linked leverage system transfers these movements to a movable needle on a dial.

Because air pressure also changes with altitude, aneroid barometers are used in many airplanes to indicate altitude. This is done by merely changing the dial to read in a unit of height rather than one of pressure. Such a barometer is called an *altimeter*.

INQ Figure 11–5   **Aneroid barometer.**

References

American Association for the Advancement of Science (AAAS). (1993). *Benchmarks for science literacy*. New York: Oxford University Press.

Baca, L. M., Baca, E., & deValenzuela, J. S. (2004). Background and rationale for bilingual special education. In L. M. Baca & H. T. Cervantes (Eds.), *The bilingual special education interface* (pp. 1–23). Upper Saddle River, NJ: Merrill/Prentice Hall.

Fradd, S. H., Lee, O., Sutman, F. X., & Saxton, M. K. (2001). Promoting science literacy with English language learners through instructional materials development: A case study. *Bilingual Research Journal, 25*(4), 417–434. Retrieved November 13, 2004, from *http://brj.asu.edu/content/vol25_no4/pdf/ar5.pdf*

Mastropieri, M., & Scruggs, T. E. (2004). *The inclusive classroom: Strategies for effective instruction* (4th ed.). Upper Saddle River, NJ: Merrill/Prentice Hall.

National Research Council (NRC). (1996). *National science education standards*. Washington, DC: National Academy Press.

Selected Trade Books: Water, Air, and Weather

For Younger Children

Aardema, V. (1981). *Bringing the rain to Kapiti Plain*. New York: Puffin Books.

Ardley, N. (1983). *Working with water*. Danbury, CT: Watts.

Bang, M. (1997). *Common ground: The water, earth, and air we share*. New York: Scholastic.

Barrett, J. (1982). *Cloudy with a chance of meatballs*. New York: Aladdin Paperbacks.

Berger, M., & Berger, G. (1993). *How's the weather? A look at weather and how it changes*. Nashville, TN: Ideals Children's Books.

Branley, F. (1986). *Sunshine makes the seasons*. New York: HarperTrophy.

Branley, F. (1987). *Air is all around you*. New York: HarperTrophy.

Branley, F. (1999). *Flash, crash, rumble, and roll*. New York: HarperCollins.

Carle, E. (1996). *Little cloud*. New York: Philomel.

Cole, J. (1986). *The magic school bus at the waterworks*. New York: Scholastic.

Cole, J. (1996). *The magic school bus wet all over: A book about the water cycle*. New York: Scholastic.

Cole, J. (2000). *The magic school bus kicks up a storm: A book about weather*. New York: Scholastic.

DeWitt, L. (1993). *What will the weather be?* New York: HarperTrophy.

Dorros, A. (1990). *Feel the wind*. New York: HarperTrophy.

Gibbons, G. (1987). *Weather forecasting*. New York: Macmillan.

Greene, C. (1991). *Caring for our air*. Springfield, NJ: Enslow.

Greene, C. (1991). *Caring for our water*. Springfield, NJ: Enslow.

Kalan, R. (1991). *Rain*. New York: Morrow.

Kirkpatrick, R. K. (1985). *Look at weather*. Austin, TX: Raintree.

Leutscher, A. (1983). *Water*. New York: Dutton.

Llewellyn, C. (1991). *First look in the air*. Milwaukee, WI: Gareth Stevens.

Lloyd, D. (1983). *Air*. New York: Dial Books.

Locker, T. (1997). *Water dance*. Orlando, FL: Harcourt Brace.

Locker, T. (2003). *Cloud dance*. San Diego, CA: Voyager.

Maki, C. (1993). *Snowflakes, sugar, and salt*. Minneapolis: Lerner.

Markle, S. (1993). *A rainy day*. New York: Orchard Books.

Martin, C. (1987). *I can be a weather forecaster*. Danbury, CT: Childrens Press.

Miller, D. (2003). *Arctic lights, arctic nights*. New York: Walker and Company.

Morrison, G. (2002). *Pond*. New York: Houghton/Mifflin, Walter Lorraine Books.

Otto, C. (1992). *That sky, that rain*. New York: Harper.

Palazzo, J. (1982). *What makes the weather?* New York: Troll Associates.

Pluckrose, H. (1987). *Think about floating and sinking*. Danbury, CT: Watts.

Schnur, S. (2000). *Spring thaw*. New York: Viking Books.

Seixas, J. S. (1987). *Water—what it is, what it does*. New York: Greenwillow Books.

Smeltzer, P., & Smeltzer, V. (1983). *Thank you for a drink of water*. Palm Beach, FL: Winston.

Swallow, S. (1991). *Air*. Danbury, CT: Watts.

Taylor, K. (1992). *Flying start science series: Water; light; action; structure*. New York: John Wiley.

Webb, A. (1987). *Water*. Danbury, CT: Watts.

Webster, V. (1982). *Weather experiments*. Danbury, CT: Childrens Press.

Wilder, L. (1995). *Winter days in the big woods*. New York: HarperCollins.

For Older Children

Arnov, B. (1980). *Water: Experiments to understand it*. New York: Lothrop, Lee & Shepard Books.

Branley, F. M. (1982). *Water for the world*. New York: Harper & Row.

Bright, M. (1991). *Polluting the oceans*. Danbury, CT: Watts.

Cosner, S. (1982). *Be your own weather forecaster*. Parsippany, NJ: Julian Messner.

De Bruin, J. (1983). *Young scientists explore the weather*. Torrance, CA: Good Apple.

Dickinson, J. (1983). *Wonders of water*. New York: Troll Associates.

Elson, D. (1997). *Weather explained*. New York: Henry Holt.

Flint, D. (1991). *Weather and climate*. Danbury, CT: Watts.

Ford, A. (1982). *Weather watch*. New York: Lothrop, Lee & Shepard Books.

Frevert, P. (1981). *Why does the weather change?* Chicago: Creative Education.

Gallant, R. A. (1987). *Rainbows, mirages, and sundogs*. New York: Macmillan.

Jeffries, L. (1983). *Air, air, air*. New York: Troll Associates.

Kiefer, I. (1981). *Poisoned land: The problem of hazardous waste*. New York: Atheneum.

McKinney, B. (1998). *A drop around the world*. Nevada City, CA: Dawn.

Mebane, R., & Rybolt, T. (1995). *Water & other liquids*. New York: Twenty-First Century Books.

Miller, C., & Berry, L. (1987). *Acid rain*. Parsippany, NJ: Julian Messner.

Murata, M. (1993). *Science is all around you: Water and light*. Minneapolis: Lerner.

Pollard, M. (1987). *Air, water, and weather*. New York: Facts on File.

Pratt, K. (1994). *A swim through the sea*. Nevada City, CA: Dawn.

Pratt-Serfini, K. J. (2001). *Salamander rain: A lake and pond journal*. Nevada City, CA: Dawn.

Riley, P. D. (1986). *Air and gases*. New York: David & Charles.

Seabrooke, S. (2004). *The world almanac for kids 2005*. New York: World Almanac.

Seymour, P. (1985). *How the weather works*. New York: Macmillan.

Smith, H. (1983). *Amazing air*. New York: Lothrop, Lee & Shepard Books.

Snodgrass, M. E. (1991). *Environmental awareness: Water pollution*. Marco, FL: Bancroft Sage.

Sorensen, V. (1956). *Miracles on maple hill*. Orlando, FL: Harcourt Brace.

Steele, P. (1991). *Wind: Causes and effects*. Danbury, CT: Watts.

Walpole, B. (1987). *Water*. Danbury, CT: Watts.

Ward, A. (1986). *Experimenting with surface tension and bubbles*. New York: David & Charles.

Wick, W. (1997). *A drop of water*. New York: Scholastic.

Wu, N. (1991). *Planet earth: Life in the oceans*. Boston: Little, Brown.

Resource Books

Agler, L. (1986). *Liquid explorations*. Berkeley, CA: Great Explorations in Math and Science.

Barber, J. (1986). *Bubble·ology*. Berkeley, CA: Great Explorations in Math and Science.

Barber, J., & Willard, C. (1994). *Bubble festival*. Berkeley, CA: Great Explorations in Math and Science.

Benjamin, R. F., Wilson, J., & Youngs, D. (2001). *Spills and ripples*. Fresno, CA: AIMS Education Foundation. (water activities)

Butzow, C. M., & Butzow, J. W. (1989). *Science through children's literature: An integrated approach*. Englewood, CO: Teacher Ideas Press. (water topics on pp. 150–157; weather topics on pp. 200–205)

Butzow, C. M., & Butzow, J. W. (1994). *Intermediate science through children's literature: Over land and sea*. Englewood, CO: Teacher Ideas Press. (weather topics on pp. 24–36; ocean and lake topics on pp. 131–169)

Deery, R. (1985). *Tornadoes and hurricanes*. Torrance, CA: Good Apple.

Fredericks, A. D., Meinbach, A. M., & Rothlein, L. (1993). *Thematic units: An integrated approach to teaching science and social studies*. New York: HarperCollins. (weather topics on pp. 153–160)

Graube, I. (1990). *Seasons thematic unit*. Huntington Beach, CA: Teacher Created Materials.

Halverson, C., Beals, K., & Strang, C. (2001). *Ocean currents*. Berkeley, CA: Great Explorations in Math and Science. (ocean, water, and wind activities)

LeCroy, B., & Holder, B. (1994). *Bookwebs: A brainstorm of ideas for the primary classroom*. Englewood, CO: Teacher Ideas Press. (air activities on pp. 97–98)

Lyons, W. (1997). *The handy weather answer book*. Detroit, MI: Visible Ink Press.

Malnor, B., & Malnor, C. (1998). *A teacher's guide to a drop around the world*. Nevada City, CA: Dawn.

Malnor, B., & Malnor, C. (1998). *A teacher's guide to a swim through the sea*. Nevada City, CA: Dawn.

Shaw, D. G., & Dybdahl, C. S. (1996). *Integrating science and language arts: A sourcebook for K–6 teachers*. Boston: Allyn & Bacon. (water cycle topic on pp. 73–78)

Watercourse & Council for Environmental Education. (1995). *Project WET*. Bozeman, MT: Author.

Western Regional Environmental Education Council. (1992). *Aquatic Project WILD*. Boulder, CO: Author.

Wiebe, A. (1990). *Soap film and bubbles*. Fresno, CA: AIMS Education Foundation.

Wiebe, A. (2002). *Weather sense: Moisture*. Fresno, CA: AIMS Education Foundation. (weather activities)

Wiebe, A. (2002). *Weather sense: Temperature, air pressure, and wind*. Fresno, CA: AIMS Education Foundation. (weather activities)

Williams, J. (1992). *USA Today: The weather book*. New York: Vintage Books.

THE EARTH IN SPACE

"The sky's the limit." "What goes up must come down." Even young children today smile at these clichés. Television, magazines, and space missions have given children a beyond-the-earth outlook unknown to most previous generations.

Outside school, however, few children learn the basic ideas and physical laws that give meaning to the motions of objects in space. We concentrate on several of these ideas and laws in this section as we examine how the earth's motions in space cause time and seasonal changes; how the relative motions of sun, earth, and moon bring about moon phases, eclipses, and tides; how size and distance are measured in the solar system and beyond; and how gravity and the laws of motion affect the movements of planets, satellites, and rockets.

Benchmarks and Standards

A child who observes the sun, moon, stars, and planets will begin to find patterns in their behavior. Seasons, tides, phases of the moon, and day and night are all relevant topics as indicated in the sample standards and benchmarks.

Sample Benchmarks (AAAS, 1993)

- Like all planets, the earth is approximately spherical in shape. The rotation of the earth on its axis every 24 hours produces the night-and-day cycle. (By Grades 3–5, p. 68)
- We live on a relatively small planet, the third from the sun. (By Grades 6–8, p. 68)

Sample Standards (NRC, 1996)

- Objects in the sky have patterns of movement. The sun, for example, appears to move across the sky in the same way every day, but its path changes slowly over the seasons. (By Grades K–4, p. 134)
- Most objects in the solar system are in regular and predictable motion. Those motions explain such phenomena as the day, the year, phases of the moon, and eclipses. (By Grades 5–8, p. 160)

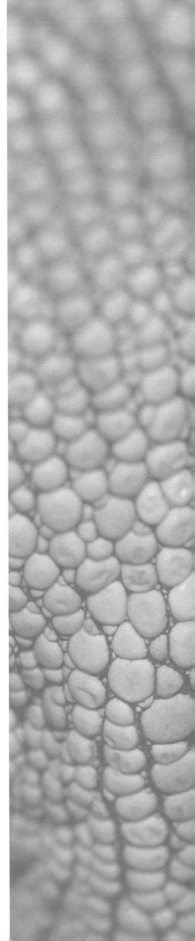

TIME AND THE SEASONS **Inquiry**

The Way the Earth Rotates

MATERIALS
• Globe
• Sunny area
• Small nail with large head
• Hammer
• Sticky tape
• Stick (1 meter, or 1 yard, long)
• Directional compass
• Pebble
• Clock

Invitation

Each day, the sun seems to follow a pattern in the sky. It seems to rise in one direction, move across the sky, and then set in the opposite direction. But the sun is relatively still. We know that it only seems to move because the earth rotates. In which direction does the earth rotate? You can find out for yourself by using a globe and then the earth itself.

Exploration

1. Get a small nail. Push the nail point through the sticky side of a small piece of tape. Fasten the nail head down to the place on the globe where you live.
2. Take the globe, hammer, and stick outdoors to a sunny area. Pound the stick upright into the ground.
3. Notice the shadow made by the stick. Position the globe so that the nail is upright and makes a shadow exactly in the same direction. (You may have to slip a book under the globe's base to keep the nail upright.)
4. Rotate the globe from west to east as shown.

Teaching Tips

Some children may need to be shown directions outdoors and on the globe. You might help them understand that north always runs from where they are to the North Pole and that south runs from there to the South Pole.

For the best shadow, the stick needs to be reasonably upright. A plumb bob made of string tied to a piece of chalk can help children align the stick if needed. You may substitute a tetherball pole for the stick. The nail, too, should be upright. If needed, a book or other object can be slipped under the globe base to make the nail vertical. If you can borrow some globes from other teachers, you might want to do this as a small-group activity.

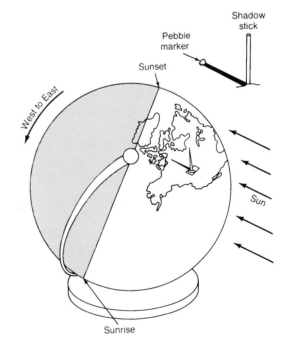

Concept Invention

1. What happens to the nail shadow if you rotate the globe a little from west to east? Make a record of the direction and length of the shadow.
2. What happens to the nail shadow if you rotate the globe a little from east to west? Make a record.

3. Put a pebble marker at the tip of your stick's shadow. Look at the shadow again 5 minutes later. In which direction did the shadow move?
4. In which direction does the earth rotate?

Concept Application

Daily shadows on the earth move from west to east. Shadow movement shows that the earth rotates the same way. Notice other shadows around you. How does their direction compare to the direction of the stick's shadow? Where will their shadows be in 1 hour? in 3 hours? Check your predictions and record what you find.

A Shadow Clock

Invitation

Before people had clocks, one way they told time was by watching shadows on sunny days. You can do that, too. But now you can use a clock to check how well you can keep time using shadows.

Exploration

1. Lay the card in a sunny place. Put the nail, pointing up, in the center of the card. Trace a small circle around the nail head. If the nail falls over, be sure to replace it inside the circle.
2. Each hour you can, trace the nail shadow with a pencil and then check a clock. Record the hour by the tip of the pencil tracing as illustrated. It is all right to carry your shadow clock back and forth, but always put it back in the same way and place.
3. Plan to check your shadow clock on the next sunny day.

MATERIALS

- Large blank file card
- Pencil
- Nail
- Clock or watch
- Sunny area

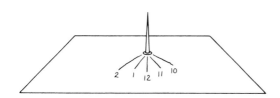

 Teaching Tips

It is essential that children align their shadow clocks exactly the same way each time. Otherwise, their pencil recordings may not coincide with additional shadows. A chalk outline or piece of tape to align an edge can be a helpful reminder. Within a week, or sooner, children will detect a difference in the shadow alignments. This difference happens because the tilted earth continues to move around the sun. The same event is responsible for the changes of seasons.

Concept Invention

1. Check the shadow clock each hour, or when you can. Notice where the shadow is. How well can you keep time by the hour?
2. Can you tell the right time on the half hour? Can you tell when it is 15 minutes before the hour? Can you tell when it is 15 minutes after the hour?
3. Will your shadow clock keep the right time for a week or longer?
4. Do the nail shadows slowly change? If so, how do they change?

Concept Application

It is possible to keep track of the time in a general way with a shadow clock; however, it gets less accurate as time goes on. Compare a shadow clock and other types of clocks (such as analog, digital, or atomic clocks). What are some advantages and disadvantages of each?

Direct Sun ———————

Invitation

How warm is slanted versus direct sunshine?

Exploration

1. Cut two same-sized pieces of cardboard.
2. Staple black paper to each piece. Staple a pocket for each thermometer as shown. Slip a thermometer into each pocket.

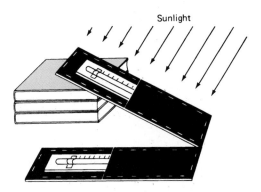

Sunlight

MATERIALS

- Cardboard
- Ruler
- Two matched thermometers
- Black paper
- Stapler
- Scissors
- Books

Teaching Tips

Your students may be unsure about how high they must prop up the direct sunlight thermometer. You might have them tape a nail head down to the cardboard. They then can tilt the cardboard until the nail no longer makes a shadow, indicating relatively vertical sunlight.

---

3. Lay one thermometer flat in the sun. It will get slanted sunshine. Prop up the other thermometer with some books so that the sun strikes it directly.
4. Look at each thermometer carefully. Be sure the temperature in neither thermometer rises so high that the thermometer breaks. After a few minutes, take out the thermometers and check the temperatures.

Concept Invention

1. Which thermometer has the higher temperature?
2. Which seems to give more heat-slanted or direct sunshine?

Adapting for Students with Exceptionalities

When experimentation involves measuring devices such as thermometers, it may be helpful to purchase large, specially made measuring instruments for adapting activities.

Concept Application

Check how far North America is from the sun during winter and summer. Also check the tilt of the earth's axis for North America during winter and summer. What does this say about direct and slanted sunlight?

Why the Earth Has Seasons ———————

Invitation

Suppose you could see the earth from outer space as it circles the sun each year. This would help you understand why the earth has seasons. But you might have to wait a long time to do that. You can use a globe and light to find out now. How can a model earth (globe) and sun (lighted bulb) be used to show seasons?

Exploration

1. Get a tilted globe. The earth rotates on a make-believe pole. The pole's north end always points toward the North Star as the earth circles the sun. (That is why globes are tilted.)
2. Label one wall "north." (You will need to keep the globe tilted toward that wall.)
3. Tape a nail head down to the place on the globe where you live.
4. Set up the globe and lamp as shown in the illustration. Darken the room.

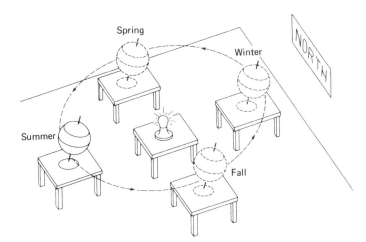

5. Begin at the summer position. Center the nail in the "sunshine" and point the North Pole toward north. Look at the nail shadow where you live. Measure and record how long it is. Notice how much daylight there is east and west of where you live.
6. Repeat step 5 at each of the other three positions.

Teaching Tips

If four globes are available, all four can be set up and used at the same time with four groups of students. Each group can rotate to a new position after a few minutes for observation and measurement. The best place from which to observe the amount of daylight and darkness at one's latitude is just above the globe's North Pole.

Concept Invention

1. During which season do you see the shortest shadow where you live? During which season do you see the longest shadow where you live? (A short shadow shows strong, direct sunshine. A long shadow shows weak, slanted sunshine.)
2. When is the longest period of sunshine where you live? When is the shortest period of sunshine? (The longer the sun shines, the warmer it gets where you live.)

MATERIALS

- Tilted globe
- Unshaded table lamp
- Small nail with large head
- Pencil and paper
- Sticky tape
- Ruler

Scaffolding for English Learners

When facilitating this activity with students, allow time to discuss how various cultures celebrate the seasons. This will provide a linguistic foundation for later learning of what causes the seasons.

Concept Application

The earth's tilted axis and revolution about the sun cause seasonal changes. During which seasons will the periods of daylight and darkness be about the same? Where and when north of you is it possible to have 24 hours of darkness or 24 hours of daylight? When and where can this happen south of you?

TIME AND THE SEASONS CONCEPTS

Because the earth is so large, compared to the size of a person, it is difficult at first to visualize the earth's motions in space. One remedy is to make the earth small compared to a person. That is what a globe model of the earth does.

Globe and Shadows

If you put a globe in the sun, the sunlight shines on one-half of the globe, as it does on one-half of the earth. If you position your town or city so that it is facing directly upward, and north on the globe faces north, the globe will face the sun as the earth does.

How will you know this is so? You can test it. Stick a small nail through a piece of sticky tape and fasten the nail head to your town on the globe. Be sure the nail is vertical. (You may have to prop up the globe base with a book or two.) Then look at the nail's shadow. You'll find it identical in direction and proportional to shadows of other objects around you. Leave the globe in place during the day, and the nail shadow will move and change length as other shadows do as the earth rotates. Or, if you want a preview of what shadows the earth objects will make, you can rotate the globe and watch the nail's shadow.

Rotation and Time

Most upper-grade students know the earth rotates, but few can tell in which direction. The sun rises in a generally eastern direction and sets in a generally western direction, with opposite shadows. Therefore, it is a west-to-east rotation.

INQ Figure 12–1 shows how people on the East Coast of the United States move into the sunlight. To them, it looks as though the sun is rising from the horizon and climbing higher as time goes by. Six hours from the time they first observe "sunrise," the sun is closest to being directly overhead. This is *midday*, or the exact middle of the daylight period. Gradually, they continue to rotate counterclockwise. Shadows grow longer. Around 6:00 P.M., it is almost twilight, and the sun appears to sink into the western horizon. The next 12 hours they spend in darkness, until once again the sun appears to rise. A complete rotation takes 24 hours, or one complete day. Of course, most of the time people in New York (or elsewhere) do not have equal parts of daylight and darkness. You know that summer days are longer than winter days, for example. We shall discuss why shortly.

INQ Figure 12–1   **The apparent motion of the sun is caused by the earth's rotation.**

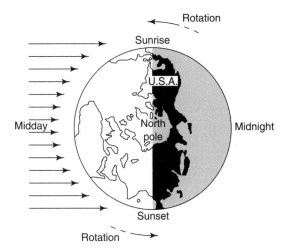

Expect some trouble with the term *day* because it has two meanings: the hours during which it is light, and the time for one complete rotation. You might use the terms *complete day* and *daylight* to distinguish the two.

Time Zones

It would be extremely inconvenient to judge time by where the sun is overhead. Every location a few kilometers east or west of another location would have a different noon-time as the sun reached its midday position, for example. Although this was not a problem in the days of slow-moving transportation, it became intolerable when railroads were established.

The problem was solved in 1833 by creating four standard time zones in the United States. INQ Figure 12–2 shows those in use today in the continental United States. We set our watches ahead going eastward and back going westward. The entire globe is now divided into 24 time zones, 15° apart. (The 15° separations came from dividing 360° by 24 hours, because the earth is a near sphere.)

The practical effect of having the same time zone for three cities hundreds of kilometers apart is shown in INQ Figure 12–3. Notice that only one city can experience midday at a given moment, although it is noon at all three cities.

Seasons

People in New York on December 21 experience about 9 hours of daylight and 15 hours of darkness. Six months later, the reverse happens. An even greater difference is found at a higher latitude, such as near Seattle, Washington (50th parallel). To see why, first examine INQ Figure 12–4. Notice that the earth's axis is tilted 23° from the plane of the earth's orbit around the sun. As the earth revolves about the sun, its axis continues to point in the same direction—toward the North Star. Check the winter position. Because of the tilt, the Northern Hemisphere is in darkness longer than it is in daylight. You can see this by checking the length of the parallels of latitude shown. In the summer position, you see the reverse. Now the same latitude is exposed to sunlight for a much longer period. At the "in between" periods of spring and fall, day and night periods are more nearly equal.

INQ Figure 12–2 The continental United States has four time zones.

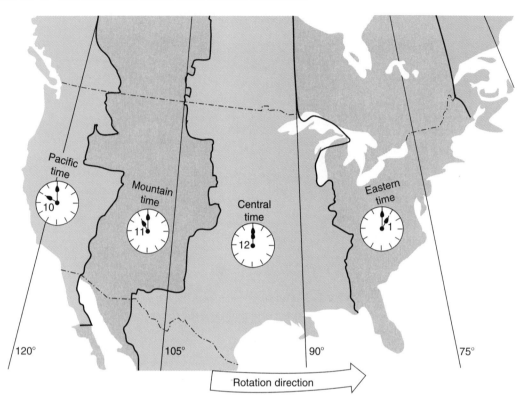

INQ Figure 12–3 Midday at one city and noon at three cities in the same time zone (not to scale).

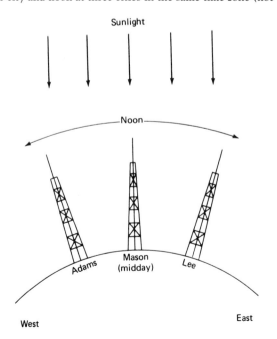

INQ Figure 12–4   The seasons. Outside figures as viewed from above. Notice the unequal periods of daylight at the 50th parallel except on March 21 (spring equinox) and September 23 (fall equinox).

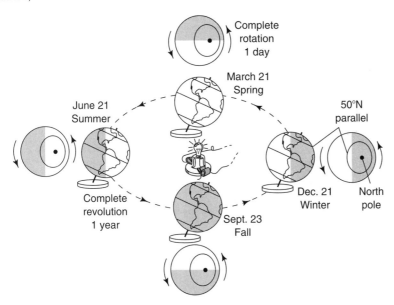

Also observe that the Southern Hemisphere has conditions opposite those in the Northern Hemisphere. While New York shivers in December, the beaches in sunny Rio de Janeiro are crowded with swimmers and sunbathers enjoying their summer.

Besides the increased length of the days, there is another reason why summers are warmer than winters. The sun's rays are more nearly overhead during summer than at other times. Note the words "more nearly overhead." Because the earth's axis is tilted, at noon the sun can never be completely vertical (at a 90° angle) north of the Tropic of Cancer or south of the Tropic of Capricorn.

If you ask children to explain why it is warmer in summer than it is in winter, don't be surprised if one replies, "The earth is closer to the sun." This answer is entirely logical even though it is wrong. In fact, the opposite is true. The earth's path (orbit) around the sun is a slightly elongated circle, or ellipse, as are nearly all the orbits of celestial bodies. In winter, we are almost 5 million kilometers (3 million miles) closer to the sun than in summer. But because this distance is small compared with the average distance, about 150 million kilometers (93 million miles), the effect is negligible.

MOON, EARTH, AND SUN INTERACTION **Inquiry**

Moon Phases

Invitation

MATERIALS

- White ball (tennis or volleyball)
- Bright window
- Daytime moon

Have you ever watched the moon over 1 or 2 weeks? If so, you know its shape seems to go through changes, or phases. You can predict what phase will show when you understand why the moon's appearance changes. Working with a moon model can help. A ball can be the moon, and your head can be the earth. Light from a bright window can be the sun. How can a model be used to show moon phases?

Exploration

1. Close all the classroom shades or curtains except for one bright window.
2. Hold the ball above eye level and face the window, as illustrated. See the dark or shadowy side of the model. This is a new moon. (A real new moon cannot be seen from the earth.)

3. Turn the model moon to the left. Stop when you are sideways to the window. This is a first-quarter moon. The moon has gone one-quarter, or one-fourth, of the way around the earth.
4. Make another quarter turn to the left. Stop when your back is to the window. Now the entire moon facing you is lighted by the sun. This is a full moon.
5. Move a quarter turn left until you are sideways to the window. This is a last-quarter moon. Compare it with the first-quarter moon. Notice that the opposite part is lighted now.
6. Move the last quarter turn to your left. This is the new moon again. From one new moon to the next takes about 4 weeks.

Teaching Tips

If a bright window is unavailable, use the light from a filmstrip projector in a dark room. To do Concept Invention step 2, a daytime moon must be visible. Consult the detailed weather section of your local newspaper for moonrise and moonset times during a period when a daytime moon is visible.

Concept Invention

1. The illustration shows eight moon phases out of order. Using your moon model, can you figure out the correct order? Start with the new moon.

2. Go outside in the sun. Point your model toward the real moon. Notice where the sun shines on the real moon. Notice where it shines on the model. How does the real-moon phase compare to the model phase?

3. How can you move your model in the sun to make other phases? (Never look at the sun; it may harm your eyes.)

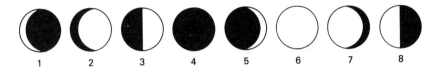

1   2   3   4   5   6   7   8

Scaffolding for English Learners

Remember not to focus on language errors that may impede concept development. For example, if the student says, "The new moon appear invisible" instead of "The new moon appears invisible," then the scientific concept is still understood despite the error in language. These language errors will be resolved naturally as the English learner progresses with language development. (See Ovando, Collier, & Combs, 2003, for a discussion of the role of error correction with English learners.)

Concept Application

Moon phases appear because one-half of the moon is lighted by sunshine as it revolves around the earth. Observe the moon now and then for a few days. Notice how its appearance changes. Keep a record. Can you predict what it will look like in 1 week? Can you predict what it will look like in 2 weeks? Draw what you think and then find out if you were correct.

An Earth–Moon Model ────────

Invitation

Astronauts have walked on the moon several times, so it is easy to think that the moon is close to the earth, even though it is far away. One way to show its distance is to make a scale model.

Exploration

1. You will need a large ball for the earth and a smaller one for the moon. The earth is about four times as wide as the moon. Measure the width of a ball by putting it between two books. Use a ruler to find the distance between the books. A basketball is about four times wider than a tennis ball.

2. The moon is about 30 earth widths away, or 10 times farther away than the distance around the earth. Wrap a string 10 times around the basketball. Cut off what is left.

MATERIALS
• Basketball
• String
• Tennis ball
• Two books
• Ruler
• Scissors
• Clay

3. Stretch the string between the "earth" and the "moon" as illustrated. This scale model shows sizes and distance compared to the real earth.

Teaching Tips

The sequence is designed to help children gain an understanding of proportion without its mathematics. After these experiences, most children should have a realistic scaled view of the earth–moon system. If you want, you might proceed directly with figures they can scale: the earth's diameter, 12,800 kilometers (8000 miles); the moon's diameter, 3200 kilometers (2000 miles); and average distance between them, 384,000 kilometers (240,000 miles).

Concept Invention

1. How can you make a scale model that is half this size?
2. Suppose you had a ball 10 centimeters (4 inches) wide to use as the earth. How large would the moon need to be? How far apart should the earth and the moon be?
3. Suppose you had a ball 5 centimeters (2 inches) wide to use as the moon. How large would the earth need to be? How far apart should the earth and the moon be?

Concept Application

Relative sizes and distance in the earth–moon system may be shown in a scale model. Suppose you wanted your whole model to be no longer than a meterstick or yardstick. How large would you make your earth and moon? How far apart would you place them?

Eclipses of the Sun and Moon ──────────

MATERIALS

- Volleyball or basketball
- Filmstrip projector
- Tennis ball
- Sticky tape
- String
- Table
- Two large index cards

Invitation

Sometimes the earth, moon, and sun are in a straight line in space. Then, something interesting may happen: The moon may block off, or eclipse, the sunlight, or the earth may block, or eclipse, the moon. You can learn how eclipses work with a model of the sun, moon, and earth. How can you use the following items—volleyball, tennis ball, and projector—to demonstrate eclipses?

Exploration

1. Set up the materials as shown. Put a basketball or volleyball on a table. This will be the "earth."
2. Use sticky tape to fasten a short string to a tennis ball. This will be the "moon."
3. Darken the room. Turn on the projector "sun." Point it toward the earth.
4. Holding the string, move the moon around the earth. Notice the shadows made by the moon and the earth.

Concept Invention

1. At what position does the moon make a shadow on the earth? (This is an eclipse of the sun.)
2. How much of the earth is covered by the moon's shadow?
3. At what position does the earth make a shadow on the moon? (This is an eclipse of the moon.)
4. How much of the moon is covered by the earth's shadow?

Teaching Tips Some students may wonder why a solar eclipse and a lunar eclipse do not occur every month. You might help them understand that the plane of the moon's orbit around the earth is somewhat tilted. Also, the two bodies are relatively much farther apart than in the model, so usually the moon's shadow misses the earth, and the earth's shadow misses the moon. The distance between the two bodies also means that the moon's shadow on earth in solar eclipses is much smaller than found in the inquiry. Remember that you should never look at the sun during a solar eclipse. The sun can quickly injure eyes.

Adapting for Students with Exceptionalities

When involving exceptional students in complex activities such as eclipses, use a variety of visual diagrams and pictures to supplement the activity and make the information understandable. For example, in the Concept Application, show students several eclipse pictures along with the basketball and tennis ball manipulations.

Concept Application

A lunar eclipse happens when the earth's shadow falls on the moon. A solar eclipse happens when the moon's shadow falls on the earth. Would more people on the earth be able to see a sun eclipse or a moon eclipse? Explain your answer. Move the moon around the earth again, but now have it go just above or below the earth. Do you see eclipses now? Explain why or why not.

MOON, EARTH, AND SUN INTERACTION CONCEPTS

Why does the moon seem to change its shape? Why do the oceans have tides? What causes eclipses? Children are curious about these things. This section presents some ways the sun, earth, and moon interact. We consider moon phases first.

Moon Phases

You know that the moon, like our earth, receives and reflects light from the hot, glowing sun. Also, the moon revolves around the earth in about 28 days. Study INQ Figure 12–5 for a moment. The drawings on the right show the earth and moon as seen from far out in space. The drawings of the moon on the left illustrate how it appears to us on the earth as it goes through each of eight different positions or phases.

Suppose we are standing on the earth in the right-hand part of this illustration. Look at position 1. This is the new moon position. The moon's face is now dark to us. Slowly, the moon moves on in its orbit. At position 2, we see a new crescent moon; at position 3,

INQ Figure 12–5   **Moon phases as seen from the earth (left); the earth and moon as seen from far out in space (right).**

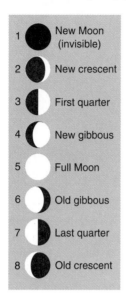

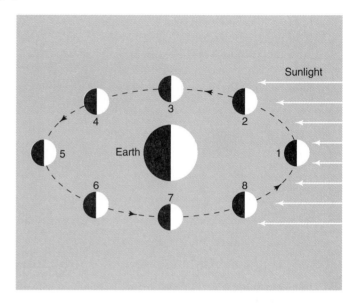

a first-quarter moon. At position 4, we see a new gibbous moon; one side is now almost fully illuminated. At position 5, the moon is full. The other positions reverse the sequence of phases from old gibbous, last quarter, old crescent, to new moon.

As the moon moves from the new to full positions, more and more of it appears to be shining; it is said to be *waxing*. But from full- to new-moon positions, less and less of its lighted part is visible from earth, so it is said to be *waning*. Compare the moon phases you actually see with those in INQ Figure 12–5.

Tides

The interaction of sun, moon, and earth also results in tides. How do tides happen? The law of universal gravitation, first formulated by the great 18th-century philosopher and scientist Sir Isaac Newton, provides much of the answer. Briefly stated, every object in the universe attracts each other; the force of this attraction depends on the mass of each object and the distance between them. (*Mass* is the amount of matter that makes up the object.)

INQ Figure 12–6

Mutual attraction between earth and moon causes ocean tides.

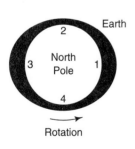

As shown in INQ Figure 12–6, the mutual attraction between earth and moon causes the ocean to bulge at position 1. This is a direct high tide. An indirect high tide appears at position 3 because it is most distant from the moon; gravitational attraction is weakest here. Also, the land surface is pulled slightly away from this region. Positions 2 and 4 have low tides because these are areas of weak attraction that furnish the extra water making up the high tides.

What causes the tides to rise and fall? Put yourself in position 1. As you rotate on the earth toward position 2, the tide will seem to *ebb*, or fall. You experience a low tide. Moving from position 2 into 3, you gradually come into the bulge. It seems as though the tide is "coming in." You experience a high tide. Rotating onward, you have another low tide before once again arriving at the direct high-tide area. In other words, the oceans tend to bulge continually in the moon's direction and opposite point, as the earth

INQ Figure 12–7 **The sun also affects tidal flows.**

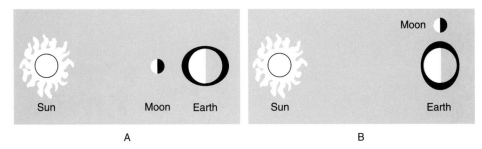

rotates. The continual bulges create the illusion that the tides are moving in and out independently.

Because the earth's rotation takes about 24 hours, high tides happen about every 12 hours. Therefore, we have one direct high tide and one indirect high tide simultaneously. Six hours elapse between low and high tides. Actually, these times are a little longer because the moon itself moves some distance in its orbit while the earth rotates. Because the tidal bulge moves in alignment with the moon as it advances, the earth must rotate an extra 52 minutes each 24 hours before it is again in the direct high-tide zone.

Twice monthly, unusually high and low tidal ranges occur called *spring tides*. High tides are very high and low tides are very low. (Incidentally, there is no connection between spring tides and the season. Perhaps the name arose because these tides appear to "spring up" so fast.) A week later, there is much less variation from high to low tides. Tides during this period are called *neap tides*.

INQ Figure 12–7 shows how these tides take place. When the sun and moon are aligned (A), the sun's added gravitational attraction causes very high spring tides. This happens during the time when the moon is in either the full- or new-moon phase. Because the sun is so far away, its tremendous mass adds only one-third to the force of gravitational attraction. When the sun and moon pull at right angles (B), we have neap tides. This happens when the moon is in its first- and last-quarter phases.

Interestingly, besides water tides, there are also huge atmospheric tides and tiny land tides. All happen through the same interaction of sun, moon, and earth. Accurate measurements show that some land portions of the earth rise and fall more than 30 centimeters (1 foot) with the tides.

Eclipses

Causes of eclipses are seen in INQ Figure 12–8. Both earth and moon cast conelike shadows. When the moon is in position 1, the tip of its shadow barely reaches the earth. Persons in this small, shadowy area see a solar eclipse. A total eclipse is never more than 272 kilometers (170 miles) across. Sunlight is cut off except for a whitish halo, called the *corona*. The shadow moves quickly over the ground because both the earth and the moon are in motion. Sunlight is never blocked for more than 8 minutes.

In position 2, the moon is eclipsed when it revolves into the earth's large shadow. Practically everyone on the earth's dark side can see a lunar eclipse, which may last for 2 hours before the moon revolves out of the earth's shadow. Several partial lunar and solar eclipses occur each year.

Notice that eclipses happen in the full- and new-moon positions. Why, then, don't they occur every few weeks? The reason is that the moon's plane of orbit is tilted about 5°

INQ Figure 12–8   **Cause of solar (1) and lunar (2) eclipses.**

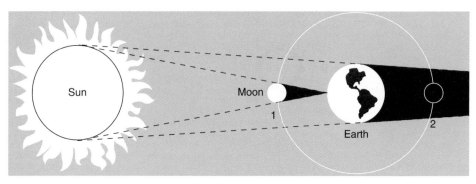

from the earth's orbital plane around the sun. This tilt usually causes the moon to pass above and below positions required for eclipses.

A 5° tilt would be only a minor deviation from the earth's orbital plane in INQ Figure 12–8, hardly enough to make a difference. In proper scale, however, this small deviation is quite significant. With a scale of 2.5 centimeters to 1600 kilometers (1 inch to 1000 miles), the earth's diameter is 20 centimeters (8 inches), and the moon's diameter is 5 centimeters (2 inches). Their distance apart is 6 meters (20 feet). The sun's diameter and distance at this scale are even more surprising. Imagine a sun model 22 meters (72 feet) across, 2.4 kilometers (1.5 miles) away!

The Earth–Moon System

We usually think of the moon revolving around the earth, but strictly speaking, this is not quite the case. The gravitational attraction of these two objects is such that they are locked together in a revolving system that has a common center of mass (barycenter). To see why this is so, look at INQ Figure 12–9. The large ball of clay represents the earth, and the small one is the moon. A short wire joins the two to simulate their gravitational attraction. If you suspend system A from the middle with a string, the much heavier earth goes down and the moon goes up. The same thing would happen if a heavy adult and a small child got on a seesaw with the fulcrum in the middle.

In system B, the balance is improved, but much the same thing happens. In system C, though, a balance is found. If you spin each model system with a twisted string, systems A and B will wobble and sway unevenly; but system C will revolve uniformly and simulate the motion of the earth–moon system. In any spinning system such as this, there is a tendency for the two objects to fly apart. The gravitational attraction between the two prevents this from happening.

In system D, the side of the earth facing the moon is strongly attracted to the moon. The water moves more easily than the solid earth, so it flows strongly toward the near side and becomes a high tide. The earth's opposite side is attracted less because it is farther away. So, the tendency of this far side of the spinning system to fly apart is countered only weakly by the weakened gravitational pull. The result is an indirect high tide.

Our model is imperfect in several ways. The earth's mass is about 80 times greater than the moon's. Also, the distance scale is wrong. If we were to use the proper scale, our short wire connector would need to be at least several feet long.

INQ Figure 12–9 The earth-moon system has a common point of balance, or center of mass, called the barycenter (distance not to scale).

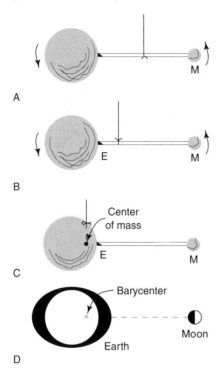

The Moon's Orbit ─────

From an earth reference position, it is natural to regard the moon as revolving in a circular path around the earth (or, more accurately, the barycenter). But motion is relative to the observer. If we could see the moon's path from far out in space, it would not look circular. Instead, it would weave in and out in a shallow, alternating pattern along the earth's orbit. (See INQ Figure 12–10.) Because the sun is in motion, a similar pathway is woven by the earth. Is it wrong, then, to say that the moon revolves around the earth and the earth around the sun? No, it is just another way of looking at the same set of facts.

Solar Wind ─────

One interesting interaction between the earth and the sun is the stream of ionized particles ejected at high speeds from the surface of the sun known as *solar wind*. Most of the current information we have about solar wind comes from the Solar and Heliospheric Observatory (SOHO) project. The International Solar Terrestrial Physics (ISTP) science

INQ Figure 12–10 The earth and moon orbits drawn to scale.

initiative is a collaborative effort by U.S., European, and Japanese space agencies to obtain coordinated, simultaneous investigations of the sun–earth space environment over an extended period of time. SOHO, one component of the ISTP program, includes a cooperative venture between the European Space Agency (ESA) and the National Aeronautics and Space Administration (NASA). Launched on December 2, 1995, the SOHO spacecraft is specifically designed to study the internal structure of the sun, the sun's outer atmosphere, and the origins of the solar wind that blows continuously outward throughout our solar system. SOHO will help scientists understand the interactions between the sun and the earth's environment.

According to SOHO scientists, solar wind is a stream of particles, primarily ionized hydrogen (electrons and protons), with a component of helium and trace amounts of heavy ions, flowing outward from the sun at speeds as high as 900 kilometers (559 miles) per second. SOHO scientists view solar wind as essentially the hot solar corona expanding into interplanetary and interstellar space. Solar wind has been detected from the sun outward past the orbit of Neptune. The stream of particles comes in two varieties. Low-speed solar wind moves about 1.5 million kilometers (932,056 miles) per hour, and high-speed solar wind moves at speeds as high as 3 million kilometers (1,864,114 miles) per hour.

As solar wind flows past the earth, it changes the shape and structure of the earth's magnetic field. Changes in solar wind can disrupt telecommunications, interfere with electrical power systems, and even damage satellites. To find out more information about SOHO, to see the current solar wind speed and other real-time data, to receive free materials, or to see related lesson plans, check the SOHO website (*http://sohowww.nascom.nasa.gov/*).

SOLAR SYSTEM AND BEYOND Inquiry

Size and Distance in the Solar System ————

Invitation

The solar system is huge. You cannot make a model that shows both size and distance at the same time. It would be too big to fit in the classroom or playground. But you can make a scale model of part of the system—the sun and the earth. It can help you understand more about distance and size in the solar system.

Exploration

1. Make a clay ball 1 centimeter (3/8 inch) wide for the earth.
2. The sun is 108 times wider than the earth, so cut out a circle 108 centimeters (43 inches) wide from yellow construction paper. (You may need to tape some sheets together.)
3. The sun is about 150 million kilometers (93 million miles) from the earth, so the two models will need to be about 116 meters (383 feet) apart.
4. Practice taking giant steps. Try to make each step 1 meter (or 1 yard) long. Then, step off the sun–earth distance on the playground.
5. Have someone hold up the model sun at one end. Hold up your tiny model earth, stuck on a pin, at the other end. Notice how far away the sun is.

> ### MATERIALS
> - Yellow construction paper
> - Clay
> - Meterstick or yardstick
> - Straight pin
> - Sticky tape
> - Playground
> - Scissors

> **Teaching Tips**
> A large circle may be drawn with a pencil tied to a string. Its radius with the current sun model would be 54 centimeters (21 inches). Many children will enjoy being challenged to extend their solar system model on a local map. Pluto will need to be placed several kilometers or miles away!

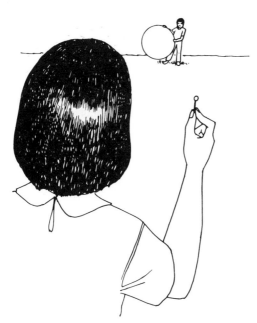

Concept Invention

1. The planet Jupiter is five times farther away from the sun than the earth. How far away (meters or feet) would Jupiter be with your model?

2. Uranus is almost 18 times farther from the sun than the earth. How far away would Uranus be with your model?
3. Pluto, the farthest planet, is more than 39 times farther away. How far would Pluto be with your model?
4. The largest of the solar system's nine planets is Jupiter. It is 11 times wider than the earth. How large would Jupiter be with your model?
5. The smallest planet is Pluto. It is only about one-third as wide as the earth. How large would it be with your model?

Adapting for Students with Exceptionalities

Check with your regional NASA Educator Resource Center for materials that can be adapted for exceptional student education (*http://www.nasa.gov/audience/foreducators/ topnav/materials/about/index.html*).

Concept Application

The large distances among planets in the solar system make it difficult to scale planet sizes and distances together in a model. Explain what would happen if you were to try to make a model of the entire solar system.

Constellations ————

MATERIALS

- Cardboard box
- Aluminum foil
- Scissors
- Black thread
- Black paint or paper
- Sticky tape
- Partner

Invitation

Most people have seen the group, or constellation, of stars called the Big Dipper. The stars make a pattern that looks like an old-fashioned water dipper. There are many more constellations of stars. But although they seem to make a pattern, they may be very different in size and millions of kilometers from each other. Seen from another angle, they may not look at all like constellations. You can find out more about what constellations are like by making a model.

Exploration

1. Cut off the top and one side of a cardboard box.
2. Cover the side and back inside with black paint or paper.
3. Snip different-sized pieces of black thread to hold your "stars."
4. Make different-sized stars from pieces of foil. Wrap each piece around a thread end. Squeeze each into a ball shape.
5. Ask someone to use tape and hang your stars in some pattern different from the one shown in the illustration. (Notice that, in the front view, this constellation looks like a **W**, but from the side looks like an upside-down **V**. If the box's side was as long as the playground, you could put the stars even farther apart. Then you would see no pattern at all from the side.)

Teaching Tips It is essential that children first view the constellation model directly from the front and from some distance. Otherwise, the activity may be less effective. The foil balls may be suspended quickly, and shifted as needed, by affixing each thread end to the box top inside with a bit of tape.

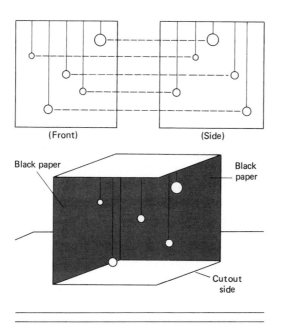

Concept Invention

1. Look at the constellation your partner has made from the front view from 15 steps away. Can you draw its shape?
2. At what distances from you are the stars? Which is the closest or next closest? Record what you think from left to right.
3. What do you think the constellation looks like from the side? Draw what you think.
4. Ask your partner to twist the box around very slightly. How, if at all, does this help you tell distances and the side pattern? How many more times must you twist the box around to tell?
5. Play a game with your partner. Each person hangs a different constellation. How many stars can you order properly by distance from you? How many side patterns can you tell from front patterns?

Concept Application

Stars of a constellation share a common direction, but they may vary greatly in size and distance from each other. Check the night sky on a clear day and record the location of stars from one constellation. Describe and name your constellation (such as the Big Dipper was named). Can your classmates locate your constellation on subsequent clear nights?

SOLAR SYSTEM AND BEYOND CONCEPTS

Planets ————

The earth is one of nine planets revolving around a medium-sized star, the sun. How did the solar system begin? Scientists are not sure. One prominent theory holds that the sun and planets may have been formed from an enormous swirling cloud of dust and gases. Slowly, gravitational attraction caused these materials to come closer together. The speed of rotation increased more and more. As rotating dust and gas particles rubbed together, much friction and heat developed. A large mass in the center became so hot that it formed into the sun. Gradually, most of the remaining materials spread out as a result of their spinning and began revolving around the sun. They slowly shrank and cooled into nine separate masses, which became planets (see INQ Figure 12–11).

Mercury

Mercury is the closest planet to the sun. It rotates very slowly, only two thirds around to one complete revolution around the sun, which takes only 88 days. Its small mass results in a very weak surface gravity. Mercury is heavily cratered from numerous collisions with meteoroids.

Mercury was explored in three flybys by the *Mariner 10* spacecraft in 1974 and 1975. During these missions, scientists found evidence there of a polar ice cap.

Venus

Venus, next in order from the sun, is enveloped in a dense atmosphere of mostly carbon dioxide and sulfuric acid. This atmosphere reflects sunlight so well that, except for the sun and Earth's moon, Venus is the brightest object in Earth's sky. Its surface temperature is very high as a result of the greenhouse effect.

NASA's *Magellan* spacecraft used radar to explore Venus's surface during its orbit from 1990 to 1994. Astronomers found volcanic lava flows, "venusquake" faults, and other features on the surface. *Mariner 2, 5,* and *10* and the *Pioneer* Venus spacecraft have all made missions to Venus.

Mars

After Earth is Mars. It has an unusual reddish appearance and polar ice caps that advance and recede with the seasons. It is more like Earth than the other planets, but its very thin

INQ Figure 12–11   **The solar system (not to scale).**

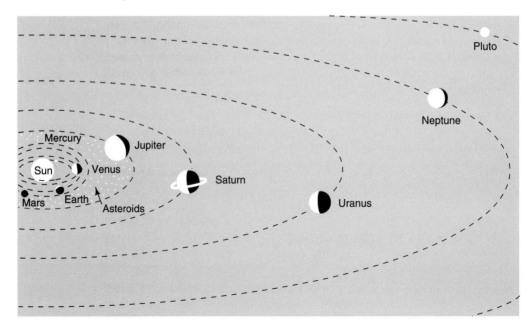

atmosphere and severe weather make it unlikely that living things are on this planet. Two tiny natural satellites, or moons, revolve speedily around Mars. *Mariner 4, 6*, and *7*, in the 1960s, explored the planet. In the 1970s, *Mariner 9* and the *Viking* missions allowed two landers to explore the planet further. Unfortunately, the landers did not find evidence of life.

On July 4, 1997, the Mars *Pathfinder* mission landed on the planet and left a mobile robot rover to explore the surface. In 1999, a polar lander was launched. The spirit and opportunity rovers have now visited Mars. A Mars Global Surveyor is scheduled to create high-resolution maps of the planet's surface. Other orbiters and landers were launched in 2001, 2003, and 2005, including a reconnaissance orbiter. Further information can be found on the Mars Exploration Program web page. New images and updated information are also available for viewing on the Internet from NASA's Jet Propulsion Laboratory's web pages.

Jupiter

Jupiter is a giant ball of hydrogen and helium gas and the largest outer planet. It is almost big enough to form into a star. In fact, Jupiter's diameter is 11 times greater than that of Earth. The Great Red Spot on Jupiter appears to be a storm that is almost three times the size of planet Earth.

NASA's *Pioneer 10* and *11* and *Voyager 1* and *2* spacecrafts explored Jupiter. It was also studied by the Jupiter-orbiting *Galileo* spacecraft.

Saturn, Uranus, Neptune, Pluto

Saturn, the second biggest planet in our solar system, is conspicuous because of its many rings. They are believed to be composed of ice and rock particles that can be as big as a house. Saturn was explored by NASA's *Pioneer 11* in the 1970s and by the *Voyager 1* and *2* spacecrafts in the 1980s. The *Cassini* spacecraft, launched in 1997, arrived at Saturn in 2004.

Uranus is about three and one half times Earth's diameter. This planet rotates on its side. The *Voyager 2* spacecraft flew by Uranus in 1986.

Neptune is the furthest of the giant outer planets in the solar system. Neptune's Great Dark Spot is a storm that is similar to Jupiter's Great Red Spot. The *Voyager 2* spacecraft flew by Neptune in 1989.

Pluto is so small and distant that it was not discovered until 1930. Its "moon," Charon, is about half the diameter and mass of Pluto. Its orbital plane is tilted sharply from those of other planets, and its orbit is so elliptical that at times the planet is closer to the sun than Neptune. Pluto is the only planet that has not been visited by spacecraft, although NASA has a mission called "New Horizons" that will be launched in 2006.

New Information on the Planets

Ancient sky-watchers were so puzzled by the changing appearance of the planets that they named them "wanderers." Long ago, all such objects were thought to be stars, which ordinarily seem fixed in space. We realize now that their differences in brightness and position from time to time occur because they revolve at different distances and speeds in their orbits around the sun.

Today, astronomers are finding new planets and are discovering more about distant bodies through the use of the Hubble Space Telescope and other space probes. For an up-to-date account of new findings, children can log on to NASA's web pages on the Internet (see the Companion Website for specific addresses). NASA's Office of Space Science Solar System Exploration Education and Outreach Forum is available to the public; it contains educational and informational resources that pertain to solar system exploration. This office provides information about the planets and other bodies contained in our solar system.

Comets, Meteors, and the Asteroid Belt

Comets are huge, unstable bodies apparently composed of gases, dust, ice, and small rocks. A few are briefly visible as they occasionally sweep near the sun and far out again in immense, highly elliptical orbits. They have so little mass that the pressure of sunlight causes a long streamer, or "tail," to flow from the comet head always in a direction opposite the sun. Like the planets, comets may have originated from the gases and dust of the solar nebula over 4 billion years ago.

Most children have seen "shooting stars." These are fragments of rock and metal, probably from broken-up asteroids and parts of comets that hurtle through interplanetary space at high speeds. Although most are no larger than a grain of sand, some weigh tons. It is estimated that billions of such *meteors*, as they are called, plunge daily into the earth's atmosphere and burn up from the heat of air friction. The few that do penetrate to the earth's surface in solid form other than dust are called *meteorites*.

Is there any danger of being struck by a meteorite? Not much. Only a few instances of anyone ever being injured are recorded. One such event happened in 1954. An Alabama woman was grazed by a 3.7-kilogram (10-pound) meteorite that crashed through her home's roof. In 1982, a 2.2-kilogram (6-pound) meteorite smashed through the roof of a home in Connecticut; no one was injured.

NASA is planning a mission to the asteroid belt that will be launched in 2005 and will reach the asteroid belt in 2008. The name of the mission is "Dawn" and it involves a new solar-electric propulsion system.

Sizes and Distances

By far the most difficult ideas in astronomy for children to grasp are the distances and sizes of objects in space. It would be helpful to their thinking if a large section of the playground could be used for scaled distance activities. Yet, even a very large area can be inadequate to demonstrate both distance and size on the same scale. At 2.54 centimeters to 12,000 kilometers (1 inch to 8000 miles), for example, Pluto would need to be located about 11 kilometers (7 miles) away!

Distances are even more astounding as we move beyond the solar system. Now, the kilometer or mile is too tiny a unit of measurement for practical purposes. You will want to acquaint students with the *light-year*, defined as the distance a beam of light travels in 1 year. At 300,000 kilometers (186,000 miles) per second, this is almost 9.5 trillion kilometers (6 trillion miles). The *parsec*, or the distance to a star that shows a parallax of 1 second of arc, is another unit of astronomical measurement that advanced students may be able to understand.

The Asteroid Belt

Between Mars and the next planet, Jupiter, is an unusually large gap containing several thousand irregularly shaped chunks of stone and metal called *asteroids* (tiny "stars") made of rock and metal that is mostly nickel and iron. Some astronomers think these may be the remains of a planet that came too close to huge Jupiter and disintegrated under its powerful gravitational attraction. Ranging from about 1.6 to 800 kilometers (1 to 500 miles) in diameter, they are invisible to the unaided eye.

Flybys of asteroids were completed in 1991 and 1993 by the *Galileo* spacecraft. In 1996, the *Near Earth Asteroid Rendezvous (NEAR)* spacecraft also explored the asteroid belt.

The Stars

When we view the stars, some seem to group into patterns, or constellations. People commonly think such stars are about the same in size and distance from the earth. But the only thing stars in a constellation typically share is a common direction. If we could view constellations from other angles (we can, very slightly, as the earth orbits the sun), most constellation patterns would disappear.

The light from our nearest star, the sun, takes about 8 minutes to reach the earth. In contrast, a distance of 4.3 light-years separates us from the next nearest star, Proxima Centauri. These stars have more than 100 billion companions clustered in an immense aggregation of stars and filmy clouds of gas and dust called the Milky Way galaxy. The shape of our galaxy is like a pocket watch, with a thickened center, standing on end (INQ Figure 12–12). It is thought to be about 100,000 light-years long and 12,000 light-years thick. The galaxy seems to be rotating slowly about its center, where the stars are most thickly concentrated.

Our galaxy is but one of millions more strewn throughout space at incomprehensible distances, containing further stars beyond reliable calculation.

Stellar Types and Evolution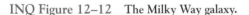

The stars we see range in size from the small, dim, *white dwarf* with a diameter that is much smaller than the sun, to the very large, very bright star known as a red *supergiant*, with a diameter hundreds of times larger than the sun. Stars change in size as part of an evolutionary process. All stars begin as a mass of cool gas. Gravity will cause the gas to contract. Eventually a high temperature and pressure condition causes a nuclear fusion chain reaction, which gives off energy, and the gas becomes a star. When the star's core runs out of hydrogen gas to transform into helium gas, it undergoes a change that puts it into a new phase of its evolution. What happens next depends on the mass of the star.

If the star was similar in mass to our sun, it will swell in size and become a large, bright red giant star. The red giant will continue nuclear fusion until all of its helium gas becomes carbon. It then shrinks in size and becomes a dim white dwarf star.

If a star is a lot more massive than the sun, it expands to a much greater size and is called a red supergiant, with brightness thousands of times greater than that of our sun. As a massive red supergiant star enters the late stage of its evolution, it explodes in a tremendous

INQ Figure 12–12   The Milky Way galaxy.

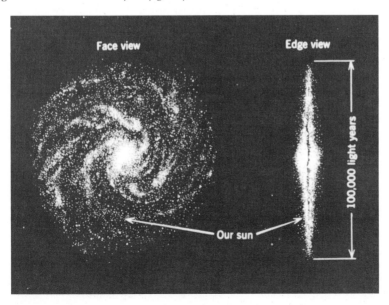

burst called a *supernova* that is visible in distant galaxies. This star will eventually contract to become a *neutron star* with an astounding density of 100 million tons per cubic centimeter (0.061 cubic inch).

If the collapsing star of a supernova has a great enough mass, then even the star's huge density cannot hold gravity back, and the supernova creates a new form that contracts forever. Eventually the gravitational force becomes so great that light cannot escape and the star disappears forever into a collapsing *black hole*.

GRAVITY AND THE LAWS OF MOTION **Inquiry**

The Sun's Gravity ———————

Invitation

Why doesn't the sun's gravity pull in the near planets?

Exploration

MATERIALS
• Strong string (2 meters, or 6 feet, long)
• Partner
• Rubber ball
• Watch with second hand
• Sewing thread spool
• Outdoor place

1. Tie one end of the string tightly to the ball. Slide the other end through the hole of a sewing spool.
2. You will be the "sun." The ball "planet" will revolve around you on the string. Hold the spool in one hand. Whirl the planet by moving the spool around. Hold the string with your other hand to keep it from slipping through the spool, as shown. (You could mark the string below the spool to easily see any slip.)
3. Feel how the ball pulls on the string. Have someone count the number of times your planet circles the sun in 15 seconds. Try to keep the string length above the spool the same.

Concept Invention

1. Try it a second time. Keep the string length the same as before, but now pull harder on the string below the spool. This increases the pull of "gravity" on your planet.
2. If the planet is to stay at the same distance, what must happen to its speed?

Concept Application

Have someone count again the number of orbits your planet makes in 15 seconds. Describe how the first and second counts compare. What do you think makes it possible for the closer planets not to be pulled into the sun?

Rockets ————

Invitation

What makes a rocket work?

Exploration

1. Thread one end of the string through a straw. Fasten that end low on a table leg. Fasten the other end high on a wall. The string should be tight.
2. Blow up the balloon. Fold over the small, open end and fasten it with a paper clip.
3. Use tape to fasten the balloon to the straw as shown.
4. Hold the balloon near the floor end of the string. Quickly remove the paper clip and let go.

MATERIALS

- Sausage-shaped balloon
- Sticky tape
- String (6 meters, or 20 feet, long)
- Paper clip
- Soda straw
- Five pennies

 Teaching **T**ips When air rushes out of the balloon, there is an equal and opposite push inside, so the balloon moves. In a rocket engine, burned fuel forms hot gases that push out through the open back of the engine. An equal and opposite push inside moves the rocket forward.

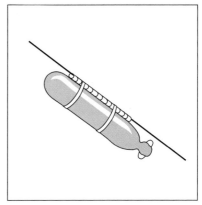

Concept Invention

1. What happens to the balloon?
2. How can you explain what happens?

Concept Application

Have a contest with teams of classmates to see whose balloon rocket can lift the most weight to a "space station." Tie one end of each string to a light fixture or other high place. Use sticky tape to fasten pennyweights to each balloon. Make some fair rules: The lower end of each string and rocket must touch the floor when the rocket is released. Each team gets two turns; the first is for practice. Observe carefully what the best rockets look like during the first trial and record this data. Also draw how your "improved" rocket will look. Use this information to prepare for the second trial. No team can change its rocket once the second trials begin. To win, here are some things to consider.

- How much air should be in the balloon? (If it breaks, you're out of the contest.)
- How long should the straw be?
- How should the straw be attached to the balloon?
- Should the string be upright or at a slant?
- What kind of string is best?
- How many pennies should be stuck on the balloon?
- Where is it best to put the pennies for balance?

GRAVITY AND THE LAWS OF MOTION CONCEPTS

Nobody knows what caused the planets to begin moving, but the reason they keep moving is readily understandable: There is almost nothing in space to stop them. But why do they circle the sun? You have already been introduced to Newton's law of gravitation. Equally important to understand is Newton's law of inertia. Briefly stated, any object at rest or in motion remains at rest or continues in motion in a straight line unless acted on by some outside force.

Anyone who has ever tried to push a heavy, stalled automobile knows how hard it is to move a heavy body at rest. It has much inertia. Anyone who has ever tried to stop a heavy, rolling automobile by pushing against it knows how difficult this is. A body in motion has the inertia of motion (momentum). The more momentum it has, the harder it is to stop it.

Causes of Orbits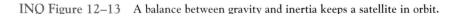

INQ Figure 12–13 shows how the laws of gravitation and inertia combine to keep objects in orbit. Although a natural satellite, our moon, is shown in this case, the same laws operate with all bodies that orbit other bodies in space.

If the moon were unaffected by our earth's powerful gravitational force, it would follow a straight path owing to its inertial momentum. Because it is affected, the moon follows a path that is a result of each factor countering the other.

A common example of this countering effect happens when a ball rolls swiftly off a table. Instead of falling straight down, the ball's inertia of momentum keeps it going nearly sideways for an instant until gravity forces it to the floor. The resultant path of its fall is an arc.

In our illustration, gravity and inertia are equally powerful. If this were not so, the moon would either be drawn into the earth or pull away from it. This is what happens to an artificial satellite that moves too slowly or too quickly. Clearly, getting a space satellite into a sustained orbit is tricky business. Its velocity and angle of entry into orbit must be

INQ Figure 12–13 A balance between gravity and inertia keeps a satellite in orbit.

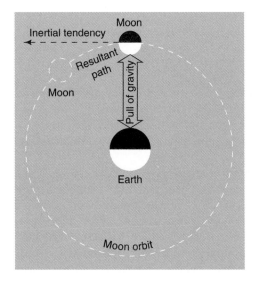

calculated closely. Because perfection in these matters is nearly impossible, most orbits are markedly elongated (elliptical).

Because gravity weakens with distance, the speed of the orbiting body must be slower as the distance from its parent body increases. This is necessary to maintain balance of the two forces. At 35,680 kilometers (22,300 miles) from the earth, for example, the proper orbital speed for a satellite results in one complete orbit each 24 hours. Because this is the period of the earth's rotation, a satellite positioned above the equator always stays in the same relative position. With several of these satellites properly spaced, television and radio signals are relayed to any place on earth.

Zero Gravity ——————

When astronauts circle the earth in a spaceship, they have no sensation of weight; the pull of gravity is balanced exactly by the counteracting inertia of motion. We sometimes experience this weightless, or *zero gravity*, condition on the earth for an instant when an elevator starts rapidly downward or an automobile goes too fast over the crown of a steep hill.

In one science lesson not long ago, a bright child asked her teacher an astute question: "If we would be weightless in an orbiting satellite, why wouldn't we be weightless on the moon?" The teacher had her reconsider the law of gravitation, especially the part that says ". . . this attraction depends on the mass of each object and the distance between them."

Because the moon has a much smaller mass than the earth, its surface gravity is only about one sixth that of the earth's. An 81-kilogram (180-pound) astronaut weighs a mere 13.5 kilograms (30 pounds) on the moon. However, the moon's mass is almost infinitely greater than that of a space vehicle. The tiny mass of a space vehicle has practically no gravity at all.

Because prolonged periods of weightlessness seem detrimental to astronauts' health, attempts are being made to design space vehicles that create a gravitylike condition. This may be done by rotating the vehicle at a carefully calculated speed. The astronauts' inertia gives them a feeling of gravity as they are slightly pressed against the spaceship's interior. An analogy is the small ball that remains stationary on the rim of a roulette wheel until it stops turning.

Rockets ——————

Through the ages, people have always yearned to explore what mysteries lie beyond the earth. Until recently, our technology had not been as advanced as our ambitions. Early devices and inventions designed for space travel included hitching a flock of geese to a wicker basket, hand-cranking propellers attached to hot-air balloons, and festooning a box with crude rockets containing gunpowder. Occasionally, such contraptions were personally occupied by their daring inventors—and some did depart from this earth, although not in the manner intended.

Because space is a near vacuum, no engine that draws oxygen from the air to burn its fuel can serve in a propulsion system. Instead, rocket engines are used; these carry their own oxygen supply. Rockets work because for every action there is an equal and opposite reaction (another of Newton's laws of motion). When a rocket pushes hot gases out of its combustion chamber (action), the gases push back (reaction) and thrust the rocket ahead.

Most rockets today are composed of multiple stages fastened together in a cluster or a tandem arrangement. The main rocket propels all the stages to a point where the rocket's fuel is expended and then it drops off. The remaining stages reach even higher velocities as the process continues, lightening the load each time. The speed of the last stage represents the accumulated sum of speeds attained by each stage. Perhaps future rockets will be efficient enough to reduce or eliminate the necessity for current cumbersome staging techniques.

Problems in Space Travel

Although modern rocketry provides the means to reach beyond the earth, travel for astronauts poses some difficult problems. As the rocket blasts off in a terrifying surge of power, the rapid acceleration pins the astronauts' bodies to the seats with crushing force.

Once beyond the earth's atmosphere, they need oxygen and sufficient pressure to keep their bodies working normally. They need some means of temperature control. Without air conduction of heat energy, the side of the spaceship facing the sun gets very hot, and the dark side gets freezing cold. Because of their weightless condition, the astronauts may eat and drink from plastic squeeze bottles.

To prevent the space vehicle from being burned to a cinder as it reenters the atmosphere, the angle and speed of reentry must be exactly right. These are only some of the problems of space travel.

With so many difficulties, why do people venture into space? Although our curiosity is one answer, of course, there are many advantages for continued space efforts. Some benefits are improved communications, surveys of earth resources, long-range weather forecasting and possible weather control, astronomers' observation posts beyond the annoying interference of the earth's atmosphere, possible answers to how the universe was formed, and improved mapping and navigation. All these benefits may help us understand and solve problems here on the earth.

Eventually will come the most important reason of all. Someday, perhaps 3 to 5 billion years from now, the sun's nuclear fuel will be largely depleted. The sun should gradually expand and engulf the inner planets in an unimaginable inferno of extinction before it finally collapses and dies out. Perhaps by then our descendants will have found a comfortable haven among the stars.

References

American Association for the Advancement of Science (AAAS). (1993). *Benchmarks for science literacy*. New York: Oxford University Press.

National Research Council (NRC). (1996). *National science education standards*. Washington, DC: National Academy Press.

Ovando, C. J., Collier, V. P., & Combs, M. C. (2003). *Bilingual and ESL classrooms: Teaching in multicultural contexts*. Boston: McGraw-Hill.

Selected Trade Books: The Earth in Space

For Younger Children

Bendick, J. (1991). *Artificial satellites: Helpers in space*. Brookfield, CT: Millbrook Press.

Bendick, J. (1991). *Comets and meteors: Visitors from space*. Brookfield, CT: Millbrook Press.

Branley, F. M. (1987). *Rockets and satellites*. New York: Harper & Row.

Branley, F. M. (1991). *The big dipper*. New York: HarperCollins.

Branley, F. M. (1998). *The planets in our solar system*. New York: HarperTrophy.

Branley, F. M. (1999). *The moon seems to change*. Topeka, KS: Econo-Clad Books.

Branley, F. M. (1999). *What makes day and night*. Topeka, KS: Econo-Clad Books.

Branley, F. M. (2000). *The International Space Station*. New York: HarperCollins.

Branley, F. M. (2000). *The sun, our nearest star*. New York: HarperCollins.

Coffelt, N. (1999). *Dogs in space*. Topeka, KS: Econo-Clad Books.

Cole, J. (1990). *The magic school bus lost in the solar system*. New York: Scholastic.

Cole, J. (1996). *The magic school bus out of this world: A book about space rocks*. New York: Scholastic.

Cole, J. (1999). *The magic school bus sees stars: A book about stars*. New York: Scholastic.

Donnelly, J. (1989). *Moonwalk: The first trip to the moon*. New York: Random House.

Fradin, D. (1984). *Spacelab*. Danbury, CT: Childrens Press.

Friskey, M. (1982). *Space shuttles*. Danbury, CT: Childrens Press.

Gorey, E., & Neumeyer, P. (1982). *Why we have day and night*. Santa Barbara, CA: Capra Press.

Hamer, M. (1983). *Night sky*. Danbury, CT: Watts.

Hasen, R. (1998). *Astronauts today*. New York: Random House.

Hort, L. (1991). *How many stars in the sky?* New York: Morrow.

Jackson, K. (1985). *The planets*. New York: Troll Associates.

Jay, M. (1987). *Planets*. Danbury, CT: Watts.

Lyon, G. (1990). *Come a tide*. New York: Orchard Books.

Polacco, P. (1996). *Meteor*. Ossining, NY: Paper Star.

Simon, S. (2004). *Space travelers*. San Francisco, CA: Seastar Publishing Co.

Stearns, C. (1998). *Where did all the water go?* Centreville, MD: Tidewater.

Weimer, T. E. (1993). *Space songs for children*. Pittsburgh, PA: Pearce-Evetts.

For Older Children

Adams, R. (1983). *Our wonderful solar system*. New York: Troll Associates.

Adler, I. (1980). *The stars: Decoding their messages*. New York: Thomas Y. Crowell.

Alexander, K. (1990). *The kid's book of space flight*. Philadelphia, PA: Running Press.

Asimov, I. (1990). *Projects in astronomy*. Milwaukee, WI: Gareth Stevens.

Asimov, I. (1991). *Ancient astronomy*. New York: Dell.

Becklake, S. (1998). *Space, stars, planets, and spacecraft*. Hillsdale, NJ: DK Publishing.

Bendick, J. (1982). *Space travel*. Danbury, CT: Watts.

Berger, M. (1983). *Bright stars, red giants, and white dwarfs*. New York: G. P. Putnam.

Branley, F. (1987). *Star guide*. New York: Harper & Row.

Buchanan, D. (1999). *Female firsts in their fields: Air and space*. Broomall, PA: Chelsea House.

Burnham, R. (2000). *The Readers' Digest children's atlas of the universe*. Pleasantville, NY: Reader's Digest Children's Books.

Cabellero, J. A. (1987). *Aerospace projects for young children*. Atlanta: Humanics.

Couper, H., & Henbest, N. (1987). *The moon*. Danbury, CT: Watts.

Dickinson, T. (1998). *Nightwatch: A practical guide to viewing the universe*. Willowdale, Ontario: Firefly Books.

Fichter, G. S. (1982). *Comets and meteors*. Danbury, CT: Watts.

Furniss, T. (1987). *Let's look at outer space*. Danbury, CT: Watts.

Gallant, R. A. (1983). *Once around the galaxy*. Danbury, CT: Watts.

Gardner, R. (1988). *Projects in space science*. Parsippany, NJ: Julian Messner.

Harris, A., & Weissman, P. (1990). *The great voyager adventure: A guided tour through the solar system*. Parsippany, NJ: Julian Messner.

Harris, R. (1999). *I can read about the sun and other stars*. Topeka, KS: Econo-Clad Books.

Kelch, J. (1990). *Small worlds: Exploring the 60 moons of our solar system*. Parsippany, NJ: Julian Messner.

Koppes, S. N. (2003). *Killer rocks from outer space: Asteroids, comets, and meteorites*. Minneapolis, MN: Carolrhoda Books/Lerner.

Lauber, P. (1982). *Journey to the planets*. New York: Crown.

Lewellen, J. (1981). *Moon, sun, and stars*. Danbury, CT: Childrens Press.

Myring, L. (1982). *Sun, moon, and planets*. Toronto, Ontario: EDC Press.

Richard, G. (1987). *Spacecraft*. Danbury, CT: Watts.

Ride, S., & O'Shaughnessy, T. (2003). *Exploring our solar system*. New York: Crown Books for Young Readers.

Ridpath, I. (1991). *Space*. Danbury, CT: Watts.

Riley, P. D. (1986). *The earth and space*. New York: David & Charles.

Shepherd, D. (1995). *Auroras: Light shows in the night sky*. Danbury, CT: Watts.

Simon, S. (1982). *The long journey from space*. New York: Crown.

Simon, S. (1984). *The moon*. Portland, OR: Four Winds.

Simon, S. (1999). *Comets, meteors, and asteroids*. Topeka, KS: Econo-Clad Books.

Vogt, G. (1982). *Mars and the inner planets*. Danbury, CT: Watts.

Vogt, G. (1987). *Space laboratories*. Danbury, CT: Watts.

Wood, R. (1991). *Thirty-nine easy astronomy experiments*. Silver Springs, MD: Tab Books.

Resource Books

AIMS Project Team. (1998). *Gravity rules!* Fresno, CA: AIMS Education Foundation.

Beals, K., Erickson, J., & Sneider, C. (2000). *Messages from space*. Berkeley, CA: Great Explorations in Math and Science. (solar system and beyond)

Butzow, C. M., & Butzow, J. W. (1989). *Science through children's literature: An integrated approach*. Englewood, CO: Teacher Ideas Press. (astronomy and outer space topics on pp. 158–168)

Engelbert, P., & Dupuis, D. (1998). *The handy space answer book*. Detroit, MI: Visible Ink Press.

Fredericks, A. D., Meinbach, A. M., & Rothlein, L. (1993). *Thematic units: An integrated approach to teaching science and social studies*. New York: HarperCollins. (earth, sun, and moon topics on pp. 161–167; space exploration on pp. 210–217)

Glaser, D., Willard, C., Beals, K., & Pompea, S. (2002). *Living with a star*. Berkeley, CA: Great Explorations in Math and Science.

Gould, A., Willard, C., & Pompea, S. (2000). *The real reasons for the seasons*. Berkeley, CA: Great Explorations in Math and Science.

Shaw, D. G., & Dybdahl, C. S. (1996). *Integrating science and language arts: A sourcebook for K–6 teachers*. Boston: Allyn & Bacon. (rocket and space travel topics on pp. 213–230)

Sneider, C. I., & Bergman, L. (Eds.). (1999). *Earth, moon, and stars*. Berkeley, CA: Great Explorations in Math and Science.

Sneider, C. I., & Bergman, L. (Eds.). (1999). *Experimenting with model rockets*. Berkeley, CA: Great Explorations in Math and Science.

Sutter, D., Gould, A., & Sneider, C. (1999). *Moons of Jupiter*. Berkeley, CA: Great Explorations in Math and Science. (reenact Galileo's telescopic study)

Wiebe, A., Cordel, B., & Hillen, J. (1994). *Out of this world*. Fresno, CA: AIMS Education Foundation.

Young, R. (2000). *Astronomy thematic unit*. Huntington Beach, CA: Teacher Created Materials.

PROFESSIONAL BIBLIOGRAPHY

GENERAL SOURCES OF ACTIVITIES

American Association for the Advancement of Science, & Walthall, B. (Ed.). (1995). *IdeAAAS: Sourcebook for science, mathematics, & technology education.* Washington, DC: Learning Team.

American Chemical Society. (2001). *The best of wonderscience* (Vol. 2). Belmont, CA: Wadsworth.

Cothron, J., Giese, R., & Rezba, R. (2002). *Science experiments by the hundreds* (2nd ed.). Dubuque, IA: Kendall/Hunt.

DeVito, A. *Creative sciencing.* Minneapolis, MN: Sagebrush Educational Resources.

Freidl, A., & Koontz, T. (2004). *Teaching science to children: An inquiry approach.* New York: McGraw-Hill Higher Education.

Sewall, S. (1990). *Hooked on science: Ready-to-use discovery activities for grades 4–8.* West Nyack, NY: Center for Applied Research in Education.

Stringer, J. (Ed.). (1996). *Science and technology ideas for the under 85.* Hatfield, Herts., UK: Association for Science Education.

Stringer, J. (Ed.). (1998). *More science and technology ideas for the under 85.* Hatfield, Herts., UK: Association for Science Education.

Strongin, H. (1991). *Science on a shoestring.* Reading, MA: Addison-Wesley.

Van Cleave, J. P. (1989–1999). *Science for every kid* (5 volumes: biology, chemistry, earth, astronomy, physics). New York: John Wiley.

OTHERS

Also visit the AIMS Education Foundation (*http://www.aimsedu.org/*), Great Explorations in Math and Science (*http://www.lhs.berkeley.edu/GEMS/ gems.html*), National Science Teachers Association (*www.nsta.org*), and the Association for Science Education (*http://www.ase.org.uk/*) for new activity books and ideas.

TEACHER PERIODICALS

Discover, 114 Fifth Ave., New York, NY 10011. (monthly; interesting, up-to-date information about developments in science; *http://www.discover.com/*)

Journal of Elementary Science Education, (*http://static.highbeam. com/j/journalofelementaryscience.education/*) (practical and theoretical articles related to elementary science teaching and learning)

Journal of Science Teacher Education, contact Jon Pederson, Association for the Education of Teachers in Science Executive Secretary, University of Oklahoma, Norman, OK 73070; *pedersenj@ou.edu*. (practical and scholarly articles related to teacher preservice, teacher in-service, and science teaching)

School Science and Mathematics, *http://oreganstate.edu/ pubs/ssm/* (monthly; nine issues a year; includes articles on methods and research)

Science, American Association for the Advancement of Science. (accurate, up-to-date nontechnical information about developments in science; *http://www.scienceonline.org/*)

Science Activities, Heldref Publications, 1319 Eighteenth Street, NW, Washington, DC 20036-1802. (10 issues a year; useful activities for teachers of the upper grades and beyond; *http://www.heldref.org*)

Science and Children, National Science Teachers Association, 1840 Wilson Blvd., Arlington, VA 22201-3000. (monthly; eight issues a year; articles of interest and practical value to elementary school teachers; *www.nsta.org/*)

Science Education, John Wiley and Sons, Inc., 605 Third Ave., New York, NY 10158. For individual subscriptions contact Jon Pederson, Association for the Education of Teachers in Science Executive Secretary, University of Oklahoma, Norman, OK 73070; *pedersenj@ou.edu.* (reports of research and essays on the teaching of elementary and secondary school science)

Science News. (weekly; brief, easy-to-read reports on current findings of scientific research; *http://www.sciencenews.org/*)

CHILDREN'S PERIODICALS

National Geographic Kids Magazine, National Geographic Society, 1145 17th St. NW, Washington, DC 20036. (monthly; articles on environmental features of interest to children; *http://www.nationalgeographic.com/world/*)

Odyssey, Cobblestone Publishing Company, 30 Grove St., Suite C, Peterborough, NH 03458. (bimonthly; full-color astronomy and space magazine for children 7–13; *http://www.odysseymagazine.com/*)

Ranger Rick Nature Magazine, National Wildlife Federation, 11100 Wildlife Center Drive, Reston, VA 20190–5362. (monthly; for children of elementary school age; interesting stories and pictures on natural subjects, including ecology; *Your Big Backyard* is for preschool and primary-level children; *http://www.nwf.org/kidzone/*)

3–2–1 Contact, Sesame Workshop, P.O. Box 2933, Boulder, CO 80322. (10 issues a year; experiments, puzzles, projects, and articles for children 8–14; *http://www.sesameworkshop.org/*)

Wonderscience, American Chemical Society, 1155 16th St., NW, Washington, DC 20036. (science activities for children; also includes *Best of Wonderscience*; *http://www.chemistry.org/portal/a/c/s/1/acsdisplay.html?DOC= education%5curriculum%5cwondsci.html* and *http://www. chemistry.org/portal/a/c/s/1/wondernetdisplay.html?DOC= wondernet\topics_list\index.html*)

PROFESSIONAL TEXTS

Abruscato, J. (2004). *Teaching children science: A discovery approach* (6th ed.). Needham Heights, MA: Allyn & Bacon/Pearson Education. (methods, activities, and content for elementary school science)

Barba, R. H. (1998). *Science in the multicultural classroom: A guide to teaching and learning* (2nd ed.). Needham Heights, MA: Allyn & Bacon. (elementary science methods)

Carin, A., & Bass, J. (2005). *Teaching science as inquiry* (10th ed.). Upper Saddle River, NJ: Merrill/Prentice Hall. (methods and activities, with emphasis on discovery teaching)

Ebenezer, J., & Conner, S. (1998). *Learning to teach science: A model for the 21st century.* Upper Saddle River, NJ: Merrill/Prentice Hall. (methods and activities, with emphasis on discovery teaching)

Esler, W. K., & Esler, M. K. (2000). *Teaching elementary science* (8th ed.). Belmont, CA: Wadsworth. (methods and subject matter; exemplifies and applies three kinds of lessons)

Gabel, D. (1993). *Introductory science skills.* Prospect Heights, IL: Waveland Press. (a laboratory approach to learning science and mathematics skills and basic chemistry)

Harlan, J., & Rivkin, M. (2004). *Science experiences for the early childhood years: An integrated affective approach* (8th ed.). Upper Saddle River, NJ: Merrill/Prentice Hall. (everyday science activities for younger children)

Howe, A. C. (2002). *Engaging children in science* (3rd ed.). Upper Saddle River, NJ: Merrill/Prentice Hall. (elementary science methods)

Krajcik, J., Czerniak, C., & Berger, C. (1999). *Teaching children science: A project-based approach.* New York: McGraw-Hill.

Lind, K. K. (1999). *Exploring science in early childhood: A developmental approach* (3rd ed.). Albany, NY: Delmar. (elementary science methods)

Martin, D. J. (2003). *Elementary science methods: A constructivist approach* (3rd ed.). Albany, NY: Delmar. (elementary science methods)

Martin, R. E., Jr., Sexton, C., & Gerlovich, J. (2005). *Teaching science for all children: Inquiry lessons for constructing understanding* (3rd ed.). Needham Heights, MA: Allyn & Bacon. (methods and content of elementary school science)

Rezba, R., Sprague, C., Fiel, R. L., & Funk, H. J. (2002). *Learning and assessing science process skills* (4th ed.). Dubuque, IA: Kendall Hunt. (process skill development and assessment)

Tolman, M. N. (2001). *Discovering elementary science: Method, content, and problem-solving activities* (3rd ed.). Needham Heights, MA: Allyn & Bacon. (elementary science methods and content)

Victor, E., & Kellough, R. (2000). *Science K-8: An integrated approach* (10th ed.). Upper Saddle River, NJ: Merrill/ Prentice Hall. (methods, content, and activities; features an extensive scope of subject matter in outline form)

AGENCIES AND SOCIETIES

The Association for Science Teacher Education (ASTE), contact Walter S. Smith and Caryl Kelley Smith, ASTE Executive Secretaries, Department of Biology, Ball State University, Muncie, IN 47306-0440, *wsmith@bsu.edu* (WSS) or *eelslake1@aol.com* (CKS and WSS) (*http:// theASTE.org*).

Computer Learning Foundation, P.O. Box 60007, Palo Alto, CA 94306-0007 (*http://www.computerlearning.org/*).

Foundation for Science and Disability, E. C. Keller, Jr., Treasurer, 236 Grand St., Morgantown, WV 26506-6057 (*http://www.as.wvu.edu/~scidis/organizations/ FSD_brochure.html*).

The Franklin Institute Science Museum, 222 North 20th Street, Philadelphia, PA 19103, (215) 448-1200 (*http://www.fi.edu/*).

International Council of Associations for Science Education (ICASE), Jack B. Holbrook, Executive Secretary, ICASE, P.O. Box 6138, Limassol, Cyprus.

National Audubon Society, 700 Broadway, New York, NY 10003, (212) 979-3000, fax (212) 979-3188 (*http://www.audubon.org/*).

National Energy Foundation, 3676 California Ave. Suite A117, Salt Lake City, UT 84104 (*http://www.nefl.org/*).

National Science Foundation, 4201 Wilson Blvd., Arlington, VA 22230 (*http://nsf.gov/*).

National Science Teachers Association, 1840 Wilson Boulevard, Arlington, VA 22201-3000, (703) 243-7100 (*http://www.nsta.org/*).

National Weather Service, 1325 East West Highway, Silver Spring, MD 20910 (*http://www.nws.noaa.gov/*).

Office of Indian Education Programs, Bureau of Indian Affairs (*http://oiep.bia.edu/*).

Society for Advancement of Chicanos and Native Americans in Science (SACNAS), P.O. Box 8526, Santa Cruz, CA 95061, (831) 459–0170 (*http://www.sacnas.org/*).

Technical Education Resource Center, 2067 Massachusetts Ave., Cambridge, MA 02140, (617) 547-0430, fax (617) 349-3535 (*http://www.terc.edu/*).

U.S. Environmental Protection Agency, Ariel Rios Bldg., 1200 Pennsylvania Ave. NW, Washington, DC 20460, (202) 272-0167 (*http://www.epa.gov/*).

U.S. Geological Survey, Information Services (*http://www.usgs.gov/*).

SCIENCE CURRICULUM PROJECTS

ACTIVITIES FOR INTEGRATING MATHEMATICS AND SCIENCE (**AIMS**)

Grades K–8. This program, developed at Fresno (California) Pacific College, was originally funded by the National Science Foundation to train a group of teachers in the rationale and methods for integrating science and mathematics in grades 5–8. The classroom testing of written materials produced such positive results that a full-fledged writing project was launched to develop additional teaching booklets. Materials are now available for K–8.

The rationale for AIMS includes these points: (a) Mathematics and science are integrated outside the classroom and so should also be integrated inside it; (b) as in the real world, a whole series of mathematics skills and science processes should be interwoven in a single activity to create a continuum of experience; (c) the materials should present questions that relate to the students' world and arouse their curiosity; (d) the materials should change students from observers to participants in the learning process; and (e) the investigations should be enjoyable because learning is more effective when the process is enjoyed.

For more information, write to AIMS Education Foundation, 1595 S. Chestnut Ave., Fresno, CA 93702-4706 (*http://www.aimsedu.org/*), 888-733-2467.

FULL OPTION SCIENCE SYSTEM (**FOSS**)

Grades K–6. The FOSS program is designed to serve both regular and most special education students in a wide cross section of schools. Developed at the Lawrence Hall of Science, in Berkeley, California, the program features several modules at each grade level that include science lesson plans in the earth, life, and physical sciences and extension activities in language, computer, and mathematics applications.

The laboratory equipment includes several package options, from complete kits to individual items. Materials assembly directions show how teacher and students can gather and construct equipment for many activities. A correlation table tells how to integrate activities with other programs and state department of education guidelines for science.

Much care is taken to have a suitable match between activities and students' ability to think at different ages. Further work has made the program easy to instruct and manage. Provisions for preparation time, ease of giving out and retrieving materials, cleanup, storage, and resupply have continually guided program developers.

The commercial distributor of FOSS is Delta Education, 80 Northwest Blvd., P.O. Box 3000, Nashua, NH 03061-3000, 800-258-1302 (*http://www.delta-ed.com/*, *http://www.lawrencehallofscience.org/foss/*).

GREAT EXPLORATIONS IN MATH AND SCIENCE (**GEMS**)

Grades Preschool–9. Gems is a growing resource for activity-based science and mathematics. Developed at the University of California at Berkeley's Lawrence Hall of Science and tested in thousands of classrooms nationwide, more than 50 GEMS teacher's guides and handbooks offer a wide spectrum of learning opportunities from preschool and kindergarten through 10th grade. GEMS guides can be integrated into your curriculum or stand on their own as a stimulating way to involve students. The GEMS series interweaves a number of educational ideas and goals. GEMS guides encompass important learning objectives, summarized on the front page of each guide, under the headings of skills, concepts, science themes, mathematics strands, and the nature of science and mathematics. Taken together, these headings help provide a summary of the unit objectives. These objectives can be directly and flexibly related to science and mathematics curricula, local and district guidelines, state frameworks, benchmarks, and the national standards. For more on flexible ways to build your own curricula using GEMS, contact the University of California, GEMS, Lawrence Hall of Science #5200, Berkeley, CA 94720-5200 (*http://lhsgems.org/gems.html*).

NATIONAL GEOGRAPHIC KIDS NETWORK

Grades 4–6. The National Geographic Kids Network is a program that has children gather data on real science problems and then use a computer network to share their data with a scientist and children in other locations. The developer is the Technical Education Resource Center (TERC) in partnership with the National Geographic Society, which publishes and distributes the program.

Each instructional unit is 6 weeks long and focuses on a central science problem. Children learn to ask questions and gather data in scientifically acceptable ways. The data are transmitted to an interested scientist who analyzes the data, answers children's questions, and then sends back an overview of all the collected information from cooperating schools. Curriculum materials include children's handbooks that have background information on the topic of study, teacher guides, and computer software. The software is made up of a word-processing program, data charts, and a computer map of North America, all of which are used to ready and transmit data. For details, write National Geographic Society, 1145 17th St. NW, Washington, DC 20036-4688 (*http://www. nationalgeographic.com/kids/*), 800-647-5463.

OUTDOOR BIOLOGY INSTRUCTIONAL STRATEGIES (OBIS)

Ages 10–15. Developed at the Lawrence Hall of Science, University of California (Berkeley), OBIS is designed for use with community youth organizations and schools that want to offer outdoor laboratory experiences. Four activity packets offer a broad selection of interesting, firsthand activities for studying ecological relationships in different environments: desert, seashore, forest, pond and stream, city lots, and local parks. Each activity card consists of background information for the leader, description of materials needed and any advance preparation required, a lesson plan, and several follow-up suggestions. Each activity can be used alone or as part of a developmental sequence. For more information see *http://www.lawrencehallofscience.org/OBIS/OBISpubs.html*, University of California, OBIS, Lawrence Hall of Science #5200, Berkeley, CA 94720-5200.

SCIENCE FOR LIFE AND LIVING

Grades K–6. The full name for this curriculum is "Teaching Relevant Activities for Concepts and Skills." The developer is the BSCS Group, a nonprofit foundation for science education.

After readiness activities at the kindergarten level, these concepts and skills form the main curriculum structure: order and organization (grade 1); change and measurement (grade 2); patterns and prediction (grade 3); systems and analysis (grade 4); energy and investigation (grade 5); and balance and decisions (grade 6). Children build their own understanding of an integrated world of science, technology, and health as they work through activities that bring out the concepts and skills.

Each complete lesson contains five consecutive phases: (a) An engagement activity begins the lesson. Children connect what they know to the current material and reveal their prior knowledge, including misconceptions. (b) Exploration follows, in which students explore the materials or environment and form a common base of experience. (c) An explanation phase gives students a chance to describe what they are learning and gives the teacher an opportunity to state the intended learning. (d) Elaboration then provides activities that extend understandings and give further chances to practice skills. (e) The last phase, evaluation, allows students and teacher to assess what has been learned.

Published materials are available from the Kendall/Hunt Publishing Company, 4050 Westmark Drive, P.O. Box 1840, Dubuque, IA 52004-1840 (*http://www. kendallhunt.com/*).

SCIENCE AND TECHNOLOGY FOR CHILDREN (STC)

Grades 1–6. The developer of the STC curriculum project is the National Science Resources Center, established in 1985 by the National Academy of Sciences and the Smithsonian Institution to improve the teaching of science and mathematics in the nation's schools. The project's mission is to increase significantly the number of schools that offer hands-on science programs to children and to interest more females and minority members in science.

Teaching units include such titles as Weather (grade K–1), The Life Cycle of Butterflies (grade 2), Plant Growth and Development (grade 3), Electric Circuits (grade 4), Microworlds (grade 5), and Magnets and Motors (grade 6). They are designed to focus on easy-to-use materials and integrate science with other areas of the curriculum. Each unit includes a teacher's guide; pupil activity booklet; description of needed materials; and annotated lists of recommended trade books, computer software, and audiovisual materials.

The developers sought to make the management of materials and activities as practical as possible. In the field testing of units, evaluation procedures monitored how well the units worked under a wide variety of classroom conditions.

For details, contact the National Science Resources Center, 901 D St. SW, Suite 704B, Washington, DC 20024 (*http://www.nsrconline.org/*).

SCIENCE CURRICULUM IMPROVEMENT STUDY (SCIS)

Grades K–6. SCIS is organized on a base of powerful and modern science concepts. Each of 12 instructional units features a central concept, with supporting subconcepts and process skills integrated into the activities.

Lessons have three parts: exploration, invention, and discovery. In the exploratory part, children are given objects to observe or manipulate. At times, these observations are guided by the teacher; otherwise, the children observe and manipulate the objects as they wish.

Explorations allow firsthand contact with the material under study and provide a basis for children to use language. At the same time, the need arises for an explanation to make sense out of what has been observed. This is taken up in the second part of the lesson sequence. After discussion, the teacher gives a definition and a word for the new concept.

This "invention" of a concept sets up the third part of the lesson. Now, children are given a variety of further experiences within which they discover many applications of the concept. These extend and reinforce their knowledge and skills.

An updated version of this program, SCIS3, is available from Delta Education, 80 Northwest Blvd., P.O. Box 3000, Nashua, NH 03061-3000 (*http://www.delta-ed.com/*).

SCIENCE IN A NUTSHELL

Grades K–8. Real fun with real science. Discover how exciting real science can be with Delta's Science in a Nutshell mini-kit series. Introduce or enhance specific science content areas in the classroom, at home, in a resource room, or in an after-school program. Clearly written, hands-on activities challenge young scientists aged 6–12 to investigate their world. Mini-kits are suitable for use with individuals or with small groups of two to three. Contact Delta Education, 80 Northwest Blvd., P.O. Box 3000, Nashua, NH 03061-3000 (*http://www.delta-ed.com/*).

WONDERSCIENCE

Wonderscience offers hands-on science activities for elementary school teachers and students. The *Best of WonderScience* was developed as a joint effort of the American Chemical Society (ACS), and the American Institute of Physics. The ACS is at toll-free 1-800-227-5558 (*http://www.chemistry.org/portal/a/c/s/1/acsdisplay.html? DOC=education%5curriculum%5cwondsci.html*).

COMMERCIAL SCIENCE SUPPLIERS

The following classifications of suppliers may not be entirely accurate, because suppliers often change offerings with business conditions. A current catalog should reveal the full scope of materials for sale in each case. Use school stationery when requesting free elementary-level catalogs. An annual, comprehensive listing of suppliers accompanies each January issue of *Science and Children*.

GENERAL SUPPLIES

Wisconsin Fast Plants Program, University of Wisconsin-Madison, Science House, 1630 Linden Drive, Madison, WI 53706, 1-800-462-7417 (*http://www.fastplants.org/_home_flash.html*), *info@fastplants.org*.

Carolina Biological Supply Company, 2700 York Road, Burlington, NC 27215 (*http://www.carolina.com/*, carolina@carolina.com, 800-334-3551.

Delta Education, 80 Northwest Blvd., P.O. Box 3000, Nashua, NH 03061-3000 (*http://www.delta-ed.com/*).

Edmund Scientific Company, 60 Pearce Ave, Tonawanda, NY 14150, 1-800-728-6999 (*http://www.edsci.com/*).

Frey Scientific Company, P.O. Box 8101, 100 Paragon Parkway, Mansfield, OH 44903, 1-800-225-3739 (*http://www.freyscientific.com/*).

Ward's Natural Science Establishment, 5100 West Henrietta Road, P.O. Box 92912, Rochester, NY 14692-9012, 800-962-2660, (*http://www.wardsci.com/*).

BALANCES

Ohaus Scale Corporation, 19A Chapin Road, P.O. Box 2033, Pine Brook, NJ 07058, 800-672-7722 ext. 7804 (*http://www.ohaus.com/*).

MICROSCOPES AND MICROPROJECTORS

Brock Optical, 1959 Barber Road, Sarasota, FL 34240, 941-342-7727 (*http://www.magiscope.com/*).

Leica Microsystems, Inc., 90 Boroline Rd., Allendale, NJ 07401, 201-236-5900 (*http://www.discovermicroscopy.com/website/sc_ead1.nsf*).

Ken-A-Vision Manufacturing Company, 5615 Raytown Road, Raytown, MO 64133 (*http://www.ken-a-vision.com/*) 800-501-7366, *info@ken-a-vision.com*.

Swift Optics, 1190 North 4th St., San Jose, CA 95112, 800-523-4544 (*http://www.swift-optics.com/*).

AQUARIA, TERRARIA, CAGES

Carolina Biological Supply Company, 2700 York Road, Burlington, NC 27215 (*http://www.carolina.com/*), carolina@carolina.com, 800-334-3551.

Delta Education, 80 Northwest Blvd., P.O. Box 3000, Nashua, NH 03061-3000 (*http://www.delta-ed.com/*).

Frey Scientific Company, P.O. Box 8101, 100 Paragon Parkway, Mansfield, OH 44903, 1-800-225-3739 (*http://www.freyscientific.com/*).

KITS AND MODELS

Delta Education, 80 Northwest Blvd., P.O. Box 3000, Nashua, NH 03061-3000 (*http://www.delta-ed.com/*).

SOFTWARE

Scholastic Software & Multimedia, 2931 East McCarty Street, Jefferson City, MO 65101, 1-800-724-6527 (*http://scholastic.com/*).

Sunburst Technology, Inc., 1550 Executive Drive, Elgin, IL 60123, 1-800-321-7511 (*http://store.sunburst.com/*).

APPENDIX D

ENVIRONMENTS AND NUTRITION FOR CLASSROOM ANIMALS

Animal[1]	Environment	Nutrition[2]
Ants	Glass terrarium or large jar with dirt (covered with black paper)	Small food scraps or dead insects
Birds	Bird cage (ensure cage is large enough for bird to move freely)	Birdseed (nutritional mix from pet store—not wild bird seed)
Butterflies and Moths	Butterfly "tent" (sold in kits) or large jar with wire screen on top with small branches	Sugar water solution
Caterpillars	Medium-sized jar with holes in lid; includes a small branch	Leaves (preferably near to where they were found)
Chameleons and Lizards	Aquarium with screened top; dirt, stones, and branches on bottom	Mealworms or live insects
Fish	Aquarium with gravel and filter (dechlorinate water before use)	Fish food from pet store (do not overfeed); brine shrimp
Frogs and Toads	Aquarium with shallow water and rocks to climb out of the water	Mealworms, small caterpillars, or live insects
Fruit Flies	Small jars with fine mesh covering	A small amount of overly ripe fruit
Guinea Pigs and Rats	Large animal cage with secure openings and an exercise wheel	Guinea pig food; small amounts of fresh fruit and vegetables
Hamsters, Gerbils, and Mice	Medium or large animal cage with secure openings and an exercise wheel	Hamster or gerbil food; small amounts of fresh fruit and vegetables
Mealworms	Wide jar or plastic bucket with screen or mesh cover	Oatmeal and small slices of fresh apple
Newts and Salamanders	Aquarium with shallow water and rocks rising above water line	Mealworms and live insects
Rabbits	Large animal cage (rabbits will chew on cage, so avoid wood)	Rabbit pellets, fresh vegetables (avoid too much lettuce)
Snakes	Terrarium with secure openings; heating device (contact pet shop)	Live mice or insects (contact pet shop for specifics)
Spiders	Glass jar covered with screen	Live insects
Tadpoles	Aquarium 1/4 filled with water and rocks above the water line	Small insects or finely chopped meat
Turtles (land)	Terrarium with nonpoisonous plants and water pool	Mealworms, insects, earthworms; finely chopped vegetables
Turtles (aquatic)	Aquarium that is mostly water covered, but with small land area	Mealworms, insects, earthworms; finely chopped vegetables

[1]Contact the National Science Teachers Association (1840 Wilson Blvd., Arlington, VA 22201-3000 for the Guidelines for Responsible Use of Animals in the Classroom.

[2]All animals require plenty of fresh water. To remove the chlorine from water, leave it standing overnight.

SUMMARY OF CHILDREN'S THINKING

Thought Process	Intuitive Thought[1]	Concrete Operations	Formal Operations
Cause and Effect	Logic often contradictory, unpredictable. Events may occur by magic or for human convenience.	Contradictions avoided. Physical objects are linked to show cause and effect. Commonsense explanations may be wrong but logical.	Can separate logic from content. Systematic control of variables possible, as well as hypothetical "thought experiments," to test ideas.
Relative Thinking	Egocentric perceptions and language. Little grasp of how vertebrates interrelate. Physical properties viewed in absolute, not relative, ways.	Perceptions of position and objects more objective. Aware of others' views. Some understanding of interrelated variables, when connected to concrete objects and pictures.	Understand relative position and motion. Can define and explain abstract concepts with other concepts or analogies. May temporarily show some egocentricity in propositions.
Classifying and Ordering	Sort one property at a time. Little or no class inclusion. Trial-and-error ordering in early part of stage.	Understand class inclusion principle. More consistent seriation with diverse objects. Can follow successive steps, less discrete thinking.	Can recombine groups into fewer, more abstract categories. Can form hierarchical systems.
Conservative Thinking	Mostly do not conserve. Perceptions dominate thinking. Center attention on one variable and do not compensate. Little or no reverse thinking.	Can reverse thinking, consider several variables and compensate. Conserve most of the Piagetian test concepts.	Conserve all of the Piagetian test concepts, with displaced and solid volume usually last.

Table based on a format suggested by Robert Mele.
[1]Intuitive thought is the last period of the preoperational stage.

STATE EDUCATION AGENCIES

Alabama
Alabama State Dept. of Education
Gordon Persons Bldg.
Montgomery, AL 36130
(*http://www.alsde.edu/*)

Alaska
State of Alaska
Dept. of Education
801 W. 10th St., Ste. 200
Juneau, AK 99801-1894
(*http://www.educ.state.ak.us/*)

Arizona
Arizona Dept. of Education
1535 W. Jefferson St.,
Phoenix, AZ 85007
(*http://www.ade.state.az.us/*)

Arkansas
Arkansas Dept. of Education
4 State Capitol Mall
Little Rock, AR 72201
(*http://arkedu.state.ar.us/*)

Bureau of Indian Affairs
Dept. of Interior, BIA
1849 C St., NW
Mail Stop 3525, Code 521, MIB
Washington, DC 20240
(*http://www.doi.gov/bureau-indian-affairs.html*)

California
State Dept. of Education
1430 N. Street
Sacramento, CA 95814
(*http://www.cde.ca.gov/*)

Colorado
Colorado Dept. of Education
201 E. Colfax Ave.
Denver, CO, 80203
(*http://www.cde.state.co.us/index_home.htm*)

Connecticut
State Dept. of Education
165 Capitol Ave.
Hartford, CT 06145
(*http://www.state.ct.us/sde/*)

Delaware
State Dept. of Public Instruction
Townsend Bldg.
401 Federal St., Suite 2
Dover, DE 19901
(*http://www.doe.state.de.us/*)

District of Columbia
Education Program
D.C. Public Schools
415 12th St., NW, Rm. 1004
Washington, DC 20004
(*http://www.k12.dc.us/dcps/home.html*)

Department of Defense
4040 N. Fairfax Dr.
Arlington, VA 22203
(*http://www.dodea.edu/*)

Florida
Florida Dept. of Education
Florida Education Center, Ste. 522
Tallahassee, FL 32399
(*http://www.fldoe.org*)

Georgia
Georgia Dept. of Education
1862 Twin Towers East
Atlanta, GA 30334
(*http://www.doe.k12.ga.us/index.asp*)

Hawaii
Education Program
1390 Miller St.
Honolulu, HI 96804
(*http://doe.k12.hi.us/*)

Idaho
Idaho State Dept. of Education
650 W. State St.
P.O. Box 83720
Boise, ID 83720-0027
(*http://www.sde.state.id.us/Dept/*)

Illinois
Illinois State Board of Education
100 N. First St.
Springfield, IL 62777-0001
(*http://www.isbe.state.il.us/*)

Indiana
Indiana Dept. of Education
Rm. 229 State House
Indianapolis, IN 46204-2798
(*http://www.doe.state.in.us/*)

Iowa
State of Iowa
Department of Education
Grimes State Office Building
Des Moines, IA 50319-0146
(*http://www.state.ia.us/educate/index.html*)

Kansas
Kansas Dept. of Education
120 S.E. 10th St.
Topeka, KS 66612-1103
(*http://www.ksbe.state.ks.us/*)

Kentucky
Kentucky Dept. of Education
Capitol Plaza Tower
500 Mero St.
Frankfort, KY 40601
(*http://www.education.ky.gov*)

Louisiana
State Dept. of Education
P.O. Box 94064
Baton Rouge, LA 70804-9064
(*http://www.louisianaschools.net/lde/
index.html*)

Maine
Maine State Dept. of Education
State House Station #23
Augusta, ME 04333
(*http://www.state.me.us/education/
homepage.htm*)

Maryland
Maryland State Dept. of Education
200 W. Baltimore St.
Baltimore, MD 21201-2595
(*http://www.marylandpublicschools.
org/msde*)

Massachusetts
Massachusetts Dept. of Education
350 Main St.
Malden, MA 02148-5023
(*http://www.doe.mass.edu/*)

Michigan
Michigan Dept. of Education
P.O. Box 30008
Lansing, MI 48909
(*http://www.michigan.gov/mde*)

Minnesota
Minnesota Dept. of Education
1500 Highway 36 West
St. Paul, MN 55113
(*http://education.state.mn.us/html/mde_
home.htm*)

Mississippi
State Dept. of Education
Walter Sillers Bldg., Ste. 501
P.O. Box 771
Jackson, MS 39205-0771
(*http://www.mde.k12.ms.us/*)

Missouri
Missouri Dept. of Education
Dept. of Elementary & Secondary
Education
P.O. Box 480
Jefferson, MO 65102
(*http://www.dese.state.mo.us/*)

Montana
Office of Public Instruction
State Capitol Bldg.
Helena, MT 59620
(*http://www.opi.state.mt.us/*)

Nebraska
Nebraska Dept. of Education
301 Centennial Mall South
P.O. Box 94987
Lincoln, NE 68509-4987
(*http://www.nde.state.ne.us/*)

Nevada
Nevada Dept. of Education
Capitol Complex
Carson City, NV 89710
(*http://www.doe.nv.gov/*)

New Hampshire
New Hampshire Dept. of Education
1010 Pleasant St.
Concord, NH 03301
(*http://www.ed.state.nh.us/*)

New Jersey
New Jersey Dept. of Education
Division of Standards and Assessment
CN 500
Trenton, NJ 08625-0500
(*http://www.state.nj.us/education/*)

New Mexico
State of New Mexico
Dept. of Education
300 Don Gaspar
Santa Fe, NM 87501-2786
(*http://sde.state.nm.us/*)

New York
New York State Education Dept.
Bureau of Professional Career
Opportunity Programs
Empire State Plaza
Cultural Education Center, Rm. 5C64
Albany, NY 12230
(*http://www.nysed.gov/*)

North Carolina
Dept. of Public Instruction
116 W. Edenton St.
Raleigh, NC 27603-1712
(*http://www.dpi.state.nc.us/*)

North Dakota
Dept. of Public Instruction
600 E. Boulevard Ave., Department 201
Bismark, ND 58505
(*http://www.dpi.state.nd.us/*)

Ohio
Ohio Dept. of Education
65 S. Front St.
Columbus, OH 43266-0208
(*http://www.ode.state.oh.us/*)

Oklahoma
State Dept. of Education
2500 N. Lincoln Blvd.
Oklahoma City, OK 73105-4599
(*http://sde.state.ok.us/*)

Oregon
Oregon Dept. of Education
700 Pringle Pkwy., S.S.
Salem, OR 97310
(*http://www.ode.state.or.us/*)

Pennsylvania
Pennsylvania Dept. of Education
8th Floor, 333 Market Street
Harrisburg, PA 17126-0333
(*http://www.pde.state.pa.us*)

Puerto Rico
Office of Education
Office 809
Dept. of Education
Hato Rey, PR 00919
(*http://www.eduportal.de.gobierno.pr/
EDUportal/*)

Rhode Island
Rhode Island Dept. of Education
255 Westminster St.
Providence, RI 02903
(*http://www.ridoe.net/*)

South Carolina
South Carolina Dept. of Education
Curriculum Section
801 Rutledge Bldg.
Columbia, SC 29201
(*http://www.myscschools.com/*)

South Dakota
Dept. of Education and Cultural
   Affairs
700 Governors Dr.
Pierre, SD 57501-2291
(*http://www.state.sd.us/deca/*)

Tennessee
Tennessee Dept. of Education
4th Floor Northwing
Cordell Hull Bldg.
Nashville, TN 37243-0388
(*http://www.state.tn.us/education/*)

Texas
Texas Education Agency
1701 N. Congress
Austin, TX 78701
(*http://www.tea.state.tx.us/*)

Utah
Utah Dept. of Education
250 East 500 South
Salt Lake City, UT 84111
(*http://www.usoe.k12.ut.us/*)

Vermont
Vermont State Dept. of Education
120 State St.
Montpelier, VT 05602
(*http://www.state.vt.us/educ/*)

Virgin Islands
Dept. of Education
No. 44-46 Kongens Gade
Charlotte Amalie,
U.S. Virgin Islands 00802
(*http://www.usvi.org/education/*)

Virginia
Virginia Dept. of Education
P.O. Box 2120
Richmond, VA 23218-2120
(*http://www.pen.k12.va.us/*)

Washington
Office of Superintendent of Public
   Instruction
P.O. Box 47200
Olympia, WA 98504-7200
(*http://www.k12.wa.us/*)

West Virginia
West Virginia Dept. of Education
1900 Kanawha Blvd. East
Charleston, WV 25305
(*http://wvde.state.wv.us/*)

Wisconsin
Dept. of Public Education
125 S. Webster St.
P.O. Box 7841
Madison, WI 53707-7841
(*http://www.dpi.state.wi.us/*)

Wyoming
State Dept. of Education
241 Hathaway Bldg.
Cheyenne, WY 82002-0050
(*http://www.k12.wy.us/*)

INDEX

Page numbers for Inquiry Unit chapters are in italics. Page numbers for the appendices are in bold.